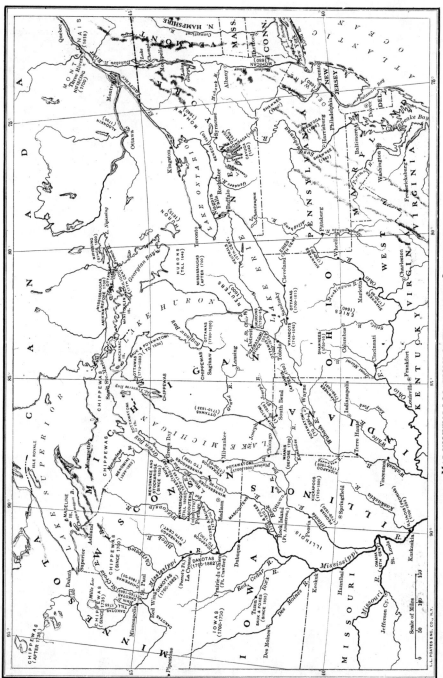

MAP SHOWING LOCATIONS OF THE LEADING INDIAN TRIBES.

TO ILLUSTRATE THE INDIAN TRIBES OF THE UPPER MISSISSIPPI VALLEY AND REGION OF THE GREAT LAKES.

L.L. POATES ENG. CO., N.Y.

THE INDIAN TRIBES OF THE UPPER MISSISSIPPI VALLEY AND REGION OF THE GREAT LAKES

as described by Nicolas Perrot, French commandant in the Northwest; Bacqueville de la Potherie, French royal commissioner to Canada;
Morrell Marston, American army officer;
and Thomas Forsyth, United States
agent at Fort Armstrong

Translated, edited, annotated,
and with bibliography and index by

EMMA HELEN BLAIR

With portraits, map, facsimiles, and views

VOLUME I

*Introduction to the Bison Books Edition
by Richard White*

University of Nebraska Press
Lincoln and London

⊛ The paper in this book meets the minimum requirements of
American National Standard for Information Sciences—Perma-
nence of Paper for Printed Library Materials, ANSI Z39.48-1984.

First Bison Books printing: 1996
Most recent printing indicated by the last digit below:
10   9   8   7   6   5   4   3   2   1

Library of Congress Cataloging-in-Publication Data
Blair, Emma Helen, d. 1911
The Indian tribes of the Upper Mississippi Valley and region of the
Great Lakes / Emma Helen Blair; introduction by Richard White.
p.   cm.
Originally published: Cleveland, Ohio: Arthur H. Clark Co., 1911.
Includes bibliographical references and index.
ISBN 0-8032-6099-7 (pbk.: alk. paper)
1. Indians of North America—Northwestern States.   2. Indians of
North America—Northwest, Old.   I. Title.
E78.N8B63   1996
977'.01—dc20
96-5129   CIP

Reprinted from the original editions by Arthur H. Clark Company,
Cleveland, Ohio. Volume 1 was published in 1911; volume 2 in
1912. As with the original, each volume begins on page 13; no
material has been omitted from this Bison Books edition.

The Contents, and Writers thereof

NICOLAS PERROT: *Memoire sur les mœurs, coustumes et religion des sauvages de l'Amerique septentrionale; publié pour la première fois par le R. P. J. Tailhan, de la Compagnie de Jésus* (Paris, 1864). Written before 1720; published by Father Tailhan from the original Ms., a careful and accurate representation of the original; NOW FIRST TRANSLATED INTO ENGLISH. It contains, besides the subjects mentioned in the above title, considerable early tribal history.

BACQUEVILLE DE LA POTHERIE: *Histoire de l'Amerique septentrionale* (Paris, 1722). Material so far as it relates to the tribes of the upper Mississippi; NOW FIRST TRANSLATED INTO ENGLISH. This writer obtained his information directly from Perrot, Louis Joliet, the Jesuit missionaries, and other reliable sources; and thus Perrot's *Memoire* is admirably supplemented with interesting accounts of his own dealings with the tribes (to whom he was long an accredited and useful agent of the French government in Quebec), and with further information regarding their early history, mutual relations, traits of character, customs, mode of life, etc.

LT.-MAJOR MORRELL MARSTON, U.S.A., military commander at Fort Armstrong (site of the present Rock Island, Ill.): Official report rendered to the special commissioner of the U.S. government to visit the Indian tribes under its care and report on their condition, in 1820. HERE PRESENTED FROM MARSTON'S ORIGINAL MS., in the library of the Wisconsin Historical Society, dated November, 1820. This account is obtained from interviews with the leading men of the tribes around Fort Armstrong, information supplied by prominent American traders among the Indians, and Marston's personal knowledge and observation during long intercourse with the western tribes. He describes their social organization, mode of life, industries, customs, beliefs, etc.; and makes valuable suggestions regarding their treatment by the government and the regulation of the Indian trade.

THOMAS FORSYTH, U.S. sub-agent among the Indians, with headquarters at Fort Armstrong: An account of the manners and customs of the Sauk and Fox Indians of Indians tradition. Original Ms., NEVER BEFORE PUBLISHED; in library of Wisconsin Historical Society; dated St. Louis, January 15, 1827. Forsyth, a son of one of the leading white traders in the northwest, spent most of his life among the western Indians, and was long a U.S. agent among them (appointed in 1812). This document was a report sent to his chief, Gen. William Clark (of the Lewis and Clark expedition). He describes the origin of the Sauks and Foxes (according to their traditions), their government and alliances, traits of character; customs in war, marriage, burial, etc.; family life, practices in sickness, beliefs, mode of life, amusements, etc.; their relations with other tribes; and their language, with a considerable vocabulary.

℀ BIOGRAPHY OF NICOLAS PERROT, prepared by the editor from the notes of Father Tailhan.

℀ INDIAN SOCIAL ORGANIZATION, mental and moral traits, and religious beliefs; and accounts of three remarkable religious movements among Indians, by various writers.

℀ LETTERS DESCRIBING THE CHARACTER AND PRESENT CONDITION of the Sioux, Potawatomi, and Winnebago tribes. Written for this work by missionaries and others.

℀ BIBLIOGRAPHY. An unusually extensive bibliography, annotated as to authority, value, field covered, etc., has been included.

℀ AN EXHAUSTIVE ANALYTICAL INDEX concludes the second volume.

Translations and Summary

THE translations from the French are made with great care for accuracy; the documents in English are faithful reproductions of the originals. All are fully annotated with special reference to the need of students for information of the best available results of modern historical and ethnological research.

THESE WRITINGS, now for the first time made accessible to readers and students, form A VALUABLE ADDITION TO OUR SCANTY LITERATURE ON THE INDIAN TRIBES OF THE UPPER MISSISSIPPI REGION.

PERROT and La Potherie describe these tribes as they were in the beginning of the eighteenth century; and Marston and Forsyth, as they found the same peoples a hundred years later. All of these documents contain information furnished by men who had spent the best part of their lives among those Indians, and whose natural ability, personal character, and official position render their accounts unusually reliable.

IT COMPRISES much new and first-hand material upon primitive beliefs, superstitions, legends, and ceremonies; feasts, songs, dances, games, and amusements; customs regarding courtship and marriage, naming of children, seclusion of women at childbirth, funerals, and mourning; clan organizations, and secret societies; mode of waging warfare, etc. There are detailed accounts of aboriginal life, in all its aspects — occupations and industries, mode of hunting, food, medical practice, ornaments, clothing. The writers who have furnished these documents were associated with the Indians in thoroughly practical, everyday business relations, which renders their sketches of native character unusually valuable; and after reading these it is much easier to understand the dealings of the Indians with English, French, and Americans, to say nothing of their own intertribal affairs. Especial interest attaches to the accounts by Marston and Forsyth, as showing the dealings of the U.S. Government with the western tribes at so early a day, and the attempt to regulate the Indian trade.

3nòian Cribes

THE more important of the tribes herein described are: Algonkins; Amikoues (or Beavers); Assiniboins; Chippewas (or Ojibwas, or Sauteurs); Crees (or Kiristinons); Foxes (or Outagamies, or Musquakies, or Rénards); Hurons; Illinois confederacy; Iowas (or Ayoës); Iroquois (including the Senecas, Onondagas, etc.; the Five Nations); Kickapoo; Mascoutens; Menominees; Miamis; Missisakis; Nepissings; Ottawas; Potawatomis; Sauks (or Sakis) Shawnees; Sioux tribes (especially the Dakotas); Winnebagoes; Wyandots (or Tobacco Hurons).

THE WORK as a whole constitutes a general history of the Indian tribes of the Northwest and region of the Great Lakes, from their first intercourse with civilization to 1825. It also furnishes much valuable material relating to the early history of the French and British in the Northwest, of Canada, and the region of the Great Lakes—the fur-traders, *coureurs de bois*, guides, explorers, etc.

THE various narratives and accounts are written in an exceedingly interesting manner, and even to the general reader are of absorbing interest. The volumes are a desirable addition to school and college libraries as collateral and supplementary reading.

"[PERROT'S] facility in acquiring the Indian languages, his natural eloquence, the blending of heroism, and hardiness, of coolness and generosity, acquired for him the confidence, and affection of a great number of tribes. His work has, therefore, a different value than the relations of the missionary fathers, regarding the Indian tribes two centuries ago."—Thomas W. Field's *Indian Bibliography*.

"This manuscript is of great importance as it throws much light on Indian trade, the *coureurs de bois*, etc."—Larned's *Literature of American History*.

"Il [La Potherie] est une autorité que l'on peut invoquer en toute sûreté. Il est un des rares militaires français qui ait témoigné de la sympathie au colon candien. Il est peut-être le seul qui lui ait rendu justice dans ses écrits."—*Transactions of the Royal Society of Canada*.

INTRODUCTION

Richard White

Emma Blair's *The Indian Tribes of the Upper Mississippi Valley and Region of the Great Lakes*, originally published in 1911, stands like some weathered landmark along a frontier trail. It is in some ways a flawed piece of scholarship—some of its selections abridged, all rather narrowly interpreted in a conventionally Turnerian way, and now dated by the editor's desire to interpret her sources as traces of the progress from savagery to civilization—but its flaws are also part of its importance and attraction. The volume marks not only a particular trail of western and Indian history, but the passage of scholars as well as explorers and agents of empire upon it. Blair includes the seventeenth-century memoir of Nicolas Perrot and the eighteenth-century history of Claude Charles Le Roy, Bacqueville de la Potherie, as well as nineteenth-century reports by Morrell Marston and Thomas Forsyth on the Sac and Fox. She also records the scholarly editing and commentary on these works in the nineteenth- and early twentieth century.

What you have before you, then, in this new Bison Books edition, is a sedimented piece of scholarship in which Blair's preface and its interpretation, as well as her editorial selection, are merely the final markings of the early twentieth century. Looking at Blair's *Indian Tribes* almost archaeologically, reading it as a palimpsest by peeling away the various layers of scholarship and authorship can serve as both an introduction to the work and a guide to using it. Since historians, unlike archaeologists, have the ability to skip directly to the bottom layer, I will begin with the people whom Blair's first authors recorded: the various Algonquian, Iroquoian and Siouan-speaking peoples of the seventeenth-century Great Lakes region whom Perrot and La Potherie, Marston, and Forsyth describe.

Blair's volume is about Indian peoples, but it is a history written by outsiders. The voices of Great Lakes Indians appear repeatedly in these accounts, particularly those of Nicolas Perrot and Claude Charles Le Roy, Bacqueville de la Potherie, but these are voices most significantly mediated and interpreted by Frenchmen and Americans, all of whom, in different ways, could claim direct experience with the people about whom they wrote. They each created histories that are in many ways unique.

Perrot and La Potherie, whose accounts form the heart of this book, are in some cases the sole source and in other cases the fullest source on the events which they record. Out of their own experience, they fashioned accounts of Indian peoples that have shaped all subsequent interpretations of the early history of contact between Europeans and Indians in the region. It is nearly impossible to write of this important era without depending on Perrot and La Potherie. They, along with the *Jesuit Relations* and other travel accounts and memoirs, form the major sources for the mid-seventeenth century before official French sources become more abundant.

Of the two Frenchmen, Nicolas Perrot is the more significant and fascinating figure. Perrot was born in France about 1644 and came to New France in 1660 as a young donné, a lay servant, of the Jesuits. The Jesuits gave him the opportunity to visit Indians and learn their languages, and after leaving the Jesuits he traveled among the Fox and Potawatomis in 1665. In 1667 he became a partner in a trading company and embarked on a career that would make him a critical mediator between Indians and French in the region. He journeyed regularly to the West until he married in 1677, but even after his marriage he spent much of his time in the Great Lakes region until 1698.[1]

Perrot played a particularly important role in the 1680s. He became what might be called a French chief—an equivalent of the medal chiefs who arose among Great Lakes Indians and gained influence through their dealing with Europeans. Much of his standing in French society came from his ability to deal with Indian peoples. He was one of Governor Le Febvre de La Barre's chosen emissaries to bring New France's western allies into the war against the Iroquois in 1684. He mediated an important peace between the Fox and the neighboring Ojibwas. He opened a fur trading post among the Sioux and served as an interpreter when the French negotiated a peace with the Onondaga chief Otreouti (La Grande Gueule). With renewed war against the Iroquois in the 1690s, Perrot played a critical role in the West, maintaining peace among the various peoples of the Great Lakes and securing their aid against the Iroquois. His last important official act was to serve as one of the interpreters in the great peace conference of 1701, which ended the wars between the French and their western allies on one side and the Iroquois on the other.

Perrot wrote his *Mémoire sur les moeurs, coustumes et relligion des sauvages de l'Amérique septentrionale* as a document designed to influence French-Indian policy that he believed had begun to go astray. Perrot wrote for a particular audience: Intendant Claude Michel Bégon. Written from notes compiled during his travels and his own memory of his experiences, the *Mémoire* is intended to inform and persuade. It is at once didactic and vivid. "There are both good and bad traits among the savages," Perrot writes, and then vividly and concretely describes them:

> When any stranger asks it from them, they could not receive him more kindly, no matter how unknown he may be; it is on their side the most friendly of welcomes, and they even go so far as to spend all their means to entertain those whom they receive. A stranger as soon as he arrives [at a cabin] is made to sit down on a mat, of the handsomest [that they have], in order to rest from his fatigue; they take off his shoes and stockings, and grease his feet and legs; and the stones are at once put in the fire, and all preparations quickly made, in order to give him a sweat. (vol. 1, 132)

Perrot's concrete details, the sense that he has been that stranger, give his didacticism its authority. And as befitting an authority, he closes the *Mémoire* with a suggested speech designed to return the western Indians to their proper relation to the French.

Perrot's purpose is important. In both his account and La Potherie's, Indians are not objects of study but rather active participants in a larger common history. They not only fascinate Perrot and La Potherie, they irritate them, deceive them, and actively pursue interests of their own that sometimes coincide with those of the French and sometimes oppose them. The authors are practical men interested in giving accounts that will allow Indians to be manipulated and put to French uses, but this very practical bent reveals how independent and difficult these peoples remain. Indians emerge as at once exotic and *sauvage* and yet also as critical participants in a common politics and economy with the French.

Perrot also played a key role in the writing of Claude Charles Le Roy de la Potherie's *Histoire de l'Amérique septentrionale*, only part of which is reproduced in Blair. La Potherie was everything Perrot was not: well-educated, endowed with important family connections (he was a relative of the minister of Marine, an important official in France) and by 1698 he was himself appointed comptroller of the Marine supervising the fortifications in Canada. Published in 1722, the *Histoire* consists of four volumes. Blair republished only part of volume 2. Perrot was the major source for La Potherie's volume 2, most of which concerns his activities among the Indians and reflects the general style of his own memoire. The other three volumes remain unpublished in English. Blair's decision not to reproduce volumes 3 and 4 is particularly unfortunate. Although not all the material in them relates to Blair's stated topic—the Indians of the Great Lakes and Upper Mississippi—these volumes do cover the Iroquois

wars in which the western Indians played such a crucial role and
the peace conference of 1701 at which La Potherie was a close observer. The western tribes were important participants in the conference. Blair's selection, then, gives us less La Potherie than Perrot
as filtered through La Potherie.[2]

It is Perrot's contribution that makes both his own memoir and
La Potherie's volume so useful, but it is Perrot's style, abetted by La
Potherie's, that makes them so difficult to use. Perrot paid little
attention to dates and it is necessary to try to contextualize the material in order to date it and place it in some order. Despite the
massive changes going on in the Great Lakes region during this time,
Perrot, and through him La Potherie, often treats a half-century of
history or more as if it all happened in a single moment.

It is this difficulty in the texts that added yet another layer to
Blair's work because her reproduction of Perrot's *Mémoire* also re-
produces much of the careful editing and annotation of Father Jules
Tailhan, who first published Perrot in French in 1864. Fr. Tailhan
was a Jesuit and a nineteenth-century editor without whom reading
and understanding Perrot would be far more difficult. Fr. Tailhan
steeped himself in Perrot. Based on the differences of style between
volume 2 of La Potherie and the other volumes, and the similarity of
volume 2 style to Perrot's, Fr. Tailhan suggested that La Potherie
based volume 2 of *Histoire* not only on conversations with Perrot but
on now-lost manuscripts and notes of Perrot.[3]

Blair reproduced Tailhan's original introduction and, more criti-
cally, his footnotes. Tailhan carefully collated Perrot's observations
with those of the Jesuit missionaries in their *Relations*. His notes in
effect bring Perrot into conversation with the Jesuits. Tailhan does
this for more than scholarly reasons. He is not only Perrot's editor,
he is his defender against an anonymous critic who challenged
Perrot's facts and interpretations in notes written in the margins of
the original manuscript. Tailhan mustered the Jesuits to support
Perrot. Blair reproduced Tailhan's marginal notes, although in a
condensed form, and the notations of the anonymous critic.

By the time Emma Helen Blair came to these manuscripts then,
there were already several layers in place. She reproduced the Indian accounts given to Perrot, his own rendering of these accounts
and his own experiences in his memoire, La Potherie's use of Perrot's
material to construct his own *Histoire*, and finally Fr. Tailhan's impressive nineteenth-century scholarship in explicating and clarify-
ing Perrot and, through him, La Potherie.

By this time Blair was an experienced editor and a well-trained
historian. She had done post-graduate work in economics and history at the University of Wisconsin between 1892 and 1894. She did
not complete her degree, but she did work with and come to admire

Frederick Jackson Turner, then in the early stages of his career. While at Wisconsin, she had taken a position as library assistant and history editor at the State Historical Society of Wisconsin. It was a treasure trove of historical sources and an important intellectual center in its own right. At the State Historical Society she had assisted Reuben Gold Thwaites in the massive job of translating and editing the *Jesuit Relations*, and then moved on to edit *The Philippine Islands, 1493–1898, 1903–1907.* Her last work would be *The Indian Tribes of the Upper Mississippi Valley and Region of the Great Lakes,* published in 1911. She died the same year.[4]

Blair created the present volume by combining Perrot (as edited by Tailhan) with selections from La Potherie and by adding two more accounts: Major Morrell Marston's 1820 report on the Sac and Fox and Thomas Forsyth's 1827 "An account of the Manners and Customs of the Sauk and Fox Nations of Indians Tradition." She provided ethnographic notes of her own, relying largely on the Smithsonian's original *Handbook of North American Indians.* And, finally, she added a set of appendices in the form of both ethnological notes and contemporary letters from "missionaries and other competent observers" that described the condition of the Sioux, Potawatomis, and Winnebagoes.

Morrell Marston was a military officer who knew the Sac and Fox by virtue of his command at Fort Armstrong on the Mississippi, but Thomas Forsyth could stand in some ways as a nineteenth-century Perrot. Born in 1771 at Detroit, in the heart of Great Lakes Indian country, he entered the fur trade in 1790. He became an important American Indian subagent during the War of 1812, helping to keep the Potawatomis neutral. He became American agent at Fort Armstrong near Rock Island in 1819 and there wrote his account of the Sac and Fox. In some regards, this account is a nineteenth-century equivalent of Perrot's *Mémoire*. It is the work of a knowledgeable outsider and describes the culture and history of a tribe critical to American policy. It is designed to produce knowledge necessary to control and manipulate the Sac and Fox, even as it recognized them as a people of importance and significance.[5]

Blair's intent was to weave the works together and render the volume "a connected and homogeneous whole." She saw the documents she reproduced as tracing the Indians of the Great Lakes from a time when "the tribes of that region [were] in a highly primitive social state, at that time entirely unaffected, or but slightly modified, by contact with European civilization" to a later period when the tribes "had become more influenced by contact with the white people, and . . . their forced exodus to the west side of the Mississippi was well under way" (vol. 1, 16–17). It is a portrayal that modern scholarship has modified considerably. Perrot and La

Potherie wrote at a time when the peoples of the region were already enmeshed in European trade networks. They already formed critical components of European alliances and were deeply affected by warfare that had disrupted and rearranged their own politics and society. Most significantly, they had been decimated by European diseases.[6]

By the time Blair combined and edited these various accounts, the older sense of the importance of Indian peoples in a common history had little place in professional historical scholarship. Blair was a conventional Turnerian, and she considered Indians less as independent actors than as obstacles in the path of a Turnerian frontier. Like nature, they existed to be subdued and improved. Their improvement is an underlying theme of this volume.

Blair seems to have conceived of her project, at least in part, as a response to both old-fashioned Indian-hating and the rising racialist interpretations of Indians in the early twentieth century. She drew on older, but still quite common, cultural evolutionary theories to argue for Indian equality. She stigmatized Indian cultures as backward and primitive, but she thought Indian peoples were equal to whites in intelligence and ability. She wanted to bring her readers to "a clearer realization that the Indian is in reality very much the same kind of being that his white brother would have been if put in the red man's place; and that we all, whether red, black, brown, yellow, or white, belong to one great human race, the work of one Creator, the children of one common Father" (vol. 1, 19). She very much believed in Indian abilities, and she very much accepted that the proof of those abilities was the extent to which Indians imitated whites. She ended her preface with a plea for support of the Indian policies of the United States government, which sought "just and humane treatment for the Indians" (vol. 1, 20).

In the end, Blair's volume was as much a product of its time as the accounts of Perrot, La Potherie, Marston, and Forsyth were of theirs. It had similar aims: it was an attempt to muster historical and ethnographic knowledge to influence policy. And, ironically, like the authors she reproduced, Blair failed. Blair's work did little to halt racialist inroads on American Indian policy and a growing conviction of Indian inferiority.[7] Blair's scholarship could not stop racism, and, in hindsight, even the programs which she so ardently approved were doing great damage. Allotment of Indian reservations led to widespread and disastrous erosion of Indian land base and to serious social dislocation. Forced education brought abuses of its own. The policies that Blair praised and that she hoped her scholarship would support came under harsh attack within twenty years.

Blair's immediate aims were frustrated, but her efforts nonetheless made available in English a set of edited documents of considerable cultural and historical importance. These accounts, first of all, continue to have an immense effect on our understanding of the societies that Europeans encountered in North America and of Indian and white contact itself. The documents allow us to get as close as we ever will to these societies. The material is fascinating in its own right, but the very sedimented nature of the book Blair created gives these accounts of Perrot, Le Potherie, and the others additional value. In reading them we can gain insight into how both scholars and the general public have culturally constructed and used Indian societies for nearly four centuries. Here are the documents which allow us to see, if we read them closely, how the cultural work of establishing and erasing difference proceeds during different times. This is a fascinating, multi-leveled book still worthy of new audiences.

NOTES

1. The basic biographical account is taken from the entry in David M. Hayne, ed., *Dictionary of Canadian Biography* (Toronto: University of Toronto Press, 1969), 2:516–20.

2. Ibid., 2:421–22.

3. Ibid., 2:423; Nicolas Perrot, *Memoir*, in Blair, *Indian Tribes*, 1:262–63.

4. *Who Was Who in America* (Chicago: A. N. Marquis Co., 1943–), 1:103.

5. For Forsyth, see *History of Indian-White Relations,* ed. Wilcomb E. Washburn, *Handbook of North American Indians*, general ed. William C. Sturtevant (Washington DC: Smithsonian Institution, 1988), 4:664.

6. Richard White, *The Middle Ground: Indians, Empires, and Republics in the Great Lakes Region, 1650–1815* (New York: Cambridge University Press, 1991).

7. See Frederick E. Hoxie, *A Final Promise: The Campaign to Assimilate the Indians, 1880–1920* (Lincoln: University of Nebraska Press, 1984).

CONTENTS OF VOLUME I

ILLUSTRATIONS TO VOLUME I

PREFACE

Among the subjects of perennial interest, not only to historical students but to the general reading public, are the customs, character, and beliefs of the North American Indians, and their relations with the white peoples who have possessed themselves of the vast territories once occupied by those aborigines. The present work is devoted to these subjects, its text presenting old French and American memoirs by writers who, having spent many years among the Indians, were most competent and reliable as authority on aboriginal life. The *Mémoire* of Nicolas Perrot (written probably during 1680 .o 1718, but not published until 1864), and La Potherie's *Histoire de l'Amérique septentrionale* (first published in 1716), have long been known to historical writers, and often cited by them; but these works are largely unknown to the reading public, as they long since passed out of print, and have never been published in English. Yet they are original sources of prime importance to students of Indian history and life; for Perrot, the most noted of the Canadian *coureurs de bois*, spent most of his life among the western tribes, and was a keen and shrewd observer – while it is his lost memoirs on Indian affairs which, as the best authorities surmise furnished material for most of La Potherie's second volume (the part of his *Histoire* which is used in the present work).

Very appropriately are these narratives of the French domination over the Indians followed by two valuable

papers on the natives after they passed under the control
of the United States; these were written a century later,
by American officials who were perhaps equally con-
versant with the Indian tribes of the Northwest Territory. One of these was Major Morrell Marston, U.S.A.,
commanding at Fort Armstrong (located at the present
Rock Island, Ill.), who in 1820 sent a report on the
Sauk and Fox tribes to Reverend Dr. Jedidiah Morse,
a special agent sent in that year by President Monroe to
investigate the conditions and needs of the Indian tribes
in the United States.   Dr. Morse's report of this mission
(published in 1822) is a most valuable storehouse of information on that subject; but it is known mainly to
historical writers, and is almost buried under nearly a
century's dust.   For the present publication I have used
the original autograph manuscript of Marston, which is
now in the Manuscript Department of the Wisconsin
State Historical Society.   This statement applies
equally to the document which follows Marston's, the
"Account of the manners and customs of the Sauk and
Fox nations" furnished (in 1827) to Gen. William
Clark, then U.S. superintendent of Indian affairs, by
Thomas Forsyth, government agent among those tribes –
a man who was considered one of the ablest of the Indian agents of his time, and was almost the counterpart
of Perrot in his understanding of Indian character, influence over the tribes, and shrewdness of judgment.   This
paper by him has never before been printed in any form.
To these documents I have added certain appendices
which, with the extensive annotations provided, supply desirable sidelights, especially on the real character
of the American Indian – all drawn from the best authorities, and presenting the subject in the light of actual
observation and scientific method.   By this treatment I

have endeavored to bring the work down to the present day, and render it a connected and homogeneous whole.

Perrot's life among the Indian tribes began as early as 1665, little more than a half-century after the founding of Quebec; and during nearly forty years he traveled and lived among the Indians – successively as engagé to the Jesuit missionaries, *coureur de bois* and trader, explorer, and agent of the Quebec government. His narrative greatly illumines the history of the relations between the French colony and the Indian tribes within its sphere of influence, and still more the character and customs of the aboriginal peoples in their primitive condition; for he was the first white visitor to several of the western tribes, and even those of the east were not yet very greatly altered by contact with Europeans. He describes the creation myths and the religious ideas of the Algonquian peoples; their occupations, modes of hunting, and sports; their marriage and burial customs; their traits of character, both good and bad. He recounts the wars between the Algonkins and Iroquois, and the expulsion of the Hurons from their ancient homes by the latter; the flight westward of the peoples defeated and ruined by the fierce Iroquois; the relations of the French with all the savage peoples; and the extension of French domination and possession toward the west. After relating various instances of treachery committed by the Hurons, he dilates on the insolence and vainglory of the savages' nature, and the impossibility of relying on them for loyalty to France; and closes by outlining the attitude and policy which the French ought to assume toward the western tribes. Father Tailhan, the first editor of Perrot, performed his task *con amore*, and was an excellent editor, even from the standpoint of our modern historical methods. He did not alter or obscure the text, or even attempt to "modernize" it; he explained all his emendations, was careful and fair in statement, and sought not his own glory; and his portrait of Perrot, as regards both character and abilities, is well drawn. His annotations were voluminous, unnecessarily so at the present time, on account of the greater accessibility of the works on which he drew; and I have therefore condensed them as much as possible, in order to obtain space for later and more scientific information – retaining, however, all that is useful to the modern reader, as well as many of Tailhan's comments on Indian character and the policy of the whites toward the dispossessed Indian tribes.

Perrot's lost writings evidently reappear in the next document here presented, the second volume of La Potherie's *Histoire de l'Amérique septentrionale*. This is occupied with the tribes west of Lake Huron, and contains much information that is nowhere else found, especially regarding the peoples along the upper Mississippi; it describes with considerable detail their customs, mode of life, and character; their early tribal history; and their relations with each other and with the French. This last feature is of especial value, as describing the nature and course of intertribal and inter-racial politics in that early period (over two centuries ago) when these great commonwealths of Michigan, Wisconsin, Illinois, Iowa, and Minnesota were still an almost unbroken wilderness, inhabited only by savage and often nomadic tribes, and explored only by a few adventurous Frenchmen – such as Perrot, La Salle, and Joliet – and a few zealous and intrepid missionaries, like Dablon, Allouez, and Marquette. These white men found the tribes of that region in a highly primitive social state, at that time entirely unaffected, or but slight-

ly modified, by contact with European civilization; and
their observations, as recorded in Perrot, La Potherie,
Charlevoix, and the Jesuit *Relations*, are invaluable as
records of early aboriginal life, customs, and beliefs, and
for the study of primitive society.

Of the same character are the relations of Marston
and Forsyth at a later period, save that in their time all
the Indian tribes had become more influenced by contact with the white people, and that their forced exodus
to the west side of the Mississippi was well under way,
before the steady pressure of white migration to the
open, fertile regions of the Central West. Marston
made diligent inquiries regarding the beliefs, customs,
mode of life, occupations, etc., of the Sauk and Fox
tribes; and he presents, besides these matters, sketches of
their leading chiefs, enumeration of the clans within the
tribes, etc. At the close of his letter, he criticizes the
government factory system, and makes suggestions as
to the best way of carrying on the Indian trade and improving the material and social condition of the Indians.

Equally interesting and valuable is Forsyth's account
of the same tribes, written seven years later; to some
extent he covers the same ground as does Marston, but
he adds much new material. He describes the relations
of the Sauk and Fox with other tribes, and with the
whites; their mode of warfare, and their military societies; their customs and mode of life; their marriage and
funeral ceremonies, and the naming and training of
children; their physical traits, and their treatment of
disease; their ideas of the universe, religious beliefs, and
mental traits; their amusements, hunting, etc. At the
end of this memoir, Forsyth presents some observations
on the language of those tribes, and a vocabulary of
considerable length.

Following these documents are three appendices: (A) a biographical sketch of Nicolas Perrot, condensed from Tailhan's notes; (B) notes by leading ethnologists on Indian social organization, mental and moral traits, religious beliefs, and some important religious movements among western tribes; (C) letters written to the editor by missionaries and other competent observers, describing the character and present condition of the Sioux, Potawatomi, and Winnebago tribes.

All these documents are of great value as original accounts of the western tribes, obtained through personal observation and inquiry by reliable and competent men, and their writings are a precious contribution to both historical and ethnological knowledge. But perhaps even more valuable to the student in those fields are the conclusions that have thus far been reached by the ethnologists of to-day, based on collected data of this sort and on their own studies of aboriginal life and thought, and considered in the light of modern science and philosophy. Much of this valuable material it has been my privilege to secure for the present work, through the generous coöperation of the Bureau of American Ethnology at Washington, the chief officials of which have kindly furnished to me not only answers to various special inquiries, but the proof-sheets of volume two, *Handbook of American Indians*, permitting me to use in my annotations, etc., such matter as I might desire. This liberality has enabled me to present to my readers the latest and most reliable information regarding many topics, which otherwise could have been obtained only by long and tedious search through many printed volumes and even in some cases would have been entirely inaccessible. With this aid, I have endeavored to round out and unify the subject as presented in the documents here published, and to place before the reader a more accurate and lifelike view of aboriginal life and character than is usually entertained by readers who know the Indian mainly through newspaper and magazine "stories," novels, and "Wild West shows." My work on these volumes will be well repaid if those who read them gain a clearer realization that the Indian is in reality very much the same kind of being that his white brother would have been if put in the red man's place; and that we all, whether red, black, brown, yellow, or white, belong to one great human race, the work of one Creator, the children of one common Father.

The deepening and growing consciousness in the world of human brotherhood, and of our responsibility toward one another, is perhaps the most cheering token of progress and upward growth in this latter day; but unfortunately one still encounters occasional survivals of the idea once current in certain quarters that "there is no good Indian except a dead one." Inhuman and brutal as this is, it has been uttered even by persons who called themselves Christians; and occasion still remains to protest against such cruel and unjust notions. Complete refutation of them is found in the many instances of noble words and deeds by Indians; in the progress made by some of the tribes in civilization and religious life; in the results of modern ethnological research and study; and in the practical application of the Golden Rule, which, translated into the vernacular, reads, "Put yourself in his place." There is of course, as every one knows, an evil side in the savage character; the history of many tribes and many individuals is blackened by duplicity, treachery, and ferocious cruelty; and there are depraved Indians, as well as good ones. But it must not be forgotten that the Indians have, with some exceptions, during most of our acquaintance with them been in the primitive stages of culture, and we can not in justice apply to them the same strictness of judgment to which we who have passed through many more centuries of evolution and progress are rightly liable; that the white man's record in the border wars and even in later dealings with the Indians, is not so spotless that we can cast all the blame on the other side; and that in no case is it right to censure all for the evil deeds of some.

The government of the United States is doing all in its power, in most cases, for the best welfare of the Indian peoples under its care; but it needs for this purpose a backing of public interest and opinion even stronger than it has thus far received, and, still more, the efforts of each individual citizen to aid, by word and deed, in securing just and humane treatment for the Indians. So long as greedy and conscienceless traders sell to them (in violation of the laws) vile whisky and shoddy or adulterated goods, so long as other unscrupulous white men take advantage of their ignorance or lack of judgment to cheat them in regard to their work or other business dealings, so long will the efforts of missionaries, government officials, and others who are trying to uplift the Indians be to a certain extent neutralized; and public opinion should be interested and strong enough to rebuke sharply all such evil acts, no matter by whom committed. I do not ask for any sentimental effusion or lavish giving in behalf of the Indians; but only for justice in all our dealings with them, and for the same humane and kind interest in improving their material and moral condition that we consider proper for the poor or ignorant classes in our white population. Let them be given a "square deal" in every way, and there is no doubt that in time they will prove themselves worthy of it.

My cordial thanks are tendered to those who have furnished information and other aid in the preparation of this work. Every contribution that I have used has been credited to its proper source, and is gratefully appreciated. Especial recognition is due to Dr. W. H. Holmes (now curator of ethnological department in U.S. National Museum) and Dr. F. W. Hodge, of the Bureau of American Ethnology, for aid and favors which I have already mentioned; Prof. Frederick J. Turner, of Harvard University (late of University of Wisconsin), for valuable criticism and suggestions; Mr. Charles E. Brown, secretary of the Wisconsin Archeological Society and curator of the State Historical Museum, for valuable aid; Dr. R. G. Thwaites, secretary of the Wisconsin State Historical Society, for permission to use some sixty pages of matter in Wisconsin *Historical Collections*, volume sixteen (translated for that work from Perrot and La Potherie by the present editor), and other courtesies; and Mr. Frank E. Stevens, Sycamore, Ill., for photograph of Fort Armstrong and various information. Thanks are also extended to Dr. W. B. Hinsdale, of the University of Michigan; Sister Lillian, S.H.N., Oneida, Wis.; Gardner P. Stickney, Milwaukee, Wis.; Hon. Francis E. Leupp, late commissioner of Indian affairs; and Dr. E. Kremers, University of Wisconsin, for various courtesies. E. H. B.

Madison, Wis., January, 1911.

MEMOIR ON THE MANNERS,

customs, and religion of the savages of
North America.   By Nicolas Perrot.

Edited and published (in French) for the first
time (Leipzig and Paris, 1864) by the Reverend
Jules Tailhan, S.J.

Now first translated into English.

Preface to the original French edition

In 1671 France, already mistress of Acadia, and of Canada as far as Lake Ontario, took possession of all the regions, discovered or to be discovered, from the Northern Sea to the Southern Sea, and from the Western Sea to Lakes Huron and Superior. Thus by a stroke of the pen, and in the presence and with the consent of some fifteen tribes hastily called together, she appropriated to herself the exclusive dominion of all North America save the English colonies bordering on the Atlantic, and Mexico, which was subject to Spain. Soon afterward (1682 and 1689), the cession of Louisiana and the Sioux country, to which the natives gave more or less actual consent, confirmed, so far as the Mississippi Valley was concerned, the somewhat disputable rights originating in that first assumption of possession. Unfortunately, the actual occupation of the territory was not commensurate with this enormous extension of nominal sovereignty. There were seven or eight thousand Frenchmen, clustered in little settlements in the towns of Quebec, Three Rivers, or Montreal, or scattered along both banks of the St. Lawrence from Cap Tourmente to the infant village of La Chine; in such condition was the colonization of Canada, even after sixty years. Further up the river, toward the west, Fort Frontenac and four or five posts of less importance, a dozen missionaries, and a few hundred *coureurs de bois*,[1] were all that reminded the

---

[1] Literally, "forest rovers" or "rangers" — preferably the former wording, since the latter is now applied to officials in the United States Forestry Service. See account of these men and their occupation, in note 164. — ED.

traveler that he was treading on French soil. On the other hand, and while the European population was receiving hardly perceptible accessions, the aboriginal race was continually diminishing with disheartening rapidity. The flourishing settlements in which Jacques Cartier in 1535 met so friendly a reception had already ceased to exist in the time of Champlain; and the numerous tribes of Hurons and Algonquins whose alliance the founder of Quebec accepted a century later [than Cartier] had, at the period of which we speak, been overwhelmed by the attacks of the Iroquois, or had entirely disappeared, or outlived their ruin only in scattered and miserable remnants. In order to find again, in the entire extent of the French possessions, even a faint image of the former power and prosperity of the savages, it was necessary in 1689 to search for it as far away as the Miamis and the Maskoutens, at the apex of the triangle which the valleys of the Mississippi and the St. Lawrence together form.

It was there, in the midst of peoples of diverse races – who had been always established in that region, the most remote from New France, or who had more recently fled thither as being an asylum inaccessible to their enemies – that Nicolas Perrot,[2] the author of the present memoir, resided almost habitually from 1665 to 1699. At first an ordinary *coureur de bois* by occupation (1665-1684), and on occasion an interpreter (1671 and 1701), he was later, under the successive governments of La Barre, Denonville, and Frontenac (1684-1699), commissioned to exercise an authority analogous to that of our chiefs of "Arab bureaus"[3] in Algeria. His famil-

---

[2] See biographical notice of Perrot, Volume II, appendix A. – ED.

[3] In 1860 the government of Algeria was reorganized. "Under the authority of the governor-general, the administration was divided between two high

iarity with the languages of the country, his natural
eloquence, and the happy mingling of bravery, sang-
froid, and generosity which formed the basis of his character – these soon won for him the esteem, confidence,
and even affection of the natives, at least so far as those
people are accessible to this last feeling. The Poutéouatamis, the Maloumins, the Outagamis, the Miamis and
Maskoutens, the Ayoës, and the Sioux accorded to him,
with the honors of the calumet, the rights and prerogatives which their own chiefs enjoyed; and not less was
his influence over the Outaouais and the Tionnontaté
Hurons. We hasten to add to his praises the fact that he
placed at the service of the [French] colony this influence, so legitimately acquired, as long as he was permitted to employ it – that is, up to the time when the
suppression of the French posts in Michigan and Wisconsin, and that of the [fur] trade,[4] broke off the relations between him and the savages.

Those long years of intimate and daily intercourse
with the western tribes had initiated Perrot in all the
secrets of their customs, their traditions, and their history. Returning to private life, and becoming master
of some leisure, he resolved to commit to writing this

functionaries, independent of each other, a lieutenant-governor and a director of
civil affairs. The former was not only commander-in-chief of the army of
Africa; he had also the administration of the military jurisdiction, exercised
through three generals of division and the 'Arab bureaus' placed under their
authority."   See Leroy-Beaulieu's *L'Algérie et la Tunisie* (Paris, 1897),
286. – ED.

[4] The fur trade of Canada was from the first a royal monopoly, usually
"farmed out" to either individuals or trading companies; but illegal traffic,
carried on by the *coureurs de bois* and even by many government officials, di-
verted much of the profit from the royal treasury, and led to numerous efforts to
restrict and punish it. Tailhan here alludes to the revocation in 1698 of the
twenty-five licenses granted by the crown (1681) to private persons to carry on
the fur trade. These were restored in 1716, but revoked three years later; and
again restored in 1726. – ED.

treasure of knowledge gradually gathered at the price of so many fatigues and dangers; and thus was composed the memoir which we are now publishing for the first time. In writing it, Perrot had in mind no other object than to enlighten confidentially the intendant of Canada [5] in regard to the real characters of the tribes in alliance with or hostile to France, and the relations which ought to be maintained with them. He therefore did not yield to the desire for making himself conspicuous, or to the inducement, at once so easy and so powerful, to vilify his equals or his superiors for the benefit of a jealous mediocrity. He relates what he knew, and what he saw with his own eyes; he relates it according to his ability, without any literary pretension, without any anxiety for the favors of a public for which he did not intend his work; and he stops writing when his supply of paper comes to an end. Moreover, he is never seen to distort the facts in order to accommodate them to the requirements of his own self-love. If he makes mistakes (and that sometimes occurs), it is in points of little importance, or in regard to a few events of which he had not been an actual witness. In short, in the memoir which he has left us the evident imperfection of its form is amply redeemed by the exactness of the information which constitutes its groundwork. The sincerity and the special knowledge of Perrot are, moreover, placed beyond any doubt by the perfect agreement which prevails between him and the best informed writers, either preceding or contemporary with him. Their accounts, not only the printed but the unpublished ones, confirm

---

[5] Referring to Claude Michel Bégon, who held office from August, 1712, to August, 1726. The intendant (usually a lawyer) had charge of the affairs of finance, justice, and police in the colony; the office was created partly to relieve the governor from those responsibilities, partly as a check on his conduct when arbitrary or illegal. As might be expected, the relations between these two officials were seldom friendly. — ED.

at nearly all points the assertions of our author. One
may be easily convinced of this, by glancing over the
notes in which I have opposed the evidence of those relations to the criticisms which some anonymous person
has written on the margins of our manuscript.[6]

It is, again, to those ancient and precious documents
that I have had recourse, whenever there has been a
question of elucidating or completing Perrot's narrative.
I have followed the same course in the notices, more or
less extensive, which it has seemed to me ought to be
devoted, either to the author himself, or to such of the
savage tribes as he mentions oftenest in his work. In
these matters, the rôle of reporter is the only one which
could be fitting for me. In order to be more faithful to
this, I have frequently substituted the full citation of
texts for the mere references whose exactness it would
sometimes have been difficult to verify. The reader will
thus have, in the more important questions, facilities for
forming his judgment from the documents themselves.

There exists but one copy (of the last century) of
Perrot's memoir, in all probability the same which was
used by Father Charlevoix,[7] and which he obtained from
Monsieur Bégon, intendant of Canada, in 1721. Our
edition is a scrupulous reproduction of that copy. When
at various times an addition or a correction has appeared
to me necessary, I have introduced it into the text, but
within brackets, retaining along with it the original reading, in order that the reader may always be able to recognize what properly belongs to Perrot. Moreover, of
these additions or corrections there is little of which I

---

[6] Notes made by this anonymous annotator will be indicated by ANON., following. — ED.

[7] Pierre F. X. de Charlevoix, a noted Jesuit historian, whose work entitled
Histoire et description générale de la Nouvelle France (Paris, 1744) is one of
our most valued authorities for the early history of New France and its
peoples. — ED.

am the author; nearly all of them appear written above the lines in the manuscript which I have employed for this edition.

In conclusion, permit me to return thanks to my friend and former colleague in the University of Québec, Monsieur the abbé Ferland; and to Monsieur Margry,[8] for a long time well known on account of his learned researches in the history of our colonies. The advice and information received from them have admirably aided me in fulfilling with fewer imperfections the task which I had assumed.   J. TAILHAN.[9]

Paris, July 3, 1864.

---

[8] Pierre Margry (1818-1894) was for many years archivist of the Ministry of Marine and Colonies at Paris, and while in that post made industrious researches in the Mss. under his charge for such as related to French exploration and colonization in North America. A selection of these was published by him (Paris, 1876-1886), under the title *Découvertes et établissements des Français dans l'ouest et dans le sud de l'Amérique septentrionale (1614-1754)*; to enable him to do this the U.S. Congress voted (1873) to subscribe for five hundred copies of the work. A large part of its contents is devoted to the achievements of La Salle, for whom Margry claimed the first discovery of the Mississippi River; a great controversy arose among historical writers and students over this question, but the best authorities have regarded the weight of evidence as favoring the priority of Marquette and Joliet in making this discovery.

Abbé J. B. A. Ferland, a prominent Canadian historian, is best known by his *Cours d'histoire du Canada* (Quebec, 1861, 1865), a valuable work displaying much historical ability, thoroughness, and conscientious scholarship. — ED.

[9] Jules Tailhan was born at Limoux, France, Jan. 6, 1816; he entered the Jesuit novitiate Oct. 17, 1841, and two years of his scholastic life were spent in the Jesuit college of Quebec. For several years he was librarian of the École de Ste. Geneviève at Paris, and long an agent there for missions abroad; and he died in that city June 26, 1891. Besides his editorship of Perrot's *Mémoire*, he wrote a few books (chiefly in his earlier years, and on theological subjects); and many articles for magazines and reviews, on matters relating to bibliography and literature and Spanish history. See Sommervogel's *Bibliothèque de la Compagnie de Jésus* (Bruxelles and Paris, 1890-1900). — ED.

I. Beliefs of the savage tribes of North America regarding the creation of the world, before Europeans had visited and associated with them

All the peoples who inhabit North America have no knowledge about the creation of the world save what they have learned from the Europeans who discovered them, and those with whom they have constant intercourse; and they give hardly any attention even to that knowledge. Among them there is no knowledge of letters or of the art of writing; and all their history of ancient times proves to be only confused and fabulous notions, which are so simple, so gross, and so ridiculous that they only deserve to be brought to light in order to show the ignorance and rudeness of those peoples.

They believe that before the earth was created there was nothing but water; that upon this vast extent of water floated a great wooden raft,[10] upon which were

---

[10] French, *cajeux*, meaning "a wooden raft or sledge;" sometimes is written *cayeux* or *caieul* in the Jesuit *Relations*. This word is still used in Canada.
— TAILHAN.

The annotations made by Tailhan on Perrot's narrative are detailed and voluminous, so much so that they occupy more space than the text itself; he carefully examined the best early authorities on the history of New France and its peoples — the *Relations* of the Jesuit missionaries; the works of Champlain, La Potherie, Charlevoix, Lafitau, and others; the *Lettres édifiantes* — and cited from these very fully whatever might throw light on Perrot's memoir. At that time these works were less widely known and less accessible than they are now, and historical students had reason for much gratitude to this learned and scholarly priest for placing before them the fruits of his researches. Since Tailhan's day, the multiplication and greater publicity of libraries and the increased activity of private collectors have made those valuable works more accessible to students; and, moreover, editions of Charlevoix, parts of

all the animals, of various kinds, which exist on earth; and the chief of these, they say, was the Great Hare. He looked about for some spot of solid ground where they could land; but as nothing could be seen on the water save swans and other river-birds, he began to be discouraged. He saw no other hope than to induce the beaver to dive, in order to bring up a little soil from the bottom of the water; and he assured the beaver, in the name of all the animals, that if he returned with even one grain of soil, he would produce from it land sufficiently spacious to contain and feed all of them. But the beaver tried to excuse himself from this undertaking, giving as his reason that he had already dived in the neighborhood of the raft without finding there any indication of a bottom. Nevertheless, he was so urgently pressed to attempt again this great enterprise that he took the risk of it and dived. He remained so long without coming to the surface that those who had entreated him to go believed that he was drowned; but finally he was seen appearing, almost dead, and motionless. Then all the other animals, seeing that he was in no condition to climb upon the raft, immediately exerted themselves to drag him up

Lettres édifiantes, and especially of the *Jesuit Relations*, in English translation, have placed these within reach of readers unacquainted with the French language. In this new edition and translation of Perrot, therefore, the editor has deemed it best to omit most of the long citations from those works, retaining, however, full references to the volumes and pages. In reading the Jesuit *Relations* (of which full sets of the original editions are even now quite rare) Tailhan used the Quebec edition; but as the various *Relations* are therein separately paged, his references to them extend in the present edition only to the chapter, which can be consulted even more easily in the Cleveland reissue (1896-1901), entitled *The Jesuit Relations and Allied Documents*. The latter edition is cited in the present annotations as *Jesuit Relations*; the former, simply as *Relation* of 1650, etc. By shortening Tailhan's annotations (in which, however, all that is really valuable has been carefully retained), more space has been secured for later and more scientific information. It may be added here that in the necessary condensation of Tailhan's notes, and of those obtained from the invaluable *Handbook of American Indians*, the exact language of each writer has been used when possible, and is enclosed in quotation marks. — ED.

Autograph Letter of Perrot

on it; and after they had carefully examined his claws and tail they found nothing thereon.

Their slight remaining hope of being able to save their lives induced them to address the otter, and entreat him to make another effort to search for a little soil at the bottom of the water. They represented to him that he would go down quite as much for his own welfare as for theirs; the otter yielded to their just expostulations, and plunged into the water. He remained at the bottom longer than the beaver had done, and returned to them in the same condition as the latter, and with as little result.

The impossibility of finding a dwelling-place where they could maintain themselves left them nothing more to hope for; when the muskrat proposed that, if they wished, he should go to try to find a bottom, and said that he also believed that he could bring up some sand from it. The animals did not depend much on this undertaking, since the beaver and the otter, who were far stronger than he, had not been able to carry it out; however, they encouraged him to go, and even promised that he should be ruler over the whole country if he succeeded in accomplishing his plan. The muskrat then jumped into the water, and boldly dived; and, after he had remained there nearly twenty-four hours he made his appearance at the edge of the raft, his belly uppermost, motionless, and his four feet tightly clenched. The other animals took hold of him, and carefully drew him up on the raft. They unclosed one of his paws, then a second, then a third, and finally the fourth one, in which there was between the claws a little grain of sand.

The Great Hare, who had promised to form a broad and spacious land, took this grain of sand, and let it fall upon the raft, when it began to increase; then

he took a part of it, and scattered this about, which
caused the mass of soil to grow larger and larger. When
it had reached the size of a mountain, he started to walk
around it, and it steadily increased in size to the extent
of his path. As soon as he thought it was large enough,
he ordered the fox to go to inspect his work, with power
to enlarge it still more; and the latter obeyed. The fox,
when he had ascertained that it was sufficiently extensive for him to secure easily his own prey, returned to
the Great Hare to inform him that the land was able to
contain and support all the animals. At this report, the
Great Hare made a tour throughout his creation and
found that it was incomplete. Since then, he has not
been willing to trust any of the other animals, and continues always to increase what he has made, by moving
without cessation around the earth. This idea causes
the savages to say, when they hear loud noises in the
hollows of the mountains, that the Great Hare is still
enlarging the earth; they pay honors to him, and regard
him as the deity who created it. Such is the information
which those peoples give us regarding the creation of the
world, which they believe to be always borne upon that
raft. As for the sea and the firmament, they assert that
these have existed for all time.[11]

[11] "The traditions collected by Perrot, in this chapter and the following,
were common to the greater part of the peoples of New France," found, with
greater or less variation, among not only the Algonquian tribes but those of the
Huron-Iroquois family (consult Charlevoix's *Histoire de la Nouvelle France*,
vol. iii, 344; *Lettres édifiantes*, Paris, ed. 1781, vol. iv, 168, 169; and Jesuit *Relations* – of 1633; of 1634, chap. iv; of 1636, part 2, chap. i). But Perrot pays
most attention to the traditions and beliefs of the Outaouais of the lake region.
"Of all the peoples above enumerated, the Outaouais alone ascribe to the Great
Hare the formation of the earth. According to them, this Great Hare (Micha-
bou, Ouisaketchak) was a man of gigantic stature, born in the island of
Michillimakinak (now Makinac, in Lake Huron), who made the first nets for
catching fish, on the model of the web woven by the spider. (*Relation* of 1670,
chap. xii; *Lett. édif.*, vol. iv, 168, 169.)" The Hurons had not this tradition
of the Great Hare as creator. The Montagnais "make him the younger brother

II. Belief of the savages regarding the creation of man

After the creation of the earth, all the other animals withdrew into the places which each kind found most suitable for obtaining therein their pasture or their prey. When the first ones died, the Great Hare caused the birth of men from their corpses, as also from those of the fishes which were found along the shores of the rivers which he had formed in creating the land. Accordingly, some of the savages derive their origin from a bear, others from a moose, and others similarly from various kinds of animals; and before they had intercourse with the Europeans they firmly believed this, persuaded that they had their being from those kinds of creatures whose origin was as above explained. Even today that notion passes among them for undoubted truth, and if there are any of them at this time who are weaned from believing this dream, it has been only by dint of laughing at them for so ridiculous a belief. You will hear them say that their villages each bear the name of the animal which has given its people their being — as that of the crane, or the bear, or of other animals. They imagine that they were created by other divinities than those which we recognize, because we have many inventions which they do not possess, as the art of writing, shooting with a gun, making gunpowder, muskets, and other things which are used by [civilized] mankind.

of the Messou or Creator, and, by a just compensation, the elder brother of the animals of his kind — that is, a hare wonderfully great and powerful; the same, very probably, who was one day put to death by a certain Tchakabesch, whose mother he had (without any doubt, through absent-mindedness) devoured. (*Relation* of 1637, chap. xi; *id.* of 1634, chap. iv.) Since I have spoken of the Outaouais, I will observe that this name properly belonged to the tribe of *Cheveux-Relevés* (Ondataouaouat); later, the French used it to designate all the other tribes of Upper Algonquins (*Relation* of 1670, chap. x)." — TAILHAN.

Those first men who formed the human race, being scattered in different parts of the land, found out that they had minds. They beheld here and there buffaloes, elks, and deer, all kinds of birds and animals, and many rivers abounding in fish. These first men, I say, whom hunger had weakened, inspired by the Great Hare with an intuitive idea, broke off a branch from a small tree, made a cord with the fibers of the nettle, scraped the bark from a piece of a bough with a sharp stone, and armed its end with another sharp stone, to serve them as an arrow; and thus they formed a bow [and arrows] with which they killed small birds. After that, they made *viretons*,[12] in order to attack the large beasts; they skinned these, and tried to eat the flesh. But as they found only the fat savory, they tried to make fire, in order to cook their meat; and, trying to get it, they took for that purpose hard wood, but without success; and [finally] they used softer wood, which yielded them fire.[13] The skins of the animals served for their covering.

---

[12] *Vireton*: "in ancient times, a cross-bow shaft, feathered spirally with thin plates of wood, horn, or iron, which gave the shaft a rotary motion in the air" (Littré). Cf. *Handbook Amer. Indians*, art. "Arrows," for illustrations and descriptions of Indian arrows, etc. — ED.

[13] "Two methods of making fire were in use among the American aborigines at the time of the discovery. The first method, by flint-and-pyrites (the progenitor of flint-and-steel) was practiced by the Eskimo and by the northern Athapascan and Algonquian tribes ranging across the continent" from Alaska to Newfoundland, "and around the entire Arctic coast, and also throughout New England; as well as by the tribes of the north Pacific coast. . . The second method, by reciprocating motion of wood on wood and igniting the ground-off particles through heat generated by friction, was widespread in America, where it was the most valued as well as the most effectual process known to the aborigines. The apparatus, in its simplest form, consists of a slender rod or drill and a lower piece or hearth, near the border of which the drill is worked by twisting between the palms, cutting a socket. From the socket a narrow canal is cut in the edge of the hearth, the function of which is to collect the powdered wood ground off by the friction of the drill, as within this wood meal the heat rises to the ignition point. This is the simplest and the most widely diffused type of fire-generating apparatus known to uncivilized man." There are various kinds of fire drill, containing considerable improvements on this simple

As hunting is not practicable in the winter on account of the deep snows, they invented a sort of racket,[14] in order to walk on this with more ease; and they constructed canoes, in order to enable them to cross the rivers.

They relate also that these men, formed as I have told, while hunting found the footprints of an enormously tall man, followed by another that was smaller. They went on into his territory, following up this trail very heedfully, and saw in the distance a large cabin; when they reached it, they were astonished at seeing there the feet and legs of a man so tall that they could not descry his head; that inspired terror in them, and constrained them to retreat. This great colossus, having wakened, cast his eyes on a freshly-made track, and this induced him to step toward it; he immediately saw the man who had discovered him, whom fear had driven to hide himself in a thicket, where he was trembling with dread. The giant said to him, "My son, why art thou afraid? Reassure thyself; I am the Great Hare, he who has caused thee and many others to be born from the dead bodies of various animals. Now I will give thee a companion." Here are the words that he used in giving the man a wife: "Thou, man," said he, "shalt hunt, and

original type. "Fire-making formed an important feature of a number of ceremonies. . . There are also many legends and myths grouped about the primitive method of obtaining fire at will. . . On the introduction of flint-and-steel and matches the art of fire-making by the old methods speedily fell into disuse among most tribes and was perpetuated only for procuring the new fire demanded by religious rites. . . Consult Dixon in *Bulletin* Amer. Museum Nat. History, vol. xvii, part 3, 1905; and Hough in *Rept.* National Museum, 1888 and 1890."—WALTER HOUGH, in *Handbook Amer. Indians*, art. "Fire-making."

[14] The racket (Fr. *raquette*) used in tennis and other European ball-games; here very naturally applied, on account of its similar construction, to the aboriginal snowshoe. The latter was in use everywhere by the northern tribes of America, and has been adopted by the white men of Canada and the United States in those regions where snows abound. See descriptions of snowshoes, in Lafitau's *Mœurs des sauvages*, vol. ii, 220-223; and Schoolcraft's *Ind. Tribes*, vol. iii, 68 (with illustrations). — ED.

make canoes, and do all things that a man must do; and
thou, woman, shalt do the cooking for thy husband, make
his shoes, dress the skins of animals, sew, and perform
all the tasks that are proper for a woman." Such is the
belief of these peoples in regard to the creation of man;
it is based only upon the most ridiculous and extravagant
notions – to which, however, they give credence as if they
were incontestable truths, although shame hinders them
from making these stories known.[15]

[15] "The Montagnais assigned quite another origin to the human race: man,
they said, was born from Messou and a female muskrat (*Relations* – of 1633;
of 1634, chap. iv). The Hurons did not suppose that our sublunary race had
been the object of a creation properly so termed; they believed that above the
sky had existed from all time a world similar to ours, peopled by men such as
we. One day a woman, named Ataentsic, fell or threw herself from it, through
a chasm which opened under her feet. At that period our earth was not yet in
existence, and everywhere, in place of it, extended an ocean without limits.
The turtle, seeing Ataentsic fall, invited all the other aquatic animals to construct an island on which to receive her, and even offered to carry upon its own
back this island which they were going to form. Ataentsic was not hurt by
her fall, and in the refuge which had been prepared for her gave birth to twin
boys, whom she called Tawiscaron and Jouskeha. The former was afterward
killed by the other, in consequence of a dispute that arose between them. (*Relations* – of 1635; of 1636, part 2, chap. i.) The Iroquois added to this, that
the posterity of Jouskeha did not go beyond the third generation, a deluge having
entirely engulfed them. In order to repeople the earth, it was necessary to
change beasts into men. (Charlevoix, *Nouv. France*, vol. iii, 345.)" But the
antiquity or the authenticity of these traditions should not be accepted without
much reserve; this is also Charlevoix's opinion (*ut supra*, 199), who is considered a careful and cautious historian. This position is supported by the
following considerations: The savages had had more or less intercourse with
the Europeans during more than a century before the missionaries and Perrot
studied their beliefs; these beliefs were handed down solely by oral tradition
(*Relation* of 1646, chap. v), in the absence of writing or pictures among the
savages; they always have been addicted to falsehood and untruth (Champlain,
Voyages, ed. 1632, part 1, 125; *Relations* – of 1634, chap. vi; of 1673, in *Relations inédites*, vol. i, 119; and various citations of similar import from Spanish
historians, in regard to the savages of Spanish America); they are incapable of
chronological calculations beyond a man's lifetime (*Relation* of Father Gravier,
20, 21). In the light of these facts, it is most probable that they had been influenced by European ideas, and had (perhaps unconsciously) incorporated these
with their genuine traditions received from their ancestors. The *Relation* of
1637 (chap. xi) says of the savages: "They vary so greatly in their beliefs that
one can have no certain knowledge of what they believe." This effect of inter-

III. Commencement of wars among the savages

Each of these men inhabited a region that belonged to him; and there they lived with their wives, and gradually multiplied. They lived in peace, until they became very numerous; having, then, multiplied in the course of time, they separated from one another, in order to live in greater comfort. They became, in consequence of this expansion, neighbors to peoples who were unknown to them, and whose language they did not understand; but the Great Hare had given to each of them a different dialect when he drew them forth from the bodies of animals. Some of them continued to live in peace, but the others began to wage war. Those who were weaker abandoned their own lands, in order to escape from the fury of their enemies; and they retreated to more distant places, where they found tribes whom they must again resist. Some devoted themselves to the cultivation of the land and produced their food – Indian corn, beans, and squashes. Those who lived by hunting were more skilful, and considered as more warlike by the others, who greatly feared and dreaded the hunters. However, neither class could dispense with the other, on account of the necessities of life [which each produced]. It was this which caused them to live much longer in peace; for the hunter obtained his grain from the tiller of the soil, and the latter procured his meat from the hunter. But eventually the young men, through

course with Europeans upon the native traditions would naturally continue and gradually develop, even to the nineteenth century. "Now this is precisely what has occurred. Today, the Outaouais and the other tribes of the West (Maloumines, Sakis, Renards, and Ouinipegs or Puans) cite, as belonging to their primitive beliefs, certain facts of which neither Perrot or the Jesuit missionaries found, even one hundred years ago, the slightest trace in the traditions of those peoples. (*Annales de la propagation de la Foi*, vol. iv, 495, 537.)" – TAILHAN.

a certain arrogance that is native to all the savages, and no longer recognizing any chief, committed murders[16] by stealth, and incited wars against their allies, who were obliged to defend themselves.

IV. First wars of the Irroquois who were neighbors to the Algonkins, with whom they lived in peace; and the occasion of their war

The country of the Irroquois was formerly the district of Montreal and Three Rivers;[17] they had as

---

[16] "*Assassin*, for *assassinat*, recurs quite often from the pen of Perrot. This expression was still in use among the French Canadians far into the eighteenth century." Instances are cited from official documents printed in Dussieux's *Canada sous la domination française*, 124, 126. — TAILHAN.

[17] "Wrong; they have never been so near neighbors as they are at present."
— ANON.

"Bacqueville de la Potherie says (*Histoire de l'Amérique septentrionale*, vol. i, 292), like Perrot: 'The Iroquois grew impatient of restraint, and . . . returned, in the following spring, to their ancient domains, which were in the vicinity of Montreal and along the river on the way up to Lake Frontenac.' The testimony of La Potherie is not to be disdained; we know, through one of his contemporaries, that he had drawn his information from the best sources. [For this] he addressed himself, by preference, to the savage chiefs in alliance with France; to Jolliet, who discovered the Mississippi; to the Jesuit fathers; and, above all, to Nicolas Perrot, whose various memoirs he has textually inserted in his second volume. (Cf. La Potherie's *Histoire*, vol. iv, 268, 269.) Here, however, has not La Potherie, following our author, confounded the *Iroquets*, anciently dwelling on the island of Montréal, with the *Iroquois*, changed into *Iroqoués* by the pronunciation then in use of the diphthong *oi*, of which frequent examples are found in Perrot — as *Illinoetz* for Illinois, Amicoués for Amicouas or Amiquois?" — TAILHAN.

The memoirs of Perrot above referred to as published by La Potherie are translated, in large part, in these volumes, immediately following the present text of Perrot. As for the Iroquets, they were an Algonquian tribe, named for their chief, who aided Champlain in his expeditions against the Iroquois (1609 and 1615); they were then living between the present Kingston and Ottawa. Formerly they had lived (1500-1530) on Montréal Island, but were driven out by the Iroquois and most of them adopted into the ranks of their conquerors. For history of this tribe, and sketch of changes in tribal supremacy on the St. Lawrence, see *Jesuit Relations* (Cleveland, 1896-1901), vol. v, 288-290; cf. other references found in index to that work. — ED.

neighbors the Algonkins,* who lived along the river of the Outaoüas, at Nepissing, on the French River, and between this last and Taronto. The Irroquois were not hunters; they cultivated the soil, and lived on the roots which it produced and the grain which they planted. The Algonkins, on the contrary, supported themselves by their hunting alone, despising agriculture as a pursuit little suited to their ambitious pride, and regarding it as infinitely beneath them – so that the Irroquois were regarded in a certain sense as their vassals. That did not hinder them from trading together; the Irroquois carried to them grain, in exchange for the dried meat and skins which the former obtained from the Algonkins. The Irroquois, as being much less warlike, could not avoid living with them on that footing; and it was necessary that there should be on their side apparent submission to the will of the Algonkins.

Once it happened, during the peace that reigned between these peoples, that the Algonkins sent word to the Irroquois of the village nearest them that the latter should go to spend the winter among them; and that during the winter they would supply their guests with fresh meat, which made better soup than the dried meat, of which the principal flavor was that of the smoke. The Irroquois accepted the offer made to them. When the season permitted, they [all] set out on a hunting trip, and wandered far into the forests, where they succeeded in killing all the beasts that they encountered within the

* Algonkins (or Algonquins): a name originally applied to a small tribe living on the Gatineau River, east of Ottawa, Que.; but later it was extended to various other tribes of the same stock, living on the upper Ottawa River and the shores of Georgian Bay and Lake Huron, as far as Sault Ste. Marie. Some of these peoples were driven by Iroquois incursions to Mackinaw and westward, and became consolidated into the tribe now known as the Ottawa. From the name Algonkin is derived "Algonquian," the appellation of the ethnic stock and linguistic family most widely diffused in all North America. – JAMES MOONEY and CYRUS THOMAS, in *Handbook Amer. Indians*.

limits of the places where they could hunt in their vicinity; then they lacked provisions, and were obliged to break camp and go farther in search of game. But as the savages can accomplish only a very short march in a day – because they have to carry with them their cabins, their children, and whatever is necessary to them, when they shift their quarters for hunting – the Algonkins chose from their best hunters six young men to go to kill game for the coming of the people from both villages; and the Irroquois engaged to add to these six of their men, who should share the game which all together killed, and who should go ahead of the two tribes, with their meat. When these twelve young men reached a place where there were indications of game, some occupied themselves in making camp, while the others worked at clearing away the snow-drifts and looking for the elk-yards.[18] Having found these, they returned to their companions; and, confident in their skill and experience in hunting, they agreed together that each Algonkin should be accompanied by an Irroquois when the animals were skinned, and that the meat of these, with the hides, should be carried to the camp.

On the next day, the Algonkins, each with an Irroquois, went out in various directions; they found many moose, which they failed to secure because at that time they used only arrows; and they were obliged to return

[18] French, *ravages*, referring to the gnawed or broken branches where the elk have fed. Both the moose and the caribou in winter, when the snows are deep, collect in small bands and form "yards." They tramp down the snow to make a hard floor, leaving it surrounded by a vertical wall of untrodden snow. They make it in a dense thicket, with abundance of shrubbery yielding the favorite food; and from the shrubs they bite the twigs and strip off the bark, even that of the large trees as far up as they can reach. When all the food in this yard is consumed, they make another, in some place where a fresh supply of food may be found. See descriptions of these yards and their formation, in *Canada Naturalist and Geologist* (Montreal, 1857), vol. i, 64, 65; and J. D. Caton's *Antelope and Deer of America* (New York, 2nd ed.; 1881?), 349. — ED.

to camp without having obtained any game. They went again to that place on the following day, but had no better success. But the Irroquois, who were careful to remember the manner in which the Algonkins made their approaches [on the game], demanded their consent to go and hunt by themselves. The Algonkins replied very haughtily that they were astounded that the Irroquois should presume to expect that they could kill beasts, since the Algonkins themselves had not been able to do so. But the Irroquois, without consulting them further on this point, set out on the morrow to do their own hunting, without the Algonkins; and finally arrived at their camp, laden with meat. The others, who had accomplished nothing, when they saw that those whom they had despised now had the advantage, resolved to take their lives, and did so; for one day, when the Irroquois were asleep, the Algonkins murdered them, and covered up their bodies with snow. As for the meat, they dried it, that it might be less heavy to carry, and went to meet their people. When they were asked what had become of their companions, they replied that the latter were all lost in the icy waters of a river which they had passed; and, in order to give more color to this falsehood, they broke a hole in a large ice-field in order to show inquirers the place where these men had been drowned. The Algonkins made a liberal division of the meat, and gave the greater part of it to the Irroquois. They encamped all together in that locality, and spent the rest of the winter there in hunting, without any tidings of the murder which had been committed there.

When the snows began to melt toward spring, the bodies of those dead men caused an insupportable stench in the camp, which led to the discovery of the murders. The Irroquois made complaint of the crime to the chief

of the Algonkins, who rendered them no justice therefor; but with a threatening countenance he told them
that he was very near driving them out of their own
country, and even entirely exterminating them, and that
it was only through pity and compassion that he spared
their lives. The Irroquois decided to retire quietly,
without making any answer to this speech of the Algonkin chief; but they immediately sent information to the
[other] Irroquois allied to them of the threats which
had just been made against them, and of the murder
that had been committed. They then resolved to take
vengeance, and not long afterward they broke the heads
of some Algonkins whom they met in a lonely place.
But, not being able to avert the consequences which this
deed drew upon them from the Algonkins, those Irroquois departed [from the Algonkins], and fled for refuge
toward Lake Erien [i. e., Erie], where the Chaoüanons [19]
dwelt; these made war on the Irroquois, and compelled
them to go to settle along Lake Ontario, which is now
called Lake Frontenac. After having maintained during several years a war against the Chaoüanons and their
allies, the Irroquois took refuge in Carolina, [20] where
they are at this time. All these hostilities were very useful in accustoming the Irroquois to war, and rendering
them able to fight with the Algonkins, who before that

[19] *Chaoüanons*: the French form of the English appellation Shawnees. When
first known by the latter people, this tribe were living in Kentucky; later, they
made frequent migrations – across the mountains into Virginia and the Carolinas;
then (about 1683) into Ohio; and, some fifteen years later, to Pennsylvania.
By the middle of the eighteenth century, most of them were in Ohio; and about
1832 they were removed by the Federal government to a reservation in Kansas.
The Shawnee dialect seems to have reached a high development, advanced
beyond other Algonquian tongues. – ED.

[20] "Since they [the Iroquois] have approached Lake Ontario, they have not
returned to the South." – ANON.

"This criticism is entirely justified; it was, in fact, the Chaouanons who,
conquered by the Iroquois, took refuge in Carolina, as Perrot himself affirms a
little farther on." – TAILHAN.

time carried terror among them. They have completed the destruction of the Algonkins, and many other tribes have proved the valor of these redoubtable enemies, who have compelled those peoples to abandon their own lands.[21]

V. Religion, or rather superstition, of the savage tribes

It cannot be said that the savages profess any doctrine; and it is certain that they do not, so to speak, follow any religion.[22] They only observe some Jewish

---

[21] "Charlevoix and La Potherie reproduce, in abridged form, the narrative of Perrot. The former remarks, with good reason, that of all the primitive history of the Iroquois and Algonquins this event is the only one the account of which has come down to us clothed with some probability — let us add, and the only one of which we have knowledge. Charlevoix does not venture to determine its time, but he supposes it to be not very remote. A passage from the *Relation* of 1660 (chap. ii) leads me to believe that this strife broke out in the second half of the sixteenth century, and that it occurred chiefly between the Agniers and the Algonquins. Every one knows that the Iroquois confederation was composed of the following five tribes: the Agniers (Mohawks, of the English), the Onneyouts (Oneidas), the Onontagués (Onondagas), the Goyogouins (Cayugas), and the Tsonnontouans (Senecas). Cf. Charlevoix's *Histoire*, vol. iii, 199; La Potherie's *Histoire*, vol. i, 289; and Ferland's *Cours d'histoire du Canada*, vol. i, 94." — TAILHAN.

[22] "The earliest and most trustworthy writers of New France are, in regard to the absence of all that is properly called religion among the diverse peoples of this region, entirely in accord with our author. 'There is no law among them, and they do not know what it is to adore God and to pray to him, living like the brute beasts.' (Champlain, *Voyages*, 126.)" (Similar opinions may be found in Biard's *Relation*, chap. viii; *Relation* of 1626; *id.* of 1648, chap. xvi; *Lett. édif.*, vol. vi, 330, and vii, 6.) "Among the savages who had any religion, it was only a coarse fetichism, the practices of which were most commonly reduced to dances, fastings, and feasts; and these were in almost every case regulated by the dream, interpreted by the sorcerers of the tribe." More detailed accounts of the superstitions of the savages are given in the relations of the missionaries, as noted in the following references: The religious ideas of the natives of Acadia are described in Biard's *Relation*; of the lower Algonquins [i.e., those on the St. Lawrence River], in the *Relation* of 1634 (chap. iv); of the Outaouais, in the *Relation* of 1667 (chap. v), and in a letter of Father Rasles (*Lett. édif.*, vol. vi, 173); of the Hurons and Iroquois in the *Relations* of 1636 (chap. iii), 1648 (chaps. xii-xvi), and 1670 (chap. ix); of the Kilistinons and

customs,[23] for they have certain feasts at which they
make no use of a knife for cutting their cooked meat,
which they devour with their teeth. The women have
also a custom, when they bring their children into the
world, of spending a month without entering the husband's cabin; and during all that time they cannot even
eat there with the men, or eat food which has been prepared by men's hands. It is for this reason that the
women cook their own food separately.[24]

The savages – I mean those who are not converted [to
Christianity] – recognize as principal divinities only the
Great Hare, the sun, and the devils. They oftenest invoke the Great Hare, because they revere and adore him
as the creator of the world; they reverence the sun as
the author of light; but if they place the devils among
their divinities, and invoke them, it is because they are
afraid of them, and in the invocations which they make

Sauteurs, in the *Relations* of 1667 (chap. xiii), and 1670 (chap. x); of the
Maloumines, or Wild Oats tribe, in the *Relation* of 1674 (in *Relations inédites*,
vol. i, 224); of the peoples who dwelt at the head of Green Bay, or Bay of the
Puants, in the *Relation* of 1672 (chap. ii); of the Illinois, in the *Relation* of
1671 (chap. iv), and a letter of Father Marest (*Lett. édif.*, vol. vi, 330); and,
finally, of the Miamis, in a letter of Father Beschefer (then unpublished, dated
Oct. 21, 1683, from which a short extract is given). "If any reader is surprised
at the silence maintained by Perrot in regard to the belief of the savages in a
supreme God or Great Spirit, I would remind him that the Outaouais, according
to the testimony of Father Allouez (who had long been associated with them),
'did not recognize any sovereign ruler of heaven and earth' (*Relation* of 1667,
chap. v). Now it is the Outaouais to whom Perrot specially devotes himself in
this part of his memoir." These citations are fortified by others from missionaries among the tribes in Spanish America. Other accounts of the religion
of the Canadian savages may be found in Charlevoix's *Histoire*, vol. iii, 343 ff.,
and in Ferland's *Cours d'histoire*, vol. i, 97 ff. – TAILHAN.

The letter by Beschefer above mentioned is published in the *Jesuit Relations*,
vol. lxii; Tailhan's citation is on pages 204-207, the paragraph relating to the
superstitions of the Miamis. – ED.

[23] "On the so-called judaical customs, see Charlevoix's *Histoire*, vol. iii,
349." – TAILHAN.

[24] For superstitious beliefs of the aborigines regarding menstruation, barren-
ness, and childbirth, see *Jesuit Relations*, vol. iii, 105, vol. ix, 111, 119, 123, 308,
309, vol. xiii, 261, vol. xv, 181, 249, vol. xvii, 213, vol. xxix, 109. – ED.

to the devils they entreat them for [the means of] life. Those among the savages whom the French call "jugglers" talk with the demon, whom they consult for [success in] war and hunting.

They have also many other divinities, to whom they pray, and whom they recognize as such, in the air, on the land, and within the earth. Those of the air are the thunder, the lightning, and in general whatever they see in the air that they cannot understand – as the moon, eclipses, and extraordinary whirlwinds. Those which are upon the land comprise all creatures that are malign and noxious – especially serpents, panthers, and other animals, and birds·like griffins; they also include in this class such creatures as have, according to their kind, unusual beauty or deformity. Lastly, those that are within the earth, [especially] the bears, who pass the winter without eating, and are nourished only by the substance which they obtain from their own navels, by sucking;[25] the savages pay the same regard to all the animals that dwell in caves, or in holes in the ground, and invoke these whenever they have, while asleep, dreamed of any of these creatures.

For invocations of this sort, they make a feast with victuals or with tobacco, to which the old men are invited; and in the presence of these they declare the dream which they had when they promised this feast to him of whom they had dreamed. Then one of the old men makes a speech, and, naming the creature to whom the feast is dedicated, addresses to it the following words: "Have pity," he says, "on him who offers to thee" (and here he names each article of food); "have pity on his

---

[25] "It is because they are so fat, that they do not need to eat; the woodchucks and the whistling marmots do not eat, any more than the bear." – ANON.

The above-mentioned animals are, respectively, *Arctomys monax* and *A. pruinosus.* – ED.

family, and grant him what he needs." All those who
are present respond with one voice, "O! O!" many times,
until the prayer is ended; and this word "O!" means
among them the same as "Be it so!" [Eng. "Amen!"]
among us. There are tribes who, in this sort of solemnities, oblige the guests to eat everything; other tribes do
not thus compel you, but you eat what you wish to, and
carry the rest to your home.

Other feasts are made among these savages in which
a sort of adoration is practiced, by not only consecrating
to the pretended divinity the viands of the feast, but laying at his feet the contents of a leather pouch which they
call their "warrior's pouch," or, in their language, their
Pindikossan;[26] in this will be found the skins of owls, of

---

[26] See description of a medicine-pouch in Le Clercq's *Relation de Gaspésie*,
346-349 (translated in *Jesuit Relations*, vol. xxii, 317, 318); cf. the latter work,
vol. lxviii, 151, 153; there are also various references to the personal manitou
or fetich — vol. xii, 15, vol. xxxi, 191, vol. lxi, 149 (its form determined by
dreams), vol. lxvi, 233, vol. lxvii, 159, 161, vol. lxviii, 147 (manitou of warriors), etc. In the State Historical Museum of Wisconsin is an interesting
specimen of the medicine-pouches used by shamans; it is perhaps a half-century
old, and formerly belonged to an old shaman of the Winnebago tribe in Wisconsin. It is made of buffalo-skin, with the hair outside, and is tied with cords
of hide; the size is about eighteen by twelve inches. It contains an otter-skin,
tanned, and painted red and yellow, on which the head, tail, and ends of paws
are carefully preserved; a pair of small gourd rattles; a white weasel-skin,
with the hair on; a little bundle of tiny bows and arrows; a bone musical instrument resembling a flageolet, with incised ornaments on the surface, and attached
to a stick that is trimmed with tufts of horsehair, feathers, etc.; a section of
some animal's bone, also incised on the surface, and adorned with small brass
hawk's-bells, strips of rabbit's skin, etc.; a medicine-tube or cupper, made of
the end of a horn, used to suck out evil spirits, etc.; and another small horn, with
lines cut around it at regular intervals, resembling the "graduate" of a modern
pharmacist. All these articles were used by the shaman in his medical practice, and all were regarded and styled "sacred." One of the skins was probably
his personal manitou.

In Perrot's text occurs the word *foignes*, which appears to be a copyist's error,
as it is not contained in the dictionaries; the original word was probably *cygnes*,
and it has accordingly been translated "swans." Several species of swan
(*Cygnus*) were found at that time about the great lakes and in the Mississippi
Valley.

The *Relation* of 1661-1662 mentions (page 11) among the birds of southern

snakes, of white swans, of perroquets and magpies, or of other animals that are very rare. They also carry therein roots or powders which serve them as medicines. Before the feast, they always fast, neither eating nor drinking until they have had a dream; and during their fast they blacken their faces, shoulders, and breasts with coals; however, they smòke tobacco. The assertion is made (but it seems incredible) that there are some of them who have fasted as long as twelve consecutive days, and others for less.[27] If the dream which they have had

United States "little paroquets, which are so numerous that we have seen some of our Iroquois return from those countries with scarfs and belts which they had made from these birds by a process of interweaving." This reminds us of the feather ornaments and mantles of the Aztecs and Hawaiians. O. T. Mason says (*Handbook Amer. Indians*, art. "Feather-work") : "The feathers of birds entered largely into the industries, decorations, war, and worship of the Indians. . . The prominent species in every area were used. . . The most striking uses of feathers were in connection with social customs and in symbolism. . . The downy feather was to the mind of the Indian a kind of bridge between the spirit world and ours. Creation and other myths spring out of feathers. Feather technic in its highest development belongs to South America, Central America, and Polynesia, but there is continuity in the processes from the northern part of America southward."— ED.

[27] "What Perrot says here of the influence of dreams on the decisions to be made by the savages when there was question of war, hunting, or sickness, cannot give the reader an adequate idea of the force and extent of this superstition. Everything was permitted, when there was a question of procuring the accomplishment of dreams. For example: an Iroquois had dreamed that he was captured by enemies, and bound to a stake in order to be burned alive; on awaking, he hastened to assemble his best friends, and caused himself to be cruelly tormented – in order that, the dream being partially verified in time of peace, he need no longer dread its full realization in time of war. On dreams, their origin according to the savages, and the superstitions to which they gave rise, the reader can consult Champlain (*Voyages*, book 3, chap. v) ; and the *Relations* – of 1648 (chap. xii), of 1633, of 1636 (chap. ii and iii), of 1642 (chap. x), of 1662 (chap. iv), of 1670 (chap. vii), of 1656 (chap. ix), of 1671 (chap. iii), of 1672 (chap. ii). As for the fastings of the savages, the special circumstances in which they imposed these on themselves, and the ceremonies with which they were accompanied, cf. *Relations* – of 1634 (chap. iii), of 1667 (chap. v and xi), of 1672 (chap. ii), of 1673 (in *Rel. inéd.*, vol. i, chap. i)."
                                                                        – TAILHAN.

"Most revelations of what was regarded by the Indians as coming from the supernatural powers were believed to be received in dreams and visions. Through them were bestowed on man magical abilities and the capacity to

is about a divinity which is either upon or within the ground, they continue to blacken themselves with coals, as has been stated; but if it is about the Great Hare, or the spirits of the air, they wash themselves, and then smear the skin with black dirt, and in the evening begin the solemnity of the feast.

The person who offers it invites two companions to attend this entertainment; and they must sing with him, in order to incline toward him the divinity of whom he has dreamed, and who is the occasion of this ceremony. Formerly, when they had no guns, they uttered as many loud cries as there were large kettles on the fire for cooking the food. Afterward, he who gives the feast begins to sing, in concert with his two assistants, who are painted [28] with vermilion or with a red dye. This

---

foresee future events, to control disease, and to become able to fill the office of priest or of leader. It was the common belief of the Indians that these dreams or visions must be sought through the observance of some rite involving more or less personal privation. . . In general the initiation of a man's personal relations to the unseen through dreams and visions took place during the fast which occurred at puberty, and the thing seen at that time became the medium of supernatural help and knowledge, and in some tribes determined his affiliations. It was his sacred object. . . Any dream of ordinary sleep in which this object appeared had meaning for him and its suggestions were heeded. . . The dreams of a man filling an important position, as the leader of a war party, were often regarded as significant, especially if he had carried with him some one of the sacred tribal objects as a medium of supernatural communication. This object was supposed to speak to him in dreams and give him directions which would insure safety and success. . . The general belief concerning dreams and visions seems to have been that the mental images seen with closed eyes were not fancies but actual glimpses of the unseen world where dwelt the generic types of all things, and where all events that were to take place in the visible world were determined and prefigured."

— ALICE C. FLETCHER, in *Handbook Amer. Indians.*

[28] "*Mattachez*, painted or variegated with one or more colors; we find also *matachez* and *matachiez*. 'My fourteenth [speech, with accompanying present] was for painting [*matachier*] his face; for it is here the custom never to go to battle without having the face painted, some with black, some with red, some with various other colors — each one possessing therein a special livery, as it were; and to these they adhere even unto death' (*Relation* of 1634). 'A skin *matachée* is a skin painted by the savages in different colors, and on which they

song is offered solely in honor of the divinity of whom the man has dreamed; for each creature, animate or inanimate, has its own special song. They continue during the evening to sing all the songs that belong to their other pretended divinities, until all the guests are assembled. When every one has arrived, the host alone recommences the song which is peculiar to the divinity of his dream.

This feast is one of dog's flesh, which [among them] is ranked as the principal and most esteemed of all viands;[29] and they serve with it several meats, as the flesh of the bear, the elk, or any other large game. If they have none of these, they supply its place with Indian corn, which they season with grease and then pour it out on the plate of each guest. You will note that, in order to render this repast a solemn one, there must be a dog, whose head is presented to the most prominent war-chief, and the other parts are given to the warriors. When the food is cooked, the kettles are taken off the fire, and one of the gentlemen [*escuyers*, ironically] goes calling aloud through the village, to make it known that the feast is ready, and that every one may come to it. The men are allowed to attend it, with their weapons, and the old men, each with his own plate. No precedence is observed in their seats, but every one takes his place without any order; strangers are welcome at the feast, as well as the people of the village; and they even serve the strangers first, and with whatever is best of the food.

depict calumets, birds, or animals' (Letter of Father Poisson, in *Lett. édif.*, vol. vi, 384). 'His face is all *mataché* with black' (La Potherie's *Histoire*, vol. ii, 12, and vol. iii, 26, 45)." — TAILHAN.

[29] "If the [flesh of the] dog was the most esteemed of all meats among the upper Algonquins and the Hurons, it was, in turn, regarded by the Montagnais as the most wretched of all" — a statement which is made in some old *Relation*, but for which the reference has been mislaid. — TAILHAN.

When every one has taken his place, the director of this ceremony (who always remains standing),[30] assisted by his two companions – and having his wife and children seated beside him, decked with the most precious ornaments that he possesses; and his two companions armed, like himself, with a javelin or else a quiver of arrows – forthwith speaks in a loud tone, to make all the guests hear him, saying that he sacrifices these viands to such and such a spirit (whom he names), and that it is to this spirit that he consecrates them. He uses such expressions as this: "I adore thee," he says, "and invoke thee,[31] in order that thou mayest favor me in the enterprise which I am undertaking, and that thou mayest take pity on me and all my family. I invoke all the spirits, both evil and good, all those of the air, of the land, and within the ground, so that they may keep me and my friends in safety, and that we may be able to return to our own country after a fortunate journey." Then all those present respond, with one voice, "O! O!" Feasts of this sort are usually made only on the occasion of a war, or of other enterprises in which they engage when on expeditions against their enemies. If any Frenchman is present among them, they do not say, "I invoke the evil spirits;" but they pretend to address only the good spirits. But the words that they use in invocations of this sort are so peculiar that there is no one but themselves who can understand them.[32] They usually have recourse to

---

[30] "Incorrect; he is seated." – ANON.

"Among the Iroquois the orator delivered while standing, or walking about, the discourse which preceded certain solemn repasts (Letter of Father Millet, in *Relation* of 1674). . . It was, perhaps, in the tribal councils that the orator spoke while seated, doubtless through respect for his hearers (Biard's *Relation*, chap. viii; cf. *Relation* of 1646, chap. v)." – TAILHAN.

[31] "He says *Maunoré*, or 'I salute thee,' and 'I invoke thee'." – ANON.

"There was a somewhat similar practice among the Hurons; see the *Relation* of 1636, chap. iii." – TAILHAN.

[32] "In incantations and in the formal speeches of priests and shamans a

all the spirits whom they believe to be most powerful, and those who may be more propitious than the others to their side; and they even imagine that they cannot avert the evils which befall them – from enemies, or sickness, or any other misfortune – if they have omitted such invocations.

When the master of the feast has ended his prayers – in the attitude above-mentioned, and [equipped] with his bow and quiver of arrows, his javelin or his dagger – he assumes the most furious aspect that he possibly can, chants his war-song, and, with every syllable that he utters, makes the most frightful contortions with his head and body that you ever saw. All this, however, proceeds rhythmically; for the voice and the body are in accord at every moment with the demonstrations of his animosity, which make it evident that his courage is continually increasing, while he walks incessantly, in accord with the tones and the cadence of his song, from end to end of the place where the feast is given. Thus he goes and comes many times, meanwhile continuing his gesticulations, and when he passes in front of the guests – who are seated flat on the ground, at both sides, and upon all spots where they can see him – they respond to his song, keeping time with it, all shouting in guttural voices, *Ouiy! Ouiy!* But what is more agreeable in the measures of their song is, that at certain places therein the singer utters two or three syllables much faster than the others; all those present do the same by responding, *Ouiy! Ouiy!* more rapidly, in the same time as the singing requires. This is so regularly observed that among five hundred people together not one will be found who fails to do thus.

All the women and children, and in general all the

---

peculiar vocabulary is sometimes used, containing many archaic and symbolic terms." – FRANZ BOAS, in *Handbook Amer. Indians*, art. "Languages."

persons in the village who are not invited to the feast, repair to it in order to be spectators of the solemnity; for this they lose their own food and drink, and often abandon their cabins, which they thus render liable to be plundered by other savages, who are naturally inclined to theft.

When the master of the feast has finished his parade and song, he resumes his place, and remains in the same position which he had before. One of his companions now relieves him; he plays the same part and character which he has seen the former enact, and after he has ended it he goes to rejoin the master of the feast. The other companion also sings in his turn, and after him all the guests, one after another, who endeavor to rival one another in assuming the most furious aspect. Some while singing fill their dishes with red-hot embers and burning coals, which they fling upon the spectators, who cry out with one voice (very loudly, but slowly), *Ouiy!* Others seize firebrands, which they hurl into the air; and there are some of them who pretend to break the heads of those present. These latter are obliged to make amends for this insult to the man whom they have feigned to strike, by making him a present of vermilion, or a knife, or some other article of like value. Only the warriors who have killed men, or have captured prisoners, are permitted to act in that fashion, those feigned attacks signifying that thus they have slain their enemies. But if it should occur that one of these actors did not give anything to the man whom he thus approached in the company, the latter would tell him before all the spectators that he had lied therein, and that he had never been able to kill any one, which would cover him with confusion.

While all these songs are going on, the warriors display haughtiness, courage, and a readiness again to overcome all the perils which they have previously encountered in the various places where they have been engaged in war. At certain moments they stop singing, and those who are present shout all together, *Ouiy!* Then they continue singing, one after another in the assembly taking each his turn; sometimes three or four appear together, taking their places at each end and in the middle of the place where the feast is held. Marching from one end to the other, they meet [and pass] without losing the least cadence of their song, or changing the contortions in their faces and bodies, even though they may be singing different songs, and with different gesticulations. Those who look on follow the singing, and respond in their turn at the moment when the dancers pass before them. For it must be known that each man has his own peculiar song, and that he cannot sing that belonging to his comrade without thus offering him an insult, which would draw a blow from a club on him who had sung the war-song of another man – which is the worst insult that can be offered to him in a gathering where he is present.[33] This song cannot be sung even after his death, on the day of the funeral, save by those in his family who take his name.[34] It is, however, per-

---

[33] Cf. *Relation* of 1636 (chap. vii), and La Potherie's *Histoire* (vol. ii, 116, 117). "On the songs of the savages, see also the *Relations* – of 1634, of 1642 (chap. x), of 1656 (chap. vii)." – TAILHAN.

[34] " 'In this country they do not, as in Europe, take family names; the children do not bear the name of the father, and not one of them has a name that is common to all the family; each person has his own name – in such manner, however, that no name is ever lost if that can be avoided. Thus, when any one of the family dies all the relatives assemble, and together decide which among them shall bear the name of the deceased, giving his name to some other person, a relative. He who takes a new name likewise assumes the responsibilities that are annexed to it, and thus he is a chief if the dead man were one. This accomplished, they restrain their tears and cease to weep for the dead; and in this manner they place him among the number of the living – saying that he is brought back to life, and has taken life in the person of him who has received

missible to sing it before its owner on other than festal
occasions, provided that the singer does not remain
seated, and that it be known that in singing this song he
was ignorant that it belonged to the other.

When every one in the assembly has sung, those who
have been assigned to serve the food at once take the
dishes of those who are strangers, fill them, and place
them before these guests; then they serve their chiefs;
and to both these classes they give the best of the food.
The other guests are served without order or distinction;
they all are seated flat on the ground, which serves them
for a table; and on it they set, between their legs, the
dishes which are carried to them. Every person there
must, above all, be furnished with his own dish; otherwise he will not have his share [of the food]. In this
they hardly ever fail, the savage being naturally too fond
of eating to be forgetful on any occasion when it is a
question of filling his stomach well.[35]

When it has been decided to make a general expedition, or to form small war-parties, the commander of

the dead man's name and rendered him immortal.' (*Relation* of 1642, chap. x).
Perrot mentions, farther on, this curious custom and the ceremonies with which
this resurrection from the dead are accompanied." — TAILHAN.

In the *Jesuit Relations* are many references to adoption for the purpose of
preserving the dead person's name; see index to that work, vol. lxii, 351, under
heading "Resuscitation." — ED.

[35] "Incorrect; for they are not gluttons, but they eat a great deal when they
need it, and they fast when they must." — ANON.

"Perrot has never denied that the savages were intrepid fasters when they
had nothing to put into their mouths, or when superstition, with them more
powerful than gluttony, imposed upon them the obligation of a temporary
abstinence; but what he affirms, and what is true, is, that on every other
occasion they ate with an appetite that the heroes of Homer might envy, and
placed at the service of their hosts a voracity which did not wear out an entire
day spent in satisfying it. On every page of the old relations is found the equivalent of what Perrot sets forth in this passage of his memoir." Citation is
made from "an anonymous and unpublished history of New France, in Latin,
written about 1637," which confirms (chap. xii) Perrot's statements. See also
Relation of 1634, chap. vi; *id.* of 1635, chap. iv; and La Potherie's *Histoire*,
vol. ii, 184. — TAILHAN.

such gives a feast similar to that which has just been
described. Those who desire attend it, in order to en-
roll their names with him; for he would not be accompanied by any persons unless he had previously entertained them. The expedition which must be made is
carried out according to his orders; and while it lasts
this commander has his face, shoulders, and breast blackened with clay or coals. He is careful also to sing his
death-song every morning, when they break camp, and
does not fail to do this until he gets beyond danger or
returns to his own village – where, if no misfortune has
befallen him, he again gives a feast to thank the spirit
who has been favorable to him on his journey; and to
this feast are invited the chief men of the village, and
those who have accompanied him in his enterprise.[36]

VI.　Continuation of the superstitions of the savages

They honor as the god of the waters the Great Panther, whom the Algonkins and others who speak the
same language call Michipissy.[37] They tell you that

[36] "There were among the savages two kinds of feasts: ordinary, at which
each guest could eat as much as he pleased of the portion that was placed before
him, and the rest he could eat or carry away, as he chose; and 'eat-all' feasts,
which must be entirely consumed on the spot, and before the company separated.
In this latter kind of repast, each of the guests must eat his portion without
leaving anything; but if his strength was unequal to his courage he was obliged
to find among the other guests one whose stomach was complaisant enough to
swallow what his own refused. On the feasts of the savages, and the etiquette
that was observed therein, cf. *Relations* – of 1634 (chap. vii and xiii), of 1637
(chap. ii), of 1642 (chap. x), of 1648 (chap. xiv); also, regarding the feasts
of the Illinois, Father Rasles (*Lett édif.*, vol. vi, 175 ff.)." Father Gravier (in
his relation of the Illinois [1694]) "tells us of a singular custom of that
people: the giver of the feast had the right to say whatever he wished to his
guests, without their being able to show resentment at it." – TAILHAN.
　The relation by Gravier here cited was published in *Jesuit Relations*, vol.
lxiv; the reference is to page 165. – ED.
[37] "The Michipissy or Great Panther, elsewhere called Michibissy or Missi-

this Michipissy always dwells in a very deep cave, and that he has a large tail; and when he goes to drink the waving of his tail stirs up high winds, but when he switches it sharply it rouses great tempests. In the journeys which they have to make, whether small or great, they utter their invocations in this manner: "Thou who art the master of the winds, favor our voyage, and give us pleasant weather." This is said while smoking a pipe of tobacco, the smoke from which they fling into the air. But before they undertake voyages that are rather long they are careful to kill some dogs with their clubs, and to hang the bodies from a tree or a pole; sometimes also they suspend thus dressed skins of elk, or moose, or deer, which they consecrate to the sun or the lake, in order to obtain fair weather.[38] If in the winter they have

---

bizi, was invoked by the Outaouais or people of the upper country, in order to obtain a good catch of sturgeons (*Relation* of 1667, chap. v; Letter of Father Rasles, in *Lett. édif.*, vol. vi, 173). It was also the object of veneration by the savage tribes near the Bay of Puans (*Relation* of 1673, chap. iv, in *Rel. inéd.*, vol. i)." — TAILHAN.

[38] "This superstition was in force among the Illinois, as is proved by the following passage from the relation by Father Gravier already cited:" [The passage here referred to may be found in *Jesuit Relations*, vol. lxiv, 187. — ED.] "The Kilistinons, who lived upon the shores of Lake Alimibegong [i.e., Nipigon — ED.], between Lake Superior and Hudson Bay, were also 'idolaters of the sun, to whom they ordinarily presented sacrifices, fastening a dog to the top of a pole, which they left hanging thus until it became rotten' (*Relation* of 1667, chap. xiii). It was the same with the Amikoués (*Relation* of 1673-1679, chap. i). Among the Maloumines, at the top of the pole was placed the image of the sun, and lower down what was offered to it in sacrifice (*Relation* of 1674, chap. v, in *Rel. inéd.*, vol. i). Finally, we know through Father Allouez (*Relation* of 1667, chap. v) that among all the peoples known under the name of Outaouais the dog was among the victims most frequently offered to the manitous." — TAILHAN. [Cf. *Jesuit Relations*, vol. lxvii, 159. — ED.]

The signification and value of sacrifice are variously conceived by different peoples, and these ideas and their progress are thus concisely summed up by Tylor, in his *Primitive Culture*: "The ruder conception, that the deity takes and values the offering for itself, gives place on the one hand to the idea of mere homage expressed by a gift, and on the other to the negative view that the virtue lies in the worshiper depriving himself of something prized. These ideas may be broadly distinguished as the gift-theory, the homage-theory, and the abnegation

to make some special journey over the ice, there is a certain spirit whom they invoke on that account, whom the

theory." It will be seen that "the gift-theory was the dominant one among Indian
tribes, yet the ordeals of such a ceremony as the Sun-dance show plainly that the
abnegation-theory occupied a prominent position in the thought of some tribes;
nor can we deny that the homage-theory was also entertained, however difficult it
may be to isolate it thoroughly from the others. In all this the differences in
point of view between North American Indians and the lower classes of so-called
civilized races on the subject of sacrifice are not very great. A far greater distinction is that between the view that sacrifice produces a change in the deity
beneficial to the worshiper, and the view that sacrifice produces a beneficial
change in the worshiper himself."

Sacrifices were most commonly offered by individuals — the person desiring
to approach the deity, the father of a family, the oldest man in the village, or
the leader of a war or hunting party. "Society and tribal rites and ceremonies
were oftener than not themselves considered as sacrifices, and thus furnish us
with examples of sacrifices participated in by large bodies of people. Not as
frequently as in the Old World, and yet occasionally (witness for instance the
White Dog ceremony of the Iroquois and the human sacrifice of the Skidi
Pawnee), there is a special national sacrifice consummated by chosen individuals to whom the title of 'priest' may very properly be applied." All superhuman beings, and all supernatural beings, objects, and forces which were supposed
to possess the least supernatural power, were the recipients of sacrifices. "In
the case of the natural objects mentioned it is to be understood that it was
not the object in any case which was thus approached, but the animating soul
of each." Offerings were also made to personal manitos, guardian spirits, etc.
"In several cases, even by Christianized Indians, sacrifices were offered to
missionaries, to the crosses which they carried or set up, and to the mission
churches." Tobacco was most widely used for a sacrifice; another important
article for this purpose was corn; next came articles of food, adornment, clothing,
and implements for hunting and fishing. Animals were sacrificed — dogs, buffalo, bears, deer, elk, etc. — a white one being usually preferred; also various
parts of their bodies. In the list must be placed fish, birds (especially the
eagle) and their feathers, beans and other valued kinds of vegetal nature;
also manufactured articles, as blankets, arrows, powder and lead, knives, guns,
utensils, etc.; and red paint was used in sacrifices, in various ways. In some
cases the funeral ceremonies of a chief or other person of rank included the
killing of servants or others, in order that their spirits might serve the dead in
the land of the departed. Mutilations were practiced (as in the Sun-dance) as
sacrifices to the deity. Songs, dances, feasts, and ceremonies generally, are also
regarded as a sort of sacrifice, since their object is to please the deity. Offerings were usually laid on or near a sacred object; on various occasions they
were thrown into the water or into fire, or on the ground, and sometimes suspended from trees or poles. "In the case of food, the idea was usually present
that supernatural beings partook only of the spirit of the food and man could
very properly devour its substance. . . At most sacrificial feasts the food was
devoured by all alike. Only occasionally do we find that function appropriated

Algonkins call Mateomek, to whom they give and offer
tobacco-smoke in like manner, entreating him to be favorable and propitious to them in their journey. But that
ceremony is practiced with much indifference, their
little fervor being very far from that which is shown in
their solemn feasts.

The Nepissings (otherwise called Nepissiniens),
Amikoüas, and all their allies assert that the Amikoüas
(which term means "descendants of the beaver") had
their origin from the corpse of the Great Beaver, whence
issued the first man of that tribe; and that this beaver
left Lake Huron, and entered the stream which is called
French River. They say that as the water grew too low
for him, he made some dams, which are now rapids and
portages. When he reached the river which has its rise
in [Lake] Nepissing, he crossed it, and followed [the
course of] many other small streams which he passed.
He then made a small dike of earth; but, seeing that the

---

by shamans, priests, or some special class of persons, as was so frequently the
case in the Old World." "Tobacco was sometimes offered loose, but oftener
in a pipe, the stem of the pipe being presented to the deity, or whiffs of smoke
directed toward him, a common formula being to offer it to the four cardinal
points, zenith, and nadir successively. . . Not infrequently the sacrifice bore
a symbolic resemblance to the object desired by the person sacrificing."

"The White Dog feast of the Iroquois was celebrated five days after the
first appearance of the new moon following the winter solstice. The harvest
feast of the Southern tribes and the corn-planting sacrifice of the Quapaw were
in the same way dependent upon the succession of the seasons." Other times
for sacrifices were determined by periods of want, war, or disease, or by other
circumstances of the people, or by custom at certain seasons. As for the
objects for which sacrifices were offered, "the sum and substance of all was, as
usual, to escape evils and secure benefits;" they were chiefly for food and health,
then came fair weather, rain, success in war, preservation of the family, etc.

The consideration of sacrifice also touches mortuary customs, "the shades of
the dead being invoked and presented with food, clothing, etc., much as in the
case of higher powers. There are many cases in which supernatural beings are
said to have been men originally, but a real worship of ancestors as such
appears to be altogether absent, in spite of the almost divine honors which were
paid dead chiefs among the Natchez." Other related subjects are incense,
taboos, confession, consecration, and atonement; also charms and magic for-
mulæ. – JOHN R. SWANTON, in *Handbook Amer. Indians.*

flood of the waters penetrated it at the sides, he was obliged to build dams at intervals, in order that he might have sufficient water for his passage. Then he came to the river which flows from Outenulkamé, where he again applied himself to building dams in the places where he did not find enough water – where there are at the present time shoals and rapids, around which one is obliged to make portages. Having thus spent several years in his travels, he chose to fill the country with the children whom he left there, and who had multiplied wherever he had passed, laboriously engaged in the little streams which he had discovered along his route; and at last he arrived below the Calumets. There he made some dams for the last time, and, retracing his steps, he saw that he had formed a fine lake; and there he died. They believe that he is buried to the north of this lake toward the place where the mountain appears to view as in the shape of a beaver, and that his tomb is there; this is the reason why they call the place where he lies "the slain beaver." When those peoples pass by that place, they invoke him and blow [tobacco] smoke into the air in order to honor his memory, and to entreat him to be favorable to them in the journey that they have to make.[39] If, when any stranger or poor widow is in need near these Amikoüas or any one of their clan, they see a branch that has been gnawed at night by some beaver, the first person who finds it at the entrance of his tent picks it up and carries it to the head of the clan, who immediately causes a supply of food to be collected for

---

[39] "This tradition of the Amikouas – or, as Perrot calls them elsewhere, the Amikoués – is related, following our author, by Charlevoix (*Histoire*, vol. iii, 283). We likewise read something similar to this in the *Relation* of 1670 (chap. xii)." – TAILHAN.

Amikwa (or Beaver People): a small Algonquian tribe encountered by the French on the north shore of Lake Huron, and later driven to Lakes Superior and Michigan by the attacks of the Iroquois; but in 1740 a remnant of them had taken refuge in Manitoulin Island. – ED.

this poor person, who has a memorial of their ancestors;
and those in the villages willingly club together to make
a present to him who has done them the honor of recall-
ing to them their origin.   They do not practice this with
the Frenchmen, since these deride them and their superstition.

VII.   Marriage among the savages

There are some savage peoples among whom persons
marry in order to live together until death; and there
are others among whom married persons separate whenever it pleases them to do so.   Those who observe this
latter maxim are the Irroquois, the Loups, and some
others.   But the Outaoüas marry their wives in order to
remain with them throughout life, unless some very
forcible reason gives the husband occasion to put away
his wife.   For without such a reason the man would expose himself to be plundered and to a thousand humilia-
tions, since she whom he had wrongfully quitted, in
order to take another wife, would go at the head of her
relatives and take from him whatever he had on his person and in his cabin; she would tear out his hair and
disfigure his face.   In a word, there is no indignity or insult which she would not heap upon him, and which she
may not lawfully inflict on him, without his being able
to oppose her therein if he does not wish to become the
butt of ignominy in the village.   When the husband does
not take another wife, the one whom he has deserted
may strip him when he comes back from hunting or
trading, leaving to him only his weapons; and she takes
away [even] these if he positively refuses to return with
her.   But when the man can prove on his side that she
has been unfaithful to him, either before or since he has
left her, he can take another wife without any one being

able to raise objection. The woman cannot at her own whim abandon her husband, since he is her master, who has bought and paid for her; even her relatives cannot take her away from him; and if she leaves him custom authorizes him to kill her, without any one blaming him for it.[40] This has often brought on war between families, when [relatives] undertook to maintain the husband's right when the woman would not consent to return to him.

---

[40] "Wrong; the most severe toward this offense are the Miamis; but they do no more than to cut off the noses from such licentious persons." — ANON.

"This contradiction is offered somewhat too lightly; for among the tribes that Perrot visited, there was at least one in which the unfaithful wife was punished by death." This was the Illinois (*Relation* of 1670, chap. xi); and other savage peoples punished adultery even more severely than did the Miamis. "It is well, however, to add that, even among the Illinois, cutting off the nose was the penalty most commonly inflicted." — TAILHAN.

"East of the Mississippi the clan and gentile systems were most highly developed. The rules against marriage within the clan or gens were strictly enforced. Descent of name and property was in the female line among the Iroquoian, Muskhogean, and southeastern Algonquian tribes, but in the male line among the Algonquians of the north and west. Among some tribes, such as the Creeks, female descent did not prevent the subjection of women. As a rule, however, women had clearly defined rights. Gifts took the place of purchase. Courtship was practically alike in all the Atlantic tribes of the Algonquian stock; though the young men sometimes managed the matter themselves, the parents generally arranged the match. A Delaware mother would bring some game killed by her son to the girl's relatives and receive an appropriate gift in return. If the marriage was agreed upon, presents of this kind were continued for a long time. A Delaware husband could put away his wife at pleasure, especially if she had no children, and a woman could leave her husband. The Hurons and the Iroquois had a perfect matriarchate, which limited freedom of choice. Proposals made to the girl's mother were submitted by her to the women's council, whose decision was final among the Hurons. Iroquois unions were arranged by the mothers without the consent or knowledge of the couple. Polygamy was permissible for a Huron, but forbidden to the Iroquois. Divorce was discreditable, but could easily be effected. The children went with the mother. Monogamy is thus found to be the prevalent form of marriage throughout the continent. The economic factor is everywhere potent, but an actual purchase is not common. The marriage bond is loose, and may, with few exceptions, be dissolved by the wife as well as by the husband. The children generally stay with their mother, and always do in tribes having maternal clans." — ROBERT H. LOWIE and LIVINGSTON FARRAND, in *Handbook Amer. Indians*.

The Irroquois, the Loups, and some other tribes do not act toward their women as the Outaoüas do; there are among them, however, some men who never leave their wives and love no other woman during life. But the greater number, especially the young men, marry in order to leave their wives whenever they please. The man and wife take each other for a hunting or trading voyage, and share equally the profit they have made therein. The husband can even agree with the wife regarding what he will give her for such time as he desires to keep her with him, under condition that she remain faithful to him; she also, after having ended the voyage, can separate from him.[41] There are some of them, however, who feel a mutual love, and always live together; these are the couples who have had children; and the latter, according to the rule of the savages, belong to the mother, since they always live with her – the boys, until they are ready to be married; and the girls, until the death of the mother. If the father should leave his wife, the children whom he has had by her would not fail, when they grew up, to treat him with contempt, and to overwhelm him with reproaches for having abandoned them in their childhood and left to their mother all the care and hardship of rearing them.[42]

[41] "All the savages take with them some women on a campaign, and they have others who remain at home with the children." — ANON.

"Simultaneous plural marriage was, as a fact, practiced by the greater number of the peoples of New France. It was in vogue in the valley of the St. Lawrence (Biard's *Relation*, chap. vi; *Relation* of 1644, chap. viii; Perrot, p. 27; La Potherie's *Histoire*, vol. ii, 31; Charlevoix's *Histoire*, vol. iii, 283), and, in the great valley of the Mississippi, among the Illinois and the Sioux, and others (*Lett. édif.*, vol. vii, 21, 22; *Relation* of 1660, chap. iii)." — TAILHAN.

[42] "Idle tales." — ANON.

"This contradiction is no more deserved than that one which is questioned in the first note to this chapter. An Illinois could not separate from his wife when he had had children by her (*Lett. édif.*, vol. vii, 21, 22). As for children taking the side of their mother against their father who had abandoned her, I read something of the same sort in Father Lafitau's *Mœurs des sauvages Amériquains*, vol. i, 189, 190." — TAILHAN.

I. *Customs in use among the savages of both North*
and South who speak the Algonkin language,
or those who spring from that stock, when
they seek a girl in marriage

Those peoples make love secretly, during a rather long
time. The youth makes the first beginning, by declaring his purpose to some one of his friends whose discretion and fidelity he knows; the girl does as much, on
her side, and chooses as confidant one of her companions,
to whom she discloses her secret. The youth, having
with him the comrade whom alone he has informed of
his love, approaches at an unseasonable hour the place
where the girl is sleeping, and informs her that he
wishes to visit her. If she consents to this, he sits down
close to her, and makes known to her, in the most deco-
rous manner, the affection that he feels toward her, and
his intention of making her his wife. If the girl does
not give a favorable reply on an occasion of this sort,
after he has made his declaration, he then withdraws;
but he returns on the next day, in the same manner as
before. He continues to visit her every night, until he
has gained her consent, given by her telling him that her
mother is mistress of her person.[43]

The young man then goes to his mother, and an-
nounces to her the name of the girl whom he is seeking

---

[43] "These love-affairs are greatly exaggerated." — ANON.

"Not so, however, in regard to what Perrot says of the custom, universally
accepted among those peoples, in pursuance of which the young men went at
night to visit the young women whom they sought in marriage. The early
missionaries frequently mention it, and continually lament the dissolute acts
which resulted from such a custom. Among other accounts of this subject the
reader may consult the *Relations*: of 1639 (chap. iv), of 1640 (chap. viii), of
1642 (chap. ii), of 1643 (chap. iv), of 1670 (chap. xi). Among some of the
Canadian tribes these nocturnal visits took place by way of pastime, without any
idea of marriage (*Relation* of 1642, chap. x)." — TAILHAN.

The reader will find in the *Jesuit Relations* (Cleveland, 1896-1901) abundant information and curious details regarding Indian customs in courtship, marriage, and divorce (see index of that work, in art. "Indians"). — ED.

in marriage, with the consent which the latter has given
him. The mother then tells his father, or, if he has none,
the uncle or nearest cousin; and the two go to visit the
girl's family, in order to propose to them the alliance
with their son. Sometimes it is sufficient to make this
proposal to the brother of the girl, who will then discuss
it with their mother; and, after having gained her consent, the relatives meet together in order to settle what
amount, whether in furs or in other goods, they will give
to provide for the young people. The mother of the
young man carries to the girl's home the half of what
shall be given her in marriage, and returns thither two
or three times to carry something in order, as she says,
to pay for the body of her future daughter-in-law. During that time all the goods are distributed among the
relatives of the girl, who reimburse the mother-in-law
for part of them with provisions, such as Indian corn
and other kinds of grain; for it is the woman who takes
care to furnish her husband with grain. The new bride
is dressed as handsomely as possible, and is accompanied
by her mother-in-law, who points out to the girl the place
near herself which she must occupy with her husband,
who is then strolling in the village. When the bride is
seated, the mother-in-law takes from her all the garments which she has on her person, and gives her others,
also some goods which she carries to the girl. The latter
then returns to her mother, who again strips her of all
her finery, and receives from her all the goods that she
has; then having dressed the girl for the last time, the
mother sends her back to her husband's house, making
her a present of some sacks of grain. Repeated visits of
this sort are sometimes made very often; but when it is
desired to end them the girl is dressed in ragged garments, and it is by this means that the marriage cere-

monies are terminated; for after that she lives with her mother-in-law, who has charge of her.

Although the savages have not, at bottom, much esteem for modesty they nevertheless surpass the Europeans in external propriety; for in all their love-affairs they never utter in conversation a word which can wound chaste feelings. There are among them some who, after being married, have remained six months or even a year without intercourse, and others the same for more or less time. The reason which they give for this is, that they marry not because of lust, but purely through affection.[44]

When the marriage has been consummated, the newly wedded go together to hunt and fish; and thence they return to the village, to the cabin of the girl's mother, and give her whatever they have brought. This mother takes a part of it to give to the mother of the youth, who is obliged to live with his mother-in-law and work for her during two years, for it is his duty to do so. During all that time, she alone is under obligation to feed and support him; and if he must give any feast she pays the expense of it.

After he has served his two years with his mother-in-law, he returns with his wife to his own mother; and

---

44 "A mere story; that does not occur except when there is only an engagement between the young people." — ANON.

"But here is what I read in the *Relation* of 1652, chap. ii: 'Those peoples ordinarily behave, during the first two, three, or four months of their married life, as if they were brother and sister, giving as a reason for their mode of conduct that they love each other with the affection of near relatives, who feel a horror of carnal actions. This love of relationship is among the pagans greater and stronger than the love of marriage, into which it degenerates. If in those first months they come to dislike each other, they part without any disturbance, remaining as they were before.' Cf. La Potherie (*Histoire*, vol. ii, 20), Lafitau (*Mœurs des sauvages*, vol. i, 514), and Gravier (*Relation de la mission de Notre Dame*)." — TAILHAN.

On this point, see *Jesuit Relations*, vol. ix, 308, vol. xviii, 177, vol. xix, 69, vol. xxxvii, 153-155, vol. xl, 229. Continence was also practiced to obtain favorable dreams (vol. xvii, 203). — ED.

when he comes back from hunting or fishing he gives his mother-in-law a part of what he has brought back for his mother. Similarly, when he returns from trading it is always the wishes of his mother-in-law to which he must pay regard; [45] and his wife is obliged to do whatever work is suitable for women, the same as if she were the servant of the house. When either the man or his wife dies, the members of the family to which the dead person belongs exhaust their means, and contribute among the relatives, to furnish peltries, merchandise, and provisions to be carried to the parents of the departed, so as to aid the latter in meeting the great expenses which they necessarily incur on that occasion. In following pages mention will be made of matters concerning the mode in which they solemnize their funerals.

If the husband dies, the wife cannot marry again unless the man is one to the liking of the mother-in-law, [46] and after two years of mourning. This period the widow observes by cutting off her hair, and not using any grease on it; she combs it as seldom as she possibly can, and it is always bristling; she also goes without vermilion, which she can no longer use on her face. Her clothing is but a wretched rag, sometimes a worn-out old blanket, sometimes a hide black with dirt, so wretched that it cannot be used for anything else. She is interdicted from visiting her friends, unless they have previously visited her or she meets them when she goes out

---

[45] "The anonymous annotator has corrected all this passage in the following manner: 'When he returns from hunting or fishing his mother gives him a part of what he has brought, for his mother-in-law; if he comes from trading, similarly, and his wife is obliged,' etc. But this correction cannot, nor should it, be accepted. It is contrary to the author's real meaning, clearly expressed in the original text. La Potherie (*Histoire*, vol. ii, 30, 31) agrees with Perrot."
— TAILHAN.

[46] "Wrong." — ANON.

"Correct, according to Charlevoix (*Histoire*, vol. iii, 376) and Lafitau (*Mœurs des sauvages*, vol. ii, 439, 440)." — TAILHAN.

to search for firewood. In the cabin she usually occupies the place which her husband had while living. In whatever place she may be, she must not show any indication of pleasure, and it is not without having to suffer pain that she must thus restrain herself; because the savages, when they see the women weeping for their departed husbands, mock them and say a thousand insulting things to them. She continues to render the same services to the parents of her husband, and yields as entire submission to all that they command her to do, as she did when he was alive. Those about her show, it is true, much consideration for her modesty and for the line of conduct which she is obliged to follow; for they take special pains not to give in the least thing any occasion for grief – either giving her food, or sending to the house of her parents, out of respect to her, the best of what they have, without either herself or her family being expected to reciprocate the gift through politeness.

When her two years of widowhood have expired, if she has strictly observed [the requirements of] her mourning, they take off her rags, and she again puts on handsome garments; she rubs vermilion on her hair and her face, and wears her earrings, her collar of glass and porcelain beads, and other trinkets which the savages consider most valuable. If one of the brothers or near relatives of her late husband loves her, he marries her; if not, she accepts [as husband] [47] some man whom she is obliged to marry, without the power to refuse him – for the parents of the deceased are masters of her body. But

[47] Fr. *sinon elle en adopte un.* Tailhan says here: "From what has been said by Perrot in the preceding paragraph, we must conclude that here the pronoun *elle* relates not to the widow, but to her mother-in-law." He evidently thinks that the latter, in default of another son, adopts one, for the purpose of providing a husband for the widowed daughter-in-law; but his antecedent for *elle* seems rather too far-fetched, since Perrot seems to mean here that a second husband for the widow is chosen for her by the mother-in-law. — ED.

if they do not provide a husband for her she cannot be hindered from marrying some other man after the period of her widowhood is ended; and in leaving to her this liberty they are obliged to recognize her fidelity by presents.

If any one of her relatives who already had one wife took the widow as his second one, his first wife would be the mistress [of the household].   If the widow were not his relative, and if he did not on his return from hunting or fishing give her a share of what he brought back, this would arouse so great jealousy between his two wives that they would begin to fight over it; and, the two families coming to mutual encounter, each to support the cause of the woman who belonged to it, very grievous accidents would occur, without any one being able to interfere to prevent them or to put an end to the quarrel.   Some chief has the right only to quiet them, when he sees that in the fray there has been bloodshed. But very often settlements thus made are not of long duration; for on the first opportunity they remind each other of the quarrel, and finally one of the two wives is constrained to quit the husband, which in such case is permitted to her.   But if he has any supplies, whether meat or fish, the wife who leaves him carries away from him, with the assistance of her mother, sisters, cousins, or nieces, all that he has, without his offering any opposition; and the quarrel begins afresh over this matter. Nevertheless, one sees among the savages many men who have two wives, and who yet live in quite harmonious manner, although not relatives – for when the women are such they always live together without any strife, all that is furnished by their husband being for the common use of their family, who cultivate the land together.   But when the wives are not of kin they work separately, and

strive to be each richer than the other in grain and produce, in order with these to make presents on both sides
and maintain friendly and pleasant relations.

When the wife dies, the husband in like manner observes his mourning. He does not weep, but he refrains
entirely from painting his face with vermilion, and puts
only a very little grease on his hair. He makes presents
to the parents of the deceased wife; if he does not lodge
with them he sends them the best part of his game or
fish, or of any other gains. It is not permitted to him to
marry again until after his two years of mourning, and
when he has spent them in the manner required. If he
is a good hunter, or has some other accomplishment, his
sister-in-law or one of her cousins is given to him in marriage; but if there are none of these he accepts a girl who
is regarded as suitable, whom he is obliged to take for
his wife, without the power of refusal; for he is prohibited from marrying again save with the knowledge
and consent of his mother-in-law, in case she is alive, or
at the will of her relatives if she is dead. If he disobeyed
this rule all the relatives of his deceased wife would
heap a thousand indignities on the woman whom he had
taken without such consent; and if he had two wives, they
would do the same to the other one. The relatives
would carry their animosity so far that the brothers or
the cousins of the deceased woman would league themselves with their comrades to carry away his new wife
and violate her; and this act would be considered by
disinterested persons as having been legitimately perpe-
trated. This is the reason why very few men are known
to make such a mistake when they marry again, since
this is the law among them, although it is not universal.

The chiefs of the villages are not under obligation to
remain widowers after six months' time, because they

cannot get along without women to serve them, and to
cultivate the lands which produce their tobacco and all
[else] that is necessary for them to be prepared to receive those who come to visit them, and strangers who
have any business regarding the tribe to place before
them.   But it is not the same with the war-chiefs, who
are, like the others, obliged to spend two years as widowers; and if such a man is not a good hunter, or if he
does not please the family of the dead woman, they content themselves with making him a present and telling
him to look for his comfort where he can find it.[48]

II.   *Practice or occupations of the men*

Among the savages the men are obliged to hunt and
fish.   They usually live along the shores of the lake
otherwise called "the fresh-water sea" [i.e., Lake Su-
perior], and they repair to it in the evening to stretch
their nets, and then in the morning to lift these out. They
are obliged to bring their venison to the door of the
cabin, and their fish to the landing-place, where they
leave it in the canoe.   It is their duty to go to find the
wood and poles suitable for building the cabin, and
roofing for the cabin which stands in the regular village,
not out in the fields; also to make the canoes, if they are
skilful enough, and to chop all the wood which they
need, as it is taken for granted that this is somewhat
rough work.   When they are on the road, it is for the

---

[48] "The *Relations* of New France, and La Potherie, Lafitau, and Charlevoix,
could furnish — besides what I have borrowed from them in the previous
notes — many more and fresh proofs in support of Perrot's veracity, and of the
accuracy of his information on all that concerns marriage among the savages
of Canada; but one must keep within bounds.   I will content myself with placing before the reader's eyes the following references: Champlain, *Voyages*,
293, 294; *Relations* — of 1639 (chap. x), of 1642 (chap. xi), of 1646 (chap. x,
and part 2, chap. ii), of 1657 (chap. xii), of 1670 (chap. xi); La Potherie,
Histoire, vol. iii, 13 ff; Charlevoix, *Histoire*, vol. iii, 284 ff." — TAILHAN.

man to carry the load if the woman finds herself too heavily burdened, or the child if it is unable to follow them; when these difficulties do not occur, he marches at his ease, carrying only his weapons.

III. *Occupations of the woman*

The obligations of the women are to carry into the cabin (of which she is the mistress) the meat which the husband leaves at the door, and to dry it; to take charge of the cooking; to go to get the fish at the landing, and clean it; to make twine, in order to provide nets for the men; to furnish firewood; to raise and harvest the grain; not to fail in supplying shoes for the entire family, and to dry those of her husband and give them to him when he needs them. The women also are obliged to go to bring water, if they have no servants in the house; to make bags* for holding the grain, and mats of rushes (either flat, or round, or long) to serve as roofing for the cabins or as mattresses. Finally, it is for them to dress the skins of the animals which the husband kills in hunting, and to make robes of those which have fur. When they are traveling, the women carry the roofing

---

* Many varieties of bags and pouches were made by the Indians of the United States and were used for a great number of purposes," especially to serve in place of pockets in garments, and for a means of transportation. "The pouch was a receptacle of flexible material for containing various objects and substances of personal use and ceremony, and was generally an adjunct of costume. The bag, larger and simpler, was used for the gathering, transportation, and storage of game and other food. The material was tawed leather of various kinds, tanned leather, rawhide, fur skins, skins of birds; the bladder, stomach, or pericardium of animals; cord of babiche, buckskin or wool, hair, bark, fiber, grass, and the like; basketry, cloth, beadwork, etc." These receptacles were of many shapes and sizes, and often were provided with flaps, or with straps or thongs for attaching them to shoulder or belt, or for suspending them from neck or forehead. "Most bags and pouches were ornamented, and in very few other belongings of the Indian were displayed such fertility of invention and such skill in the execution of the decorative and symbolic designs." — WALTER HOUGH, in *Handbook Amer. Indians.*

for the cabin, if there is no canoe. They apply themselves to fashioning dishes of bark, and their husbands
make the wooden dishes. They fabricate many curious
little articles which are much in demand by our French
people, and which they even send to France as rarities.[49]

IV. *Of the children*

When a child, either boy or girl, has reached the age
of five or six months, the father and mother make a feast
with the best provisions that they have, to which they
invite a juggler with five or six of his disciples. This
juggler is one of those who formerly offered sacrifices
[to their divinities]; he will be described in the following pages. The father of the family addresses him, and
tells him that he is invited in order to pierce the nose
and ears of his child; and that he is offering this feast to
the sun, or to some other pretended divinity whose name
he mentions, entreating that divinity to take pity on his
child and preserve its life. The juggler then replies,
according to custom, and makes his invocation to the
spirit whom the father has chosen. Food is presented to
this man and his disciples, and if any is left they are
permitted to carry it away with them. When they have
finished their meal, the mother of the child places before
the guests some peltries, kettles, or other wares, and

---

[49] "All that Perrot says here of the occupations, and of the respective shares
of the man and the woman in the tasks of the household, has been reproduced
by Charlevoix (*Histoire*, vol. iii, 331-334), and is in entire accord with the
details given upon the same subject, not only by Champlain (*Voyages*, 292, 293)
but by the *Relations* of early missionaries. See especially those of 1633 and of
1634 (chap. v); also Charlevoix (*ut supra*), and Father Lafitau (*Mœurs des
sauvages*, vol. ii, 3, 63 ff., 106 ff). Among the Illinois it was very nearly the
same, except that the women there worked still more (*Lett. édif.*, vol. vi, 179,
329). Further on, we see that the Huron men, as an exception to the custom in
force among all the other savage tribes in Canada, shared with their women
the labors of the fields. Among the Tounika of Louisiana the men took as their
part all the toilsome labors, and left to their women only the care of the household (Gravier, *Voyage*, 30)." — TAILHAN.

places her child in the arms of the juggler, who gives it to one of his disciples to hold. After he has ended his song in honor of the spirit invoked, he takes from his pouch a flat bodkin made of a bone, and a stout awl,[50] and with the former pierces both ears of the child, and with the awl its nose. He fills the wounds in the ears with little rolls of bark, and in the nose he places the end of a small quill, and leaves it there until the wound is healed by a certain ointment with which he dresses it. When it has healed, he places in the aperture some down of the swan or the wild goose.

This child has for a cradle a very light piece of board, which is ornamented at the head with glass beads or bells, or with porcelain beads either round or long. If the father is a good hunter, he has all his adornments * placed on the cradle; when the child is a boy, a bow is attached to it; but if it is a girl, only the mere ornaments are on it. When the child cries, its mother quiets it by singing a song that describes the duties of a man, for her

---

[50] "The aboriginal American awl is a sharpened stick, bone, stone, or piece of metal, used as a perforator in sewing. It was universal among Indians from the earliest times, and is one of the familiar archæologic objects recovered from excavations in prehistoric sites." The awl was used to make perforations through which thread of sinew or other sewing material was passed when skins for moccasins, clothing, tents, etc., were sewed, and in quillwork, beadwork, and basket work. Other uses for awls were for making holes for pegs in woodwork, as a gauge in canoe-making, for shredding sinew, for graving, etc.," and various implements resembling awls were used for many other purposes. "The awl was so indispensable in everyday work that it was usually carried on the person, and many kinds of sheaths and cases were made for holding it;" these were of various materials, and often handsomely ornamented. — WALTER HOUGH, in *Handbook Amer. Indians.*

The primitive tools and implements used by the aborigines were of course early replaced by the improved articles of European manufacture. — ED.

* The text here, and in the last clause of this period, reads *apiffements,* which is probably a copyist's error in the Ms. used by Tailhan. The word should be *attifements,* which is not found in the lexicons, but was doubtless coined by Perrot (or else was current in his day) from *attifer,* meaning "to adorn or bedeck the person." — CRAWFORD LINDSAY, official translator for the Legislature of Quebec.

boy; and those of a woman, for her daughter. As soon as the child begins to walk, a little bow with stiff straws is given to a boy, so that he may amuse himself by shooting them. When he has grown a little larger, they give him little arrows of very light weight; but when he has once attained the age of eight or ten years he occupies himself with hunting squirrels and small birds. Thus he is trained and rendered capable of becoming some day skilful in hunting. Such is the method pursued by the upper tribes; those down here no longer use this sort of circumcisions, and do not call in jugglers to make them; the father, or some friend of the family, performs this ceremony without any further formality.

VIII. Of funerals among the savages of the upper country, and the manner in which they perform the obsequies

When an Outaoüas, or other savage [of that region] is at the point of death, he is decked with all the ornaments owned by the family – I mean, among his kindred and his connections by marriage. They dress his hair with red paint mixed with grease, and paint his body and his face red with vermilion; they put on him one of his handsomest shirts, if he has such, and he is clad with a jacket and a blanket, as richly as possible; he is, in a word, as properly garbed as if he had to conduct the most solemn ceremony. They take care to adorn the place where he is [lying] with necklaces of porcelain and glass beads (both round and long), or other trinkets. His weapons lie beside him, and at his feet generally all articles that he has used in war during his life. All his relatives – and, above all, the jugglers – are near him. When the sick man seems to be in agony, and struggles to yield up his last breath, the women

and girls among his relations, with others who are hired
[for this purpose], betake themselves to mourning, and
begin to sing doleful songs, in which mention is made
of the degrees of relationship which they have with the
sufferer. But if he seems to be recovering, and to regain consciousness, the women cease their weeping;
but they recommence their cries and lamentations whenever the patient relapses into convulsions or faintness.
When he is dead (or a moment before he expires), they
raise him to a sitting position, his back supported, [to
look] as if he were alive. I will say here, in passing,
that I have seen some savages whose death-agonies
lasted more than twenty-four hours, the sick man making fearful grimaces and contortions, and rolling his
eyes in the most frightful manner; you would have believed that the soul of the dying man beheld and
dreaded some enemy, although he was lying there without recognizing us, and almost dead. The corpse remains thus sitting until the next day, and is kept in this
position both day and night by the relatives and friends
who go to visit the family; they are also assisted from
time to time by some old man, who takes his place near
the women who are relatives of the dead man. [One of
them] begins her mournful song, while she weeps hot
tears; all the others join her therein, but they cease to
sing at the same time when she does; and then a present
is given to her – a piece of meat, a dish of corn, or some
other article.

As for the men, they do not weep, for that would be
unworthy of them; the father alone makes it evident, by
a doleful song, that there is no longer anything in the
world which can console him for the death of his son.
A brother follows the same practice for his elder brother,
when he has received from the latter during his life vis-

ible marks of tenderness and affection. In such case, the brother takes his place naked, his face smeared with charcoal, mingled with a few red lines. He holds in his hands his bow and arrows, as if he intended at the start to go against some enemy; and, singing a song in a most furious tone, he runs like a lunatic through the open places, the streets, and the cabins of the village, without shedding a tear. By this extraordinary performance he makes known to all who see him how great is his sorrow for the death of his brother; this softens the hearts of his neighbors, and obliges them to provide among themselves a present, which they come to offer to the dead. In the speech with which they accompany this gift they declare that it is made in order to wipe away the tears of his relatives; and that the mat which they give him is for him to lie on, or [that they give] a piece of bark* to shelter his corpse from the injurious effects of the weather.

When the time comes for burying the corpse, they go to find the persons designated for this office; and a scaffold is erected seven or eight feet high, which serves the

* "Among the resources of nature utilized by the tribes of North America bark was of prime importance. It was stripped from trees at the right season by hacking all around and taking it off in sheets of desired length. The inner bark of cedar, elm, and other trees was in some localities torn into strips, shredded, twisted, and spun or woven. The bark of wild flax (*Apocynum*) and the *Asclepias* were made into soft textiles. Bark had a multitude of functions. . . It supplied many tribes with an article of diet in the spring, their period of greatest need. . . For gathering, carrying, garnering, preparing, and serving food, the bark of birch, elm, pine, and other trees was so handy as to discourage the potter's art among non-sedentary tribes. It was wrought into yarn, twine, rope, wallets, baskets, mats, canoes, cooking-pots for hot stones, dishes for serving, vessels for storing, and many textile utensils connected with the consumption of food in ordinary and social life." Bark was also used for the roofs and sides of dwellings, and was woven into matting for floors, beds, and partitions; and from it were made trays and boxes, cradles, and coffins. The thin inner bark was used as materials for clothing. Bark furnished materials for basketry, dyeing, implements for hunting and fishing, tribal records, and ceremonial usages. — OTIS T. MASON, in *Handbook Amer. Indians.*

dead in place of a grave – or, if he is placed in the
ground, they dig for him a grave only four or five feet
deep. During all this time, the family of him whose
funeral is solemnized exert all their energies to bring
him grain, or peltries, or other goods, [which they place]
either on the scaffold or near the grave; and when one
or the other is completed they carry thither the corpse,
in the same position which it had at death, and clothed
with the same fine apparel. Near him are his weapons,
and at his feet all the articles which had been placed
there before his death. When the funeral ceremonies
have been performed and the body buried, the family
make liberal payment to those who took part therein, by
giving them a kettle or some porcelain necklaces for
their trouble.[51]

---

[51] "The disposal of the dead by the Indians may be classed under the heads
'Burial' and 'Cremation.' The usual mode of burial among North American
Indians has been by inhumation, or interment in pits, graves, or holes in the
ground, in stone cists, in mounds, beneath or in cabin, wigwams, houses, or
lodges, or in caves. . . Embalmment and mummification were practiced to a
limited extent; the former chiefly in Virginia, the Carolinas, and Florida, and
the latter in Alaska. . . Scaffold and tree burial was practiced in Wisconsin,
Minnesota, the Dakotas, Montana, etc., by the Chippewa, Sioux . . . and
other Indians. The burial mounds of Wisconsin indicate this mode of disposing
of the dead in former times, as the skeletons were buried after the removal of
the flesh, and the bones frequently indicate long exposure to the air. . . It
was also the custom among the Indians of the Lake region to have at certain
periods what may be termed communal burials, in which the bodies or skeletons
of a district were removed from their temporary burial places and deposited
with much ceremony in a single large pit" (see Brebeuf's account, in *Jesuit Relations*, vol. x, 279-311, of "the solemn feast of the dead"). "Cremation was
formerly practiced by a number of tribes of the Pacific slope. The ancient
inhabitants of southern Arizona practiced cremation in addition to house burial,
the ashes of the cremated dead being placed in urns; but among the modern
Pueblos, especially those most affected by Spanish missionaries, burials are
made in cemeteries in the villages. The ceremonies attending and following
burial were various. The use of fire was common, and it was also a very general custom to place food, articles especially prized by or of interest to the dead,
and sometimes articles having a symbolic signification, in or near the grave.
Scarifying the body, cutting the hair, and blackening the face by the mourners
were common customs, as, in some tribes, were feasts and dancing at a death or
funeral. As a rule the bereaved relatives observed some kind of mourning for

All the people in the village are obliged to attend the funeral procession; and, when all is over, one man among them all steps forward, who holds in his hand a little wooden rod, as large as one's finger and some five inches long, which he throws into the midst of the crowd, for him who can catch it. When it has fallen into some person's hand the rest try to snatch it from him; if it falls on the ground every one tries to reach it to pick it up, pulling and pushing each other so violently that in less than half an hour it has passed through the hands of all those who are present. If at last any one of the crowd can get possession of it, and display it to them without any one taking it from him, he sells it for a fixed price to the first person who desires to buy it; this price will be very often a kettle, a gun, or a blanket. The by-standers are then notified to be present again, on some day appointed, for a similar ceremony; and this is done, sometimes quite often, as I have just related.

After this diversion, public notice is given that there is another prize, to be given to the best runner among the young men. The goal of this race is indicated, [and the course is marked out] from the place where the runners must start to that which they are to reach. All the young men adorn themselves, and form in a long row on the open plain. At the first call of the man who is to give the signal, they commence to run, at some distance from the village, and the first one who arrives there carries away the prize.

a certain period, as cutting the hair, discarding ornaments, and neglecting the personal appearance, carrying a bundle representing the husband (among the Chippewa, etc.), or the bones of the dead husband (among some northern Athapascan tribes), and wailing morning and night in solitary places. It was a custom among some tribes to change the name of the family of the deceased, and to drop the name of the dead in whatever connection." See especially Yarrow's "Mortuary Customs of the North American Indians," in the first *Report* of the Bureau of Amer. Ethnology. — CYRUS THOMAS, in *Handbook Amer. Indians*, art. "Mortuary Customs."

A few days afterward the relatives of the dead man give a feast of meat and corn, to which are invited all the villagers who are not connected with them by marriage and who are descended from other families than their own – and especially those persons who have made presents to the dead. They also invite, if any such are found, strangers who have come from other villages; and they inform all the guests that it is the dead man who gives them this feast. If it is one of meat, they take a piece of this, as well as of other kinds of food, which they must place upon the grave; and the women, girls, and children are permitted to eat these morsels, but not the grown men, for these must regard such act as unworthy of them. At this feast each is free to eat what he wishes, and to carry the rest [of his portion] home with him. Considerable presents in goods are given to all those strangers who have previously made presents to the dead person; but these are not given to his own tribesmen. The guests are then thanked for having remembered the dead, and congratulated on their charitable dispositions.[52]

II. *The mourning of the savages, in general*

I have already described the mourning of husbands and of wives, each for the other; but not all the savages who are under obligation to observe the general mourning put grease or vermilion on the face and hair. If it

---

[52] "With the description given by Perrot of burial and mourning among the savages may be compared what is said on the same subject by Biard (*Relation*, chap. viii), Champlain (*Voyages*, 303), and, among the *Relations* of New France, those of 1636 (chap. viii) and of 1639 (chap. x). It is these sources from which all the historians of Canada have drawn – La Potherie (*Histoire*, vol. ii, 43-45), Lafitau (*Mœurs des sauvages*, vol. ii, 388 ff.), Charlevoix (*Histoire*, vol. iii, 371-376), and Monsieur Ferland (*Cours d'histoire*, vol. i, 101, 102). The Illinois did not inter their dead. The corpse, carefully wrapped in skins, was attached by the head and feet to the upper part of trees (*Lett. édif.*, vol. vi, 178, 179)." – TAILHAN.

is a chief who has died, his near relative may not converse, save in a very low tone with that one of his friends who is commissioned to express his wishes; he is obliged to avoid social intercourse and worldly conversation; he may, however, be present at feasts to which he is invited, but may not utter a word while there. When presents are brought to him for the dead man, that [official] friend receives them and returns thanks for him. It must be noted that the children and young people of both sexes are not under obligation to this general mourning; it is only adult persons who cannot excuse themselves from it. It lasts a whole year, at the end of which time the relatives assemble to adopt a person who is qualified to assume the office of the dead chief, and who must be of the same rank. As for women, girls, or boys, a similar usage prevails, [the adopted one being] of the same age and sex [as the dead]. Then they adorn themselves and paint themselves with vermilion, each person remaining in his place in the cabin. The parents of the departed man or woman are present therein, also clad with the best garments that they possess.

At the outset, three persons are requested to sing, and to beat the drum,[53] keeping time with the measure of their song. The person, whether man or woman, who has been adopted immediately enters the cabin of the departed, dancing; and after he has offered presents, composed of peltries or other goods, to the nearest relative of the deceased person whose place the newcomer has taken, he continues dancing all day to the sound of that instrument, which is ordinarily the guide for the dancing of the savages. During this time the parents of the departed stop him occasionally in his dancing, to place some adornments on his body or his neck; or else

---

[53] This drum is described in the *Relation* of 1634, chap. iv. — TAILHAN.

they present to him a blanket, shirt, or cloak; and they paint him with vermilion, and adorn him as handsomely as they can. When the dance is ended, they give him food, with various presents, in memory of him whose place he has taken, in whose behalf he danced and appeared on this solemn occasion. This man, or this woman, assures the family that he or she will always be ready to render them all the services which shall be within their power—whether to cook and serve the food at their feasts, or to discharge any commissions which may be entrusted to them. In fine, these who are adopted yield themselves to serve as attendants or servants of the family; moreover, when they have anything of value they carry the greater part of it to their master; and they regard themselves as united to this family, as much as if they were actually kindred.[54]

---

[54] The reasons for adopting a living person to take the place of the dead — thus, in Indian phrase, "bringing back the dead to life" — are given in the *Relation* of 1642, chap. xii. See also those of 1636 (chap. viii), of 1644 (chap. xiv), of 1646 (chap. x), and of 1669 (chap. vii). — TAILHAN.

Adoption was "an almost universal political and social institution which originally dealt only with persons but later with families, clans or gentes, bands, and tribes. It had its beginnings far back in the history of primitive society and, after passing through many forms and losing much ceremonial garb, appears to-day in the civilized institution of naturalization. In the primitive mind the fundamental motive underlying adoption was to defeat the evil purpose of death to remove a member of a kinship group, by actually replacing in person the lost or dead member." By a fiction of law, the personality as well as the political status might be changed by adoption, as when two sisters were adopted into different clans. "From the political adoption of the Tuscarora by the Five Nations, about 1726, it is evident that tribes, families, clans, and groups of people could be adopted like persons." The person adopted received a personal name and a kinship name (as "son" or "uncle"), and even a fictitious age might be conferred on him. In the Iroquois League, there were various grades of adoption for other peoples admitted to the confederacy, by which they were made probationers for citizenship, which would be granted after they had received sufficient tutelage. This adoption of tribes was practiced by the Iroquois in order to recruit the great losses incurred in their many wars.
— J. N. B. HEWITT, in *Handbook Amer. Indians.*

III.   *The manner in which the savages celebrate the feast of their dead*

If the savages intend to celebrate the feast of their dead, they take care to make the necessary provision for it beforehand.   When they return from their trade with the Europeans, they carry back with them the articles which suit them for this purpose; and in their houses they lay in a store of meat, corn, peltries, and other goods.   When they return from their hunting, all those of the village come together to solemnize this feast. After resolving to do so, they send deputies from their own people into all the neighboring villages that are allied with them, and even as far away as a hundred leagues or more, to invite those people to attend this feast. In entreating them to be present at it, they designate the time which had been fixed for its solemnization.   The greater part of the men in those villages who are invited to this feast set out, a number in each canoe, and these together provide a small fund with which to offer a common present to the village which has invited them, on their arrival there. Those who have invited them make ready for their coming a large cabin, stoutly built and well covered, for lodging and entertaining all those whom they expect. As soon as all the people have arrived, they take their places, each nation separately from the others, at the ends and in the middle of the cabin, and, thus assembled, they offer their presents and lay aside their [outer] garments, saying that messengers have come to invite them to pay their respects to the shades and the memory of the departed in that village; and immediately they begin to dance to the noise of a drum and of a gourd which contains some small pebbles, both keeping the same time. They dance from one end to the other of the cabin, returning after one another, in single file, around three spruce-trees or three cornstalks which are set up there. During these dances, people are at work preparing the meal; they kill dogs, and have these cooked with other viands which are speedily prepared. When all is ready, they make the guests rest a little while, and after all the dances are ended the repast is served.

I omitted to state that as soon as the hosts call for the dances to stop they take from their guests the presents which they have made, and all their garments; and in exchange for these the visitors are given, by those who invited them, other articles of clothing which are more valuable. If the hosts have just returned [from the trading],[55] these are shirts, coats, jackets, stockings, new blankets, or [packages of] paints and vermilion, even though the guests have brought only old garments – perhaps greasy skins, or robes [made from the skins] of beavers, wild-cats, bears, and other animals.

When those who are invited from the other villages have all arrived, the same entry and the same reception are provided for the people of each village. When all are assembled, they are expected to dance all at the same time during three consecutive days; and during this period one of the hosts invites to a feast at his own house about twenty persons, who are chosen and sent out by their own people. But instead of serving food at this feast, it is presents which are offered to the guests, such as kettles, hatchets, and other articles from the trade; there is, however, nothing to eat. The presents which they have received belong in common to the tribesmen; if these were articles of food, they can eat them, which accordingly they do very punctually, for their appetites

---

[55] "There is evidently a lacuna of several words here. As there is, in this passage mention of presents of which the European origin could not be doubted, I have restored the mutilated phrase thus: *S'ils reviennent de la traitte, ce sont,* etc." — TAILHAN.

never fail them. Another of the hosts will do the same
for other dancers, who will be invited to come to his
house, and see how his people treat [their guests] – until
all those of the [entertaining] village have in turn given
feasts of this sort. During [these] three days they lavish
all that they possess in trade-goods or other articles; and
they reduce themselves to such an extreme of poverty
that they do not even reserve for themselves a single
hatchet or knife. Very often they keep back for their
own use only one old kettle; and the sole object for which
they incur all this expenditure is, that they may render
the souls of the departed more happy and more highly
respected in the country of the dead. For the savages
believe that they are under the strictest obligation to
perform, in the honors which they pay to their dead, all
that I have related, and that it is only this sort of lavish
spending which can fully secure rest for the departed
souls; for it is the custom among those people to give
whatever they possess, without reservation, in the ceremonies of funerals or of other superstitions. There are
still some of those savages who have sucked the milk of
religion, who nevertheless have not wholly laid aside
ideas of this sort, and who bury with the corpse whatever
belonged to the person during his life. Solemnities of
this kind for the dead were formerly celebrated every
year, each tribe being alternately hosts and guests; but
for several years past this has been no longer the custom,
except among some few [villages]. The Frenchmen
who have gone among them have made them realize
that these useless extravagances of theirs were ruining
their families, and reducing them to a lack of even the
necessities of life.[56]

---

[56] Regarding the great feast of the dead, among not only the Hurons but
the upper Algonquins, cf. Champlain, *Voyages*, 303, 304; the *Relations* of 1636
(chap. ix) and of 1642 (chap. xii); La Potherie, *Histoire*, vol. ii, 47; Lafitau,

IX. Belief of the unconverted savages in regard to the immortality of the soul, and the place where the departed dwell forever

All the savages who are not converted believe that the soul is immortal;[57] but they maintain that when it is separated from the body it goes to a beautiful and fertile land, where the climate is neither cold nor hot, but agreeably temperate. They say that that land abounds with animals and birds of every kind, and that the hunters while going through it are never in danger of hunger, having only to choose what animals they will attack, to obtain food. They tell us that this beautiful country is very far away, beyond this earth; and it is for this reason that they place on the scaffolds or in the graves of the dead, at their funerals, provisions and weapons, believing that the souls will find again in the other world, for their use, and especially in the voyage which they must make thither, whatever shall be given to them in this world.

They believe, furthermore, that as soon as the soul has left the body it enters this charming country,[58] and that, after having traveled many days, it encounters on its

Mœurs des sauvages, vol. ii, 446-457; Charlevoix, *Histoire*, vol. iii, 377, 378.
— TAILHAN.

[57] The early writers fully confirm the strength and universality of this belief, among the savage tribes of America, in the immortality of the soul. See Cartier, *Seconde navigation*, chap. x, 50 (Quebec, 1843); Champlain, *Voyages*, 127; Biard, *Relation*, chap. viii; Lallemand in *Relation* of 1626; *Relations* — of 1634 (chap. iv), of 1636 (chap. ii), of 1637 (chap. xi), of 1639 (chap. x); *Lett. édif.*, vol. vii, 11, 12. "I know of but a single exception to this general consent. The Péouaroua Illinois declared to Father Gravier that man perished utterly, and that, if the soul survived, we would see the dead return to the earth (*Relation de la mission de Notre Dame*)." — TAILHAN.

[58] Cf. various passages in the *Relation* of 1636, chap. ii and ix. — TAILHAN.

Cf. traditions among the (modern) Winnebagoes, recorded in Wis. *Hist. Collections*, vol. xiii, 467. — ED.

route a very rapid river, over which there is only a slender tree-trunk by way of bridge; and that in passing over this it bends so much that the soul is in danger of being swept away by the flood of waters. They assert that if unfortunately this mishap occurs, the soul will be drowned; but that all these perils are escaped when once the souls have reached the country of the dead. They believe also that the souls of young people, of either sex, have nothing to fear, because they are so vigorous; but it is not the same with those of the old people and the infants who have no assistance from other souls in this dangerous crossing, and it is this which very often causes them to perish.

They relate to us, moreover, that this same river abounds with fish, more in number than can be imagined. There are sturgeons and other kinds of fish in great numbers, which the souls kill with blows of their hatchets and clubs, so that they can roast these fish while on their journey, for they no longer find therein any game. After they have traveled a long time, in front of them appears a very steep mountain, which closes their path and compels them to seek another; but they do not find any way open, and it is only after experiencing great suffering that they finally arrive at this fearful passage. There two pestles of prodigious size, which in turn rise and fall without ceasing, form an obstacle most difficult to overcome; for death is absolutely inevitable if while making the passage one is unfortunately caught under [them] – I mean, while one of the two pestles is falling.[59] But the souls are very careful in watching for that fortunate

---

[59] "A contradictory statement; for if the soul is immortal it cannot be killed, either by the water or by the pestle." – ANON.

"Certainly; but it is not a question of finding a logical procedure in the assertions of savages. The real question reduces itself to ascertaining whether this belief actually existed among them, and not whether it is reasonable or absurd." – TAILHAN.

moment when they can clear a passage so dangerous; yet many fail in it, especially those of old persons and little children, who are less vigorous and move through it more slowly.

When the souls have once escaped from this peril, they enter a delightful country, in which excellent fruits are found in abundance; and the ground seems to be covered with all kinds of flowers, the odor of which is so admirable that it delights their hearts and charms their imaginations. The short remaining distance which they must traverse before arriving in the place where the sound of the drum and the gourds – marking time for [the steps of] the dead, to give them pleasure – falls agreeably on their ears, urges them on to hasten directly thither with great eagerness. The nearer they approach it, always the louder becomes this sound; and the joy which the dancers express by their continual exclamations serves to delight the souls still more. When they are very near the place where the ball is held, part of the dead men separate from the others in order to meet the newcomers, and assure them of the great pleasure which their arrival generally gives to the entire assembly. The souls are conducted into the place where the dance is held, and are cordially received by all who are there; and they find there innumerable viands, of all flavors, everything of the most delicious taste, and prepared in the best manner. It is for them to choose whatever pleases them, and to satisfy their appetites; and when they have finished eating they go to mingle with the others – to dance and make merry forever, without being any longer subject to sorrow, anxiety, or infirmities, or to any of the vicissitudes of mortal life.

Such is the opinion of the savages in regard to the immortality of the soul. It is a mere dream, although one

of the most absurd that can be invented; and they give
[credit] to it with so much obstinacy that, when one
tries to make them see its extravagance, they answer to
Europeans who talk thus with them that we [white men]
have a special country for our dead; and that they, having been created by spirits who dwelt together in friendly intercourse and were all good friends, had selected in
the other world a country different from their own.
They maintain that this is an undoubted truth, and that
they have learned it from their ancestors. These forefathers once went so far in a military expedition that,
after they had found the end and farthest limit of the
earth, they passed through this gate of the pestles which
I have just described, before entering that beautiful
country; and then they heard at a little distance the
sounds of beating the drums and rattling the gourds.
Their curiosity having induced them to go forward, in
order to ascertain what this was, they were discovered by
the dead, who came toward them; and then, when they
tried to flee, they were quickly overtaken and conducted
into the cabins of these inhabitants of the other world,
who received them with the utmost good-will. Afterward they escorted these men as far as the gateway of the
pestles, which stopped their motion, to enable them to
pass without danger; and the dead men, in leaving them
there, told them not to come back again until after they
should die, lest some evil should happen to them.[60]

[60] Cf. La Potherie, *Histoire*, vol. ii, 45; Charlevoix, *Histoire*, vol. iii, 351-
353; Lafitau, *Mœurs des sauvages*, vol. i, 401-404, 409, 410. — TAILHAN.

X. The games and amusements of the savages

I. *The game of crosse*

The savages have several kinds of games, in which they take delight. They are naturally so addicted to these that they will give up their food and drink, not only to play but to watch the game. There is among them a certain game, called crosse,[61] which has much likeness to our game of long tennis. Their custom in playing it is to oppose tribe to tribe; and if one of these is more numerous than the other, men are drawn from it to render the other equal to it [in strength]. You will see them all equipped with the crosse – which is a light club, having at one end a broad flat part that is netted like a [tennis] racket; the ball that they use in playing is of wood, and shaped very nearly like a turkey's egg. The goals for the game are marked in an open level space; these goals face east and west, south and north. In order to win the game, one of the two parties must send its ball, by driving it [with the racket], beyond the goals that face east and west; and the other [must send] its ball beyond those to the south and north. If the party which has once won sends the ball again beyond the east and west goals from the side that it had to win, it is obliged to recommence the game, and to accept the goals of the opposing party; but if it should succeed in winning a second time, it would have accomplished nothing – for, as the parties are equal in strength, and are quits, they always begin the game again in order to act

---

[61] See mention of this game – which, with some modifications, became "lacrosse," the national game of Canada – in *Jesuit Relations*, vol. x, 185-187 (played for sick), 197, 231, 326-328, vol. xiv, 47, vol. xv, 155, 179 (in memory of dead). – Ed.

the part of conqueror; and that party which wins carries away what has been staked on the game.

Men, women, boys, and girls are received into the parties which are formed; and they bet against one another for larger or smaller amounts, each according to his means.

These games usually begin after the melting of the winter's ice, and last until seed-time. In the afternoon all the players may be seen, painted with vermilion and decked with ornaments. Each party has its leader, who makes an address, announcing to his players the hour that has been appointed for beginning the games. All assemble in a body, in the middle of the place [selected], and one of the leaders of the two parties, holding the ball in his hand, tosses it into the air. Each player undertakes to send it in the direction in which he must drive it; if it falls to the ground, he endeavors to draw it toward him with his crosse; and, if it is sent outside the crowd of players, the more alert distinguish themselves from the others by closely following it. You will hear the din that they make by striking one another, while they strive to ward off the blows in order to send the ball in a favorable direction. If one of them keeps it between his feet, without allowing it to escape, it is for him to avoid the blows that his adversaries rain incessantly upon his feet; and, if he happens to be wounded in this encounter, that is his own affair. Some of them are seen who [thus] have had their legs or arms broken, and some even have been killed. It is very common to see among them men crippled for the rest of their lives, and who were hurt in games of this sort only as the result of their own obstinacy.[62] When such accidents occur, the player

[62] "Wrong; neither arms nor legs were ever broken, still less were men killed." — ANON.

"Between the anonymous writer and Perrot, who spent forty years of his life

who is so unfortunate as to be hurt retires quietly from the game, if he is in a condition to walk; but, if his injuries will not permit this, his relatives convey him to the cabin, and the game always goes on as if nothing were the matter, until it is finished.

As for the runners, when the parties are equally strong they will sometimes spend an afternoon without either side gaining the advantage over the other; but sometimes, too, one of them will bear away the two victories which it must have in order to win the game. In this sport of racing, you would say that they looked like two opposing parties who meant to fight together. This exercise has much to do with rendering the savages agile, and ready to ward adroitly any blow from a club in the hands of an enemy, when they find themselves entangled in combat; and if one were not told beforehand that they were playing, one would certainly believe that they were fighting together in the open field.[63] Whatever mishap this sport may occasion, they attribute it to the luck of the game, and they feel no hatred to one another. The trouble falls on the injured persons, who nevertheless put on as contented an aspect as if nothing had happened to them, thus making it appear that they have great courage, and are men. The party that has won carries away what its members staked, and the profit that it has made, and that without any objection on either side when it is a question of paying [the bets], no matter what kind of game it may be. However, if any person who does not belong to the party, or who has not made any bet, should drive the ball to the advantage of one of the

in the midst of the savages, the reader will pronounce sentence. I only add that Charlevoix (*Histoire*, vol. iii, 319) applies to this game the epithet 'dangerous;'" and that La Potherie, in describing its consequences (*Histoire*, vol. ii, 126, 127), borrows from Perrot the very sentences to which the anonymous writer objects. — TAILHAN.

[63] "Not so; it is easy to understand that they are playing." — ANON.

two parties, one of the players whom the blow does not favor would attack this man, demanding of him whether this were any of his business, and why he was meddling in it. They have often come to blows over this point, and if some chief did not reconcile them there would be bloodshed, and even some one would be killed. The best way to prevent this disorderly conduct is to begin the game over again, with the consent of those who are winning; for if they refuse to do so, the responsibility rests on them. But when some one of the influential men interposes, it is not difficult to adjust their dispute and induce them to conform to his decision.

II. *The game of straws*

At the game of straws the savages lose not only all that they possess, but even that which belongs to their comrades. Here is an account of this game. They take for this sport a certain number of straws, or of the stems of a special plant, which is not so thick as the cord [used] for a salmon-net, and with these they make little sticks, all alike in length and thickness; the length is about eleven inches, and the number is uneven. After turning and mingling these in their hands, they lay them on a piece of skin or of blanket; and he who must begin the game, holding in his hand an awl (or more commonly a small pointed bone), makes contortions of his arms and body, continually saying *Chok! Chok!*–a word which has no meaning in their language, but which serves to make known his desire to play well and to be fortunate in the game. Then with this awl or small pointed bone he thrusts into some part of the [pile of] straws, and takes away a number of them as he pleases; his opponent takes those which remain on the cloth, and with inconceivable quickness counts them, by tens, without making any mistake; then he who has the uneven number has made a lucky hit.

Sometimes they play with seeds which grow on the trees, which closely resemble little beans.[64] Each takes a certain number of these for [indicating] the value of the goods which he wishes to stake – that is, a gun, a blanket, or some other article. The player who at the beginning of the game finds that he has nine straws in his hand has won all, and draws what has been staked. If he finds that he has a number not even, below nine, it is in his power to double [the stakes?], and to honor the game with what suits him. For this purpose he lays down at any place in the game, as he chooses, one straw, and three, five, or seven [of them] on other spots; for the number nine, it is always taken for granted, predominates over all the others. In short, he who finds nine straws in his hand usually draws all that has been staked. Beside the straws which lie on the cloth are the seeds with which the players have honored the game; and you must note that they always place more of these on the nine than on all the others.

When the players have made their bets, he who has been lucky often takes the straws and turns them endwise in his hands, and then places them on the table, saying *Chank!* which means "nine;" and the other, who has the awl or the little bone in his hand, draws off [part of] the straws, in such place as he prefers, and takes as many of them as he pleases, as has been already stated, and the other takes the rest of them. If the last to take them

---

[64] The seeds thus used as counters may have been those of the honey locust (*Gleditschia triacanthos*), or of the Kentucky coffee-tree (*Gymnocladus dioica*). – A. B. STOUT, botanist, University of Wisconsin.

The Indians commonly use as dice, in the bowl-game, the flattish stones of the wild plum (*Prunus americana*). The Virginia Indians employed for this purpose the hard, flat seeds of the persimmon (*Diospyros virginiana*).

— WM. R. GERARD.

prefers to leave them, his adversary is obliged to take
them; and, each counting them by tens, he who has the
uneven number has won, and takes whatever has been
staked. But if it happens that the winner has only one
straw more than the other man, he takes only those seeds
which represent that straw. For example, the number
three is greater than two, by one; five is superior to
three, and seven to five; but nine surpasses all.

If several persons are playing and one of them finds
five in his hand, they play four at a time, two against two,
or fewer if they cannot make up the number of four
players; one pair wins the seeds which stand for the five
straws, and the other [the] seeds which are at stake for
the three straws and for one. When any one has not in
his hand the uneven number of those which remain on
the cloth – that is, one and three – after they have carefully counted the straws by tens, when he has not the
nine he is obliged to double what he has staked, even if
he might have in his hand five or seven straws; and his
play counts for nothing. He is obliged also to form two
other piles of straws; in one he places five and in
the other seven straws, with as many seeds as he pleases.
When he has laid these on the cloth, his opponents in
their turn prick off [straws], and then he takes those
which are left; by that time there are some of the players
who are lucky, nevertheless each one takes for himself
only the seeds which are designated for the number of
straws [which he has], and he who has nine takes only
the seeds laid down for the nine straws. When another
player draws away seven straws, he takes the rest; for
three straws and for one it is all the same, but not for
[numbers] higher than these.[65]

<hr>

[65] "Lafitau says (*Mœurs des sauvages*, vol. ii, 351) of this description by
Perrot: 'I would gladly have inserted it here, but it is so obscure that it is
almost unintelligible. No one of the other Canadian French whom I have met

It should be noted that, after they have lost the game which lies before them, they continue playing upon their promises [to pay], if the players declare that they [still] have possessions, even though these are not in their hands. But when one continues to be unlucky, the winner may refuse [to accept] seeds from the loser for the value which he requires from the latter, and may oblige him to go to find the goods themselves, refusing to play any longer until he sees these, nor can any retort to this be made. The loser will immediately tell one of his comrades to bring the goods to him, and if his ill-luck continues he will lose everything that he owns. One of his comrades then relieves him and takes his place, stating what he intends to risk on the game to the winner, who then accepts seeds for the value [of the bet].

This game lasts sometimes three or four days. When any one of the party who loses wins back all, and he who has hitherto been lucky in play comes to lose not only the profit which he had made but what of his own property he had staked, another of his comrades also takes his place, and everything goes on as before, until one of

has been able to give me an account of it; and all that I have been able to learn is, that after having divided these straws they take them into their hands with inconceivable dexterity; that the odd number is always lucky, and the number nine superior to all the others; that the division of the straws causes the game to run high or low, and doubles the stakes, according to the different numbers, until the game is won; and the contest is sometimes so spirited, when some of the villages are playing against the others, that it lasts two or three days. Although all passes peaceably, and with apparent good faith, there is nevertheless much cheating and sleight-of-hand in the game.' Like him, Charlevoix admits (*Histoire*, vol. iii, 318) that he had understood nothing in all the explanations of this game; and La Potherie acknowledges (*Histoire*, vol. iii, 23) that its mechanism is not easy to understand. I have not been more fortunate than my predecessors, and the game of straws remains for me an undecipherable enigma." — TAILHAN.

The above citations will serve to explain any obscurity which may appear in Perrot's text. It has been translated as accurately as is possible; but the present editor can claim no further illumination for its difficulties than the above-cited authorities possessed. — ED.

the two parties is entirely ruined. Thus the contest comes to an end among those people, it being a rule with the savages that they cannot quit the game until one side or the other has lost everything. It is for this reason that they cannot dispense with furnishing revenge to all those of a party, decisively, one after another, as I have just stated. In the game they have liberty to play on their own account, as they please; and if there happened to be a quarrel over this – I mean between the winners and the losers, each supported by those of his own party – they would come to blows, in which there would be bloodshed, and it would be very difficult to reconcile them. If the disposition of the winner is such as to be calm while he loses, and he feigns to overlook the many adroit tricks and the cheating which they very often practice in playing, he is praised and esteemed by every one; while he who has tried to cheat is blamed by every one, and there is no one who wishes to play with him, unless he ignominiously restores what he has unlawfully won.

This game of straws is usually held in the cabins of chiefs, which are large and are, so to speak, the academy of the savages; and there are seen all the young men, making up opposing sides, and the older men as spectators of their games. If the player fancies that he has had luck in picking off the straws, and that he has on his side the uneven number, holding them in one hand he strikes [the table] with the other; and when he has made the count of them by tens, without saying a word he makes it known by a sign that he has won, by taking for himself the seeds which have been staked, when he sees that he against whom he is playing has not as many of them. If one of the players tries to object that the straws could not have been correctly counted, they hand them over to two of the spectators to count them; and the one who has really won always sweeps off his straws, without saying anything, and takes possession of the articles at stake. All of this passes without any dispute, and with great fairness. You will note that this game is not at all one for women, and that it is only the men who engage in it.

III. *Game of dice*

The savages have also a certain game of dice, in which the dice-box is a wooden dish, quite round, empty, and very smooth on both sides. The dice are composed of six small flat bones, in shape closely resembling a plum-stone; these are quite smooth, with one of the sides colored black, red, green, or blue, and the other usually white, or of some other color than the former side. They place these dice in the dish, and, holding it by both sides, jerk it upward, causing the dice within to leap and bounce around. Then, having slammed the bottom of the dish against the table, while the dice are rolling about they immediately strike their own chests or shoulders with sharp blows, saying, "Dice! dice! dice!" until the dice stop moving. When five or six of these are found with the same color on the [upper] face, a player sweeps off the seeds which represent his agreement with the other party; if the loser and his comrades have nothing more to wager, the winning side takes all that is at stake. Entire villages have been known to wager each its entire wealth against another at this game, and to lose it all. They also present challenges;[66] and when one party happens to throw a pair-royal of six all the men

[66] "*Momon,* or *mommon,* a challenge given over a cast of dice. On the game of dice, or bowl, cf. *Relation* of 1636 (chap. ix), and that of 1639 (chap. viii); La Potherie, *Histoire,* vol. iii, 22; Lafitau, *Mœurs des sauvages,* vol. ii, 339-342; Charlevoix, *Histoire,* vol. iii, 260, 261. . . . If what Perrot says of the passion for gaming among these same savages, and the disorders which followed in its train, needed confirmation, it would be sufficient to read what is narrated of them in the *Relations* of 1636 (chap. ii and ix) and 1639 (chap. x)." — TAILHAN.

and women of the tribe that is backing them rise to their
feet and dance, keeping time to the sound of the gourd
rattles. The entire affair goes off without any dispute.

The girls and women play at this game, but they very
often have eight dice, and do not use the dish for it, as
the men do; they only lay down a blanket, and throw the
dice on it with their hands.[67]

XI.   The usual food of the savages, and their hunting

I.   *The usual food of the savages*

The kinds of food which the savages like best, and
which they make most effort to obtain, are the Indian
corn, the kidney-bean, and the squash. If they are without these, they think that they are fasting, no matter what
abundance of meat and fish they may have in their stores,
the Indian corn being to them what bread is to Frenchmen. The Algonkins, however, and all the northern
tribes, who do not cultivate the soil, do not lay up corn;
but when it is given to them while they are out hunting
they regard it as a [special] treat.

Those peoples commonly live only by hunting or fishing; they have moose, caribous, and bears, but the beaver
is the most common of all their game. They consider
themselves very fortunate in their hunting expeditions
when they encounter some rabbits, martens, or par-
tridges, from which to make a soup; and without what
we call *tripe de roche* [68]—which you would say is a spe-

---

[67] On the game of dice (also called "of dish," or "of bowl"), see *Jesuit Relations*, vol. x, 185-187, 197, vol. xiv, 81, 285, vol. xv, 155, vol. xvii, 159, 201-205,
242. Gambling was a universal vice connected with all these games described
by Perrot. — ED.

[68] *Tripe de roche* is the Canadian term ("ironically given" — CLAPIN) for a
species of edible lichen (*Umbilicaria dillenii*) growing on rocks; often mentioned by early explorers. The Jesuit André describes the method of cooking

cies of gray moss, dry, and resembling *oublies*;[69] and which of itself has only an earthy taste, and the flavor of the soup in which it is cooked – most of their families would perish of hunger. Some of these have been known who were compelled to eat their own children, and others whom starvation has entirely destroyed. For the northern country is the most sterile region in the world, since in many places one will not find a single bird to hunt; however, they gather there plenty of blueberries[70] in the months of August and September, which they are careful to dry and keep for a time of need.

The Chiripinons or Assiniboüalas sow in their marshes some wild oats,[71] which they harvest; but they can trans-

it, and says, "It is necessary to close one's eyes when one begins to eat it" (*Jesuit Relations*, vol. lv, 151). – ED.

[69] *Oublie*, one of the wafers used to stick papers together; it is evident that he compares *tripe de roche* to these wafers, as regards its nutritive value. It also resembles them in being gluey or gelatinous. This lichen (also called "famine bread") is used as food in the northern wilds only when people are absolutely starving, although it has some nutritive value. – CRAWFORD LINDSAY.

[70] *Bluet*: the well-known "blueberry" (*Vaccinium canadense*), which formed an important and valued article of food among the northern Indians. See La Potherie's *Histoire*, vol. ii, 57; and *Jesuit Relations*, vol. xvi, 191, 258, 259, vol. xxxviii, 243, vol. xlviii, 165, vol. lix, 69, 71, 306, vol. lxxi, 373. – ED.

[71] "In this passage of our manuscript the words *Chiripinons ou* have been crossed out, and for them have been substituted, *Cristinaux, nation différente des Assiniboils.* Moreover, one reads on the margin the following annotation, 'The wild oats grows without sowing.'" The manner of gathering this grain is described by Father Marquette, in the relation of his voyages and discoveries. – TAILHAN.

This "wild oats" refers to the grain known as wild rice (*Zizania aquatica*), which grows in marshes and shallow streams and lakes from the Rocky Mountains to the Atlantic, and from latitude 52° to the Gulf states; it is especially abundant in Wisconsin and eastern Minnesota. Its Algonquian name is *manó mīn*, meaning "good berry;" and there are many other names – Indian, English, and French – extant for this well-known grain. The Menomini tribe, found on the shore of Green Bay by Nicollet in 1634, have always been known as the "Wild-rice Indians," which is simply the translation of their own name, *Omanominewak* – called by the French writers Malhominis, Maloumines, etc. The wild rice is claimed to be even more nutritious than any of our cereal grains, including even maize. The only full and thorough account of it yet published is A. E. Jenks's "Wild Rice Gatherers of the Upper Lakes," in 19th *Report* of the Bureau of Amer. Ethnology, 1011-1160: therein are given the

port this grain to their homes only in the season of navigation. As their canoes are very small, and heavily loaded with their children and the produce of their hunting, they have very often been reduced almost to starvation on account of being too far distant from their *caches** and their own country.

II. *The manner in which the northern tribes hunt the beaver*

The peoples of the north hunt for beaver in the winter, with an ice-chisel [*tranche*] and a snare made of cords of hide. They begin by breaking a hole in the lodge into

history, description, habitat, and uses of this grain; the Indian tribes using it; methods of cultivating, harvesting, and cooking it; etc. The author says (p. 1019) of this study: "It has thrown light upon the almost constant warfare between the Dakota and Ojibwa Indians for two hundred and fifty years. It has shed light also upon the fur trade in a territory unexcelled in the richness of its furs, yet almost inaccessible had it not been for the wild rice which furnished such nourishing and wholesome support to the traders and hunters." See also the excellent paper of Gardner P. Stickney, "Indian Use of Wild Rice," in *Amer. Anthropologist*, vol. ix, 115-121. It appears that some efforts have been made to introduce wild rice into the market, as a cereal for American consumption; but these were unsuccessful, on account of the general (and somewhat foolish) prejudice against grains lacking in whiteness – the wild rice being green or almost black in color. – ED.

* "The storage of articles and supplies appears to have been quite general throughout America, and the practice of caching, or hiding, things not less so. The extent of this custom indicates its ancient origin, a belief strengthened by the discovery of large deposits of articles of stone which in many cases show partial disintegration and other indications of great age. . . The season, the temperature, the locality, and the time required to make a cache were important considerations. Some things, when time allowed, were sewed in skins and suspended on trees or hidden in hollow tree trunks; others were buried under shelving rocks or in carefully prepared holes in the ground. Owing to seasonal journeys of large numbers of persons in search of food or other supplies, many things had to be left behind which, because of their weight or bulk, would add to the difficulty of movement. Caching was resorted to in order to prevent the hidden things from being disturbed by wild beasts, stones often being piled over the cache; or, when the deposit was of food or clothing, fires were built in order that the ashes should hide surface indications and thus keep enemies from disturbing the deposit; or, in other cases, the sod was carefully removed and replaced after the cache was completed; or, if the land was sandy,

which this animal goes for refuge; and they break down the dams [72] which it has been careful to build in order to retain the water in the marsh. After they have thus drained away the water during the night, the savages lay their snare, which is made like a pouch, as large as the place through which the beaver must necessarily pass, for there is no other – the ice, and the dams which the animal made in the autumn, no longer permitting it to ascend or descend the stream. The animal is therefore constrained to abandon its dwelling, or to repair the breach which has already been made in its wall; for this snare, as has been stated, occupies the passageway,[73] and its shape is like that of a purse, with a cord in its end which is drawn together to close the snare. The beaver, then attempting to descend to the bottom of the water, enters this snare that is stretched for it; and the man who is stationed upon the ice, perceiving [by the motion of the net] that it is captured, draws in the net, and breaks the animal's head. They always secure it in the same way; and such is the manner in which the beavers are killed. If the bank of the swamp were not steep and were on a level with the water, it would be much easier to destroy them; for then it would only be necessary to

water was poured over the surface to conceal indications of the ground having been disturbed. The term *cache* has been adopted from the French *cacher*, 'to hide,' and has been very generally adopted by the whites, who have not been slow to accept and practice this primitive method of hiding things intended to be reclaimed." – J. D. McGuire, in *Handbook Amer. Indians*, art. "Storage and caching."

[72] "They break open the lodge, and not the dam, for the net, but especially when they wish to trap the animal in the places where he is accustomed to go." – Anon.

[73] "Wrong; this net is not stretched in the passage to the water, but in the place through which the beaver must pass to come to his lodge when he is hunted in other places. It is also stretched at the entrance to a place to which they know the animal has gone to hide itself, and where a barrier has been made with stakes driven into the ice; in this barrier is left an opening, in which the net is stretched." – Anon.

break into their lodges to compel the animals to come out from them.

The noise which the hunters make by sharply striking the handles of their tools [upon the ice] enables the beavers [74] [sc. hunters?] to recognize by the variations in the sound that there are cavities under the ice; and the animals try to take refuge in these in order to regain their breath, for the fright which has been given them has greatly harassed them. After they have rested there for some time, they try to return to their dwellings or to reach some other place of safety; then all the hunters observe entire silence, and quit making a noise, but they continue to walk about very cautiously, with sharp sticks in their hands, looking for the places where they see the water in motion, because they think that the beaver may be there. They immediately close the entrance to its hole, and knowing, by the sticks which it tries to force aside, the moment when it tries to leave the hole, they immediately spear it with a sharp blade fastened to the end of a stake. [75]

III. *Chase of the caribou, moose, and other animals*

Hunting the caribous is usually practiced on the great flat plains [*savanes*]; [76] and at the outset they surround

---

[74] "Wrong." — ANON.

"It is really to the hunters, not to the beavers, that the resonance of the tool-handle [struck] against the ice indicates the cavities in which the animals have gone to seek refuge; moreover, I am much inclined to believe that the copyist has by mistake substituted here the word *castors* for *chasseurs* which was found in the original." — TAILHAN.

[75] "The beaver is never speared in the winter; it is seized by the hand through a hole that has been made in the ice — through which the hunter knows that the beaver is near, by the motion which it causes in the water." — ANON.

In the *Relation* of 1634 (chap. ix) is "a more complete and especially a more intelligible description of the beaver-hunt;" cf. La Potherie, *Histoire*, vol. i, 134. — TAILHAN.

[76] "All these savages . . . are known in the French relations by the

the game with trees and poles planted at intervals, in
which they stretch snares of rawhide, which enclose a
narrow passage purposely left. When all these snares
have been prepared, they go far away, marching abreast
and uttering loud yells; this unusual noise frightens the
animals and drives them to flight on every side; no
longer knowing which way to go, they encounter this
obstruction which has been made ready in their course.
Not being able to clear it, they are compelled to follow
it until they reach the passage in which the snares are
laid with running knots, which seize them by the neck.
It is in vain that they strive to escape; rather, they tear
up the stakes [of the snare] and drag these with them
as far as the larger trees; in short, their utmost efforts
to extricate themselves only serve to strangle them more
quickly.[77]

The moose are hunted in about the same manner, especially when the savages are in a region where these
animals are numerous; or else they endeavor to take them
by surprise and kill them with guns or arrows. But in
the winter, when the snows are deep, they have sharp
blades on long handles for killing the moose by coursing
them. On the other hand, the elk can be captured only
with a snare.[78]

The Kiristinons,[79] who often frequent the region along

generic name of Savanois [i.e., Meadow people], because the country that they
inhabit is low, swampy, thinly wooded; and because in Canada those wet lands
that are good for nothing are called Savanes" (Charlevoix, *Histoire*, vol. iii,
181). – TAILHAN.

[77] See Champlain's description of this sort of hunting, in *Voyages*, page 266;
it is more clear and easily understood than Perrot's. See also Charlevoix's
Histoire, vol. iii, 128, 129. – TAILHAN.

[78] For description of elk-hunting by the savages, see *Relation* of 1634, chap.
ix. – TAILHAN.

[79] The Cree, a name "contracted from Kristinaux, French form of *Keniste-
noag*, given as one of their own names: an important Algonquian tribe of British
America whose former habitat was in Manitoba and Assiniboia, between Red

the shores of Lake Superior and the great rivers, where moose are more commonly found, have another method of hunting them.   First, they embark on the water, two men in each canoe, and keep at a certain distance from one another; their dogs are on the land, and enter a little distance into the depths of the forest to seek their game. As soon as the dogs have found the trail, they never quit it until they have found the moose; and the wonderful instinct which they possess of remembering in what place their masters are leads them to drive on the game directly to that quarter, continually pursuing them until the moose are constrained to dash into the water. The savages, who are [now] on the shore listening intently for the barking of their dogs, at once enter their canoes [again], and attack and slay the moose.

The marten [skins] that are most valued and handsome are those from the north; the fur on them is more

---

and Saskatchewan Rivers. . . A portion of the Cree, as appears from the tradition given by Lacombe (*Dict. Lang. Cris*), inhabited for a time the region about Red River, intermingled with the Chippewa and Maskegon, but were attracted to the plains by the buffalo, the Cree like the Chippewa being essentially a forest people.   Many bands of Cree were virtually nomads, their movements being governed largely by the food supply.   The Cree are closely related, linguistically and otherwise, to the Chippewa. . . At some comparatively recent time the Assiniboin, a branch of the Sioux, in consequence of a quarrel broke away from their brethren and sought alliance with the Cree.   The latter received them cordially and granted them a home in their territory, thereby forming friendly relations that have continued to the present day.   The united tribes attacked and drove southwestward the Siksika and allied tribes who formerly dwelt along the Saskatchewan.   The enmity between these tribes and both the Siksika and the Sioux has ever since continued."   The history of the Cree, who have always been friendly to both the French and the English, "consists almost wholly of their contests with neighboring tribes and their relations with the Hudson Bay Company. . . In more recent years, since game has become scarce, they have lived chiefly in scattered bands, depending largely on trade with the agents of the Hudson Bay Co.   At present they are gathered chiefly in bands on various reserves in Manitoba, mostly with the Chippewa." Their numbers were greatly reduced by smallpox in 1786 and 1838; in 1776 the Cree proper were estimated at about 15,000.   "There are now about 10,000 in Manitoba (7,000 under agencies), and about 5,000 roving in Northwest Territory; total, 15,000." — JAMES MOONEY and CYRUS THOMAS, in *Handbook Amer. Indians.*

black than brown; and the trade in these is one of the best carried on in that country.

The savages called Saulteurs[80] are at the south of Lake Superior, and hunt the beaver and the moose. They also go fishing, and catch excellent fish; and they harvest some Indian corn, although not in so great quantity as do the tribes on the shores of Lake Huron, who live in open or prairie country. Martens are found there, and even if the caribou is not seen there they have by way of compensation many other animals in abundance, which they kill with great ease. Moreover, they have for neighbors and friends the Sioux, on whose lands they hunt, when they wish, buffaloes, elk, and deer,[81] and

[80] The *Relation* of 1670 thus describes (chap. x) the Sault de Sainte-Marie [i.e., the rapids of St. Mary's River; popularly known as "the Soo"]: "What is commonly known as the Sault is not, properly speaking, a descent or fall of water from a considerable height; but it is an exceedingly violent current of the waters from Lake Superior, which being checked by a great number of rocks that dispute their passage, form a dangerous cascade, half a league broad — all those waters descending, and precipitating themselves one upon another, as if on a staircase, over the great rocks that obstruct the river. This place is three leagues below Lake Superior, and twelve leagues above the lake of the Hurons — all this distance forming a beautiful river, divided by many islands. . . The earliest and native inhabitants of this place are those who call themselves Pahouitingonach . . . whom the French call Saulteurs, because it is these people who live at the Sault as in their own country, the other tribes being there only by loan, as it were."

"The Sauteurs of to-day apply to themselves no other name than that of Odgiboweke (Otjibwek, Odjibewais), from which the English have called them Chippewais. These peoples of Algonquin stock have almost entirely abandoned their ancient dwelling at Saut-Sainte Marie. They form the most numerous part of the savage population dispersed through the vast British possessions of the Northwest, and dwell not far from the line that separates those possessions from the American territory. Their lives are spent in waging war against the Sioux, their neighbors on the south, in hunting the bison, and most of all in exploiting the liberality of the Bois-Brulés of the Red River (who are Canadian-Sauteur mixed-bloods). The tribe of Sauteurs, wrote in 1851 a missionary to those regions (*Rapport sur les missions du diocèse de Québec*, no. 9, 111; Québec), 'is in general the most slothful and mendicant people whom I know. They are the scourge of the mixed-bloods, who are industrious in hunting, and courageous in enduring its fatigues; so the Sauteurs beset them, in order to live almost exclusively at their expense.' " — TAILHAN.

[81] French, *cerfs, biches, chevreüils*; and in the sentence at the beginning of

other game, which they take by surprise with the discharge of guns and arrows.

There are yet other tribes along Lakes Huron and Illinois who possess lands sufficiently cleared to obtain from them all the grain that they can need, and who live in great comfort with [this and] the produce of their fishing; but when they wish to go to hunt beaver or any other animal they are compelled to go to a great distance. The seasons which they usually take for hunting are the autumn and winter, because at that time the pelts of the animals are better than at others. For capturing these they use snares, in which for bait there is a branch of a tree which they call "the trembling tree;" [82] the animals are very fond of this, and in trying to reach the inner end of the snare, where the bait is placed, they step upon a trigger, which lets fall a heavy weight on the animal's back and kills it.

They hunt all the other beasts with guns, although they have also arrows, but they are not so skilful in using these weapons as are the people of the north and of the prairies, because the use of firearms is not so general among them as in those tribes; and because in the distant regions to which they are accustomed to go for

---

this paragraph is mentioned (as in many other places) the *élan*. There is some confusion in various writers in the use of these words and of their English equivalents, and sometimes it is difficult to identify them precisely. On the authority of Crawford Lindsay and C. Hart Merriam (late chief of U.S. Biological Survey), I have regularly translated *cerf* as "elk" (*Cervus canadensis*, or *C. wapiti;* also called "wapiti"); *élan* as "moose" (*C. alces*, or *Alces americanus*; also called "moose deer"); *chevreüil* as "deer" (*Odocoileus virginianus*, or *Cervus virginianus*; the red or Virginia deer). The caribou (*C. tarandus*, or *Tarandus hastalis*) is allied to the reindeer. These four apparently include all the species of *Cervus* in Canada and the northern United States east of the Rocky Mts. The name *biche*, as found in dictionaries, seems to mean the doe of the red deer; but J. D. Caton says, in *Antelope and Deer of America* (N.Y., 1881, second edition) that the elk or wapiti (presumably the female) is called *la biche* by the Canadian French. — ED.

[82] The American (or "quaking") aspen or poplar (*Aspen* — or *Populus* — *tremuloides*), called *bois blanc* ("whitewood") by the French Canadians. — ED.

RAPIDS OF ST. MARY'S RIVER

hunting there are bears, elk, deer, wild-cats, beaver, some *pekans*,[83] and otters. If they go to the west or toward the south they find there buffalo but few moose,[84] for of all the animals which I have just enumerated few live where there are moose; and for this reason the savages run great risk of fasting at times. Martens are also very common there; and when the beaver cannot supply the deficiency of moose, they are exposed, when there is so little snow that they are prevented from running down the moose, to famine – all the more certain because it is very difficult to overcome those animals by surprise.

IV. *Natural productions of the prairies; game and wild beasts that are encountered there*

The savage peoples who inhabit the prairies have lifelong good-fortune; animals and birds are found there in great numbers, with numberless rivers abounding in fish. Those people are naturally very industrious, and devote themselves to the cultivation of the soil, which is very fertile for Indian corn. It produces also beans, squashes (both small and large) of excellent flavor, fruits, and many kinds of roots. They have in especial a certain method of preparing squashes with the Indian corn cooked while in its milk, which they mix and cook together and then dry, [a food] which has a very sweet taste. Finally, melons grow there which have a juice no less agreeable than refreshing.

The various kinds of animals that the country fur-

[83] *Pekan*: a French-Canadian name for the animal called "fisher," "black fox," and "black (or wild) cat" (*Mustela pennanti*); its fur was esteemed by Europeans. — ED.

[84] "This entire passage is not very clear. I think that Perrot meant to say that the savages of Lake Huron and the Lake of the Illinois (Lake Michigan) hunt not only the beaver, but also 'all the other beasts,' because 'in the distant hunting expeditions on which they are accustomed to go, there are bears, moose,' etc." — TAILHAN.

nishes are: buffaloes, elk, bears, lynxes, raccoons, and panthers,[85] whose flesh is very good for food. There are also beavers, and black and gray wolves, whose skins serve as their garments; and still other animals which also they use for food. The birds or fowls of the rivers and swamps are: swans,[86] bustards, wild geese, and ducks of all kinds. Pelicans are very common, but they have an oily flavor, whether alive or dead, which is so disagreeable that it is impossible to eat them.

The land birds are: turkeys, pheasants, quails, pigeons, and curlew[87] like large hens, of excellent flavor. In that region are found still other birds, especially innumerable cranes. The people of that country generally use guns and bows in hunting; and in the marshes they drain them, and use the ice-chisel.

Toward the north, the animals all have very rich fur; but as one goes southward, where the winter does not last long, as soon as it is over the furs cease to be as valuable.

[85] *Tygres*: referring to the panther or cougar (*Felis cougar*). The name "catamount" is a nuisance, being used differently by various authors, sometimes being applied to the panther or cougar, sometimes to the Canada lynx (*Lynx canadensis*; French, *chat cervier*). It should be restricted to the panther. — C. HART MERRIAM, late chief of U.S. Biological Survey.

[86] Of the swan (*Cygnus*, or *Olor*), two species were commonly found in the northern and central states: *C. americanus* (or *ferus*), the American or whistling swan; and *C. buccinator*, the trumpeter swan. The American white pelican (*Pelecanus erythrorhyncus*) is described in *Jesuit Relations*, vol. lv, 197, 199, 321. The wild goose (*Anser anser*) is said to be the wild stock of the domesticated goose — Leonhard Stejneger, in *Riverside Natural History* (Boston, 1884). The name *outarde* (English, "bustard") was given by the French Canadians to the Canada goose (*Anser*, or *Branta, canadensis*). All of these wild water-birds, which formerly abounded in the United States and Canada, are now rare or unknown in the long-settled eastern regions, and are found in abundance only in remote parts of the west and north where settlements are yet few and scattered. — ED.

[87] "There exist in Canada and the United States two species of curlew [*corbigeaux ou courlis*]: the long-beaked curlew (*Numenius longirostris*, Aud.) and the northern curlew (*Numenius hudsonicus*, Aud.). What Perrot says of the prairie curlew may be understood of one as well as of the other. Cf. J. M. Lemoine's *Ornithologie du Canada*, 356, 357 (Québec, 1861, second edition)." — TAILHAN.

In that region the heat is as great as in the islands of the south or in Provence; and it is a country abounding in parroquets. But if we push into the north, as far as the entrance to Ouisconching [i.e., Wisconsin River], the winter there is extremely cold and long. That is where the beaver-skins are the best, and where hunting lasts for a longer time in the year.

The savages have in their country various kinds of roots. That which they call [blank in text], meaning "bear's root," [88] is an actual poison if it is eaten raw; but they cut it in very thin slices, and cook it in an oven* during three days and nights; thus by heat they cause the acrid substance which renders it poisonous to evaporate in steam, and it then becomes what is commonly called cassava root.

Also in winter they dig from under the ice, or where there is much mud and little water, a certain root, of better quality than that which I have just mentioned; but it is only found in the Louisiana country, some fifteen leagues above the entrance to the Ouisconching. The savages call this root, in their own language, *poke-*

[88] *Racine de l'ours*: This, from Perrot's description, was the "Indian turnip" (*Arisæma triphyllum*), the crown of which is very acrid when fresh, but loses this quality when boiled or roasted, in which state it was sometimes eaten by the Indians. It yields one-fourth of its weight of a pure amylaceous matter, like starch, arrowroot, or cassava. If the French name is a translation of the Indian, the corm may be the *makopin*, or "bear-root," of the Ojibwa.
　　　　　　　　　　　　　　　　　　— WILLIAM R. GERARD, New York City.

* "The pit oven, consisting of a hole excavated in the ground, heated with fire, and then filled with food which was covered over and allowed to cook, was general in America, though as a rule it was employed only occasionally, and principally for cooking vegetal substances. This method was found necessary to render acrid or poisonous foods harmless and starchy foods saccharine, and as a preliminary in drying and preserving food for winter use. Rude camp devices, such as baking in a cavity in the ashes, sometimes incasing in clay the substance to be cooked, were in common use; simple pit ovens, charged according to a definite plan, and ovens with a draft hole, the latter occurring among the Pueblos, comprise the varieties of this invention in northern America." — WALTER HOUGH, in *Handbook Amer. Indians.*

koretch ;[89] and the French give it no other name, because nothing at all resembling it is seen in Europe. It has the appearance of a root, about half as thick as one's arm, or a little more; it also has firm flesh, and externally resembles an arm; in one word, you would say at sight of these roots, that they are certainly great radishes. But cut it across the two ends, and it is no longer the same thing; for you find inside it a cavity in the middle, extending throughout its length, around which are five or six other and smaller cavities, which also run from end to end. To eat it, you must cook it over a brazier, and you will find that it tastes like chestnuts. The savages are accustomed to make provision of this root; they cut it into pieces and string them on a cord, in order to dry them in the smoke. When these pieces are thoroughly dry, and hard as wood, they put them into bags, and keep them as long as they wish. If they boil their meat in a kettle, they also cook therein this root, which thus becomes soft; and, when they wish to eat, it answers for bread with their meat. It is always better with consid-

---

[89] This was the rhizome of *Nelumbo lutea*, called by the Oto and Quapaw *tarowa* and *taluwa* ("hollow root"), and by the Ojibwa tribes *wâgipin* or *wargipin* ("crooked root"). Both the rhizome and the seeds ("water chinkapins") are used as food by the Indians wherever the plant grows. — WM. R. GERARD.

Several clumps of *Nelumbo* lately grew (and may be still present) in Rice Lake and Mud Lake, two small isolated lakes west of Lake Koshkonong, Wis. They were there when the earliest settlers of that locality arrived, and are supposed to have been introduced by Indians, although no one knows when or by what tribe; and botanical works state that the plant was introduced in that region by Indians, although no actual proof of this is adduced.
— ARLOW B. STOUT, Univ. of Wisconsin.

" 'The *Pokékoretch* of Perrot is without any doubt the *Nelumbium luteum*, an aquatic plant with a cylindrical and fleshy root; its flower measures from 6 to 20 pouces [the pouce = 1⅛ inches], in diameter, and floats on the surface of the water. Both the roots and the seeds are eaten; the latter are of the size of a hazelnut, and have the taste of the chestnut; they are much sought by the savages.' I owe this note and the two following to the courtesy of Monsieur [Ovide] Brunet, professor of botany in Laval University, Québec. This plant may be one described by Father Marquette in his *Récit des voyages*, section vii." — TAILHAN.

erable grease; for although this root is very sweet and has a good flavor, it sticks to the throat in swallowing and goes down with difficulty, because it is very dry. The women gather this root, and recognize it by the dried stem, which appears sticking up above the ice. The shape [of the flower] is like a crown, of red color; it is as large as the bottom of a plate, and is full of seeds in every way resembling hazelnuts; and when these are roasted under hot cinders they taste just like chestnuts.

That country also produces potatoes; some are as large as an egg, others have the size of one's fist, or a little more. They boil these in water by a slow fire during twenty-four hours; when they are thoroughly cooked, you will find in them an excellent flavor, much resembling that of prunes – which are cooked in the same way in France, to be served with dessert.[90]

The tribes of the prairies also find in certain places lands that are fertile, and kept moist by the streams that water them, whereon grow onions of the size of one's thumb. The root is like a leek, and the plant which grows from it resembles the salsify. This onion, I say, is so exceedingly acrid that, if one tried to swallow it, it would all at once wither the tongue, the throat, and the inside of the mouth; I do not know, however, whether it would have the same injurious effect on the inside of the body. But this difficulty hardly ever occurs, for as

[90] This was the so-called "Indian potato" (*Apios tuberosa*).
— WM. R. GERARD.

There is no true potato native in Wisconsin; but *Solanum jamesii* is found west of the Rockies. The plant alluded to is probably *Apios tuberosa*.
— A. B. STOUT.

"The potato [*pomme de terre*] which is here mentioned is no other than the *Psoralea esculenta*, a plant of the leguminous family, which abounds in the elevated plains of the Missouri, and on the hills in the vicinity of Saint Louis. The Canadian voyageurs called it 'prairie apple' or 'turnip' [*pomme ou navet de prairie*]. The savages always boil it before eating it, although this root has not a disagreeable taste even when raw." — BRUNET (cited by Tailhan).

soon as one takes it into the mouth he spits it out; and
one imagines that it is a certain wild garlic, which is
quite common in the same places, and has also an insupportable acridness.[91]

When the savages lay in a store of these onions, with
which the ground is covered, they first build an oven,
upon which they place the onions, covering them with
a thick layer of grass; and by means of the heat which the
fire communicates to them the acrid quality leaves them,
nor are they damaged by the flames; and after they have
been dried in the sun they become an excellent article of
food. Their abundance, however, counts for nothing,
although the agreeable taste which one finds in them
often induces him to satisfy his appetite with them; for
nothing in the world is more indigestible and more [sc.
less?] nourishing. You feel a load on your chest, your
belly as hard as a drum, and colic pains which last two
or three days. When one is forewarned of this effect,
he refrains from eating much of this root. I speak from
experience, having been taken unawares by it; and after
the distress which I experienced from it I have no
longer any desire to taste it.

The prairies inhabited by the Illinois produce various
fruits, such as medlars, large mulberries, plums, and
abundance of nuts, as in France; and many other fruits.[92]
As for the nuts, some are found as large as a hen['s egg],

---

[91] Several species of *Allium* are found wild in the West — *A. trioceum*, or
wild leek; *A. cernum*, wild onion; *A. canadense*, wild garlic. The second of
these may have been the one described in the text. — ARLOW B. STOUT.

"The data (too slight) which end the two preceding paragraphs, on the
specific characteristics of the 'onion' of Perrot incline me to believe that he refers
to a species of *Allium*, probably *A. canadense*. The Cherokees, who are neighbors of the Illinois, very willingly use it as food." — BRUNET (cited by Tailhan).

This was probably the common wild garlic (*Allium canadense*). Plants of
the genus *Allium* found but little favor with the Indians as articles of food.
— WM. R. GERARD.

[92] In regard to the natural productions of the prairies, cf. Father Marquette's

which are so bitter and oily that they are good for nothing for eating. There are also strawberries in abundance, raspberries, and potatoes. But the people further north, as far up as Ouisconching, have no longer these medlars, and those who are still farther away are without these nuts like those of France; with these exceptions, they have all the other fruits of which mention has just been made.

V. *Hunting the buffalo*

I have already remarked that the savages of the prairies live in a happy land, on account of the great numbers of animals of all kinds that they have about them, and the grains, fruits, and roots which the soil there produces in abundance; but I have said nothing of the customs which they practice in their hunting expeditions or of the manner in which they pursue the chase, especially that of the buffalo.

The savages set out in the autumn, after they have gathered the harvest, to go hunting; and they do not return to their villages until the month of March, in order to plant the grain on their lands. As soon as this is done, they go hunting again, and do not return until the month of July, which is the time when the rutting season of the buffalo begins.

description of them, in *Récit des voyages*, section vii. He there mentions a sort of nut, which seems to be similar to this nut of which Perrot speaks; but the latter says that it is worthless for eating, while Marquette says that it is very good when ripe — which may be "purely a matter of taste." Other information regarding those fruits, etc., may be found in a letter by Father Gabriel Marest, in *Lett. édif.*, vol. vi, 327. — TAILHAN.

Mesles was the old French name for the fruit of the medlar, a tree not found in this country. Perhaps the fruit here mentioned by Perrot was the persimmon, which Capt. John Smith likened to a medlar. The nut mentioned by Perrot was possibly that of *Carya porcina* (the "pig-nut"), which attains a length of two inches; it is oily, and sweet at the first taste. The "bitter-nut" (*C. amara*; name applied also to *C. cordiformis*) is barely an inch long. — WM. R. GERARD.

The people of an entire village go together to this hunting, and, if there are not enough of them, they unite with those of another village, and that for two reasons: the first, in order to defend themselves against the attacks which their enemies might make against them; and the other, that thus they may be able to drive in a greater number of animals.

They assemble at nightfall on the eve of their departure, and choose among their number the man whom they consider most capable of being the director of the expedition. This is usually one of the more prominent war chiefs; he takes for adjutants all the other chiefs, and agrees with them on all the rules that should be laid down for the procedure that they must observe in order to hunt the buffaloes.

On the same day, one of the leading men makes a harangue before all the assembly, in which he makes known the orders that have been issued in regard to the limits which shall be observed in this hunt, and the punishments ordained for those persons who overstep them. He declares that these orders provide for depriving the disobedient of their weapons, breaking their bows and arrows, tearing down their cabins, and plundering them of property found therein; and this law is inexorable among them. The reason which obliges them to employ so much severity and strictness against those who fail to obey the rule is, that if any of them during the hunt were to pass beyond the prescribed limits all the game would escape them by flight, and the village would be in danger of perishing from hunger. All the chiefs are generally subject to this law; and even if he who is [appointed] over all the rest should commit this fault, he would be punished with the same rigor as any other man, without regard to his authority. In case he re-

fused to submit to it, all the young men – who are, so
to speak, his prop – would unite against him, and lay
violent hands on all persons who should come forward
to take his part.

This headman of the chiefs, with his adjutants, forms
the necessary detachments to go out scouting on the
[various] routes; and if these men suspect that there is
any danger for their people they come back over their
path in order to cover their tracks and to prevent any
attack by the enemy.

When the village has a large number of young men
able to bear arms they divide these into three bodies:
one takes its route to the right, another that to the left,
and half of the third party is divided between the two
former ones. One of these latter parties goes away [from
its main column] a league or thereabout to the right, and
the other remains on the left, both parties forming, each
on its own side, a long file; then they set out, in single
file, and continue their march until they judge that their
line of men is sufficiently long for them to advance into
the depths [of the forest]. As they begin their march at
midnight, one of the parties waits until dawn, while the
others pursue their way; and after they have marched a
league or more another party waits again for daylight;
the rest march [until] after another half-league has been
covered, and likewise wait. When the day has at last
begun, this third party which had separated to the right
and the left with the two others pushes its way farther;
and as soon as the rising sun has dried off the dew on the
ground, the parties on the right and the left, being in
sight of each other, come together in [one] file, and close
up the end of the circuit which they intend to surround.

They commence at once by setting fire to the dried
herbage which is abundant in those prairies; those who

occupy the flanks do the same; and at that moment the entire village breaks camp, with all the old men and young boys – who divide themselves equally on both sides, move away to a distance, and keep the hunting parties in sight so that they can act with the latter, so that the fires can be lighted on all four sides at once and gradually communicate the flames from one to another. That produces the same effect to the sight as four ranks of palisades, in which the buffaloes are enclosed. When the savages see that the animals are trying to get outside of it, in order to escape the fires which surround them on all sides (and this is the one thing in the world which they most fear), they run at them and compel them to reënter the enclosure; and they avail themselves of this method to kill all the beasts. It is asserted that there are some villages which have secured as many as fifteen hundred buffaloes, and others more or fewer, according to the number of men in each and the size of the enclosure which they make in their hunting.[93] For that country is nothing but plains, except only some small islands, to

[93] "Remains of the early species of the bison are found from Alaska to Georgia, but the range of the present type (*Bison americanus*) was chiefly between the Rocky and Allegheny Mountains." The first authentic account of this animal was that of Cabeza de Vaca, who saw the bison on the plains of Texas (*ca.* 1530). At that time the herds ranged from northern Mexico northwestward from the Rio Grande to British Columbia, through the valleys of the Saskatchewan and Red Rivers, thence (to the west of Lakes Winnipeg and Superior, and south of Lakes Michigan and Erie) to the vicinity of Niagara, thence southward through the western portion of the Atlantic Southern States, and into northern Mississippi and Louisiana. All the tribes within this range depended largely on the buffalo for food and clothing, and this dependence, with the influence of the habits of the animal, profoundly affected tribal customs and religious rites. This is more clearly seen in the tribes west of the Mississippi, where the people were in constant contact with the buffalo during the summer and winter migrations of the great northern and southern herds. These great herds were composed of innumerable smaller ones of a few thousand each, for the buffalo was never solitary except by accident. This habit affected the manner of hunting and led to the organization of hunting parties under a leader and to the establishment of rules to insure an equal chance to every member of

which they are accustomed to go and encamp for the
purpose of drying their store of meat.

The elk and the deer are quite often caught in these
circles of fire, but make their escape; and the savages

the party. . . The annual summer hunting party generally consisted of the
entire tribe. As the main supply of meats and pelts was to be obtained, religious
rites were observed throughout the time," with severe penalties for disobedience
of prescribed rules. This tribal or ceremonial hunt occurred in the summer
months, "when the animals were fat and their hair thin, the flesh being then in
the best condition for food and the pelts easiest to dress on both sides for the
making of clothing, shields, packs, bags, ropes, snowshoes, tent, and boat covers.
The meat was cut into thin sheets and strips and hung upon a framework of
poles to dry in the sun. When fully 'jerked' it was folded up and put into
parfleche packs to keep for winter use. A cow was estimated to yield about
forty-five pounds of dried meat and fifty pounds of pemmican, besides the
marrow, which was preserved in bladder skins, and the tallow, which was
poured into skin bags." The sinews, horns, and hair of the animal were used
in various ways, and even its dried excrements supplied fuel to the dwellers
on the treeless plains. "The buffalo was supposed to be the instructor of
doctors who dealt with the treatment of wounds, teaching them in dreams
where to find healing plants and the manner of their use. The multifarious
benefits derived from the animal brought the buffalo into close touch with the
people: it figured as a gentile totem, its appearance and movements were
referred to in gentile names, its habits gave designations to the months, and it
became the symbol of the leader and the type of long life and plenty; ceremonies
were held in its honor, myths recounted its creation, and its folk-tales delighted
old and young. The practical extinction of the buffalo with the last quarter
of the nineteenth century gave a death-blow to the ancient culture of the tribes
living within its range." — ALICE C. FLETCHER, in *Handbook Amer. Indians.*

In the Chicago *Record-Herald* for Jan. 17, 1909, is an interesting account
by William E. Curtis of the present numbers, habitat, and condition of the few
buffalo yet remaining in North America, compiled from data obtained from
the U.S. Department of Agriculture and the American Bison Society — an
association organized at New York in December, 1905, to take measures to
secure the preservation of the buffalo; its president is William T. Hornaday,
superintendent of the zoölogical gardens in Central Park of that city. This
officer has compiled a census of the American buffaloes known to exist on Jan. 1,
1908, which shows their numbers as follows: In Canada 476, in the United
States 1,116, in Europe 130, all in captivity; and of wild animals 25 in the
United States and 300 in Canada — a total of 2,047 pure-blooded bison. Besides
these, there are a considerable number of "cattaloes," the product of a cross
between the bison and the domestic breed of cattle — in the United States 260,
in Canada 57, in Europe 28. As experience shows that the bison does not breed
well in captivity, it has been thought best to provide for them a permanent open
range, and a tract of land for this purpose was selected by the American Bison
Society in Missoula County, Montana. — ED.

usually follow up only those animals that they are certain of killing or of capturing by surprise.

The people of the village then encamp in the place [that they find] most convenient, and nearest to the scene of the carnage. This camp being established, the game is divided among the families, each receiving what its hunters have slain; some have more and others less, according to the number of men in each; but the whole is distributed by the decisions of the chiefs, with great equity and justice. Each of these families strips the hides from the animals that fall to its share, and the people remain in the camp until all their store of meat is thoroughly dried. They are very careful to gnaw the bones of the animals so clean that no meat whatever is left on them. They finish [skinning the game] before noon, and the rest of the day is sufficient for preparing the meat [for drying].

The Illinois and their neighbors have no lack of wood for drying their meat; but the Ayoës [94] and the Panys [95]

---

[94] "The Ayoës, neighbors and allies of the Sioux, resided between 44° and 45° north latitude, at twelve days' journey beyond the Mississippi. They figure in one of the *Relations* of New France under the name of Aiaoua, or Mascouteins Nadouessi (*Relation* of 1673-1679, chap. iii). Charlevoix (*Histoire*, vol. iii, 396) calls them Aiouez." See La Potherie's account (*Histoire*, vol. ii, 182-184) of Perrot's first meeting with this people (in 1685). "In 1836 the old-time alliance of the Ayoës and the Sioux no longer existed. I read the following in a letter by Father Van Quickemborne, of the Society of Jesus, missionary among the Poutéouatomis and the Kickabous (*Annales de la propagation de la Foi*, vol. x, 130): 'Rumors of war have disturbed us for several days. An incursion by the northern Sioux is announced; and they are reported to be already the conquerors of the Sacks [Sakis, Ousakis] and the Aiouais.' These last and the Sakis lived united, in 1836, at a place thirty miles north of Leavenworth, in Kansas (cf. *Annales, ut supra*, 132)." — TAILHAN.

[95] "The *Panys* of Perrot, *Panis* of Charlevoix (*Histoire*, vol. iii, 212), *Panismaha* of the *Lett. édif.* (vol. vi, 327), and *Pawnees* of the Anglo-American historians and geographers, wandered about the shores and to the southwest of the Missouri; and they extended very far toward New Mexico (Charlevoix, *ut supra*). Father Vivier (*Lett. édif., ut supra*) classes them also among the Missourian tribes. Even to-day [1864] their hunting-grounds extend to the north of the Platte River in Nebraska. In 1837 their population attained the

generally use only the well-dried dung of the buffaloes, as wood is extremely scarce among them.

Thus you see how these tribes carry on their hunting expeditions, and they are always ready and able to defend their families against their enemies; for the families are always, on the march, placed on the flanks, which are protected on the right and the left by the warriors, and sheltered from the attacks that might be made on them. Besides that, there is nothing to fear behind them, for the men sent out to reconnoiter defend them at the rear, and on such occasions serve them as a rear-guard. It is impossible, therefore, for the enemy to appear without the entire troop knowing it, by means of the alarm-cry which each utters to the next one, and by the prompt assistance of the warriors, who immediately hasten to oppose the enemy. The women and children are out of danger; the warriors make a bold stand, and are very seldom driven back.

---

number of ten thousand souls (*Annales de la propagation de la Foi*, vol. xi, 394)." — TAILHAN.

Pani is but a variant of Pawnee, the name of a confederacy belonging to the Caddoan family, which migrated slowly toward the northeast, the Pawnee tribes finally establishing themselves "in the valley of Platte River, Nebraska, which territory, their traditions say, was acquired by conquest." In the nineteenth century, "the trail to the southwest, and later that across the continent, ran partly through Pawnee land, and the increasing travel and the settlement of the country brought about many changes. Through all the vicissitudes of the nineteenth century the Pawnee never made war against the United States," but often under severe provocation waited for the government to redress their wrongs, and their men served as scouts in the United States army during the Indian hostilities. By various treaties (1833-1876) they ceded their lands in Nebraska to the government; and in 1876 they "removed to Oklahoma, where they now live. In 1892 they took their lands in severalty and became citizens of the United States." Their numbers have steadily diminished since 1860, and in 1906 there were but 649 survivors. The name Pawnee "is probably derived from *pariki*, 'a horn,' a term used to designate the peculiar manner of dressing the scalp-lock, by which the hair was stiffened with paint and fat, and made to stand erect and look like a horn." The name was also applied to Indian slaves in the seventeenth and eighteenth centuries, perhaps because the Pawnees at first furnished most of these slaves. — ALICE C. FLETCHER, in *Handbook Amer. Indians*.

In their winter hunts they follow the same rules; but
the snow with which the ground is entirely covered prevents them from making the fires spread, and thus obtaining the same success as in other seasons of the year.
As for their [hunting] laws, they are under the same
obligation to observe them; but they are unavoidably
compelled to arrange a much longer line of men to form
the circuit with which it is necessary to surround the
buffaloes. If any one of the animals finds an opening
for forcing its way through them, they run to meet it
to prevent its flight; or else they follow behind the game
so swiftly that they always slay many of the beasts.

It is only the skin on the bellies of the cows and that
of the yearling calves which the savages use for making
their garments; but the hides of the bulls are used for
[making] bucklers, with which they ward off their
enemies' arrows and the blows of clubs. When they
wish to dress this hide, they cut off a sufficient piece of it,
and, after thoroughly scraping both sides of it, they boil
it a moment in water, and then take it out of the kettle.
Then they stretch it on a hoop of the same size as the
buckler that they intend to make, and when it is entirely
dry it becomes as hard as the heavy leather used for the
soles of shoes. When the savages wish to cut it for
stretching, they take pains beforehand to make it as
nearly round in shape as they can; and when it is quite
dry they remove the superfluous leather attached to the
hoop [on the outer edge]. In this manner they make the
bucklers which they carry to war.

VI.   *Manner in which the savages hunt the bear in
winter*

Toward the end of autumn the bears seek a place
where they find shelter from the rigors of the winter

season; it may be in a hollow place in a rock, or under the roots of a tree, or in a hollow log, or else in a hole that the bear digs in the ground. If the animal is very large, it will select the roots of the largest it can find among the fallen trees, and cover them over with a quantity of spruce-branches, in order to entrench itself therein.

This animal is in rut in the month of July, at which time it becomes so lean, and the flesh so insipid and disagreeable in flavor, that it is impossible to eat it; but when that period has passed, the bear has instinctive knowledge of the fruits that can restore it to good condition—such as raspberries, hazelnuts, walnuts, crab-apples, plums, acorns, beechnuts, berries, and other fruits, each according to its season. As soon as the winter has come, the bear makes its retreat in a place least exposed to the cold; and although it eats nothing during all that season it is nevertheless able to retain the fat which has been supplied to it by the fruits on which it fed during the autumn.

The savages apply themselves to hunting the bear in the season when the elk and deer are lean. A war-chief will make up a party of young men, to whom he will give a feast; but note here that the givers of the feast[96] may not eat of it; it is for them to see that the others eat enough. This chief, I say, declares before all the assembly that he desires to go on a bear-hunt, and invites them to accompany him, telling them the day on which

---

[96] " 'Those of the feast,' that is, the chief who gives the feast; for he alone, among the company, abstained from taking part in the repast — at least, this is what Charlevoix affirms (*Histoire*, vol. iii, 116). This usage is still in force among some of the tribes of English America: 'When their supplies of food are abundant, they [the savages of Lake Abbitibbi] sometimes make feasts in honor of the great Manito . . . he who gives the feast has the right to sing during the entire time while the feast lasts; but he is not permitted to eat' (*Rapport sur les missions de Québec*, no. 2, 52)." — TAILHAN.

he has decided to set out. It must be understood that
this feast is sometimes preceded by a fast of eight days,
without eating or drinking, in order that the bear may
be favorable to the chief and those of his party – meaning
that he desires to find and kill some bears, without incurring any injury to himself or his people.

The day of their departure having arrived, he as-
sembles all his men, who, like himself, have their faces
blackened with coal; and all remain fasting until evening, when they eat, but only a little. They set out the
next morning, and at the start the chief of the party begins to station his men so as to make a circuit of about a
quarter or a half of a league, and to complete the en-
closing line which was planned at the very place from
which they departed. They beat up and then range
through the tract of land which is thus enclosed; and
they carefully examine all the trees, roots, and rocky
places which are within their circuit, and kill the bears
which may be found there. As soon as they kill one,
they light a pipe and, thrusting it into the animal's
throat, they blow the smoke out through its nostrils.
They cut the string that is under the tongue, and wrap
it in a piece of cloth in order to keep it with great care.
After they have carefully examined and traversed all
the places within this enclosure, the chief forms still
another circuit, if the weather permits; and his men
search through this in the same manner as I have already described.

After that, they are occupied in skinning the bears, and
the flesh they carry to their camp. If among these animals they find one that is unusually larger and longer
than the others, it is roasted in the same manner as a
pig is, and set aside for a solemn feast on their arrival
at the village. When the animal is skinned, they re-

move all the fat, and cut it into quarters. When all the men have eaten at the camp, at evening each one takes from his pouch all the tongue-strings that he has, which are placed over a brazier with great respect and many invocations – the hunters firmly believing that if these pieces while broiling make a squeaking sound (which never fails to occur), or curl and twist, they will kill more bears. If, on the contrary, no sound is made in the cooking, and the heat does not cause the strings to move, they say that their hunting will be worth little.

It is their custom to hunt on the next day as on the first, to blacken themselves with coal, and to observe their fasting until evening. They also have the habit of washing themselves before their meal, with the notion that, if they failed to do so, they would transgress rules absolutely necessary for obtaining success in hunting bears; and that, these animals being hidden in their holes, the hunters could not discover them, or else would run great risk of being devoured by them. They conduct this hunt with arrows, and not with guns, because the noise [of the latter] would frighten those who were not far away, or prevent them from leaving their lairs.[97]

This hunt lasts sometimes eight days or more; then they return to their village, to which they convey their meat – I mean, the carcasses cut into quarters; and the whole is divided up among the families. If there is among them any stranger, or any of their allies, they also make a present of meat to such.

If the hunt is successful, they invite some near-by villages, and for that purpose they set aside two or three

---

[97] "It was actually when the bear left its lair that the savages killed it" (see *Relation* of 1634, chap. ix). Cf. Father Allouez, in *Relation* of 1676, chap. iii. "These animals were extraordinarily numerous to the west of Green Bay and Lake Michigan. In one single campaign, one village of Poutéouatomis killed more than five hundred of them" (see Allouez, *ut supra*). – TAILHAN.

carcasses to give to these neighbors. A larger share in the spoils of the chase is given [to those persons] who receive the strangers at their houses to entertain them and to make special feasts for them.

As for the great bear which they had roasted, as has already been stated, a solemn feast of it is made by the chief of the hunting party. This animal is carried to him entire, not even excepting its intestines, and twenty men are invited to this banquet. They cut off the hide of this beast in pieces three or four fingers long; they make a sort of dressing composed of chunks of fat; as for the intestines, both large and small, these remain as they are. They borrow the great kettles which are reserved for feasts of this sort – which always remain outside, and are brought into the cabin only when used on such occasions. Those gentlemen take care to cook the flesh, the head, the haslet, and the entrails of the bear; but the blood is prepared separately, seasoned with the grease from the fat of the animal, which is melted out beforehand. When all is cooked and ready to eat, the chief cooks take as many wooden sticks as there are persons to be invited, and demand from the giver of the feast the names of those whom he wishes to invite; and when he has named them one of these sticks is carried to each guest, with the declaration that he is invited to a feast at the house of [So-and-so]. They do not fail to go thither, each carrying his own dish, and on their arrival take their places. If there are strangers in the room, they are placed next to the giver of the feast; if not, the chiefs have that place. The host has a divinity, supposed [to be chosen] at his pleasure, to whom he dedicates the feast; and his assistants serve all the guests present. There are only three or four who must without fail eat the head, blood, and haslet of the bear; and each of the others [must eat] a slice of the fat a brasse[98] in length (which is distributed among them as equally as possible), if they are to expect the god of the earth to grant to the village his favor and abundance of his blessings. They are still further obliged to drink among them all the oil or grease which floats on the broth after the meat is cooked, and they swallow it as if it were wine. It is not without making great efforts that they come to the end [of the feast]; and when they cannot chew any longer, and the morsels cannot pass their throats, they take some spoonfuls of the broth to make these slip down. There are some of them who die from such excesses, and others who are scarcely able to recover from them; see to what extremes pride and gluttony carry those peoples. For if they have eaten everything they are congratulated thereon, and the spectators come to tell them, by way of praise, that they are [indeed] men; they reply to all these civilities by saying that it is only the proper thing for brave men to do their duty on such an occasion.

When the hunters arrive at the village, if they are loaded all the children, as far away as they can descry them, shout aloud their joy at the sight, with repeated exclamations of *Kous! Kous!* and do this without stopping until the hunters have laid down their loads at the doors of their cabins. Such is always the practice at the arrival of the hunters. For as soon as one [of the children] raises an outcry the rest run out of their houses in order to second him, and the fathers and mothers even strive to urge them on in their shouts.[99]

---

[98] The *brasse* was a linear measure of five old-French feet, or 1.62 metres, equivalent to 5.318 English feet. — ED.

[99] "Very singular ceremonies preceded, accompanied, and followed the feast in which the Montagnais (the lower Algonquins) ate the bear killed in their hunting" (see *Relation* of 1635, chap. iv; *id.* of 1637, chap. xi). "The Montagnais, converted to Catholicism, long ago renounced all these superstitious prac-

XII. Moral traits of the savages

There are both good and bad traits among the savages. The most praiseworthy are their hospitality and the harmony which prevails between them and the persons connected with them. They have also many faults: ambition, vengeance, self-interest, and vainglory entirely possess their hearts. They follow three principles which induce them to plunge with excess into all kinds of vices.

I. *The hospitality of the savages*

The hospitality that they exercise surpasses all that which is general among the Europeans. When any stranger asks it from them, they could not receive him more kindly, no matter how unknown he may be; it is on their side the most friendly of welcomes, and they even go so far as to spend all their means to entertain those whom they receive. A stranger as soon as he arrives [at a cabin] is made to sit down on a mat, of the handsomest [that they have], in order to rest from his fatigue; they take off his shoes and stockings, and grease his feet and legs; and the stones are at once put in the fire, and all preparations quickly made, in order to give him a sweat.[100] The master of the family, and some

---

tices. To-day, when they have slain a bear they make with it a feast to which they invite all their friends, and at which the fat of this animal constitutes the most esteemed viand. The head of the bear is exposed at the top of a pole, in the same place where it was killed. It is a trophy erected by the hunters in order to make known to all who pass that way their good success. Cf. *Missions de Québec*, 11th rep., 63, 94. . . Among the peoples of the Bay of Puans, the head of the slain bear received the adoration of the guests occupied with eating its body" (*Relation* of 1672, chap. ii). "The Miamis ate the bear at the beginning [of the feast], and afterward they adored its skin" (see Father Allouez in *Relation* of 1674, chap. xii). "The customs of Finland also establish the great honors paid to the bear slain by the hunters — a usage doubtless originating in various countries from the terror which this powerful animal inspires, and from the benefits obtained by the family from hunting it." — TAILHAN.

[100] See description of this sweating process in *Relation* of 1634, chap. vi —

other men who are prominent in the community, go with him into the place where the sweat is given, and allow him to lack for nothing therein. The kettle is over the fire, so as to provide food for him when he comes out of the sweat; and if the cabin in which he lodges is not very well supplied with provisions, search is made through-

"another point of resemblance to the northern peoples of Eastern Russia."
— TAILHAN.

"Few practices were so universal among the Indians as the sweat-bath, probably known to every tribe north of Mexico, although along the northwest coast south of the Eskimo territory it seems to have been superseded by bathing in the sea. The sweat-lodge is to this day common in most Indian villages and camps. The type of the ordinary sweat-house seems to have been everywhere the same. Willow rods or other pliant stems were stuck into the ground and bent and fastened with withes into a hemispherical or oblong framework, which usually was large enough to accommodate several persons. A hole conveniently near the door was dug, into which stones, usually heated outside, were dropped by means of forked sticks. These were sprinkled with water to furnish steam. A temporary covering of blankets or skins made the inclosure tight. This was the sweat-house in its simplest form. . . In no tribe was the sweat-lodge made except according to prescribed rules. In permanent villages a more roomy and substantial house was made. . . Among the Indian tribes methods of sweating seem to have been everywhere very similar. After a half-hour or more spent in the steaming air of the sweat-house, the bather plunged into the cold water of a stream, when one was near, and thus the function ended."

"There seem to have been three distinct purposes for which sweating was practiced. First, it was a purely religious rite or ceremony for the purpose of purifying the body and propitiating spirits. A sweat-bath was always undergone by warriors preparing for war, among many tribes, by boys at the puberty age; and, perhaps generally, before any serious or hazardous undertaking. Such ceremonial baths were almost always attended by scarification or the mutilation of some part of the body. . . No doubt the offering of prayers in the sweat-house for success in various enterprises was a general custom. The religious motive probably gave rise to the practice, and it was by far the most important in the estimation of the Indian. Second, sweating was important in medical practice for the cure of disease. The underlying idea was doubtless analogous to its religious and ceremonial use, since it was intended to influence disease spirits, and was usually prescribed by the shaman, who sang outside and invoked the spirits while the patient was in the sweat-house. . . Third, it was often purely social and hygienic. A number of individuals entered the sweat-house together, apparently actuated only by social instinct and appreciation of the luxury of a steam bath." Among some tribes this was "an almost daily custom, frequently having no other purpose than to give pleasure. It is probable that this practice is modern and that the sweat-bath has lost something of its primitive importance and sacredness." — H. W. HENSHAW, in *Handbook Amer. Indians*.

out the village for the best food for him.   I mean here
the best grain and the best quality of meat which can be
found, for which the man in whose house the stranger is
accommodated afterward pays, often at four times what
it is usually worth.   While the guest is eating, all the
leading people come to pay him visits.   If he is clad in
cloth garments, they take from him his clothing, and instead they give him furs, of their handsomest and most
valued, to clothe him from head to foot.   He is invited
to all the feasts that are given in the village, and in conversation they inquire of him for some news from his
own part of the country.   If he knows of nothing new,
he draws on his imagination for it; and even if he lies
no one would venture to contradict him, even supposing
that they were quite certain of facts contrary to his
stories.   There is but one person alone of the entire assembly who converses with the stranger; all the rest keep
silence, with the reserve and modesty that are prescribed
for a novice in a religious order, in which he is obliged
to maintain this behavior under penalty of the severe
measures belonging to the most strict rule on this point.
When the stranger shows a desire to return whence he
came, they load him with what is most suitable for his
journey; if he is inclined to prefer peltries to other
goods, these are given to him.   They are just as liberal
toward those who give them nothing as to those who
carry [presents] to them.

   This sort of reception is ordinary among the savages;
in point of hospitality, it is only the Abenakis, and those
who live with the French people, who have become
somewhat less liberal, on account of the advice that our
people have given them by placing before them the obligations resting on them to preserve what they have.   At
the present time, it is evident that these savages are fully
as selfish and avaricious as formerly they were hospit-

able. Although they are no less haughty than they were
before, they have fallen very low in sordidness, even so
far as to beg; and notwithstanding all that, the most
singular thing is, that they not only consider themselves
so necessary to those who aid them to live, but regard
those very persons as their inferiors and incapable of
excelling them. Those of the savages who have not been
too much humored [by the French] are attached to the
ancient custom of their ancestors, and among themselves
are very compassionate. If any one of them is in want,
they at once unite their efforts to assist him. When there
has been scarcity of grain among their allies, they have
invited the latter to come to them for it. They are very
tender-hearted in regard to sick people, for they employ
all means in their power, and give all that they can, to
relieve the sufferings of these. If there is any child captured from their enemies whose life has been spared,
and whose master allows him to suffer for lack of food,
they give him something to eat.

When a stranger to whom they have given hospitality
wishes to go home and is ready to depart, the host who
has received him packs up his belongings, and gives him
the best things that he has in his cabin – whether in peltries, trade-goods, or provisions – that may be necessary
to the guest on his journey. Although such generosity
may be astonishing, it must be admitted that ambition is
more the motive for it than is charity. One hears them
boast incessantly of the agreeable manner with which
they receive people into their houses, and of the gifts that
they bestow on their guests – although it is not denied
that this is done smilingly and with all possible gra-
ciousness.[101]

---

[101] "Most of the *Relations* – those, for example, of 1634 (chap. v and xiii),
of 1635, of 1636 (chap. vi), and, finally, of 1673 (chap. ii) – bestow the same

II. *Of the harmony among the savages*

The harmony which subsists among the savages is in truth displayed not only by their words, but in their actual conduct. The chiefs who are most influential and well-to-do are on an equal footing with the poorest, and even with the boys – with whom they converse as they do with persons of discretion. They warmly support and [even] take in hand the cause of one another among friends; and when there are any disputes they proceed therein with great moderation. They expose themselves as little as possible to personal encounters and disputes together;[102] and if there is any person who deserves a reprimand, this is given to him with great mildness. The old men treat the young men as sons, and these call the old men their "fathers." Seldom are there quarrels between them. When some erring person has committed an evil deed through a hasty and choleric disposition, the entire village takes an interest in the settlement of the

praise on the hospitality of the savages as does Perrot. 'Hospitality,' it is said in the last-named *Relation* just cited, 'is a moral virtue which is very common among the savages.' If, then, one chances on certain passages (*Relation* of 1634, chap. vi) where the contrary seems to be affirmed, it must be understood of savages spoiled by the neighborhood of Europeans, and initiated by them into the meanest calculations of cupidity. It must, however, be admitted that savage hospitality seems to have been frequently blind lavishness, by which one man expected to retaliate upon another; it was quite as much extravagant display of comradeship, and heedlessness of the future, as cordial liberality. 'A savage will observe that the kettle is over the fire at his neighbor's house, or that the latter is actually eating his meal, and he will go, without ceremony and without being invited, to sit down there and eat as if he were in his own house; and . . . he returns home without taking into account the favor that he has just received – because, in his eyes, it is not a favor. The next day, another man will do the same by him' (*Missions de Québec*, 12th rep., 66)."
— TAILHAN.

[102] "The harmony among the members of the same tribe, and especially among those of the same family, was and still is truly admirable among the savages. Perrot, in his depiction of this for us, falls short of the reality." See *Relation* of 1636, part 2, chap. vi; and an especially interesting example of fraternal love, in *Relation* of 1648, chap. x; cf. also *Relation* of 1634, chap. v.
— TAILHAN.

affair; they contribute together to render satisfaction to
the injured party, who finds no difficulty in laying aside
the vengeance which he had proposed to take on the
offender; and they seldom refuse to accept the decision
of any prominent man who intervenes in the affair.
Sometimes there are some of them who positively insist on the death of the guilty person; and if the old men
come to an agreement about it those who are inclined to
vengeance will not say a word, but will not fail, at the
first opportunity, to break the head of some relative or
tribesman of the murderer – or of several, according to
the number of people who have been slain. For if they
killed more [than that number], that would be the means
of arousing a war; instead, they only return blow for
blow, and are quits for it by the presents which they
make – as they say, to wipe away the blood [that was
shed].   If the first one slain was a man, his death will
be avenged upon a son of the murderer. When affairs
are settled, they are satisfied on both sides, as has been
said.

If any person encounters a grievous accident or a
great misfortune, the entire village takes an interest in
it, and goes to console him. The men perform this duty
for the men, and the women fulfil it for one another
among themselves. Visits of this sort are paid to the
afflicted person without conversation. The visitor fills
his pipe with tobacco and presents it to the other to
smoke; after he has smoked it for a little while he returns it to the person who gave it to him, so that the latter
also may smoke. This method of smoking by turns lasts
for some time, and then he who came to console returns
to his own house; and on his departure the sufferer
thanks him for the kindly interest in his troubles which
his visitor has shown. You must know that custom or-

dains that visits of this sort must be serious, and made
in silence; the reason which they give for this is, that if
they should use their voices for condolence on these occasions they would cause such agitation in the mind of him
who was in affliction that it would excite him to vengeance for the injury, or on the person who had wronged
him.

III. *Justice among the savages*

When savages have committed theft and are discovered, they are compelled to make restitution, or to give
satisfaction for the theft with other goods in case these
stolen are spent. If there should be failure to render this
satisfaction, the man who had been robbed would gather
several of his comrades, and would go – entirely naked,
as if he were marching against his enemies, and carrying
his bow and arrows – into the cabin of the thief, where he
plunders and seizes everything that belongs to him; nor
does the guilty man dare to say a word, but keeps his
head bowed down between his knees. But if he feels
that he is innocent of the crime of which he is accused,
he rushes to seize his weapons, and tries to oppose this
pillage. The spectators who are present hold back those
who are most hot-headed; but if there were only the
parties concerned the affair would not pass by without
bloodshed, or some one being killed. If, on the contrary,
the accused were innocent and had killed his man [while
defending his property], it would not be necessary for
him to make satisfaction; for his innocence would shelter
him from all evil results. But when he is really a
criminal he himself utters his own condemnation, and
never denies the fact, and he quietly suffers when three
or four times the amount of what he stole is taken away
from him. If among his goods there were any article
that he had borrowed, its owner comes forward to re-

claim what belongs to him, which is surrendered to him without any objection, the savages never appropriating anything of what does not pertain to them.[103]

When one of their connections commits a murder and is discovered to be its author, all the old men come together, make up among themselves a considerable present, and send it by deputies, in order to come to an agreement regarding means to arrest vengeance; for they all are involved in that vengeance, so far as it concerns in particular the leading persons of the offended tribe. The deputies, on their arrival at the place to which they were sent, enter with their presents the cabin of the murdered person; and the reception given to them is similar to that previously described when writing of the sweat-house. After the envoys have eaten what is offered to them, they produce their presents in the middle of the cabin, and demand that all the chiefs be called in to hear them; and when all have come they speak as follows:

"We are here to confess to you the crime committed by one of our young men upon So-and-so" (and then they name the man who was slain). "Our village does not approve the [act of the] murderer. You know that you have been our allies for a long time, and that your ancestors and ours presented the calumets to each other to smoke together" (they mention the year). "Since that time our villages have always aided each other against such and such a nation, with whom we were at war. You are not ignorant that our dead are in the other world, in the same place as yours; and if Heaven has permitted that one deluded man has overthrown or

---

[103] Observe the attitude of the Hurons (although they were very thievish) toward this offense, as mentioned in *Relation* of 1636, chap. vi; and "the village near which a theft has been committed is responsible for it, if the actual offender cannot be detected (*Relation* of 1637, part 2, chap. i)." — TAILHAN.

broken the union which our ancestors had with you, and which we have always maintained, we have therefore come with the design of averting your just resentment. While you are waiting for a more complete satisfaction, this present which we offer you is to wipe away your tears; that one is to lay a mat under the corpse of your dead; and this other, to lay on him a sheet of bark to cover him and shield him from the bad effects of the weather."

If the relatives of the dead man should be unwilling to hear any talk of satisfaction, and should take the resolution of positively obtaining vengeance for their loss, several of the old men would intervene with presents, in order to become mediators. They would argue that the people were placing themselves on the verge of having a war, with most grievous consequences, and, entreating the afflicted ones to have pity on their land, would warn them that when war was once kindled there would no longer be safety in any place; that many innocent persons would be sacrificed; that warriors attack indiscriminately all whom they encounter while on the warpath; that there would be no longer any peace or confidence between neighbors; and that, in short, they would behold desolation so great that brother would slay brother and cousin slay cousin, and that they would be their own destroyers; for as the ties of marriage and alliance are so strongly knit together, each man considers himself as a member no longer of the village where he was born, but of that one in which he has settled.

If the distressed relatives steadily persist in trying to obtain vengeance, and if the village is a large one and inclined to support their contention, the chiefs are detailed to confer with the principal men among the murderer's relatives, who are continually on their guard. These envoys set forth, when there is no way of settling the difficulty, that they are in danger of the destruction, for the sake of one man, of an entire village, [and that] by allies who cease to be such when they declare themselves enemies, and who are certainly very strong. They therefore induce the relatives, by dint of presents, to deliver the guilty man to his own comrades, who break his head and then cut it off to send it to the dead man's relatives. After that, presents are made on both sides in order to complete the arrangement.[104]

IV. *Of the ambition and vainglory of the savages*

All the savages generally display much vainglory in their actions, whether good or bad. They are as vain of debauchery as of valor; of the excesses and insolent acts that they commit when drunken, as of the chase; and of lewdness, as of generosity. When they choose to glorify themselves for the good that they have done, or the services that they have rendered to any one, they use audacious taunts; and in order to praise themselves for things that are worthy of reproach, they employ language and a certain manner of speaking that are so ridiculous and intolerable that nothing more would be needed, among Europeans, to excite quarrels. You would be astonished at seeing them get ready [for some

---

[104] "It is no longer a question of presents when the head of the culprit has been cut off; but this happens so rarely that one might say it did not exist."
— ANON.

"Poisoners taken in the act, or those who were suspected of having by their sorceries caused the death of any one, were killed without any form of trial (*Relation* of 1635). As for other murderers, they were usually under obligation only to pay the price of blood to the relatives of the victim; and yet it was not they, but their village or their tribe, which must furnish this amount. Hardly ever was this price refused." See *Relation* of 1636, chap. vi; also that of 1648, chap. xvii; in the latter, Ragueneau says, "In one word, it is the crime that is punished." — TAILHAN.

occasion]; they do not know what posture to assume; I believe that if they had a mirror before their eyes[105] they would change their appearance every quarter of an hour. Are they occupied with their hair, they arrange it over and over again, in the most elaborate manner that they can devise. They are no less fantastic in making up their faces with different colors, which they are continually applying thereon. In one word, ambition is one of the strongest passions which animate them.

V. *Of the vengeance of the savages*

The vengeance of the savages is more often inspired by ambition than by courage, for there are no people in the world more cowardly than they are.[106] That is made

[105] "That is something which they are never without." — ANON.

It is said of the Outaouais that they always "carry a mirror in the hand, and very often gaze at themselves to admire their grotesque ornaments" (*Annales de la propagation de la Foi*, vol. iv, 543). "In order to witness similar ridiculous performances, it is not absolutely necessary to go so far as among the savages." — TAILHAN.

[106] "Perrot here seems to me much too severe, his European prejudices not permitting to render to the savage's valor the justice which is due him. From the fact that those peoples do not understand courage in our way, it does not follow that we can accuse them of cowardice. They are almost as brave as the heroes of Homer. It is success that they seek above all else; moreover, when they see fortune turning against them and find that one path is still open to flight, they do not hesitate to take it — not so much through fear of death as because they have gone to war in order to carry away the scalp of their enemy, and not to leave their own with him. They hold, therefore, in slight esteem those deaths so glorious to the modern mode of thinking, which might have been averted by seasonable precaution." But they have actually displayed almost incredible bravery in some battles (see especially the account of an assault by Iroquois on Fort Richelieu, in *Relation* of 1642, chap. xi), and in numberless cases of death by torture at the hands of a pitiless enemy. "That the courage of those peoples may need to be aroused by motives of vengeance, of honor, or of self-interest, I willingly admit on the testimony of Perrot; but what civilized man is not a savage in this respect? Such motives were not lacking among them, bravery being held in high esteem among our Indians; and, united with liberality, it alone could secure any influence among them. The extraordinary value which they placed on it, may even furnish us a tolerably plausible explanation of the horrible torments that they inflicted on their prisoners of war. Among some of those tribes, one would think, it was actually their main pur-

sufficiently evident in their fits of passion by the trembling with which their bodies are seized, and the pallor
which would appear upon their faces if these were not
covered with black, red, or other colors. They expose
themselves to danger with great rashness;[107] it is that
which renders them so enterprising; for if ambition excites them to vengeance they will go stealthily to kill a
man in the midst of his friends, and to confront an
ambuscade, even though they are sure that they can
never retur ɩ from the undertaking.[108] They are so bold
that they will approach a hostile camp so near that they
can count their foes.[109] But all these extraordinary displays of courage are maintained only through vainglory,
or from a passion to attract praises to themselves, either
during life or after death. Notwithstanding, the reproach has quite often been cast on them that they had
been cowardly enough to suffer injuries and let them
go unpunished; the reason is, that [in such cases] ambition had no share, for there is no extreme to which their

---

pose to force the captive to dishonor himself and his tribe by yielding to the
violence of the tortures, and betraying his weakness by tears and groans unworthy of a brave man. But this refinement of vengeance hardly ever attained
its object. Then — that is, when the victim had, by his unshakable fortitude,
mocked the hopes of his butchers, they consoled themselves by devouring his
heart and drinking his blood, to the end that they might thus appropriate to
themselves his invincible courage, which they were forced to admire. Besides,
it was this last result which was almost exclusively sought. Accordingly,
only prisoners of distinction were subjected to these torments, since their
known intrepidity dissipated even the shadow of a doubt on this point. Cf.
Simon, *Noticias historiales de la conquista de Tierra-Firme*, not. ii, 82, and
not. iv, 315, 322." — TAILHAN.

[107] "Wrong; there is no temerity among them." — ANON.

"It is evident from the preceding note that the valor of the savage is sometimes accompanied by a daring which borders on temerity; farther on in
Perrot's own account may be seen instances of this (chap. xvi) ;" see also *Relation* of 1670, chap. vi. — TAILHAN.

[108] "Wrong." — ANON.

"I would be quite inclined to think that this time the criticism is correct."
                                                          — TAILHAN.

[109] "By favor of the night and of some woodland." — ANON.

passion for it does not carry them, even to desperation, and to treachery in order to take their revenge.

VI. *Among the savages, self-interest dominates* [*even*] *ambition and vengeance*

Although ambition and vengeance are two passions which imperiously possess the minds of the savages, self-interest carries them still further, and has far more ascendency over them.   There is no disgrace or injury which they do not overlook if those who have insulted them indemnify them with goods of sufficient value.[110] They will sell the lives of their nearest relatives, and will even consent to permit their friends to be killed.   They will tolerate (although they are jealous) the prostitution of their wives, the violation of their daughters and their sisters.   They will engage in unjust wars, and will break treaties of peace with [other] peoples without good cause.   Self-interest corrupts them, and renders them capable of every kind of evil deed; they make it their chief idol, as being that one in which they place all their confidence.[111]   This maxim renders, in their view, all projects which they form by it in all cases glorious, however base and treacherous these may be; and

---

[110] "Exaggeration." — ANON.

"We see, however, even here (page 102), the Outaouais violating, for the sake of wretched lucre, the most sacred laws of hospitality, by delivering to the Hurons a Sioux chief who was united to their own chief by an alliance the most intimate that can exist between two Indians of different tribes.   It would seem to me almost certain that Perrot, in drawing in his memoirs this portrait (certainly not a flattering one) of savages in general had especially in view the great family of the Illinois.   In order to be convinced of this, one has only to compare with the text of our author what Father Marest wrote of this same people at the same period (*Lett. édif.*, vol. vi, 322). . .   In short, it is evident that, generally speaking, the savages are neither brutes nor heroes, nor altogether men, but great children — who most often allow themselves to be carried away by the first impression, good or bad, when self-interest does not decide them."
— TAILHAN.

[111] "Some are capable of cowardice of this sort, but few." — ANON.

besides glorying in such things they never fail to accomplish them, so far as is within their power, as will be seen by what follows.

VII.   *Subordination is not a maxim among the savages*

The savage does not know what it is to obey. It is more often necessary to entreat him than to command him; he nevertheless yields to all demands made upon him – especially when he fancies that there is either glory or profit to be expected therefrom, and then he comes forward of his own accord and offers his aid. The father does not venture to exercise authority over his son, nor does the chief dare to give commands to his soldier – he will mildly entreat; and if any one is stubborn in regard to some [proposed] movement, it is necessary to flatter him in order to dissuade him, otherwise he will go further [in his opposition]. If the chiefs possess some influence over them, it is only through the liberal presents and the feasts which they give to their men, and here is the reason which induces them to pay respect to their chiefs; for it is characteristic of the savages always to incline to the side of those who give them most and who flatter them most.[112]

---

[112] "Among the savages of New France, the principle of independence was absolute; and it recognized in no authority the right to impose limits on it. Each tribe, and in each tribe every village, and in each village every family, and in each family every individual, all considered themselves free to act according to their own pleasure, without ever having to render account to any one. It is equally correct to say that the Hurons, the Iroquois, and the Algonquins had no government. Their chiefs enjoyed no power except in military and hunting expeditions, in which, moreover, they were followed only by those persons who were very desirous to go. In all other circumstances their only means for securing obedience was persuasion, and even this method did not always succeed. . . If a murder were committed, if a peace solemnly pledged with another people were violated by the caprice of a single individual, the chiefs must not undertake to punish the offender directly; that would have been to ascribe to themselves a jurisdiction over him which they did not even dream of claiming. Presents were offered to the injured party, to 'cover the

XIII. Continuation of the war between the Algonkins and the Irroquois, which has been carried on against many other tribes

I have made remarks on the subject of the war by the Algonkins against the Irroquois, at the beginning of this memoir; and [have stated] that the Irroquois, having been compelled to abandon Lake Erie, had retired to Lake Ontario, which at present bears the name of Lake Frontenac; and that they had always remained there or in its vicinity, after they had driven out the Chaoüanons and their allies toward Carolina.

In the raids which the Irroquois made in that period they carried away many families from among their enemies, and spared the lives of the children, who became, when grown, so many warriors in their service. The victories which they had gained over those tribes prompted some of the latter to take revenge for the murders which the Irroquois had committed on their people, in which they had been too shamefully treated. They marched therefore against the Irroquois and routed many of them, but the latter soon avenged themselves for this, for, as the Algonkins had attacked them only with small parties, their defeats had not been of great importance.[113] It is certain that the lack of subordina-

---

dead,' or to restore the peace, and all was said — a custom which we meet also in the nations who invaded the Roman empire in the fifth century. The greatest punishment that could be inflicted on the guilty person was, not to defend him, and to allow those whom he had injured freedom to take vengeance on him at their own risk and peril." See *Relations* — of 1634, of 1637 (chap. xiii), of 1648 (chap. x). "It was not altogether thus with the tribes scattered through the valley of the Mississippi. Among some of these — for example, the Miamis and the Natchez — the chiefs possessed far more extensive power, and sometimes even unlimited; but that was only an exception. Cf. Perrot (chap. xx), *Relation* of 1671 (chap. iv), and *Lett. édif.* (vol. vii, 9 ff.)." — TAILHAN.

[113] "This passage of Perrot is very obscure. As the phrases of which it is

tion which has always prevailed among that [Algonkin] people has been a reason why they have not destroyed that of the Irroquois; do we not see every day that the largest [war-]parties among them will not listen to any commands, and that the chiefs, each giving orders according to his own judgment, cause their plans to miscarry?

This war lasted until the peace which Messieurs Tracy and de Courcelles granted [1666] to the Aniez when they went to make war on those peoples, whose courage had terrified the Irroquois;[114] it was among the French that this peace ceased to be permanent, when Monsieur the Marquis [de] Denonville marched [1687]

---

composed can be applied alike to the Iroquois or to the Algonquins, they offer only an equivocal and perplexed meaning. Among all the explanations that can be furnished, this appears to me most probable: the Algonquins marched against the Iroquois parties, who had taken the war-path in order to avenge the murder of their tribesmen, and defeated many of them; but the Iroquois did not delay in taking their revenge. Having been attacked, in the first encounters, only by small bands of Algonquins, their defeats could not be very bloody ones, and consequently could not greatly weaken them. Cf. La Potherie, *Histoire*, vol. i, 293." — TAILHAN.

[114] " 'Whose courage had terrified the Iroquois.' Grammatically, these words can be understood only of the Agniers, one of the five confederated Iroquois tribes. But then how could the courage of the Agniers frighten the friends and allies of that warlike people? Because their courage, that is, their presumptuous audacity and their violence, imposed fear on the rest of the confederation, and hindered the conclusion of the peace with the French. This would be quite in accord with what the *Relation* of 1648 (chap. vii) states, of the fear inspired by the Agniers in their own countrymen: 'What has caused, it is said, the Onnontaeronnon [the Iroquois of Onnontagué; the Onondagas] to entertain thoughts of peace is . . . secondly, the fear that they feel lest the Annieronnon [the Agniers, or Mohawks] — who become insolent in their victories, and who render themselves insupportable even to their allies — may become too strong, and in time tyrannize over them.' Perhaps also this member of the sentence should be referred to Messieurs de Tracy and de Courcelles, whose courage frightened the Iroquois, and constrained them to demand peace. It would not be the first time, in this memoir, when the grammatical construction and the author's meaning openly contradicted each other. Perrot, as is known, did not pride himself on literary skill; he was more practiced in affairs than in rules of syntax. Account must also be taken of the uncertainty in which we remain over the correct reading of a text of which the original is lost and of which but a single copy remains to us." — TAILHAN

against the S[on]nontoäns. However, Monsieur de la
Barre afterward [1684] led an expedition against the
Onontagués, with whom he concluded a peace.[115]

XIV. Defeat and flight of the Hurons, driven out of their own country

The French having discovered this country [of Can-
ada], the news of their settlement [in it] spread from
tribe to tribe. The Algonkins were living, as I have
previously remarked, along the river of the Outaoüas,[116]
and the Hurons were in their own ancient country.[117]
These latter, after having been at war with the Irroquois,
made peace with them [1624]. Missionaries were
granted to a party of them who came [to the French set-
tlements], and a detachment of soldiers to defend them
in case they were attacked [1644]. The Irroquois stirred
up war against one of the Huron villages, and laid it
waste. They maintained peace with another village of
the same people, but seized a third by surprise and
ruined it, as they had the first. Those of the Hurons who
could escape separated; some went toward the Illinois,
and the others went down [the St. Lawrence] to the
[French] colony, with the missionaries and the soldiers
who were compelled to abandon their stations [1650-
1651].

This defeat spread terror among the Outaoüas and
their allies, who were at Sankinon, at Thunder Bay,
and at Manitoaletz and Michillimakinak. They went

---

[115] "Monsieur de la Barre made his expedition before Monsieur Denonville
had come to this country; it is Monsieur de Callières who concluded the peace
which Monsieur Denonville had broken." — ANON.

"In the detailed narration of these events which we read farther on, Perrot
has restored the order of the facts, here by oversight confused." — TAILHAN.

[116] "In Three Rivers and at Montréal." — ANON.

[117] "Between Lake Huron and Lake Ontario." — ANON.

to dwell together among the Hurons, on the island which
we call Huron Island.[118] The Irroquois remained at
peace with another village, established at Detroit, of sav-

[118] "Huron Island, located at the entrance to the Bay of Puans, in Lake
Michigan, now figures on the American maps under the name of Pottowatomie
Island — and with good reason, since the Poutéouatamis were its first inhabitants.
But at the period when the Outaouais Algonquins of Sankinon and Anse-au-
tonnerre (Saginaw and Thunder Bays, on the western shore of Lake Huron), and
of Michillimakinak and Manitoaletz (Mackinaw and Manitouline, two islands
in the same lake), took refuge there, the Poutéouatamis had already left it.
Indeed, it is evident from a comparison of Perrot's narrative with that of La
Potherie that, on departing from Huron Island, the Algonquins and their allies
retreated into Michigan (the present state of Wisconsin and northwestern section
of Michigan), and settled among the Poutéouatamis, at a day's journey (seven
or eight leagues) from the abode which their fear of the Iroquois forced them
to abandon. The Poutéouatamis welcomed the fugitives with all the more
kindness since they belonged to the same race, speaking the same language, and
were animated with the same hatred against the Iroquois, who in former times
had driven them also from their native land — that is, from the immense
peninsula which to-day forms the eastern division of Michigan (*Relation* of
1667, chap. ix; *id.* of 1671, third part, and chap. v). This first migration of
the Poutéouatamis must have been made about 1636 at latest, for after 1637 or
1638 we find them established in the neighborhood of the Puans, and consequently
near the bay to which the latter tribe gave their name (*Relation* of 1640, chap.
x). In the course of the following years they spread along the shores of that
same bay, the inner end of which they were occupying in 1671 (*Relation* of
1671, *ut supra*), having also again taken possession of Huron Island, and some
of their bands being dispersed over the neighboring mainland, at the entrance
of the bay. At least this is what Father Allouez seems to indicate when, on
the one hand, he places the country of the Poutéouatamis in the Lake of the
Illinois or Lake Michigan (*Relation* of 1667, chap. ix), which is literally true
of Huron Island only; and, on the other, he mentions a village of that same
people situated on one of the shores of the bay, eight leagues from an Ousaki
village built on the opposite shore (*Relation* of 1670, chap. xii). Now the bay
is no wider than its entrance (Marquette, *Récit des voyages*, chap. i). Warriors, hunters, and fishers, the Poutéouatamis were of all the western savages
the most docile, and the most friendly to the French. Their natural politeness
and their kind attentions extended even to strangers, which is very rare among
those peoples (*Relation* of 1667, *ut supra*). Finally (and this is the most complete encomium on their energetic vitality), they have thus far resisted the
method, as efficacious as hypocritical, which the Anglo-Saxon race has so pro-
fitably employed to rid itself of so many other tribes. They have been poisoned
with rum and brandy; fraudulent treaties have been imposed on them, by
threats or by misrepresentations, which despoiled them of their territory, almost
without compensation. Thus they have been driven back from one region to
another, [till they are] far beyond the Mississippi, in a corner of Kansas, from

ages who were called "Neutral Hurons," because they
did not embrace the interests of their allies, but maintained an attitude of neutrality. The Irroquois, however, compelled these people to abandon Detroit and
settle in the Irroquois country. Thus they augmented
their own strength, not only by the many children whom
they took captive, but by the great number of Neutral
Hurons whom they carried to their own country; and it
was at that time that they made so many raids against
the Algonkins that the latter were compelled to seek
shelter among the French of the [Canadian] colony.
The Nipissings made a stand in their villages during
several years; but they were finally obliged to flee far

---

which the flood of invaders will, without doubt, again drive them; but all has
been useless, and they obstinately persist in living. A day will come, however,
when they, [with patience] worn out by so many injustices and outrages, will
endeavor to take in their own way a revenge too well deserved; then all will
be ended. On these incorrigible Redskins, bold enough to scalp some of the
Pale-faces who have so long oppressed, plundered, or even murdered them, will
be let loose five or six thousand militiamen, and a "heroic" general who has to
repair his reputation; grape-shot will be poured on them without pity, and
those whom the cannon shall have spared will be hanged by way of an example. [If you doubt this] inquire first for the tribes of Oregon, or the Sioux
of Minnesota." — TAILHAN.

See description of the Bay of Puans (Baie Verte, or Green Bay) and its
apparent tides, in Marquette's *Récit des voyages* (chap. i), and an account of
Father André's observations thereon in *Relation* of 1676. "Some recent observations have confirmed the truth of all that precedes. In fact, see what I find in
the *Correspondant* of October, 1862 (vol. lvii of the collection, p. 257, note 2):
'Mr. Graham has just verified the fact of lunar tides in Lake Michigan, in
America.' " — TAILHAN.

In 1849 Increase A. Lapham made observations which indicated regular tides
in Lake Michigan, apparently the first scientific discovery of this phenomenon.
(See G. G. Meade's *Report of Survey of Northern Lakes, 1861*, pp. 313, 361.)
This matter again received attention in 1871, observations being made at Milwaukee which showed semi-diurnal tides at that point — solar of 4/100 and
lunar of 8/100 of a foot. At the same time was investigated the phenomenon
of irregular oscillations (or seiches) in the surface-level; these appeared to be
caused by "oscillations of the barometer, either local or general, and by the
accompanying winds, periodicity arising in some cases by reflection from an
opposite shore." (See detailed account by C. B. Comstock in *id.*, 1872, pp.
7-16). — ED.

northward to Alimibegon [Nepigon]; and the savages who had been neighbors to the Hurons fled, with those along the Outaoüas River, to Three Rivers.

The Irroquois, elated by the advantage which they had gained over their enemies in thus compelling them to take flight, and finding no other bones to gnaw, made several attacks upon the Algonkins and even upon the French, taking several captives who were afterward restored to their homes. That was succeeded by more than one treaty of peace, which proved to be of short duration. The early relations of these events describe them quite fully; accordingly I do not expatiate upon them here, but limit myself to an account of only such things as they have òmitted, and which I have learned from the lips of the old men among the Outaoüa tribes.

The following year [1653], the Irroquois sent another expedition, which counted 800 men, to attack the Outaoüas; but those tribes, feeling sure that the enemy had ascertained the place where they had established themselves, and would certainly make another attack against them, had taken the precaution to send out one of their scouting parties, who went as far as the former country of the Hurons, from which they had been driven. These men descried the Irroquois party who were marching against them, and hastened back to carry the news of this incursion to their own people at that [Huron] Island. They immediately abandoned that place and retreated to Méchingan, where they constructed a fort, resolving to await there the enemy. The Irroquois [came to that region, but] were unable to accomplish anything during the first two years. They made further efforts to succeed, and put in the field a little army, as it were, intending to destroy the villages of that new settlement, at which a considerable extent of land had been already cleared. But the Outaoüas had time enough to harvest their grain before the arrival of the enemy; for they were always careful to keep scouts on the watch, in order not to be taken by surprise, and the scouts saw the enemy in time. The Irroquois finally arrived one morning before the fort, which appeared to them impregnable. In their army were many Hurons who were the offspring of the people whom they had come to attack – men whose mothers had escaped from the ruin of their tribe when the Irroquois had invaded their former country. The enemy had at the time not much food, because they found very little game on the route which they had thus far followed. Deliberations were held, and propositions for a treaty of peace were made. One of these was that the Hurons who were in the Irroquois army should be given up, which was heeded and granted. In order to settle upon the terms of the treaty, it was agreed that six of their chiefs should enter the fort of the Hurons, and that the latter should, in exchange, give six of their men as hostages. A treaty of peace was accordingly made and concluded between them. The Outaoüas and Hurons made presents of food to the Irroquois, and also traded with them for blankets and porcelain collars.[119] The latter remained in camp for several days to rest their warriors, but when they entered the fort only a few at a time were admitted, and these were drawn by the Outaoüas over the palisades by ropes.

The Outaoüas sent word to the Irroquois army before their departure that they wished to present to each of their men a loaf of corn-bread; but they prepared a poison to mix with the bread. When the loaves were baked, they were sent to the Irroquois; but a Huron

---

[119] "Porcelain" was the Canadian-French term for the shell, glass, or porcelain beads used as money and ornaments by the Indians — the "wampum" of English writers. — Ed.

woman who had an Irroquois husband knew the secret, and warned her son not to eat any of the bread, because it had been poisoned. The son immediately informed the Irroquois of this; they threw the bread to their dogs, who died after eating it. They needed no more to assure them of the conspiracy against them, and determined to go away without provisions. They concluded to divide their forces into two parties; one of these embarked from that place,[120] and were defeated by the Saulteurs, Missisakis, and people of the Otter tribe (who are called in their own tongue Mikikoüet),[121] but few of the Irroquois escaping. The main force pushed farther on, and soon

[120] "Our manuscript here presents a gap which I do not attempt to fill. I thought at first that I could do so, by reading this passage thus: [*Dont l'un relascha de l'autre côté du lac*]; but the space left blank by the copyist is so small that it deprives of all probability this attempt at restoring the text. What is certain is, that of the two Iroquois parties one returned on their march, and, crossing the Bay of Puans and the lake of the Illinois, took the road to their own country, going along the shores of Lake Huron (where they were surprised and defeated by the Saulteurs, Mississakis, and Mikikouets); the other pushed farther on, toward the southwest, and penetrated as far as the territory of the Illinois, where they too were entirely routed. This conclusion is reached by comparing the narratives of Perrot and La Potherie (*Histoire*, vol. ii, 54). We note, however, that this latter writer, by an evident *quiproquo*, makes those of the Iroquois go to the Illinois whose route, after their departure from the country of the Poutéouatamis, followed the shores of Lake Huron — which is absurd; for, in order to reach Lake Huron from Michigan, they must of necessity have turned their backs on the Illinois, and on the vast prairies where, it is claimed, they had encountered that people." — TAILHAN.

[121] "It has been previously seen (chap. xi, note [80]) that the Sauteurs, or Chippewais, who in former times inhabited that portion of western Michigan which is bathed by the waters of the three lakes — Michigan, Superior, and Huron — have almost entirely abandoned it. Part of them were obliged, several years ago, to migrate, whether they would or no, beyond the Mississippi; others now reside on the great island of Manitouline; and some have not yet been able to resign themselves to leaving their ancient territory (*Annales de la propagation de la Foi*, vol. vi, 69). The Mississakis had their settlements on the northern shore of Lake Huron, not far from Manitouline Island (*Relation* of 1648, chap. x; *id.* of 1671, third part, and chap. ii; La Potherie, *Histoire*, vol. ii, 60). About 1720, some of their families resided at Fort Frontenac; their villages were also found on the western shore of Lake Ontario, at Niagara, and at Détroit (Charlevoix, *Histoire*, vol. iii, 195). Beyond this I have nothing more to say of the Mississakis, save that 'this people, besides the multiplicity of wives

found themselves among the buffaloes. If the Outaoüas had been as courageous as the Hurons, and had pursued the enemy, they could without doubt have defeated them, considering their slender supply of food. But the Irroquois, when they had secured abundance of provisions, steadily advanced until they encountered a small Illinoët village; [122] they killed the women and children

and the superstitions which are common to them and to the other savages, are the boldest and most arrogant of all those around us' (*Relation* of 1673, chap. ii). Of the Mikikoués (or Otter People) no other mention is made of them, either in Perrot or anywhere else. The old *Relations*, in especial, say not a word of this tribe. Perhaps some error has slipped into our manuscript, and the copyist may have written Mikikoués instead of Nikikoués — an Algonquin tribe, who dwelt on the north shore of Lake Huron, between the Mississakis and the Amikoués (*Relation* of 1648, chap. x; *id.* of 1658, chap. v). Father Beschefer, too, associates the Nikikoués with the two other peoples whom I have just named (unpublished *Relation* of 1682). It is quite surprising that Perrot does not mention the Amikoués in his narrative, since, according to the *Relation* of 1671 (chap. ii) it was their chief who took the principal part in the victory obtained by the Sauteurs, the Mississakis, and the Otter People over the Iroquois who were returning to their own country after their unsuccessful expedition to the Poutéouatami country. We likewise read there that these Iroquois were defeated on the lands of these very Amikoués, and that but one of them escaped out of one hundred and twenty. This exploit brought such glory to that chief that, three years after his death, when his son desired to honor his memory by reviving his name, more than sixteen hundred warriors from all the neighboring tribes responded to the son's appeal, and assisted at the feasts celebrated on this occasion (*Relation* of 1671, *ut supra*)." — TAILHAN.

122 Here the text reads *brigade*; but it must be an error for *bourgade*, since La Potherie (*Histoire*, vol. ii, 55) mentions it as *un petit village d'Illinois*.
— TAILHAN.

"The Illinois [a name with many variants; signifying "the men"] were still, at this epoch, one of the most powerful peoples in New France. Their sixty villages contained twenty thousand warriors, and from one hundred to one hundred and twenty thousand inhabitants — not including the Miamis, who could furnish a quota of eight thousand warriors (*Relation* of 1658, chap. v; *id.* of 1660, chap. iii). But from 1667 all was quite changed; those numerous and flourishing villages, dispeopled by war, had been reduced at first to ten, then to two (*Relation* of 1667, chap. xi; *id.* of 1670, chap. xi) — or to eight, according to another *Relation* (that of 1671, third part) — which counted no more than eight or nine thousand inhabitants (*Relation* of 1670, *ut supra*). They spoke a dialect of the Algonquin language, very different from the mother-tongue — but not so much so that the Illinois and the Algonquins could not, with a little practice, understand each other (*Relation* of 1667, chap. xi; *Voyage* of Father Marquette). This great and powerful nation was subdivided into a certain

therein, for the men fled toward their own people, who
were not very far from that place. The Illinoëts imme-

number of tribes; here are the names of some among them:" the Kikabous, or
Kikapous; the Kaskaskias; the Kaokia; the Tamarois, or Tamarohas; the
Kouivakouintanouas; the Negaouichiriniouek (the Negaouich Illinois?), neighbors of the Poutéouatamis; the Peorias; the Moüingoüena; the Mitchigamias,
who of all the Illinois were the most distant toward the south; the Kitchigamich,
or Ketchegamins, "who spoke the same language as the Kikapou Illinois, and
therefore with some probability can be regarded as belonging to the same
stock;" the Maskoutens, or Fire People, classed among the Illinois for the same
reason; the Miamis, or Oumiamis (the Algonquin prefix *ou* being equivalent
to our article), composed of several distinct peoples. See various references
to these peoples and tribes in the *Jesuit Relations*; also in Charlevoix's *Histoire*,
vol. ii, 484, and vol. iii, 188, 392; La Potherie's *Histoire*, vol. ii, 261; and
Annales de la propagation de la Foi, vol. x, 137, 138. "The Illinois extended
their raids and their hunting over an immense territory, of which the present
state of Illinois represents only a part;" it extended from the Fox River of
Wisconsin and Lake Michigan to the Miami and the Ohio Rivers, and westward
to the Mississippi, which they occupied from the thirty-third to the fortieth
parallel (Marquette). "But these limits were never closely drawn; they varied,
to the east and especially the west, at the dictation of events (see *Relation* of
1671, third part)." It was the Sioux (or Nadouessi) "whose continual hostilities seem to have forced the Illinois to their first migration toward Lake
Michigan (see *Relation* of 1667, chap. xi)."
   The war between the Iroquois and the Illinois (1656-1667) brought on the
ruin of the latter people, and those who escaped took refuge beyond the Mississippi. Later (1666) the peace imposed on the Iroquois by the power of
France reopened to the Illinois the doors of their own country; but many of
them did not profit by the opportunity which was offered to them, or did so
quite late. In 1674 there were, as yet, on the banks of the river of the Illinois,
only the single tribe of Kaskaskias; they numbered seventy-four lodges and
nearly three thousand souls (Marquette, *Voyages*). Seven other tribes rejoined
the first one in 1676, and formed with it a village of three hundred and fifty
lodges, which contained at least eleven thousand inhabitants (*ibid.*); for among
the Illinois four or five fires were combined in each lodge, and each fire was
always for two families (*Lett. édif.*, vol. vi, 175). Toward 1693 or 1694 the
Illinois people were divided among eleven villages, of which one alone contained
three hundred cabins or twelve hundred fires (*ibid.*); but from 1712 these villages were reduced to three, situated at immense distances from one another, in
a territory of two thousand square leagues (*id.*, 325, 328). To-day one would
seek in vain for a single Illinois savage in the greater part of those vast regions.
By a cleverly combined mingling of violence and fraud the United States has
taken possession of that territory, and brutally expelled from it its ancient
owners (Letter of Father Thébaud, in *Annales de la propagation de la Foi*,
vol. xvi, 450). Here again the Anglo-Americans have done what, according
to the testimony of the missionaries, they do everywhere else; after having demoralized the savage, and deprived him of his possessions, they have driven

diately assembled their forces, and hastened after the
Irroquois, who had no suspicion of an enemy; overtak-
ing the enemy at nightfall, the Illinoëts later attacked
them, and slew many of them. Other Illinoët villages,
who were hunting at various places in that vicinity, having learned what had occurred, hastened to find their
tribesmen, who had just dealt a blow at the Irroquois.

him from his native land as if he were a wild beast (*Missions du diocèse de
Québec*, no. xii, 70, 1859). I have previously cited the somewhat unfavorable
judgment pronounced over our savages by one of their most zealous missionaries
[Father Marest; see reference in note 110]; it is therefore my duty, in strict
justice, to acknowledge here that their first apostles paint them in more flattering
colors" (see mention of the traits of the Illinois in *Relation* of 1667, chap. xii;
id. of 1671, chap. iv; Marquette's *Voyages*). In attempting to reconcile these
varying opinions, we must "take into account the demoralization produced
among these Indians, in half a century, by their relations with the Europeans
and by the trade in brandy; and, in the lavish praises of the Illinois by Fathers
Allouez and Marquette, must make allowance for the illusions of that charity
which believeth all things, hopeth all things, and thinketh no evil, until the
last extremity. One finds, nevertheless, in the relation of the second of these
missionaries an indication, unfortunately too clear, of the immorality with which
our Illinois were later reproached. To be convinced of this, it is sufficient to
compare the 'mystery' described by Father Marquette (*Voyages*) with what is
related of an identical custom, in vogue among other savage peoples, by many
historians, both Spanish and French. . . But these moral infirmities of the
Illinois, even as great ones as are supposed, ought not to make us Frenchmen
forget the invariable fidelity of these savages to our country. Entering their
hearts at the same time as did the Catholic faith, this devotion to France never
once deviated, from the end of the seventeenth century to the treaty of Paris
(1763), which handed over our North American colonies to England. When our
cause was hopelessly lost, and when, in execution of this shameful treaty, the
English commissary presented himself (1765) to take possession of Fort Chartres
and the country of the Illinois, those Indians could not resign themselves to this
peace and this change [of rulers]. The chief of the Kaskaskias, speaking in his
own name, and in that of the Missourites and the Osages, his allies, declared
to the French commandant that in all their tribes there was not one man who
willingly submitted to it." (See his speech in Bancroft's *History of the United
States*, vol. iv, chap. xviii.) "Indeed, it was these faithful and devoted allies
who, two years before, had sorrowfully repeated to the commandant of Fort
Chartres, 'Father, do not abandon thy children; not one Englishman will penetrate as far as this while the red man lives. . . Our hearts are with the
French; we detest the English, and we will kill them all' (*id.*, chap. vii).
Would not one say that a secret presentiment made them recognize in these
newcomers the approaching authors of their final and irreparable ruin?"
— TAILHAN.

Assembling all their warriors, they encouraged one another, made a hasty march, surprised the enemy, and utterly defeated them in battle; for there were very few of the Irroquois who returned to their own villages. This was the first acquaintance of the Illinoëts with the Irroquois; it proved baneful to them, but they have well avenged themselves for it.

XV. Flight of the Hurons and Outaoüas into the Micissypy region

In the following year [1656] the Outaoüas descended in a body to Three Rivers. Missionaries were allotted to them: the Hurons had Father Garot, and the Outaoüas had Father Mesnard, with five Frenchmen who accompanied them. Father Garot was slain by the war-party of the Flemish Bastard,[123] who had embarked with the Hurons on the Lake of Two Mountains, where he had caused a fort to be built; but, having allowed the main body of the Outaoüas and Saulteurs (who were much better canoemen than the Hurons) to go ahead, the Irroquois came up with them, although [they had

[123] "Perrot is mistaken; Father Mesnard did not go among the Outaouais until 1660. Father Garreau had for a companion in 1656 Father Dreuillette; and the latter, after the catastrophe on the Lake of Two Mountains, seeing himself abandoned by the savages, returned to the Colony with the few Frenchmen who had followed him (*Relation* of 1656, chap. xv)." Some oversight of the copyist has misplaced the parts of this sentence; but the facts of the case render the sense plain, that Father Garreau had embarked with the Hurons, and that he was slain by the band of the Flemish Bastard, who had built the fort. That noted chief "was son of a Hollander and an Iroquois woman. The tribe of Agniers, to whom he belonged through his mother, chose him for one of their chiefs. The Lake of Two Mountains is formed by an expansion of the Outaouais River, near its discharge into the Saint Lawrence. North of this lake extends the seigniory of the same name, belonging to the [Sulpitian] seminary of Montreal. It is in this seigniory that the gentlemen of Saint Sulpice established, near the beginning of the last [i.e., the seventeenth] century, two villages of Christian Iroquois and Algonquins, which still exist to-day, and count a thousand inhabitants." — TAILHAN.

started] far behind the Hurons, defeated them, and took
many of them captive. The Irroquois and the French
were then at peace. The Flemish Bastard had the body
of the father conveyed to Montreal, which at that time
was already founded [in 1642]. As soon as he had arrived he was asked why he had fired on the father, but
replied that neither he nor his people had killed him.
He said that the murderer was a Frenchman, who, having deserted from Montreal, had come to join the Bastard's party at the time when he went to lay ambuscades
for the Outaoüas, who intended to ascend the River des
Prairies. This Frenchman was handed over to the governor and shot to death, for lack of an executioner.[124]

The Flemish Bastard brought many Huron prisoners,
whom he tortured by burning their fingers, without any
opposition from the side of the French; and when he
returned to his own village he spared their lives. They
will never forget the manner in which, on that occasion,
we abandoned them to the mercy of their enemies. They
also will remember forever how little effort the French
made to oppose the Irroquois when the latter, in time of
peace [May, 1656], carried away the Hurons who dwelt
on Orléans Island, and made them pass in canoes before
Quebec and Three Rivers, meanwhile [compelling
them] to sing, in order to increase their mortification.
But in revenge the Outaoüas have since then sought
every opportunity to betray the French, although they
pretend to be our devoted friends; they treat the French

124 Perrot is the only one among the early chroniclers of events in New
France who has placed on a Frenchman the guilt of having slain Father Garreau; those writers evidently suppressed this fact, so discreditable for any
Frenchman. But this murderer is probably the man mentioned in the *Relation*
of 1656 (chap. xvi) as a French renegade who had joined the Iroquois, and
who by a curious retribution of fate was led, by the dying missionary himself, to
repent of his errors; he was afterward betrayed to the French by an Iroquois,
taken to Quebec, and executed by the authorities. — TAILHAN.

thus through policy and fear, for they do not trust any people, as will be more fully shown in the conclusion of this memoir.

When all the Outaoüas were dispersed toward the [great] lakes, the Saulteurs and the Missisakis fled northward, and finally to Kionconan [i.e., Keweenaw], for lack of game. Then the Outaoüas, fearing that they were not strong enough to repel the incursions of the Irroquois, who had gained information of the place in which the former had established themselves, sought refuge in the Micissypy region, which is now called Loüisianna. They ascended that river to a place about twelve leagues from the Ouisconching, where they came to another river, which is named for the Ayoës [Iowas]. They followed this stream to its source, and there encountered peoples who received them cordially. But as they did not find, in all that region which they traversed, any place suitable for a settlement – since the country was entirely destitute of woods, and contained only prairies and level plains, although buffaloes and other animals were found there in abundance – they retraced the same route by which they had come; and, having again reached the shores of the Loüisianna River, they continued to ascend it. Before they had gone far, they dispersed in various directions to pursue the chase; I will mention only one of their bands, whom the Scioux encountered, captured, and carried away to their villages. The Scioux, who had no acquaintance with the firearms and other implements which they saw among the strangers – for they themselves use only knives and hatchets of stone and flint[125]– hoped that these new peoples who had come near them would share with them

125 In the text, *de cousteaux de pierre de moulange, de haches et de cailloux*; this last phrase should probably read, *et de haches de caillou*, as indicating the

the commodities which they possessed; and, believing that the latter were spirits, because they were acquainted with the use of iron – an article which was utterly unlike the stone and other things which they used – conducted them, as I have said, to their own villages, and delivered the prisoners to their own people.

The Outaoüas and Hurons gave the Scioux, in turn, a friendly reception, but did not make them presents of much value. The Scioux returned to their own country, with some small articles which they had received from the Outaoüas, and shared these with their allies in other villages, giving to some hatchets, and to others knives or awls. All those villages sent deputies to those of the Outaoüas; as soon as they arrived there, they began, according to their custom, to weep over every person they met,[126] in order to manifest the lively joy which they felt

materials of the weapons used by the Sioux. The *pierre de moulange* means *pierre de meule* or *meulière*, that is, millstone-grit; the former phrase is still in use in Canada with that meaning. – TAILHAN.

Axes of stone were in general use by the tribes of North America, save along the Pacific coast, where specimens are seldom found. They varied from thirty pounds to one ounce in weight, the majority ranging from one to six pounds; they were usually fastened to handles by withes and cords, which were kept in place by grooves or notches cut in the stone. These implements were quickly superseded by the iron axes introduced and furnished to the Indians by the Europeans. – W. H. HOLMES and GERARD FOWKE, in *Handbook Amer. Indians*.

126 "The Dacotahs, or Sioux, were in the seventeenth century what they are still to-day, one of the most powerful and most numerous savage peoples of North America. They were divided into two great sections, the eastern or sedentary Sioux, and the western or nomadic Sioux. The former inhabited, on both banks of the Upper Mississippi, the territory of which Perrot farther on outlines for us the limits. The old *Relations* of New France designate them under the name Nadoüessis (Nadoüessiouek, and Nadoüessioux). . . The nomadic Sioux, dispersed through the immense plains of the West to the north of the Missouri, extended their inroads and their hunting as far as the Rocky Mountains. The tribe among them nearest to the Nadoüessioux figures in the *Relation* of 1660 (chap. iii) under the name of Poualaks, or 'warriors.'" "Perrot in his memoir notices only the eastern Sioux (the Nadoüessioux of the *Relations*), and from what he says of them it is easy to judge that that people were greatly superior, in moral qualities, to the various tribes of either the Algonquin or the Huron-Iroquois stock. As brave as any one of those tribes, the Sioux were more faithful to their promises, friends to peace, benevolent and

in meeting them; and they entreated the strangers to have pity on them, and to share with them that iron, which they regarded as a divinity. The Outaoüas, see-

hospitable to strangers, humane to their conquered and captive enemies — to whom they almost always gave their liberty, and whom they did not commence to torture until the law of retaliation (from which a savage never considers himself dispensed) rendered it a sacred duty to them. The *Relations* of New France are, in reference to the Sioux, entirely in accord with Perrot; and their testimony is here all the less suspicious because it concerns a people who were implacable enemies of the tribes who were evangelized by the religious of the Society of Jesus, the authors of those relations." (See the *Relation* of 1667, chap. xii; *id.* of 1671, third part; *id.* of 1674, chap. ix). "To this proved bravery the Sioux — less perfidious than the Iroquois, to whom their courage made them equal — united an inviolable fidelity to their sworn promise, a moderation which did not permit them to attack until after they had been first assailed (*Relation* of 1670, chap. xi), and, in war, a generous conduct far above that of the Hurons and the Algonquins. Satisfied with having obtained the victory, they most often gave freedom to the prisoners taken in battle (*Relation* of 1671, chap. iv). All this will doubtless surprise readers who are accustomed, giving credence to modern writers, to picture to themselves the Sioux under a different aspect. Certainly it is a far cry from these people, such as Perrot and the *Relations* of New France display to us, to the Sioux of the American journals — as cowardly as cruel, as perfidious as vindictive. But as peoples, like individuals, are subject to deplorable transformations, how can one be surprised if the Sioux of to-day have no longer anything in common with those of former times? Perhaps also, in the moment when they are being exterminated in order to punish them for their cruelties, and especially in order to cleanse more quickly the house which others wish to occupy, in the portrait which has been depicted for us the features have been coarsened or distorted and the colors laid on too heavily. Such procedure is much practiced, and the wisdom of nations has long taken it into account."

"The Sioux tilled the soil after the manner of the Hurons; but they cultivated hardly anything besides tobacco and a little maize (*Relation* of 1642, chap. xii). . . In order that each man might gather his harvest in peace, without encroaching on any other, the Sioux divided among themselves the marshes and the lakes in which the wild oats grew (*Relation* of 1671, chap. iv). As their country was poorly supplied with trees, neither they nor the Poualaks covered their lodges with sheets of bark, as did the savages of the Saint Lawrence; but they used for this elk-skins very well dressed, and so skilfully sewed together that no cold penetrated through them. Some of them, more industrious, built for themselves 'houses of sticky earth [*terre grasse*], very much as the swallows build their nests.' They burned mineral coal (*Relation* of 1660, chap. iii; *id.* of 1667, chap. xii)." Polygamy was in great honor among them, each Sioux having seven or eight wives (*Relation* of 1660, chap. iii). Hardly any other worship was known to them than that of the calumet (*Relation* of 1670, chap. xi). In their battles they used almost exclusively the bow and arrows, and

ing these people weeping over all who approached them, began to feel contempt for them, and regarded them as people far inferior to themselves, and as incapable even of waging war. They gave to the envoys

that with so much skill and rapidity that in a moment the air was full of their darts — 'especially when, after the manner of the Parthians, they turn about while fleeing; for it is then that they shoot their arrows so quickly that they are to be feared no less in their flight than in their attack' (*Relation* of 1671, chap. iv). Finally, their language differs in every way from that of the Hurons and that of the Algonquins (*id.* of 1670 and 1671, *ut supra*). All that has just been said is true of the Poualaks as well as of the Nadoüessioux or sedentary Sioux. Between these different divisions of the one people there never existed more than two points of unlikeness, and those purely accidental: one, that the Nadoüessioux lived in a territory of which the limits were nearly fixed (Perrot, 88); the other, that they had some knowledge of navigation, to which the Poualaks and the rest of the Siouan tribes were strangers." See Father Marest's account in 1712 (*Lett. édif.*, vol. vi, 372).

"Nothing is more difficult than to fix even approximately the figures of the Siouan population in the seventeenth century; all that can be said is, that it must have risen to a very high number. The *Relations*, indeed, assign to the Nadoüessioux forty villages, to the Poualaks at least thirty, and to the Assinipoualaks thirty (*Relation* of 1656, chap. xiv; *id.* of 1658, chap. v; *id.* of 1660, chap. iii; *id.* of 1671, third part) — without mentioning the Ayoës, who very probably belonged to the Siouan people. . . That admitted, it would be necessary, as a very natural result, to include in the reckoning the Ouinipegous or Puans [i.e., the Winnebagoes], a people who were formerly very numerous (*Relation* of 1667, chap. x; *id.* of 1640, chap. x), but, later, almost entirely exterminated by the Illinois (*Relation* of 1670, chap. xii); and they spoke the same language as did the Ayoës or Aiouas (*Relation* of 1676). Even as concerns the eastern Sioux, or Nadoüessioux, the figures given by the *Relations* may be regarded as much below the real numbers. . . In 1829 a missionary computed at ten thousand the number of men able to bear arms among the Sioux residing in the vicinity of Fort Saint Peter on the upper Mississippi; and at twenty-five or thirty thousand the number of women and children. This latter figure is probably inadequate; it is thirty or forty thousand that he must have meant (*Annales de la propagation de la Foi*, vol. iv, 536). Another missionary allows to the Sioux only eight thousand souls in all (*id.*, vol. viii, 311, 312); and a third (*id.*, vol. xxiv, 423), three thousand lodges and thirty thousand souls."

— Tailhan.

The houses of earth mentioned in the *Relation* of 1660 probably refer to the earth lodges constructed by the Omaha, Osage, Pawnee, and other tribes; see description and illustrations of these in *Handbook Amer. Indians*, art. "Earth lodge" and "Habitations." In the northwest, and especially in the Dakotas, there are extensive beds of lignite, of good quality; the settlers obtain much fuel from these in some localities, where it can be easily dug from the ground, the strata often outcropping above the surface. — Ed.

a few trifles, such as knives and awls; the Scioux declared that they placed great value on these, lifting their eyes to the sky,[127] and blessing it for having guided to their country these peoples, who were able to furnish them so powerful aid in ameliorating their wretched condition. The Outaoüas fired some guns which they had; and the report of these weapons so terrified the Scioux that they imagined it was the thunder or the lightning, of which the Outaoüas had made themselves masters in order to exterminate whomsoever they would. The Scioux, whenever they encountered the Hurons and Outaoüas, loaded them with endearing terms, and showed the utmost submissiveness, in order to touch them with compassion and obtain from them some benefits; but the Outaoüas had even less esteem for them when they persisted in maintaining before them this humiliating attitude.

The Outaoüas finally decided to select the island called Pelée [128] as the place of their settlement; and they spent several years there in peace, often receiving visits from the Scioux. But on one occasion it happened that a hunting-party of Hurons encountered and slew some Scioux. The Scioux, missing their people, did not know what had become of them; but after a few days they found their corpses, from which the heads had been sev-

---

[127] Among most of the Indian tribes, the sky was revered not only as the residence of a deity, but (by a sort of personification) as the deity himself, and was often invoked, especially at councils; the sun also was regarded as a deity. See *Jesuit Relations*, vol. x, 159-165, 195, 273, vol. xviii, 211, vol. xxiii, 55, vol. xxxiii, 225, vol. xxxix, 15, vol. xlvi, 43, vol. lxviii, 155. — ED.

[128] "Pelée [i.e., Bald] Island is situated in the Mississippi, three leagues below the mouth of the Sainte-Croix River, and at the entrance to the Lake of Bon-Secours (now Lake Pepin). Its surface was entirely bare of trees, which in early days caused the name to be given to it under which it is designated by Perrot and by Charlevoix (*Histoire*, vol. iii, 398). — TAILHAN.

Its location was at the upper end of Lake Pepin, opposite Red Wing, Minn. Charlevoix says (*ut supra*): "The French of Canada have often made it the center of their trade in those western regions." — ED.

ered. Hastily returning to their village, to carry this sad news, they met on the way some Hurons, whom they made prisoners; but when they reached home the chiefs liberated the captives and sent them back to their own people. The Hurons, so rash as to imagine that the Scioux were incapable of resisting them without iron weapons and firearms, conspired with the Outaoüas to undertake a war against them, purposing to drive the Scioux from their own country in order that they themselves might thus secure a greater territory in which to seek their living. The Outaoüas and Hurons accordingly united their forces and marched against the Scioux. They believed that as soon as they appeared the latter would flee, but they were greatly deceived, for the Scioux sustained their attack, and even repulsed them; and, if they had not retreated, they would have been utterly routed by the great number of men who came from other villages to the aid of their allies. The Outaoüas were pursued even to their settlement, where they were obliged to erect a wretched fort; this, however, was sufficient to compel the Scioux to retire, as they did not dare to attack it.

The continual incursions made by the Scioux forced the Outaoüas to flee.[129] They had become acquainted

---

[129] "Perrot adds no chronological indication to his curious narrative of the Huron and Outaouais migrations. We will endeavor to fill this gap, by having recourse to the contemporaneous *Relations*. In that of 1672 (chap. iv) see first, briefly described, the main events of that flight;" the Hurons, driven from their own country by the Iroquois, fled to Michilimackinac, thence to the islands at the mouth of Green Bay, and finally to the western end of Lake Superior, where also the Ottawas took refuge. Alarmed at the hostile attitude assumed by the Sioux toward them, they resolved to return (1671) to Michilimakinac. "Thus less than twenty years (from 1652 or 1653 to 1671) had been sufficient to bring back the Hurons and the Outaouais to their starting point; for these latter also returned, in 1671, to Manitoualine Island, and later to Saguinan, which they had left at the same time when the Hurons abandoned Missilimakinac (*Relation* of 1671, third part, chap. iv; Charlevoix, *Histoire*, vol. iii, 279). The flight of these peoples to the Huron Islands cannot be placed later

with a stream which is called Black River; they entered its waters and, ascending to its source, the Hurons found there a place suitable for fortifying themselves and establishing their village. The Outaoüas pushed farther on, and proceeded as far as Lake Superior, where they fixed their abode at Chagouamikon [Chequamegon]. The Scioux, seeing that their enemies had departed, remained quietly, without pursuing them farther; but the

than 1653; for the *Relation* of the following year (of 1654, chap. iv) shows us that they were settled there, and were sending from those distant regions one of their parties to trade at Montréal and Three Rivers. In 1657 the Hurons and the Outaouais, who a few years before had abandoned those islands in order to penetrate farther within the Méchingan of Perrot (now western Michigan and Wisconsin), were residing, the former on the shore of the Bay of Puans, among the Pouteouatamis, where they had victoriously repulsed the attack of the Iroquois; the latter, among the Ouinipegous or Puans, and among the Maloumines (*Relation* of 1658, chap. v). . . From the beginning of 1660, the Outaouais inhabited Point Chagouamigon, as well as the islands that belong to it on the southern shore of Lake Superior (*Relation* of 1661, chap. iii; *id.* of 1664, chap. i). The Hurons, at the same period, kept themselves in hiding near the sources of the Black River, at six days' journey (forty or fifty leagues) from the same lake, and seven or eight days from the Bay of Puans (*Relation* of 1660, chap. iii). These two peoples were visited in 1659 by two French traders, who pushing farther ahead, formed an alliance with the Sioux (*ibid.*). It is, therefore, between the years 1657 and 1660 that the events related by Perrot must have taken place, from the flight of the Hurons and Outaouais to the Mississippi until their first disputes with the Sioux, followed by a new migration, which was not to be the last one (Perrot, chap. xv). The Hurons were still occupying the same location toward the end of 1661 (*Relation* of 1663, chap. vii) but their sojourn there was not very long. In 1665 Father Allouez found the two tribes reunited at the Point (*Relation* of 1667, chap. iii, vi, vii, viii). Four years later the number of savages at Chagouamigon was fifteen hundred, of whom five hundred were Christian Hurons of the Tobacco tribe. The rest were composed of pagan Hurons and of Algonquins who had accompanied their flight, belonging to the Sinagaux, Kiskakon, and Keinouché Outaouais (*Relation* of 1667, chap. vii; *id.* of 1670, chap. xi). In estimating at forty or fifty leagues the six days' journey which separated Lake Superior from the residence of the Hurons (*Relation* of 1660, chap. iii), I have only applied the rule therefor indicated by Father Dreuillettes in the *Relation* of 1658 (chap. v): 'You will also see the new routes for going to the North Sea [i.e., Hudson Bay] . . . with the distances in leagues, according to the number of days' journeys which the savages spend therein — which I place at fifteen leagues a day in going down-stream, on account of the swiftness of the currents, and seven or eight leagues in going up-stream.' " — TAILHAN.

Hurons were not willing to keep the peace, and sent out several hostile bands against the Scioux. These expeditions had very little success; and, moreover, drew upon them frequent raids from the Scioux, which compelled them to abandon their fort, with great loss of their men, and go to join the Outaoüas at Chagouamikon.

As soon as they arrived there, they planned to form a war-party of a hundred men, to march against the Scioux and avenge themselves. It is to be observed that the country where the latter dwell is nothing but lakes and marshes, full of wild oats; these are separated from one another by narrow tongues of land, which extend from one lake to another not more than thirty or forty paces at most, and sometimes five or six, or a little more. These lakes and marshes form a tract more than fifty leagues square, and are traversed by no river save that of Loüisianna [the Mississippi]; its course lies through the midst of them, and part of their waters discharge into it. Other waters fall into the Ste. Croix River, which is situated northeast of them, at no great distance. Still other marshes and lakes are situated to the west of the St. Pierre [Peter] River, into which their waters flow. Consequently, the Scioux are inaccessible in so swampy a country, and cannot be destroyed by enemies who have not canoes, as they have, with which to pursue them. Moreover, in those quarters only five or six families live together as one body, forming a small village; and all the others do the same, removed from one another at certain distances, in order to be near enough to be able to lend a helping hand at the first alarm. If any one of these little villages be attacked, the enemy can inflict very little damage upon it, for all its neighbors immediately assemble, and give prompt aid wherever it is needed. Their method of navigation in lakes of this kind is, to push through [130] the wild oats with their canoes, and, carrying these from lake to lake, compel the fleeing enemy to turn about [and thus bewilder him]; they, meanwhile, pass from one lake to another until they clear them all and reach the firm ground.

The hundred Hurons became involved among these swamps, and without canoes; they were discovered by some Scioux, who hastened to spread the alarm everywhere. That was a numerous people, scattered along all the borders of the marshes, in which they gathered abundance of wild oats; this grain is the food of those people, and tastes better than does rice. More than 3,000 Scioux came together from every side, and besieged the Hurons. The loud noise, the clamor, and the yells with which the air resounded showed them plainly that they were surrounded on all sides; and that their only resource was to make head against the Scioux (who were eagerly striving to discover their location), unless they could find some place by which they could retreat. In this straitened condition, they concluded that they could not do better than to hide among the wild oats, where the water and mud reached their chins. Accordingly, they dispersed in various directions, taking great pains to avoid noise in their progress. The Scioux, who were sharply searching for them, and only longed to meet them in battle, found very few of them, and were persuaded that they themselves were entirely hidden by the wild oats; but they were greatly astonished at seeing only the trail made in leaving the lake, and no trace of the Hurons' entrance.[131] They bethought them of this

---

[130] In the text we read *devant*, which is apparently a copyist's error for *dedans.* — TAILHAN.

[131] This sentence follows the original text of the Ms., which was, however, printed otherwise by Tailhan, under the impression that the words *sortie* and *entrée* had been transposed by oversight of either the author or the copyist.

device: they stretched across the narrow strips of land [between the lakes] the nets used in capturing beavers; and to these they attached small bells, which they had obtained from the Outaoüas and their allies in the visits which they had made to those tribes, as above related. They divided their forces into numerous detachments, in order to guard all the passages, and watched by day and night, supposing that the Hurons would take the first opportunity to escape from the danger which threatened them. This scheme indeed succeeded; for the Hurons slipped out under cover of the darkness, creeping on all fours, not suspecting this sort of ambuscade; they struck their heads against the nets, which they could not escape, and thus set the bells to ringing.[132] The Scioux, lying in ambush, made prisoners of them as soon as they stepped on land. Thus from all that band but one man escaped; he was called in his own language Le Froid ["he who is cold"]. This same man died not a long time ago.[133]

The captives were conducted to the nearest village, where the people from all the others were assembled in order to share among them the prey. It must be observed that the Scioux, although they are not as warlike

Later, in writing his annotations, he concluded that he had made a mistake, and explains the Ms. reading thus: "By a stratagem familiar to savages, and in order the better to throw off the track the Sioux who were pursuing them, the Hurons entered the lakes of wild rice by walking backward, thus leaving only the traces of their departure." — ED.

[132] Cf. Radisson's device for the protection of himself and Groseilliers at Chequamegon — "a long cord tyed wth some small bells, w[ch] weare senteryes" (Wis. *Hist. Colls.*, vol. xi, 73). — ED.

[133] "This disastrous expedition followed the arrival of the Hurons at Chagouamigon (Perrot, 88), consequently it could not have occurred before 1662. However, it preceded, perhaps by a few years, the visit that the chief of the Sinagaux Outaouais paid to the Sioux in 1665 or 1666 (Perrot, 91 and 99); it is therefore very probable that the defeat of the Hurons by the Sioux belongs to either 1662 or 1663. Charlevoix (*Histoire*, vol. i, 346) and La Potherie (*Histoire*, vol. ii, 217, 218) have borrowed from Perrot the narrative of this event, but without endeavoring to assign to it an exact date." — TAILHAN.

or as crafty as the other tribes,[134] are not, like them, cannibals. They eat neither dogs nor human flesh; they are not even as cruel as the other savages, for they do not put to death the captives whom they take from their enemies, except when their own people are burned by the enemy. They were naturally indulgent, and are so now, for they send home the greater number of those whom they have captured. The usual torture which they inflict upon those whom they have doomed to death is, to fasten them to trees or stakes, and let their boys shoot arrows at them; neither the warriors, nor any men, nor the women, took part in this. But, as soon as

[134] "Our Ms. bears here, written over the lines, the following correction: 'It must be observed that the Sioux, although they are not so warlike, are more crafty than the other peoples,' etc. But nothing in Perrot seems to me to necessitate or to authorize this change." The following lines, at first sight, would indicate that the Canadian savages were habitually addicted to cannibalism; but in fact they practiced it only occasionally — and with different motives from those of most cannibals. With this restricting consideration, "it must be acknowledged that the accusation made by Perrot against our savages is entirely well-founded. . . But there is a point which seems to me very worthy of notice; it is the contrast which, in this respect, existed in primitive times between almost all of the peoples in the Mississippi region and all of the other peoples, both savage and civilized, of New France and Mexico. We have previously observed what humanity the Sioux displayed toward their prisoners of war. The numerous tribes of Illinois, who occupied over so vast an extent the valley of the Mississippi below the Sioux, reduced their enemies to slavery and sold them to the neighboring tribes; but it is not known that, before their wars with the Iroquois, they tortured or killed their captives; we are even certain of the contrary (*Relation* of 1670, chap. xi; *Voyages* of Father Marquette, vol. i, section 6; *Lett. édif.*, vol. vi, 182, 183). If we continue to descend the Mississippi we encounter, after the Illinois and the Natchez, the Houmas, still more gentle and kind to their captives than were the Illinois and the Sioux. When at the end of an expedition with successful result the Houma warriors made their solemn entry into their village, all the women of the tribe came to weep over the conquered, condoling with them for having been captured; and afterward they treated them as well as they did their own children, if not better (Gravier, *Voyage*). . . To return to the peoples of the Misssisippi, I must admit that the Natchez condemned to the fire those enemies whom the fate of battle cast into their power (*Lett. édif.*, vol. vii, 26); but we do not know whether this custom — the existence of which was made known to us for the first time only in 1712 — was not of recent institution among them, and the result of retaliation for a long time provoked, as among the Sioux and the Illinois." — TAILHAN.

they saw their own people burned, they resolved to do the same by way of reprisal; even in this, however, they do not behave with as much cruelty as do their enemies – either because some motive of pity or compassion will not permit them to behold such suffering, or because they believe that only despair can make the captives sing during their torments with so much fortitude and bravery, if it may be so called. On this account they speedily kill their captives with clubs.

The Scioux, having shared the prisoners, sent back part of them, and made the others objects for their sport – delivering them, as I said, to their boys to be shot to death with arrows; their bodies were then cast upon the dung-heap. Those whose lives they spared were condemned to see their comrades die, and were then sent home. Having arrived there, they gave a faithful account of all that had occurred, and said that, having seen the numbers of the Scioux, they believed it impossible to destroy them. The Outaoüas listened very attentively to the relations of these new arrivals, but, as they were not very brave warriors, they were not willing to make any hostile attempt; and the Hurons, recognizing the smallness of their numbers, made up their minds to meditate revenge no longer, but to live peaceably at Chagouamikon, [which they did] during several years. In all that time they were not molested by the Scioux, who gave all their attention to waging war against the Kiristinons [Crees], the Assiniboüles, and all the nations of the north; they ruined those tribes, and have been in turn ruined by them. For all those tribes are, at the present time, reduced to very small numbers: the Scioux, who formerly had more than seven or eight thousand men, seem to be those who travel by canoe,[135]

---

[135] "The text of Perrot here seems to me to be so badly treated that I do not even attempt to discover the real meaning. All that I think I understand in

instead of which the other tribes of the prairies cannot all together form, to-day, a body of more than a hundred men or so, at most. It is true that the Renards, the Maskoutechs, and the Kikapous have greatly contributed to defend them, and not the other tribes.

Father Mesnard,[136] who had been assigned to the

this sentence is, that the Sioux — not only those who travel by canoe, but those of the plains — destroyed their enemies, but not without themselves experiencing losses so considerable that they were reduced almost to nothing." — TAILHAN.

"Immediately in touch with the skin-boat countries all around the Arctic, from Labrador to Kodiak in Alaska and southward to the line of the white birch, eastward of the Rocky Mountains, and including the country of the great lakes, existed the birch-bark canoe. With framework of light spruce wood, the covering or sheathing of bits of tough bark sewed together and made watertight by means of melted pitch, these boats are interesting subjects of study, as the exigencies of travel and portage, the quality of the material, and traditional ideas produce different forms in different areas. . . From the northern boundary of the United States (at least from the streams emptying into the St. Lawrence), southward along the Atlantic slope, dugout canoes, or pirogues, were the instruments of navigation. On the Missouri River and elsewhere a small tub-shaped craft of willow frame covered with rawhide, with no division of bow or stern, locally known as the bull-boat, was used by Sioux, Mandan, Arikara, and Hidatsa women for carrying their goods down or across the rivers. It was so light that when one was emptied a woman could take it on her back and make her way across the land." — OTIS T. MASON, in *Handbook Amer. Indians.*

The name Missouri is generally understood to mean "great muddy," referring to the turbid waters of the river Missouri; but an interesting statement is made by Thomas Forsyth on this point, among some scattered memoranda in the book containing his "Memoir on the Sac and Fox Indians" (*q.v., post,* vol. II). He says: "Missouri is a corruption of the Indian word Miss-sou-ly i.e., Canoe, and that nation of Indians were called by other Indians (particularly the Ninne-ways [Illinois] Indians who resided east of the Mississippi) Miss-sou-li-au, that is 'Canoe men,' as they done all their travelling in canoes." — ED.

[136] René Ménard was born at Paris in 1604 or 1605, and entered the Jesuit order in 1624; he came to Canada in 1640, and spent the next nine years as a missionary to the Hurons (in their ancient abode near Georgian Bay). After those Indians were driven westward by the Iroquois in 1649, Ménard was stationed at Three Rivers, Canada, during some seven years, and then spent two years among the Iroquois. In 1660 he was sent from Montreal with a party of Ottawas to their home on Lake Superior, and spent the winter with them, where he suffered great hardships and was harshly treated by the Indians. In the summer of 1661, hearing that some Hurons were encamped near the headwaters of Black River in Wisconsin, he set out to visit them; but near the end of the journey he lost his way and was seen no more — probably dying of hunger in the forest, or slain by some Indian. See *Jesuit Relations,* vol. xviii, 256, 257,

Outaoüas [1660] as a missionary, accompanied by some Frenchmen who were going to trade with that people, was abandoned by all the men whom he had with him — excepting one, who even until death rendered to the father all the services and aid that he could look for. This father followed the Outaoüas to the lake of the Illinoëts, and in their flight into the Loüisianna region even beyond the Black River.

It was there that only one solitary Frenchman remained as companion to this missionary, and that all the others left him. This Frenchman, I say, carefully followed the route and made portages in the same places as did the Outaoüas, never turning aside from the same river that they followed. One day [in August, 1661] he was in a swift current, which swept him away in his canoe; in order to aid him the father left his own canoe, and did not take the right path to reach him. The father entered a path that had been trodden by the [wild] animals, and, attempting to regain the right one, became entangled in a labyrinth of trees and lost his way. The Frenchman, after he had with great difficulty ascended that rapid, waited for the good father; and, as the latter did not come, he resolved to go in search of him. In the woods he called to the father, shouting as loudly as he could, for several days, hoping to find him, but without avail. On the way, however, he encountered a Sakis who was carrying the missionary's kettle, and who told his news to the Frenchman — assuring the latter that he had found the father's tracks far inland [from the river], but that he had not seen the father himself. He said that he had also found the tracks of several other persons, who were going toward the Scioux; and he even declared that he thought the Scioux

vol. xlvi, 297, vol. lxxi, 144; also H. C. Campbell's monograph on Ménard, in Parkman Club *Pubs.* (Milwaukee), no. 11. — ED.

must have killed the father, or that he had been captured by them. In fact, the missionary's breviary and
cassock were found, several years afterward, among that
people, who displayed those articles at their feasts, consecrating to them their best viands.

The Outaoüas, having settled at Chagouamikon, there
applied themselves to the cultivation of Indian corn and
squashes, on which, with the fish they could catch, they
subsisted. They searched along the lake to find whether
other tribes were there, and encountered the Saulteurs
who had fled northwards, and with them some Frenchmen, who had followed them to Chagouamikon in
order to settle there. Part of the Saulteurs had gone
toward Kionconan [Keweenaw], and reported that they
had seen many tribes; that beavers were exceedingly
abundant there; that they did not all return together
because they had left their people at the north; that the
latter intended to dwell here, but without a fixed residence, purposing to roam in all directions; and that the
Nepissings and Amikouets were at Alimibegon.

At these tidings, the Outaoüas went away toward the
north, and sought to carry on trade* with those tribes
[1662], who gave them all their beaver robes for old

* "Evidences of widespread commerce and rude media of exchange in North
America are found in ancient shell-heaps, mounds, and graves, the objects having passed from hand to hand often many times. Overland, this trade was done
on foot, the only domestic animal for long-distance transportation being the dog,
used as a pack beast and for the travois and the sled. In this respect the north
temperate zone of America was in marvelous contrast with the same latitudes
of the Old World, where most of the commercial animals originated." But the
lack of animals was made up by using the water routes, especially the great
river-systems, navigable for canoes, in which neighboring waters are connected
for traffic by easy portages. "The North American continent is divided into
culture areas in a way conducive to primitive commerce. Certain resources
of particular areas were in universal demand, such as copper, jade, soapstone,
obsidian, mica, paint stones, and shells for decoration and money, as dentalium,
abalone, conus, olivella, and clam shells." The Atlantic slope from Labrador to
Georgia, the special home of Algonquian and Iroquoian tribes, produced abundance of animal life, and the salt-water bays and inlets yielded marine creatures

knives, blunted awls, wretched nets, and kettles used until they were past service. For these they were most humbly thanked; and those people declared that they were under great obligations to the Outaoüas for having had compassion upon them and having shared with them the merchandise which they had obtained from the French. In acknowledgment of this, they presented to them many packages of peltries, hoping that their visitors would not fail to come to them every year, and to bring them the like aid in trade-goods. They assured the Outaoüas, at parting, that they would go on a hunting expedition [to make ready] for their coming; that they would be present, without fail, at the rendezvous agreed upon; and that they would surely wait for them there.

In the following year [1663] the Outaoüas and all the

----

and aquatic birds in profusion, for food supplies, at the same time stimulating easy transportation and commerce. "The great lakes and the St. Lawrence, moreover, placed the tribes about them in touch with the copper mines of Lake Superior. Through this enlarging influence the Iroquois were ennobled and became the leading family of this area. A medium of exchange was invented in the shape of wampum, made from clam shells. The mounds of the southern portion of this slope reveal artifacts of copper, obsidian, and shell, which must have been transported commercially from afar along the water highways in birch-bark canoes and in dugouts. The Mississippi area was a vast receiving depot of commerce, having easy touch with other areas about it by means of portages between the headwaters of innumerable streams," which connected it with those areas from Chesapeake Bay to Columbia River. "The mounds reveal dentalium shells from the Pacific, obsidian from the Rockies, copper from Lake Superior, pipes of catlinite and black steatite from Minnesota and Canada, and objects from the Atlantic. . . Commerce was greatly stimulated through the coming of the whites by the introduction of domestic animals, especially horses, mules, donkeys, cattle, sheep, goats, poultry; by the vastly enlarged demand for skins of animals, ivory, fish, and native manufactures; by offering in exchange iron tools and implements, woven goods, and other European products desired by the Indians. The effects of this stimulated trade were profound, for both good and evil. Indians were drawn far from home. The Iroquois, for example, traveled with the fur traders into northwestern Canada. Many kinds of Indian handiwork have entered into world commerce. . . In ancient times there were intertribal laws of commerce, and to its agents were guaranteed freedom and safety." — OTIS T. MASON, in *Handbook Amer. Indians.*

other tribes who were trading with the French were going down in a body to Quebec. They did so not without fear, for they imagined that the Irroquois were in ambuscade everywhere. However, they did not encounter the enemy until they reached Cape Massacre (which is the locality of the latest land-grants), below Saint Ours; and in that place there were sixteen Irroquois, who carried away an [Algonkin] canoe, and eight men who were paddling it, in the sight of all the Outaoüa fleet. This fleet, I say, very far from giving chase to so weak an enemy, was on the point of returning home, and abandoning their own [cargo of] peltries as well as that which the Frenchmen had shipped with them. It is certain that the French had much difficulty in dissuading them from this idea, and that without [this effort] they would have carried out the resolution that they had made to return directly home. On their arrival at Quebec, the chief of the Outaoüas was put in prison, with irons on his feet, for having abandoned the missionary who had lost his way. All his people gave valuable presents in order to have him set at liberty; and as soon as they obtained him they traded their peltries and returned to their own village, with two Frenchmen whom they carried with them.

At the end of two years [1665] they came down to the Colony to get the articles which they needed. They were overtaken, at the portage of the Calumets, by a party of Irroquois who were waiting for them, where the latter had built a wretched fort of stakes—which might have been torn down with the hands if the Outaoüas had had the courage to approach it, since the stakes were not very heavy. Their only endeavor was to fell some trees upon the fort, but this was unsuccessful, so they invested it. After they had been thus besieged during five days, without being taken, the Irroquois held a parley with the Outaoüas, and told them to continue their journey in entire safety, protesting that they would not follow them. But the latter did not place much confidence in this, and came very near throwing their peltries on the ground, and likewise abandoning those of the Frenchmen who had embarked with them, whom the Outaoüas had carried [to the upper country] in the preceding years. They were exhorted to do nothing of that sort, and the men from the Colony induced them by liberal promises to carry their merchandise thither. By dint of urging, they consented to go down to Three Rivers, on the way casting into the river the greater part of their own peltries, in order to save those of the Frenchmen – who, having received what belonged to them, hid themselves until the departure of the savages. This trick drew upon them a thousand reproaches and insults from the Outaoüas.

In pointing out to you that the Hurons, when they abandoned their own country [dispersed] – some to return to the [French] colony, and the others to find a refuge farther on – I neglected to state that those who went down to the Colony [1650] had for their missionary, Father l'Allemand,[137] and that a detachment of French soldiers was designated to receive them. Be-

---

[137] "The remnants of the Huron missions were conducted to Québec by Father Paul Ragueneau; no Father Lallemand figures in the narratives of that sorrowful migration (*Relation* of 1650, chap. viii, ix). Neither the *Relation* of 1650 nor Charlevoix alludes to the misadventure of the father charged with guiding to Québec the fugitive Hurons; Perrot alone has preserved for us the memory of it. But the silence of the former and the error into which the latter has fallen as to the name of the missionary who was ill-treated by Le Borgne of the island, are not sufficient grounds for entirely rejecting the story of our author. The Creuse River is one of the numerous affluents of the Outaouais; a little below its mouth is encountered the island of Allumettes (called also Le Borgne's Island, for the reason assigned by the author), and still farther down the island of Grand Calumet, and the rapids and the portage of the same name." — TAILHAN.

tween Creuse River and the Calumets there is a large island, commonly named Isle du Borgne, otherwise called Isle des Allumettes. It is named Isle du Borgne because the chief of the Algonkin village which was established there was a one-eyed man. He had under his command there four hundred warriors, and was regarded as the terror of all the peoples, even of the Irroquois. This chief gathered a certain toll from all travelers who went down to the French colony, for permission to pass by that place, and without it he would not allow them to go any farther. It was therefore necessary to submit to his demands, whether ascending or descending [the river]; and in order to find him one was obliged to go by way of the main channel, which is toward the south of the island; the lesser channel, which is much shorter, is at the north. When the Hurons reached the upper end of the island, they intended to pass by the village, according to custom, to wait upon the chief and ask his permission to pass by [his village]; but Father l'Allemand told them that the French, being masters of the country, were not obliged to do that, and persuaded them to follow the small channel. Le Borgne was soon informed of this, and sent all his warriors to bring all the Hurons to the village; and after they were asked the reason why they had planned to pass without his permission they excused themselves by saying that it was Father l'Allemand who had prevented them from asking it, and that he had made them believe that the French were the masters of the nations. Le Borgne seized Father l'Allemand and had him suspended from a tree by the arm-pits, telling him that the French were not the masters of his country; and that in it he alone was acknowledged as chief, and they [all] were under his authority.

In the following year he went down to the Colony,
making his men carry him into and out of his canoe,
and never taking a step without being escorted by his
guards; but that did not prevent him from being arrested and placed in a dungeon. The savages of his
following tried to make some disturbance, in order to
get him out of prison; but the authorities immediately
put themselves on the defensive, and sent word to the
savages to behave themselves. In short, the only attitude that they could take was that of submission, and
of humiliating themselves with offers of presents in
order to obtain the freedom of their chief, who was released a few days afterward.

See what the French accomplished in the first establishment of the Colony, although it was then of very
little importance in the world. They have been able to
preserve and maintain the glory of the nation against
the savages (who were incomparably stronger and more
numerous at that time than they are now), since, if I
dare say it, we were their masters. Did we not oblige
them to recognize this by valuable presents, which were
acknowledged only by very ordinary ones? and did not
we even inform them, in offering these, that it was done
only through compassion for their miserable condition?
On the other hand, in this present time of ours they desire to dominate us and be our superiors; they even regard us as people who are in some manner dependent
on them. I will explain what has given rise to this
presumption [of theirs], and how it will be difficult to
remove it from their minds.

The Outaoüas and other tribes lived peaceably for
many years in the country where they had taken refuge
to escape from being annoyed by the Scioux. An Irroquois party came one day to Sault-Sainte-Marie [1662],

to look for a village to eat; they were confident that, having carried terror among all the other savages, whom they had driven from their native lands, they would make themselves feared as soon as they came in sight. The hundred Irroquois men who composed this party went above Sault-Sainte-Marie, and proceeded to encamp at the mouth of Lake Superior, five leagues or thereabout from the rapids; and there they descried fires along the high hills at the north, not far distant from them; they sent scouts in that direction, to ascertain who might be there.

Some Saulteurs, Outaoüas, Nepissings, and Amikouëts had left their settlement and come hither to hunt elk in the neighborhood of this Sault, and to carry on their fishing for the great whitefish, or salmon, which they catch there in abundance, in the midst of the boiling waters of those rapids. Hardly any place is known where this fish is so large or so fat as those which are found here. These people were scattered about, hunting, when one of them perceived the smoke from the camp of the Irroquois. They gave warning to one another, and rallied together to the number of a hundred men. They elected for chief of their party a Saulteur, who well deserved to be thus honored; for he had a thorough knowledge of the region where they were, having lived in it before the war with the Irroquois.

This chief first of all sent out a canoe to reconnoiter, which was seen by the Irroquois who had been detailed for the same purpose; but the latter, believing that they had not been perceived, remained motionless, for fear of failing in their [intended] attack, and apprehensive that the Algonkins, if these happened to escape from their clutches, would go to warn the entire village, whose people would immediately take to flight. The

Saulteurs advanced, and proceeded as far as the camp
of the Irroquois without being discovered; a very dense
forest favored them, so that they had opportunity to
count the enemy and the women whom they had with
them. The intention and plan of the people who were
encamped there was, to carry away the [inhabitants of
the] villages, one place after another, remaining in each
[long enough] to consume the provisions which they
would find there, and doing the same with regard to the
others.

The scouting party of the Saulteurs, having succeeded
therein, returned to their camp to report the discovery
that they had just made. Their people immediately
embarked, and proceeded all night without being able
to reach the place where the Irroquois were; they passed
it, however, in a very thick fog, without being perceived
by any one. They had gained knowledge of a little cove,
quite deep, the head of which was in the rear of the
[Irroquois] camp; they gained that location, and concluded that they must defer the attack on the enemy
until the next day. During the night they made their
approaches, and posted themselves on a small but steep
bank of earth, some five or six feet high, at the base of
which were the tents of the Irroquois, who were sleeping very tranquilly. Their dogs, scenting the ambushed
Saulteurs, were beguiled by a little meat that was thrown
to them, in order to prevent them from barking; and
when the light of day began to appear sufficiently for
discharging their arrows with effect, the assailants
uttered their usual war-cries. The Irroquois awoke,
and, trying to hasten to seize their arms, they were
pierced by the shots that were fired at them from every
side, and were forced to face about by the enormous
number of arrows that were showered upon them. When

the Saulteurs had finished shooting them (I mean the men), they leaped down from the bank, [and] entered the tents of their enemies, with clubs in their hands. It was then that the Saulteur youth gave way, and fled toward their canoes, while the men dealt their blows everywhere, and one could know by their yells whenever they killed an Irroquois. Those who tried to flee toward the shore were fiercely attacked; the Saulteur youth, who had not seconded their elders in the fight, regained their courage when they heard the cries of victory uttered by the latter, and rushed to meet those Irroquois who had been routed, and finished the slaughter, none of the enemy escaping. You see how complete their victory was.[138]

The Irroquois who had been sent out as scouts returned to their camp a few days after this defeat, expecting to join their people there; but when they found only headless corpses on the ground, and the bones of those whose flesh had been eaten, they made diligent haste to carry back to their own country this dismal news. It is said that the Irroquois have not dared since that time to enter the Lake Superior [country]; but in truth they have never set any limits [to their operations] in waging war, and, as pitiless man-eaters, they have always taken pleasure in drinking the blood and eating the flesh of all the different tribes, going to seek their prey even to the confines of America.

After the defeat of the Irroquois, the Saulteurs and their companions returned in triumph to Kionconan and Chagouamikon. They dwelt there in peace always, until some Hurons who had gone to hunt on the borders of the Scioux country (for Chagouamikon is not far away

---

[138] "The *Relation* of 1663 (chap. iv) ascribes all the honor of this victory to the Sauteurs, and informs us, besides, that the Iroquois war-party was composed of Agniers and Onneiouths" [i.e., Mohawks and Oneidas]. — TAILHAN.

from there), cutting across the country in a straight line, [a distance of] fifty to sixty leagues, [captured some of the Scioux], whom they carried away to the [Saulteur] villages alive, as they were not desirous of killing them. The people received these captives very kindly, and especially the Outaoüas, who loaded them with presents, Although they did not seem very appreciative of their welcome, it is certain that they would have been thrown into the kettle if it had not been for the Outaoüas. When the Scioux wished to return home, Sinagos, the Outaoüa chief, accompanied them [1665-1666], with his men and four Frenchmen. On their arrival in the Scioux country, and during all the time that they spent there, many kind attentions were offered to them; but they did not bring back a large stock of peltries, because those people are accustomed to roast their beavers [whole], in order to eat them.

Honors were heaped on Chief Sinagos, and they sang the calumet[139] for him–which is one of the notable

---

[139] See description of the calumet in Marquette's *Récit de Voyages* (section 6). "To employ the calumet for 'talking with strangers,' was the same as what Perrot calls here 'singing the calumet to them.' Observe how the Ayoës, allies of the Sioux, sang it to our author" (La Potherie, *Histoire*, vol. ii, 185). "The song or dance of the calumet was also held in great honor among the Illinois;" see Father Allouez's account of it in *Relation* of 1667, chap. xi. Cf. Marquette's *Voyages*, vol. i, section 6; this has been reproduced almost textually by La Potherie (*Histoire*, vol. ii, 16-20). – TAILHAN.

Calumet (a Norman-French word, originally derived from Low Lat. *calamellus*, dimin. of *calamus*, "reed") : "Either one of two highly symbolic shafts of reed or wood, about two inches broad, one-fourth inch thick, and eighteen inches to four feet long – the one representing the male, the other the female shaft, usually perforated for a pathway for the breath or spirit, painted with diverse symbolic colors and adorned with various symbolic objects, and which may or may not have a pipe bowl to contain tobacco for making a sacred offering of its benevolent smoke to the gods. In modern usage the term usually includes the pipe. Its coloring and degree of adornment varied somewhat from tribe to tribe, and were largely governed by the occasion for which the calumet was used. From the meager descriptions of the calumet and its uses it would seem that it has a ceremonially symbolic history independent of that of the pipe; and that when the pipe became an altar, by its employment for burning

CALUMET SONG

marks of distinction conferred by them, for they render him who has had that honor a son of the tribe, and naturalize him as such. When the calumet is presented and sung to him, obedience is due to him from the people of the tribe. The calumet constrains and pledges those who have sung it to follow to war the man in whose honor it has been sung; but the same obligation

sacrificial tobacco to the gods, convenience and convention united the already highly symbolic calumet shafts and the sacrificial tobacco altar, the pipe-bowl; hence it became one of the most profoundly sacred objects known to the Indians of northern America. . . The calumet was employed by ambassadors and travelers as a passport; it was used in ceremonies designed to conciliate foreign and hostile nations and to conclude lasting peace to ratify the alliance of friendly tribes; to secure favorable weather for journeys; to bring needed rain; and to attest contracts and treaties which could not be violated without incurring the wrath of the gods. The use of the calumet was inculcated by religious precept and example. A chant and a dance have become known as the chant and the dance of the calumet; together they were employed as an invocation to one or more of the gods. . . The dance and the chant were rather in honor of the calumet than with the calumet. . . J. O. Dorsey asserts that the Omaha and cognate names for this dance and chant signify 'to make sacred kinship,' but not 'to dance.' This is the key to the esoteric significance of the use of the calumet. The one for whom the dance for the calumet was performed became thereby the adopted son of the performer. . . From Dorsey's account of the Omaha calumets it is evident that they are together the most highly organized emblems known to religious observances anywhere; and it is further in evidence that the pipe is an accessory rather than the dominant or chief object in this highly complex synthetic symbol of the source, reproduction and conservation of life. . . By smoking together in the calumet the contracting parties intend to invoke the sun and the other gods as witnesses to the mutual obligations assumed by the parties, and as a guaranty the one to the other that they shall be fulfilled. This is accomplished by blowing the smoke toward the sky, the four world-quarters, and the earth, with a suitable invocation. . . There were calumets for commerce and trade and for other social and political purposes, but the most important were those designed for war and those for peace and brotherhood. . . The use of the calumet, sometimes called 'peace pipe' and 'war pipe,' was widespread in the Mississippi Valley generally," from the Chippewa and Cheyenne in the north to the Choctaw and Natchez in the south; "in the Ohio and St. Lawrence Valleys and southward its use is not so definitely shown." — J. N. B. HEWITT, in *Handbook Amer. Indians*.

A document written (1744) by the Jesuit missionary Jacques Eustache le Sueur states that the calumet dance was introduced in 1720 by emissaries from the Foxes among his Abenaki converts on the St. Lawrence, in order to seduce the latter from their French alliance; see Wis. *Hist. Colls.*, vol. xvii, 194-200. — ED.

does not rest upon him. The calumet halts the warriors belonging to the tribe of those who have sung it, and arrests the vengeance which they could lawfully take for their tribesmen who have been slain. The calumet also compels the suspension of hostilities and secures the reception of deputies from hostile tribes who undertake to visit those whose people have been recently slain by theirs. It is, in one word, the calumet which has authority to confirm everything, and which renders solemn oaths binding. The savages believe that the sun gave it to the Panys, and that since then it has been communicated from village to village as far as the Outaoüas. They have so much respect and veneration for it that he who has violated the law of the calumet is regarded by them as disloyal and traitorous; they assert that he has committed a crime which cannot be pardoned. In former times this was the obstinate contention of the savages, and they are still of the same opinion; but that does not hinder them from committing acts of treachery while employing the calumet. Those of the prairies have the utmost attachment for it, and regard it as a sacred thing. Never did they betray the pledge that they had given to those who sang it, when that nation dealt a blow against their own – unless he who had sung it should perfidiously take part in the attack made upon them. That would be the basest of all traitorous acts, because it would break the calumet in pieces and disrupt the union which had been contracted through its agency.

I have just said that the Scioux sang the calumet to Chief Sinagos; this ceremony was performed in their villages with authority and solemnity. All the chiefs were present, and gave their consent to an inviolable peace. After that solemnity, Chief Sinagos, with his people and the Frenchmen who had gone with him, returned to Chagouamikon, assuring the Scioux that he would revisit them the following year. This he failed to do, even in the second year afterward; and the Scioux did not know what had caused him to break his promise. It happened, however [1669-1670], that some Hurons, having gone to hunt far toward the Scioux country, were captured by some young men of that nation, and taken to their village. The chief, who had sung the calumet to Sinagos, was greatly incensed at seeing these prisoners, and made it his business to protect them; he almost attacked those who had captured them, and nearly caused war between his villages and theirs. He took possession of the captives, and set them at liberty. On the next day, this chief sent one of them to Chagouamikon, in order to assure the Hurons that he had not been to blame in the late affair; that the attack had been made by some misguided young men, who were not even of his own tribe; and that in a few days he himself would conduct to their homes the captives whom he had retained in his village. That Huron, whom he had sent to Chagouamikon to assure his tribesmen of the Scioux chief's sincere good-will, told them – either because he chose to lie, or because some one instigated him to do so – that the Scioux had made prisoners of him and his companions; that he had fortunately escaped from their hands; and that he did not know, since his departure, whether his comrades were still alive or had been put to death.

The Scioux chief who had sung the calumet to Sinagos chose to go in person to restore the Huron captives to their people. He departed from his village with them; but when they came near Chagouamikon they deserted him. Having reached their friends, they declared that they had just escaped from death by flight. The

Scioux chief, not seeing those persons the next morning, was much surprised; he nevertheless persisted in his resolution and continued on his way, reaching the village on the same day. Not daring, however, to go among the Hurons, whom he distrusted, he entered the cabin of Chief Sinagos, to whom he had sung the calumet, who, with all the Outaoüas, received him very cordially. He explained to them that he had set the Hurons free; he had four companions, including a woman. The Hurons – crafty, and the most treacherous of all the savage tribes – when they could not persuade the Outaoüas to deliver the Scioux to them, concluded to see what could be done by presents; and by the agency of these they gained over Chief Sinagos, whose house the Scioux had entered. Such was their success that they corrupted him; and all the Outaoüas, following his example, were so carried away that they had the inhumanity to throw the Scioux into the kettle and eat them. At the same time, abandoning their villages, they went to live at Michillimakinak and Manitoaletz [1670-1671]. The next year they went down to Montreal, and bought, in exchange for their peltries, only guns and munitions of war – intending to march against the Scioux, build a fort in their country, and wage war against them during the entire winter. Returning home after this trading expedition, they hastily gathered in their grain-crops, and all departed in a body to march against the Scioux. Their forces were increased along the route; for Chief Sinagos had for a brother-in-law the chief of the Sakis, who resided at the Bay; and the Poutéouatamis and the Renards were his allies. As the Outaoüas had brought with them all the goods which they had obtained in trade with the French, they made presents of these to the Poutéouatamis, Sakis, and Renards, who formed a body of over a thousand men, all having guns or other powerful weapons of defense.

As soon as they arrived in the Scioux country, they fell upon some little villages, putting the men to flight and carrying away the women and children whom they found there. This blow was so quickly dealt that they had not time to reconnoiter or to erect fortifications. The fugitives quickly carried the alarm to the neighboring villages, the men of which hastened in crowds to fall upon their enemies, and so vigorously attacked them that they took to flight, and abandoned the fort which they had commenced. The Scioux pursued them without intermission, and slew them in great numbers, for their terror was so overwhelming that in their flight they had thrown away their weapons; besides, they were stripped of all their belongings, and some of them had only a wretched deerskin for covering. In a word, nearly all of them perished – by fighting, by hunger, or by the rigor of the climate. The Renards, the Kiskaouets,[140] and the Poutéouatamis, tribes less inured to war than the others, were the only ones whose loss was not so great in this enterprise; and that because they took to their heels at the beginning of the combat. The Hurons, the Sinagos, and the Sakis distinguished themselves on this occasion and, by the courageous resistance that they made, greatly aided the fugitives by giving them time to get the start of the enemy. At the end, the disorder among them was so great that they ate one another [1671-1672].

The two chiefs of the party were made prisoners, and Sinagos was recognized as the man to whom they had sung the calumet; they reproached him with his perfidy

---

[140] The Kishkakons, the Bear clan of the Ottawas. In 1658 they were dwelling near the mouth of Green Bay, twenty years later at Mackinac; still later they lived along the St. Mary's River; and in 1736 they were divided between Mackinac and Detroit. — ED.

in having eaten the very man who had adopted him into his own nation.   They were, however, unwilling to burn either him or his brother-in-law; but they made him go to a repast, and, cutting pieces of flesh from his thighs and all other parts of his body, broiled these and gave them to him to eat – informing Sinagos that, as he had eaten so much human flesh and shown himself so greedy for it, he might now satiate himself upon it by eating his own.   His brother-in-law received the same treatment; and this was all the nourishment that they received until they died.   As for the other prisoners, they were all shot to death with arrows, except a Panys[141] who belonged to the chief of those savages; and he was sent back to his own country that he might faithfully report what he had seen and the justice that had been administered.[142]

XVI.   War of the Algonkins against the Irroquois

I will here resume the detailed account which I interrupted, concerning the war of the Algonkins against the Irroquois.

I.   *The Irroquois Attack the Algonkins and the French*

The Irroquois, having routed the Hurons and driven away many tribes into distant regions, beheld themselves

---

[141] Captives taken in war were generally enslaved, and these slaves were also transferred to the whites, especially to the French. So many were obtained (largely by the Illinois) from the Pawnees that the Indian slaves were everywhere known as the Panis. Slavery in Canada was not legally abolished until 1834. – ED.

[142] "Two reasons have induced me to place in 1665-1666 the coming of the Sioux to Chagouamigon, followed by their return to their own country with the chief of the Sinagaux and the four Frenchmen of whom Perrot speaks: The first is, that in that year some Sioux certainly visited Point de Saint-Esprit (*Relation* of 1667, chap. xii) ; the second, that according to the relation of events, as it is given by our author, at least four or five years elapsed between this

masters of all the surrounding territories, and had no more cause for fear, save the Algonkins. They therefore devoted themselves solely to the destruction of that people, and went down into their country in order to wage war there. But the Algonkins, as they did not feel strong enough to defend themselves against those who came to attack them, sought an asylum in the [French] colony; they were pursued thither. Then the French united with the Hurons who had escaped from the carnage which had been made in their ancient fatherland, and took up the cause of the Algonkins. During this entire war many detachments were sent out, both small and large, who sometimes were victorious and sometimes defeated. When the Irroquois, treacherous and crafty, saw that they could not easily succeed in their schemes, they demanded peace. But, even though the negotiations on this subject were well advanced, they did not cease to commit acts of hostility and to kill with clubs, when they were least expected; they took the ground that the peace concerned only one of their villages, and that consequently all the others could undoubtedly wage war as before. We have even known the people of a village with which we were at peace to become members of those villages who were not thus peaceable. If they found themselves captives, and were asked why they joined our enemies, they would say that, being present by chance in a village where a war-party was being formed, they had enlisted with the chief who commanded it. These reasons were only specious ones, and rendered it very evident that they were steadily persisting in their design of waging war.

visit and the abandonment of Chagouamigon in 1670-1671 by the Hurons and Ottawas. The *Relations* of New France mention in various places the quarrels of these two latter tribes with the Sioux; but they do not enter at all into detail." — TAILHAN.

Many treaties of peace of this sort have been made, in which the Algonkins have never consented to be included, being persuaded of the malignancy and bad faith of the Irroquois, who have never had any other idea than that of absolutely destroying them. They have nevertheless consented to some peaces that have been made; but, to tell the truth, there has never been any real benefit from these, since the Irroquois have very often used them the better to cover up their game, and to deal their blows with more security.

II. *Defeat of the Hurons*

The treaty of peace being made between the Algonkins and the Irroquois, the latter made up from all their villages a large expedition to come to wage war in the Colony, and to carry away the Hurons settled in a village at the extremity of the island of Orléans, who had some cultivated lands there. It must be understood that there was not then any French settlement from Three Rivers to Cap Rouge; and that this party came down by the Richelieu River, which now is called Sorel. The Irroquois went past Three Rivers at night, without being discovered, and descended [the river] to Quebec, where they had the same fortune; and then they proceeded toward the lands of the Hurons, in order to prepare their ambuscades there. They resolved to wait until the next day [May 18, 1656], that they might more completely take the Hurons by surprise when the latter went out to work on their lands – because at that time they would all be outside of their fort. Those poor people, who had not the least expectation of this blow, and who relied upon the peace which existed between them and the Irroquois, at the usual hour went out, both men and women, to work on their lands; for among that people, who are naturally industrious, the men assist the women in their work, contrary to the custom of the savages. As soon as the Irroquois thought that all of them had gone away, they took possession of the land between the fort and the Hurons, in order to prevent the latter from taking refuge within it, and made prisoners of nearly all the people of that village. The manner in which this affair took place was plainly seen from Quebec.

The Irroquois, having thus rendered themselves masters of the Hurons, compelled them to embark in their canoes, and they passed in front of Quebec in open day, meanwhile obliging the captives to sing while passing, in order to humiliate them still more. That caused murmurings among the citizens, and every one was astonished that the French did not curb the insolence of the Irroquois by cannonading their canoes, which proceeded side by side, in military array; but they did not attempt to do anything, on account (as they said) of the missionaries who were among the Irroquois, whom they would certainly, on account of that, have handed over to the most cruel tortures. I will not dwell longer on this subject, the [*Jesuit*] *Relations* having made sufficient mention of it.

Meanwhile the Irroquois returned home triumphant; they put to death part of the prisoners, and granted life to the others – who, with their posterity, will remember that they were abandoned by the French to the mercy of their enemies.

III.   *Defeat of the Algonkins by the Irroquois*

The Irroquois no longer set their minds on anything so much as on the destruction of the Algonkins, who were of all their enemies the most formidable. They had reduced the Hurons to a condition in which they could no longer inspire fear, and regarded the French as a people who were not acquainted with their mode of warfare and were incapable of vanquishing them, not knowing [how to make] their way through the forests of the country.

The friendly reception that was given to the Irroquois when they came in large bodies to Quebec to treat of peace led them to imagine that we feared them; if they came in small squads, the French gave them clothing, and spoiled them with the presents that they gave them. This idea induced them to conclude peace once more with the Algonkins. The two peoples exchanged collars with each other, and made solemn declaration of the inviolable union between them, promising that they would not fail, in the following winter, to meet together in order to cement the bond.

The Algonkins, all of whose villages were in the vicinity of Three Rivers, set out at the usual time for their winter hunt, and separated into two bands; one took its route along Nicolet River, and the other toward the Ouabmachis.[143] In those regions there were a great number of elk, and the snow was very favorable for hunting that game; for they could, without taking much trouble, by coursing kill as many elk as they would find.

It is said that an Algonkin named Piskaret, who was the terror of the Irroquois, and whose valor they knew well, entered one of his enemies' villages, killed an entire family with his club, and then took refuge in one of their woodpiles. The following night, he did the

---

[143] "Perrot writes by turns *Ouabmakis* and *Ouabmachis*; I have adopted Ouabmachis, preferring it as more closely approaching the *Ouamachis* of Charlevoix. The true form seems to me to be *Oumachiche*, from which, by cutting off the Algonquin article *ou* will be formed *Machiche*, the name at present borne by this river. The Machiche rises north of the Saint Lawrence, and flows into the part of that river which is called Lake St. Peter." — TAILHAN.

same in another house, and, having deprived the dead
of their scalps, hid himself in the same retreat. But the
third time when he attempted to perform an exploit
like the two preceding, he was discovered, and obliged
to flee. He was naturally agile and nimble, and steadily
kept considerably in advance of his pursuers; and for
this reason he took it into his head to wait for them until
evening. Seeing that the night was approaching, he hid
himself in the hollow of a tree. Those who had been
running after him thought that he was far ahead, and,
no longer hoping to overtake him, occupied themselves
with making a fire not far from his retreat, and encamped there. When he saw that they were sound
asleep, he broke the heads of them all, and came back
laden with their scalps.

It is also related that on another occasion he, with four
other men, attacked five Irroquois canoes, which he
capsized by firing, not at the men within them, but at
the bottoms of their canoes, with bar-shot; these filled
the canoes with water, and made them overset. Then
rushing upon the enemies he killed them all, except some
prisoners whom they were carrying away for the amusement of their village. This exploit was performed in
the broad part of the mouth of Sorel River, in the
middle of the stream. These extraordinary deeds, and
many others of the same sort, rendered this man redoubtable among the Irroquois.

The Algonkins tell us that this Piskaret was a very
brave man; and that he placed great confidence in [the
strength of] his heart and his legs. He set out one day
from the Nicolet River to go hunting beyond St. François River; and as he was returning home, laden with
the muzzles and tongues of elks, he saw behind him six
Irroquois, who had descried him before he saw them,

and who carried a flag. As they marched they were singing the peace-song, by which they made it known that they were coming with the intention of confirming the peace. The Algonkin intrepidly approached them, and, sitting down with them, lighted his pipe and gave them some tobacco. In the conversation that they had together, he informed them that his village was on the Nicolet River, and in it were one-half of the Algonkins encamped in a body, the other half being on the Ouabmachis River. The Irroquois in turn informed him of what had brought them into the region where they then were, and told him that they were going to visit their father Ononthio, and to congratulate the Algonkins. After they had paid each other, on both sides, attentions and expressions of regard, they arose to continue their journey, and immediately one of the six Irroquois placed on his own shoulders the load that the Algonkin had to carry; it is the custom of the savages to act thus with those whom they greatly honor and respect. They all marched abreast, the Algonkin in the midst of them; but there was one of the company who lagged behind, and who, allowing them to go a little way ahead, afterward quickly rejoined them, and killed the Algonkin (who had no suspicion of him) with his club.

These Irroquois of whom I have just spoken had been detached from a large party (of nearly a thousand men), to go scouting; having slain the Algonkin, they hastened with all speed to inform their people of all that they had learned. As soon as the Irroquois heard this, they resolved to divide their men into two bodies, of whom one should go to carry away the Algonkins at Nicolet, and the other to seize those on the Ouabmachis River; and this plan was carried out at daybreak the next morning. Some Algonkins escaped from their clutches, but the greater part of them were captured or massacred.

After such an overthrow, the Irroquois had no longer anything to fear, finding themselves everywhere victorious; for the few Algonkins who still remained were not capable, [even if] united together, of destroying a single village of their enemies. All the harm that they could do to the Irroquois, therefore, was to knock on the head those whom they might encounter alone. They entreated the Poissons Blancs to aid them – a tribe who, with other Algonkins, are settled above the river of Three Rivers; and they induced a village of Montagnais from the Saguenay to come to Sillery. The Mikmaks of Accadia promised to aid them; the Nepissings united with them; and all together formed parties who numbered four or five hundred men. But the dissensions which prevailed among them broke up all their measures, and caused the failure of everything that they had planned; for, as I have already remarked, the Algonkins have never been willing to endure any subordination. Courage and haughtiness alone inspire them to action in their battles, and these traits have prevented them from saving themselves in the losses that they have incurred; and although the Irroquois were much more numerous the Algonkins would have routed them if they had acted in full concert, as they are much better warriors than the Irroquois.

This war continued until the arrival in this country of the regiment of Carignan [1665]. The late Monsieur Le Moine was captured in the same year by the Outaoüas [sc. Irroquois], and carried home by them.[144] For

144 "This Le Moine of whom Perrot speaks must be the same as Charles Le Moine, sieur de Longueil, the head of one of the most illustrious families of New France. In the passage that concerns him I have proposed to substitute the word 'Irroquois' for 'Outaouais,' which appears in the text. The Ottawas, friends of the French and their allies in the war that was then desolating the colony, could not cherish hostile intentions against one of the bravest defenders of their own cause, make him a prisoner, and condemn him to the fire. All that is very naturally explained [as occurring] among the Iroquois. It is with-

several years they had already contemplated putting him to death if he happened to be captured. He had great personal courage, and was feared by all the savages. People have related that one old [Irroquois] woman even dried pieces of bark for nearly ten years, in order to burn him. When he arrived [in their country] they sentenced him to the stake; but when they were going to burn him one of the leading men of their tribe arrived, who obtained his deliverance, and, accompanied by several other chiefs, brought him to Montréal.

On their arrival there they saw Monsieur de Courcelles, governor-general of the country, and all the troops who had recently come from France; and the French were eagerly expecting Monsieur de Tracy, who had taken the route by the islands of Guadeloupe – of which, as well as of this colony, his Majesty had appointed him viceroy. These Outaoüa [*sc.* Irroquois] envoys were greatly astonished at seeing so many soldiers, to whom orders were given to divide their numbers among the settlements, in order to defend the inhabitants of New France; and in the same year the detachments were made that were necessary to work on the construction of the forts at Sorel and Chambly.

The Irroquois ambassadors reached Montreal at the same time, in order to make pretended negotiations for a peace similar to those which they had made before; but when they saw the reënforcements which had

out any doubt Charles Le Moine and his captivity to whom the following passage of the *Relation* of 1666 refers" (in chap. ii, a passage relating to a French gentleman captured by the Iroquois and taken to their country, but afterward released). – TAILHAN.

The above conjecture and emendation by Tailhan are entirely correct. Charles le Moyne (who came to Canada about 1641) was captured by the Iroquois in 1665, and escaped death as here related. For his public services he was ennobled (1668) by Louis XIV. Among his children were Pierre, sieur d'Iberville, and Jean Baptiste, sieur de Bienville, famous for the exploration and first colonization of the present Louisiana and Mississippi. – ED.

arrived in the country they changed their tune and talked more sincerely.

This news spread throughout all the villages of the savage tribes. The Tsonontouans and the Goyogouans united with the Onontagués to make their peace with the French, and with the tribes down here, [which lasted] until the war which was waged against the Tsonontouans.

IV. *Expeditions of the French against the Irroquois*

The ambassadors of the Onontagués, the Goyogouans, and the Tsonontouans declared that their allies were not willing, ever since that same winter, to make peace with us; this compelled Monsieur de Courcelles to march against them, at the head of five hundred men and a considerable number of Canadians. The guides could not discover the road to their villages; they led the party to Corlard, where they found only one cabin of Irroquois [February, 1666]. The Flemish Bastard was also there, with a party of Aniez, whose chief he was. Some skirmishes took place with the advanced posts, and many gunshots were fired on both sides; but the enemy were repulsed. The commander of our troops left his post, trying to pursue those who had come to attack him; he was thus left with four men besides himself, without its being possible to succor him. Monsieur de Courcelles, finding that he was almost out of provisions, turned back in retreat for the first time, and was joined by a hundred Algonkins who, hunting in that vicinity, learned that he was there, and came to proffer him their services; but as he was not in a condition to be able to undertake anything against the enemy, he thanked them and continued his journey.

This expedition, although it made no progress, certainly intimidated the Aniez and Anoyés [i.e., Mohawks and Oneidas], who had with them some prisoners of ours – among them Monsieur de Noirolle, a nephew of Monsieur de Tracy. Monsieur de Chasy, his cousin,[145] was killed north of the fort of La Motte on Lake Champlain. At the end of this campaign the Aniez held councils among themselves, and took measures for surrendering the prisoners and demanding peace.

Monsieur de Tracy despatched in the following summer [May, 1666] a party of three hundred men, French and Algonkins, who met on the way the Flemish Bastard, having with him Monsieur de Noirolle and three other Frenchmen; one of these latter was wounded in the heel, and Monsieur de Courcelles recommended him, on departing, to Sieur Corlard.[146] The French and Algonkins of the advance-guard seized and bound the Flemish Bastard and two of his men; but as soon as

---

[145] "Monsieur de Chasy was the nephew and not the cousin of Monsieur de Tracy. Perrot himself has corrected this mistake a little farther on."
— TAILHAN.

Monsieur de Tracy's cousin is called De Lérole in the "Journal des Jésuites." Perrot was at that time (1665, 1666) trading in Wisconsin, and, forty-two years after these events, he gives in this chapter of his memoir a brief recital of them, from memory; we should therefore not be surprised that he has fallen into some errors as to dates. — TAILHAN (additional note, p. 341).

[146] "Arendt van Corlaer (Corlar and Corlart in the *Relations* and in Perrot) was about 1640 the commander of a small fort built by the Dutch six leagues from Orange (the present Albany, N.Y.). The savages, and the French following their example, called by his name at first the post where he had resided, and then the governors (successively Dutch and English) of New Belgium, which later became New York. One of these latter, Governor Dongan, in his report of February 22, 1687, to the Board of Trade explained this custom by the affection which this good man had inspired in the Indians who had dealings with him (*Docum. Hist. of New York*, vol. i, 156). Influenced by similar motives, the savages of Canada gave to all the governors of the colony the name of Ononthio (i.e., 'great mountain'), which was only the translation into their language of the name of Montmagny, the successor of Champlain; they also used this epithet to designate the King, but united with it the adjective 'Great' ('Great Ononthio')." — TAILHAN.

the main body of the troops had arrived on the scene –
who had hastened their pace at hearing the outcries and
hootings of the Algonkins – Monsieur de Sorel, the commander-in-chief, made them unbind the prisoners. The
Algonkins showed their discontent at this, and were
inclined to use insolent language to the commander;
for they desired that these Irroquois should be burned.
But Monsieur de Sorel answered them sharply, with so
much spirit and firmness that they had no words with
which to answer him. You will note that when these
men were seized they declared that they were coming
as ambassadors to treat of an adjustment [of their relations with us]; and that it was for this reason that Monsieur de Sorel dealt thus with them.

He brought these ambassadors with him to Quebec,
and presented them to Monsieur de Tracy, who sent one
of them back to his own country with a letter for Monsieur Corlard – in which he assured him of his promise
[to the Irroquois], in order to induce them all to come
in security to the colony, saying that they would be
kindly received there.

A prominent war-chief left the country of the Aniez
about the same time – I mean, a month before the Flemish Bastard left it – having under his command thirty
warriors, who were bringing back to Montréal the
French prisoners whom they had. He went with his
men to encamp at the Prairie de la Magdeleine (where
there was not yet any settlement), and found there some
Onontagués who had been hunting during the winter,
the better to persuade the French of the stability of that
peace which they had just concluded together. They
informed this newly-arrived party that the Flemish Bastard was at Quebec, in order to conclude the peace there.

When this chief heard that news, he would not go

any farther; he allowed his party to rest themselves there, and embarked with the Onontagués, who carried him to Montréal. When he arrived there a batteau was despatched, in which he took his place to go to Quebec; on his arrival there, he found the peace concluded. Monsieur de Tracy received him very kindly, and often had him eat, with the Flemish Bastard, at his own table; for this chief was a man of high standing and esteem among the savages of his tribe.

One day Monsieur de Tracy, giving a dinner, mentioned at the table how keenly he felt the loss of Monsieur his nephew, which had just occurred; but said that the public good had, notwithstanding, obliged him to grant to the Flemish Bastard the peace which he had asked for. That was enough to make this haughty chief of the Aniez understand the sorrow which Monsieur de Tracy felt at the death of Monsieur de Chasy (whom this chief had slain), and to constrain him, as a matter of propriety, to abate his arrogance. But, far from compassionating the grief which his host made evident, before him and all the company this chief raised his arm, loudly boasting that it was his hand that had broken the youth's head. This preposterous insolence broke off the peace that Monsieur de Tracy had granted to the Flemish Bastard; and, telling this talkative chief that he would never kill any more Frenchmen, he had him seized and bound. Then, without placing him in prison, he sent for the executioner, and gave orders that the murderer should be strangled in the presence of the Flemish Bastard; and a little while afterward he set out [October, 1666], at the head of fourteen hundred men – soldiers, Canadians, and Algonkins – accompanied by Monsieur de Courcelles, to march against the Aniez. He had left at Sorel, on the way, the Flemish Bastard (whom he sent home after this campaign), who was employed in burning and throwing into the river the Indian corn belonging to four villages; as a result, more than four hundred souls died from hunger during the winter. Those who survived wandered about here and there, and went to beg for food among the Onontagués; the latter refused to give it, and jeered at them, telling them that the wild northeast wind had destroyed their grain through their own fault.

At the end of the campaign the Flemish Bastard was sent home; and when he arrived there he found entire desolation. The Aniez were continually imagining that they had the French in the neighborhood of their villages; they insisted that he should retrace his steps, and go back to entreat peace in earnest. With very little delay, then, he returned to Quebec, where he protested, with all the guarantees that the French wished to exact from him, that he desired to obtain peace; that he would remain as a hostage; and that he himself would come to live, with his family in the colony, in order to prove the sincerity which led him to come to ask for peace. These arguments were heard with favor; moreover, he did not fail to fulfil what he had promised, for many of the same tribe, following his example, came to settle at Montréal, without, however, cultivating any land there. They dispersed themselves from the river of the Outaoüas as far as Creuse River, where the hunting of beaver, otter, elk, and moose is very common; and they were seen in the spring and autumn seasons coming down to the colony, laden with so great a quantity of peltries that the price of these fell by more than a half in France.

XVII. Murders committed against Irroquois

I. *The first murder*

Some soldiers of the Carignan regiment took it into their heads to range the woods with the Irroquois, and to follow them everywhere in their hunting expeditions. They provided themselves with plenty of brandy, and went away without telling this to any one, making known their departure to one of their officers only – who even aided them in making their preparations for this trip, in the hope of securing some share [of the profits] therein.

Five of these soldiers, who were already accustomed to voyages of this sort, and who knew the route by this [Outaoüas] river, and the places where the Irroquois were accustomed to hunt, set out at night, and arrived at Pointe Claire in Lake St. Louis; and there they found an Irroquois, who had his canoe full of moose-skins. These soldiers asked him if he would drink a draught of brandy, but he answered "no." Seeing, however, that they invited him to drink without paying for it, and without [apparent] selfish motive, he accepted the offer that they made him; that led him to drink more of the brandy, and, by dint of urging him, he took so much that he became dead-drunk. These soldiers, seeing that he had lost his reason and his senses, fastened a stone to his neck and flung him into the water, in the broad part of the lake. The other Irroquois who had been out hunting returned to Montréal, and some time afterward asked [these soldiers] if they had not seen him, but the latter answered "no;" his comrades therefore believed that he had been drowned along the rapids of the Outaoüas River.

These savages, however, when either going to or re-

turning from a hunt, perceived a corpse floating on the
water – either because the cord which served to attach
the stone to his neck had broken, or because the stone
was not heavy enough. They went directly toward this
corpse, and recognized the man of whom there were no
tidings. They conveyed it to Montréal, and in the complaints that they made they set forth that in their hunting parties there had been no other savages besides
themselves, and that consequently there were no others
than Frenchmen who could have slain their comrade.
Close search was made to find the authors of this deed,
but without success.

The soldiers, after committing this murder, carried
the peltries in the night to their officer, and made him
believe that they had been trading with some Irroquois
who were returning from their hunt. This officer gave
the hides in payment to some person; for it was the custom in the country to use peltries instead of money.[147]
The person who obtained them from this officer had
likewise given them to some one else, and in this manner they had passed through several hands. It happened that a Frenchman, having one of them, carried
it to the house of a merchant, at which were present some
Irroquois; and they recognized it by the special mark
which each of them places on his own pelts. Immediately they seized it, in order to carry it to the commandant of the city. The Frenchman was summoned,

---

[147] Regarding the use of peltries as money, see *Jesuit Relations*, vol. ix, 173-
177, 205; xxi, 123; xxii, 241; xxxvii, 71; lx, 291, 305; lxix, 127, 245-249, 259-
263. See also J. R. Swanton's article "Exchange" in *Handbook Amer. Indians*,
where he enumerates the chief articles used among the aborigines as standards
of value, with their equivalents in money, etc. The beaver pelt was "the basis
of all trade between the French of Canada and the Indians," from the beginning
of that intercourse; and in the great fur regions of Canada it also remained
such between the English and the Indians. "Up to the present time everything
is valued in 'skins,' meaning beaver skins; but the term has come to have a
fixed value of fifty cents in Canadian money." – Ed.

and questioned to ascertain from whom he had received
this hide; and he named the person who had given it to
him.   He too was sent for, and likewise named the
person from whom he had received it; and by this means
it was learned that the hide had come in the first place
from the house where the officer lived.   Search was
made there, and many hides with the same mark were
found in it, which were recognized as the property of
the murdered savage.   These proofs left no further
reason to doubt that he had been slain by some soldiers.
At that time, those soldiers had gone away again to trade
in brandy on the Outaoüas River, after having repaid
to the officer the first advance, also the last one, that he
made them, by the remainder of the plunder from the
Irroquois whom they had murdered.   Orders were
given to the officer to arrest these men as soon as they
should return, or to notify [the commandant], in order
to punish them and render justice to the Irroquois; for
already the latter were heard to utter their discontent.
They intimated that their indignation was great enough
to renew the war, if there had been a failure to render
them satisfaction for this murder.

II.   *Justice rendered to the Irroquois for the above-
mentioned murder*

The authors of this crime, not having any shelter
more certain than the house of their officer, arrived
there in the night; they were arrested there, and thrown
into prison.   The military council having assembled to
try their case, they confessed at the first interrogation
the crime of which they were accused; and all five were
condemned to be put to death, in the presence of the
Irroquois.

They were led out, and all five were bound each to a

post. The Irroquois were astonished at the ample justice that was rendered to them, and entreated mercy for
four of them; because, as they had lost only one man, it
was not just, they said, to kill five for him, but one
only [ought to die]. They were given to understand that
the five were equally criminal, and without any exception merited death. The Irroquois, who were not expecting so extensive a satisfaction, redoubled their entreaties to obtain mercy for four, and for this purpose
made presents of porcelain collars; but the French did
not listen to them, and all five men were shot to death
[1669].

The justice which on this occasion was rendered to
the Irroquois was published in all their villages, whose
people [therefore] had great confidence in the French;
and many of their families, influenced by so splendid a
reparation, came down into the colony and remained
there, [attracted] by the abundance of game and the
other necessities of life that they found there for living
comfortably.

III. *Another murder*

Some years afterward eleven Irroquois were hunting
south of the Lake of Two Mountains, toward the end of
the island of Montréal, and carried on trade with a
merchant who went to find them there. This trader took
with him a very intelligent Canadian, who was thoroughly acquainted with the language of the Irroquois,
and was highly esteemed by them. These Irroquois,
having found out where his lodging was, went to visit
him; he entertained them, and assured them that he
would not fail to visit them in their winter camp. He
did not forget this; for he set out one day, accompanied
by a merchant and his servant, and reached the camp.
All three were very hospitably received, and all the

more cordially because they had taken care to carry with them some brandy, of which they made a present to the savages. The Irroquois having drunk it until they had lost their wits, the Frenchmen murdered them for the sake of plundering them. This murder was discovered, and the murderers, having been warned by their friends to be gone, escaped so well, each in his own way, that it was impossible to arrest them.[148]

---

[148] "As these two murders were committed in the course of a single year (*Relation* of 1670, chap. vi, ix; Charlevoix, *Histoire*, vol. i, 425, 426), Perrot's 'few years' must necessarily be changed to 'few months.' These abominable crimes, occurring successively in a colony where until then they had been unknown, must have made certain governors of that time understand how fatal was this trade in brandy, which they stubbornly protected through a false policy, and especially through opposition to the ecclesiastical authority, which forbade that trade. As a matter of fact, the most evident result of this infamous commerce has always been the demoralization of the Europeans who conducted it, and the degradation, ruin, and death of the savages. Accordingly, the honorable and Protestant Company of Hudson Bay, actuated by higher motives than those blind and jealous Catholic [governors], has for many years absolutely prohibited the brandy trade throughout the extent of the immense regions subject to its jurisdiction. And it has been possible, since then, to establish a period of halt in the movement of depopulation which threatened to bring, before long, the complete extinction of the aboriginal tribes (*Missions de Québec*, tenth report, 36, 107; thirteenth report, 137). I have spoken of demoralization, ruin, and death; but there is no exaggeration in this language. The reader may judge of this by the following extract from an anonymous document addressed in 1705 to the Comte de Pontchartrain (*Mémoire historique sur les mauvais effets de la réunion des castors dans une même main*; this document is found in the Archives of the Marine): 'There are many of these *coureurs de bois* who, with the view to enrich themselves all at once, make nearly all their commerce center around the brandy-trade. Every one knows the passion of the savages for this liquor, and the fatal effects that it produces on them. Experience, as old as the Colony, teaches us that they drink it only to intoxicate themselves, without having ever been able to understand by what fatal charm this surprising effect can be produced. The village or the cabin in which the savages drink brandy is an image of hell: fire [i.e., burning brands or coals flung by the drunkards] flies in all directions; blows with hatchets and knives make the blood flow on all sides; and all the place resounds with frightful yells and cries. They bite off each other's noses, and tear away their ears; wherever their teeth are fixed, they carry away the morsel [of flesh]. The father and the mother throw their babes upon the hot coals or into the boiling kettles. They commit a thousand abominations – the mother with her sons, the father with his daughters, the brothers with their sisters. They roll about on the cinders and coals, and in blood. In this frightful condition they fall

The Irroquois, [knowing] the close search that was
being made everywhere in order to render them justice,
and no longer doubting that the French were in earnest,

asleep among one another; the fumes of the brandy pass away, and the next
morning they awake disfigured, dejected, and bewildered at the disorder in
which they find themselves. Entirely savage as they are, they nevertheless feel
horrified at their condition; and many of them repent, and form the resolution
to drink no more in future. Some Frenchmen, unworthy to bear that name,
solicit them to begin again. The latter find immense profits in this infamous
commerce, because, when they have once intoxicated the savages, they plunder
them of even the clothes, weapons, and other articles which they had previously
sold to the savages. Some of these Frenchmen have been known to acknowledge,
with sorrow and tokens of repentance, that they had obtained more than 15,000
livres' worth of beaver-skins with a single cask of brandy which did not cost
them 200 livres; but that, while returning from their voyages, their cabin had
taken fire while they were asleep, and all their beaver-skins and the rest of their
equipment were consumed. There are, besides, a hundred instances of the
curse of God on those who carry on this odious commerce; and not one of them
is known whose affairs have ended prosperously. . . His Majesty has, at
various times, issued wise regulations opposed to this evil commerce; but avarice,
greed for gain, jealousy of authority, and false policy, have always found
means to elude them.' These disorders, with the same features, are still reproduced to-day wherever the dealers in strong liquors can penetrate. See what
was written in 1839 by a missionary on the Missouri, who cannot be suspected
of having drawn his inspiration from the preceding memoir: 'The deplorable
excess in liquors . . . will end, I fear, by entailing the total ruin of the
tribe; for war, pestilence, and famine are its inevitable results. Some Americans without conscience are inundating the country with their fatal liquors; and
the government, which alone can put an end to a traffic so immoral, thus far has
opposed it only by severe laws, but not with efficacious measures. . . One
must be a witness to the orgies of these people in order to understand to what
excess their brutal passion can carry them. Once the bounds of temperance are
passed, their blood is inflamed, and a sort of rage consumes them. . . At first
there are songs of joy, but soon arise cries and yells, followed by altercations. A
combat is begun with the strokes of knives, and ended with blows from clubs.
Very often blood is mingled with their libations, and murder seasons the feast.
Above all else, the combatants strive to cut off each other's noses; it is for them
an exploit of which they boast' (*Annales de la propagation de la Foi*, vol. xiii,
52, 53). Cf. J. Long's *Voyage and Travels*, 97, 111, of the French translation
(Paris, the year II). For the rest, the savages are under no illusion as to
the real cause of their degradation and their misfortunes. Once some agent
(I forget his name) of the President of the United States assembled in council
the Ouinipegous or Puans, that he might make known to them the order to
quit their ancient abodes — where, it was claimed, they had become a permanent
cause of trouble and scandal by their bad conduct. The great orator and head
chief of the tribe made a speech, and said, among other very sensible remarks:
'In order to avoid being just toward us, they accuse us of being the most per-

on account of the complete satisfaction that had been made to them in the case of the preceding murder, manifested no resentment for this last crime. They still continued to hunt along the Outaoüas River, having with them some Frenchmen who carried on a good business [in trading with them], and of whom they took excellent care. They requested more Frenchmen from Monsieur de Courcelles, in order that, if some Outaoüas came down [to the colony] who were ignorant of the peace, no strife or bloodshed might occur.

XVIII.   Terror of the Outaoüas at the sight of the Irroquois who were hunting along the river

More than nine hundred Outaoüas came down to Montréal in canoes;[149] in this number there were five of us Frenchmen [1670]. It must be understood that in that period those peoples [of the upper country] were very cowardly, and little used to war. While on our voyage we found, past [Lake] Nepissing, some Nepissing canoes which were coming back from Montréal; this induced us to stop and encamp, in order to get some

verse people under the sun. If this reproach were cast at us by Indians, I would show that it is exaggerated; but it is the white men who apply it to us, and I confine myself to replying that the blame recoils on them. Why impute to us vices which you yourselves have encouraged? Why do you come to the very doors of our cabins to tempt us with your brandy, so destructive to our tribe? If there are crimes committed among us, it is the result of drunkenness; and who makes us drunken? Who? they are greedy men, who sell us poison and plunder us to pay for it' (*Annales de la propagation de la Foi*, vol. xvii, 490). In fact, brandy is for the savages a veritable poison; strychnine or arsenic would kill them more quickly, but not more surely." — TAILHAN.

149 "The Ottawa fleet, according to the *Relation* of 1679 (chap. i), comprised only ninety canoes, manned by four hundred men. That is very different from the nine hundred Ottawas of Perrot. But it is easy to explain this disagreement, more apparent than real, by regarding these ninety canoes as a part of the entire fleet — which we are authorized to do by the phrase 'the last bands,' which the *Relation* uses to designate them." — TAILHAN.

news from the colony. They assured us that there were several bands of Irroquois, escorted by some Frenchmen, who were hunting in the vicinity of the river, and who had given them a very hospitable reception, offering them provisions to refresh themselves. That large body [of Outaoüas], in their apprehension, were already afraid of what has just been related, and even were ready to give up [their journey]; but, as the Outaoüas had great confidence in me and looked on me as their friend, I persuaded them to continue their voyage — except some canoes of Saulteurs, Missisakis, and Kiristinons who slipped away and returned to their own homes. When we had descended the Calumets we met, a little below the [rapids of the] Chats, Monsieur de la Salle,[150] who was hunting with five or six Frenchmen and ten or twelve Irroquois.

That great fleet of Outaoüas appeared already shaking with terror at this sight, and desired to give up their voyage entirely on hearing the report made by the Frenchmen, who told them that there were still several other bands of Irroquois who were hunting farther down [the river]. I could not prevent myself then from reproaching them for their cowardice; and, having reassured them, they continued their route, for there was not room [in that place] for their camp. It was there-

---

[150] "Robert Cavelier de la Salle, who was born at Rouen in 1633, and died at the hand of an assassin in Texas, March 16, 1687, played a very important part in New France. At first a Jesuit, then a voyageur, he was still but little known when (in 1670) he was encountered by Perrot on the shore of the Ottawa. He had, however, in the preceding year been the first to descend the Ohio River, as far as the falls which interrupt its navigation (Margry, 'Les Normands dans l'Ohio et le Mississippi,' *Journal général de l'instruction publique,* supp., August 20, 1862). Thirteen years later (1682) he finished the discovery of the Mississippi, commenced by Joliet and Father Marquette in 1673." Margry maintains (*ut supra*) that La Salle had preceded them in this discovery, but this assertion seems inadmissible; and various contemporary documents and reliable historians are cited to disprove it. — TAILHAN.

212 NICOLAS PERROT [Vol.

fore necessary to paddle all night, and to leave all the loaded canoes afloat, in order that we might proceed the next morning. Two hours before daylight, all the fleet in departing took the broad part of the river, and slipped along about daylight without making any noise. We had in the early morning a heavy fog, so dense that it prevented us from seeing our canoes; but the sun in rising scattered it, and we observed opposite us a camp of seven Irroquois, with whom were five or six soldiers.

At that time the greater part of the Outaoüas had already gone past [this camp]. The Irroquois did not move from their fires; it was only the Frenchmen who came toward us and called to us; but not one of the canoes would halt; on the contrary, they exerted themselves to paddle more vigorously. Nevertheless, I compelled the canoe in which I was to land. The soldiers made me eat and drink with them; my canoemen were continually urging me to embark, for it was a long day's work that we must perform. The sun was about to set when the main body came down in a line along the rapids. My canoe was among the foremost in our group of thirty—of which some had come to land, and others were yet on the water. There were also some in the rapids, who could not ascend, or force their way against the current, for whom we must wait.

Two leagues farther down, repeated volleys of musket-shots were fired, the smoke from which we saw rise in the air. This alarm constrained all the Outaoüas to range themselves in a squadron, and those who had landed felt obliged to reëmbark, despite all that I could do to prevent them, and they overtook the main body. They made the resolution to abandon everything and take to flight; and I did all in my power to dissuade them from this course. The men in my canoe were al-

ready unnerved [by their terror]. I hastened to meet
them all, and proposed to them to give me a canoe, so
that I could take the lead and go to the place where
the guns were fired; and I urged on the Frenchmen
(who were no less overcome by fear than were the savages) to accompany me. I endeavored to make them
recover from the terror that had seized them, by assuring them that the Irroquois, as a proof of their sincerity,
had some Frenchmen with them. I gained the front of
the main fleet, and managed so well that they consented
to follow me. As my canoe neared land, toward evening, the Irroquois fired a last volley, in order to salute
us. Most of the Outaoüas, on recognizing that it was
only to pay us honors that the guns were fired, recovered
their courage and came to land, but without unloading
their peltries. This band was composed of twelve Irroquois, who had with them two soldiers from Montréal,
whom I knew. The Outaoüas were still trembling, and
were resolved to travel all night until they could reach
the first French houses, not believing themselves safe
among these dozen Irroquois—who without doubt
would have been very friendly and entertained them,
if they had had some game to give them.

When the Outaoüas saw the Irroquois asleep, they all
embarked about midnight, and my canoe alone remained. My canoemen, however, did not cease to call
me, in order that I should [also] embark; but I was
sleeping so soundly, with those two Frenchmen, that I
did not hear the summons. One of my canoemen ven-
tured to come to awaken me, but so gently that you
would have said that he was going to surprise a sentinel.
He whispered in my ear that it was time to embark, and
that the entire fleet was already far ahead. I immediately arose, in order to go with him; and at daybreak it was

apparently [still] out of our sight. They all paddled vigorously, and did not wait for us until they reached the Grande Anse, in Lake St. Louis. About two hours after noon, we set out to go to Montréal, and then the Outaoüas began to take breath and, when we reached that place, to feel that they were entirely safe.[151]

XIX. Sedition stirred up, in an unexpected manner, by the Outaoüas at Montréal.

The trading of the Outaoüas with the French was well advanced (it was usually carried on in the town-hall of Montréal, where they are accustomed to display their merchandise), when it happened that a savage of the above-named people stole some article from a French soldier, without the latter being aware of it. The sentinel – who had orders to keep watch on those who were trading, in order that they might not be molested, and that no mischief be done – saw the theft committed; he notified the man to whom the wrong had just been done, who immediately rushed upon the thief and tried to snatch from him some fragments of beaver-skin that he held. The savage resisted him, the sentinel advanced in order to check those who had tried to strike the savage, and presented the end of his gun in order to hold back the people who were trying to rush on him in a crowd. The sentinel urged the savage to give back what he had seen him take. Many of the lookers-on thought that men had been wantonly knocked down, and undertook to rush headlong upon the soldier; and they actually took away his gun. When he saw that he was disarmed, he drew his sword. The man who had committed the theft tried to grasp him and take away his sword, but, as he could

---

[151] "La Potherie gives (*Histoire*, vol. ii, 114-120) a much more circumstantial relation of this voyage." – TAILHAN.

CARTE
du Gouvernement du
MONTRÉAL.

Saut du trou   Saut du Buisson
Rapides
R. des Prairies
Lac des a
Momtagne
S. Gabriere
Mac quercü
S.
chute
chute
Chateauguai a
R. des Prairies
Mirion du
La Chine
S. Pierre
Saut
S.
Louis des
Iroquois
Prairie de la
Magdelaine
Montreal
S. Marie
Isle
Jesus
pointe au fable
R. Nicolet
bout du Lac
Longueil
Fointe trembler
la Chernaye
Tremblay
Boucherville
Cap Varenne
R. de la Somption
Repentigni
Pointe du Lac
Tonnancour
Cap S.
Michel
Isl. Sulpice
Vercheres
les corne
Contre cœur
S. ours
Cap
massacre
la Valerie
R. Quammachiche
Ru. de Richelieu ou des Iroquois
Soret
Antaua
daubrai
R. Macquarge
Les Filles a
Richelleu
Fort des Iroquois
R. S. Froçois
Lac S. Pierre
R. des Loup

JURISDICTION OF MONTREAL

not accomplish this, he received a sword-blow on his arm. Then the soldier turned the point of his weapon toward every one who attempted to come near him. Immediately the Outaoüas came up, with their arms in their hands. I also hastened to the place as soon as I possibly could; several chiefs with whom I was acquainted joined me; and we checked the outbreak that was beginning.

Monsieur de la Motte,[152] a man of courage and honor, was then in command at Montréal; his company was the only one of the Carignan regiment that remained in the country. Having been notified that all his soldiers and those of the [militia] guard were in the town-hall, he ordered the drums to beat to call them together; and he marched at the head of the troops, in order to oblige every one to perform his duty; but when he arrived, the riot was quelled. He perceived (without knowing me) that I was talking energetically to the savages, and easily recognized that I understood their language. He spoke to me, inquiring where the chiefs were; I showed them to him, and he at once had them arrested and led to his house; I contrived to follow them, so as to learn the outcome of this affair. At the same time all the soldiers of the garrison, who in all numbered sixty men, were stationed along the palisades; they were commanded by a sergeant, who had orders to fire on the first Outaoüas who might seem to be attempting any disturbance.

A [certain] person of high standing, who desired to go up to the Outaoüa country by availing himself of the return of this fleet, was present. Monsieur de la Motte asked him to inquire from these people, in their own

---

[152] "Monsieur de la Motte (or Mothe), captain in the regiment of Carignan-Sallières, came to Canada in 1665 with his regiment. In that same year, or at the beginning of the following one, he built Fort Sainte-Anne on one of the islands of Lake Champlain (*Relation* of 1666, chap. iii), and was slain in a battle with the Iroquois, September 22, 1690." — TAILHAN.

language, what reason they had for stirring up such a
tumult. They made their complaint, with an artless relation of the truth; but this new interpreter repeated it
[to la Motte] otherwise, in order to gratify the savages,
and made it appear that in reality the soldier was to
blame for the whole affair. Monsieur de la Motte—
who had long been a captain, and whose services commanded respect—ordered the second sergeant of his company to go to find the sentinel, and to have him immediately placed on the wooden horse,[153] with weights of
two hundred pounds on his feet.

As I had heard that the savage blamed himself in
what he had just related, and that he had frankly admitted how the affair had occurred, I could not refrain
from making protest at this; and I stoutly declared
that, according to the very deposition which the savage
had just made, the soldier was innocent, and that he did
not deserve the punishment that had been decreed, since
the interpreter had explained the matter otherwise than
it [really] was. Monsieur de la Motte, irritated at the
soldier, hastily walked into his own room without paying any attention to what I had just said. I repeated
once more [the real truth of] the case, and made the
ensign of the company listen to me. The interpreter,
without seeming to hear me, mistrusted that the officer
would not fail to relate and explain the matter to Monsieur de la Motte; so he immediately burst into a passion and inveighed against me, and demanded justice for

---

[153] Referring to an instrument of torture known as the *chevalet* — "a sort of
wooden horse with a sharp back, on which soldiers who had committed disorderly acts were placed with cannon-balls attached to their feet" (Littré). It
was a cruel punishment, and men sometimes received serious physical injuries
from it. In this connection, note the curious statement (London *Weekly Times*,
Dec. 14, 1909) that on Dec. 14, 1909, the Manx legislative council "struck out
the proposal to repeal the obsolete ecclesiastical ordinance that children pulling
horses' tails should be set on a wooden horse for two hours and whipped." — ED.

the contradiction which I had just given him in regard
to the false interpretation. I walked up to him, in the
presence of Monsieur de la Motte, and maintained
that he had wrongly explained the statement of the savage; that I understood the savage language; and that
this person, in interpreting it, had not stated what the
savage had just confessed.

Monsieur de la Motte, who had suspended his judgment in regard to the soldier, sent for him and, after
interrogating him, ordered him to state exactly how the
whole affair had occurred. He made the same relation
that the savage had given, and in the manner that I have
just stated. Monsieur de la Motte then turned to the
person who had not told the truth about it, and contented
himself with making some remarks to humiliate him;
and then he sent away the soldier and the chiefs whom
he had placed under arrest.

The trading of the Outaoüas was nearing its end when
a canoe arrived at Montréal sent by Monsieur de Courcelles, with orders to send down to Quebec all the chiefs
of that people, and those of the Irroquois, in order to
conclude the peace between them.

Monsieur de la Motte, having received these orders,
sent for me and ordered me to embark with the Outaoüas, who made objections to going; but they were
obliged to obey, against their will. The Irroquois did
not seem to feel any repugnance to going.

When the Outaoüa chiefs found that they were forced
to embark in the vessel assigned for their voyage, they
sent all their people back to their homes, and had their
own canoes follow them. An officer and twelve soldiers
were commanded to escort them as far as the place where
we made our first encampment after leaving Montréal.
They entreated me to ask the officer that they might be

permitted to embark in their own canoes, to which he consented; and we arrived safely at Quebec [July, 1670]. There the friends of the man to whom I had given the lie at Montréal made every effort to make trouble for me with Monsieur de Courcelles, and to prevent me from being the interpreter [in the peace conference]. But Monsieur de la Motte had written [to him] in my favor, and guaranteed my reliability and fidelity, so that my enemies received no hearing. There was some person who tried to find fault with the interpretation that I had made, and to insist that it was not correct; but he was entirely put to confusion in this attempt, for my version was generally received as truthful.

XX. Arrival of the Intendant Monsieur de Talon, having orders to cause the insignia of France to be planted in the country of the Outaoüas, and to take possession of it in the name of the king

The first ships from France arrived at Quebec while all the chiefs were there. Monsieur de Courcelles received letters from Monsieur de Talon, who wrote to him how serviceable it was to secure some Frenchmen who had gone among the Outaoüas and knew their language, so that these could go up there and take possession of their country in the name of the king. Monsieur de Courcelles at once cast his eyes on me, and had me remain at Quebec until the return of Monsieur the intendant.

When he arrived there, he asked me if I would decide to go up to the Outaoüas in the capacity of an interpreter, and to escort a deputy whom he would station there to take possession of their country. I informed him that I was always ready to obey him, and offered him my services. I then set out with Sieur de Saint Lusson, his deputy, and we arrived at Montréal, where we remained until the beginning of the month of October [1670]. We were obliged, in this voyage, to spend the winter with the Amikoüets; the Saulteurs also wintered in the same quarter, and went hunting. They secured more than two thousand four hundred moose, in an island called Isle des Outaoüas,[154] which is forty leagues in length, and includes the stretch of Lake Huron from the part opposite the St. François River as far as the river of the Missisakis, on the route to Michillimakinak. This extraordinary catch of game was, however, only made with snares.[155]

I notified these peoples to proceed to the Saulteur country in the springtime, as early as they could, in order to hear the message from the king that Sieur Saint Lusson was carrying to them and to all the tribes. I also sent some [Saulteur] savages to tell those in the north that they too must not fail to proceed to their country. I went with a sledge,[156] and carried behind me

[154] "Perrot here designates, under the name 'island of the Ottawas,' the great island of Manitouline, the primitive residence of the Ottawas properly so called (Ondataouaouat, Cheveux Relevés). It is still inhabited by the remains of that tribe, and by a few hundred Sauteurs." — TAILHAN.

[155] "Although devices for inducing animals to effect self-imprisonment, self-arrest, or suicide differ from hunting weapons in that the victim is the active agent, the two classes merge into each other. The Indians had land, water, and air traps; and these acted by tension, ratchet, gravity, spring, point, or blade. They were self-set, ever-set, victim-set, or man-set, and were released, when necessary, either by the hunter out of sight or by the victim. The following list embraces all varieties of traps used by the Indians north of Mexico, and they were very clever in making them effective without the use of metal: A, Inclosing traps – (a) pen, (b) cage, (c) pit, (d) door; B, Arresting traps – (e) meshes, (f) hooks, (g) nooses, (h) clutches; C, Killing traps – (i) weights, (k) piercers, (l) knives." — O. T. MASON, in Handbook Amer. Indians.

[156] "The Eskimo and the Indians north of lat. 40° used as a vehicle for travel and transportation, complementary to the skin boat and the bark canoe, the sled drawn by man and dog over snow and ice. . . Sleds differ in construction, shape, and use according to the materials, the ingenuity of the people, the nature of the ice and snow, the journeys to be made, and the loads to be

a canoe from the other side of the island, in which I embarked; for it is to be noted that the lake never freezes, except on the coast where we wintered – and not at all, out from the shore, on account of the continual waves which the wind causes there. We set out from that place to go toward the bay of the Renards and Miamis,[157] which is not far distant; and I summoned all the chiefs to come to Sault Sainte Marie, where we were to plant the stake and fasten to it the arms of France, in order to take possession of the Outaoüas' country. It was the year 1669 [*sc.* 1671] when that took place.[158]

On the fifth of the month of May I reached Sault Sainte Marie with the principal chiefs of the Pouté-

---

hauled. . . The parts of a sled are the runners, shoes, crossbars, handles, lashings, lines, traces, toggles, packing, webbing, and braces. These belong to the fully-equipped sled, which is a marvel of convenience, but some of them may be wanting. There are four plans of construction besides numerous makeshifts: (1) The bed lashed to solid runners; (2) the bed on pairs of bent sticks spliced together or arched and fastened below to runners; (3) the bed resting on a square mortised frame, probably an introduced type; (4) the bed flat on the ground, the toboggan." – O. T. MASON, in *Handbook Amer. Indians.*

See Le Jeune's description of the most primitive type of Montagnais sledge (of the toboggan type), in *Jesuit Relations*, vol. vii, 109. From the Indians the sled was adopted, with variations and modifications, by the early settlers of Canada, who called this conveyance *train*; it is still in use in many parts of the Dominion. See Warburton Pike's description of it in his *Barren Ground of Northern Canada* (London, 1892), p. 90: "We used the ordinary traveling sleighs of the North: two smooth pieces of birch, some seven feet in length, with the front ends curled completely over and joined together with cross slats secured with *babiche* [strips of moose-hide] into a total width of sixteen inches." – ED.

[157] This refers to the Bay of Puans, or Green Bay, near which these tribes had lived for several years. See *Relation* of 1671, chap. v; *id.* of 1673, chap. i; Marquette's *Voyage*, section 3; La Potherie, *Histoire*, vol. ii, 125. – TAILHAN.

[158] "Possession of the Ottawa country was not taken until a year after the return of Talon to New France, in July, 1670 (Perrot, 125, 126). Perrot (or his copyist) therefore makes an error of two years in assigning the year 1669 as the date of that ceremony. At the end of the very document recording that taking of possession, a copy of which belongs to the archives of the Marine, we read, 'Done at Sainte-Marie-du-Sault, on the 14th day of June, in the year of grace 1671.' The *Relation* of that year (part 3) erroneously dates it on the 4th day of June." – TAILHAN.

oüatamis, Sakis, Puans, and Malhominis; those of the Renards, Mascouetechs, Kikabous, and Miamis did not go farther than the Bay. Among these latter was the head chief of the Miamis, named Tetinchoua, who, as if he had been the king, kept in his cabin day and night forty young men as a body-guard.[159] The village that he governed was one of four to five thousand warriors; he was, in a word, feared and respected by all his neighbors. It is said, however, that he had a very mild disposition; and that he never had any conversation except with his lieutenants or the men with whom he held counsel, who were commissioned with his orders. The Poutéoüatamis did not venture, out of consideration for him, to expose him to making this voyage, dreading for him the fatigue in the canoe, and fearing that he might become ill. They represented to him that, if any accident happened to him, his tribe would consider them responsible for it, and on that account would attack them. He then yielded to their arguments, and even requested them to act for him in the coming transaction, just as he would do for them if he were the one to go. I had explained to them the nature of this business, and why they were summoned.

---

[159] "Father Charlevoix gives a narrative (*Histoire*, vol. i, 437, 438), as taken from Perrot's memoirs, of the reception of that traveler by the great chief of the Miamis which is not found elsewhere save in La Potherie (*Histoire*, vol. ii, 125, 126). The former historian has some hesitation in vouching for the rigorous exactness of the details which we read in Perrot regarding the respect and deference of the Miamis for their great chief; but he would have been less timid if he had, at the moment when he wrote, recalled the following passage from Father Dablon, an eye-witness of what he narrates:" (see *Relation* of 1671, chap. v). The other tribes of the Illinois, however, displayed the same independent and even intractable disposition as all the other savages of the northern regions (cf. *Lett. édif.*, vol. vi, 321); yet the southern tribes among whom Hernando de Soto passed were like the Miamis in this respect: "The chiefs of tribes there generally enjoyed prerogatives of honor and authority which were equal, if not superior, to those of the great chief of the Miamis" (see Oviedo, *Historia de Indias*, vol. i, book xvii, 560, 561, 564, 567).—TAILHAN.

On my arrival [at Sault Sainte Marie], I found not
only the chiefs from the north, but also all the Kiristinons, Monsonis, and whole villages of their neighbors.
The chiefs of the Nepissings were also there, [with]
those of the Amikoüets, and all the Saulteurs who were
settled in the same quarter. The stake was planted in
their presence, and the arms of France were attached to
it with the consent of all the tribes – who, as they could
not write, gave presents for their signatures, affirming
thus that they placed themselves under the protection of
the king, and in subjection to him. The official report
of this taking possession was then drawn up, on which I
placed my signature as interpreter, with that of Sieur
de Saint Lusson, the deputy; the reverend missionary
fathers Dablon, Allouez, Dreuillette, and Marquet[160]

[160] All these were noted Jesuit missionaries. The eldest among them was
Gabriel Dreuillettes (born in 1610), who entered the Jesuit order at the age
of eighteen, and came to Canada in 1643. He was a missionary among the
wandering Algonkin tribes on the St. Lawrence, and the Abenaki tribes of
Maine, during nearly twenty years. In 1661 he went with Dablon on a mission
to the Cree tribes, and ten years later was in charge of the Jesuit mission at
Sault Ste. Marie. He died at Quebec, April 8, 1681.

Claude Dablon (born in 1618 or 1619) entered the order at the age of twenty,
and came to Canada in 1655. For two years he labored in the Iroquois mission,
then spent a year among the Cree about Hudson Bay, and some six years in the
settlements on the St. Lawrence; in 1668 he went with Marquette to the Algonkin tribes about Lake Superior. From 1671 he held responsible positions
in his order, which called for his residence at Quebec – where he died in 1697.

Claude Jean Allouez (born in 1622) became a Jesuit when seventeen years
old, and joined the Canada mission in 1658. After seven years' labor in the
St. Lawrence settlements, he went among the Ottawas of Lake Superior; and
spent the rest of his life among the northwestern tribes. He died in August,
1689, while engaged in these missionary labors. The official announcement of
his death credited him with having instructed more than 100,000 savages, over
10,000 of whom he baptized.

Jacques Marquette, who came to Canada (1666) at the age of twenty-nine,
is especially notable for his voyage of exploration with Louis Joliet (1673-1674),
in which they discovered the Mississippi River and followed its course as far
as the Arkansas. Previously to this, Marquette had labored among the Ottawas at Chequamegon and the Hurons at Mackinac; and in October, 1674, he
went to found a mission among the Kaskaskias of Illinois. He was forced by
illness to abandon this work, and died (May 18, 1675) while on his way back

signed it farther down; and, below these, the Frenchmen who were then trading in those quarters. That
[proceeding] was transacted according to the instructions given by Monsieur Talon. After that, all those
peoples returned to their respective abodes, and lived
many years without any trouble in any quarter.

I have forgotten to mention that the Hurons and the
Outaoüas did not arrive until after the taking of possession, because they had fled from Chagouamikon for
having eaten the Scioux, as I have previously related.
We conferred with them on what had just been done,
and they, as the other tribes had done, consented to all
that had been agreed and concluded.[161]

---

to Mackinac. Wisconsin is represented in the Capitol at Washington, D.C., by
a statue of Marquette. In the *Jesuit Relations* (vol. lxi, 400-403) may be found
an illustration of a recently-discovered portrait which is thought to be that of
the missionary-explorer; also (vol. lix) his journal and letters. — ED.

[161] "The *Relation* of 1671 (part 3) and La Potherie (*Histoire*, 128-130) contain many details of this taking of possession that are omitted by Perrot; I
refer the reader to those writings, and content myself with giving here the
(unpublished) official report of that ceremony, after the copy, somewhat incorrect, deposited in the archives of the Marine. I have restored the orthography,
either correct or probable, of certain names more or less maltreated by the copyist, and have placed these readings in brackets, next to those of the text. The
passages suppressed and indicated by leaders present nothing of historical
interest; they are nothing more than formulas or tedious repetitions. . . One
century had not passed away when there remained no other trace of the French
domination in that part of America than this sheet of paper which had formerly
verified its establishment. If one compares the list of the tribes which came to
Sainte-Marie-du-Sault, as we read it in this document, with that which the
author of our memoir furnishes, one is surprised at not finding therein the same
names. This is the result of the multiplicity of names given by the savages
to the same tribe, or to the diversity of forms which sometimes were assumed
by the same name. . . In closing, I will point out a slight error by Perrot.
Father Marquette did not figure among the witnesses to the taking of possession; he was at that time with the Hurons and Ottawas, who did not arrive
at the Sault until after the ceremony. In our text, therefore, it is necessary to
substitute for the name of Father Marquette that of Father André, which is found
in the official report of Monsieur de Saint Lusson among those of other witnesses, which follow the name of the delegate [of Monsieur Talon]." — TAILHAN.

XXI.   The Irroquois, being no longer at war with the French or with their allies, carry hostilities among the Andastes and the Chaoüanons

The Irroquois could no longer make war on their neighbors, having been compelled by force of arms to put an end to all their cruelties; they therefore sought to carry it into the country of the Andastes and the Chaoüanons,[162] whom they routed in several encounters. From these tribes they considerably augmented their own forces, by the great numbers of children or other prisoners whose lives they spared.   The Andastes were entirely ruined; and the few who remained surrendered themselves by private agreement.   They were received among the Tsonontouans, where they are at the present time.

Monsieur de Courcelles, having secured the general peace with the Irroquois, resolved to visit Lake Ontario. He went thither with a few men, and arrived [1671] at Kataracouy,[163] which is the name by which Fort Fron-

---

[162] "The Andastes 'are people speaking the Huron language who live in Virginia' (*Relation* of 1646, chap. vi).   Their war against the Iroquois, commenced about 1659, continued a long time (from 1657 to 1673) with varied fortune of success and reverses, and was ended by their complete destruction. (Cf. *Relation* of 1672, chap. vi.)   The Chaouanons, driven from the shores of Lake Erie by the Iroquois, sought a refuge farther south, in a country which Perrot calls Carolina.   In 1673 they inhabited the valley of the Ohio (Marquette, *Voyages*).   Some remnants of this tribe resided in 1835 in Kansas, south of the river from which that territory has taken its name (*Annales de la propagation de la Foi*, vol. x, 132); and at that period they were distinguished by a stage of civilization that was relatively quite advanced (*id.*, vol. ix, 91)." — TAILHAN.

The name Andastes included several tribes located south of the Iroquois Five Nations, in what is now Pennsylvania; they were akin to the Iroquois by race and language.   The Dutch colonists of New York called these tribes Minquas; and the English, Susquehannocks or Conestogas.   They were at war with the Iroquois during some seventy-five years, but were finally conquered and incorporated among their victors (about 1675).   Regarding the Chaouanons, or Shawnees, see note 19. — ED.

[163] Kataracoui was the Indian name for the locality which is the site of the

tenac is [now] called. He summoned the Irroquois, who had [orders] to assemble there all together, so that he might lay before them his intention to build a fort. They consented to this, and some presents were given to them, for which they gave others in return. In the same autumn, a little before this, Monsieur de Courcelles was recalled [to France], and relieved by Monsieur de Frontenac, who caused this fort to be built in the following summer, and bestowed on it his own name; and he did not fail to go thither to spend some months of the year. He summoned thither the chiefs of all the Irroquois nations, and always maintained harmony between them and the savages of the upper country – until some Irroquois warriors who came from Chaoüanonk, where they had accomplished nothing, carried away five families of Renards, and a chief who had gone to solicit aid in the war which that tribe were then waging against the Illinois. That was the cause of the Irroquois destroying an Illinois village, and making attacks everywhere indiscriminately. I have written a memoir on the subject of these wars, which you, Monseigneur, have; and for that reason I have given no account of it in this memoir.

All the unjust raids which the Irroquois made everywhere did not draw Monsieur de Frontenac into making war on them; he foresaw the evil results of that. As soon as a blow was struck he was notified of it by presents on the part of those who had first dealt it, and others from those who had been attacked. He was able to quiet all, although the Irroquois steadily became stronger and stronger by means of the great numbers of captives whom they continued to make among their enemies.

Monsieur de Frontenac gave to various persons per-

present town of Kingston, Ont. – an important place for both commercial and
military purposes. – ED.

mits [164] for the trade which was carried on in the upper country, among the savages who are outside of the [regular trade of the] colony. I also obtained one,

[164] "The trade in peltries outside of Canada was vested in a company which held the absolute monopoly of it. As for the trade with the savages, it was permitted only in the towns of Quebec, Three Rivers, and Montreal; in order to engage in trade outside of these places, a permit must be had, furnished by the governor-general of the colony. These permits (of which the king had fixed the number at twenty-five) were granted to the noble families who had least wealth, or to such colonists as the government wished to recompense for their services. It is, without doubt, by this latter right that Perrot obtained his permit, through the agent of Monsieur Bellinzani — not Belgralie, as erroneously written in our manuscript — one of the principal officials in the ministry of the Marine under the great Colbert. The holder could, at his own pleasure, use the permit obtained, or sell it to a third party; and in every case it conferred upon its owner the right to send or to take among the savages a canoe laden with merchandise, in exchange for which the latter gave their peltries. On returning [to the Colony], the net profit was divided into two equal parts, of which one was paid to the owner of the permit, and the other to the voyageurs or *coureurs de bois* who managed the canoe and traded with the tribes (La Potherie, *Histoire*, vol. ii, 142). I extract from a memoir already cited [that of 1705, sent to Pontchartrain, see *footnote* 148] the following picture of the life, full of dangers, toils, and adventures, which was led by these Canadian voyageurs, of whom Perrot still remains one of the most famous:

" 'These *coureurs de bois* are always young men in the prime of life; for advanced years cannot endure the fatigues of this occupation. Some of them are of good family, and others are merely habitants, or the sons of habitants; and still others have no vocation, and are called volunteers; but the desire for gain is common to all these men. Some carry their own merchandise among the savages; others borrow the goods from the merchants. Some of them carry on this trade in behalf of private persons who give them wages; others have an interest, and take risks, with the merchants. As all Canada is only one vast forest, without any roads, they could not travel by land; they make their voyages on the rivers and the lakes, in canoes which ordinarily contain each three men. These canoes are made of sheets of birchbark, smoothly stretched over very light and slender ribs of cedar wood; their structure closely resembles that of the Venetian gondolas. They are divided into six, seven, or eight sections by light wooden bars, which strengthen and hold together the two sides of the canoe. . . As an entire canoe cannot be made with a single sheet of bark, the pieces which compose it are sewed together with the roots of the sprucetree, which are more flexible and white than the osier; and these seams are coated with a gum which the savages obtain from the spruce. . . The savages, and especially their women, excel in the art of making these canoes, but few Frenchmen succeed in it. . . The *coureurs de bois* themselves propel their canoes, with small paddles of hard wood, very light and smooth; the man at the rear of the canoe guides it, which is the part of their calling that requires skill. The two other men paddle ahead. . . A canoe properly man-through the favor and recommendation of Monsieur Bellinzani, secretary of Monsieur de Colbert.

It was about the same time when Monsieur de Ches-

aged can make more than fifteen leagues a day in still water; it goes farther if descending the current of a river, but a less distance when it ascends against the current. . . When they meet rapids or waterfalls which cannot be passed with the canoe, they go ashore, and unload the bales . . . these, as well as the canoe, are carried on their backs and shoulders . . . until they have passed the fall or rapids, and find the river suitable for again embarking on it; and this is called "making portages." . . When there is a favorable wind, this is a great help to the canoeman, who does not neglect to hoist a sail (with which each canoe is provided for use on such occasions), and to pitch his tent on shore, where he lands every evening in order to eat and sleep; that is called "cabining" [*cabaner*]. In such a canoe these three men embark, at Quebec or Montreal, to go 300, 400, and even 500 leagues from the colony, to procure beaver-skins among savages whom very often they have never seen. All their provisions consist of a small quantity of biscuit, with pease, Indian corn, and some kegs of brandy; and they are soon reduced to obtaining their food only from the game and fish that they find on their way. . . It often happens that the hunting and fishing are not successful, and they are reduced to very punctual fasting, and have nothing to eat save a kind of moss . . . which they call *tripe de roche* ["rock tripe"]. When they are returning from their voyages, or are going from one tribe to another, and have nothing to eat, they have recourse to their Indian moccasins and to the pelts which they have procured in trade, with which they make a paste for their food. . . As not much time is necessary for carrying on this traffic, the life of the *coureurs de bois* is a perpetual idleness, which leads them into all kinds of debauchery. They sleep, they smoke, they drink brandy at whatever cost; and often they seduce the wives and the daughters of the savages. . . Gambling, drunkenness, and women often consume both the capital and the profits of their voyages. They live in entire independence; they do not have to render account to any one for their actions; they recognize neither superior nor judge, neither laws nor police, nor any subordination.' " — TAILHAN.

About this time the court revoked the congés; these were a score of permissions which his Majesty had granted to the families of the poorer gentlemen to go trading among the Outaouaks, and which the governor-general distributed to the persons whom he thought most in need of them. A congé was, then, a permission for one year to take into the Outaouak country a canoe with eight men, loaded with merchandise. Those who did not care to go up thither would sell their congés for a sum varying from eight to twelve hundred francs. The buyer would choose three voyageurs, to whom he gave a thousand écus' worth of goods, which he rated high; these goods would produce about twelve thousand francs' profit. The owner of the congé had the half of this profit, besides his principal; and the voyageurs shared the rest. Those people usually resorted to Michilimakinak, or else went among those nations who, they believed, had most peltries. So many abuses crept in with all these favors from the Prince that persons who were entitled to but one year extended that term, and

neau, intendant of the country, wrote letters against Monsieur de Frontenac, and sent word to the court that he was bestowing permissions upon his own dependants only. His letters obtained credence, and it was forbidden to issue these permits to any one thereafter.

The Canadians, seeing themselves deprived of these privileges, grew lax [in their obedience to the government], and believed that the privileges were rightfully theirs; and that was the reason why most of the young men in the country left it, and returned only by stealth to obtain trade-goods, and bringing back peltries, which were secretly sold. This traffic opened the eyes of the merchants, who found it greatly to their own advantage; they advanced to these young men the goods that were necessary for their voyage, some of them being opposed to the issue of the orders mentioned above. As a result, these Canadians made themselves like unto the savages, whose dissolute conduct they copied so well that they forgot what was due from them to French subordination and discipline, and, if I may venture to say so, to even the Christian religion. In order to prevent this lawlessness when it commenced, punishment should have been administered from the beginning to such as com-

others went thither as they would. As a result, beaver-pelts became so abundant that the Farmers of the West [i.e., the Company of the West Indies] could with difficulty find sale for them in France, or a market in foreign countries. On the other hand, Monsieur de la Salle, seeing his projects thwarted by the disorderly commerce which some unauthorized Frenchmen were coming into those quarters to carry on, ordered his men to plunder them; and, at an assemblage of the savages convened by him, he begged them not to trade with any one who was not provided with one of the commissions issued by him. He took this action because the trade which he carried on was really the means of maintaining those peoples, and because he could not succeed in his discoveries if he did not attach them to himself. He took all necessary precautions to prevent the abuses which might be occasioned by the orders which he had given; but they were nevertheless certain to occur; for the savages, extending their range up to the places where trade was free, plundered all, indifferently, whom they found roving in those quarters. — LA POTHERIE (*Histoire*, tome ii, 142, 143).

mitted offenses by transgressing the orders of the king.
The court, having been informed that this evil was not
diminishing, sent to Monsieur de Frontenac a decree of
amnesty [for those offenders], which he made public in
the Outaoüas country – to which he sent Monsieur de
Villeraye for this purpose, and stationed him there as
commandant in those regions.

The Irroquois then began to make raids on the Illinois
and other tribes, for their forces were continually increasing. They even undertook to go against the Outaoüas and Nepissings, from whom they took many captives. Monsieur de Frontenac, having gone to visit the
fort which he had caused to be built, as soon as he
arrived there had all the Irroquois chiefs assembled;
and he talked with them in such fashion that they surrendered their captives, and remained quiet, promising
to make no more raids on our allies who are included in
the peace. Nevertheless, Monsieur de Frontenac was
continually urged to make war on them; but he foresaw
that, if once it were kindled, it would not be extinguished very soon; he therefore contented himself with
intimidating them by [threats of] war in his speeches
to them, and succeeded therein.

Continual disputes arose between him and Monsieur
du Chesneau through the suggestions made by their dependants on both sides. The king, having been informed of this, recalled both of them to France, and
sent over Monsieur de la Barre to relieve Monsieur de
Frontenac, and Monsieur de Meule in place of Monsieur du Chesneau. This recall, to the detriment of the
country, was caused by the ill-considered counsel that
was given to each of those officials.

Messieurs de la Barre and de Meules, having relieved
them [1682], were persuaded by the ecclesiastics to

make war against the Irroquois; the merchants also, who were considering not so much the destruction of that people as their own interests, on their side urged him on to declare war. They did not foresee that, in rendering the Irroquois their enemy, they could not bring those savages back to them when they pleased. They fancied that as soon as the French made their appearance the Irroquois would beg for mercy from them; that it would be easy to establish warehouses and construct vessels on Lake Ontario and in the Lake of the Outaoüas; and that the war was a means for finding wealth. All these counselors succeeded in causing this war to be undertaken.

XXII. War undertaken by Monsieur de la Barre against the Irroquois

Monsieur de la Barre, having finally resolved on the war which he had been persuaded to make against the Irroquois [1684], sent presents to the Outaoüas tribes inviting them to come to join him at Fort Frontenac, in order that they might, united together, destroy the village of the Onontaguez. Monsieur de la Durantaye was ordered to command the Outaoüas, and for his second in command he was given Monsieur de Lude; he sent notification of this to the latter at Kamalastigouia,[165] at the furthest end of Lake Superior, where he was stationed. Monsieur de la Durantaye had all the Frenchmen called in who were in the vicinity of Michillimakinak. All

---

[165] "In this passage of our manuscript one may read indifferently *Kamalestgauda* or *Kamalesigauda*; but farther on this same name appears again, very plainly written, under the form *Kamalastigouia*, which for that reason I have adopted. A petition from Du Luth (in archives of the Marine) in which he made application in 1693 for the concession of this post, of which the exact location is unknown to me, has the form *Kamanastigouian*." — TAILHAN.

This place (the name also written Kaministiquoia) was near the present Port Arthur, Ont. — ED.

his people being brought together, he sent out the tomahawk [166] to present it to the Saulteurs, Missisakis, and
other tribes who dwelt about Lakes Huron and Superior, but there was not one of them who would accept
it. He had it carried among the tribes of the Bay, who
likewise refused it.

Monsieur de la Barre had given me a permit to go to
trade among the Outaoüas. On my way to the Bay I
met, five leagues from Michillimakinak, the deputies
who were going to invite the tribes of that Bay with the
tomahawk and presents; but when they returned they
reported that not one of the tribes had been willing to
give their consent to the war, or to accept the presents
that had been offered to them. The envoys went among
the Hurons, who accepted the tomahawk; the Outa-

---

[166] " 'The *casse-tête* ["head-breaker"] or tomahawk is a sort of war-hatchet,
which is the symbol of a war that is declared. The custom is, to present it
with formality in the middle of a dance, in which each person is animated by
all the most frightful emotions which fury can inspire' (La Potherie, *Histoire*,
vol. ii, 157). This weapon was at first a sort of club, formed from the root of
a tree or from some other very hard wood, two and a half feet long, squared on
the sides, and enlarged or rounded off at its extremity. Later, the savages substituted for this a small iron hatchet, to which they gave the same name (Lafitau,
Mœurs des sauvages, vol. ii, 196, 197; Charlevoix, *Histoire*, vol. iii, 238)."
    — TAILHAN.

"Tomahawk" is the name applied to a sort of weapon in common use
among the Algonquian tribes of the eastern United States, and probably came
into English through the early colonists, from the dialect of Virginian tribes;
it is common to widely scattered peoples, being found as far west as the Cree.
"A common conception of the tomahawk is that it was the aboriginal representative of the European hatchet — that is to say, a cutting tool — and in
colonial times and even later the name was generally applied, apparently
through misapprehension, to the metal hatchet. The etymology of the word
[meaning, an instrument to strike with] would seem, however, that the name
was applied originally to a striking instrument or weapon of the club type,
rather than to an edged implement. An examination of the literature of the
subject confirms this conclusion." This weapon seems to have been originally
a club, some three feet long, with a knob at the end, sometimes made more
effective by inserting in it a spike of bone or flint. The French called it
casse-tête, "head-breaker." After the Indians obtained metal hatchets from
the Europeans the name tomahawk was often applied to these.
    — W. H. HOLMES, in *Handbook Amer. Indians.*

oüas, the Kikapous, and the Sinagos refused to hear them speak.

Monsieur de Lude arrived, the following night, from Kamalastigouia, and learned that none of the tribes, except the Hurons, had consented to go out on the warpath. In the morning he was told that I was at Michillimakinak; he sent for me, and told me that no one could, better than I, induce the tribes to unite with us in this war, [as he was] persuaded of the ascendency that I possessed over their minds. I set out therefore, one Sunday, after I had heard holy mass, to go among those peoples; they listened to me, and accepted the tomahawk and the presents. They only asked me for a few days to repair their canoes, and to make their preparations for joining us; they were given a week in which to get ready. At the end of that time they arrived [at Michillimakinak], and we all departed together; but the Outaoüas did not come until three hours later, at Sakinang [i.e., Saginaw] – to the number of four hundred men, including the chiefs and old men. After their departure, a canoe was sent to inform the tribes at the Bay that we all had set out from Michillimakinak; and that I had induced peoples who had refused to accept the tomahawk and the presents to unite with us in the war. I told them that they had always looked on me as their father, and that I was to march at the head of the Outaoüas, who were doing quite right in following me. One of the chiefs then spoke, and declared to all the villages that it was their duty to take an interest in this war, and to go to it, since I was taking part in it. He declared that he and his family would not allow me to expose myself to danger unless they were there too, and he set out without making any preparations. He was followed by a hundred young men; all the rest would

PIPE AND TOMAHAWK DANCE (Ojibwa)

have accompanied him if there had been [enough] canoes.

The Outaoüas having joined us, Messieurs our commanders gave them into my care. An unforeseen accident which occurred on the third day of our journey frightened them, and made them look on it as a bad omen for the war which we were going to carry on. There was a French soldier who unawares let his gun go off, and was killed by the shot; this sad occurrence filled their imaginations with notions unfavorable to our enterprise, but I beguiled them from these ideas.

When we arrived at the islands of the Détroit,[167] they drove a herd of elk into the water; a young man who sat in the middle of a canoe, attempting to fire at them, broke the arm of his brother who was paddling in the front part of the same canoe. This second accident made such an impression on the Outaoüas that they were going to turn back, if I had not persuaded the father of the wounded man to make a public declaration that he had left his own country with the sole intention of perishing with his weapons in his hand against the Irroquois. The young man actually died from his wound; and his brother lived only a short time after this, on account of the chagrin and sorrow that he felt [over his carelessness]. Notwithstanding, the Outaoüas could not evade continuing their route.

The people from the Bay whom I have previously mentioned joined us at two leagues' distance from Longue Pointe on Lake Erien; and they informed the Outaoüas that if they remained long absent from their women the latter would starve, as they did not know the method for catching fish. They desired therefore to

---

[167] "Perrot here gives the name of Détroit ['the strait'] to the river formed by the discharge of Lake Huron into Lake Erie. Cf. Charlevoix, *Histoire*, vol. iii, 255, 256." — TAILHAN

return home; but I opposed this purpose, telling them
that there was cowardice in such a resolution. At first
they were angry at me, and roughly answered that they
would show me what they could do. At that time we
were detained in that place by bad weather[168] for seven
or eight days; and we had taken care to send out some
Frenchmen thence to make a reconnaissance toward the
country of the Irroquois.

At this reproach [of mine], the Outaoüas also sent
out some of their men by land, who reached the region
to which we had sent our men to get intelligence of
the enemies; but they did not meet each other until
some time later. The Outaoüas while marching amused
themselves by whistling and counterfeiting the call of
the elk, until the Frenchmen (who were not very far
from them) believed that there really were elk there;
and they went farther into the woods, going toward the
place where they had heard the sounds. When they had
come quite near, one of those at the front spied something white in a thicket, and thought that he saw the
breast of an elk; this led him to fire his gun, with which
he wounded an Outaoüa who was wearing a shirt, and
pierced the shirt of the man behind this one.

This last blow gave the finishing stroke to their belief
that they had good reason to abandon us; there were even
some of them who were bold enough to say that they
must fight against us, because we were already beginning

---

[168] "Perrot does not name the tribe from the Bay who came to Long Point
to join the other savages who were *dégradés* — that is, detained in that place
by bad weather; but La Potherie (*Histoire*, vol. ii, 159, 160) informs us that
it was the Outagamis. In a 'Memoir of the payments made by Sieur de la
Durantaye to the Ottawas for the service of the king and the execution of the
orders of Monsieur de la Barre in the years 1683-1684' (in the archives of
the Marine) appears the following item: 'Given to the Puans, the Saquis, the
Outagamis, and the Malominis, on August 20, in my behalf, by Sieur Nicolas
Perrot in order to invite them to go to Montreal, eleven pounds of tobacco, at
eight francs a pound.' " — TAILHAN.

to kill them. By my arguments I won over the wounded
man and his uncle, who assured the Outaoüas that his
nephew was not dead, although he had been wounded;
that he wished to go further in order to die; and that he
had left his own country with this design. He added,
addressing them directly, that they could nevertheless
give up the enterprise if they so wished; but that, as for
himself and his nephew, they would follow the French
everywhere. His speech produced so good an effect that
they continued their march with us.

At last we arrived at Niagara, where Monsieur de la
Durantaye commissioned me to inform the Outaoüas, in
presenting to them the tomahawk, that the three barks
belonging to Fort Frontenac would be there at our arrival, laden with three hundred guns for arming them, and
with other military supplies, and all the food they would
want. I told him my opinion regarding this, which was,
not to entangle himself with assurances of this sort, and
that it would be time to say this when we reached that
place, in case that such abundance were found there;
because, if matters went otherwise and they found that
they had been deceived, it would be no longer possible
to keep them in hand. Despite all my arguments, he
positively insisted that I must carry out his orders as
above.

When we arrived there, we found no vessel; I di-
verted their minds, however, during two or three days,
by making them believe [that contrary winds] had prevented the barks from coming. Time passed, and nothing came; that made them murmur. They began to tell
me that I had deceived them, and that the French were
intending to betray them and deliver them into the hands
of the Irroquois, who would [now] have no difficulty in
carrying away their wives and children. The com-

manders and the Frenchmen no longer knew what to
say about it; they held consultations, and called together
the chiefs and all the elders of the tribes, to whom they
declared that it was necessary to take the route toward
the north side of the lake [Ontario], and go straight to
Fort Frontenac; that they would find Monsieur de la
Barre there, or, if he had not yet arrived, they would
wait there for him; and if they learned that he had advanced from that place, they would follow him, because
his arrival would protect us from the attacks of the
enemy. The savages, who are creatures of contradiction, always desiring to be masters of their own acts,
said that it was necessary to take the [route to the]
south, and march straight to the country of the Tsonontouans.[169] They stubbornly maintained this, despite

[169] *Tsonnontouan*, a corrupted form of the Iroquois name (signifying "People
of the Great Mountain") for the westernmost tribe in their League — who
were called by the Dutch *Sinnekens* (apparently the Mohegan translation of the
Iroquois name), a term at first applied to all the Iroquois tribes save the Mohawks, but finally restricted to the westernmost one, and anglicized to the form
Senecas, by which name they are still known. When first encountered by the
French, "they occupied that part of western New York between Seneca Lake
and Geneva River, having their council fire at Tsonontowan, near Naples, in
Ontario County. After the political destruction of the Erie and Neuters, about
the middle of the seventeenth century, the Seneca and other Iroquois people
carried their settlements westward to Lake Erie and southward along the
Allegheny into Pennsylvania. They also received into their tribe a portion of
these conquered peoples, by which accessions they became the largest tribe of
the confederation and one of the most important. They are now chiefly settled
on the Allegany, Cattaraugus, and Tonawanda reservations, N.Y. A portion
of them remained under British jurisdiction after the declaration of peace
and live on Grand River reservation, Ontario. Various local bands have been
known as Buffalo, Tonawanda, and Cornplanter Indians, and the Mingo
(formerly in Ohio) have become officially known as Seneca from the large
number of that tribe among them. No considerable number of the Seneca ever
joined the Catholic Iroquois colonies. In the third quarter of the sixteenth
century the Seneca was the last but one of the Iroquois tribes to give its suf-
frage in favor of the abolishment of murder and war, the suppression of
cannibalism, and the establishment of the principles upon which the League of
the Iroquois was founded. However, a large division of the tribe did not at
once adopt the course of the main body, but on obtaining some coveted privileges and prerogatives the recalcitrant body was admitted a constituent member

whatever good arguments could be employed to make
them change their resolution. I went into their camp to
confer with all the chiefs, to whom I showed that it was
too great a risk to expose themselves to, in such an enterprise, and that we would certainly be defeated, in place
of securing our safety by taking the other course. I
talked with all of them individually, one after another;
and after the answers they gave me I saw that there were
only a few men among them who stubbornly maintained
that opinion; and the reason why they were so hard to
move was, because of the reproach of cowardice which I
had previously flung at them – while as for the rest I was
not wrong. All the savages likewise told me the same
thing, even though I might say no more to them about
it. I returned to Messieurs our commanders to tell them
what I had just heard, and to assure them that terror

in the structure of the league. . . The political history of the Seneca is largely
that of the League of the Iroquois, although owing to petty jealousies among
the tribes the Seneca (like the others) sometimes acted independently in their
dealings with aliens. But their independent action appears never to have been
a serious and deliberate rupture of the bonds uniting them with the federal
government of the League, thus vindicating the wisdom and foresight of its
founders in permitting every tribe to retain and exercise a large measure of
autonomy in the structure of the federal government. It was sometimes apparently imperative that one of the tribes should enter into a treaty or other
compact with its enemies, while the others might still maintain a hostile attitude toward the alien contracting party." The Iroquois were at war, during
most of their early history, with the Algonquian peoples about them, both on
the north and the south, and sometimes extended their hostile incursions even as
far as Labrador and Illinois respectively, the Senecas being especially active
against tribes west of their own region; and it was mainly they who ruined
and dispersed the Huron tribes (1648-1649), and subjugated the Neuters (1651)
and the Erie (1656). "In 1657 the Seneca, in carrying out the policy of the
League to adopt conquered tribes upon submission and the expressed desire to
live under the form of government established by the League, had thus incorporated eleven different tribes into their body politic. . . The earliest estimates of the numbers of the Seneca, in 1660 and 1677, give them about
5,000. . . In 1908 those in New York numbered 2,736 on the three reservations, which, with those on Grand River, would probably give them 3,000 in all.
The proportion of Seneca now among the 4,052 Iroquois at Caughnawaga, St.
Regis, and Oka cannot be estimated." – J. N. B. HEWITT, in *Handbook of
Amer. Indians*, art. "Seneca."

abode in the camp of the Outaoüas, and that they were afraid we would take the route by way of the country of Tsonontouans. I proposed an expedient, which was, to publish in their camp that, as we had controlled the advance as far as Niagara, we would for the present confer on them the power of directing it; that we were ready to follow them in the direction that they [thought best]; and that we would regulate [our motions] by the first canoe that should depart. They agreed to what I have just stated, and immediately all the French canoes were launched, and the baggage was placed in them.

When all that was accomplished, I called out in their camp, "Now do you direct the course;" and at once all those who were not numbered with the obstinate ones embarked, taking the route to the north, and followed us.

Thirty or thereabouts of the stubborn ones did not stir from their camp during the rest of the day; they sent two men out as scouts toward the country of the Irroquois. These men discovered a bark under sail, and immediately returned to notify their people, who sent us advice of it by a canoe.

The next day we reached Niagara, where the bark arrived; but it had nothing [for us] except letters from Monsieur de la Barre. In these he informed us that it had been necessary for him to make peace, on account of the disease which had broken out in his camp; this had caused the deaths of nearly nine hundred Frenchmen, and of as many more savages who had accompanied him.* Although Monsieur de la Barre had followed the advice of many persons in undertaking this expedition, they were the first to write letters to the court

---

* "It is impossible that Monsieur de la Barre's army, eleven hundred men strong (Charlevoix, *Histoire*, vol. i, 489, 490), should lose eighteen hundred of them by sickness. The copyist has probably added here a zero to the figure written in the original." — TAILHAN (additional note, page 338 of his edition).

against him, and to declare that he was no longer capable of conducting a war. He was, in fact, recalled in the following year, and relieved by Monsieur [de] Denonville [August, 1685].

I did not return to the Outaoüas immediately after the campaign; I did not go there until the following spring, in consequence of the news which were received through the voyageurs, who reported that the men of Monsieur de la Salle were making trouble for the Frenchmen who went [up there relying] on their permits from Bay des Puans as far as the Illinois; and that they even carried away the property of the traders.[170]

XXIII. Campaign of Monsieur Denonville against the Irroquois

I was sent to that bay, carrying a commission to be commander-in-chief there, and in the regions further toward the west, and even of those which I might be able to discover.[171] Monsieur de la Durantaye then re-

---

[170] "Cf. La Potherie, *Histoire*, vol. ii, 143. In 1685, while La Salle at the head of a new expedition landed on the coast of Texas, his lieutenant in the country of the Illinois, Chevalier de Tonty, continued the interdiction to the *coureurs de bois* of trade with the savages of those regions. Monsieur de Denonville wrote thus to the Marquis de Seignelay: 'I have been told that Monsieur de Tonty will not allow our Frenchmen to go trading in the Illinois country. If the king has given that country to Monsieur de la Salle alone, it would be proper that you should have the goodness to notify me of that fact, to the end that I may conform to the orders of his Majesty' (letter of September 13, 1685; in archives of the Marine)." — TAILHAN.

[171] "In the spring of 1685 Perrot arrived at the post of Saint François Xavier, on the Bay of Puans, and took possession of the command which Monsieur de la Barre had just entrusted to him; and almost immediately he set out on a journey to the country of the Sioux, the most remote of all the lands which were under his jurisdiction. On August 1 of the same year, Monsieur de Denonville, the new governor of Canada, arrived at Quebec, charged by the [French] minister, among other things, to oppose all new expeditions, and those to remote regions — as we learn from himself in a letter of September 13 to the Marquis de Seignelay (in the archives of the Marine): 'There are some of our Frenchmen who are among the Outaouas, who say that they have

lieved Monsieur de la Valtrie, who had been commanding officer there in the Irroquois campaign.

I had no sooner arrived in the region where I was to
govern than I received orders from Monsieur Denonville to go back with all the Frenchmen whom I had.
I was unable to do so without abandoning the goods
which I had been compelled to borrow from the mer-

orders from Monsieur de la Barre to go to the Mississippi. I know that it is
not your intention to allow our Frenchmen to ramble so far away; and I will
do my best to bring them back.' This explains to us the command given to
Perrot to return to the Bay, with all those who had followed him to the
Mississippi. It was not long before the Marquis de Seignelay changed his
ideas entirely; and Perrot, who was recalled in 1685 from the country of the
Sioux, received four years later a definite order to take possession of it in the
name of the King." In fulfilment of this order, Perrot formally took possession
for France of "the Bay of Puants, the lake and rivers of the Outagamis and
Maskoutins, the river of Ouiskonche and that of Missisipi, the country of the
Nadouesioux, the Sainte Croix River and [that of] Saint Peter, and other places
farther removed." Among the witnesses were Father Joseph J. Marest, a Jesuit
missionary then among the Dakotas, the voyageur Le Sueur, and Boisguillot, commandant (under Perrot) "of the French in the vicinity of the Ouiskonche on the
Mississipi." The act of taking possession is in the archives of the Marine; it
is dated at the post of Saint Antoine (anglicized as St. Anthony), May 8, 1689.
"To maintain peace and friendly relations among the savages, and between
them and the Canadian traders or *coureurs de bois*; to reëstablish harmony
where it was disturbed; to go in quest of new countries, and to engage
their inhabitants in alliance with France; and finally, in time of war to bring
together the French and the friendly tribes, and march at their head: such were
the principal functions of the command entrusted to Perrot, as we can assure
ourselves by our memoir (pages 139, 146), by the act above cited, and by the
following lines from a letter by the Marquis de Denonville to Monsieur de la
Durantaye (June 6, 1686; in archives of the Marine): 'If Nicolas Perrot
could call together some savages, in order to add them to [the forces of] Monsieur du Lhude (Du Lhut) when the time for that shall come, he would have
to plan for that at an early date.'" Apparently the office conferred upon Perrot
by La Barre — that of commander-in-chief of the Bay and the lands adjoining —
left him responsible to the governor only; but in the following autumn Denonville, the new governor, placed under La Durantaye's authority, as commandant
at Michillimakinak, all the Frenchmen who were then in the upper lake region
(letters of Denonville to Seignelay, Oct. 12, 1685, and June 12, 1686; in archives of the Marine). The same arrangement prevailed under Frontenac.
As Perrot set out for his voyage to the Bay, he heard of the war begun between
the Outagamis on one side, and the Sioux and Chippewas on the other. He
hastened to Michillimakinak, with instructions from La Barre to pacify the
hostile tribes, which he succeeded in doing, and then went to the Bay (La
Potherie, *Histoire*, vol. ii, 166-186). — TAILHAN.

chants for my voyage. At that time I was in the country of the Scioux, where the ice had broken up all our canoes, and I was compelled to spend the summer there; meanwhile I devoted myself to procuring boats so that I could go to Michillimakinak, but the canoes did not reach me until the autumn [1686].

In the beginning of the winter I received other orders, to call together all the Frenchmen and savages whom I should find within my reach and along my route, in order to go with them to [a place] near the lake where the Tsonontouans are settled. Immediately I set out, and I invited the Miamis [to go] to this war, which they promised me to do; but the Loups, who were their neighbors, dissuaded them from it, making them believe that the French intended to betray them, and to make the Irroquois eat them when they joined the former.

I went by land to the village of the Miamis, who were about sixty leagues distant from my post; and I returned by land, the same as I had gone. I learned on the road, before arriving there, that a body of fifteen hundred men from the tribes of the Bay – Renards, Maskouetechs, Kikapous – who were going to war against the Scioux, intended to pillage my stock of merchandise, knowing that I was not there; and that they were planning to do the same to the Frenchmen further up, and to kill them. Some of them had come, therefore, as spies to my post, to find out the condition of affairs there, under the pretext of trading for powder; and they carried back to the camp [of the warriors above-mentioned] the information that within the fort[172] they had seen only four persons.

When I returned thither the next day, two others of

---

[172] "Perrot's fort was located on the left bank of the Mississippi, eighty or ninety leagues from the mouth of the Wisconsin, and not far from the Pelée

those savages came to the fort, who found me there. I told them that I must talk with their chiefs, of whom I named to them seven or eight of the more prominent. They returned to their camp, and the very men whom I had named to them came to visit me.

The sentinel who was on duty notified me of their arrival. I had always taken care to keep the gate of the fort closed; I had it opened in order that they might enter, and conducted them into my cabin. They saw there many guns in good condition, provided with good flints and locks. The two spies who had previously come had likewise seen the guns. I made them believe that we [Frenchmen] numbered forty men, not counting those whom I had sent out to hunt. They believed this, just as I said it, because the men whom they had seen there, going into a cabin, quickly changed their clothing and again appeared before them.

I had some food given to them, and meanwhile I re-proached them for their treacherous purpose of trying

Island which has been already mentioned. (Cf. Charlevoix, *Histoire*, vol. iii, 398.)" — TAILHAN.

In 1888 were discovered, at a spot about one mile north of the present Trempealeau, Wis., relics which apparently indicated the site of an early French post; and it is supposed that this was Perrot's headquarters during the winter season of 1685-1686. (Cf. note 128 in this volume.) For location of forts erected by him in Wisconsin, see Wis. *Hist. Colls.*, vol. x, 59-63, 299-372, 504-506; for view of the site near Trempealeau, see vol. xvi, 164. — ED.

The discovery of the Mississippi in 1673, and the explorations of La Salle in Louisiana a few years later, opened the way for the French to establish trading-posts, military stations, and colonies in the great Mississippi Valley and the region of the Great Lakes. The trading-posts of the English were mainly in the great northwest beyond Lake Superior (under the control of the Hudson Bay company), and to the south of the French "sphere of influence;" but in this latter region trade gradually pushed its way to the west and north until there were frequent clashes and much jealousy between the French and English traders. "The trading post was generally a large square inclosed by a stockade; diagonally at two corners were turrets, with openings for small cannon and rifles in each turret so as to defend two sides of the wall. Within the stockade were the store-houses, quarters for the men, and a room for general trade." — ALICE C. FLETCHER, in *Handbook Amer. Indians*.

Site of Perrot's Fort, 1685-1686

to plunder my goods and kill the Frenchmen. I told them of every point in their conspiracy. I also made them understand that they were at that moment at my disposal, but that I was not a traitor, like them; and that my only demand from them was, to give up the war that they were on the way to undertake, and rather to turn their arms against the Irroquois. [I added that] two sentinels were all the time stationed at the two bastions of the fort, both having many guns at hand, and relays were on duty all night long. These savages confessed to me that they had been plotting; I made them some presents, in order to induce them to obey me, and received from them, verbally, all sorts of amends.

The next day the main body of that band arrived, and they thought that they could enter [the fort] all at once; I held the chiefs in my power within it, and I warned them that they were dead men at the first act of violence that their men should commit, for we would begin with them. My Frenchmen, under arms, kept well on their guard. There were some of the chiefs whom I detained, who climbed up on the gate of the fort, and called out to their men that matters were amicably settled between them and us. They entreated me to buy their peltries in exchange for ammunition, so that they could go hunting for buffalo. I had them enter by turns, and, after I had traded with them for what they had, they separated, each to his allotted place, to carry on their hunt. A few days afterward, I set out with two Frenchmen, to go across the country to the Bay; and at every turn I encountered some of those savages, who showed me the best roads and entertained me very hospitably. When I reached the Bay, I held conferences with the tribes there. In the spring [1687] I set out with all the young men, and arrived at Michillimakinak one afternoon. Monsieur de la Durantaye had gone away in the morning with the Frenchmen, who had not been able to make the Outaoüas resolve to go on the war-path. As soon as they saw me, they told me to wait for them a few days, since they were intending to go away with me; they said that their canoes were not in good condition, and that when these were ready they would follow the French. I believed them, and waited for them during a week. Monsieur de la Durantaye arrested thirty Englishmen who had come to trade with the Outaoüas, and confiscated all their goods; and he caused the best part of these, and especially their brandy, to be distributed among the Outaoüas. Those savages had preserved a keg of it, containing twenty-five *pots*,[173] in order to get my men drunk and contrive to entice them away; they did what they could and gave my men a keg full; but I was informed of it, and had the keg staved in before me, and the brandy poured out upon the ground.[174]

I embarked with my people, after I had sharply upbraided the Outaoüas; and I joined Monsieur de la Durantaye, who had met Monsieur de Tonty at the fort of Monsieur de Lude, located at Détroit. They had arrested thirty more Englishmen, and were on the point of going back [to Michillimakinak] if I had not arrived; for sixty Englishmen had already become too

---

[173] The *pot* is a measure containing two French pints, equivalent to 3.29 English pints. — ED.

[174] Cf. La Potherie's somewhat fuller account (*Histoire*, vol. ii, 201-204). Denonville wrote to Seignelay (letter of Aug. 25, 1687; in archives of Marine): "It is certain that if these two parties of Englishmen had not been seized and plundered, and if their brandies and other merchandise had been carried into Missilimakinak, all our Frenchmen would have had their throats cut in a revolt of all the Hurons and Outaouas, which would have been imitated by all the other tribes farther west. This is a fact known to all our Frenchmen, by reason of the presents which the former had sent secretly to all the distant savages." — TAILHAN.

many enemies for them, and had narrowly escaped being killed by the very savages who had accompanied them, inasmuch as the Frenchmen had become intoxicated on the liquor that they had plundered from the Englishmen; and that would have occurred, if the officers had not kept the prisoners under guard. They feared that the Irroquois, having information of their advance, would prepare ambuscades for them; and that, if the English joined the enemy, they might be defeated. My arrival caused them to resume their voyage the next morning, without any fear, on account of the assistance furnished to them by my party; and at the end of two days we reached Niagara, where we threw up an intrenchment to defend ourselves from the Irroquois if they came to attack us. We spent several days in that place; the Outaoüas and Hurons joined us there, who reached us by land from Thehegagon, and left their canoes opposite, in Lake Huron. They decided to follow [us], when they saw that the tribes at the Bay had refused to believe them; for it would have been a cause for shame to them not to be present in an encounter with the enemy, if any such had occurred when they had seen their allies pass by their place of abode.

We there received orders from Monsieur Denonville, and advanced toward the Tsonontouans; and our people arrived there at the same time when he did.

Monsieur Denonville, having caused an intrenchment to be constructed on the shore of the lake [Ontario], marched with his troops against the villages; and, at half a league from the nearest one, fought against eight hundred Irroquois, who were in ambuscade and were beaten back [July, 1687]. On the next day our people encamped in the village itself, and laid waste all the cleared lands about it. During that time

the Hurons and Outaoüas led astray the savages down
here [i.e., in Lower Canada], and induced them to consent to that notion [of not continuing the war].

Monsieur Denonville ordered me to harangue them
and reproach them for their cowardice in refusing to
continue their victories.   I induced them to follow us
everywhere.

The campaign being accomplished, I went down to
the colony with Monsieur Denonville in order that I
might, as a mediator, ask from him peace for the Irroquois with the French and all the savage allies.   Although word of this was sent to the Outaoüas, and they
were forbidden, in the governor's name, to go to war,
they did so, in spite of Monsieur de la Durantaye.

I have set down in the memoirs which I have presented to you, Monseigneur, what is of usual occurrence
among those peoples, who always desire what we do not,
and who take sides through [a spirit of] contradiction.
In order to succeed with them, it is necessary to know
how to manage them; otherwise it is difficult to do anything with them.

You will readily understand, by these memoirs, that
the savages are by nature treacherous, above all the Hurons and the Outaoüas.   I have related many examples
of their treachery, and I would never come to an end if
I undertook to expatiate thereon.   It will be sufficient
that I here cite a few more of such instances, which have
not been hitherto set down.

XXIV.   Huron treachery, rendered abortive, against all the Outaoüa tribes

The Rat,[175] who died at Montréal, [August 2, 1701],
went to see the Irroquois and proposed to them the de-

---

175 "Kondiaronk, or 'the Rat,' chief of the Petun Hurons, gave throughout

struction of the Outaoüa tribes [1689]. They agreed together that the Irroquois should come with a large force to Michillimakinak, and that they should send scouts ahead to observe and examine the places in which they could attack the Outaoüas. It was resolved that the Hurons should occupy the flank of the fort; that the Rat should confer with all the tribes at the Bay and the Saulteurs, and invite them, in behalf of the Irroquois (who would not fail to come there to see them), to repair to this fort in order to confirm more thoroughly the peace which they had made together, and which the governor had made them conclude; but that it was proper and even necessary to form another and a new one among themselves, independently of that one, which would be more substantial and assured [than the governor's]. The Irroquois, in order to persuade them more easily to this, had given presents of collars to the Rat, in order that he might offer them to the other Outaoüa

the course of his long career numerous proofs of bravery and political ability. No one perhaps among the savage chiefs of New France, excepting Pontiac — who equaled and even surpassed him — deserves to be compared with him. Toward the end of his life he seemed to become more closely attached to the French cause, and died regretted and lamented by all. In the histories of Canada may be found much detailed information regarding this illustrious leader, who had nothing of the savage save in name and apparel." — TAILHAN.

Adario, a Tionontate chief, was also known as Kondiaronk and Sastaretsi. The French authorities in 1688 persuaded him to lead an expedition against the Iroquois, but on the road he learned that the latter were on the point of concluding peace with the French. Exasperated at this, he captured the Iroquois envoys on their road to Montreal, and told them that the French had commissioned him to kill them; but he set them at liberty, save one, and told them to take revenge on the French. He then brought about the execution of this captive by the French commander at Michillimackinac. These transactions, with Adario's falsehoods, so angered the Iroquois that they planned and carried out the fearful massacre of the French at and near Montreal, Aug. 25, 1689, and ravaged the settlements on the St. Lawrence. In later years, however, Adario was converted to the Christian faith by a Jesuit missionary, and became a friend to the French. He died at Montreal in 1701, while he was negotiating a peace between the Iroquois and the tribes of the upper country. — ED.

tribes when they should be assembled. They furnished to the latter much stronger assurances besides, by sending them word that they could [thus] secure a good stronghold; for it was the purpose of the Irroquois, according to the measures that they had taken, to render the Hurons masters of a stockade which they were to undermine. By this method the assault was sure [of success], because the Hurons fired off only powder. This treachery was at last disclosed; for an Aniez who came to Michillimakinak to trade met at Sakinang some Amikoüets and other savages, who received him as a friend and even gave him some peltries. They were so kind to him that he could not refrain from revealing this conspiracy to the chief of the Amikoüets (whose name was Aumanimek), one of my good friends – who, knowing that I was to go up from Montréal to the Outaoüas, waited for me, in order to winter with me at the place where, on those voyages, it is necessary to halt, so as to spend the winter there.

I arrived at his place of abode, and immediately we set out to go to the bay of the Puans; and on the way to Michillimakinak he made known to me the treacherous plan [of the Hurons]. I informed the reverend Fathers [there] of what he had told me; and they employed me to tell the Rat – but without naming the Aniez, or the chief of the Amikoüets – that he was the author of this plot. They sent for him, and told him that they had learned, from the lips of the Irroquois themselves, the design that the latter entertained of destroying the Outaoüa peoples. The Fathers, in order to convict him more forcibly, told him the means which had been agreed upon for the success of his scheme, and all that he had planned in order the better to deceive them; he could not deny it, and the whole plan fell through.

It is well known that the Hurons have always sought the destruction of the tribes in the upper country, and that they have never been strongly attached to the French; but they have not dared to declare their feelings openly. When they have had war with the Irroquois, it has been only in appearance, for in reality they were at peace with the latter; and they have protested to the Irroquois that we held them as captives in the colony, and that they carried arms against the Irroquois only by compulsion, without being able to do otherwise, since they were in the midst of the French and the Outaoüas, who would have caused them annoyance and trouble if they had refused to obey.

After the campaign of Monsieur Denonville against the Tsonontouans, deputies [from the Hurons] arrived among them to make their excuses because they had accompanied the French army. The Tsonontouans made answer that the Hurons did not come until the grass had grown tall, and when only the tops of their heads could be seen – meaning that they had not come to warn them of their misfortune until it had happened. The Hurons told them that they must have had information of it beforehand, through an Aniez whom they had sent. It is true, moreover, that two Aniez arrived at Michillimakinak, just as the [French] voyageurs were about to depart to join the army below, in the Tsonontouan country. The commanders had confidence in the fidelity of one of the two, against the opinion of all their followers; and this man deserted us when eight leagues from the [Tsonontouan] village. Without that, we would have found the enemy at home; for when we reached the shore of the lake they began to take flight and to burn their village.

XXV.　Another piece of Huron treachery

The Hurons, seeing that Monsieur de Louvigny (who was commander-in-chief[176]) was, together with the Outaoüas, unwilling that the Hurons should change [the location of] their village – knowing perfectly well that their only purpose in quitting that place was, that they might go to give themselves up to the Irroquois – separated; and half of them went to live with the Miamis on the Saint Joseph River.[177] Monsieur de Louvigny having been recalled by that time, we had for commandant in his place Monsieur de la Motte [1695].[178]

At that time I was at the Bay, from which place I sent sixty men (as I have set down in my other memoirs), who were followed by Hurons and Outaoüas, and who went rather to warn the Irroquois than to make

[176] "Monsieur de la Porte Louvigny was first appointed commandant at Michillimakinak in the month of April, 1690. He arrived there toward the end of July or the first of August in the same year, and remained in that post until some time in 1694, when he was recalled by the Count de Frontenac, and replaced by Monsieur de la Mothe-Cadillac. Later (in 1712) he was ordered to go back and resume [the French] possession of that post, which had been abandoned for several years." – TAILHAN.

[177] "In 1693 Count de Frontenac sent Monsieur de Courtemanche to reside, in the capacity of commandant, among the Miamis of Saint Joseph; and he wrote to the minister (letter of Oct. 15, 1693; in the archives of the Marine): 'His presence among those savages (who have great confidence in him), and his good management, will be very useful in preventing the English from intruding there, as I have been informed they are planning to do.' " – TAILHAN.

[178] "This refers to Monsieur de la Mothe-Cadillac, who held commands at Michillimakinak, at Detroit, and in Louisiana, successively." – TAILHAN.

Antoine de la Mothe-Cadillac came to America when a young man, and settled in Acadia. Losing all his property there by English invasions (1690-1691), he removed to Quebec and entered the Canadian military service, receiving a command therein from Frontenac. During 1694-1697 he was commandant at Mackinac, and in 1701 established the post of Detroit, which he governed for ten years. From 1712 to 1715 he was governor of Louisiana; and he died in France, Oct. 18, 1730. His "Relation: Missilimakinak, etc." is printed in Margry's *Découvertes et établissements des Français* (Paris, 1876-1886), vol. v, 75-132. – ED.

war on them; they found, nevertheless, that they were compelled to fight, as I have previously related.

Since the establishment of Détroit, have not the Hurons conspired to murder the Frenchmen who garrisoned that place, commanded by Monsieur de la Motte [1704 or 1707]? and if their plots have been eluded it is only by the vigilance [of the French] in keeping on their guard.[179]

[179] "Perrot doubtless alludes to the plot formed against Detroit, in 1708, by the Hurons, the Miamis, and some Iroquois (Charlevoix, *Histoire*, vol. ii, 322, 324). Like Perrot, Messieurs de Vaudreuil and Raudot attributed the main part in this affair to the Petun Hurons; they wrote thus to the minister (joint despatch of November 14, 1708): 'Le Pesant [an Ottawa chief] was received at Detroit by Monsieur de la Mothe, and the Hurons and Miamis were so incensed at seeing him there that in the spring of 1708 those two tribes, with a score of Iroquois who were returning from a raid into the plains country, laid a plot to massacre Monsieur de la Mothe and all the Frenchmen who were in the fort, as well as the Ottawa savages settled there.' I should, in this connection, observe that the various acts of treachery, actual or attempted, of which Perrot here accuses the Huron peoples (and to which we shall have to give attention farther on) ought to be imputed only to the tribe of which I have just spoken. The other Hurons, who took refuge at Lorette, near Quebec, rendered their service to France until the last, with unshaken devotion and courage. Even to-day they are French in language and religion. According to the latest Canadian census (1861) the Hurons at New Lorette number 261, all Catholics; but this has not prevented certain magazines from announcing (1862) the death of the last of the Hurons. As for the Petun Hurons, they were, like so many other tribes, forced to leave Michigan, and to go into exile beyond the Mississippi, into what is called 'the Indian Territory.'"
— TAILHAN.

When the great Huron confederacy of tribes dwelling around Lake Simcoe and south and east of Georgian Bay was ruined and dispersed by the Iroquois in 1649, a part of the fugitive Hurons took shelter with the Tionontati — called by the French "Huron de Pétun" ("Tobacco Hurons") because they cultivated the tobacco — a people of kindred race who resided not far westward from the Huron country. They too were attacked in the same year by the fierce Iroquois, and one of their towns destroyed; the rest of the Tionontati, with the refugee Hurons, fled for safety westward from place to place, reaching northern Wisconsin (about 1657), and the Illinois country by 1659; they were kindly received by the Algonquian tribes, but soon incurred the hostility of the Sioux, and retreated to Chequamegon Bay, where they settled among the Ottawas. These fugitives were all classed by the French as "Hurons," and known by that name under the French régime — dwelling at Michillimackinac after 1670, from which place they gradually scattered to Detroit and various places in the region of Lake Erie. After the English conquest of Canada,

XXVI.   Treachery of the Outaoüas toward the French

Many times, also, have the Outaoüas been known to plot against the Frenchmen who were trading with them.   Have they not, to my knowledge, presented the dagger to all the tribes of the upper country, in order to incite them to become accomplices in the foul attempt that they longed to make, and to urge them on to massacre those [Frenchmen] who were trading with them?   I speak as an eyewitness, for I caused their enterprise to miscarry.[180]

It is known that they murdered the Miami chiefs who had come to confer with the French at Détroit, and whom they attacked on that occasion [1706].   When the Illinois, aided by the French, fought against the Renards, were not they [i.e., the Hurons] ready to massacre the French, if the Renards had [not] been entirely defeated [1712]?   It is an indisputable fact that they slew some Irroquois who had put themselves under the protection of the fort at Katarakouy [1704].   Have not we seen the Irroquois help to burn some Sakis who had been captured by them?[181]

these Hurons became known as Wyandots (a corruption of their own original appellation, Wendat); and they acquired great influence among the northwestern tribes.   In 1842 they removed to Kansas, and in 1867 were placed on a reservation still occupied by them in northeastern Oklahoma.

— J. N. B. HEWITT, in *Handbook Amer. Indians*, art. "Hurons."

[180] "The historians of Canada say nothing, to my knowledge, of this conspiracy by the Outaouais against the *coureurs de bois* of the colony." — TAILHAN.

[181] "In regard to the massacre of the Miami chiefs by the Outaouais, the defeat of the Outagamis by the French and the Illinois, and the murder of the Iroquois chiefs at Katarakouy, the reader may turn to Charlevoix (*Histoire*, vol. ii, 292, 307-309, 365-372).   In the same history will also be found some details regarding the murder of three Frenchmen by the Miamis of Saint Joseph (*ibid.*, 322, 323).   From 1675 discord prevailed between the Miamis and the Illinois (Letter and journal of Father Marquette), and there was a new outbreak of it in 1687 (Ms. *Mémoire sur l'estat présent du Canada*) . . .

The Miamis have slain Frenchmen, the Illinois likewise, the Saulteurs the same, as also the people of the
north. On their part there has been only conspiracy
against us, without our having made any movement to

the two tribes, however, in 1691 were reconciled, and marched together against
the Iroquois (*Journal* of Sieur de Courtemanche; in the archives of the
Marine)." The murders and treacherous acts ascribed by Perrot to the western
tribes must not be too literally understood as such; usually the murders were
mere reprisals, and often had only too good reason. Denonville wrote to Seignelay (Letter of June 12, 1686; in archives of the Marine): "It is a marvel
that the savages have not killed them all with their clubs, to protect themselves
from the acts of violence which they have suffered from the French." This
explains the seizure of Perrot's property by the Miamis, and their threat to
burn him; it was by way of retaliation for attacks made on them by some
French *coureurs de bois*. As for plots and treason, it must be remembered that
the Indians often found it necessary to deal for themselves with enemies from
whom the colonial government was either unable or unwilling to protect them;
that they sometimes had reason to fear the results of greater friendship between
the French and the Iroquois; that very often they sought commercial relations
with the English, as being much more advantageous to them than were their
dealings with the Canadian merchants; and that those tribes were allies, not
subjects, of France, so that their actions just mentioned could not properly be
called intrigues or treachery. It must not be forgotten, also, that with very
few exceptions the Indian tribes of the west remained faithful to the cause of
France until the end of the French domination in America. Frontenac, Denonville, and other French officials had the same distrust of the Indians as Perrot;
but the latter governor admitted that they were attracted to the English by
the better market thus afforded for the sale of their peltries. As proof of this,
is cited a Ms. dated 1689, in the archives of the Marine, showing the difference
in prices at Orange [Albany] and Montreal; for one beaver-skin an Indian
received at Orange forty pounds of lead, or a red blanket, or a large overcoat,
or four shirts, or six pairs of hose, while at Montreal each of these items cost
him two pelts, and even three for the above quantity of lead. A gun cost two
pelts at Orange, and five at Montreal; and one pelt procured for the Indian
eight pounds of gunpowder from the English, while the French demanded
four for that quantity. "The other petty wares which the savages buy in
trade from the French are given to them by the English as part of the bargain.
The English give six *pots* of brandy for one beaver-skin; this is rum, or
guildive (otherwise sugar-cane brandy), which they import from the islands
of America [i.e., the West Indies]. The French have no standard [of price]
for the brandy trade; some give more, and others less, but they never go so
high as one *pot* for one beaver-skin. . . It is to be noted that the English
make no difference as regards the quality of the beaver-skins, which they buy
all at the same price — which is more than fifty per cent higher than the French
give; and, besides, there is more than one hundred per cent difference in the
value of their trade and that of ours." — TAILHAN.

avenge ourselves. What conclusions may not one draw from the result? Ought we not to conjecture that [even] if the Renards were entirely overthrown (which they are not yet) still other wars would arise; and that the assistance which these traitors obtain from the colony, in order to aid in destroying them, will conduce only to the same destruction for the French? and then they will destroy one another. For there is not a savage tribe which does not bear ill-will to some other. The Miamis and the Illinois hate each other reciprocally; the Irroquois have malicious feelings toward the Outaoüas and the Saulteurs; and it is the same with the other tribes. There is not one of those peoples that does not consider itself justified in waging war against the others; accordingly, we can only expect successive and inevitable wars, unless we [do something to] prevent them. But I fear that we are preparing too late to prevent these wars, and that the fire is kindled so brightly that it cannot be extinguished, on account of the aid which the French continue to furnish to other tribes out of consideration for that of the Hurons, who are more treacherous and crafty than all the others; for they would no [longer] be in existence if the French had not protected them, although they have many times incurred our indignation. Such, therefore, are the matters on which I can give you information; I would enlarge somewhat further on them if [my supply of] paper had permitted it. But you can, as a result of what I have [here] set down, easily understand what are the traits of the savages. The instance of the Tsonontouans will readily convince you that it is impossible to depend on any of the tribes; and that it is much better to let them settle their quarrels among themselves than to meddle therein, unless this is to reconcile them. Such arrangements as had [already] been

adroitly made would have instilled in their minds notions of fear and subordination; because the Renards,
who are almost destroyed, would have only waited for
the disobedience of any one of their enemies to join themselves to the people whom the enemy had tried to attack.
Thus the Renards, timorous and defeated, would have
been forced to agree to the peace, and the others would
find themselves compelled to accept it.

It may be objected to this that all the tribes would
be ranged on the side of the English. Alas! are not they
[already] thus ranged? Where are the peoples who do
not allow themselves to be attracted by cheap merchandise? Do the Hurons, in whom we have most confidence, furnish many peltries to Détroit and Montréal?
Do not they prefer to carry their furs to the English,
and do not they give them to the Miamis? Do not the
Illinoetz go among those [English] who are established
in Louysianne? It is, then, a weak argument to be
brought forward, when one means that the tribes would
go to give themselves up to the Irroquois; since the latter are more friendly toward the Renards (who are on
good terms with the Irroquois) than to any other of the
peoples whom they have ruined since the peace concluded between them and the French.[182] It is also an

---

[182] "Even when they were at peace with the French, the Iroquois attacked
without scruple the savages allied with us; and it is thus that they dealt with
the Illinois in the course of the years 1674-1679. They were urged on in this
by the English colonists of Boston, Manhattan [New York], and Orange [Al-
bany], who saw therein a means for enlarging their territories, or at the very
least of assuring to themselves the monopoly of the peltries. The Count de
Frontenac and the Marquis de Denonville complain bitterly of this in their
despatches; and the latter is especially astonished that such practices were permitted at a time when the closest friendship reigned between the two crowns
of France and England. But of what importance were the most solemn treaties
to those merchants? those who, in order to force the western tribes to implore
their mediation with the Iroquois, and to win it by carrying to them their
precious furs, went so far as to set at naught the reiterated prohibitions of their
own sovereign. More than that, they were seen — always to the same end — to

argument that has no foundation, to try to maintain that the tribes will place themselves under the rule of the English because they carry their peltries to that people – which it would have been easy to prevent if we had showed less condescension to them and had not been so ready to comply with their humors; it is this which is the source of their arrogant notion that the French cannot get along without them, and that we could not maintain ourselves in the Colony without the assistance that they give us.

I hope that you will be pleased, Monseigneur, to examine this memoir and the others which I have had the honor to place before you; [183] and that in reflecting thereon you will recognize that, at the establishment of

treat their own brethren of Virginia as they had treated the French of Canada. Indeed we know – and it is the Marquis de Denonville who tells us of it (Letter of Aug. 10, 1688; in archives of the Marine) – that for a long time past they 'maintained war with those of Virginia, for fear that the Iroquois might trade with the latter. I know that the merchants of Orange have given presents to the Iroquois for that. If then they are faithless to their own countrymen, how will they be trustworthy with us?' " – TAILHAN.

[183] "The bishop of Quebec, the governor, and the intendant were the only persons in the colony who had right to the title of Monseigneur; it is therefore one of these three personages that Perrot here addresses. But the first two must be dismissed from our consideration: one, on account of his being, by his vocation, a stranger to most of the questions discussed in these memoirs; the other (the Marquis de Vaudreuil), because the author speaks of him a little farther on (page 266) in the third person. It must therefore be the intendant, Monsieur Bégon, for whom Perrot composed these relations; moreover, it was from the hands of this magistrate that, three years later (1720-1721), Father Charlevoix received the manuscript of the present memoir (see his Histoire, vol. ii, pp. lx, lxi). The other memoirs which Perrot had sent to the intendant of Canada, and to which he refers for fuller details regarding the events which he only mentions here, contained a narrative of the war by the Iroquois against the tribes of the upper country and the Illinois, as well as the frequent acts of treachery of which the savages – and more especially the Hurons and the Ottawas – were guilty (Perrot, 129, 130, 143, 146). I am strongly inclined to believe that La Potherie has inserted the greater part of these relations in the second volume of his history. It is, in fact, to be noted that (1) La Potherie was acquainted with Perrot in Canada, and that he received from him the most exact information (Histoire, vol. ii, 87; vol. iv, 268; (2) his second volume, almost throughout, could have been written only by means of the data

the Colony, we began at the outset to assert our authority over the savages (although at that time it contained very few Frenchmen), and we were careful to maintain ourselves in that superiority, despite all the changes that might occur – notwithstanding that the savages were then more numerous and more barbarous – I mean, more brutish – than they now are. But to-day, when they are weaker and more humanized, they try to be masters over us; and already they push their insolence so far as to flatter themselves, if I may say so, that they have a right to lay down the law for us, for they see that we tolerate them and leave them in immunity. If the French, instead of that, had made them understand as they should the obligations under which they are to us, the assistance that we have given them, and that, in a word, the continuance of their maintenance and protection is in our power, they would feel more respect, regard, and obedience toward their benefactors.

XXVII. Of the insolence and vainglory of the savages, and what has given rise to it

All the savages who trade with the French are such only in name; equally with ourselves, they are bent on availing themselves of everything that they see and understand can be to their advantage. Ambition and vainglory are, as I have already stated, the supreme passions that sway them. They see the French commit, through self-interest, a thousand mean acts before their

furnished by Perrot, whose voyages, adventures, and even numerous harangues to the savages are recounted therein at great length; (3) the style in this same volume, save in a very small number of pages, is very noticeably different from that of the three others, and by its loose, incorrect, and perplexing constructions it most often recalls, if I am not mistaken, the style of Perrot – which cannot be explained on the hypothesis of merely verbal communications made by the latter to La Potherie." – TAILHAN.

eyes, every day, in order to be numbered among their friends and to acquire their peltries—not only in the Colony, but also in their own country.[184] They perceive that the commandants, like the rest, trade with them; for among the savages it is the custom of the chiefs to give freely, and this [trading by officials] seems to them so much the more odious. They are so presumptuous as to believe that we dare [not] chastise them, or make their families feel our anger, when they commit any fault; for they, however culpable, see that they are supported by influential persons, and that a Frenchman—very often innocent, and justified by the law—is punished on account of quarrels that he has had with them. That results in their abusing Frenchmen, and especially when they see punishment inflicted on the person against whom they have made complaints. The interpreters, or else those who direct them, are very often the cause of this, through the unfair partiality which such persons usually have for them. Such acts of injustice, even though in their favor, make them feel so great a contempt for us that they regard those of the French nation as wretched menials and the most miser-

---

[184] A *Mémoire historique* in the archives of the Marine, on the beaver-trade monopoly and its detrimental effects, says: "The *coureurs de bois* often committed a thousand base acts with the savages in order to obtain their beaver-skins; they followed them even in their hunting expeditions, and did not even give them time to dry and prepare their pelts. They endured the stinging jeers, the contempt, and sometimes the blows of those savages, who were lost in wonder at covetousness so sordid, and at seeing the French come from so great a distance, with so much fatigue and expense, in order to gather up dirty and foul-smelling beaver-skins, with which they clothed themselves, and which they no longer valued. . . In order to understand fully the meaning of this last phrase, it is necessary to remember that the beaver-skins most in demand by the French were those which they designated by the name *castor gras d'hiver* ["greasy winter pelts"] — that is, the skins of beavers killed during the winter, and of which the savages had made robes for themselves, which they had worn long enough to render them greasy, by their sweat penetrating to the roots of the fur (another Ms. in those archives, on 'the leasing of the Western Domain;' and cf. La Potherie, *Histoire*, vol. i, 136)." — TAILHAN.

able people in the world.   See how we have managed them for some time past!

Some of them have become so haughty that it is necessary to treat them at the present time with a sort of submissiveness.   If they talk with the authorities of the country, it is in a manner so lofty and imperious that the latter would not dare, as it were, [to refuse] what the savages have to demand; and if they did not obtain it they would not fear to display their resentment.   In earlier days we did not let ourselves govern [them] in this fashion; we knew how to indulge them in a proper way, and when they deserved it, whether in the colony or in their own country; we were likewise strict in punishing them when they were in fault.   I have cited several examples of this sort in this memoir.   But how many times I have compelled them to submit, when they have spoken evil of Monsieur the governor, and to go to him with presents, confessing their fault!   When they have undertaken to plot some undertaking against the [welfare of the] state, I have obliged them to desist from it.   This memoir bears witness to this in many places; and if any one undertakes to find fault with what I advance I am ready to prove its truth – making them thoroughly understand that all which I have related is entirely accurate, by the testimony of two hundred persons worthy of confidence, who have seen and known what I have accomplished in their country – I mean, that of the savage tribes – for the glory and the benefit of the colony.

Do we not continually see Frenchmen, before our very eyes, who were only worthless menials – but who, after having run away to the woods, amassed wealth which they as quickly dissipated – thrust themselves forward to relate marvelous tales to the authorities, who have given credence to them, and, thinking to act for the best according to the statements made to them by such men, have brought all the affairs [of the frontiers] to ruin, and have reduced them to so pitiable a condition that it will be very difficult to restore them [to their former state]? It has been proposed, as a beginning, to destroy the Renards, in order to cause everything to flourish; I have presented to Monseigneur de Vaudreuil a memoir on this subject, which has been thwarted, since it has not produced its [intended] effect. He has recognized, by the consequences, that what I set forth therein has come to pass, to the detriment of the colony. I desire that all may go well, but I fear the contrary; and I dread lest the proverb used in the world may prove true – that is, that the end will crown the work, to the advantage of some others than of the colony. I am unwilling to write down what I foresee, for fear of [causing] trouble to some persons who bear me ill-will, and who nevertheless would in the long run admit that I had told the truth.

When I had the honor of being commissioned to take charge of the management of the savages, liberty was allowed me to tell them my opinions [frankly]; but there are some jealous persons who have accused me of being too harsh toward them. But when I have talked seriously to the savages they have been seen to come to render submission, and to show their repentance for their fault.

When seven of the Outaoüa tribes took sides with the Irroquois, Monsieur de Louvigny sent me to put a stop to that [1690 or 1694]. I made them understand that they were going to give themselves up to people who would eventually destroy them; and that, if their father Onontio had not sustained them, they would be all de-

stroyed by this time.[185]   I set forth to them the treachery
which the Irroquois had shown to the Hurons at the
time when the Miamis aided in destroying them, and
united with them without showing any regard for the
peace which they had formed together.

When the English have tried to entice them by presents (which they have accepted) I have made them
understand that they were going to become allies of perfidious people, who had corrupted part of the tribes who
came in their way; and that, after they had made the
men tipsy, they had sacrificed and carried away their
wives and children in order to send them into distant
islands, from which they never came back.[186]   I told
them that, as they well knew, the Irroquois were like
children of the English, and, in concert with the latter,
would not have failed to destroy them if their father
Onontio had not protected and defended them; and that
the cheapness of their goods was only a bait of which
the English availed themselves to become their masters,
and to deliver them as a prey to the Irroquois.   When
they have tried to invent reasons for beginning war, have
I not explained to them that this would disturb the tranquillity of their families, and that they ought rather to
defend these and themselves against the Irroquois, who
are altogether enemies to them?

In all their enterprises for evil, have they not yielded
to my opinion that they should desist therefrom?   In
the absence of my superiors, I have always talked with

---

[185] "This mission, with which Perrot was charged by Monsieur de Louvigny
(between 1690 and 1694), must not be confounded with that which was confided
to him directly by the Count de Frontenac in the month of April, 1690, and of
which we shall speak farther on.   The latter was addressed to all the tribes
then residing at Michillimakinak or in its vicinity." — TAILHAN.

[186] "Bancroft makes mention (*History of U.S.*, vol. i, chap. v) of savages
being sold as slaves by the English of Connecticut, New Hampshire, the Carolinas, and Virginia." — TAILHAN.

the savages [as] in my own right; and it is this which has given opportunity to the envious to speak evil of me; moreover, it is from this [malicious interference] that have proceeded all the untoward events that have since occurred.

If I had gone up with Monsieur de Louvigny [1716, 1717], I would have flattered myself that I could induce the Renards to ask for peace, even though our allies were not inclined to it.

XXVIII. Harangue which ought to have been made to all the Outaoüa Tribes, in order to bind them to the peace with the Renards and their allies

"Listen, my children," says our father Onontio, "listen," he says: "I have the grief of hearing every year the reports and accounts of massacres that are committed in your country by your destroying one another; I look in horror at the blood that has been shed, and which will yet be spilled. If I do not put an end to it, I am certain that in a short time you all will be exterminated, and that I shall no longer have any children. I love you and your families, and I desire that they [continue to] live.

"Thou, Outaoüack, art making war on the Renard, who has spared thy life, taking thy part against the Miamis when thou didst go hunting on the upper Black River;[187] for he would have killed thee if it had not been for the Renard and the Kikapou, who opposed his purpose.

---

[187] "The Black River has its source in a lake [Lake Morrison, in Taylor County] in the state of Wisconsin; and, after flowing through a part of that state from N.E. to S.W., falls into the Mississippi between 44° 5′ and 44° 15′ north latitude." — TAILHAN.

"Thou, Saulteur, hast in the same time saved the lives of all the people who lived at Mamekagan, when Chingouabé entreated the Miamis to go to eat his dogs. He was ready to betray and eat thee if the Renard, whom thou regardest as thine enemy, had been willing to agree to thy destruction. Nevertheless, thou hast slain him; he has only taken vengeance when thou hast constrained him to do so; but he has willingly restored to thee thy people, and thou still detainest his men.

"Thou, Miamis, knowest that the Renard has never waged war against thee; but he sustained and aided thee in defending thyself when thou wast routed by the Scioux.[188]

"Thou,[189] [Maskouten?], art not ignorant that thy chiefs died from a malady, when the Renard went to avenge the Miamis of the Crane,[190] who would have been ruined by the Scioux if the Renard had not taken pity

[188] "Chingouabé, chief of the Sauteurs who were settled at Chagouamigon, figures in that capacity among the deputies of the tribes from the upper country to whom the Count de Frontenac gave audience on July 18 and 29, 1695. From his speech on that occasion it is evident that at that time the Sioux were at war with the Outagamis and the Maskoutens, and that the Sauteurs were inclined to take sides with the Sioux against the latter tribes (*Relation* of 1694-1695; in archives of the Marine). Unfortunately, this does not throw much light on the events to which Perrot alludes in this passage. The one that follows is much more clear, and finds its confirmation in contemporaneous monuments, or in the early historians of Canada. These show us (1) that in 1697 the Sioux had already twice chastised the Miamis (*Relation de ce qui s'est passé au Canada en 1696, 1697*; in archives of the Marine); (2) that about the same period the Outagamis with the Miamis were waging war against the Sioux (La Potherie, *Histoire*, vol. ii, 343-352); (3) that the same thing was about to occur again in 1701, when Monsieur de Courtemanche (sent by Monsieur de Callières, governor of New France) put a stop to the expedition that was ready to begin its march (Letter of Callières, Oct. 1, 1701)." — TAILHAN.

[189] "The name is left blank in the Ms. This passage refers, I think, to the Maskoutens, of whom a great number were swept away by a contagious malady at the time (1690) vaguely indicated by the author (La Potherie, *Histoire*, vol. ii, 249, 250)." — TAILHAN.

[190] "I leave to those persons who are versed in the Illinois or the Miami language the care of finding, among the savage names given to the tribes of this latter people, the one which corresponds to the French appellation of

on them. He won their good-will by presents, and confirmed the alliance that thou didst contract with him;
and with him thou hast never had war, any more than
with the Kikapou, who has always dwelt in the same
village with thee. On the contrary, the other Miamis
have slain the relatives of thy people, this winter.

"Thou, Illinoëts, hast never had war with the Renard,
or with the Kikapou; thou didst, notwithstanding, attack him when he was at Détroit. He defended himself,
and you have slain each other; thou didst take thy
revenge when he was defeated at Détroit, and when he
returned to his own country. He captured one of thy
chiefs, whom he sent back; and thou didst break the
heads of his envoys; thou shouldst be content.

"Thou, Pouteoüatamis, thy tribe is half Sakis; the
Sakis are in part Renards; thy cousins and thy brothers-
in-law are Renards and Sakis. Pirimon and Ouenemek,
who are thy chiefs, and who weep over the murders that
are committed in thy families, one against another, these
men are of the Sakis. I love you all," says your father
Onontio, "and I desire to extinguish the fires of war,
which are burning so high that, besides those people
who have been [already] consumed by them from all of
you, they will not fail to consume all who remain, on
both sides, if I do not extinguish them.

"Thou, Huron, be content; thou hast lost thy people,
but thou shouldst [not?] be avenged. Thou art too

'Miamis of the Crane,' by which Perrot here designates one among those
tribes." — TAILHAN.

Perrot here alludes to the Crane clan of the Miami, the principal division
of that tribe; they are called Atchatchakangouen by Allouez (*Jesuit Relations*,
vol. lviii, 40, 41), and Tchidüakoüingoües by La Potherie, *Histoire*, vol. ii,
261). Mooney says of them (*Handbook Amer. Indians*, 107): "On account
of the hostility of the Illinois they removed west of the Mississippi, where they
were attacked by the Sioux; and they afterward settled near the Jesuit mission
at Green Bay, and moved thence into Illinois and Indiana with the rest of the
tribe." — ED.

cruel; remember what thou hast done against me and against my children thine allies, when I have come forward for thee against all, and when I protected thee – and if I had not shielded thee thou wouldst no longer be alive. Thou didst endeavor to betray me on a certain occasion, and I pardoned thee, in order to secure thy gratitude.

"Thou, Outaoüack, didst slay the Miamis at Détroit, who were under my protection; and thou didst, at the same time, assassinate some Frenchmen there and elsewhere.

"Thou, Saulteur, hast likewise slain some Frenchmen; and thou, Missisakis, hast done the same. But I have swallowed the grief that I felt over my dead, and have not chastised thee; and thou, Miamis, likewise; I have pardoned all. Indeed, far from taking my vengeance, I have aided you against the Irroquois, who was one of my faithful children, whom you have slain; but he has never made any disturbance since the latest agreement of peace, which I obliged him to make with you, and without which all of you would have been destroyed. For he was quite able to ruin you, without obtaining from me more than my willingness and consent. On the contrary, in order to maintain you I have furnished not only the assistance of my military power, but also my young men, who have been everywhere slain for your sake. I have even aided you against the Renard, who has never slain my young men.

"I ordain, my children, that you put an end to this war; and if any one disobeys me I shall declare myself against him, and for the Renard."[191]

[If this had been done], all the tribes would have

---

[191] "The colonial government followed an entirely opposite policy, and declared itself against the Outagamis, but it was never able either to reduce them to submission or to destroy them wholly." — TAILHAN.

consented to peace. This is why we ought not to fear reproaching them for their faults, any more than to remind them of the services that we have rendered to them; for it is characteristic of the savage not to forget the benefit that has been conferred upon him, on the occasions that have arisen.

Here then, Monseigneur, are my humble ideas, which would have had their good results if I had accompanied Monsieur de Louvigny. As for the Renards, I would certainly have managed affairs with them.

The scarcity of paper does not permit me to give fuller examples of this sort of harangue, as I would have been able to if I were not destitute of paper.

HISTORY OF THE SAVAGE PEO-

ples who are allies of New France. By Claude Charles Le Roy, Bacqueville de la Potherie [192] [from his *Histoire de l'Amérique septentrionale* (Paris, 1753), tome ii and iv].

The second volume of the above work is here presented for the first time in English translation, partly in full and partly in synopsis – the latter indicated by bracketed paragraphs.

---

[192] Claude Charles Le Roy, Bacqueville de la Potherie was born in the West-Indian island of Guadeloupe, about 1668. His family was allied to the noted one of Pontchartrain; and La Potherie obtained thus appointments in the marine service from 1689 on. The first important one was a post in the squadron sent under the noted commander Le Moyne d'Iberville (1697) to drive the English out of Hudson Bay. In the following year La Potherie was appointed comptroller-general of the marine and fortifications in Canada, the first incumbent of a newly-created post. In 1700 he married a lady belonging to one of the leading Canadian families, and apparently intended to settle permanently in that colony; but in the following year the deaths of his father and brother recalled him to Guadeloupe. Almost nothing is known of his subsequent life, save that both he and his wife had died by the year 1738; and before the end of the century the family had disappeared from Canada. See J. Edmond Roy's biography of La Potherie, and description of his work, in *Proceedings and Transactions* of the Royal Society of Canada, second series, vol. iii, 3-44. Therein Roy has neglected to account for the appellation "Bacqueville" in La Potherie's name; but he cites a document (dated 1738) in which that writer's son is called "seigneur de Bacqueville et de la Touche en Touraine," apparently showing that an estate of that name in France belonged to the family from which he sprang. – ED.

HISTORY OF THE SAVAGE PEOPLES WHO ARE ALLIES OF NEW FRANCE

Chapters I-VII

[These chapters, up to page 60, are devoted to an account of the beliefs, customs, mode of life, etc., of the Indian tribes then known to the French of Canada, with an enumeration of those peoples, and brief mention of the first acquaintance of the French with those who lived east of Lake Huron. Most of this is so similar to Perrot's account that to translate it here would be useless repetition. Accordingly, the narrative begins at page 60, with the tribes which properly are included within the field of the present work.]

The Sauteurs, who live beyond the Missisakis, take their name from a fall of water which forms the discharge of Lake Superior into Lake Huron, through extensive rapids of which the ebullitions are extremely violent. Those people are very skilful in a fishery which they carry on there, of fish which are white, and as large as salmon.[193] The savages surmount all those ter-

---

[193] The noted whitefish of the lakes (*Coregonus albus*); it was called by the Chippewa *atikameg* (meaning "caribou fish"), from which one of the Montagnais tribes was called Attikamegues (the Poissons-blancs, or "whitefish," by the French). Another species (*C. tullibee*) is found in the great lakes and rivers of N.W. Canada; it is of inferior quality, with watery flesh, and is known as "mongrel whitefish," also as *toulibi* or *tulibee*, corruptions of the Chippewa word *otonabi.* – A. F. CHAMBERLAIN, in *Handbook Amer. Indians.*

In the *Proceedings* of the U.S. National Museum for 1909 (vol. xxxvi, 171, 172) is a note on this fish by David S. Jordan and B. W. Evermann, to the following effect: The common whitefish of Lake Superior is the so-called "Labrador whitefish" (*Coregonus labradoricus*), characteristic of the Canadian

rible cascades, into which they cast a net[194] which resembles a bag, a little more than half an ell in width and an ell deep, attached to a wooden fork about fifteen feet long. They cast their nets headlong into the boiling waters, in which they maintain their position, letting their canoes drift while sliding backward. The tumult of the waters in which they are floating seems to them only a diversion; they see in it the fish, heaped up on one another, that are endeavoring to force their way through the rapids; and when they feel their nets heavy they draw them in. It is only they, the Missisakis, and the Nepiciriniens who can practice this fishery, although some Frenchmen imitate them. This kind of fish is large, has firm flesh, and is very nourishing. The savages dry it over a fire, on wooden frames placed high above, and keep it for winter. They carry on an extensive traffic in this fish at Michillimakinak, where both the savages and the French buy it at a high price. This [Sauteur] tribe is divided: part of them have remained at home to live on this delicious fish in autumn, and they

---

lakes generally, and only this kind is found at Sault Ste. Marie; it is apparently distinct from the whitefish of Lakes Erie and Ontario. "The Lake Superior whitefish must stand as *Coregonus clupeiformis*; the whitefish of Lake Erie is *C. albus*." — ED.

[194] Nets, netting, or network were used throughout northern America by its natives — for the capture of animals (differing according to the creature to be caught, the form, or the function), "for the lacings of snowshoes and lacrosse sticks, for carrying-frames and wallets, for netted caps, for the foundation of feather work," etc. "These were made from animal tissues and vegetal fibers — wool and hair, hide, sinew, and intestines; roots, stems, bast, bark, and leaves. Animal skins were cut into long delicate strips, while sinew and vegetal fibers were separated into filaments, and these twisted, twined, or braided and made into openwork meshes by a series of technical processes ranging from the simplest weaving or coiling without foundation to regular knotting." They were made most often by the women's hands, but also with many forms of the seine needle, or shuttle; and the meshing shows a variety of processes. Holmes has shown, in his studies of ancient American pottery, that netting was used to provide ornament on vessels of clay, by molding them in it; and the same forms of netting are used in ancient garments, especially those into which feathers were woven. — OTIS T. MASON, in *Handbook Amer. Indians*.

seek their food in Lake Huron during the winter; the others have gone away to two localities on Lake Superior, in order to live on the game which is very abundant there. Those who left their natal soil made an alliance with the Nadouaissioux, who were not very solicitous for the friendship of any one whomsoever; but, because they could obtain French merchandise only through the agency of the Sauteurs, they made a treaty of peace with the latter by which they were mutually bound to give their daughters in marriage on both sides. That was a strong bond for the maintenance of entire harmony.

The Nadouaissioux, who have their village on the upper Missisipi about the latitude of 46°,[195] divided

---

[195] "The Siouan family is the most populous linguistic family north of Mexico, next to the Algonquian." The name is taken from Sioux, an appellation of the Dakota (the largest and best-known tribal group of the family) abbreviated from *Nadouessioux*, a French corruption of the name (*Nadowe-is-iw*) given them by the Chippewa; it signifies "snake" or adder, and metaphorically "enemy." "Before changes of domicile took place among them, resulting from the contact with whites, the principal body extended from the west bank of the Mississippi northward from the Arkansa nearly to the Rocky Mountains, except for certain sections held by the Pawnee, Arikara, Cheyenne, Arapaho, Blackfeet, Comanche, and Kiowa. The Dakota proper also occupied territory on the east side of the river, from the mouth of the Wisconsin to Mille Lacs; and the Winnebago were about the lake of that name and the head of Green Bay. Northward Siouan tribes extended some distance into Canada, in the direction of Lake Winnipeg. A second group of Siouan tribes, embracing the Catawba, Sara or Cheraw, Saponi, Tutelo, and several others, occupied the central part of North Carolina and South Carolina and the piedmont region of Virginia; while a third, of which the Biloxi were the most prominent representatives, dwelt in Mississippi along the Gulf coast. . . The Dakota formerly inhabited the forest region of southern Minnesota, and do not seem to have gone out upon the plains until hard pressed by the Chippewa, who had been supplied with guns by the French. According to every fragment of evidence, traditional and otherwise, the so-called Chiwere tribes — Iowa, Oto, and Missouri — separated from the Winnebago or else moved westward to the Missouri from the same region. . . As to the more remote migrations that must have taken place in such a widely scattered stock, different theories are held. By some it is supposed that the various sections of the family have become dispersed from a district near that occupied by the Winnebago, or, on the basis of traditions recorded by Gallatin and Long, from some point on the

their territory and their hunting-grounds with the Sauteurs. The abundance of beaver and deer made the
latter gradually forget their native land. They spent

north side of the great lakes. By others a region close to the eastern Siouans
[of Virginia and Carolina] is considered their primitive home, whence the
Dhegiha [the Omaha, Ponca, Osage, Kansa, and Quapaw] moved westward
down the Ohio, while the Dakota, Winnebago, and cognate tribes kept a more
northerly course near the great lakes. . . The earliest notice of the main northwestern group is probably that in the Jesuit *Relation* of 1640, where mention is
made of the Winnebago, Dakota, and Assiniboin. As early as 1658 the Jesuit
missionaries had learned of the existence of thirty Dakota villages in the
region north from the Potawatomi mission at St. Michael, about the head of
Green Bay, Wis. In 1680 Father Hennepin was taken prisoner by the same
tribe. In 1804-1805 Lewis and Clark passed through the center of this region
and encountered most of the Siouan tribes. Afterward expeditions into and
through their country were numerous; traders settled among them in numbers,
and were followed in course of time by permanent settlers, who pressed them
into narrower and narrower areas until they were finally removed to Indian
Territory or confined to reservations in the Dakotas, Nebraska, and Montana.
Throughout all this period the Dakota proved themselves most consistently
hostile to the intruders. . . Later still the Ghost-dance religion spread among
the northern Siouan tribes and culminated in the affair of Wounded Knee,
Dec. 29, 1890."

"It is well-nigh impossible to make statements of the customs and habits of
these people that will be true for the entire group. Nearly all the eastern tribes
and most of the southern tribes belonging to the western group raised corn;
but the Dakota (except some of the eastern bands) and the Crows depended
almost entirely on the buffalo and other game animals, the buffalo entering very
deeply into the economic and religious life of all the tribes of this section. In
the east the habitations were bark and mat wigwams, but on the plains earth
lodges and skin tipis were used. Formerly they had no domestic animals except
dogs, which were utilized in transporting the tipis and all other family belongings, including children; but later their places were largely taken by
horses, the introduction of which constituted a new epoch in the life of all
Plains tribes, facilitating their migratory movements and the pursuit of the
buffalo, and doubtless contributing largely to the ultimate extinction of that
animal. Taking the reports of the United States and Canadian Indian offices
as a basis and making a small allowance for bands or individuals not here
enumerated, the total number of Indians belonging to the Siouan stock may be
placed at about 40,800. The Tutelo, Biloxi, and probably the rest of the
eastern Siouan tribes were organized internally into clans with maternal
descent; the Dakota, Mandan, Hidatsa, and Crow consisted of many non-totemic
bands or villages, and the rest of the tribes of totemic gentes. The Siouan
family is divided as follows:" 1, Dakota-Assiniboin group; 2, Dhegiha
group; 3, Chiwere group; 4, Winnebago; 5, Mandan; 6, Hidatsa group; 7,
Biloxi group; 8, Eastern division (of which but a few scattered remnants
survive). — J. R. SWANTON, in *Handbook Amer. Indians*.

the winter in the woods to carry on their hunting; and in the spring they visit Lake Superior, on the shore of which they plant corn and squashes. There they spend the summer in great peace, without being disturbed by any neighbor, although the Nadouaissioux are at war with the people of the north. The Sauteurs are neutral; and the tribe that goes to war always takes care beforehand that there is no Sauteur [involved in it]. Their harvest being gathered, they return to their hunting-grounds.*

Those who have remained at the Saut, their native country, leave their villages twice a year. In the month of June they disperse in all directions along Lake Huron, as also do the Missisakis and the Otter People.[196] This lake has rocky shores, and is full of

---

* The reason for this frequentation of the Lake Superior shore by the Indians for the cultivation of corn and other crops may be found in the following description by G. W. Perry in *Transactions* of Wisconsin State Horticultural Society for 1877, pp. 178, 179: "The south shore of Lake Superior, in Wisconsin, rises rapidly from the level of the lake to the dividing ridge which separates the waters of the Gulfs of St. Lawrence and Mexico, an average distance of less than twenty miles, the elevation ranging from five hundred feet in Douglas County to perhaps twelve hundred in the eastern portion of Ashland County. The soil on the northern slope is clay to the depth of sixty feet in Douglas County; sand overlying clay, in Bayfield County; and in Ashland, a loam of sand and clay. The clay generally carries so much lime as to be unfit for brick, but this defect is compensated by its greatly increased fertility. Every indigenous plant grows with amazing rapidity, in the long days of the short, fierce summers; while all grasses and cereals, including the hardier varieties of corn, yield abundantly, crops of superior quality." Keweenaw Point is some sixty miles long, and only five miles wide at its extremity; it varies in height from 700 to 1,000 feet, and is nearly surrounded by water. Here "the soil is sandy loam, and never freezes, being protected by six feet of snow, and is very fertile — the long days of summer (nineteen hours of daylight at the solstice) seeming to force the growth of every plant adapted to the locality. Here is the very paradise of the strawberry and the red raspberry, the service-berry, wild cherry, gooseberry, and huckleberries of four distinct varieties, all indigenous."
— ED.

[196] The Missisauga (Missisakis) were originally part of the Chippewa; they dwelt along the north shore of Lake Huron, and gradually drifted southward into the ancient Huron country between Georgian Bay and Lake Erie. About 1746-1750 they aided the Iroquois against the French, and most of them were

small islands abounding in blueberries. While there they gather sheets of bark from the trees for making their canoes and building their cabins. The water of the lake is very clear, and they can see the fish in it at a depth of twenty-five feet. While the children are gathering a store of blueberries, the men are busy in spearing sturgeon. When the grain [that they have planted] is nearly ripe, they return home. At the approach of winter they resort to the shores of the lake to kill beavers and moose, and do not return thence until the spring, in order to plant their Indian corn.

Such is the occupation of those peoples, who could live in great comfort if they were economical; but all the savages, especially all the Sauteurs, are so fond of eating that they take little heed for the morrow, and there are many of them who die of hunger. They never lay by anything whatever; if any food remains, it is because they have not been able to eat all of it in the day. They are even so proud, when some stranger comes among them, as to give him even the last morsel of food, in order to make it appear that they are not in poverty; but they do not hesitate to complain of hunger when they see Frenchmen whom they know to be well supplied with provisions. The Sauteurs were redoubtable to their enemies. They were the first to defeat the Irroquois, who to the number of a hundred warriors came to take possession of one of their villages. Hear-

driven out of their country by the latter, and settled at first near Detroit, and later in western New York, near the Senecas; but their alliance with the Iroquois lasted only till the outbreak of the French and Indian War a few years later. Those who still remain live north of Lake Erie, and in 1906 numbered 810. Part of these, living in the township of New Credit (which is entirely an Indian settlement) "are the most advanced of the Missisauga and represent one of the most successful attempts of any American Indian group to assimilate the culture of the whites. The Indian inhabitants have often won prizes against white competitors at the agricultural fairs." — JAMES MOONEY and CYRUS THOMAS, in *Handbook Amer. Indians.*

ing of the enemy's march, fifty Sauteur fighting men
went to meet them who, under the cover of a very dense
fog, entirely defeated them, although their young men
gave way [in the battle], and only thirty men remained;
and they had for arms only arrows and tomahawks, while
the Irroquois relied much on their firearms. The Sauteurs dealt quite heavy blows on the Nadouaissioux when
those tribes were at war; but since the peace was made
the bravest warriors are dead, and the rest have degener-
ated from the valor of their ancestors, and devote
themselves solely to the destruction of wild animals.

The Hurons, Outaoüaks, Cinagos, Kiskakons, and
Nansouaketons usually make their abode at Michilimakinak,[197] and leave the greater part of their families
there during the winter, when they are away hunting;

[197] Ottawa (meaning "traders"), "a term common to the Cree, Algonkin,
Nipissing, Montagnais, Ottawa, and Chippewa, and applied to the Ottawa"
because "they were noted among their neighbors as intertribal traders and
barterers." The Jesuit *Relation* of 1667 states that "the Ottawa (Outaoüacs)
claimed that the great river (Ottawa?) belonged to them, and that no other
nation might navigate it without their consent;" therefore all those who went
down to trade with the French, although of different tribes, "bore the name
Ottawa, under whose auspices the journey was undertaken. . . According to
tradition the Ottawa, Chippewa, and Potawatomi tribes of the Algonquian
family were formerly one people who came from some point north of the great
lakes and separated at Mackinaw, Mich. The Ottawa were located by the
earliest writers and also by tradition on Manitoulin Island, and also the
north and south shores of Georgian Bay." They fled westward from the
attacks of the Iroquois in the middle of the seventeenth century, and spent
some twenty years in northern Wisconsin; in 1670-1671 they returned to Manitoulin Island; but by 1680 most of them had joined the Hurons at Mackinaw,
whence they gradually spread down Lake Huron and along the east shore of
Lake Michigan, and even into the region adjoining Chicago; and their villages
were mingled with those of their old allies the Hurons, along the south shore
of Lake Erie. The Ottawa were prominent in all the Indian wars up to 1812,
and the noted Pontiac, leader in the war of 1763 around Detroit, was a chief
of their tribe. Some of them removed to Canada after the cessation of hostilities between the United States and Great Britain; those along the west shore
of Lake Michigan ceded their lands to the United States by the Chicago treaty
of Sept. 26, 1833, and agreed to remove to lands granted them in northeastern Kansas; those in northern Ohio went west of the Mississippi about
1832, and are now living in Oklahoma; but the great body of the Ottawa

for these they reserve the slenderest provision of grain, and sell the rest at a high price.

Michilimakinak, which is three hundred and sixty leagues from Quebec, is the general meeting-place for all the French who go to trade with stranger tribes; it is the landing-place and refuge of all the savages who trade their peltries. The savages who dwell there do not need to go hunting in order to obtain all the comforts of life. When they choose to work, they make canoes of birch-bark, which they sell two at three hundred livres each. They get a shirt for two sheets of bark for cabins. The sale of their French strawberries and other fruits produces means for procuring their ornaments, which consist of vermilion and glass and porcelain beads. They make a profit on everything. They catch whitefish, herring, and trout four to five feet long. All the tribes land at this place, in order to trade their peltries there. In summer the young men go hunting, a distance of

---

"remained in the lower peninsula of Michigan, where they are still found scattered in a number of small villages and settlements. . . Charlevoix says the Ottawa were one of the rudest nations of Canada, cruel and barbarous to an unusual degree, and sometimes guilty of cannibalism. Bacqueville de la Potherie says they were formerly very rude, but by intercourse with the Hurons they have become more intelligent, imitating their valor, making themselves formidable to all the tribes with whom they were at enmity, and respected by those with whom they were in alliance. It was said of them in 1859: 'This people is still advancing in agricultural pursuits; they may be said to have entirely abandoned the chase; all of them live in good, comfortable log cabins; have fields inclosed with rail fences, and own domestic animals.' The Ottawa were expert canoemen; as a means of defense they sometimes built forts, probably similar to those of the Hurons." In the latter part of the seventeenth century there were four divisions of this tribe: Kiskakon, Sinago, Nassawaketon (French, Gens de la Fourche, "people of the Fork"), and Sable; and another is sometimes named the Keinouche (or "Pickerel"), on the south shore of Lake Superior. "The population of the different Ottawa groups is not known with certainty. In 1906 the Chippewa and Ottawa on Manitoulin and Cockburn Islands, Canada, were 1,497, of whom about half were Ottawa; there were 197 under the Seneca school, Okla., and in Michigan 5,587 scattered Chippewa and Ottawa in 1900, of whom about two-thirds are Ottawa. The total therefore is about 4,700." — JAMES MOONEY and J. N. B. HEWITT, in *Handbook Amer. Indians*.

thirty to forty leagues, and return laden with game; in autumn they depart for the winter hunt (which is the best [time of the year] for the skins and furs), and return in the spring laden with beavers, pelts, various kinds of fat, and the flesh of bears and deer. They sell all of which they have more than enough. They would be exceedingly well-to-do if they were economical; but most of them have the same traits as the Sauteurs.

The Hurons are more provident; they think of the future, and they support their families. As they are sober, it is seldom that they suffer from poverty. This tribe is very politic, treacherous in their actions, and proud in all their behavior; they have more intellect than all the other savages. The Hurons are liberal; they show delicacy in their conversation, and they speak with precision. The others try to imitate them. They are insinuating, and are seldom cheated by any person whatsoever in any of their undertakings. The Outaoüaks, who are their neighbors, have imitated their customs and their rules of conduct; these people were at first very rude, but by intercourse with the Hurons they have become much more intelligent. They have imitated the valor of the latter, and have made themselves feared by all the tribes who are their enemies, and looked up to by those who are their allies.

Michilimakinak, according to the old men, is the place where Michapous sojourned longest. There is a mountain on the shore of the lake which has the shape of a hare; they believe that this was the place of his abode, and they call this mountain Michapous.[198] It is

---

[198] Manabozho, Messou, Michabo are among the synonyms of Nanabozho, "the demiurge of the cosmologic traditions of the Algonquian tribes." He is "apparently the impersonation of life, the active quickening power of life — of life manifested and embodied in the myriad forms of sentient and physical nature. He is therefore reputed to possess not only the power to live, but also the correlative power of renewing his own life and of quickening and there-

there, as they say, that he showed men how to make
fishing-nets, and where he placed the most fish. There
is an island, two leagues from the shore, which is very

fore creating life in others. He impersonates life in an unlimited series of
diverse personalities which represent various phases and conditions of life, and
the histories of the life and acts of these separate individualities form an entire
circle of traditions and myths which, when compared one with another, are
sometimes apparently contradictory and incongruous, relating, as these stories
do, to the unrelated objects and subjects in nature. The conception named
Nanabozho exercises the diverse functions of many persons, and he likewise
suffers their pains and needs. He is this life struggling with the many forms
of want, misfortune, and death that come to the bodies and beings of nature."
The true character of this concept has been misconceived. Comparison is made
between the Chippewa Nanabozho and the Iroquois Te'horon'hiawa'k'ho^n,
showing that they are nearly identical. "In Potawatomi and cognate tradition Nanabozho is the eldest of male quadruplets, the beloved Chipiapoos
being the second, Wabosso the third, and Chakekenapok the fourth. They were
begotten by a great primal being, who had come to earth, and were born of a
reputed daughter of the children of men. Nanabozho was the professed and
active friend of the human race. The mild and gentle but unfortunate Chipiapoos became the warder of the dead, the ruler of the country of the manes,
after this transformation. Wabosso ('Maker of White'), seeing the sunlight,
went to the Northland, where, assuming the form of a white hare, he is regarded as possessing most potent manito or *orenda*. [Under art. "Orenda," this
term is defined as "the Iroquois name of the active force, principle, or magic
power which was assumed by the inchoate reasoning of primitive man to be
inherent in every body and being of nature and in every personified attribute,
property, or activity, belonging to each of these and conceived to be the active
cause or force, or dynamic energy, involved in every operation or phenomenon
of nature, in any manner affecting or controlling the welfare of man. This
hypothetic principle was conceived to be immaterial, occult, impersonal, mysterious in mode of action, limited in function and efficiency, and not at all
omnipotent, local and not omnipresent, and ever embodied or immanent in some
object, although it was believed that it could be transferred, attracted, acquired,
increased, suppressed, or enthralled by the orenda of occult ritualistic formulas
endowed with more potency. . . So to obtain his needs man must gain the
goodwill of each one of a thousand controlling minds by prayer, sacrifice, some
acceptable offering, or propitiatory act, in order to influence the exercise in
his behalf of the orenda or magic power which he believed was controlled by
the particular being invoked. . . In the cosmogonic legends, the sum of
the operations of this hypothetic magic power constitutes the story of the phenomena of nature and the biography of the gods, in all the planes of human
culture." — J. N. B. HEWITT.]

"Lastly, Chakekenapok, named from chert, flint, or firestone (fire?), was the
impersonation originally of winter, and in coming into this world ruthlessly
caused the death of his mother." He is destroyed by his brother Nanabozho, in
anger for the death of their mother, and the fragments of his body become

View of Michilimackinack

lofty; they say that he left there some spirits, whom they call *Imakinagos*. As the inhabitants of this island are large and strong, this island has taken its name from those spirits; and it is called Michilimakinak, as who should say *Micha-Imakinak* – for in the Outaoüak language *micha* means "great," "stout," and "much." This place is a strait, which separates Lake Huron from Méchéygan, otherwise "Lake of the Illinois." The currents which come and go in this strait form a flow and ebb, which is not regular, however. These currents flow so rapidly that when the wind blows all the nets which are stretched [in the stream] are torn out or destroyed; and in high winds ice-floes have been seen to move against the currents, as swiftly as if they had been swept along by a torrent.

When the savages of those regions make a feast of fish, they invoke those spirits, who they say live under this island – thanking them for their liberality, and entreating them to take care always of their families; and asking them to keep their nets from harm and to preserve their canoes from surging waves. Those who are present at this feast utter, all together, [a long drawn]

huge rocks, and masses of flint or chert. "Before the Indians knew the art of fire-making Nanabozho taught them the art of making hatchets, lances, and arrowpoints." He dwelt with Chipiapoos in a land distant from that of men, and both were beneficent and powerful divinities. Through jealousy the evil manitos of the air, earth, and waters plotted to destroy the brothers, and succeeded in drowning Chipiapoos in one of the great lakes. Great was the wrath of Nanabozho, which was finally pacified by some of the good manitos, who initiated him into the mysteries of the grand medicine. Afterward the manitos brought back the lost Chipiapoos, but he was required to go to rule the country of the departed spirits; and Nanabozho again descended upon earth, and initiated all his human family into the medicine mysteries. He created animals for the food and raiment of men, and useful plants to cure sickness; and destroyed many ferocious monsters that would have endangered human life. Then he went to dwell on an ice-island in the far north, and placed at the four points of the compass beneficent beings who provide for man the light, heat, rain, and snow that are needed for his welfare." – J. N. B. HEWITT, in *Handbook Amer. Indians*, art. "Nanabozho."

Ho! which is a giving of thanks; they are very exact in offering this prayer.   Our Frenchmen have made so much sport of this custom that they do not venture to practice it openly in the presence of our people; but it is always noticed that they mutter something between their teeth which resembles the prayer that they offer to these spirits of the island.

From this strait, which is five leagues long, one goes to the Lake of the Islinois, known under the name of Méchéygan, which is the route by which one reaches the Islinois, who are in possession of the most beautiful regions that can be seen [anywhere].   This lake is one hundred and eighty leagues long by thirty wide.   Its shores are sandy; usually that on the north side is followed to reach the Bay of Puans.

This bay takes its name from the Ouénibegons,[199] [a

---

[199] A variant of Ouinipigou, the Algonkin name of a tribe now known as Winnebago. Le Jeune explains the meaning of this name and of the French translation of it, *Nation des Puans* (*Jesuit Relations*, vol. xviii, 231): "Some of the French call them the 'Nation of Stinkards' (*Puans*), because the Algonquin word *ouinipeg* signifies 'bad-smelling water,' and they apply this name to the water of the salt sea — so that these people are called Ouinipigou because they come from the shores of a sea about which we have no knowledge; and hence they ought to be called not the 'Nation of Stinkards,' but 'Nation of the Sea.'"   The Winnebago are of Siouan stock (see note 195), their Siouan name being Ho-tcañ'-ga-ra, sometimes written Ochungra or Otchagra; in the westward prehistoric migration of that people this branch separated from the rest, on the east side of the Mississippi, and moved northward into Wisconsin, where they finally settled about Lake Winnebago.   Cyrus Thomas says (*Handbook Amer. Indians*, 612): "Traditional and linguistic evidence proves that the Iowa sprang from the Winnebago stem, which appears to have been the mother stock of some other of the southwestern Siouan tribes."   The Winnebago were apparently located in Wisconsin before the coming of the Chippewa and other Algonquian tribes thither, and for many years were on hostile terms with the latter.   During the Fox wars they were for a considerable time allies of the Sauk and Foxes, but later were won over to the French side.   A hundred of their warriors went, under Langlade's command, to fight against the British (1755-1759); but in the Revolutionary War they aided the British against the Americans (also in the War of 1812-1815), and received presents from them as late as 1820.   Many of them were followers of Tecumseh and the Prophet, and their warriors fought at Tippecanoe.   After peace was restored, dissensions

word] which means Puans [i.e., "stinkards"]. This
name is explained less disagreeably in the language of
the savages, for they call it the "salt-water bay" rather
than the "bay of stinkards" – although among them
those terms mean almost the same thing. They also give
the same name to the sea, a fact which has occasioned

---

arose between the Wisconsin tribes over lands claimed by them; but by the
treaty of Little Lake Butte des Morts, August 11, 1827, the Winnebago, Menominee, and the immigrant tribes from New York ceded their lands in the
Fox River valley, and the Winnebago those in the lead region, to the United
States. On Nov. 1, 1837, a treaty was concluded at Washington with the
Winnebago by which they ceded all their lands east of the Mississippi and
agreed to move upon a tract of land in northeastern Iowa; but the tribe refused
to confirm this agreement, saying that their envoys had no right to make it.
Part of the tribe were forcibly removed thither in 1840, and later were again
removed to southern Minnesota. After the "Sioux massacre" (1862) they
were again removed, simply to pacify the frightened white inhabitants of
Minnesota, this time to South Dakota, near Pierre. But they did not like this
place, and many of them gradually made their way to the Omaha reservation
in northeastern Nebraska; there lands were granted them, or purchased from the
Omaha, and they have since remained there, cultivating their lands and displaying much thrift and industry. Meanwhile many of the tribe (more than
1,000) had remained in Wisconsin, and in 1873 the government attempted to
remove these people to Nebraska. Several hundred of them were sent thither,
against their will; the removal was even more cruel than previous ones, many
dying on the way or after reaching their destination. Many others made their
way back to Wisconsin, and joined their tribesmen who were still there. Since
then, they have been left undisturbed, and annual payments have been made
to them by the government; and homesteads have been provided for them,
chiefly in Jackson, Adams, Marathon, and Shawano Counties (in Central Wisconsin). They live mainly by picking berries, fishing, and hunting, and cultivate their lands to a limited extent. In 1887 the number of Winnebago enrolled
in Wisconsin was about 1,500; in 1907 they numbered 1,180, and there were
2,613 in Nebraska. Much of the information in this note is obtained from the
interesting and carefully prepared account given by Publius V. Lawson, "The
Winnebago Tribe," in the Wisconsin *Archeologist*, July, 1907. Therein he
presents also a series of "outline sketches of the chiefs" of the tribe, gathered
from the Wis. *Hist. Colls.* and other authorities; also portraits of several, illustrations of Winnebago implements, etc., and a map showing location of their
villages.

See also the account of this tribe in *Handbook of Amer. Indians*, by J. O.
Dorsey and Paul Radin; it describes especially their social organization and
religious ceremonies. Their population is given therein as 1,063 in Nebraska
and 1,270 in Wisconsin (in 1910). Dr. Radin is engaged in a careful and
detailed study of this tribe for the Bureau of American Ethnology. — ED.

very careful search to be made in order to ascertain if there are not in those quarters some salt-water springs, such as there are among the Iroquois; but thus far nothing of this sort has been found. It is believed that this name was given to the bay on account of the quantities of mud and mire which are encountered there [along its shores?], from which continually arise unwholesome vapors, which cause the most terrible and frequent thunders that can be heard [anywhere]. In this bay is observed a regular rise and fall of the waters, almost like that of the sea. I will gladly leave to the philosophers the inquiry whether these tides are occasioned by the winds, or by some other cause; and whether there are winds which are precursors of the moon, and attached to its retinue, which consequently agitate this lake and produce its flow and ebb whenever the moon rises above the horizon. What we can say with certainty is, that when the water is very calm, it is easily seen to rise and fall according to the course of the moon – although it is not denied that these movements might be caused by winds that are far away, and which, by pressure on the middle of the lake, cause the waters along its shores to rise and fall in the manner which is visible.[200]

This bay is forty leagues in depth; its width at the entrance is eight or ten leagues, gradually diminishing

[200] The apparent tides in Lake Michigan and Green Bay were often noticed by early explorers and writers, especially by the Jesuit missionaries (after 1670). They were chiefly mentioned by Louis André, who observed them at Mackinac, "so regular, and again so irregular" (*Jesuit Relations*, lv, 163-165); in Green Bay, where he was convinced that they were caused by the moon (*id.*, lvi, 137-139); and in Fox River (*id.*, lvii, 301-305). Marquette also mentions them, in 1673 and 1675 (*id.*, lix, 99, 179). These observers, and some in the nineteenth century, thought that these apparent tides were more or less affected and perhaps caused by the currents or the varying depth of the waters, the configuration of the shores, the direction and force of winds, etc. For more recent explanation, see page 150, *footnote.* — ED.

until at the farthest end it is but two leagues wide. The mouth is closed by seven islands, which must be doubled in voyaging to the Islinois. The bay is on the northwestern side of the lake, and extends toward the southwest; at the entrance is a small village, composed of people gathered from various nations – who, wishing to commend themselves to their neighbors, have cleared some lands there, and affect to entertain all who pass that way. Liberality is a characteristic greatly admired among the savages; and it is the proper thing for the chiefs to lavish all their possessions, if they desire to be esteemed. Accordingly, they have exerted themselves to receive strangers hospitably, who find among them whatever provisions are in season; and they like nothing better than to hear that others are praising their generosity.

The Pouteouatemis, Sakis, and Malhominis [201] dwell

---

[201] One of the variants of the name now given to this tribe, Menominee (meaning the "Wild-rice People" – see note 71). When first known to the whites these Indians were living on the Menominee River and Bay de Noque, on the southern side of the upper Michigan peninsula; and it was in the former locality that Nicolet visited them (about 1634), and where they remained until the middle of the nineteenth century. They have generally been a peaceful tribe, save that in earlier days they were often on hostile terms with their Algonquian neighbors. Although rather indolent, they are generally honest, and not so given to intemperance as the Indians of many other tribes. At various times from 1831 to 1856, the Menominee ceded lands occupied by them to the United States; and in exchange for these they received (May 12, 1854) a reservation on the Wolf River, in Shawano County, Wis. Their present population is about 1,600. – JAMES MOONEY and CYRUS THOMAS, in *Handbook Amer. Indians.*

Sauk (Sakis), a name derived from *Osawkiwag*, "people of the yellow earth" (Hewitt); they belong to the Central group of the Algonquian family. "There is no satisfactory reference to them till they are spoken of as dwelling south of the Straits of Mackinaw." Their claim, confirmed by other tribes (the Potawatomi, Ottawa, and Chippewa), is that their home was once about Saginaw Bay, from which they were driven by those tribes. "In the early part of the 18th century they were found by the French west of Lake Michigan, dwelling south of the Foxes, who were then about Green Bay. . . It is more probable that they came round Lake Michigan by way of the south. From earliest accounts it seems that the Sauk and Foxes were on very intimate

there; and there are four cabins, the remains of the Nadouaichs, a tribe which has been entirely destroyed

terms with each other. They were probably but two divisions of the same people who had been separated by some cause, probably by defeat at the hands of their enemies." They seem to have been greatly disliked by their savage neighbors, and later by the French. They were almost always at war with the adjoining tribes, most of whom were friendly to the French; and they refused to join the military operations of the latter; "there is no doubt that these early Fox wars had a good deal to do with weakening the cause of the French in the struggle with the English to gain control of the continent." In the latter part of the eighteenth century the Sauk and Foxes were "living together practically as one people, and occupying an extensive territory in what is now southern Wisconsin, northwestern Illinois, and northeastern Missouri."

A Sauk band wintering near St. Louis made an agreement (about 1804) "by which the Sauk and Foxes were to relinquish all claim to their territory in Wisconsin, Illinois, and Missouri;" but those tribes were only angered by this transaction, and the Foxes were so incensed at the Sauk that they gradually withdrew from them and moved over the Mississippi into their hunting grounds in Iowa. "Other agreements were entered into with the three divisions of these people before the treaty of 1804 was finally carried out. Out of all this, in connection with the general unrest of the tribes of this region, rose the so-called Black Hawk War. It is customary to lay the cause of this conflict to the refusal of the Sauk to comply with the terms of agreement they had entered into with the government with reference particularly to the lands on Rock River in Illinois." Their hostilities with the whites were short and unequal; they were defeated, and sought refuge among the Foxes in Iowa. This result was partly due to tribal jealousies; the Winnebago delivered up Black Hawk to the government authorities and the Potawatomi deserted to the side of the whites. "This conflict practically broke the power of the Sauk and Foxes. They united again in Iowa, this time to avenge themselves against the Sioux, Omaha, and Menominee, whom they chastised in lively fashion, but not enough to satisfy their desires. So constantly harassed were the Sioux that they finally left Iowa altogether, and the Menominee withdrew northward where they continued to remain. In 1837 the Sauk and Foxes made the last of their various cessions of Iowa lands, and were given in exchange a tract across the Missouri in Kansas. Here they remained practically as one people for about twenty years." But they were separated by internal dissensions, due largely to the Sauk leader Keokuk, and lived in separate villages. About 1858 most of the Foxes removed to Iowa; they finally found a place on Iowa River, near Tama City, where they bought a small tract of land, to which additions have been made at various times, until now they hold over 3,000 acres in common. "They have nothing more to do with the Sauk politically. In 1867 the Sauk ceded their lands in Kansas and were given lands in exchange in Indian Territory. In 1889 they took up lands in severalty and sold the remainder to the government. The total number of the Sauk is fewer than 600, of whom about 100 are in Kansas and Nebraska, and about 500 in Oklahoma. The Foxes in Iowa number about 350." — WILLIAM JONES, in *Handbook Amer. Indians.*

by the Iroquois. In former times, the Puans were the
masters of this bay, and of a great extent of adjoining
country. This nation was a populous one, very redoubtable, and spared no one; they violated all the laws
of nature; they were sodomites, and even had intercourse with beasts. If any stranger came among them,
he was cooked in their kettles. The Malhominis were
the only tribe who maintained relations with them,
[and] they did not dare even to complain of their
tyranny. Those tribes believed themselves the most
powerful in the universe; they declared war on all nations whom they could discover, although they had only
stone knives and hatchets. They did not desire to have
commerce with the French. The Outaouaks, notwithstanding, sent to them envoys, whom they had the
cruelty to eat. This crime incensed all the nations, who
formed a union with the Outaouaks, on account of the
protection accorded to them by the latter under the
auspices of the French, from whom they received
weapons and all sorts of merchandise. They made frequent expeditions against the Puans, who were giving
them much trouble; and then followed civil wars among
the Puans—who reproached one another for their ill-
fortune, brought upon them by the perfidy of those who
had slain the envoys, since the latter had brought them
knives, bodkins, and many other useful articles, of which
they had had no previous knowledge. When they found
that they were being vigorously attacked, they were compelled to unite all their forces in one village, where they
numbered four or five thousand men; but maladies
wrought among them more devastation than even the
war did, and the exhalations from the rotting corpses
caused great mortality. They could not bury the dead,
and were soon reduced to fifteen hundred men. Despite all these misfortunes, they sent a party of five

hundred warriors against the Outagamis, who dwelt on
the other shore of the lake;[202] but all those men perished,

[202] This is one of various appellations of the tribe now known as Foxes
(a name which, as often happened, was erroneously transferred from a clan
to the tribe). Their own name for themselves is Měsh-kwa 'kihŭgⁱ, meaning
(like the Hebrew name Adam) "red earth," referring to their legend of
creation. They are mentioned by various writers as Musquakies, Outagamis,
and Renards (the French appellation), each name having many variant or
corrupted forms. They were known to the Chippewa and other Algonquian
tribes as Utŭgamig, "people of the other shore." When first known to the
whites the Foxes lived about Lake Winnebago, or along the Fox and Wolf
Rivers. They were closely related to the Sauk (see preceding note), and probably both were only branches from one original stem; so it is probable that
their early migrations were closely correspondent. They were a restless, fierce
tribe, and were almost always at war with some of their Algonquian neighbors,
or with the French; they carried on war frequently with the Illinois tribes,
and finally (aided by the Sauk) drove them from their own country, and took
possession of it. In 1746 the Foxes were living at the Little Lake Butte des
Morts, just below the present Neenah and Menasha, Wis.; and they exacted
tribute from every trader who passed them, plundering every one who refused
to pay. Incensed at this treatment, the French, aided by the Chippewa, Potawatomi, and Menominee, attacked the Foxes, and after two sharp battles drove
them down the Wisconsin River, where they settled, about twenty miles above
Prairie du Chien. About 1780 the Foxes and the Sioux attacked the Chippewa
at St. Croix Falls, where the Foxes were almost annihilated. The remnant of
them united with the Sauk, and they practically make one tribe, although each
retains its identity. Their mode of life, customs, etc., are those of the tribes
of the eastern woodlands, somewhat modified by those of the plains. "There
is probably no other Algonquian community within the limits of the United
States, unless it be that of the Mexican band of Kickapoo in Oklahoma, where
a more primitive state of society exists." Most of the estimates before 1850
make their numbers 1,500 to 2,000 souls; since that time they have been enumerated together with the Sauk. "The 345 'Sauk and Fox of Mississippi' still
(1905) in Iowa are said to be all Foxes." There are also 82 Sauk and Foxes
among the Kickapoos of Kansas. — JAMES MOONEY and CYRUS THOMAS, in
Handbook Amer. Indians.

The Sauk and Foxes were concerned in the so-called "Black Hawk War" of
1832, occasioned by what they considered a fraudulent treaty and cession of
their lands and villages in Iowa to white men; they were defeated, and transported to Kansas. Driven by homesickness, the Foxes made their way back to
Iowa, and settled on the banks of the Iowa, near the present Tama City;
and gradually they have acquired there some 3,000 acres of land, on which
they live in considerable comfort and prosperity. For a minute and admirable
study of this people, their mode of life, their customs and beliefs, see the valuable monograph written by Miss Mary Alicia Owen (who for many years
has been personally and intimately acquainted with this tribe), "The Folk-Lore
of the Musquakie Indians" (London, 1904), which forms vol. li of the publi-

while making that journey, by a tempest which arose.
Their enemies were moved by this disaster, and said that
the gods ought to be satisfied with so many punishments; so they ceased making war on those who remained. All these scourges, which ought to have gone
home to their consciences, seemed only to increase their
iniquities. All savages who have not yet embraced the
Christian faith have the notion that the souls of the departed, especially of those who have been slain, can not
rest in peace unless their relatives avenge their death;
it is necessary, therefore, to sacrifice victims to their
shades, if their friends wish to solace them. This belief, which animated those barbarians, inspired in them
an ardent desire to satisfy the manes of their ancestors,
or to perish utterly; but, seeing that this was impossible
for them, they were obliged to check their resentment—
they felt too humiliated in the sight of all the nations
to dare undertake any such enterprise. The despair,
the cruel memory of their losses, and the destitution to
which they were reduced, made it still more difficult
for them to find favorable opportunities for providing
their subsistence; the frequent raids of their enemies had
even dispersed the game; and famine was the last
scourge that attacked them.

Then the Islinois,[203] touched with compassion for

cations of the British Folk-lore Society. To that society Miss Owen presented
a large and valuable collection made by her, of beadwork and ceremonial
implements obtained from the Foxes; the book is illustrated with plates (some
being colored facsimiles) showing the designs in their beadwork. — ED.

[203] Illinois (the French form of their own appellation, *Iliniwek*, meaning
"people who are men") was the name of a "confederacy of Algonquian tribes,
formerly occupying southern Wisconsin, northern Illinois, and sections of Iowa
and Missouri, comprising the Cahokia, Kaskaskia, Michigamea, Moingwena,
Peoria, and Tamaroa." From 1660 to 1670, Jesuit missionaries found some of
them living at the Mascoutin village on the upper Fox River, and even
visiting the Indians at Lake Superior for purposes of trade. Some of their
villages were situated in Iowa on the shore of the Mississippi; but the greater

these unfortunates, sent five hundred men, among whom
were fifty of the most prominent persons in their nation,
to carry them a liberal supply of provisions. Those
man-eaters received them at first with the utmost gratitude; but at the same time they meditated taking revenge
for their loss by the sacrifice which they meant to make
of the Islinois to the shades of their dead. Accordingly,
they erected a great cabin in which to lodge these new
guests. As it is a custom among the savages to provide
dances and public games on splendid occasions, the
Puans made ready for a dance expressly for their guests.
While the Islinois were engaged in dancing, the Puans
cut their bow-strings, and immediately flung themselves
upon the Islinois, massacred them, not sparing one man,
and made a general feast of their flesh; the enclosure of

part of the tribes belonging to the confederacy lived in northern Illinois, chiefly
on the Illinois River. In the village of Kaskaskia (then on the Illinois River,
in the present LaSalle County), Marquette found (1673) 74 cabins, all of one
tribe only; various missionaries who visited the place between 1680 and 1692
estimated the population at from 300 to 400 cabins, or 6,500 to 9,000 souls, belonging to eight tribes. "The Illinois were almost constantly harassed by the
Sioux, Foxes, and other northern tribes; it was probably on this account that
they concentrated, about the time of La Salle's visit, on the Illinois River.
About the same time the Iroquois waged war against them, which lasted several
years, and greatly reduced their numbers, while liquor obtained from the
French tended still further to weaken them. About the year 1750 they were
still estimated at from 1,500 to 2,000 souls. The murder of the celebrated chief
Pontiac by a Kaskaskia Indian, about 1769, provoked the vengeance of the
Lake tribes on the Illinois; and a war of extermination was begun which,
in a few years, reduced them to a mere handful, who took refuge with the
French settlers at Kaskaskia, while the Sauk, Foxes, Kickapoo, and Potawatomi
took possession of their country. In 1778 the Kaskaskia still numbered 210,
living in a village three miles north of Kaskaskia, while the Peoria and Michigamea together numbered 170 on the Mississippi, a few miles farther up. Both
bands had become demoralized and generally worthless through the use of
liquor. In 1800 there were only 150 left. In 1833 the survivors, represented
by the Kaskaskia and Peoria, sold their lands in Illinois and removed west of
the Mississippi, and are now in the northeast corner of Oklahoma, consolidated
with the Wea and Piankashaw." In 1885 but 149 remained of all these
tribes, and even these were much mixed with white blood. In 1905 their
number was 195. So far as can be judged from the early writers, the Illinois
seem to have been timid, fickle, and treacherous. — JAMES MOONEY and CYRUS
THOMAS, in Handbook Amer. Indians.

Winnebago Wigwams

that cabin, and the melancholy remains of the victims, may still be seen. The Puans rightly judged that all the nations would league themselves together to take vengeance for the massacre of the Islinois and for their own cruel ingratitude toward that people, and resolved to abandon the place which they were occupying. But, before they took that final step, each reproached himself for that crime; some dreamed at night that their families were being carried away, and others thought that they saw on every side frightful spectres, who threatened them. They took refuge in an island, which has since been swept away by the ice-floes.

The Islinois, finding that their people did not return, sent out some men to bring news of them. They arrived at the Puan village, which they found abandoned; but from it they descried the smoke from the one which had just been established in that island. The Islinois saw only the ruins of the cabins, and the bones of many human beings which, they concluded, were those of their own people. When they carried back to their country this sad news, only weeping and lamentation were heard; they sent word of their loss to their allies, who offered to assist them. The Puans, who knew that the Islinois did not use canoes, were sure that in that island they were safe from all affronts. The Islinois were every day consoled by those who had learned of their disaster; and from every side they received presents which wiped away their tears. They consulted together whether they should immediately attempt hostilities against their enemies. Their wisest men said that they ought, in accordance with the custom of their ancestors, to spend one year, or even more, in mourning, to move the Great Spirit; that he had chastised them because they had not offered enough sacrifices to him; that he would, notwithstanding, have pity on them if they were not impatient; and that he would chastise the Puans for so black a deed. They deferred hostilities until the second year, when they assembled a large body of men from all the nations who were interested in the undertaking; and they set out in the winter season, in order not to fail therein. Having reached the island over the ice, they found only the cabins, in which there still remained some fire; the Puans had gone to their hunt on the day before, and were traveling in a body, that they might not, in any emergency, be surprised by the Islinois. The army of the latter followed these hunters, and on the sixth day descried their village, to which they laid seige. So vigorous was their attack that they killed, wounded, or made prisoners all the Puans, except a few who escaped, and who reached the Malhominis' village, but severely wounded by arrows.

The Islinois returned to their country, well avenged; they had, however, the generosity to spare the lives of many women and children, part of whom remained among them, while others had liberty to go whither they pleased. A few years ago, they [the Puans] numbered possibly one hundred and fifty warriors. These savages have no mutual fellow-feeling; they have caused their own ruin, and have been obliged to divide their forces. They are naturally very impatient of control, and very irascible; a little matter excites them; and they are great braggarts. They are, however, well built, and are brave soldiers, who do not know what danger is; and they are subtle and crafty in war. Although they are convinced that their ancestors drew upon themselves the enmity of all the surrounding nations, they cannot be humble; on the contrary, they are the first to affront those who are with them. Their women are extremely laborious; they are neat in their houses, but very disgusting about their food. These people are very fond of the French, who always protect them; without that support, they would have been long ago utterly destroyed, for none of their neighbors could endure them on account of their behavior and their insupportable haughtiness. Some years ago, the Outagamis, Maskoutechs, Kikabous,[204] Sakis, and Miamis were almost defeated by them; they have [now] become somewhat more tractable. Some of the Pouteouatemis, Sakis, and Outagamis have taken wives among them, and have given them their own daughters.

The Pouteouatemis are their neighbors; the behavior of these people is very affable and cordial, and they make great efforts to gain the good opinion of persons

[204] The Kickapoo are "a tribe of the central Algonquian group, forming a division with the Sauk and Foxes, with whom they have close ethnic and linguistic connection. The relation of this division is rather with the Miami, Shawnee, Menominee, and Peoria than with the Chippewa, Potawatomi, and Ottawa." Apparently Allouez was the first white man to encounter them (1667-1670); they were then near the Fox-Wisconsin portage. At some time before 1700 they had dwelt on the Kickapoo River of Wisconsin. In the early part of the eighteenth century at least part of the tribe were living somewhere about Milwaukee River. After the destruction of the Illinois confederacy (about 1765), the Kickapoo appropriated part of the conquered territory — at first settling at Peoria, Ill., then gradually moving on to the Sangamon and Wabash Rivers. In the War of 1812 they fought with Tecumseh against the Americans, and many followed Black Hawk in the contest of 1832. In 1809 and 1819 they ceded to the United States their lands in Illinois and Indiana, and afterward removed to Missouri and thence to Kansas. A large number of the Kickapoo went, in 1852 and 1863, to Texas and thence to Mexico, which caused them to be known as "Mexican Kickapoo." "In 1873 a number were brought back and settled in Indian Territory. Others have come in since, but the remainder, constituting at present nearly half the tribe, are now settled on a reservation, granted them by the Mexican government, in the Santa Rosa mountains of eastern Chihuahua." In 1759 the population of the Kickapoo was estimated at 3,000; since that time they have steadily diminished. "Those in the United States in 1905 were officially reported at 432, of whom 247 were in Oklahoma and 185 in Kansas. There are supposed to be about 400 or more in Mexico. Within the last two years there has been considerable effort by private parties to procure the removal of the Oklahoma band also to Mexico."
— JAMES MOONEY and WILLIAM JONES, in *Handbook Amer. Indians.*

who come among them. They are very intelligent; they
have an inclination for raillery; their physical appearance is good; and they are great talkers. When they set
their minds on anything, it is not easy to turn them from
it. The old men are prudent, sensible, and deliberate;
it is seldom that they undertake any unseasonable enterprise. As they receive strangers very kindly, they
are delighted when reciprocal attentions are paid to
them. They have so good an opinion of themselves that
they regard other nations as inferior to them. They
have made themselves arbiters for the tribes about the
bay, and for all their neighbors; and they strive to preserve for themselves that reputation in every direction.[205] Their ambition to please everybody has of

[205] Potawatomi (originally meaning "people of the place of the fire;" also
called "Fire Nation"), an Algonquian tribe, "first encountered on the islands
of Green Bay, Wis., and at its head. According to the traditions of all three
tribes the Potawatomi, Chippewa, and Ottawa were originally one people, and
seem to have reached the region about the upper end of Lake Huron together.
Here they separated, but the three have always formed a loose confederacy, or
have acted in concert, and in 1846 those removed beyond the Mississippi,
asserting their former connection, asked to be again united. Warren conjectured that it had been less than three centuries since the Chippewa became
disconnected as a distinct tribe from the Ottawa and Potawatomi." It is
apparently the Potawatomi of whom Champlain heard (in 1616), named by the
Hurons Asistagueronons, and dwelling on the western shore of Lake Huron.
In the Jesuit *Relation* for 1640 the Potawatomi are spoken of as living in the
vicinity of the Winnebago, doubtless driven west by the Iroquois; but in the
following year they were at Sault Ste. Marie, having taken refuge with the
Saulteurs (Chippewa) there from the incursions of the Sioux. In 1667 many
of them were at Chequamegon Bay; and in 1670 they had again resorted to
the islands in Green Bay. Moving still further southward, by 1700 they had
become established on Milwaukee River, at Chicago, and on St. Joseph River;
and by 1800 they "were in possession of the country around the head of Lake
Michigan, from Milwaukee River to Grand River in Michigan, extending
southwest over a large part of northern Illinois, east across Michigan to Lake
Erie, and south in Indiana to the Wabash, and as far down as Pine Creek.
Within this territory they had about fifty villages." Those who lived in
Illinois and Wisconsin were known as the Prairie band, or Maskotens — which
appellation caused some writers to confuse them with the other Algonquian tribe
"People of the Prairie," in latter times known as Mascoutens. The Potawatomi were active allies of the French until the peace of 1763, and afterward
of the British until 1815. Gradually they removed westward, as the American

course caused among them jealousy and divorce; for their families are scattered to the right and to the left along the Méchéygan [i.e., Lake Michigan]. With a view of gaining for themselves special esteem, they make presents of all their possessions, stripping themselves of even necessary articles, in their eager desire to be accounted liberal. Most of the merchandise for which the Outaoüas trade with the French is carried among these people.

The Sakis have always been neighbors of the Pouteouatemis, and have even built a village with them. They separated from each other some years ago, as neither tribe could endure to be subordinate; this feeling is general among all the savages, and each man is master of his own actions, no one daring to contradict him. These peoples are not intelligent, and are of brutal nature and unruly disposition; but they have a good physique, and are quite good-looking for savages; they are thieves and liars, great chatterers, good hunters, and very poor canoemen.

The Malhominis are no more than forty in number;

settlements increased — some, however, going to Canada — until, in 1846, all those west of the Mississippi were united on a reservation in southern Kansas. Many of them — having in 1861 taken lands in severalty — removed in 1868 to Indian Territory. "A considerable body, part of the Prairie band, is still in Wisconsin; and another band, the Potawatomi of Huron, is in lower Michigan." (This last band took lands in severalty and became citizens, by 1886.) The Potawatomi are described by early writers as being very friendly to the French, well disposed toward the Christian religion, and more humane and civilized than other tribes; and their women were more reserved and modest than those of most other tribes. Polygamy was common among them. Those on Milwaukee River (who were then considerably intermixed with Sauk and Winnebago) were in 1825 described as being lazy, and much inclined to gambling and debauchery. "The tribe probably never much exceeded 3,000 souls, and most estimates place them far below that number." In 1906 those in the United States were reported to number 2,443, mostly of the "Citizen" group in Oklahoma. Those in Canada are all in Ontario, and number about 220, most of them on Walpole Island in Lake St. Clair. — JAMES MOONEY, in *Handbook Amer. Indians.*

they raise a little Indian corn, but live upon game and sturgeons; they are skillful navigators. If the Sauteurs are adroit in catching the whitefish at the Sault, the Malhominis are no less so in spearing the sturgeon in their river. For this purpose they use only small canoes, very light, in which they stand upright, and in the middle of the current spear the sturgeon with an iron-pointed pole; only canoes are to be seen, morning and evening. They are good-natured people, not very keen of intellect; selfish to the last degree, and consequently characterized by a sordid avarice; but they are brave warriors.

All these tribes at the bay are most favorably situated; the country is a beautiful one, and they have fertile fields planted with Indian corn. Game is abundant at all seasons, and in winter they hunt bears and beavers; they hunt deer at all times, and they even fish for wild-fowl. I will explain my remark; in autumn there is a prodigious abundance of ducks, both black and white, of excellent flavor, and the savages stretch nets in certain places where these fowl alight to feed upon the wild rice. Then advancing silently in their canoes, they draw them up alongside of the nets, in which the birds have been caught. They also capture pigeons in their nets, in the summer. They make in the woods wide paths, in which they spread large nets, in the shape of a bag, wide open, and attached at each side to the trees; and they make a little hut of branches, in which they hide. When the pigeons in their flight get within this open space, the savages pull a small cord which is drawn through the edge of the net, and thus capture sometimes five or six hundred birds in one morning, especially in windy weather.[206] All the year round they

---

[206] The Indian practice of capturing wild fowl in nets is also described by Dablon in the *Relation* of 1671-1672 (*Jesuit Relations*, vol. lvi, 121). The

fish for sturgeon, and for herring in the autumn; and in winter they have fruits. Although their rivers are deep, they close the stream with a sort of hurdle, leaving open places through which the fish can pass; in these spaces they set a sort of net which they can cast or draw in when they please; and several small cords are attached, which, although they seem to close the opening, nevertheless afford passage to the fish. The savages are apprised of the entrance of the fish into the net by a little bell which they fasten on the upper part of it; [207] when this sounds, they pull in their fish. This fishery suffices to maintain large villages; they also gather wild rice

passenger pigeon (*Ectopistes migratoria*) was even in recent times a notable feature in the wild life of the northwest. Many persons now living can remember seeing flocks of these birds so numerous and crowded as to obscure the sunlight, and requiring several hours to pass a given point. But they were recklessly slaughtered by the early settlers, as well as by the less intelligent Indians; and afterward many pot-hunters made it a regular business to trap and shoot the pigeons for the city markets. In consequence of these enemies the species is now exterminated — a painful illustration of the selfishness and greed of men who ought to know better, and from whom better things might have been expected; for the early settlers of the states carved from the northwest territory were mainly American people of exceptional intelligence and character. In a private letter dated March 13, 1909, C. Hart Merriam, then chief of the U.S. Biological Survey, says: "We fear that the passenger pigeon is extinct, although I am not sure that this is the case, and still have a lingering hope that a few of the birds still exist." H. W. Henshaw, present chief of the same bureau, says (in a letter of Dec. 22, 1910): "I am afraid that it is only too true that the last surviving individual of our passenger pigeon is the one in the Cincinnati Zoölogical Garden. The efforts to preserve this beautiful species were begun much too late." — ED.

[207] "Metal bells were in common use in middle America in pre-Columbian times, but they are rarely found north of the Rio Grande, either in possession of the tribes or on ancient sites; but bells were certainly known to the Pueblos and possibly to the mound-builders before the arrival of the whites. The rattle made of shells of various kinds or modeled in clay passed naturally into the bell as soon as metal or other particularly resonant materials were available for their manufacture." Of copper bells "many specimens must have reached Florida from Mexico and Central America in early Columbian times; and it is well known that bells of copper or bronze were employed in trade with the tribes by the English colonists, numerous examples of which have been obtained from mounds and burial places." — W. H. HOLMES, in *Handbook Amer. Indians*.

and acorns; accordingly, the peoples of the bay can live in the utmost comfort.

The Mantouechs, [208] who formerly composed a large village, resided about forty leagues inland, north of the bay. They were the most warlike people in all North America, and when they went out on the war-path the other tribes trembled. It was never possible to conquer them; however, all the [other] tribes, jealous of their power, leagued against them, and through the treachery of the Malhominis (who called themselves their friends) they were massacred – taken by surprise, in the same way as the Islinois were by the Puans – and only the women and children remained, who were made slaves.

Chapter VIII

[Summary of pages 81-85: The Iroquois had always, since the first coming of the French to Canada, been hostile to the Algonkin tribes, and were continually making raids on them; the latter were from the outset friendly to the French, who "needed those people, in order to maintain themselves at Quebec," and both accordingly rendered aid to each other against the Iroquois, the common enemy. But in 1665 arrived a new viceroy of the French possessions in America, Marquis de Tracy; he brought not only new colonists for Canada, but a regiment of French regular troops, with whom he was able to send a powerful punitive expedition against the Iroquois in their own country – inflicting so severe chastisement on them that he compelled them to sue for

---

[208] The Mantouek were "a tribe, possibly the Mdewakanton Sioux or its Matantonwan division, known to the French missionaries; placed by the Jesuit *Relation* of 1640 north of a small lake west of Sault Ste. Marie, and by the *Relation* of 1658 with the Nadouechiouek [i.e., Dakota], the two having forty towns ten days' travel northwest of the mission St. Michael of the Potawatomi." — *Handbook Amer. Indians.*

peace. Two years later (after the viceroy's return to France) two of his relatives and another French officer were wantonly slain by the treacherous Iroquois while out hunting. The governor, M. de Courcelles, at once threatened them with war unless they delivered up the murderer; they were alarmed at this, and sent forty of their warriors with Agariata, who had slain the French-men. This man, notwithstanding the entreaties and lamentations of his followers, was hanged in their pres-ence — a punishment which they had never before seen; and the Iroquois were so terrified that they maintained peace with the French until 1683, when war again broke out.]

All the Outaouak peoples were in alarm. While we were waging war with the Iroquois, those tribes who dwelt about Lake Huron fled for refuge to Chagoüa-mikon, which is on Lake Superior; they came down to Montreal only when they wished to sell their peltries, and then, trembling [with dread of the enemy]. The trade was not yet opened with the Outaouaks. The name of the French people gradually became known in that region, and some of the French made their way into those places where they believed that they could make some profit; it was a Peru for them. The sav-ages could not understand why these men came so far to search for their worn-out beaver robes; meanwhile they admired all the wares brought to them by the French, which they regarded as extremely precious. The knives, the hatchets, the iron weapons above all, could not be sufficiently praised; and the guns so astonished them that they declared that there was a spirit within the gun, which caused the loud noise made when it was fired. It is a fact that an Esquimau from Cape Digue, at 60° latitude, in the strait of Hudson Bay, displayed so

much surprise to me when he saw a *gode*[209] suddenly
fall, covered with blood, as the result of a gunshot, that
he stood motionless with the wonder caused by a thing
which seemed to him so extraordinary.   The Frenchmen
who traded with the Canadian tribes were often amused
at seeing those people in raptures of this sort.   The savages often took them [the Frenchmen] for spirits and
gods; if any tribe had some Frenchmen among them,
that was sufficient to make them feel safe from any injuries by their neighbors; and the French became mediators in all their quarrels.   The detailed conversations
which I have had with many voyageurs in those countries have supplied me with material for my accounts
of those peoples; all that they have told me about them
has so uniformly agreed that I have felt obliged to give
the public some idea of that vast region.

Sieur Perot has best known those peoples; the gover-
nors-general of Canada have always employed him in
all their schemes; and his acquaintance with the savage
tongues, his experience, and his mental ability have enabled him to make discoveries which gave opportunity
to Monsieur de la Salle to push forward all those explorations in which he achieved so great success.   It
was through his agency that the Mississippi became
known.   He rendered very important services to the

---

[209] *Gode* is defined by Bescherelle as the name of a small sea-bird on the
coast of Brittany; [the name was probably applied by the French explorers or
fishermen to some bird in Canada resembling it].   Mr. C. E. Dionne, the curator of the museum of Laval University at Quebec, says in his *Oiseaux du
Canada* that the name *gode* now belongs to the common murre or razor-billed
auk (*Alca torda*), and adds: "This bird, which is popularly called *gode*, fre-
quents the shores and islands of the north Atlantic, where it very commonly
makes its appearance.   On the American continent it is occasionally seen in
winter as far south as North Carolina.   It is common in the St. Lawrence
River and Gulf." — CRAWFORD LINDSAY, official translator for the legislature of
Quebec.

Cape "Digue" is Cape Diggs, at the northeast corner of Hudson Bay. — ED.

Colony, made known the glory of the king [of France] among those peoples, and induced them to form an alliance with us. On one occasion, among the Pouteouatemis, he was regarded as a god. Curiosity induced him to form the acquaintance of this nation, who dwelt at the foot of the Bay of Puans. They had heard of the French, and their desire to become acquainted with them in order to secure the trade with them had induced these savages to go down to Montreal, under the guidance of a wandering Outaouak who was glad to conduct them thither. The French had been described to them as covered with hair (the savages have no beards), and they believed that we were of a different species from other men. They were astonished to see that we were made like themselves, and regarded it as a present that the sky and the spirits had made them in permitting one of the celestial beings to enter their land. The old men solemnly smoked a calumet and came into his presence, offering it to him as homage that they rendered to him. After he had smoked the calumet, it was presented by the chief to his tribesmen, who all offered it in turn to one another, blowing from their mouths the tobacco-smoke over him as if it were incense. They said to him: "Thou art one of the chief spirits, since thou usest iron; it is for thee to rule and protect all men. Praised be the Sun, who has instructed thee and sent thee to our country." They adored him as a god; they took his knives and hatchets and incensed them with the tobacco-smoke from their mouths; and they presented to him so many kinds of food that he could not taste them all. "It is a spirit," they said; "these provisions that he has not tasted are not worthy of his lips." When he left the room, they insisted on carrying him upon their shoulders; the way over which he passed was made clear; they did [not]

dare look in his face; and the women and children
watched him from a distance. "He is a spirit," they
said; "let us show our affection for him, and he will have
pity on us." The savage who had introduced him to
this tribe was, in acknowledgment thereof, treated as a
captain. Perot was careful not to receive all these acts
of adoration, although, it is true, he accepted these
honors so far as the interests of religion were not concerned. He told them that he was not what they
thought, but only a Frenchman; that the real Spirit who
had made all had given to the French the knowledge of
iron, and the ability to handle it as if it were paste. He
said that that Spirit, desiring to show his pity for his
creatures, had permitted the French nation to settle in
their country in order to remove them from the blindness in which they had dwelt, as they had not known the
true God, the author of nature, whom the French
adored; that, when they had established a friendship
with the French, they would receive from the latter all
possible assistance; and that he had come to facilitate
acquaintance between them by the discoveries of the
various tribes which he was making. And, as the beaver
was valued by his people, he wished to ascertain whether
there were not a good opportunity for them to carry on
trade therein.

At that time there was war between that tribe and
their neighbors, the Malhominis. The latter, while
hunting with the Outagamis, had by mistake slain a
Pouteouatemi, who was on his way to the Outagamis.
The Pouteouatemis, incensed at this affront, deliberately tomahawked a Malhomini who was among the Puans.
In the Pouteouatemi village there were only women and
old men, as the young men had gone for the first time to
trade at Montreal; and there was reason to fear that

the Malhominis would profit by that mischance. Perot, who was desirous of making their acquaintance, offered to mediate a peace between them. When he had arrived within half a league of the [Malhomini] village, he sent a man to tell them that a Frenchman was coming to visit them; this news caused universal joy. All the youths came at once to meet him, bearing their weapons and their warlike adornments, all marching in file, with frightful contortions and yells; this was the most honorable reception that they thought it possible to give him. He was not uneasy, but fired a gun in the air as far away as he could see them; this noise, which seemed to them so extraordinary, caused them to halt suddenly, gazing at the sun in most ludicrous attitudes. After he had made them understand that he had come not to disturb their repose, but to form an alliance with them, they approached him with many gesticulations. The calumet was presented to him; and, when he was ready to proceed to the village, one of the savages stooped down in order to carry Perot upon his shoulders; but his interpreter assured them that he had refused such honors among many tribes. He was escorted with assiduous attentions; they vied with one another in clearing the path, and in breaking off the branches of trees which hung in the way. The women and children, who had heard "the spirit" (for thus they call a gun), had fled into the woods. The men assembled in the cabin of the leading war chief, where they danced the calumet to the sound of the drum. He had them all assemble next day, and made them a speech in nearly these words: "Men, the true Spirit who has created all men desires to put an end to your miseries. Your ancestors would not listen to him; they always followed natural impulses alone, without remembering that they had

their being from him. He created them to live in
peace with their fellow-men. He does not like war or
disunion; he desires that men, to whom he has given
reason, should remember that they all are brothers, and
that they have only one God, who has formed them to
do only his will. He has given them dominion over
the animals, and at the same time has forbidden them to
make any attacks on one another. He has given the
Frenchmen iron, in order to distribute it among those
peoples who have not the use of it, if they are willing
to live as men, and not as beasts. He is angry that you
are at war with the Pouteouatemis; even though it
seemed that they had a right to avenge themselves on
your young man who was among the Puans, God is
nevertheless offended at them, for he forbids vengeance,
and commands union and peace. The sun has never
been very bright on your horizon; you have always been
wrapped in the shadows of a dark and miserable existence, never having enjoyed the true light of day, as
the French do. Here is a gun, which I place before
you to defend you from those who may attack you; if
you have enemies, it will cause them terror. Here is a
porcelain collar, by which I bind you to my body; what
will you have to fear, if you unite yourselves to us, who
make guns and hatchets, and who knead iron as you do
pitch? I have united myself with the Pouteouatemis, on
whom you are planning to make war. I have come to
embrace all the men whom Onontio ["Monsieur de
Coursel" – La Potherie], the chief of all the French
who have settled in this country, has told me to join together, in order to take them under his protection.
Would you refuse his support, and kill one another
when he desires to establish peace between you? The
Pouteouatemis are expecting many articles suited to war

from the hands of Onontio. You have been so evenly matched [with them; but now] would you abandon your families to the mercy of their [fire]arms, and be at war with them against the will of the French? I come to make the discovery of [new] tribes, only to return here with my brothers, who will come with me among those people who are willing to unite themselves to us. Could you hunt in peace if we give [weapons of] iron to those who furnish us beaver-skins? You are angry against the Pouteouatemis, whom you regard as your enemies, but they are in much greater number than you; and I am much afraid that the prairie people will at the same time form a league against you."

The Father of the Malhomini who had been murdered by the Pouteouatemis arose and took the collar that Perot had given him; he lighted his calumet, and presented it to him, and then gave it to the chief and all who were present, who smoked it in turn; then he began to sing, holding the calumet in one hand, and the collar in the other. He went out of the cabin while he sang, and, presenting the calumet and collar toward the sun, he walked sometimes backwards, sometimes forward; he made the circuit of his own cabin, went past a great number of those in the village, and finally returned to that of the chief. There he declared that he attached himself wholly to the French; that he believed in the living Spirit, who had, in behalf of all the spirits, domination over all other men, who were inferior to him; that all his tribe had the same sentiments; and that they asked only the protection of the French, from whom they hoped for life and for obtaining all that is necessary to man.

The Pouteouatemis were very impatient to learn the fate of their people who had gone trading to Montreal;

they feared that the French might treat them badly, or
that they would be defeated by the Iroquois. Accordingly, they had recourse to Perot's guide, who was a
master juggler. That false prophet built himself a little
tower of poles, and therein chanted several songs,
through which he invoked all the infernal spirits to tell
him where the Pouteouatemis were. The reply was
that they were at the Oulamanistik River,[210] which is
three days' journey from their village; that they had
been well received by the French; and that they were
bringing a large supply of merchandise. This oracle
would have been believed if Perot, who knew that his
interpreter had played the juggler, had not declared that
he was a liar. The latter came to Perot, and heaped
upon him loud reproaches, complaining that he did not
at all realize what hardships his interpreter had encountered in this voyage, and that it was Perot's fault
that he had not been recompensed for his prediction.
The old men begged that Perot himself would relieve
them from their anxiety. After telling them that such
knowledge belonged only to God, he made a calculation,
from the day of their departure, of the stay that they
would probably make at Montreal, and of the time when
their return might be expected; and determined very
nearly the time when they could reach home. Fifteen
days later, a man fishing for sturgeon came to the village in great fright, to warn them that he had seen a
canoe, from which several gunshots had proceeded; this
was enough to make them believe that the Iroquois were
coming against them. Disorder prevailed throughout
the village; they were ready to flee into the woods or to
shut themselves into their fort. There was no probability that these were Iroquois, who usually make their

---

[210] The Manistique River, which, with its tributaries, waters Schoolcraft
County, Michigan. — ED.

attacks by stealth; Perot conjectured that they were
probably their own men, who were thus displaying their
joy as they came near the village. In fact, a young man
who had been sent out as a scout came back, in breath-
less haste, and reported that it was their own people who
were returning. If their terror had caused general consternation, this good news caused no less joy throughout
the village. Two chiefs, who had seen Perot blow into
his gun at the time of the first alarm, came to let him
know of the arrival of their people, and begged him always to consult his gun. All were eager to receive the
fleet. As they approached, the new-comers discharged
a salvo of musketry, followed by shouts and yells, and
continued their firing as they came toward the village.
When they were two or three hundred paces from the
shore, the chief rose in his canoe and harangued the old
men who stood at the water's edge; he gave an account
of the favorable reception which had been accorded
them at Montreal. An old man informed them, meanwhile praising the sky and the sun who had thus favored
them, that there was a Frenchman in the village who
had protected them in several times of danger; at this,
the Pouteouatemis suddenly flung themselves into the
water, to show their joy at so pleasing an occurrence.
They had taken pleasure in painting [matacher] themselves in a very peculiar manner; and the French garments, which had been intended to make them more
comfortable, disfigured them in a ludicrous fashion.
They carried Perot with them, whether or no he would,
in a scarlet blanket (Monsieur de la Salle was also honored with a like triumph at Huron Island), and made
him go around the fort, while they marched in double
files in front and behind him, with guns over their
shoulders, often firing volleys. This cortege arrived at

the cabin of the chief who had led the band, where all the old men were assembled; and a great feast of sturgeon was served. This chief then related a more detailed account of his voyage, and gave a very correct idea of French usages. He described how the trade was carried on; he spoke with enthusiasm of what he had seen in the houses, especially of the cooking; and he did not forget to exalt Onontio,[211] who had called them his children and had regaled them with bread, prunes, and raisins, which seemed to them great delicacies.

Chapter IX

Those peoples were so delighted with the alliance that they had just made that they sent deputies in every direction to inform the Islinois, Miamis,[212] Outagamis,

---

[211] Onontio was the Huron-Iroquois appellation of the governor of Canada; it was afterward extended to the governor of New York, and even to the king of France. — ED.

[212] The Miami were an Algonquian tribe, first mentioned (*Relation* of 1658) as living near the mouth of Green Bay; when first seen by the French (in Perrot's visits, 1668 and 1670) they were living at the headwaters of the Fox River — part of them, at least, living with the Mascoutens in a palisaded village there. "Soon after this, the Miami parted from the Mascoutens, and formed new settlements at the south end of Lake Michigan and on Kalamazoo River, Mich. The settlements at the south end of the lake were at Chicago and on St. Joseph River, where missions were established late in the seventeenth century." Those at Chicago were probably the Indians found there by Marquette and some others whom those writers called Wea. The Miami first found in Wisconsin must have been but a part of the tribe, which seems to have occupied territory in northeastern Illinois, northern Indiana, and western Ohio. Their chief village on St. Joseph River was said to be fifteen leagues inland; in 1703 they had also a village at Detroit, and in 1711 at Kekionga (on the Maumee; the seat of the Miami proper), and at Ouiatanon (on the Wabash; the headquarters of the Wea branch). By the encroachments of the northern tribes the Miami were driven from the St. Joseph River and the region northwest of the Wabash, and colonies of them moved eastward to the Miami and Scioto Rivers; but after the peace of 1763 they abandoned these settlements and retired to Indiana. "They took a prominent part in all the Indian wars in Ohio valley until the close of the War of 1812. Soon afterward they began to sell their lands, and by 1827 had disposed of most of their holdings in Indiana and had agreed to remove to Kansas, whence they went

Maskoutechs, and Kikabous that they had been at Montreal, whence they had brought much merchandise; they besought those tribes to visit them and bring them beavers. Those tribes were too far away to profit by this at first; only the Outagamis came to establish themselves for the winter at a place thirty leagues from the bay, in order to share in the benefit of the goods which they could obtain from the Pouteouatemis. Their hope that some Frenchmen would come from Chagouamikon induced them to accumulate as many beavers as possible. The Pouteouatemis took the southern part of the bay, the Sakis the northern; the Puans, as they could not fish, had gone into the woods to live on deer and bears. When the Outagamis had formed a village of more than six hundred cabins, they sent to the Sakis, at the beginning of spring, to let them know of the new establishment that they had formed.[213] The latter sent them some chiefs, with presents, to ask them to remain in this new settlement; they were accompanied by some Frenchmen. They found a large village, but destitute of everything.

later to Indian Territory, where the remnant still resides." One of their bands, however, continued to reside on a reservation in Wabash County, Ind., until 1872, when the land was divided among the survivors, then numbering about 300. Early writers praise the mildness, politeness, and sedateness of the Miami, and their respect and obedience to their chiefs, who had much more authority than those of other Algonquian tribes. It is impossible to make satisfactory statements of the population of the Miami, since they have been so frequently confused with the Wea and Piankashaw tribes. They have rapidly decreased since their removal to the west. "Only 57 Miami were officially known in Indian Territory in 1885, while the Wea and Piankashaw were confederated with the remnant of the Illinois under the name of Peoria, the whole body numbering but 149; these increased to 191 in 1903. The total number of Miami in 1905 in Indian Territory was 124; in Indiana, in 1900, there were 243; the latter, however, are greatly mixed with white blood. Including individuals scattered among other tribes, the whole number is probably 400."
— JAMES MOONEY and CYRUS THOMAS, in Handbook Amer. Indians.
[213] The location of this Outagami village is a matter of dispute, and thus far cannot be positively identified; but most probably it was in Waupaca County, Wis., somewhere on the Little Wolf River. Various local historical writers have placed it near Mukwa, Manawa, or New London. — ED.

Those people had only five or six hatchets, which had
no edge, and they used these, by turns, for cutting their
wood; they had hardly one knife or one bodkin to a
cabin, and cut their meat with the stones [214] which they
used for arrows; and they scaled their fish with mussel-
shells.   Want rendered them so hideous that they
aroused compassion.   Although their bodies were large,
they seemed deformed in shape; they had very disagreeable faces, brutish voices, and evil aspects.   They were

[214] "Primitive men doubtless first used stones in their natural form for throwing, striking, and abrading; but, as use continued, a certain amount of ad-
ventitious shaping of the stones employed necessarily took place, and this
probably suggested and led to intentional shaping.   Men early learned to frac-
ture brittle stones to obtain cutting, scraping, and perforating implements; and
flaking, pecking, cutting, scraping, and grinding processes served later to
modify shapes and to increase the convenience, effectiveness, and beauty of
implements.   Much has been learned of the course of progress in the stone-
shaping arts from the prehistoric remains of Europe; and studies of the work
of the native American tribes, past and present, are supplying data for a much
more complete understanding of this important branch of primitive activity."
At the time of the discovery, "the Americans north of Mexico were still well
within the stone stage of culture.   Metal had come somewhat into use, but in
no part of the country had it in a very full measure taken the place of stone.
According to the most approved views regarding Old World culture history
the metal age was not definitely ushered in until bronze and iron came into
common use, not only as shaping implements but as shaped product."   The
tribes of middle America had with stone implements constructed handsome
buildings and excellent sculptures, but north of Mexico only the Pueblo group
had made intelligent and extensive use of stone in building, except for the
limited use made of it by the mound-builders, the Eskimo and some others;
sculpture, however, was employed by many other tribes on objects used for
purposes of utility, adornment, and religion.   A great variety of stones were
utilized by the primitive workers, including several semi-precious kinds.   "The
processes employed in shaping these materials by the American tribes, and for
that matter, by the whole primitive world, are: (1) fracturing processes,
variously known as breaking, spalling, chipping, flaking; (2) crumbling processes, as battering, pecking; (3) incising or cutting processes; (4) abrading
processes, as sawing, drilling, scraping, and grinding; and (5) polishing processes. . .   The knowledge acquired in recent years through experiments in
stone-shaping processes has led unfortunately to the manufacture of fraudulent
imitations of aboriginal implements and sculptures for commercial purposes,
and so great is the skill acquired in some cases that it is extremely difficult
to detect the spurious work; thus there is much risk in purchasing objects whose
pedigree is not fully ascertained." — W. H. HOLMES, in *Handbook Amer. Indians.*

continually begging from our Frenchmen who went among them, for those savages imagined that whatever their visitors possessed ought to be given to them gratis; everything aroused their desires, and yet they had few beavers to sell. The French thought it prudent to leave to the Sakis for the winter the trade in peltries with the Outagamis, as they could carry it on with the former more quietly in the autumn.

All the tribes at the bay went to their villages after the winter, to sow their grain. A dispute occurred between two Frenchmen and an old man, who was one of the leading men among the Pouteouatemis; the former demanded payment for the goods; but he did not show much inclination to pay; sharp words arose on both sides, and they came to blows. The Frenchmen were vigorously attacked by the savages, and a third man came to the aid of his comrades. The confusion increased; that Frenchman tore the pendants from the ears of a savage, and gave him a blow in the belly which felled him so rudely that with difficulty could he rise again. At the same time the Frenchman received a blow from a war-club on his head, which caused him to fall motionless. There were great disputes among the savages in regard to the Frenchman who had just been wounded, who had rendered many services to the village. There were three families interested in this contention – those of the Red Carp, of the Black Carp, and of the Bear.[215] The head of the Bear family – an intimate friend of the Frenchman, and whose son-in-law was the chief of the Sakis – seized a hatchet, and declared

---

[215] These "families" were simply the tribal divisions now known as "clans" or "gentes;" they have been characteristic of savage society in all times and countries. Each clan had its distinctive symbol, usually a fish, bird, or other animal. — Ed.

"An American Indian clan or gens is an intertribal exogamic group of persons either actually or theoretically consanguine, organized to promote

that he would perish with the Frenchman, whom the people of the Red Carp had slain. The Saki chief, hearing the voice of his father-in-law, called his own men to arms; the Bear family did the same; and the

their social and political welfare, the members being usually denoted by a common class name derived generally from some fact relating to the habitat of the group or to its usual tutelary being. In the clan lineal descent, inheritance of personal and common property, and the hereditary right to public office and trust are traced through the female line, while in the gens they devolve through the male line. Clan and gentile organizations are by no means universal among the North American tribes; and totemism, the possession or even the worship of personal or communal totems by individuals or groups of persons, is not an essential feature of clan and gentile organizations. . . Consanguine kinship among the Iroquoian and Muskhogean tribes is traced through the blood of the woman only, and membership in a clan constitutes citizenship in the tribe, conferring certain social, political, and religious privileges, duties, and rights that are denied to aliens. By the legal fiction of adoption the blood of the alien might be changed into one of the strains of Iroquoian blood, and thus citizenship in the tribe could be conferred on a person of alien lineage." The primary social unit among these peoples is the family, comprising all the male and female progeny of a woman and of all her female descendants in the female line and of such other persons as may be adopted into this group; its head is usually the eldest woman in it. It may be composed of one or more firesides, and one or more families may (and usually do) constitute a clan; and all its land is the exclusive property of its women. Among the rights and privileges of the clans are: the right to a common clan name (which is usually that of an animal, bird, reptile, or natural object that may formerly have been regarded as a guardian deity); representation in the tribal council; its share in the communal property of the tribe; protection by the tribe; certain songs and religious observances; clan councils; adoption of aliens; a common burying-ground; the election or impeachment of chiefs by its women; a share in the religious ceremonies and public festivals of the tribe; etc. Their duties: the obligation not to marry within the clan; that of redeeming the life of a clan member which has become forfeited for homicide; to aid and defend fellow-members, and to avenge their deaths; to replace by other persons their clansmen lost or killed. "Clans and gentes are generally organized into phratries and phratries into tribes. Usually only two phratries are found in the modern organization of the tribes. . . One or more clans may compose a phratry. The clans of the phratries are regarded as brothers one to another and cousins to the other members of the phratry, and are so addressed. . . The phratry is the unit of organization of the people for ceremonial and other assemblages and festival, but as a phratry it has no officers; the chiefs and elders of the clans composing it serve as its directors." The government of a clan or gens seems to be developed from that of the family group, and in turn gives rise to the tribal government; and a confederation, such as the Iroquois League, is governed on the same principle. — J. N. B. HEWITT, in *Handbook Amer. Indians.*

wounded Frenchman began to recover consciousness. He calmed the Sakis, who were greatly enraged; but the savage who had maltreated him was compelled to abandon the village. These same Frenchmen's lives were in danger on still another occasion. One of them, who was amusing himself with some arrows, told a Saki who was bathing at the water's edge to ward off the shaft that he was going to let fly at him. The savage, who held a small piece of cloth, told him to shoot; but he was not adroit enough to avoid the arrow, which wounded him in the shoulder. He immediately called out that the Frenchman had slain him; but another Frenchman hastened to the savage, made him enter his cabin, and drew out the arrow. He was pacified by giving him a knife, a little vermilion to paint his face, and a piece of tobacco. This present was effectual; for when, at the Saki's cry, several of his comrades came, ready to avenge him on the spot, the wounded man cried, "What are you about? I am healed. Metaminens" (which means "little Indian corn" – this name they had given to the Frenchman, who was Perot himself) "has tied my hands by this ointment which you see upon my wound, and I have no more anger," at the same time showing the present that Perot had given him. This presence of mind checked the disturbance that was about to arise.

The Miamis, the Maskoutechs, the Kikabous, and fifteen cabins of Islinois came toward the bay in the following summer, and made their clearings thirty miles away, beside the Outagamis, toward the south. These peoples, for whom the Iroquois were looking, had gone southward along the Mississippi after the combat which I have mentioned.[216] Before that flight, they had seen

---

[216] Apparently a reference to the overthrow of the Winnebago by the Illinois, described in chapter vii. — ED.

knives and hatchets in the hands of the Hurons who had
had dealings with the French, which induced them to as-
sociate themselves with the tribes who already had some
union with us. They are very sportive when among
their own people, but grave before strangers; well built;
lacking in intelligence, and dull of apprehension; easily
persuaded; vain in language and behavior, and extremely selfish. They consider themselves much braver
than their neighbors; they are great liars, employing
every kind of baseness to accomplish their ends; but
they are industrious, indefatigable, and excellent pe-
destrians. For this last reason, they are called Metousce-
prinioueks, which in their language means "Walkers."

After they had planted their fields in this new settlement, they went to hunt cattle.[217] They wished to entertain the people at the bay; so they sent envoys to ask
the Pouteouatemis to visit them, and to bring the
Frenchmen, if they were still with them. But those
savages were careful not to let their guests know how
desirous their neighbors were to become acquainted
with the French; so they went away without telling the
latter, and came back at the end of a fortnight, loaded
with meat and grease. With them were some of those
new settlers, who were greatly surprised to see the
French – whom they reproached for not having come to
visit them with the Pouteouatemis. The French saw
plainly that the latter were jealous, and they recognized
the importance of becoming acquainted with those
peoples, who had come to the bay on purpose to trade
more conveniently with us. The Pouteouatemis, when
they saw that the French desired to go away with a Miami and a Maskoutech, made representations to them
that there were no beavers among those people – who,

---

[217] Buffaloes (see note 93) are here meant; they were usually called "wild
cattle" or "wild cows" by the early French explorers and writers. – Ed.

moreover, were very boorish – and even that they were in great danger of being plundered. The French took their departure, notwithstanding these tales, and in five days reached the vicinity of the village.[218] The Maskoutech sent ahead the Miami, who had a gun, with orders to fire it when he arrived there; the report of the gun was heard soon afterward. Hardly had they reached the shore when a venerable old man appeared, and a woman carrying a bag in which was a clay pot[219] filled with cornmeal porridge. More than two hundred

[218] The location of this Mascouten village is uncertain. There have been numerous attempts to identify it, the proposed sites ranging from Corning, Columbia County, to Rushford, Winnebago County; but the majority locate it in Green Lake County, perhaps the most probable conjecture being at or near Berlin. See *Jesuit Relations*, vol. liv; *Amer. Cath. Hist. Researches*, vol. xii, 31-34, 76-80, and vol. xiv, 98-100; and Wis. *Hist. Colls.*, vol. xvi, 42. – Ed.

[219] "Many of the more cultured American tribes were skilful potters. . . Within the area of the United States the art had made very considerable advance in two cultured centers – the Pueblo region of the southwest and the great mound province of the Mississippi Valley and the Gulf States. Over the remainder of North America, north of Mexico, the potter's art was limited to the making of rude utensils or was practically unknown. The Pueblo tribes of New Mexico and Arizona, as well as some of the adjacent tribes to lesser extent, still practise the art in its aboriginal form, and the Cherokee and Catawba of North and South Carolina have not yet ceased to manufacture utensils of clay, although the shapes have been much modified by contact with the whites. The Choctaw of Mississippi and the Mandan of the middle Missouri valley have but recently abandoned the art." Pottery is an art not available among nomads, and needs the sedentary life for its development. "The introduction or rise of the potter's art among primitive peoples is believed to correspond somewhat closely with the initial stages of barbarism; but this idea must be liberally interpreted, as some tribes well advanced toward higher barbarism are without it. The clay used was mixed with various tempering ingredients, such as sand or pulverized stone, potsherds, and shells; the shapes were extremely varied and generally were worked out by the hand, aided by simple modeling tools. The building of the vessel, the principal product of the potter's art, varied with the different tribes. Usually a bit of the clay was shaped into a disk for the base, and the walls were carried up by adding strips of clay until the rim was reached. When the strips were long they were carried around as a spiral coil. As the height increased the clay was allowed to set sufficiently to support the added weight. . . As a rule, the baking was done in open or smothered fires or in extremely crude furnaces, and the paste remained comparatively soft. In Central America a variety of ware was made with hard paste somewhat resembling our stoneware. Notwithstanding the remark-

stout young men came upon the scene; their hair was
adorned with headdresses of various sorts, and their

able aptness of the Americans in this art, and their great skill in modeling,
they had not achieved the wheel, nor had they fully mastered the art of
glazing. . . Women were the potters, and the product consisted mainly
of vessels for household use, although the most cultured tribes made and decorated vases for exclusively ceremonial purposes. In some communities a wide
range of articles was made, the plastic nature of the material having led to
the shaping of many fanciful forms. . . The ornamentation of vases included
the modeling of various life forms in the round and in relief, and incising,
imprinting, and stamping designs of many kinds in the soft clay. The more
advanced potters employed color in surface finish and in executing various designs. The designs were often geometric and primitive in type, but in many
sections life forms were introduced in great variety and profusion, and these
were no doubt often symbolic, having definite relation to the use of the object,
ceremonial or otherwise. Unbroken examples of earthenware are preserved
mainly through burial with the dead, and the numerous specimens in our
collections were obtained mostly from burial places. On inhabited sites the
vessels are usually broken, but even in this form they are of great value to
the archeologist for the reason that they contain markings or other features
peculiar to the tribes concerned in their manufacture. . . The tribes of the
plains did not practise the art save in its simplest forms, but the ancient
tribes of the middle and lower Mississippi Valley and the Gulf states were
excellent potters. The forms of the vessels and the styles of decoration are
exceedingly varied, and indicate a remarkable predilection for the modeling
of life forms — men, beasts, birds, and fishes; and the grotesque was much
affected. Aside from plastic embellishment, the vases were decorated in color,
and more especially in incised and stamped designs, those on the Gulf coast
presenting slight suggestions of the influence of the semi-civilized cultures of
Yucatan, Mexico, and the West Indies. The pottery of the tribes of the north
Atlantic states and Canada consists mainly of simple culinary utensils, mostly
round or conical bodied bowls and pots decorated with angular incised lines and
textile imprintings. The best examples are recovered from burial places in
central-southern New York and northern Pennsylvania — the region occupied
from the earliest times by the Iroquois. The clay tobacco pipes of this section
are unusually interesting, and display decided skill in modeling, although this
work has been influenced to some extent by the presence of the whites (Holmes).
The practical absence of pottery in the Pacific states and British Columbia is
noteworthy. . . The early and very general use of basketry and of stone
vessels in this region may have operated to retard the development of the potter's art. North of the Canadian boundary conditions were not favorable to
the development of this art, although specimens of rude earthenware are obtained from mounds and other sites" in certain regions. "The pottery of eastern
United States is reviewed at considerable length in the 20th Annual *Report*
(1903) of the Bureau of American Ethnology, with many illustrations and
numerous references (Holmes) ; and the publications of Mr. Clarence B. Moore
on his explorations in the Southern States contain much new and important

bodies were covered with tattooing in black, representing many kinds of figures; * they carried arrows and warclubs, and wore girdles and leggings of braided work. The old man held in his hand a calumet of red stone, with a long stick at the end; this was ornamented in its

information, with many illustrations. The varied ware of the Pueblo country is described in reports of the Bureau by J. and M. C. Stevenson, Cushing, Holmes, and Fewkes; by Hough in the National Museum reports, and by Nordenskjold in his work on the Cliff Dwellers of the Mesa Verde."
— W. H. HOLMES, in *Handbook Amer. Indians.*

* "Tattooing is a form of picture-writing more widespread than any other and perhaps more commonly practised. Originating in very ancient times, it persists to-day among certain classes of civilized peoples. Besides the permanent marking of the body by means of coloring matter introduced under the skin, tattooing includes scarification and body painting. Whether the practice of tattoo had its origin in a desire for personal adornment, or, as concluded by Spencer and others, as a means of tribal marks, its final purposes and significance among our Indians were found by Mallery to be various and to include the following: tribal, clan, and family marks; to distinguish between free and slave, high and low; as certificates of bravery in passing prescribed ordeals or in war; as religious symbols; as a therapeutic remedy or a prophylactic; as a certificate of marriage in the case of women, or of marriageable condition; as a personal mark, in distinction to a tribal mark; as a charm; to inspire fear in an enemy; to render the skin impervious to weapons; to bring good fortune; and as the design of a secret society." — H. W. HENSHAW, in *Handbook Amer. Indians,* art. "Pictographs." (For full and detailed description of this custom (with illustrations), see Garrick Mallery's papers on picture-writing in the fourth and tenth *Reports* of the Bureau of Ethnology.)

"Vases have been found in the mounds of the middle Mississippi Valley showing the human face with tattoo marks, some of the designs combining geometric and totemic figures. As tattooing gave a permanent line, it served a different purpose from decoration by paint. Among men it marked personal achievement, some special office, symbolized a vision from the supernatural powers, or served some practical purpose [as sometimes a mark on the arm for the purpose of measuring]. Among women the tattooing was more social in its significance," and the designs used therein are closely connected with those employed in pottery and basket-work. "The Chippewa sometimes resorted to tattooing as a means of curing pain, as the toothache. The process of tattooing was always attended with more or less ceremony; chants or songs frequently accompanied the actual work, and many superstitions were attached to the manner in which the one operated upon bore the pain or made recovery. Most tribes had one or more persons expert in the art who received large fees for their services." Among the Plains tribes steel needles were used; before these were introduced, sharp flints served the purpose. "The dyes injected to give color to the design varied in different parts of the country."
— ALICE C. FLETCHER, in *Handbook Amer. Indians.*

whole length with the heads of birds, flame-colored, and had in the middle a bunch of feathers colored a bright red, which resembled a great fan. As soon as he espied the leader of the Frenchmen, he presented to him the calumet, on the side next to the sun; and uttered words which were apparently addressed to all the spirits whom those peoples adore. The old man held it sometimes toward the east, and sometimes toward the west; then toward the sun; now he would stick the end in the ground, and then he would turn the calumet around him, looking at it as if he were trying to point out the whole earth, with expressions which gave the Frenchman to understand that he had compassion on all men. Then he rubbed with his hands Perot's head, back, legs, and feet, and sometimes his own body. This welcome lasted a long time, during which the old man made a harangue, after the fashion of a prayer, all to assure the Frenchman of the joy which all in the village felt at his arrival.

One of the men spread upon the grass a large painted ox-skin, the hair on which was as soft as silk, on which he and his comrade were made to sit. The old man struck two pieces of wood together, to obtain fire from it; but as it was wet he could not light it. The Frenchman drew forth his own fire-steel, and immediately made fire with tinder. The old man uttered loud exclamations about the iron, which seemed to him a spirit; the calumet was lighted, and each man smoked; then they must eat porridge and dried meat, and suck the juice of the green corn. Again the calumet was filled, and those who smoked blew the tobacco-smoke into the Frenchman's face, as the greatest honor that they could render him; he saw himself smoked [*boucaner*] like meat, but said not a word. This ceremony ended, a skin was spread for the Frenchman's comrade. The savages thought that it was their duty to carry the French guests; but the latter informed the Maskoutechs that, as they could shape the iron, they had strength to walk, so they were left at liberty. On the way, they rested again, and the same honors were paid to him as at the first meeting. Continuing their route, they halted near a high hill, at the summit of which was the village; they made their fourth halt here, and the ceremonies were repeated. The great chief of the Miamis came to meet them, at the head of more than three thousand men, accompanied by the chiefs of other tribes who formed part of the village. Each of these chiefs had a calumet, as handsome as that of the old man; they were entirely naked, wearing only shoes, which were artistically embroidered like buskins;[220] they sang, as they approached, the calumet song, which they uttered in

---

[220] Probably this was the embroidery with porcupine quills which formerly was so much in vogue among the northern Indians; an important reason for its decline is the fact that the porcupine (*Erethizon dorsatus*) has been almost exterminated in many regions. — ED.

Among the arts practiced by Indian women was that of embroidery worked with quills, usually those of the porcupine, sometimes those of bird feathers; "in both cases the stiffness of the quill limits freedom of design, making necessary straight lines and angular figures. The gathering of the raw materials, the hunting of porcupines or the capture of birds, was the task of the men, who also in some tribes prepared the dyes. Sorting and coloring the quills, tracing the design on dressed skin or birchbark, and the embroidering were exclusively the work of women." The dyes, which varied in different parts of the country, were compounded variously of roots, whole plants, and buds and bark of trees. The quills were usually steeped in concoctions of these until a uniform color was obtained — red, yellow, green, blue, or black." The porcupine quills were always flattened for this work, by pressing the edge between the forefinger and thumb-nail. The designs were drawn or painted on the skin or bark by means of a sort of stencil pattern, drawn on skin, bark, or paper, and cut through to form the stencil. "A woman who was skilled or had a natural gift for drawing would copy a design by the freehand method, except that she had first made some measurements in order that the pattern should be in its proper place and proportions. Some even composed designs, both the forms and the arrangement of colors, and worked them out as they embroidered. Among most tribes the awl was the only instrument used in quill-working; but the Cheyenne, Arapaho, and Sioux, the principal quill-

cadence. When they reached the Frenchmen, they continued their songs, meanwhile bending their knees, in turn, almost to the ground. They presented the calu-

---

working tribes, had a specially shaped bone for flattening, bending, and smoothing." — JAMES MOONEY.

"All designs in quillwork were made up of wide or narrow lines, each composed of a series of upright stitches lying close together. . . The stems of pipes were decorated with fine flattened quills, closely woven into a long and very narrow braid, which was wound about the wooden stem. Different colors were sometimes so disposed along the length of these braids that when they were wound around the stem they made squares or other figures. . . Porcupine quills were employed for embroidery from Maine to Virginia and west to the Rocky Mountains north of the Arkansas River. "Quills seem to have been an article of barter; hence their use was not confined to regions where the animal abounded. This style of decoration was generally put on tobacco and tinder bags, workbags, knife and paint-stick cases, cradles, amulets, the bands of burden straps, tunics, shirts, leggings, belts, arm and leg bands, moccasins, robes, and sometimes on the trappings of horses. All such objects were of dressed skin. Receptacles and other articles made of birch bark also were frequently embroidered with quills. Nearly every tribe has its peculiar cut for moccasins, often also its special style of ornamentation, and these were carefully observed by the workers. The dress of the men was more ornate than that of the women, and the decorations the women put on the former were generally related to man's employments — hunting and war. The figures were frequently designed by the men, and a man very often designated what particular figure he desired a woman to embroider on his garment. Some designs belonged exclusively to women; there were, moreover, some that were common to both sexes. The decorative figures worked on the garments of children not infrequently expressed a prayer for safety, long life, and prosperity, and usually were symbolic. There was considerable borrowing of designs by the women through the medium of gifts exchanged between tribes during ceremonial observances or visits, and thus figures that were sacred symbols in some tribes came to be used merely as ornaments by others. Some of the designs in quillwork were undoubtedly originated by men, while others were invented by women. These were frequently credited to dreams sent by the spider, who, according to certain tribal mythic traditions, was the instructor of women in the art of embroidery. Technical skill as well as unlimited patience was required to make even, smooth, and fine porcupine quillwork, and proficiency could be acquired only by practice and nice attention to details. The art seems to have reached its highest development among those tribes where the food supply was abundant and the men were the principal providers — conditions that made it possible for the women to have the leisure necessary for them to become adept in the working of quills. This art, which formerly flourished over a wide area, is rapidly dying out. It is doubtful whether any woman at the present day could duplicate the fine embroidery of a hundred years ago." — ALICE C. FLETCHER, in *Handbook Amer. Indians.*

met to the sun, with the same genuflexions, and then they came back to the principal Frenchman, with many gesticulations. Some played upon instruments the calumet songs, and others sang them, holding the calumet in the mouth without lighting it. A war chief raised Perot upon his shoulders, and, accompanied by all the musicians, conducted him to the village. The Maskoutech who had been his guide offered him to the Miamis, to be lodged among them; they very amiably declined, being unwilling to deprive the Maskoutechs of the pleasure of possessing a Frenchman who had consented to come under their auspices. At last he was taken to the cabin of the chief of the Maskoutechs;[221] as he en-

[221] Mascoutens (meaning "little prairie people") is "a term used by some early writers in a collective and indefinite sense to designate the Algonquian tribes living on the prairies of Wisconsin and Illinois . . . the name (*Mashko'tens*) is at present applied by the Potawatomi to that part of the tribe officially known as the 'Prairie band' and formerly residing on the prairies of northern Illinois." According to Ottawa tradition there was in early days a tribe called Mushkodainsug (or Mascoutens) on the east shore of Lake Michigan, who were driven by enemies farther southward, together with an allied tribe who are thought to have been the Sauk (to whom the Mascoutens were evidently closely related); and these are supposed to have entered Wisconsin together, passing around the southern end of Lake Michigan. Perrot was the first Frenchman to visit them; he was followed by Allouez (1670) and Marquette (1673), who both found them in this same village on the Fox River, living with the Miami and Kickapoo. In 1680 the Mascoutens are mentioned as living on Lake Winnebago and the Milwaukee River (probably two different bands who had wandered thither). In 1712 the upper Mascoutens and the Kickapoo joined the Foxes against the French; but at the siege of Detroit in the same year these tribes were attacked by other Indians, allies of the French, and nearly a thousand of them were killed or captured. "In 1718 the Mascoutens and Kickapoo were living together in a single village on Rock River, Ill., and were estimated together at 200 men. In 1736 the Mascoutens are mentioned as numbering 60 warriors, living with the Kickapoo on Fox River, Wis., and having the wolf and deer totems. These are among the existing gentes of the Sauk and Foxes. They were last mentioned as living in Wisconsin between 1770 and 1780; and the last definite notice of them mentions those on the Wabash in connection with the Piankashaw and Kickapoo. "After this the Mascoutens disappear from history, the northern group having probably been absorbed by the Sauk and Fox confederacy, and the southern group by the Kickapoo. Notwithstanding some commendatory ex-

tered, the lighted calumet was presented to him, which he smoked; and fifty guardsmen were provided for him, who prevented the crowd from annoying him. A grand repast was served, the various courses of which reminded one of feeding-troughs rather than dishes; the food was seasoned with the fat of the wild ox. The guards took good care that provisions should be brought often, for they profited thereby.

On the next day, the Frenchman gave them, as presents, a gun and a kettle; and made them the following speech, which was suited to their character: "Men, I admire your youths; although they have since their birth seen only shadows, they seem to me as fine-looking as those who are born in regions where the sun always displays his glory. I would not have believed that the earth, the mother of all men, could have furnished you the means of subsistence when you did not possess the light of the Frenchman, who supplies its influences to many peoples; I believe that you will become another nation when you become acquainted with him. I am the dawn of that light, which is beginning to appear in your lands, as it were, that which precedes the sun, who will soon shine brightly and will cause you to be born again, as if in another land, where you will find, more easily and in greater abundance, all that can be necessary to man. I see this fine village filled with young men, who are, I am sure, as courageous as they are well built; and who will, without doubt, not fear their enemies if they carry French weapons. It is for these young men that I leave my gun, which they must regard as the pledge of my esteem for their valor; they must use it

pressions by one or two of the early missionaries, the Mascoutens, like the Kickapoo, bore a reputation for treachery and deceit, but, like the Foxes, appear to have been warlike and restless." — JAMES MOONEY and CYRUS THOMAS, in *Handbook Amer. Indians.*

if they are attacked. It will also be more satisfactory in hunting cattle and other animals than are all the arrows that you use. To you who are old men I leave my kettle; I carry it everywhere without fear of breaking it. You will cook in it the meat that your young men bring from the chase, and the food which you offer to the Frenchmen who come to visit you." He tossed a dozen awls and knives to the women, and said to them: "Throw aside your bone bodkins; these French awls will be much easier to use. These knives will be more useful to you in killing beavers and in cutting your meat than are the pieces of stone that you use." Then, throwing to them some rassade:[222] "See; these will better adorn your children and girls than do their usual ornaments."

[222] *Rassade* was a French term for beads of the round sort; they were made of porcelain and of glass, both white and in various colors. The long tubular beads were known as *canons*. — Ed.

Beads, of many kinds and materials, formed a valued class of ornaments among the Indians. "All were made from mineral, vegetal, or animal substances; and after the discovery the introduction of beads of glass or porcelain, as well as that of metal tools for making the old varieties, greatly multiplied their employment." They were of many sizes and shapes — round, tubular, or flat; and some of the cylinders were several inches long. Seeds, nuts, and sections of stems and roots were used as beads; but "far the largest share of beads were made from animal materials — shell, bone, horn, teeth, claws, and ivory." In their manufacture much taste and manual skill were developed. They were used for personal adornment in many forms and combinations, and formed a prominent feature in the embellishment of ceremonial costumes; and were "attached to bark and wooden vessels, matting, basketry, and other textiles. They were woven into fabrics or wrought into network. . . They were also largely employed as gifts and as money, also as tokens and in records of hunts or of important events, such as treaties. They were conspicuous accessories in the councils of war and peace, in the conventional expression of tribal symbolism, and in traditional story-telling, and were offered in worship. They were regarded as insignia of functions, and were buried, often in vast quantities, with the dead." In the eastern part of Canada and the United States beads were largely made from shells. "In the north small white and purple cylinders, called wampum, served for ornament and were used in elaborate treaty belts and as a money standard, also flat disks an inch or more in width being bored through their long diameters. The Cherokee name for beads and money is the same. Subsequently imitated by the colonists, these beads received a fixed value. The mound-builders and other tribes of the

The Miamis said, by way of excuse for not having any beaver-skins, that they had until then roasted those animals.

That alliance began, therefore, through the agency of Sieur Perot. A week later the savages made a solemn feast, to thank the sun for having conducted him to their village. In the cabin of the great chief of the Miamis an altar had been erected, on which he had caused to be placed a Pindiikosan. This is a warrior's pouch, filled with medicinal herbs wrapped in the skins of animals, the rarest that they can find; it usually contains all that inspires their dreams. Perot, who did not approve this altar, told the great chief that he adored a God who forbade him to eat things sacrificed to evil spirits or to the skins of animals. They were greatly surprised at this, and asked if he would eat provided they shut up their Manitous; this he consented to do. The chief begged Perot to consecrate him to his Spirit, whom he would thenceforth acknowledge; he said that he would prefer that Spirit to his own, who had not taught them to make hatchets, kettles, and all else that men need; and he hoped that by adoring him they would obtain all the knowledge that the French had. This chief governed his people as a sort of sovereign; he had his guards, and whatever he said or ordered was regarded as law.

Mississippi Valley and the Gulf States used pearls, and beads of shells, seeds, and rolled copper. Canine teeth of the elk were most highly esteemed, recently being worth fifty cents to one dollar each. They were carefully saved, and a garment covered with them was valued at as much as six hundred or eight hundred dollars. . . After the colonization cradles and articles of skin were profusely covered with beadwork replete with symbolism."
— OTIS T. MASON, in *Handbook Amer. Indians.*

"The true needle with an eye was extremely rare among the Indians, the awl being the universal implement for sewing. The needle and needle-case came to be generally employed only after the advent of the whites, although bone needles three to five inches long are common in Ontario and the Iroquois area of New York." — WALTER HOUGH, in *Handbook Amer. Indians.*

The Pouteouatemis, jealous that the French had found the way to the Miamis, secretly sent a slave to the latter, who said many unkind things about the French; he said that the Pouteouatemis held them in the utmost contempt, and regarded them as dogs. The French, who had heard all these abusive remarks, put him into a condition where he could say no more outrageous things; the Miamis regarded the spectacle with great tranquillity. When it was time to return to the bay, the chiefs sent all their young men to escort the Frenchmen thither, and made them many presents. The Pouteouatemis, having learned of the Frenchman's arrival, came to assure him of the interest they felt in his safe return, and were very impatient to know whether the tribes from whom he had come had treated him well. But when they heard the reproaches which he uttered for their sending a slave who had said most ungenerous things regarding the French nation, they attempted to make an explanation of their conduct, but fully justified the poor opinion which he already had of them. The savages have this characteristic, that they find a way to free themselves from blame in any evil undertaking, or to make it succeed without seeming to have taken part in it.

Chapter X

It was for the interest of the Pouteouatemis to keep on good terms with the French; and they had been too well received at Montreal not to return thither. Indeed, after having presented to Perot a bag of Indian corn, that he might, they said, "eat and swallow the suspicion that he felt toward them," and five beaver robes to serve as an emetic for the ill-will and vengeance which he might retain in his heart, they sent some of their people on a journey to Montreal. When they came in sight of Michilimakinak, which then was frequented only by them and the Iroquois, they perceived smoke. While they were trying to ascertain what this meant, they encountered two Iroquois, and saw another canoe off shore. Each party was alarmed at the other; as for the Iroquois, they took to flight, while the Pouteouatemis, plying their paddles against contrary winds, fled to their own village; they felt an extraordinary anxiety, for they knew not what measures to take for protection against the Iroquois. All the peoples of the bay experienced the same perplexity. Their terror was greatly increased when, a fortnight later, they saw large fires on the other shore of the bay, and heard many gun-shots. As a climax to their fears, the scouts whom they had sent out brought back the news that they had seen at night many canoes made in Iroquois fashion, in one of which was a gun, and a blanket of Iroquois material; and some men, who were sleeping by a fire. All those canoes came in sight the next morning, and each one fled, at the top of his speed, into the forest; only the most courageous took the risk of awaiting, with resolute air, the Iroquois in their fort, where they had good firearms. As we were at peace with the Iroquois, some of the bolder spirits among our Frenchmen offered to go to meet that so-called army, in order to learn the motive which could have impelled them to come to wage war against the allies of Onontio. They were greatly surprised to find that it was a fleet of Outaouaks, who had come to trade; these people had, while traveling across the country, built some canoes which resembled those of the Iroquois. The men whom the Pouteouatemis had seen at Michilimakinak were really Iroquois; but they had feared falling into the hands of the Pouteouatemis quite as much

as the latter had feared them. The Iroquois, while
fleeing, fell into an ambuscade of forty Sauteurs, who
carried them away to the Sauteur village; they had come
from a raid against the Chaouanons [223] near Carolina,

[223] The French form of Shawnee (an Algonkin name meaning "south-
erners"), "formerly a leading tribe of South Carolina, Tennessee, Pennsylvania, and Ohio. By reason of the indefinite character of their name, their
wandering habits, their connection with other tribes, and because of their
interior position away from the traveled routes of early days, the Shawnee
were long a stumbling block in the way of investigators. . . The tradition
of the Delawares, as embodied in the *Walum Olum*, makes themselves, the
Shawnee, and the Nanticoke, originally one people, the separation having
taken place after the traditional expulsion of the Talligewi (Cherokee) from
the north, it being stated that the Shawnee went south. The close similarity
of dialect would bear out the statement as to relationship. Beyond this it is
useless to theorize on the origin of the Shawnee or to strive to assign them any
earlier location than that in which they were first known and where their
oldest traditions place them — the Cumberland basin in Tennessee, with an
outlying colony on the middle Savannah in South Carolina. In this position,
as their name may imply, they were the southern advance-guard of the
Algonquian stock. Their real history begins in 1669-1670. They were then
living in two bodies at a considerable distance apart, and these two divisions
were not fully united until nearly a century later, when the tribe settled in
Ohio. The attempt to reconcile conflicting statements without a knowledge of
this fact has occasioned much of the confusion in regard to the Shawnee. The
apparent anomaly of a tribe living in two divisions at such a distance from
each other is explained when we remember that the intervening territory was
occupied by the Cherokee, who were at that time the friends of the Shawnee.
The evidence afforded by the mounds shows that the two tribes lived together
for a considerable period, both in South Carolina and Tennessee, and it is a
matter of history that the Cherokee claimed the country vacated by the Shawnee
in both states after the removal of the latter to the north. . . The Shawnee
of South Carolina, who appear to have been the Piqua division of the tribe,
were known to the early settlers of that state as Savannahs, that being nearly
the form of the name in use among the neighboring Muskhogean tribes." The
Shawnee removed to the north apparently through dissatisfaction with the
English colonists, who were allies of the Catawba, enemies of the Shawnee;
"their removal from South Carolina was gradual, beginning about 1677 and
continuing at intervals through a period of more than thirty years. . . Permission to settle on the Delaware was granted by the colonial government
on condition of their making peace with the Iroquois, who then received them
as 'brothers,' while the Delawares acknowledged them as their 'second sons,'
i.e., grandsons. The Shawnee to-day refer to the Delawares as their grand-
fathers. From this it is evident that the Shawnee were never conquered by the
Iroquois, and, in fact, we find the western band a few years previously assist-
ing the Miami against the latter." Some of the migrating Shawnee joined

and had brought with them a captive from that tribe, whom they were going to burn. The Sauteurs set him at liberty, and enabled him to return to the bay by entrusting him to the Sakis. This man gave them marvelous notions of the South Sea, from which his village was distant only five days' journey – near a great river which, coming from the Islinois, discharges its waters into that sea.[224] The tribes of the bay sent him home with much merchandise, urging him to persuade his tribesmen to come and visit them.

These peoples held several councils, to deliberate whether they should go down to Montreal; they hesitated at first, because they had so few beavers. As the savages give everything to their mouths, they preferred

---

the Mohican and became a part of that tribe; and those who had settled on the Delaware afterward removed to the Wyoming Valley, and formed their village near the present town of Wyoming. The Delawares and Munsee followed them in 1742, and made their village on the opposite bank of the Susquehanna; about fifteen years later the Shawnee quarreled with the Delawares, and joined their tribesmen on the upper Ohio, soon becoming allies of the French. The Cumberland (or western) division of the Shawnee seem never to have crossed the Alleghanies to the eastward. Their principal village was on the Cumberland River, near the present Nashville, Tenn. "They seem also to have ranged northeastward to the Kentucky River, and southward to the Tennessee. It will thus be seen that they were not isolated from the great body of the Algonquian tribes, as has frequently been represented to have been the case, but simply occupied an interior position, adjoining the kindred Illinois and Miami, with whom they kept up constant communication. . . These western Shawnee are mentioned about the year 1672 as being harassed by the Iroquois, and also as allies of the Andastes, or Conestoga, who were themselves at war with the Iroquois;" and the two tribes were probably allies against the Iroquois. It is in 1684 that we find the first reliable mention of the Shawnee (evidently the western bands) in the country north of the Ohio; and they finally abandoned the Cumberland Valley soon after 1714, in consequence of a war between them and the Cherokee and Chickasaw – finally (about 1730) collecting along the north bank of the Ohio, from the Allegheny to the Scioto. Soon after 1750 they were joined by their kindred from the Susquehanna, the first time in their history when the divisions were united. – *Handbook Amer. Indians.*

[224] A reference to the Gulf of Mexico and the Mississippi River – then, however, supposed to flow into the Pacific Ocean (then called the South Sea). – ED.

to devote themselves to hunting such wild beasts as could furnish subsistence for their families, rather than seek beavers, of which there were not enough; they preferred the needs of life to those of the state. Nevertheless, they reflected that if they allowed the Frenchmen to go away without themselves going down to trade, it might happen that the latter would thereafter attach themselves to some other tribes; or, if they should afterward go to Montreal, the governor would feel resentment against them because they had not escorted these Frenchmen thither. They decided that they would go with the Frenchmen; preparations for this were accordingly made, and a solemn feast was held; and on the eve of their departure a volley of musketry was fired in the village. Three men sang incessantly, all night long, in a cabin, invoking their spirits from time to time. They began with the song of Michabous; then they came to that of the god of lakes, rivers, and forests, begging the winds, the thunder, the storms, and the tempests to be favorable to them during the voyage. The next day, the crier went through the village, inviting the men to the cabin where the feast was to be prepared. They found no difficulty in going thither, each furnished with his Ouragan and Mikouen ["his dish and spoon" – La Potherie]. The three musicians of the previous night began to sing; one was placed at the entrance of the cabin, another in the middle, and the third at its end; they were armed with quivers, bows, and arrows, and their faces and entire bodies were blackened with coal. While the people sat in this assembly, in the utmost quiet, twenty young men – entirely naked, elaborately painted [matachez] * and wearing girdles of otter-skin,

---

* "The tribes north of Mexico, as well as those of every part of the continent except, perhaps, the higher arctic regions, delighted in the use of color. It was very generally employed for embellishing the person and in applying

to which were attached the skins of crows, with their plumage, and gourds – lifted from the fires ten great kettles; then the singing ceased. The first of these actors next sang his war-song, keeping time with it in a dance from one end to the other of the cabin, while all the savages cried in deep guttural tones, "Hay, hay!" When the musician ended, all the others uttered a loud yell, in which their voices gradually died away, much as a loud noise disappears among the mountains. Then the second and the third musicians repeated, in turn, the same performance; and, in a word, nearly all the savages did the same, in alternation – each singing his own song, but no one venturing to repeat that of another, unless he were willing deliberately to offend the one who had composed the song, or unless the latter were dead (in order to exalt, as it were, the dead man's name by appropriating his song). During this, their looks were accompanied with gestures and violent movements; and some of them took hatchets, with which they pretended to strike the women and children who were watching them. Some took firebrands, which they tossed about everywhere; others filled their dishes with red-hot coals, which they threw at each other. It is difficult to make the reader understand the details of feasts of this sort, unless he has himself seen them. I was present at a like entertainment among the Iroquois at the Sault of Mon-

---

decorative and symbolic designs to habitations, sculptures, masks, shields, articles of bark, skin, pottery, etc., in executing pictographs upon natural surfaces of many kinds, as on cliffs and the walls of caverns, and in preparing the symbolic embellishments of altars and the sacred chambers. Color was applied to the person for decorative purposes as an essential feature of the toilet; for impressing beholders with admiration or fear; for purposes of obscurity and deception; in applying tribal, personal, or other denotive devices; in the application of symbolic designs, especially on ceremonial occasions; and as a means of protection from insects and the sun. The native love of color and skill in its use were manifested especially in decorative work." The pigments were both mineral and vegetal, and the aborigines were skilled in preparing them. — W. H. HOLMES, in *Handbook Amer. Indians*, art. "Painting."

treal, and it seemed as if I were in the midst of hell. After most of those who had been invited to this pleasant festival had sung, the chief of the feast, who had given the dance, sang a second time; and he said at the end of his song (which he improvised) that he was going to Montreal with the Frenchmen, and was on that account offering these prayers to their God, entreating him to be propitious to him on the voyage, and to render him acceptable to the French nation. The young men who had taken off the kettles took all the dishes, which they filled with food, while the three chanters [*chantres de la nuit*, "night-birds"] repeated their first songs, not finishing their concert until everything had been eaten – a feat which did not take long to accomplish. An old man arose and congratulated, in the most affable manner, the chief of the feast on the project which he had formed, and encouraged the young men to follow him. All those who wished to go on the voyage laid down a stick; there were enough people to man thirty canoes. At the Sault, they joined seventy other canoes, of various tribes, all of whom formed a single fleet.

These voyageurs, passing through the Nepicing [Lake], found only a few Nepicirinien [225] old men, and some women and children, the young men being at Montreal for trading. Those people concealed the resentment that they felt at not hearing any mention [by their

---

[225] The Nipissing (an Algonquian tribe) lived about the lake of that name (meaning "little water or lake") until about 1650, when they were attacked by the Iroquois and many of their number slain; then they fled to Lake Nipigon for a time. By 1671 they had returned to Lake Nipissing, and later part of the tribe went to Three Rivers, and some settled at Oka (where they still live), the village of the converted Iroquois. They were a comparatively unwarlike people, firm friends to the French, and ready to accept the teachings of the Catholic missionaries. They were semi-nomadic, spending the winters among the Hurons to fish and hunt; cultivated the soil but little, and traded with the northern tribes. — JAMES MOONEY, in *Handbook Amer. Indians.*

visitors] of paying their toll, because there were some Frenchmen, whom they were therefore very willing to treat with consideration; meanwhile they entertained the latter, as they were the most prominent men in the fleet. The guests halted an entire day, in order to conform to the usual custom of the savages who accord to their allies this right of hospitality. Next day the fleet passed through the Nepicing, and on the following day they descried some people in canoes, who uttered cries for the dead. All the fleet made for the shore, in order to wait for them; they reported that the pest was making great havoc in our colony, and they said too much about it not to frighten the more credulous of the travelers, who desired to give up their voyage. The Outaouaks, who saw all the canoes of these false alarmists arrive gradually, were surprised that they were in so good condition, and that they were so laden with merchandise. The [real] motive of those people was, to obtain at a moderate price, for themselves, the peltries belonging to the others, in order to spare themselves from going out hunting; but they did not dare to disclose their design. The savages are sufficiently politic not to seem to distrust one another; and in regard to news that is announced to them they always suspend their opinions, without letting it appear that often they think the informant is not telling the truth.

Le Brochet and Le Talon, two of the most prominent of the Outaouak chiefs, mistrusting that the Nepiciriniens might be longing to beguile the Kristinaux and the inland tribes, in order to plunder them or else compel them to pay the toll, inquired of some Frenchmen if there was any probability that the pest was at Montreal. The Outaouaks were undeceived. The Mississakis, the Kristinaux, and the Gens de Terre, easy to persuade,

yielded to the opinion of the Nepiciriniens; and the coolness of their behavior was very apparent. A Nepicirinien, meanwhile, encountering a Frenchman, told him
that every one was dying [in the colony]; and the
Frenchman answered him jestingly: "What! the French,
who are enlightened people, and who know what
is suitable for the cure of every kind of disease,
they are all dying; and you who are ignorant
are living?" The Nepicirinien replied to him. "Our
spirits have preserved us." "Your spirits," the Frenchman answered, "are incapable of that, and are no
better able to do you any good. It is the God of
the French who has done everything for you, and who
supplies your needs, although you do not deserve
it. You are liars; you are trying to deceive and
abuse the people who come down the river, so as to
plunder them, as you have always done. As the number
of men in this fleet is so great as to hinder you from doing
that, you are making them afraid, by trying to persuade
them that all the French people are dying from an
imaginary disease. Know that Onontio sent me a letter
when I was at the bay, in which he ordered me to have
all the tribes go down [to Montreal], as he wished to
see them." And, drawing from his pocket an old piece
of paper on which there was writing, which he feigned
to be from Monsieur Coursel, he said to him: "[You
may] oppose [this voyage], Nepicirinien; but if this
fleet goes back I shall continue my journey;" and the
Frenchman declared that he would make known to
Onontio the opposition that the other had made to this
fleet, and how he had hindered the accomplishment of
Onontio's purpose. The Nepiciriniens disguised their
knavish tricks as best they could, and said that in fact the
maladies had ceased when they left [the colony].

All those peoples went down to Montreal, where they
were not very well satisfied with the trading; the great
quantity of peltries caused the buyers to try to get them
very cheaply. Moreover, not only had the Nepiciriniens carried away the greater part of the merchandise,
but those who held the rest of it tried to make their profits from an opportunity so favorable; the savages
murmured at this, and even a disturbance occurred; they
cudgeled a sentinel, whose gun they took away, and
broke his sword. Some chiefs, who had caused this se-
dition, were arrested. A number of Iroquois who had
come to negotiate a peace, delighted at this hubbub, were
very desirous that the minds of people should be further
exasperated, so that they could secure an opportunity of
coming to hostilities with those tribes; they all hastened
at the report of the disturbance, and offered their services to the French. The Outaouaks, who as yet had no
acquaintance with firearms, saw very plainly that they
were not the stronger party. The Pouteouatemis were
the most discreet, and, although they were not entangled
in the midst of these troubles, they were continually
dreading lest some disagreeable consequences would
happen to them. As at that time a general peace with
the Iroquois was being discussed, the commandant at
Montreal made the Outaouaks go down to Quebec, that
they might be witnesses of what should take place for
the benefit of all the allied tribes. The Pouteouatemis,
who had as yet visited the colony but once, were very
glad at being included in this visit.

Chapter XI

The peace was made, accordingly, in 1666; and people
began to enjoy this tranquillity, which enabled every
one to live prosperously on his own lands, and to trade

among our allies with safety. In truth, nothing was more melancholy than to dwell in the continual anxiety that one might have his scalp torn off at the door of his own house, or be carried away from it among those barbarians, who burned the most of their captives.

It was, besides, for the interest of the colony to make known the glory of the king among all the peoples of the south, of the west, and of the north. The alliance which was beginning to gain footing could not better be strengthened than by assuring them, in their own country, of inviolable protection; and in fact, a little while after those peoples had gone back to their own country, Monsieur Talon, the intendant of Canada, sent thither in 1667 a delegate, with Sieur Perot, who was considered the most competent man to conduct this business. They set out with orders to go to take possession, in the name of the king, of all the country of the Outaouaks. The Saut de Sainte Marie, about the 46th degree of latitude, was the place where the general assemblies of all the tribes were held, and thus there was no locality where this matter could be transacted with more éclat. They spent five or six months in notifying the tribes, but none consented except the Puans. Perot decided to go among them himself; but he met Father Aloüet, a Jesuit, who had wintered there [at the Bay], with some Frenchmen, who had encountered there all possible annoyances. Those peoples had been so offended because the French at Montreal had sold them merchandise at an excessive price that, in order to recoup themselves, they sold their beaver pelts at a triple price to the Frenchmen who went among them. But Perot, without heeding the affronts that his compatriots had received from them, concluded to go there. He arrived at the bay in that same year in the month of May, and, finding that they were out fish-

ing, he invited them to return to their village, where he
had something important to communicate to them.
After they had reached the village, he explained to them
the motive which had brought him among them; and
they consented, without making any objection, to be
present at the [ceremony of] taking possession. It was
still necessary to interest the Outagamis, the Miamis,
the Maskoutechs, the Kikabous, and the Islinois in the
plan. The Pouteouatemis gave him an escort, because
the Nadouaissioux had, several days before, [killed]
twelve Maskoutechs who were fishing along their river.
When he was four leagues distant from their village, he
made known to them his arrival; and the chief of the
Miamis immediately gave orders that his people should
go in warlike array to receive Perot at a place half a
league away. At once they marched, in order of battle,
decked with handsome ornaments of feathers, and
armed with quivers, bows, arrows, and clubs, as if they
had intended to fight a battle. They all marched in
single file, their clubs uplifted, and from time to time
uttered yells. The Pouteouatemis, having perceived this
advance, told him that the Miamis were receiving him
in martial fashion, and that he must imitate them. Immediately he placed himself at their head, and they
rushed upon the Miamis with their guns loaded with
powder, as if to check their advance. The head of the
file of Miamis passed to the left, making a circuit of
five hundred paces in order to surround them, each man
keeping at the same distance from those in front and behind him; the head of the file joined the rear, and the
Pouteouatemis found themselves all hemmed in. The
Miamis, uttering a terrible yell, suddenly came pouring
upon them, firing all those arrows above their heads;
and when they were almost near enough to deal each

other blows, the Miamis came on as if to attack them with their clubs. The Pouteouatemis fired a volley from their muskets, preceded by frightful cries, over the others, and then all mingled together. Such was the reception by those peoples, who then, with the calumets, made their guests enter the village.

The Frenchman went to the house of the chief of all those tribes, and the others were scattered among the houses of the Miamis. The chief of the Miamis commanded fifty warriors to act as a guard and wait upon him; and several days later entertained him with the game of crosse, in this manner.

More than two thousand persons assembled in a great plain, each with his racket; and a wooden ball, as large as a tennis-ball, was thrown into the air. Then all that could be seen was the flourishes and motion through the air of all those rackets, which made a noise like that of weapons which is heard in a battle. Half of all those savages endeavored to send the ball in the direction of the northwest, the length of the plain, and the others tried to make it go to the southeast; the strife, which lasted half an hour, was doubtful. Games of this sort are usually followed by broken heads, arms, and legs; and often persons are killed therein without any other injury occurring to them. This exercise ended, a woman came to him, in the utmost grief at the sickness of her son; and she asked the Frenchman if, since he was a spirit, he had not power to heal him. The sick man was attacked by a pain in the stomach, through having eaten too much at a feast (which is only too common among them); Perot gave him a dose of theriac.[226] This remedy was so beneficial that at once it was reported among

---

[226] Theriacs were a kind of medicine highly esteemed during the middle ages; they were composed of opium, flavored with nutmeg, cardamom, cinnamon, and mace — or sometimes with saffron and ambergris. — ED.

them that he had brought a dead person to life. The result was, that the great chief and two of the most prominent men among them came to awaken the Frenchman during the night, and made him a present of ten beaver robes, in order to induce him to give them some of this remedy. He excused himself, saying that he had very little of it, and refused the robes. Moreover, he told them that he could not do without the remedy in a voyage wherein he might encounter so many dangers, but they begged it from him even more urgently; and they asked him to permit them at least to smell it. This odor seemed to them so delightful that they believed that they would almost become immortal by rubbing the chest with this remedy. The Frenchman was compelled to accept the robes, so as not to make the chief more angry. It is their custom to make presents to those who have spirits (thus they call remedies), which they believed could not produce their effect if one refused their presents. The Frenchman therefore gave them half of the theriac that he had.

It was time to return to the Pouteouatemis; the great chief, accompanied by fifty warriors, intended to go to attend this act of taking possession, but the wind grew so violent upon the lake that they were compelled to give up the voyage. The chief asked the Pouteouatemis to act and respond for him, and for the peoples who were united to his own.

All the chiefs of the bay, those of Lake Huron and Lake Superior, and the people of the north, not to mention several other tribes, came to the Saut at the end of May. These peoples being assembled, a stake was planted, and presents were made to them in behalf of his majesty. They were asked if they would acknowledge, as his subjects, the great Onontio of the French, our sovereign and our king, who offered them his protection; and, if they had not yet decided [to do that], never to acknowledge any other monarch than him. All the chiefs replied, by reciprocal presents, that they held nothing dearer than the alliance with the French and the special regard of their great chief, who lived beyond that great lake the ocean; and they implored his support, without which they could no longer maintain life. Sieur Perot, at the same time causing the soil to be dug into three times, said to them: "I take possession of this country in the name of him whom we call our king; this land is his, and all these peoples who hear me are his subjects, whom he will protect as his own children; he desires that they live in peace, and he will take in hand their affairs. If any enemies rise up against them, he will destroy them; if his children have any disputes among themselves, he desires to be the judge in these."

The [governor's] delegate then attached to the stake an iron plate on which the arms of the king were painted; he drew up an official report of the transaction, which he made all the peoples sign [by their chiefs], who for their signatures depict the insignia of their families; some of them drew a beaver, others an otter, a sturgeon, a deer, or an elk. Other reports were drawn up, which were signed only by the Frenchmen who took part in the act. One of these was dextrously slipped between the wood and the iron plate, which remained there but a short time; for hardly had the crowd separated when they drew out the nails from the plate, flung the document into the fire, and again fastened up the arms of the king—fearing that the written paper was a spell, which would cause the deaths of all those who dwelt in or should visit that district. The delegate had

orders to go, after the act of taking possession, to make
the discovery of a copper mine at Lake Superior, in the
river Antonagan; but his conduct in this enterprise was
so irregular, to use no stronger expression, that I will
content myself with stating that he was sent to Cadie,[227]
in order to send him back to France.

The discovery of the Southern Sea was an undertaking on which Monsieur Talon had set his heart, and he
cast his eyes on Sieur Joliet to make this attempt.   He
had traveled in the Outaouak country; and the knowledge of those regions which he already possessed was
sufficient to give him enough guidance to make this
discovery.   His voyage was one long series of adventures, which alone would fill a volume; but, to cut the
matter short, he penetrated as far as the Akancas, who
dwell three hundred leagues from the mouth of the
Mississippi.[228]   The Illinois who had accompanied him
brought him back by another route, shorter by two hundred leagues, and had him enter the Saint Joseph River,
where Monsieur de la Sale had begun a settlement.

The renown of the French was then made known in
the most remote countries; and it was something altogether extraordinary to the peoples therein to hear
frequent mention of a new nation, so opulent, from
which they obtained so many advantages.   What did
not the Chaouanons undertake, on the mere report of
the man who had been delivered from the hands of the
Iroquois, and whom the Pouteouatemis sent back to his
home laden with French merchandise!   They knew that
among those [northern] tribes there were some people

227 Cadie is only a shortened form of Acadie (Acadia), a name somewhat
vaguely applied at first, but generally referring to Nova Scotia. — ED.

228 An allusion to the voyage (1673) of Joliet and Marquette, who discovered the Mississippi River and explored its course as far as the Arkansas. — ED.

who were called French, who had shown themselves
more sociable than those of their own region, and who
were furnishing all sorts of merchandise. This was
enough to induce them to profit by this advantage; and
forty warriors actually departed, to settle near the Pouteouatemis. During their journey they surprised some
Iroquois who were going to make an attack at the Bay of
Puans; and of these they killed or captured several.
They passed through a village of Miamis, who welcomed them in so friendly a manner that they could not
refrain from giving them their Iroquois captives. The
Miamis sent these captives to the Outagamis to be eaten,
in reprisal for the Iroquois having carried away, a short
time before, the people of five [Miami?] cabins. The
Outagamis, seeing that this conjuncture was favorable
for making an exchange of captives, sent an embassy to
the Iroquois.

When the ambassador had crossed [Lake] Micheigan,
he encountered eight hundred Iroquois who were coming as a war-party, to attack the first village that they
might light upon. The Iroquois then could not forbear
to calm their resentment; they promised the ambassador
that from that time there would be a barrier between his
people and allies, and their own; and that the river of
Chigagon [229] should be the limit of their raids. They
sent him back with presents, giving him as companions
one of their principal men with a young warrior; and

[229] Chicago (a Sauk-Fox appellation derived from *shekagua*, "skunk") was
an important locality from an early date; a Miami village was situated there
when the first French explorers visited that region, and it was the seat of the
Jesuit mission of St. Joseph. Chicago was also the name of a chief of the
Illinois about 1725. — *Handbook Amer. Indians.*

Cadillac says in his "Relation of Missilimakinak" (1718), section v: "The
post of Chicagou comes next. The name means *Rivière de l'ail* [Garlic
River], because it produces that plant in very great quantities, wild and without cultivation." This may refer to the wild garlic (*Allium*); but some writers
suppose it to mean skunk-cabbage (*Symplocarpus fœtidus*). — ED.

at the same time they turned their weapons against the Chaouanons.

This [Iroquois] chief passed through the Miamis, the Maskoutechs, and the Kikabous, where he was received with the honors of the calumet, and loaded with presents of beaver-skins. Those peoples deputed two Miamis to accompany him on his return, in order to treat with the Iroquois for peace. He came among the Outagamis, who exerted themselves to give him proofs of their esteem; and finally he arrived at the bay, where the tribes did not fail to show him the happiness that they felt at his being one of their friends. They presented to him peltries, and two large canoes for transporting the presents which he had received on every side. The Miamis who accompanied the Iroquois followed the lake, and passed the grand Portage of Ganateitiagon, by which they reached Lake Frontenac and Kenté, where there was a French mission and a large village of Iroquois.[230] They went from there to Fort Frontenac, where Monsieur de la Sale was; he gave them many presents, assuring them that he was going to visit them in their own country.

That army of Iroquois was divided into two; six hundred went against the Chaouanons, and two hundred followed the river of Chigagon – where they encountered some Islinois who were returning from Michilimakinak with some Outaouaks, and captured or killed nineteen of them. The Islinois, when they heard of this blow, checked their resentment; they could have gone to attack the Iroquois, but they sent to Onontio (who at

---

[230] On Quinté (Kenté) Bay, on the north side of Lake Ontario, there was a colony of Cayugas, among whom the Sulpitians of Montreal founded a mission (1668); five years later the Recollect fathers took charge of this field (*Jesuit Relations*, vol. l, 326, and vol. li, 290). Fort Frontenac was at the site of the present Kingston, Ont., a place which was called Katarakoui by the Iroquois. — ED.

the time was Monsieur de Frontenac, who had arrived in Canada in 1672), a package of beaver-skins, by which they made complaint that the Iroquois had violated the peace. They said that, through fear of displeasing him, they had refrained from going to find the Iroquois and fighting them; but, nevertheless, they asked him for justice. This new governor sent them a collar by Monsieur de la Forest,[231] who directed them to defend themselves in case they were again attacked; but he told them not to set out on the war-path to encounter the enemy in their own country.

It is useless to make peace with the Iroquois; when they can surprise any one alone, they grant him no quarter.

Chapters XII-XIV

[SYNOPSIS: Chapter xii relates the proceedings of Chevalier de la Salle; in 1676 he visited all the great lakes except Superior, and established friendly relations with the tribes about their shores. On Lake Michigan he constructed a fort, as a center for trading with the Indians; and he shipped a large consignment of pelts to Montréal. In August, 1679, he embarked from Niagara with much merchandise, on a ship which he built there, and safely arrived at Michilimakinak. The Indians were alarmed at this success, forming the idea that if the French could come among them with ships their freedom would be in peril, and that the French would make slaves of them. They dissembled their anger, however, and plotted secretly to destroy the ship,

[231] Guillaume de la Forest was a lieutenant of La Salle, and held command for him at Fort Frontenac until 1685, when he joined Henri de Tonty in Illinois. These two officers obtained permission to engage in the fur trade, which was revoked in 1702, and La Forest was ordered back to Canada. In 1710 he replaced Cadillac as commandant at Detroit, where he died four years later. — ED.

kill all the French, and place themselves under the protection of the English. "They sent deputies in all haste to the Islinois, and to the tribes who dwelt along the route, to advise them to beware of the French. They sent this word to those peoples: 'We are dead; our families and yours will be henceforth reduced to servitude by the French, who will make them cultivate the ground, and without doubt will yoke them as they do their cattle. They have come to Michilimakinak in a fort that floats on the water, which cannot be entered unless they are taken by surprise. This fort has wings, which it can [use] when it sets out to destroy any people. It is to go to the Islinois by way of the lakes, and all the French who trade here are going into their great canoe; and they will be strong enough to make slaves of us all, unless we prevent their undertaking. We are acquainted with the English, who furnish merchandise to us at a more reasonable price than the French do. The French mean to betray us, and lord it over us. These presents – which we send you secretly, so that we may not be discovered – are daggers for massacring all the French who are among you, and for informing you that we will do the same to those who are with us.' The chief of the Sauteurs was more sensible than all those peoples who had sent him presents [asking him] to join that same conspiracy. His reply to them was: 'You are children. You do not know the Englishman, who is the father of the Iroquois – against whom Onontio our father has undertaken war, and whom he has compelled to demand peace; and what he has thus done is only to protect us from the Englishman's barbarous treatment. When you shall have carried out this reckless move which you are proposing, see if the Iroquois will not avail himself of the opportunity to satiate his fury, and his passion for destroying all the peoples; and if his father, who will be more partial to him than to us, will not abandon us to the kettle of the Iroquois. I know the French governor, who has never betrayed me, and I do not trust the Englishman.' It is astonishing that Monsieur de la Sale' had no knowledge of all the schemes that were plotted against him. He traded for all the peltries of those peoples, which he placed aboard his bark; and he left in the vessel only five or six Frenchmen, to whom he gave orders to return [to Niagara] with the first favorable weather; for his part, he continued his journey in canoes, in order to join the men whom he had left at the river of Saint Joseph. Hardly was the bark under sail when a storm arose, which drove it into a small bay, five or six leagues from the anchorage which it had left. The Outaouak deputies who had inveigled the Islinois into their conspiracy, returning, perceived the bark, and went on board. The pilot received them with entire good-will; but the opportunity seemed to them at the moment too advantageous to miss their stroke. They slew all the Frenchmen [footnote, "In 1679"], carried away all the goods that suited them, and burned the bark. It had cost more than forty thousand francs, [and] as much in merchandise, tools, peltries, outfit, rigging, and furniture. Monsieur de la Sale, who, after the tokens of esteem and friendship which those peoples had given him, had never suspected such perfidy, believed that his ship had been wrecked. The savages, on their part, considered themselves freed from a burden which to them seemed heavy; but they did not recognize in it their own good fortune."

[Chapter xiii relates La Salle's adventures in Illinois – his establishment on the Illinois River,[232] his ex-

---

[232] This post of La Salle's was called Fort St. Louis, and was built on the lofty height called "Starved Rock," near the present Utica, Ill. — ED.

pedition down the Mississippi (in 1681), and return to
France (1683). The Iroquois raided the Illinois country, treacherously breaking the peace they had concluded
with the French and their allies; and the tribes thus
wronged were consequently irritated against the French,
La Salle having assured them of the good behavior of
the Iroquois. At Green Bay (chapter xiv) many Indians died from the ravages of an epidemic, and the
superstitious people laid the blame for this on the missionaries there, whose destruction they began to plot.
A Frenchman (apparently Perrot) so successfully exerted his influence with the savages, at the same time
reproaching them for the murder of some servants of
the mission, that he induced them to promise that satisfaction should be made therefor, and the danger to the
mission was averted.   In the same winter [footnote, "In
1683"] a conference was held in the Outagami village,
attended by some Frenchmen who, with some Chippewa
from the Sault, had come to demand from the Outagamis satisfaction for their retention of certain captives.
On this occasion, the following speech was made (again
by Perrot, presumably): "Listen, Outagamis, to what
I am going to tell you. I have learned that you are very
desirous to eat the flesh of Frenchmen. I have come,
with these young men whom you see, to satisfy you; put
us into your kettles, and gorge yourselves with the meat
that you have been wanting." Then, drawing his sword
from his scabbard, he showed them his body, and continued: "My flesh is white and savory, but it is very
salt; if you eat it, I do not think that it will pass the
Adam's-apple without being vomited." The foremost
war chief at once answered, "What child is there who
would eat his father, from whom he has received life?
Thou hast given birth to us, for thou didst bring us the

first iron; and now thou tellest us to eat thee." The
Frenchman replied to him: "Thou art right in saying
that I gave thee birth; for when I came to thy village
all of you were in wretched condition, like people who
do not know where to halt, and who come forth from the
deepest part of the earth. Now, when you are living in
peace, and are enjoying the light which I have obtained
for you, you are desiring to trouble the country, to kill
the Sauteurs, and to bring low those whom I adopted
before I did you. Vomit up your prey; give me back
my body, which you wish to put into your kettle; and
fear lest the fumes which will rise from it, if you cook
it, will stir up vapors that will form stormy clouds
which will extend over your village—which will be in
a moment consumed by the flames and lightnings that
will issue from them; and these will be followed by a
shower of hail, which will fall with so much violence
on your families that not one of them will be safe. You
forget that your ancestors and yourselves have been vag-
abonds until now; are you weary of living in comfort?
Vomit up [your prey]. Believe your father, who will
not abandon you until you compel him to do so. Listen
to my words, and I will settle this unpleasant affair
(which you have brought on yourselves) with the Sauteurs." Nothing more was necessary to secure the return of the captives. On another occasion, "a Saki hung
up the war-kettle, against the opinion of all the chiefs
of his tribe. Some of his party entered the cabin of a
Frenchman, who was lying on his bed. Suspecting that
they came to say adieu to him, he pretended to snore;
the others waited for the moment when he could be
awakened. The Frenchman, suddenly arousing, like a
man who comes out of a heavy sleep, said aloud, in the
Saki language, 'The Sakis who are going to war will be

defeated.' Those warriors asked him what was the
cause of his agitation. He told them that he had just
dreamed that he saw, in the plains north of the Missisipi, on this side of the Sioux village, a camp of Nadouaissioux, in which there was a lighted fire, and a
great troop of black dogs, and some white dogs. These
animals, meeting there, had a fight, and the black dogs
devoured the white ones, except the largest one, who
remained the last one alive, and he was entirely exhausted. He said that he himself had tried to escape
from their jaws, but all the black dogs rushed toward
him to devour him; and the fear of being actually torn
in pieces had caused him to awake, with the startled appearance which they had just remarked. This fiction
had more effect than all the solicitations of those chiefs,
who could not prevent this war-party, formed so un-
seasonably; for those young warriors went about relating the danger of the Frenchmen; they interpreted the
sense [of this dream] by representing the Nadouaissioux
as the black dogs, and the Sakis as the white ones; and
they did not fail to say that the spirit had availed himself of the Frenchman, in this emergency, to turn them
aside from an enterprise which without doubt would
have been fatal to them." The rest of the chapter is
occupied with an account of the expedition against the
Iroquois country by Governor la Barre, evidently drawn
from Perrot's relation in his *Mémoire*.]

Chapter XV

The name of Frenchman was rendered worthy of
respect in all places; and the more remote peoples who
had profited by the advantages of alliance with the
French experienced a great change from the former condition in which they were; when they waged war against

some tribes who were unknown to us, they were able to end it to their own advantage by favor of the arms that they had obtained from us. The more discoveries we made, the more we desired to make. The north was known to us, and the south gradually became so; but it still remained to penetrate into the west, where, as we had knowledge, many peoples dwelt. Monsieur de la Barre in the spring [footnote, "1683"] sent twenty Frenchmen to attempt this enterprise, under the direction of Sieur Perrot, to whom he gave letters-patent as commandant of that region. When they had gone fifty leagues from Montreal, they met some Outaouaks, who were coming down to that city; and usage demanded that travelers who met each other should land on the shore, in order to give mutual information of the news on both sides. These Outaouaks said that the Sauteur tribe had been destroyed by the Outagamis, and that they themselves were going to Onontio, their father, to ask him for [fire]arms, in exchange for peltries, in order to avenge the Sauteurs. Although those peoples might often have quarrels, it was nevertheless to the interest of the colony to prevent them from destroying one another. The commander of these twenty Frenchmen sent information of this matter to Monsieur de la Barre, who wrote to the Jesuit fathers and the commandant at Michilimakinak to prevent the Outaouaks from making any attack on the Outagamis. The Outaouaks, rightly suspecting that Monsieur de la Barre was not favorable to their designs, and that all the letters entrusted to them might furnish obstacles thereto, burned the letters, excepting the one which was addressed to Perrot, because they imagined that, as he was a friend to them, he at least would favor them in their schemes. All that they said to the Jesuits on their arrival was, that Onontio had [given] them the Outagamis "for broth." The very opposite was learned from the letter which Perrot received, in which Monsieur de la Barre expressly forbade that the Outaouaks should commit hostile acts against the Outagamis, and directed him to settle their dispute.

A Sauteur chief had a daughter eighteen years old, who had been for a year a slave among the Outagamis, and whom he could not redeem. In this wretched situation, the dread which he felt that, if he made any attempt to demand the girl, he himself would be burned by them, took away his courage; [but now] he resolved to do it, and joined our Frenchmen. All the tribes at the bay had carried to the Outagamis a great many presents, in order to ransom this girl, but nothing had been sufficient to move them; it was even feared that she would be sacrificed to the shades of the great chief whom the Sauteurs had slain. This afflicted father found no consolation in any of the places through which he passed, because the people there told him that the Frenchmen, as they were not, like themselves, relatives of the Outagamis, could never get possession of his daughter. Perrot made him remain at the bay, for fear that the Outagamis would snatch him away from the French and put him on the gridiron. As soon as he arrived at their village they approached him, all bursting into tears, and relating to him the treachery of the Sauteurs and the Nadouaissious. They told him that their great chief had been killed in the fight, with fifty-six of their men; and that, although they had only two hundred men, they had routed the enemies, who numbered eight hundred fighting men. This discourse gave him an opportunity to speak of that girl; and, having called them to an assembly, he spoke to them as follows:

"Old men, chiefs, and young men of the Outagamis, listen to me. I have had information that, in order to form a solid peace between the Sauteurs and Nadouais- sious, through a conference which we had together, the former had invited the latter to put you and your fam- ilies into their kettles. It is the Spirit who created all who has made known to us the peril in which you have been; and we have prayed him to take pity on you, ask- ing that his almighty power may deliver you from the treachery of your enemies, who have not obtained any of your spoils, nor the scalps of your dead. He has made you masters of the field of battle; you have made pris- oners of their men, and you have cut off the heads of those whom you have slain, which is the final proof of a savage's valor. You ought not to ascribe the victory to your own bravery; it is that Spirit who has fought for you whom you ought to acknowledge as your deliverer. What do you mean to do with this Sauteur girl whom you have so long kept back? Is keeping her here likely to appease your anger against her people? She belongs to me, and I demand her from you. I am your father, and it is the Spirit who has employed me to come among you, as the first Frenchman who has opened the door of your cabin. All these peoples of the bay, who are my children, are your brothers; foreseeing your refusal, they dread the evils that threaten you. Swallow your desire for vengeance, if you desire to live." While talking to them, he held his calumet in his hand; he held it to the mouth of the brother of the great chief, to have him smoke, but the latter refused it; then he presented it to others, who accepted it. Then he filled it with tobacco, and again presented it to the first man, as many as three times; but he refused it, as he had done before, which constrained Perrot to leave the room instantly, very indignant. The Outagamis are of two lineages; those of one call themselves Renards, and the others are of the Red-earth family.[233] The man who refused the calumet was chief of the Renards, who had taken the place of his brother. The chief of the Red Earth followed Perrot, and conducted him into his own cabin, where he called together all the old men and warriors of his tribe, and spoke to them thus:

"You have heard your father Metaminens" (that is the name by which he was known), "who desires to give us life, and our brothers the Renards are trying to take it away from us, desiring us to be forsaken by the Spirit, to whom they refuse a slave girl. Bring me some kettles, and I will talk to them; I will prove their good-will, and I will see if they will refuse me. I have always been the prop of their village, and my father and dead brother have always exposed themselves to danger in their behalf, having lost many young men in order to defend them; if they refuse me, I will let another use my fire, and I will abandon them to the fury of their enemies."

After these kettles and some merchandise had been brought to him, he took his calumet and with a retinue of his lieutenants entered the cabin of that stubborn man, and said to him: "My comrade, behold the calu-

---

[233] Cf. this statement with that in Major Marston's letter of 1820 (which immediately follows La Potherie's account); there, as in various other authorities, the names Fox and Renard are applied to the Musquaki, their own appellation for their tribe. The apparent discrepancy is explained by William Jones (*Handbook Amer. Indians*, 472) as a misunderstanding by the French who first met some of the Fox clan, and thereafter applied the name of the clan to the whole tribe. Hewitt says (*ut supra*, art. "Squawkihow"): "The signification of *Muskwaki* is 'red earth,' and may have been originally employed in contradistinction to *Osauaki* or *Osawki*, 'yellow earth,' the base of the tribal name 'Sauk.'" Miss Owen confirms this statement thus (*Folk-Lore of the Musquakie Indians*, 18): "'Musquakie' means 'Fox,' whether reference is made to the animal or the tribesman, in Saukie, Kickapoo, and Musquakie, though the Saukies say jokingly that Geechee Manito-ah ["the Great Spirit"] made the Saukie out of yellow clay and the Squawkie out of red." — ED.

met of our ancestors who are dead. When any emergencies occurred in our village, they offered it to thy ancestors, who never refused it. I offer it to thee, filled with these kettles, and I entreat thee to take pity on our children, and to give that Sauteur girl to Metaminens, who has asked thee for her." The chief of the Renards smoked, and had all his relatives smoke.[234] The chief of the Red Earth returned to his cabin and told Sieur Perrot, the commandant, that the affair was settled, and that he would have the Sauteur girl. During the night a storm arose, so violent that it seemed as if the entire machinery of the world was broken up; a heavy rain, with lightning and thunder, made so great a tumult that they thought they were lost men. As all the savages are naturally superstitious, they imagined that the Spirit was incensed at them. In the village nothing was heard save the complaints of the old men, who said: "What art thou thinking of, Onkimaoüassam? dost thou intend to cause the death of thy children? Dost thou love the Sauteur girl better than the families of thy own village? Didst not thou understand what was said to thee by Metaminens, who loves us and desires to give us life?

[234] Smoking was found among the aborigines of America by the earliest discoverers. The natives took the fumes of tobacco as a cure for disease. "Tobacco or some mixture thereof was invariably smoked in councils with the whites and on other solemn occasions. No important undertaking was entered upon without deliberation and discussion in a solemn council at which the pipe was smoked by all present. The remarkable similarity in smoking customs throughout the continent proves the great antiquity of the practice." It was used much like incense, and was offered to idols by women as well as men; and this practice was also observed as a compliment to distinguished visitors. "In religious ceremonies in general the priest usually blows the smoke over the altar to the world-quarters." Sometimes the decoration of pipes and their stems has great ceremonial and ethnic significance. "Every individual engaged in war, hunting, fishing, or husbandry, and every clan and phratry made supplication to the gods by means of smoke, which was believed to bring good and arrest evil, to give protection from enemies, to bring game or fish, allay storms, and protect one while journeying." — JOSEPH D. McGUIRE, in *Handbook Amer. Indians.*

Cleanse thy mat from this filth, which will infect our land." Their fright had driven them so beside themselves, that they believed that the Spirit was going to engulf them in ruin. Onkimaoüassam himself no longer knew where he was. He was subdued, and no longer dared appear before Metaminens – who was delighted at this fear, because he well knew that it was the certain means for his obtaining that slave quickly, without the aid of any one whatever.

Onkimaoüassam went to the chief of the Red Earth, and asked him to take the girl from him, saying, "I do not dare to go before Metaminens; here is the Sauteur girl; take her." The other answered him, "It is for thee to give her up, in order that he may think that the offer comes from thee, and so not bear thee so much ill-will." Meanwhile the rain fell without ceasing; they entered the cabin of Perrot with the girl, entreating him to check this scourge which menaced them, and to prevent the Sauteurs and their allies from making war on them any longer. He returned them thanks by a present of tobacco and a kettle, at the time when he saw that very soon the rain was going to stop – telling them that this kettle would serve them for a roof to shelter them from the rain, and that they should smoke their pipes in peace, without fearing that the Spirit would punish them. Perrot, not considering himself a sufficiently good prophet to make the rain cease, rightly judged that if he remained much longer with his prisoner the aspect of affairs might change. He took leave of them, notwithstanding the bad weather, promising them that it would clear up before he arrived at the bay. After having sent the Sauteur his daughter, he went back across the country, in order to deter the people of that tribe from attacking the Outagamis in case they had that intention.

He informed them that he had taken the girl out of the kettle of the Renards, having delivered up his own body to their rage; that he was going to live among the Renards in order to assure them that the former tribe should not make any move [against them]; that he took care, therefore, not to act heedlessly; and that if people were indiscreet enough to try to exasperate the minds of the Renards, they would break his head. He told the Sauteur that, if he were slain by them, he might expect that the French would avenge Perrot's death on himself and on his tribe; and he gave him twelve brasses of tobacco, that he might present it to his chiefs [at home]. The chiefs at the bay were not a little surprised at the success obtained by the Frenchman; and they declared that one needed to be a spirit, like him, to obtain what all the peoples of the bay had not been able to accomplish with all their presents.

The curiosity of our Frenchmen whom Monsieur de la Barre had sent out was greatly excited by all the conversations which the savages held with them. The only talk at the bay was of new tribes, who were unknown to us. Some said that they had been in a country which lay between the south and the west; and others were arriving from the latter direction, where they had seen beautiful lands, and from which they had brought stones, blue and green, resembling the turquoise,[235] which they wore fastened in their noses and ears. There were some of them who had seen horses, and men re-

---

[235] "Stones of greenish hue were highly valued by the American aborigines, and this was due, apparently, to the association of certain religious notions with the color." Turquoise is found in many localities in the southwestern states, and was mined by the natives in pre-Spanish times in New Mexico and Arizona. "The turquoise is highly prized by the present tribes of the arid region, and is ground into beads and pendants, which are pierced by the aid of primitive drills; and is made into settings for mosaic work."
— W. H. HOLMES, in *Handbook Amer. Indians.*

sembling the French; it must be that these were the
Spaniards of New Mexico. Still others said that they
had traded hatchets with persons who, they said, were
in a house that walked upon the water, at the mouth of
the river of the Assiniboüels,[236] which is at the Northern
Sea of the west. The river of the Assiniboüels flows
northward into the Bay of Husson [i.e., Hudson]; it is
near Fort Nelson.

All these reports aroused [the desire] to attempt some
discovery of importance. The Frenchmen therefore set
out from the Bay of Puans with some savages who had
accompanied Islinois warriors in the west, where they
had been making raids. At their arrival opposite the
Miamis and Maskoutechs, they met fifty Sokokis[237]
and Loups, from those who had been with Monsieur de

[236] The Assiniboin (Assinipoualaks, etc.) are "a large Siouan tribe, originally constituting a part of the Yanktonai," from whom they appear to have
separated early in the seventeenth century, and probably in the region about
the headwaters of the Mississippi, whence they moved northward and joined
the Cree. As early as 1670 they were located about Lake Winnipeg, and a
century later they were scattered along the Saskatchewan and Assiniboin Rivers.
Up to 1836 they numbered from 1,000 to 1,200 lodges, trading on the Missouri
River, when the smallpox reduced them to less than 400 lodges, and in 1856
there were only 250 lodges. They now number some 2,500, of whom somewhat
less than half are on reservations in Montana; the rest are in Canadian territory. They have always been nomadic in their mode of life, and usually at
enmity with other tribes — always warring with the Dakota, until brought
under control of the whites. — JAMES MOONEY and CYRUS THOMAS, in *Handbook
Amer. Indians.*

[237] The Sokoki were a tribe connected with the Abnaki, and probably
a part of the confederacy; authorities differ somewhat, but the best evidence
seems to place them in the Abnaki group. They were found by Champlain in
1604 at the mouth of Saco River. After King Philip's War (1675) part of the
Sokoki fled to the Hudson River; and in 1725 the rest of the tribe retired to
St. Francis, Canada, with some of their allied tribes. — JAMES MOONEY, in
Handbook Amer. Indians.

"Loups" was the French translation of "Mahican" (both meaning "wolf"),
the name of an Algonquian tribe closely connected with the Delawares; they
dwelt on both sides of the upper Hudson River, and eastward into Massachusetts — in which locality those converted to the Christian faith were known as
Stockbridges, their descendants now living in Wisconsin. With this exception,
the Mahican have lost their tribal identity. — ED.

la Salle in his voyage of discovery—who, not daring to remain on the war-path of the Islinois, had retired to the bay, in order to hunt beavers there. The great chief of the Miamis, when he knew that Perrot was only three-quarters of a league from his village, came to meet him, in order to invite him to rest in his cabin. This chief told Perrot, in the midst of a feast which he made for him, that his tribe desired to settle near the Frenchman's fire, and begged him to point out to them its location. Perrot told him that he was going to establish himself on the upper Missisipi, this side of the Nadouaissious, where he would serve as a barrier to them, because he knew that they had hostilities with that people. He made presents to the Miamis, the Maskoutechs, and the Kikabouks, of twelve brasses of tobacco, and gave them some kettles. By this present he informed them that they could feel sure that those peoples would not commit any act of hostility, but that they must be cautious hereafter about raising the club against them; that they ought to fasten their hatchets to the sun, because, if they made the least hostile attack on the others, the Nadouaissious would unquestionably believe that the Miamis had settled so near to them only to render easy to their enemies the means of ruining and destroying them; that, as for the rest, if any of the Miamis wished to come to light their fire near him, he would always receive them with great pleasure. In presenting to them the two kettles, he told them that Onontio had abandoned the Islinois to the Iroquois, who would pass by way of Chigagon; and that, if the Miamis went hunting, they should do so along the Missisipi farther down, in order to avoid falling into the hands of the Iroquois.

These Frenchmen again embarked with the Sokokis, and, having arrived at the portage which must be made

in order to enter a river that falls into the Missisipi, they
met thirteen Hurons who, knowing their intention of
making an establishment in the Nadouaissious country,
undertook to thwart it and to fight with them, so as to
deprive the French of the liberty to trade, and prevent
them from furnishing [fire]arms and other munitions to
the Nadouaissious. The Hurons tried to get ahead of
them in this voyage, but were entirely prevented from
doing so, and they would have fared ill if the Sokokis
had not appeased the resentment of the French. The
latter continued their route until they reached the river,
and there they took measures for endeavoring to discover some [new] tribes. This was an undertaking of
considerable difficulty, because in that region beyond
the Missisipi there are plains of vast extent, entirely un-
inhabited, in which only wild animals are found. It was
agreed that the Puans should make the first discovery;
they promised that the French should have word from
them within forty days, and that, as soon as the latter
perceived great fires on those plains they might be assured that a tribe had been found; and this signal was to
be used by both parties. It is the custom of the peoples
who inhabit this continent that, when they go hunting
in spring and autumn, they light fires on those prairies,
so that they can ascertain each other's location. The
fire becomes so strong, especially when the wind rises,
and when the nights are dark, that it is visible forty
leagues away. Those plains abound with an infinite
number of cattle, which are much larger than those of
Europe, and are commonly called "Islinois cattle;" their
hair is quite curly, and finer than silk, and hats have
been made from it in France which are as handsome as
those of beaver.[238] When the savages wish to take many

[238] Another reference to the buffalo. In the *Jesuit Relations* are several interesting mentions of this animal's wool or hair. Marest wrote from Kaskaskia

of these animals they shut them in with a ring of their fires, which burn the trees, and from which the animals cannot escape. While the Puans crossed those lands, taking their course toward the west and southwest, the French ascended the river in canoes, toward the west; the latter found a place where there was timber, which served them for building a fort, and they took up their quarters at the foot of a mountain, behind which was a great prairie, abounding in wild beasts. At the end of thirty days they descried fires, which were far away; and they also lighted fires, [by which] the Puans knew that the French had established their post.

About eleven days after this signal, some deputies came in behalf of the Ayoës,[239] who gave notice that [the

in 1712 (vol. lxvi, 231) that the Illinois made with it leggings, girdles, and bags; and he extols its fineness. Cords or ropes were also made of it (vol. lxviii, 133). Joliet told Dablon that from this wool could be made cloth, "much finer than most of that which we bring from France" (vol. lviii, 107).
— ED.

[239] The Ayoës live at a considerable distance beyond the Missisipi, toward the forty-third degree of latitude. — LA POTHERIE.

The Iowa are one of the southwestern Siouan tribes, of the Chiwere group (see note 195), and of Winnebago origin (see note 199). "Iowa chiefs informed Dorsey in 1883 that their people and the Oto, Missouri, Omaha, and Ponca 'once formed part of the Winnebago nation;'" and the traditions of those tribes relate that at an early period they all came with the Winnebago from their common home north of the great lakes — the Winnebago stopping on the shore of Lake Michigan, attracted by the abundance of fish, while the others continued southwestward to the Mississippi River. Here the Iowa separated from the main group, and received their name of Pahoja ("Gray Snow"); and near the mouth of Rock River seem to have halted for a time. Thence they moved, successively, up the Mississippi through Iowa to southwestern Minnesota; through Nebraska, Iowa, Missouri; and thence to Missouri River, opposite Fort Leavenworth, where they were living in 1848. In 1824 they ceded all their lands in Missouri, and in 1836 were assigned a reservation in northeastern Kansas; thence a part of the tribe moved later to another tract in Central Oklahoma, which by agreement in 1890 was allotted to them in severalty. Their numbers have varied greatly at different times; in 1760 they were estimated at 1,100 souls, and in 1804 at 800 (a smallpox epidemic having ravaged the tribe the year before); in 1829, at 1,000, and in 1843 at 470. In 1905 the number in Kansas was 225, and in Oklahoma 89. The Iowa appear to have been cultivators of the soil at an early date, and had a reputation for great

people of] their village were approaching, with the intention of settling near the French. The interview with these newcomers was held in so peculiar a manner that it furnished cause for laughter. They approached the Frenchman [i.e., Perrot], weeping hot tears, which they let fall into their hands along with saliva, and with other filth which issued from their noses, with which they rubbed the heads, faces, and garments of the French; all these caresses made their stomachs revolt. On the part of those savages there were only shouts and yells, which were quieted by giving them some knives and awls. At last, after having made a great commotion, in order to make themselves understood – which they could not do, not having any interpreter – they went back [to their people]. Four others of their men came, at the end of a few days, of whom there was one who spoke Islinois; this man said that their village was nine leagues distant, on the bank of the river, and the French went there to find them. At their arrival the women fled; some gained the hills, and others rushed into the woods which extended along the river, weeping, and raising their hands toward the sun. Twenty prominent men presented the calumet to Perrot, and carried him upon a buffalo-skin into the cabin of the chief, who walked at the head of this procession. When they had taken their places on the mat, this chief began to weep over Perrot's head, bathing it with his tears, and with moisture that dripped from his mouth and nose; and those who carried the guest did the same to him. These tears ended, the calumet was again presented to him; and the chief caused a great earthen pot, which was filled with tongues of buffaloes, to be placed over the fire. These were

industry; also they hunted the buffalo, and made and sold the "redstone" (catlinite) pipes. — J. O. DORSEY and CYRUS THOMAS, in *Handbook Amer. Indians.*

taken out as soon as they began to boil, and were cut into small pieces, of which the chief took one and placed it in his guest's mouth; Perrot tried to take one for himself, but the chief refused until he had given it to him, for it is their custom to place the morsels in the guest's mouth, when he is a captain, until the third time, before they offer the dish.   He could not forbear spitting out this morsel, which was still all bloody (those same tongues were cooked that night in an iron pot) ; immediately some men, in great surprise, took their calumet, and perfumed them with tobacco-smoke. Never in the world were seen greater weepers than those peoples; their approach is accompanied with tears, and their adieu is the same.   They have a very artless manner, also broad chests and deep voices.   They are extremely courageous and good-hearted.   They often kill cattle and deer while running after them.   They are howlers; they eat meat raw, or only warm it over the fire.   They are never satiated, for when they have any food they eat night and day; but when they have none they fast very tranquilly.   They are very hospitable, and are never more delighted than when they are entertaining strangers.

Their eagerness to obtain French merchandise induced them to go away to hunt beaver during the winter; and for this purpose they penetrated far inland.   After they had ended their hunt forty Ayoës came to trade at the French fort; and Perrot returned with them to their village, where he was hospitably received.   The chief asked him if he were willing to accept the calumet, which they wished to sing for him; to this he consented. This is an honor which is granted only to those whom they regard as great captains.*   He sat down on a hand-

* For description of the calumet, see *footnote* 139.

some buffalo-skin, and three Ayoës stood behind him
who held his body; meanwhile other persons sang, holding calumets in their hands, and keeping these in motion to the cadence of their songs. The man who held
Perrot in his arms also performed in the same manner,
and they spent a great part of the night in singing the
calumet. They also told him that they were going to
pass the rest of the winter in hunting beaver, hoping to
go in the spring to visit him at his fort; and at the same
time they chose him, by the calumet which they left
with him, for the chief of all the tribe. The Frenchmen
returned to their fort, where they found a Maskoutech
and a Kikabouc, who informed them that the people of
their villages had followed them; and that they were at
a place eighteen leagues above there, on the bank of the
river. They reported that some Frenchmen had invited
the Miamis to settle at Chigagon, to which place they
had gone despite the warning that had been given them,
that the Iroquois were to go thither in order to descend
thence against the Islinois; but that, as for their people,
they had considered it more expedient to come to look
for Perrot and his men, entreating the Frenchmen to
direct them in what place they should light their fires.
Two days later, Perrot set out with them, and the people
were full of joy at seeing him; he lodged at the house of
Kikirinous, the chief of the Maskoutechs, who feasted
him on a large bear which the chief had caused to be
boiled whole. This chief asked from him the possession
of a river which watered a beautiful region that lay not
far from the place where they were; and at the same
time he asked for protection for all the families of their
tribes, and that the Nadoüaissioux might be kept from
annoying them. [He said that] they were making a
peace with the latter, the petitioner himself being its

mediator; and assured Perrot that he would bring hither a large village of Islinois, whose promise he had obtained. Perrot hardly dared to rely upon their promise, because he knew that most of them were man-eaters, who loved the flesh of men better than that of animals.[240] He told them that he did not like to have those people for neighbors; that he was sure that they were asking to settle near him with the intention of making some raids on the Ayoës, when the latter were least expecting it; and that he could not, moreover, make up his mind to hinder the Nadoüaissioux from annoying his present visitors. They told him that they were surprised that he should doubt his own children; that he was their father, and the Ayoës their younger brothers, and therefore the latter could not strike them without striking him also, since he laid them in his bosom; and that they had sucked the same milk which they desired again to suck. They entreated him to give them in return some [fire]arms and munitions. The Frenchman, having no answer to give them, had them smoke in his calumet, and told them that this was his breast which he had al-

---

[240] Cannibalism (a word derived from *Carib* through Spanish corruption) has been practiced in one form or another among probably all peoples at some period of their tribal life; and we have historical records of its occurrence among many of the tribes north of Mexico — whether as a matter of ceremony, of hunger, or even of taste. Among the tribes who thus practiced it were: the Algonkin, Iroquois, Assiniboin, Cree, Foxes, Miami, Ottawa, Chippewa, Illinois, Kickapoo, Sioux, and Winnebago; the Mohawk and some of the southern tribes were known to their neighbors as "man-eaters." Cannibalism was sometimes accidental, from necessity as a result of famine; "the second and prevalent form of cannibalism was a part of war custom and was based principally on the belief that bravery and other desirable qualities of an enemy would pass, through actual ingestion of a part of his body, into that of the consumer. Such qualities were supposed to have their special seat in the heart, hence this organ was chiefly sought;" it belonged usually to the warriors. "The idea of eating any other human being than a brave enemy was to most Indians repulsive. . . Among the Iroquois, according to one of the Jesuit fathers, the eating of captives was considered a religious duty." — A. HRDLICKA, in *Handbook Amer. Indians.*

ways presented to them to give them nourishment; that he was going soon to give suck to the Nadoüaissioux; and that the latter had only to come and carry them away, if they so desired, at the very time when these people might swear to destroy them. He promised to restrain the Nadoüaissioux if the latter came in war against them, and that if they did not obey his orders he would declare himself their enemy, provided that these people did not betray him. They went hunting the rest of the winter – for large game rather than for beaver, in order to provide food for their women and children.

Some Frenchmen went to notify the Nadoüaissioux not to make any mistakes in their pursuit of game when they should encounter some Sokokis who were hunting beaver along the river. They found on the ice twenty-four canoes of Nadoüaissioux, delighted to see these Frenchmen; and the latter returned to their village to carry this news.

THE INDIAN TRIBES OF
THE UPPER MISSISSIPPI VALLEY AND
REGION OF THE GREAT LAKES

VIEW OF FORT ARMSTRONG

THE INDIAN TRIBES OF THE UPPER MISSISSIPPI VALLEY AND REGION OF THE GREAT LAKES

as described by Nicolas Perrot, French commandant in the Northwest; Bacqueville de la Potherie, French royal commissioner to Canada;
Morrell Marston, American army officer;
and Thomas Forsyth, United States
agent at Fort Armstrong

Translated, edited, annotated,
and with bibliography and index by

EMMA HELEN BLAIR

With portraits, map, facsimiles, and views

VOLUME II

CONTENTS OF VOLUME II

ILLUSTRATIONS TO VOLUME II

HISTORY OF THE SAVAGE PEO-
ples who are allies of New France. By
Claude Charles Le Roy, Bacqueville
de la Potherie [from his *Histoire
de l'Amérique septentrionale* (Paris,
1753), tome ii and iv].

Continued and Completed from volume I

Chapter XVI

Some time afterward, three men were seen, running in great haste, and uttering the cries for the dead. As they approached the fort, they were heard to say that all the Miamis were dead; that the Iroquois had defeated them at Chigagon, to which place they had been summoned [by] some Frenchmen; and that those who were left intended to take revenge on the latter. They were brought into the fort, and pipes were given them to smoke; and gradually they regained their senses. After they had eaten a good meal, and had painted themselves with vermilion, they were questioned in regard to all the details of this news; now see in what manner the youngest of them spoke in addressing Perrot.

"When thou didst make a present this autumn to Apichagan, the chief of the Miamis, he himself set out the next day to notify all the Miamis and our people of what thou hadst told him; and he made them consent to follow thee, after he had secured the promise of all the men. Two Frenchmen had sent presents to the Miamis, to tell them that Onontio wished them to settle at Chekagou. Apichagan opposed this, and said that his people had already been slain at the river of Saint Joseph, when Monsieur de la Salle made them settle there. The Frenchmen have been the cause of the death of those whom thou lovest as thy own children; whom thou didst not induce to come to thy house, and whom thou didst warn only not to trouble themselves carrying arms against those among whom thou wast going; and whom thou didst tell that if they went to Chigagon they would be eaten by the Iroquois. At that time he prevented his people from believing the Frenchmen, to whom he sent deputies a second time, to tell them not to look for the Miamis. The Frenchmen again sent some of their men, who declared to Apichagan on the part of Onontio that he would be abandoned if he did not obey Onontio's voice, which of course disquieted the chief. He said, nevertheless, 'Follow Metaminens; if my people do not put their trust in him, they will seek death. Follow him; it is he who gives us life and who has prevented our families from being involved in the same ruin with those who have been at Chigagon.' When the Miamis reached that place the Frenchmen told them to go hunting there; and our people began to regret that they had not followed Metaminens. They dispersed in all directions to carry on their hunting, and [then] returned to the fort which the Frenchmen had built, to ascertain what they required. Some families who could not reach the fort as the others did were surprised by an army of Iroquois; and in this encounter a chief of the Miamis was captured who, in his death-song, asked his enemies to spare his life, assuring them that if they would grant it, he would deliver up his own village to them; so they released him.

"Some hunters, belonging to those families who had not gone to Chigagon, on their way back to their cabins saw from afar a large encampment; they concluded that their people had been defeated, and fled to the fort to carry the news of this. The Miamis who were there consulted together whether they should resist an assault or take to flight. A Sokoki who was among them told them not to trust the French, who were friends of the Iro-

quois. The Miamis believed him, and fled in all directions. The Iroquois came to that place, under the guidance of that Miami chief who had promised to betray
his village to them. They found there only four Frenchmen who came from the Islinois, whom they did not
molest, the Miamis having deserted – and even the commander of the French, who had been afraid to remain
there. The Iroquois followed at the heels of the people
of the village, and captured in general all the women
and children, except one woman, and some men who
abandoned their families."

The Ayoës came to the fort of the French [i.e., Perrot's], on their return from hunting beaver, and, not
finding the commandant, who had gone to the Nadoüaissioux, they sent a chief to entreat him to go to the fort.
Four Islinois met him on the way, who (although they
were enemies of the Ayoës) came to ask him to send back
four of their children, whom some Frenchmen held captive. The Ayoës had the peculiar trait that, far from
doing ill to their enemies, they entertained them, and,
weeping over them, entreated the Islinois to let them
enjoy the advantages which they could look for from the
French, without being molested by their tribesmen; and
these Islinois were sent back to the Frenchmen, who
were expecting the Nadoüaissioux. When the latter,
who also were at war with the Islinois, perceived these
envoys, they tried to fling themselves on the Islinois canoes in order to seize them; but the Frenchmen who
were conducting them kept at a distance from the shore
of the river, so as to avoid such a blunder. The other
Frenchmen who were there for trade hastened toward
their comrades; the affair was, however, settled, and
four Nadoüaissioux took the Islinois upon their shoulders and carried them to the land, informing them that

they spared them out of consideration for the Frenchmen, to whom they were indebted for life. The defeat of the Miamis at Chigagon was an event to be keenly felt by all the peoples of those quarters; and messengers were sent to the bay to ascertain the particulars of it, and to get some news of the colony. The Freshmen reported that what had been said about it was true, and that a hundred savages—Miamis, Maskoutechs, Pouteoüatemis, and Outagamis—had pursued the Iroquois, hatchet in hand, with so much fury that they had slain a hundred of the enemy, recaptured half of their own people, and put to rout the Iroquois, who even would have been destroyed if the victors had continued to pursue them. The messengers said that the Miamis were at the bay, and that they had very badly treated Father Allöüet, a Jesuit, who had prompted their going to Chigagon, as they imputed to him the loss of their people.

Monsieur the Marquis de Denonville, who was at that time the governor-general, desired to avenge these people, in order to remove the opinion that they entertained that we had the design of sacrificing them to the Iroquois. He sent orders to the French commandant who was among the Outaoüaks to call all the tribes together and get them to join his army which was at Niagara, to the end that all might go against the Tsonnontouans.

The commandant of the west was also ordered to enlist the tribes who were in his district, mainly the Miamis. That officer, having put his affairs in order, made known to some Frenchmen whom he left to guard his fort the conduct that they were to observe during his absence, and proceeded to the [Miami] village that was down the Missisipi, in order to induce them to take up arms against the Iroquois; he traveled sixty leagues on the plains, without other guide than the fires and the clouds of smoke that he saw. When he arrived among the Miamis he offered to them the club in behalf of Onontio, with several presents, and said to them: "The cries of your dead have been heard by your father Onontio, who, desiring to take pity on you, has resolved to sacrifice his young men in order to destroy the man-eater who has devoured you. He sends you his club, and tells you to smite unweariedly him who has snatched away your children. They pitch their tents outside of his kettle, crying to you, 'Avenge us! avenge us!' He must disgorge and vomit by force your flesh which is in his stomach, which he will not be able to digest—Onontio will not allow him leisure for that. If your children have been his dogs and slaves, his women must in their turn become ours." All the Miamis accepted the club,[1] and assured him that, since their father intended to assist them, they all would die for his interests.

This Frenchman, returning to his fort, perceived on the way so much smoke that he believed it was [made by] an army of our allies who were marching against the Nadoüaissioux, who might while passing carry away his men; and that constrained him to travel by longer stages. Fortunately he met a Maskoutech chief, who, not having found him at the fort, had come to meet him, in order to inform him that the Outagamis, the Kika-

---

[1] "Every tribe in America used clubs, but after the adoption of more effectual weapons, as the bow and lance, clubs became in many cases merely a part of the costume, or were relegated to ceremonial, domestic, and special functions. There was great variety in the forms of this weapon or instrument. Most clubs were designed for warfare." The Siouan tribes, and some of the Plains tribes, used the club with a fixed stone head; the northern Sioux, the Sauk, Fox, and some other Algonquian tribes, a musket-shaped club; while a flat, curved club with a knobbed head (French, *casse-tête*) was used by some Sioux, and by the Chippewa, Menominee, and other timber Algonquians. "Clubs of this type are often set with spikes, lance-heads, knife-blades, or the like, and the elk-horn with sharpened prongs belongs to this class."—WALTER HOUGH, in *Handbook Amer. Indians.*

bous, the Maskoutechs, and all the peoples of the bay
were to meet together in order to come and plunder his
warehouses, in order to obtain [fire]arms and munitions
for destroying the Nadoüaissioux; and that they had
resolved to break into the fort and kill all the Frenchmen, if the latter made the least objection to this. This
news obliged him to go thither immediately. Three
spies had left the place on the very day of his arrival,
who had used the pretext of trading some beaver-skins;
they reported at their camp that they had seen only six
Frenchmen, and, the commandant not being there, that
would be enough to persuade them to undertake the
execution of their scheme. On the next day, two others
of them came, who played the same part. The French
had taken the precaution to place guns, all loaded, at
the doors of the cabins. When the savages tried to enter
any cabin, our men discovered the secret of making them
find there men who had changed their garments to different ones. The savages asked, while speaking of one
thing or another, how many Frenchmen were in the
fort; and the reply was, that they numbered forty, and
that we were expecting every moment those of our men
who were on the other side of the river hunting buffalo.
All those loaded guns gave them something to think
about, and they were told that all these weapons were
always ready in case people came to molest the French;
and likewise that, as the latter were on a highway, they
always kept vigilant watch, knowing that the savages
were very reckless. They were told to bring to the fort
a chief from each tribe, because the French had something to communicate to them; and that if any greater
number of them came near the fort, the guns would be
fired at them. Six chiefs of those tribes came, whose
bows and arrows were taken away from them at the

gate. They were taken into the cabin of the commandant, who gave them [tobacco] to smoke, and regaled
them. When they saw all those loaded guns, they asked
him if he were afraid of his children; he answered them
that he did not trouble himself much at such things, and
that he was a man who could kill others. They replied
to him, "It seems that thou art angry at us." The commandant answered: "I am not angry, although I have
reason to be. The Spirit has informed me of your intention; you intend to plunder my goods and put me
into the kettle, in order to advance against the Nadoüaissioux. He has told me to keep on my guard, and that
he will assist me if you affront me." Then they stood
stock-still and acknowledged to him that it was true;
but they said that he was a very indulgent father to
them, and that they were going to break up all the plans
of their young men. Perrot had them sleep in the fort
that night. The next day, early in the morning, their
army was seen, part of whom came to cry out that they
wished to trade. The commandant, who had only fifteen men, seized these chiefs, and told them that he was
going to have their heads broken if they did not make
their warriors retire; and at the same time the bastions
were manned. One of those chiefs climbed above the gate
of the fort, and cried, "Go no farther, young men; you
are dead; the spirits have warned Metaminens of your
resolution." Some of them tried to advance, and he said
to them, "If I go to you, I will break your heads;" and
they all retreated. The lack of provisions harassed
them, and the French took pity on them; they had at the
time only provisions which were beginning to smell, but
gave these to the savages, who divided the food among
themselves. The commandant made them a present of
two guns, two kettles, and some tobacco, in order to

close to them, he said, the gate by which they were going
to enter the Nadoüaissioux country, contending that they
should thereafter turn their weapons against the Iroquois, and that they should avail themselves of Onontio's
bow to shoot at his enemy, and of his club to lay violent
hands on the Iroquois families. They represented to
him that they would suffer greatly before they could
reach the Iroquois country, as they had no gunpowder
for hunting; and they entreated him to give them some
in exchange for the few beaver-skins that were left in
their hands. For this purpose the chiefs of each tribe
were permitted to enter the fort, one after another. All
being quite pacified, the French undertook to call together as many of the tribes as they could, to join the
French army which was going against the Iroquois. The
Pouteoüatemis, the Malhominis, and the Puans willingly offered their aid. The Outagamis, the Kikabous, and
the Maskoutechs, who were not accustomed to travel in
canoes, united with the Miamis, who were to proceed to
the strait which separates Lake Herier [i.e., Erie] from
the Lake of the Hurons, where there was a French fort,
in which they were to find supplies for going to Niagara.

The Outagamis and the Maskoutechs, having held
their war-feast, went in quest of another small village
of the same tribe which was on their route; they wished
to invite its warriors to join their party. At the time
some Loups and Sokokis were there, intimate friends of
the Iroquois; they dissuaded the people from this enterprise. They said that Onontio intended to put them into
the kettle of the Iroquois, under pretext of avenging the
deaths of the Miamis; that three thousand Frenchmen
would indeed be at Niagara, but that there was reason
to fear that all of them would unite together with the
Iroquois, and that, having unanimously sworn the ruin

of the allies, they would unquestionably come to carry away the wives and children of the latter in all their villages. Those peoples blindly believed all that was said to them, and refused to expose themselves in a situation which seemed to them very dubious. The French pressed forward in their journey, and arrived at Michili-makinak, where they found the Outaoüaks, who had been unwilling to follow those who inhabited that quarter [i.e., the Sauteurs]; and of our men only a small number remained there, for the guard of the entrances [to the fort].

The Outaoüaks received the Pouteouatemis in military fashion; they assembled together behind a slope on which they made a camp. The fleet of the Pouteouatemis making its appearance at an eighth of a league from land, the Outaoüaks – naked, and having no other ornaments than their bows and arrows – marched abreast, and formed a sort of battalion. At a certain distance from the water they suddenly began to defile, uttering cries from time to time. The Pouteouatemis, on their part, set themselves in battle array, in order to make their landing. When the rear of the Outaouaks was opposite the Pouteouatemis, whose ranks were close to one another, they paddled more slowly. When they were at a gunshot from the land, the Frenchmen who were joined with the Outaouaks first fired a volley at them, without balls; the Outaouaks followed them with loud shouts of "Sassakoue!" and the Pouteouatemis uttered theirs. Then on both sides they reloaded their arms, and a second volley was fired. Finally, when the landing must be made, the Outaouaks rushed into the water, clubs in their hands; the Pouteouatemis at once darted ahead in their canoes, and came rushing on the others, carrying their clubs. Then no further order was maintained; all was pell-mell, and the Outaouaks lifted up their canoes, which they bore to the land. Such was this reception, which on a very serious occasion would have cost much bloodshed. The Outaouaks conducted the chiefs into their cabins, where the guests were regaled.

Although they gave them a friendly welcome, the Outaouaks did not at first know what measures to take in order to turn aside these newcomers from their enterprise, to the end of excusing themselves from joining the latter. They entreated the guests to wait a few days, so that all might embark together. Meanwhile a canoe arrived, which brought instructions from Monsieur de Denonville for the march, and for the junction of the French army with that of the allies. This canoe had descried some Englishmen, who were coming to Michilimakinak in order to get possession of the commerce; they had imagined that the French were indiscrete enough to abandon during this time the most advantageous post of the entire trade.

Three hundred Frenchmen, commanded by an officer, went out to meet them. The Hurons, when informed of this proceeding, without seeming to take notice of it, went to join the English, with the intention of aiding them; the Outaouaks remained neutral. The Chief Nansouakoüet alone took sides with the French, with thirty of his men. The Hurons, fearing that the Outaouaks, who were much more numerous than they in the village, would lay violent hands on their families, did not dare to fight as they had resolved; so that the French seized the English and their goods, and brought them to Michilimakinak. They had brought a large quantity of brandy, persuaded that this was the strongest attraction for gaining the regard of the savages—who drank a great deal of it, with which the greater number became intoxicated so deeply, that several of them died. There was reason to fear that the rest of the brandy would be distributed to the Pouteouatemis; [in that case] there would have been a disorderly scene, which would have prevented the departure of all those savages, who longed for nothing more than to signalize themselves against the Iroquois. One of the Frenchmen who had brought them then said to them: "This is the time when you must show that you are courageous; you have listened implicitly to the voice of your father Onontio, who exhorts you to the war with the Iroquois, who wish to destroy you. Thus far you have not distinguished yourselves from the other tribes, who have made you believe whatever they have wished, and who have regarded you as much inferior to themselves. Now it is necessary that you make yourselves known, and the occasion is favorable for that. The Outaouaks are only seeking to delay matters, which will prevent them from seeing the destruction of the Iroquois. We are taking part in your glory, and we would be sorry if you were not witnesses of the battle which will be fought against the Tsonnontouans. You are fighting men; you can give the lie to your allies who are not so courageous as you; and be sure that Onontio will know very well how to recognize your valor. It is partly us Frenchmen, partly men of the Pouteouatemis and from the bay, and others of your own number, who urge you not to drink brandy; it fetters the strength of the man, and renders him spiritless and incapable of action. The Englishman is the father of the Iroquois. This liquor is perhaps poisoned; moreover, you have just seen how many Outaouaks are dead from [drinking] it."

The chiefs were well pleased with this discourse, and

inspired among their young men great aversion for the brandy. The Outaouaks, however, deferred their departure, and imperceptibly beguiled those peoples. They assembled them together without the knowledge of the Jesuit fathers and the French commandant. They presented to them a keg of brandy holding twenty-five quarts [pots], and said to them: "We all are brothers, who ought to form only one body, and possess but one and the same spirit. The French invite us to go to war against the Iroquois; they wish to use us in order to make us their slaves. After we have aided in destroying the enemy, the French will do with us what they do with their cattle, which they put to the plow and make them cultivate the land. Let us leave them to act alone; they will not succeed in defeating the Iroquois; this is the means for being always our own masters. Here is a keg of brandy, to persuade you regarding these propositions, which we hope that you will carry out."

The warriors rose, with great composure, without replying, having left to the Outaouaks the keg of brandy; and they went to find two others of the principal Frenchmen who had accompanied them, whom they informed of all that had occurred. The latter went to address them the next morning before light, and encouraged them to persist in their good sentiments. The Outaouaks continually returned to the charge; they again sent the keg of brandy to the Pouteouatemis, who were longing to drink from it—for one can say that it is the most delicious beverage with which they can be regaled—nevertheless, they did not dare to taste it. They went to find those Frenchmen, and related to them this new occurrence. The Frenchmen, annoyed at all these solicitations by the Outaouaks, entered the Pouteouatemi cabin in which the brandy was; and the savage therein asked them what they wished the savages to do with it. The Frenchmen answered, while breaking open the keg with a hatchet, "Look here; this is what you ought to do with it. You must do the same with the Iroquois when you are in the fight; you must beat them with your clubs, you must slay them without sparing [even] the infants in the cradle. Put pitch on your canoes this morning; we are embarking, and we wait for no one." The Outaouaks, seeing that the canoes were ready, asked for a day's time in order to join the expedition; but our people took no notice of them. The fleet of the Pouteouatemis therefore set out, in good order, always having scouts out, who protected the advance. [From this point (top of page 205) to the top of page 209, is briefly told the campaign against the Iroquois, which is more fully related by Perrot in the *Mémoire*. – ED.]

The French voyageurs who had been among the allies came to Montreal in order to purchase there new merchandise; and at the same time the news came that the church of the [Jesuit] missionaries at the bay, and a part of their buildings, had been burned. There were some Frenchmen who met great losses in this fire; Sieur Perrot lost in it more than forty thousand francs' worth of beaver-skins.

The auxiliary troops, returning to their own country, made the report of their campaign; and they imparted a great idea of the valor of Onontio, who had forced the Iroquois themselves to set fire to their villages at the first news of his arrival. The Loups and Sokokis, who had given so bad an impression about the French to certain peoples, adroitly retreated from these warriors, in order not to be themselves treated like the Iroquois; they went by way of a small river which empties into the Missisipi, and [thus] reached their native country. All those who had taken sides with them repented of having done so. One hundred Miamis set out with the deliberate intention of making amends for the fault that they had committed in not having taken part in the general march; they were sure that they would at least find, in a certain hunting-ground, some party of Iroquois weakened with hunger and misfortunes. They proceeded to the road going to Niagara, where they found the French garrison dead from hunger, except seven or eight persons; this mischance hindered them from going farther. They guarded this fort during the winter, until the surviving Frenchmen had been withdrawn from it.

Thirteen Maskoutechs, impatient to find out whether what the Loups and Sokokis had said to them also against the French were true, set out during the general march in order to obtain information as to the truth of that report; and they met three Miami slaves who, in the rout of the Iroquois, had made their escape. The Maskoutechs, returning with these women, found two Frenchmen who were coming from the Islinois, laden with beaver-skins; they slew these men, and burned their bodies, in order to hide their murder; they also killed the Miamis and burned them and carried away their scalps.[2] When they arrived at their own village, they

[2] The practice of scalping was not common to all the American tribes. "The custom was not general, and in most regions where found was not even ancient. The trophy did not include any part of the skull or even the whole scalp. The operation was not fatal. The scalp was not always evidence of the killing of an enemy, but was sometimes taken from a victim who was allowed to live. It was not always taken by the same warrior who had killed or wounded the victim. It was not always preserved by the victor. The warrior's honors were not measured by the number of his scalps. The scalp dance was performed, and the scalps carried therein, not by the men, but by the women." In earlier times, throughout most of America the trophy was the head itself. "The spread of the scalping practice over a great part of central and western United States was a direct result of the encouragement in the

uttered three cries for the dead, such as are usually
made when they carry back [news of] some advantage
gained over the enemy. They gave to their chiefs these
three scalps, which they said were those of Iroquois,
and two guns, which they did not acknowledge to be
those of the Frenchmen. Those chiefs sent these things
to the Miamis, who, in acknowledgment, gave them several presents. Other Frenchmen who came back from
the Islinois recognized the guns of their comrades, and
not having any news of the latter, accused the Miamis
of having murdered them. The latter defended themselves, saying that the Maskoutechs had made them a
present of the guns, with three Iroquois scalps. Then
the Frenchmen made them profuse apologies for the
suspicion that they had felt that the Miamis had caused
the deaths of those two Frenchmen; and they supposed
that their friends had fallen into the power of the Iroquois, whom the Maskoutechs had met on their way.

Monsieur the Marquis de Denonville, who had humiliated the most haughty and redoubtable tribe in all
America, had no thought save to render happy the people whose government the king had entrusted to him;
he was certain that the [Indian] trade could not be better maintained than by sending back to the Outaouaks
all the voyageurs who had left [there] their property in
order to go to Tsonnontouan. He also despatched forty
Frenchmen to the Nadoüaissioux, the most remote tribe,
who could not carry on trade with us as easily as could
the other tribes; the Outagamis had boasted of excluding
them from access to us. These last-mentioned Frenchmen, on their arrival at Michillimakinak, learned that

shape of scalp bounties offered by the colonial and more recent governments,
even down to within the last fifty years, the scalp itself being superior to the
head as a trophy by reason of its lighter weight and greater adaptability to
display and ornamentation." — JAMES MOONEY, in *Handbook Amer. Indians.*

the Hurons had defeated a party of forty Iroquois, the greater number of whom they had captured, but had spared their lives. All the peoples of that region were greatly alarmed at an attack which the Outagamis had made on the Sauteurs. The former people, having learned that the French were at the Bay of Puans, sent three deputies to Monsieur du Luth,[3] a captain of the troops, to entreat him to come among them. He answered them that he would not concern himself about them, or settle their quarrels with the Sauteurs; that the French were going to pass through their river, and that they had three hundred loaded guns to fire at them if they tried to place the least obstacle in his way. They tried to justify themselves, by saying that their allies, jealous of them, had made every effort to render them odious to the French nation. They said that it was true that some war-party of their young men, going to fight against the Nadoüaissioux, had encountered on the enemy's territory some Sauteurs, from whom they had taken three girls and a young man; that when the people of the bay asked them for these captives they had not been able to refuse them, because the chiefs were waiting for the Frenchman in order to send back the captives to him. That commandant told them that he would not make known his opinions to them, since they had so often deceived him; and he continued his journey toward the Nadoüaissioux. A little while afterward he saw a canoe with five men, who came paddling as hard as they could. They were the chiefs of the Outagamis, who

---

[3] Daniel Greysolon du Luth (Lhut) was especially prominent among Northwestern explorers. An officer in the army of France, he came to Canada about 1676; two years later, he conducted a French expedition into the Sioux country. He spent nearly ten years in explorations (mainly beyond Lake Superior) and fur-trading; he was for a time commandant of the Northwest. In 1689, he had returned to the St. Lawrence; he died in 1710. The city of Duluth, Minn., was named for him. — ED.

came alongside of his boat with expressions so full of grief that he could not forbear from going to their village; the reply that he had made to the three deputies had caused so great consternation that they were inconsolable at it. It was to their interest to stand well in the opinion of the French, from whom they were receiving all possible assistance; and because they could only expect, as soon as the [French] trade with them had ceased, to become the objects of opprobrium and the victims of their neighbors. The commandant entered the cabin of the chief, who had a deer placed in the kettle; when it boiled, the kettle and some of the raw meat were placed before him, to regale all the Frenchmen. The commandant disdained to taste it, because this meat, he said, did not suit him, and when the Outagamis became reasonable he would have some of it. They understood very well the meaning of this compliment. They immediately brought in the three girls and the young Sauteur. The chief began to speak, saying: "See how the Outagami can be reasonable, and be minded as he is therein. He spits out the meat which he had intended to eat, for he has remembered that thou hadst forbidden it to him; and while it is between his teeth he spits it out, and entreats thee to send it back to the place where he seized it." The Frenchman told him that they had done well in preserving the captives; that he remembered the club that had been given to them in behalf of their father Onontio, and that in giving it he had told them that hereafter they should use it only against the Iroquois. He told them that they themselves had assured him that they would join the Frenchmen at Détroit; but that now they were using the club on his own body, and maltreating the families of the Sauteurs who had gone with the French to war. He warned them to be no longer foolish and wild; and said that he would once more settle this business. He told them to remain quiet, and said that the Sauteurs would obey him, since they had not killed any one, and were restoring the people of the Outagamis. He directed the latter to hunt beavers, and told them that, if they wished to be protected by Onontio, they must apply themselves to making war against the Iroquois only. Some Frenchmen were left with them to maintain the trade, and the rest embarked.

The Pouteouatemis cut across the country, to reach more quickly a portage [4] which lies between a river that goes down to the bay, and that of Ouiskonch, which falls into the Missisipi (about the forty-third degree of latitude), in order to receive there these Frenchmen. When the latter were twelve leagues from the portage, they were stopped by the ice-floes. The Pouteouatemis, impatient to find out what had happened to them, came to meet them, and found them in a series of ice-floes from which they had great difficulty in extricating themselves; and immediately those savages sent to their village to call out two hundred men, for the purpose of carrying all the merchandise over to the shore of the Ouiskonch River, which was no longer covered with ice. The French then went to the Nadoüaissioux country, ascending the Missisipi. The Sauteurs were notified that the French had taken away their daughters from the hands of the Outagamis; and four of them came to the bay, where the girls were, to get them, and displayed to the Frenchmen all possible gratitude; they had reason

---

[4] Alluding to the noted Fox-Wisconsin portage, long famous in the early history of exploration and trade in the Northwest; there, in the rainy season, the waters of those two great rivers flowed into each other, and the comparatively easy "carry" between them made those streams the natural (and the only practicable) route of travel between Green Bay and the Mississippi. At that point of transfer has arisen the modern city of Portage. — ED.

to be highly pleased. But a very sad misfortune again befell them; this was, that when they had almost reached home some Outagamis who were prowling about attacked them, without knowing who they were. Terror overcame them, and caused them to abandon the three girls. The Outagamis did not dare to conduct the girls to the Sauteurs, for fear of being devoured; and, unwilling to expose them, alone, to losing their way in the woods, they carried the girls home with them, considering them as free.

As soon as the Nadoüaissioux saw that the rivers were navigable they went down to the post of the Frenchmen, and carried back the commandant to their village, where he was received with pomp, after their fashion. He was carried on a robe of beaver-skins, accompanied by a great retinue of people who carried each a calumet, singing the songs of alliance and of the calumet. He was carried about the village, and led into the cabin of the chief. As those peoples have the knack of weeping and of laughing when they choose, several of them immediately came to weep over his head, with the same tenderness which the Ayoës showed to him at the first time when he went among them.[5] However, these tears do not enervate their spirits, and they are very good warriors; they even have the reputation of being the bravest in all those regions. They are at war with all the tribes, excepting

---

[5] Note Cadillac's remarks concerning the Sioux, in his "Relation of Missilimakinak," section v: "Indeed, it seldom happens that a Sioux is taken alive; because, as soon as they see that they can no longer resist, they kill themselves, considering that they are not worthy to live when once bound, vanquished, and made slaves. It is rather surprising that people so brave and warlike as these should nevertheless be able to shed tears at will, and so abundantly that it can hardly be imagined. I think that it could not be believed without being seen; for they are sometimes observed to laugh, sing, and amuse themselves, when, at the same time, one would say that their eyes are like gutters filled by a heavy shower; and, as soon as they have wept, they again become as joyful as before, whether their joy be real or false." — ED.

the Sauteurs and the Ayoës; and even these last named very often have disputes with them. Hardly does the day begin when the Nadoüaissioux bathe in their river, and they even do the same with their children in swaddling-clothes; their reason is, that thus they gradually accustom themselves to be in readiness at the least alarm. They are of tall stature, and their women are extremely ugly; they regard the latter as slaves. The men are, moreover, jealous and very susceptible to suspicions; from this arise many quarrels, and the greater part of the time they get into general fights among themselves, which are not quieted until after much bloodshed. They are very adroit in [managing] their canoes; they fight even to the death when they are surrounded by their enemies, and when they have an opportunity to make their escape they are very agile. Their country is a labyrinth of marshes, which in summer protects them from molestation by their enemies; if one [journeying] by canoe is entangled in it, he cannot find his way; to go to their village, one must be a Nadoüaissioux, or have long experience in that country, in order to reach his destination. The Hurons have reason to remember an exceedingly pleasant adventure which befell a hundred of their warriors, who had gone to wage war on those people. These Hurons, being embarrassed in a marsh, were discovered; they saw the Nadoüaissioux, who surrounded them, and hid themselves as best they could in the rushes, leaving only their heads above the water, so that they could breathe. The Nadoüaissioux, not knowing what had become of them, stretched beaver-nets on the strips of land which separated their marshes, and to these attached little bells. The Hurons, imagining that the night-time would be very favorable for extricating themselves from this situation, found themselves entangled among all these nets. The Nadoüaissioux, who were in ambush, heard the sound of the bells and attacked the Hurons, of whom none could save himself except one, whom they sent back to his own country to carry the news of the affair. They are very lustful. They live on wild oats, which is very abundant in their marshes. Their country has also the utmost abundance of beavers. The Kristinaux, who also are accustomed to navigation, and their other enemies often compel them to take refuge in places where they have no other food than acorns, roots, and the bark of trees.

One of their chiefs, seeing that very few French were left in the fort (which is near them) when all the tribes marched against the Iroquois, raised a party of one hundred warriors in order to plunder the fort. This Frenchman displayed, on his return, the anger that he felt because they had acted so badly during his absence. The [other] chiefs had not been concerned in that plan, and came very near killing that chief; he was regarded, at least after that, with great contempt. When the renewal of the alliance was made the Frenchmen went back to their fort. There was one of them who complained, on going away, that a box of merchandise had been stolen from him; it was quite difficult to ascertain who had committed this theft, and recourse was had to a very odd stratagem. The commandant told one of his men to pretend to get some water in a cup in which he had put some brandy. As it was evident that there was no [other] means of recovering the box, they were threatened with the burning and drying up the waters in their marshes; and to strengthen the effect of these menaces, that brandy was set on fire. They were so terrified that they imagined that everything was going to destruction; the merchandise was recovered, and then the French

returned to their fort. The Outagamis who had changed
their village [site] established themselves on the Missisipi after they separated (at the portages of the River
Ouiskonch) from the Frenchmen, who had taken the
route to the Nadoüaissioux.

The chief came to find the French commandant, in
order to ask him to negotiate a peace with the Nadoüaissioux. Some of the latter tribe came to trade their
peltries at the French fort, where they saw this chief,
whom they recognized as an Outagami. The Nadoüaissioux seemed surprised at this encounter; and at the
same time they formed the idea (but without showing
it) that the French were forming some evil plot against
their tribe. The commandant reassured them, and, presenting to them the calumet, said that this was the chief
of the Outagamis, whom the French regarded as their
brother ever since his tribe had been discovered; and
that this chief ought not to be an object of suspicion,
since he had even come to propose peace with them
through the mediation of the French. "Smoke," said
this Frenchman, "my calumet; it is the breast with which
Onontio suckles his children." The Nadoüaissioux
asked him to have this chief smoke, and he did so; but,
although the calumet is the symbol of union and reconciliation, the Outagami did not fail to experience em-
barrassment in this situation. He afterward declared
that he did not feel very safe at that time. When he had
smoked, the Nadoüaissioux did the same; but they would
not come to any decision, because, as they were not
chiefs, they must notify their captains of this matter.
They nevertheless expressed to him their regret that his
tribe had been so easily influenced by the solicitations of
the Sauteurs, who had corrupted them with presents,
and who had caused the rupture of the peace which they

had concluded. This negotiation could not be finished on account of the speedy departure of the French, who had orders to return to the colony. Just as they set out, the chiefs of the Nadoüaissioux arrived, and brought the calumet of peace – which would have been concluded if our Frenchmen at their departure had dared to entrust to them the chief of the Outagamis. The Outagamis had always kept the three Sauteur girls of whom I have already spoken. Their dread of losing entirely the good graces of the French – who were greatly displeased at the hostilities which that tribe had committed against the Sauteurs – obliged them to forestall the latter by the relation which they made of all the circumstances attending the sojourn [among them] of the Sauteurs' daughters. It was evident that they were not to blame, and they were charged to convey the girls back to their own people.

The Iroquois, having been extremely harassed at Tsonnontouan by Monsieur the Marquis de Denonville, entreated the English to negotiate peace for them with him; and it was for the interest of that nation that no one should disturb the tranquillity of their neighbors. As peace still prevailed throughout Europe, the English did not dare to declare themselves in favor of the Iroquois; they felt, however, very deeply the manner in which the French treated those savages, without daring to take their part or support them. The French commander, who had in view only the tranquillity of his allies and of the peoples under his government, informed the English that he would willingly grant peace to the Iroquois on condition that his allies [also] should be included in it. He despatched his orders in every direction to the end that the club should be hung up, and that all the war-parties that might be raised against the

Iroquois should be halted. Besides this, presents were sent to all the tribes, as a pledge of the good-will which the French displayed toward them in a condition of affairs which so greatly concerned their interests. The Outaouaks were so incensed against the Iroquois that they took no notice of these orders, and carried on war against them more than ever. The Islinois were more discreet, for as soon as they received the orders of Onontio they tied up the hatchet; and as they were not willing to remain thus in inaction they marched, to the number of twelve hundred warriors, against the Ozages and the Accances[15] (who are in the lower Missisipi country), and carried away captive the people of a village there. The neighboring peoples, having been apprised of this raid, united together and attacked the Islinois with such spirit that the latter were compelled to retreat with loss. This repulse was very detrimental to them in the course of time. The Outaouaks, who had followed their own caprice without consulting the French commandants who were at Michilimakinak, brought back some captives; and at night the cries for the dead were heard abroad. The next day the smoke in their camp was seen at the island of Michilimakinak; and they sent a canoe to inform the village of the blow that they had just struck. The Jesuit fathers hastened thither, in

---

15 The Osage are a Siouan tribe, one of the Dhegiha group, and are very closely related to the Kansa. According to their traditions, these tribes in their migration westward, "divided at the mouth of Osage River, the Osage moving up that stream and the Omaha and Ponca crossing Missouri River and proceeding northward, while the Kansa ascended the Missouri on the south side to Kansas River." — *Handbook Amer. Indians.*

Dorsey in his "Migrations of the Siouan Tribes" (*Amer. Naturalist*, vol. xx, 211-222) says that the entire Dhegiha group lived together (before their separation above noted), near the Ohio River, and were called "Arkansa" by the Illinois tribes. "Accances" of our text is the same as Akansa, Akansea, Kanza, etc., of the early writers, especially Marquette; but these refer to the Quapaw, another tribe of the above group. They, with the Osage and Kansa, are now on reservations in (the former) Indian Territory. — ED.

order to try to secure for the slaves exemption from the
volley of blows with clubs to which the captives were
usually treated on their arrival; but all their solicitations could not move the Outaouaks, and even served
only to exasperate them. The canoes, which were close
together, made their appearance; there was only one
man paddling in each, while all the warriors responded
to the songs of the slaves, [16] who stood upright, each hav-

---

[16] "It may be doubted whether slavery, though so widespread as to have
been almost universal, existed anywhere among very primitive peoples, since
society must reach a certain state of organization before it can find lodgment.
It appears, however, among peoples whose status is far below that of civilization." The region of the northwest coast "formed the stronghold of the
institution. As we pass to the eastward the practice of slavery becomes modified, and finally its place is taken by a very different custom. . . Investigation of slavery among the tribes of the great plains and the Atlantic slope
is difficult. Scattered through early histories are references to the subject, but
such accounts are usually devoid of details, and the context often proves them
to be based on erroneous conceptions. . . The early French and Spanish
histories, it is true, abound in allusions to Indian slaves, even specifying the
tribes from which they were taken; but the terms 'slave' and 'prisoner' were
used interchangeably in almost every such instance. . . With the exception of
the area above mentioned [the N.W. coast], traces of true slavery are wanting
throughout the region north of Mexico. In its place is found another institution that has been often mistaken for it. Among the North American Indians
a state of periodic intertribal warfare seems to have existed. . . In consequence of such warfare tribes dwindled through the loss of men, women, and
children killed or taken captive. Natural increase was not sufficient to make
good such losses; for, while Indian women were prolific, the loss of children
by disease, especially in early infancy, was very great. Hence arose the
institution of adoption. Men, women, and children, especially the two latter
classes, were everywhere considered the chief spoils of war. When men
enough had been tortured and killed to glut the savage passions of the conquerors, the rest of the captives were adopted, after certain preliminaries, into
the several gentes, each newly adopted member taking the place of a lost
husband, wife, son, or daughter, and being invested with the latter's rights,
privileges, and duties. It was indeed a common practice, too, for small parties
to go out for the avowed purpose of taking a captive to be adopted in the place
of a deceased member of the family. John Tanner, a white boy thus captured
and adopted by the Chippewa, wrote a narrative of his Indian life that is a
mine of valuable and interesting information. Adoption also occasionally
took place on a large scale, as when the Tuscarora were formally adopted as
kindred by the Seneca, and thus secured a place in the Iroquois League; or
when, after the Pequot War, part of the surviving Pequot were incorporated
into the Narraganset tribe by some form of adoption, and part into the Mo-

ing a wand in his hand. There were special marks on each, to indicate those who had captured him. Gradually they approached the shore, with measured advance. When they were near the land the chief of the party rose in his canoe and harangued all the old men, who were waiting for the warriors at the edge of the water in order to receive them; and having made a recital to them of his campaign he told them that he placed in their hands the captives whom he had taken. An old man on the shore responded, and congratulated them in

hegan." Under certain conditions, the practice of adopting prisoners of war might gradually be transformed into slavery, and it is possible that slave-holding tribes may have substituted adoption; the latter seems to have prevailed wherever slavery did not exist. Those who were actually slaves had no social status in the tribe, whether they had been captured in war or purchased; but "the adopted person was in every respect the peer of his fellow-tribesmen," and had the same opportunity for advancement or office that would have belonged to the person in whose place he was adopted – unless he were a poor hunter or a coward, in which case he was despised and ill-treated. "It was the usual custom to depose the coward from man's estate, and, in native metaphor, to 'make a woman' of him. Such persons associated ever after with the women, and aided them in their tasks." Female captives might become the legal wives of men in their captors' tribe; but such women were probably often the objects of jealousy in the husband's other wives. White captives were often adopted into Indian tribes, but after the beginning of the border wars were most often held for ransom, or sometimes sold in European settlements for a cash payment. "The practice of redeeming captives was favored by the missionaries and settlers with a view to mitigating the hardships of Indian warfare. The spread of Indian slavery among the tribes of the central region was in part due to the efforts of the French missionaries to induce their red allies to substitute a mild condition of servitude for their accustomed practice of indiscriminate massacre, torture, and cannibalism (see Dunn's *Indiana*; 1905)." White captives were always ready to escape, and were welcomed back by their friends, "whereas in the case of the Indian, adoption severed all former social and tribal ties. The adopted Indian warrior was forever debarred from returning to his own people, by whom he would not have been received. His fate was thenceforth inextricably interwoven with that of his new kinsmen." Runaway negroes early came into the possession of the southern tribes, and thus were slaves; but they often married the Indians and were otherwise treated like members of the tribe. Europeans made a practice of enslaving or selling into slavery captive Indians, many of whom were shipped to the West Indies. "In the early days of the colonies the enslavement of Indians by settlers seems to have been general." – H. W. HENSHAW, in *Handbook Amer. Indians*.

most complaisant terms. Finally the warriors stepped ashore, all naked, abandoning to pillage, according to their custom, all their booty. An old man came, at the head of nine men, to conduct the captives to a place at one side; there were five old men and four youths. The women and the children immediately ranged themselves in rows, very much as is done when some soldier is flogged through the lines. The young captives, who were very agile, quickly passed through; but the old men were so hardly used that they bled profusely. The former were awarded to masters, who spared their lives; but the old men were condemned to the flames. They were placed on the Manilion, which is the place where the captives are burned, until the chiefs had decided to which tribe they should be handed over. The Jesuit fathers and the commandants were greatly embarrassed, in so delicate a situation; for they feared that the five Iroquois tribes would complain of the little care which the French took of their people at the very time when there was discussion of a general peace. They sent a large collar of porcelain to redeem the captives; the Outaouaks insolently replied that they would be masters of their own actions, without depending on any one whatsoever. Sieur Perrot, who was at Michilimakinak with the three Sauteur girls, had a strong ascendency over the minds of those peoples; and he was called upon to make in person the demand for the captives. He went to the cabin of their council of war, with a collar, accompanied by those persons who had presented the first one. He passed in front of the Manilion, on which the prisoners, who awaited their fate, were singing; he made them sit down, and told them to cease their songs. Some Outaouaks roughly ordered them to continue; but Perrot replied to these that he intended that the captives should be silent, and he actually silenced their guards, telling the slaves that soon he would be the master of their bodies. He entered the council, where he found all the old men, who had already pronounced sentence; one was to be burned at the Bay of Puans, the second at the Saut, and the three others at Michilimakinak. Perrot was not disconcerted by that; he hung his porcelain collar to a pole when he entered, and addressed them nearly in this manner:

"I come to cut the cords on the dogs; I am not willing that they should be eaten. I have pity on them, since my father Onontio takes pity on them, and even has commanded me to do so. You Outaouaks are like bears who have been tamed; when one gives them a little freedom, they will no longer recognize those who have reared them. You no longer remember the protection of Onontio, without which you would not possess any country; I am maintaining you in it, and you are living in peace. When he asks from you a few tokens of obedience, you wish to lord it over him, and to eat the flesh of those people, whom he will not abandon to you. Take care lest you are unable to swallow them, and lest Onontio snatch them by force from between your teeth. I speak to you as a brother; and I think that I am taking pity on your children when I cut the bonds of your captives."

This discourse did not seem very compelling for obtaining a favor of this sort; nevertheless, it had all the success that one could desire. Indeed, one of the chiefs began to speak, and said: "See, it is the master of the land who speaks; his canoe is always full of captives whom he sets free, and how can we refuse him?" They sent word immediately to bring the captives, to whom they granted life in open council.

The liberty which these five old men came to enjoy

was a result of chance, or rather of caprice. One must be very politic in order to manage those peoples, who so easily stray from their duty; they should not be flattered much, and likewise should not be reduced to despair. They are managed only by solid and convincing arguments, which must be gently placed before them, but without sparing those people when they are in the wrong; but it is necessary to keep them up with hopes, making them understand that they will be rewarded when they have deserved it.

As all the tribes were to send deputies to Montreal, to be present at the general peace, the Outaouaks thought it opportune to send to Monsieur de Denonville two of those liberated captives, to the end that so authentic an example of their generosity might shine in the general council. They desired that Perrot should let the captives be seen beforehand in their own country, in order thus to induce the Five Nations to commit no further act of hostility against them, but to be very cautious to use this means without the order of the general. He told them that he did not know of any open door among the Iroquois except that indicated by the ordinary road, which was the only one by which he could enter; and that ever since he had had access to the cabin of Onontio, and had warmed himself at his fire, he would go, if Onontio wished to open the door of the Iroquois, to carry his message to all of his villages if he should command him to do so. The Outaouaks were pleased with these arguments; they recommended to him the interests of their tribe, and entreated him to be their spokesman in the general council. They gave him Petite Racine [i.e., "Little Root"], one of their chiefs, who had orders only to make a report of all the deliberations; and they assured him that, if unfortunately he were killed on the

journey through the Iroquois country, they would
avenge his death, and that they would never consent to a
peace until they had first sacrificed to his spirit many of
the Iroquois families. This was in truth the most convincing proof of the esteem which they felt for him.
But the affairs of the colony entirely changed their aspect; if the most powerful states are sometimes subject
to revolutions, we say that distant countries, [even] the
most stable, are also exposed to cruel catastrophes. Indeed Canada, which had never been so flourishing, suddenly found itself, so to speak, the prey of its enemies.
All the tribes who heard the French name mentioned
wished only for means of forming alliance with our nation; and those who were already known to us found
that it was very agreeable to be under our protection.
On the other hand, its enemies found themselves humiliated in the sight of an infinite number of peoples.
Even the English, affected by the disaster to their
friends, in some sort implored the good graces of him
who had chastised the latter. Nothing, therefore, was
more glorious for the Marquis de Denonville, but nothing was more touching than the occasion when he beheld
utter desolation in the center of his government. It was
then that the Iroquois came suddenly to the island of
Montreal, to the number of fifteen hundred warriors;
they put to the sword all that they encountered in the
space of seven leagues.[17] They rendered themselves

17 This refers to the sudden raid made by the Iroquois against the island
of Montreal in 1689; on Aug. 25 of that year 1,500 of those savages surprised
the village of Lachine, near Montreal, and slew or took captive all its inhabitants; and thence they ravaged the entire island with fire and sword. This
fearful disaster caused terror in all the French settlements, and made many of
the friendly tribes waver in their allegiance to France; but in the same year
Count de Frontenac was sent to Canada for a second term as governor, and
his able rule soon restored peace and safety. This Iroquois raid was doubtless
caused by resentment on the part of the Five Nations at Denonville's punitive
expedition into their country in 1687, and still more by his treacherous seizure

masters of the open country by using the cover of the woods; and no person could set foot on the land along the river who was not captured or killed. They spread themselves on every side with the same rapidity as does a torrent. Nothing could resist the fury of those barbarians, no matter what action was taken to furnish aid to those whom our people saw carried away [into captivity], or to resist the various parties of the enemy. The French were compelled to shut themselves at once within two wretched little forts; and if the Flemings had not warned them to be very careful to remain close to the forts it may be said that the enemy would have made an end of them with the same facility that they did of all the settlements that they ravaged. The open counry was laid waste; the ground was everywhere covered with corpses, and the Iroquois carried away six-score captives, most of whom were burned; but these are misfortunes which ought not to cause the least damage to the glory of a general. It is not surprising that the savages came to make incursions and raids into so vast a region. The skill of these peoples is, to avoid combats in open country, because they do not know how to offer battle or make evolutions therein; their manner of conducting battles is altogether different from that of Europe. The forests are the most secure retreats, in which they fight advantageously; for it is agreed that these fifteen hundred warriors would have cut to pieces more than six thousand men, if the latter should advance into the mountainous country where the savages were. There are no troops of the sort that are in Europe who could succeed in such an enterprise, not only in equal but even in far superior numbers.

of a number of their chiefs, whom he sent to work on the galleys in France — an act which violated the law of nations even the most primitive, and was both dastardly and cruel. — ED.

Chapter XVII

La Petite Racine ["Little Root"], who had come [to Montreal] on behalf of his tribe to be a witness of all that should take place in the general peace council, found an altogether extraordinary change in the condition of affairs; he traded the peltries that he had brought down, and promptly returned home. Monsieur Denonville despatched with him a canoe, by which he sent his orders to Monsieur de la Durantaye, commandant at Michilimakinak. This chief, on his return, caused universal alarm. The Outaouaks informed all the tribes of the devastation that had been inflicted upon the French, and entreated all the chiefs to come to Michilimakinak, that they might consult together upon the measures that ought to be taken regarding the wretched condition into which they were going to be plunged. They resolved in their general council to send to Tsonnontouan some deputies, with two of those Iroquois old men whom they had set free, in order to assure the Iroquois that they would have no further connection with the French, and that they desired to maintain with the Iroquois a close alliance.

The Hurons feigned not to join in the revolt of the Outaouaks; the policy of those peoples is so shrewd that it is difficult to penetrate its secrets. When they undertake any enterprise of importance against a nation whom they fear, especially against the French, they seem to form two parties—one conspiring for and the other opposing it; if the former succeed in their projects, the latter approve and sustain what has been done; if their designs are thwarted, they retire to the other side. Accordingly, they always attain their objects. But such was not the case in this emergency; they were so terrified by La Petite Racine's report that neither the Jesuits nor the commandant could pacify those people – who reproached them, with the most atrocious insults, saying that the French had abused them. Matters reached so pitiable a condition that Monsieur de la Durantaye had need of all his experience and good management to keep his fort and maintain the interests of the colony – an undertaking that any other man would have abandoned; for the savages are fickle, take umbrage at everything, are time-serving, and are seldom friends except as caprice and self-interest induce them to act as such; it is necessary to take them on their weak side, and to profit by certain moments when one can penetrate their designs.

Soon afterward, Monsieur the Marquis de Denonville was recalled to court, his majesty having appointed him sub-governor to Monsieur the Duke of Bourgogne [i.e., Burgundy]. Monsieur the Count de Frontenac succeeded him, and arrived in Canada at the end of October, 1689. Monsieur de la Durantaye, who had remained at Michilimakinak, despatched a canoe to the new governor, to acquaint him with all the movements of the Outaouaks, and, as he held only a temporary command in the post which he was occupying, Monsieur de Frontenac sent Monsieur de Louvigni to relieve him. That governor was of opinion, at the outset, that it was desirable to make known his arrival to all the tribes; Perrot was the man whom he selected for that purpose; he ordered him, at the same time, to make every effort to pacify the troubles that the Outaouaks might have occasioned in those regions. He was accordingly despatched with Monsieur de Louvigni, who cut to pieces, at fifty leagues from Montreal, a party of sixty Iroquois; three of these he sent as prisoners to Monsieur de Frontenac,

and another he took with him. He also carried away
many scalps, in order to show them to the Outaouaks, in
the hope of bringing about a reconciliation with them;
but those peoples had already secured the start of him,
lest they should draw upon themselves the indignation
of the Iroquois. On the route the French learned,
through the Missisakis, that La Petite Racine had gone
as ambassador to the Iroquois with two chiefs; that
nothing had been heard about them since, except that
it was said that one of them was yet to depart. This news
induced Monsieur de Louvigni to send Perrot with two
canoes to Michilimakinak, to inform the French of his
arrival. As soon as he came in sight of the place, he
displayed the white flag, and his men uttered loud shouts
of "Vive le Roi!" The French judged, by that, that
some good news had come from Montreal. The Outaouaks ran to the edge of the shore, not in the least understanding all these outcries; as they were thoroughly persuaded that our affairs were in very bad condition, they
were so politic as to say that they would receive in warlike fashion the French who were on the way. They
were warned that our usages were different from theirs;
we were unwilling that they should swarm into our canoes to pillage them, as is their custom in regard to
nations who come back victorious from any military expedition, abandoning whatever is in their canoes; we
preferred that they should be content with receiving
presents. Warning was sent to Monsieur de Louvigni
that he would be received in military array, with all the
Frenchmen whom he was bringing; all sorts of precautions were taken lest we should be duped by those peoples, who were capable of laying violent hands on us
when we were least expecting such action. The canoes
came into view, at their head the one in which was the

Iroquois slave; according to custom, he was made to
sing, all the time standing upright. The Nepiciriniens
who had accompanied the Frenchmen responded with
them, keeping time, by loud shouts of "Sassakoue!" followed by volleys of musketry. A hundred Frenchmen
of Michilimakinak were stationed, under arms, on the
water's edge at the foot of their village; they had only
powder in their guns, but had taken the precaution to
place bullets in their mouths. The fleet, which proceeded in regular array, as if it were going to make a
descent on an enemy's country, gradually came near.
When the canoes neared the village of the Outaouaks, [18]
they halted, and the Iroquois was made to sing; a volley
of musket-shots, to which the Outaouaks responded, accompanied his song. The fleet crossed, in nearly a
straight line, to the French village, but did not at once
come to land. The Outaouaks hastened, all in battle
array, to the landing-place, while the men in the canoes
replied to the prisoner's songs with loud yells and firing
of guns, as also did the French of Michilimakinak. At
last, when it was necessary to go on shore, Monsieur de
Louvigni had his men load their guns with ball, and
disembark with weapons ready; the Outaouaks stood at
a little distance on the shore, without making any further
demonstration.

The Hurons—who, although they have been at all
times very unreliable, had seemed greatly attached to
our interests amid the general conspiracy of the Outaouaks—demanded the slave, in order to have him
burned; [19] the other tribes were jealous of that prefer-

---

[18] The French post of Michilimackinac then stood on the mainland, at the
site of the present St. Ignace. There were three separate villages, those of
the French, Hurons, and Ottawas. A detailed map, showing these, is found in
La Hontan's *Voyages* (ed. 1741, Amsterdam, tome i, 156); this is reproduced
in Wis. *Hist. Colls.*, vol. xvi, 136. — ED.

[19] "The treatment accorded captives was governed by those limited ethical

ence. The Huron chiefs, who were very politic, after
many deliberations warned their people not to put him
in the kettle; their object in this was to render them-

---

concepts which went hand in hand with clan, gentile, and other consanguineal
organizations of Indian society. From the members of his own consanguineal
group, or what was considered such, certain ethical duties were exacted of an
Indian which could not be neglected without destroying the fabric of society or
outlawing the transgressor. Toward other clans, gentes, or bands of the same
tribe his actions were also governed by well recognized customs and usages
which had grown up during ages of intercourse; but with remote bands or
tribes good relations were assured only by some formal peace-making ceremony. A peace of this kind was very tenuous, however, especially where there
had been a long-standing feud, and might be broken in an instant. Toward
a person belonging to some tribe with which there was neither war nor peace,
the attitude was governed largely by the interest of the moment. . . If the
stranger belonged to a clan or gens represented in the tribe he was among, the
members of that clan or gens usually greeted him as a brother and extended
their protection over him. Another defense for the stranger was—what with
civilized people is one of the best guaranties against war—the fear of disturbing or deflecting trade. . . If nothing were to be had from the stranger,
he might be entirely ignored. And, finally, the existence of a higher ethical
feeling toward strangers, even when there was apparently no self-interest to
be served in hospitality, is often in evidence. . . At the same time the
attitude assumed toward a person thrown among Indians too far from his own
people to be protected by any ulterior hopes or fears on the part of his captors
was usually that of master to slave. . . The majority of captives, however,
were those taken in war. These were considered to have forfeited their lives and
to have been actually dead as to their previous existence. It was often thought
that the captive's supernatural helper had been destroyed or made to submit
to that of the captor, though where not put to death with torture to satisfy the
victor's desire for revenge and to give the captive an opportunity to show his
fortitude, he might in a way be reborn by undergoing a form of adoption.
It is learned from the numerous accounts of white persons who had been taken
by Indians that the principal hardships they endured were due to the rapid
movements of their captors in order to escape pursuers, and the continual
threats to which they were subjected," threats which were, however, seldom
carried out; and a certain amount of consideration was often shown toward
captive women and children. "It is worthy of remark that the honor of a
white woman was almost always respected by her captors among the tribes
east of the Mississippi; but west of that limit, on the plains, in the Columbia
River region, and in the southwest, the contrary was often the case." The
disposal of the captives taken by war-parties varied in many ways. Running
the gauntlet, dancing for the entertainment of their captors, tortures of various
kinds, and often burning at the stake (sometimes accompanied by cannibalism),
were among the methods of their reception in the enemy's country; but the
majority were regarded and treated as slaves by their captors, being sometimes

selves acceptable to the Iroquois, in case peace should be made with that people, by the distinguished service which they would have rendered to one of their chiefs by saving him from the fire; but we very plainly saw their design. The Outaouaks, who were greatly offended, could not refrain from saying that it would be necessary to eat him. That Iroquois was surprised that a mere handful of Hurons, whom his own people had enslaved, should have prevailed on an occasion of such importance.

The father who was missionary to the Hurons, foreseeing that this affair might have results which would be prejudicial to his cares for their instruction, demanded permission to go to their village that he might constrain them to find some way by which the resentment of the French might be appeased. He told them that the latter peremptorily ordered them to put the Iroquois in the kettle and that, if they did not do so, the French must come to take him away from them and place him in their own fort. Some Outaouaks who happened to be present at the council said that the French were right. The Hurons then saw themselves constrained to beg the father to tell the French, on their behalf, that they asked for a little delay, in order that they might bind him to the stake. They did this, and began to burn his fingers; but the slave displayed so great lack of courage, by the tears that he shed, that they judged him unworthy to die a warrior's death, and despatched him with their weapons.

The chiefs of all the nations at Michilimakinak were

<hr />

sold to other tribes, and sometimes ransomed (especially when whites). Often a captive was adopted to take the place of some person who had died, and thus was liberated from slavery. Most women and children were preserved and adopted; and the Iroquois adopted entire bands or even tribes in order to recruit their own population. — JOHN R. SWANTON, in *Handbook Amer. Indians.* [Cf. vol. i, *footnote* 134. — ED.]

summoned to meet at the house of the Jesuit fathers; and before each one was placed a present of guns, ammunition, and tobacco. Our envoy represented to them their short-sightedness in abandoning the interests of the French nation to embrace those of the Iroquois, whose only desire was for such a rupture. They were told that Onontio, who had every reason to abandon them, was nevertheless touched with compassion for his children, whom he desired to bring back to himself; and that he had sent the band of Frenchmen who had just arrived among them, striving to restore to the right path their minds, which had gone astray. That those houses burned on Montreal Island by the Iroquois, and the few corpses that they had seen in the unexpected invasion which the latter had made there, ought not to have such an effect on their minds as to persuade them that all was lost in the colony; that the Iroquois would not derive much profit from a blow which would far more redound to their shame than to the glory of true warriors, since they had come at that very time to ask for peace. That the French nation was more numerous than they imagined; that they must look upon it as a great river which never ran dry, and whose course could not be checked by any barrier. That they ought to regard the five Iroquois nations as five cabins of muskrats in a marsh which the French would soon drain off, and then burn them there; that they could be satisfied that the hundred women and children who had been treacherously carried away would be replaced by many soldiers, whom the great Onontio, the king of France, would send to avenge them. That since our Onontio of Canada, the Count de Frontenac, had arrived at Quebec, he had made the English feel the strength of his arms, by the various war-parties that he had sent into their country;

that even the Nepiciriniens who had recently come up to Michilimakinak with Monsieur de Louvigni had given us no little aid in putting five large English villages to fire and sword; that Onontio was powerful enough to destroy the Iroquois, the English, and their allies. Finally, if any one of these tribes undertook to declare themselves in favor of the Iroquois, he gave them liberty to do so, but he would not consent that those who wielded the war-club to maintain their own interests should hereafter dwell upon his lands; that, if they preferred to be Iroquois, we would become their enemies; and that it would be seen, without any further explanations, who should remain master of the country.

The chief of the Cinagos, rising in the council, spoke in these terms: "My brother the Outaouak, vomit forth thy hateful feelings and all thy plots. Return to thy father, who stretches out his arms, and who is, moreover, not unable to protect thee." Nothing more was needed to overturn all the schemes of the malcontents. The chiefs of each nation protested that they would undertake no action against the will of their father. But, whatever assurance they gave of their fidelity, most of them, seeing their designs foiled, sought to thwart us by other subterfuges. They did not dare, it is true, to carry out their resolution – either because they were unwilling to risk a combat with the French, who were only waiting for a final decision; or because they did not know how they could transport their families to the Iroquois country – but all their desire was for the time when they could open the way for a large troop from that nation who could carry them away. They decided, however, in a secret conclave that they would send to the Iroquois the same deputies on whom they had previously agreed; and that, if their departure should un-

fortunately be discovered, the old men should disown
them. This mystery was not kept so hidden that we did
not receive warning of it. A Sauteur came to warn
Perrot of their intention; one of their deputies entering
his cabin a little later, he reproached him for it. But, as
the savage is by nature an enemy of deceit, this man
could not long disguise his sentiments; and he admitted
that his brother was at the head of that embassy. Monsieur de Louvigni did not hesitate to call together all the
chiefs, whom he sharply rebuked for their faithlessness.
The Outaouaks thought that they could exculpate themselves by casting all the blame upon the man who was to
go away. Messengers were sent for him, and never did
a man seem more ashamed than he when he saw that he
must appear before the council; he entered the place
with the utmost mortification in his face. His brother
said to him: "Our chiefs are throwing the stone at
thee, and they say that they know nothing about thy departure for the Iroquois." Perrot took up the word,
saying: "My brother, how is this? I thought that thou
wast the supporter of the French who are at Michilimakinak. When the attack was made at Tsonnontouan,
all the Outaouaks gave way; thou alone, with two others,
didst second the French. At all times thou hast kept
nothing for thyself; when thou hadst anything thou
gavest it to the French, whom thou didst love as thine
own brothers; yet now thou wouldst, against the wishes
of thy tribe, betray us. Onontio, who remembers thee,
has told me to reward thee; I do not think that thou art
capable of opposing his wishes." He gave the man a
brasse of tobacco and a shirt, and continued: "See what
he has given me to show thee that he remembers thee.
Although thou hast done wrong, I will give thee something to smoke, so that thou mayest vomit up or swallow

whatever thou hast intended to do against him; and thy body, which is soiled by treason, shall be made clean by this shirt, which will make it white." That chief was so overcome with sorrow that it was a long time before he could speak; he recovered himself somewhat, and, addressing the old men, with an air full of pride and contempt, said to them: "Employ me in future, old men, when you undertake to plot anything against my father — he who remembers me, and against whom I have taken sides. I belong wholly to him; and never will I take part against the French." Then turning toward Perrot, he said to him: "I will not lie to thee. When thou didst arrive, I went near thee, intending to embrace thee; but thou didst regard me unkindly. I thought that thou hadst abandoned me, because I had been to the Iroquois with La Petite Racine. When thou didst speak to the tribes, I withdrew, in order to divert them from the design that we all had of giving ourselves to the Iroquois. They did not dare to oppose thee; but at night they held a council in a cabin (from which they turned out all the women and children), to which I was summoned. They deputed me to return to the Iroquois, and I believed that thou hadst a grudge against me; those reasons constrained me to yield to what they demanded from me."

Those peoples could no longer maintain their evil design; the explanations that had just been made checked its progress; but they always kept up a very surly feeling against the French nation, and, although they saw that they were unable to compass their object, they did not fail again to stir up opposition against us, in order to annoy us. The jealousy that they felt because we made presents of a few gold-trimmed jackets to some Hurons, who had appeared to be our friends in this af-

fair, inspired in them a new stratagem. They knew that
the Miamis, our allies, were at war with the Iroquois;
and they resolved to attack the former, who did not mis-
trust their design, that they might force the Miamis
themselves to make peace with the Iroquois. The Sauteur who had already ascertained that the Outaouaks
had intended to send deputies to the Iroquois also
learned that two canoes were to go to break heads among
the Miamis; but we again broke up their plans, and prevented this act.

The Outagamis and the Maskoutechs, wishing to second the Outaouaks at the time when they took sides with
the Iroquois – who had sent them a large collar, in order
to thank them for having restored to them five chiefs
whom they had captured when on a hostile expedition
against the Islinois – resolved, to do the Iroquois a pleasure, to massacre all the French who were coming down
from the country of the Nadouaissioux. They persuaded themselves that they would, by such a massacre,
attract to themselves the friendship of that haughty
nation, who had appeared greatly pleased when the
Outagamis had sent back to them five slaves of their nation, whom the Miamis had given to them to eat.

The arrival of the French at Michilimakinak was
heard of at La Baye. The chief of the Puans, a man of
sense, who greatly loved our nation, resolved to thwart
the plot to kill our people. He went to find the Outagamis, and made them believe that Onontio had sent La
Petit Bled d'Inde [i.e., Perrot] with three hundred Iroquois from the Sault, as many more Abenaquis, [20] all the

<hr/>

[20] Abnaki (a term derived from Algonkin words meaning "east-land," or
"morning-land"), "a name used by the English and French to designate an
Algonquian confederacy centering in the present state of Maine, and by the
Algonquian tribes to include all those of their own stock resident on the Atlantic
seaboard, more particularly the 'Abnaki' in the north and the Delawares in the
south. . . In later times, after the main body of the Abnaki had removed

Nepiciriniens, and six hundred Frenchmen, to revenge himself for their evil project. The Outagamis precipitately quitted their ambuscade, and went back to their village. This chief, who was afraid that they would learn of his ruse, went to meet Perrot at the entrance of the bay; the latter promised to keep his secret, and presented to him a gold-trimmed jacket. A contrary wind compelled them to halt there for a time, and Perrot had an opportunity to become acquainted with all that had occurred at the bay. The Outagamis had taken thither their hatchets, which were dulled and broken, and had compelled a Jesuit brother to repair them; their chief held a naked sword, ready to kill him, while he worked. The brother tried to represent to them their folly, but was so maltreated that he had to take to his bed. The chief then prepared ambuscades, in order to await the French who were to return from the country of the Nadouaissioux. All the peoples of the bay had, it is true, good reason to complain, because our people had gone to carry to their enemies all kinds of munitions of war; and one could not be astonished that we had so much difficulty in managing all those people. Perrot sent back the Puan chief to the Outagamis, to tell them on his behalf that he had learned of their design against his young men, and would punish them for it; and, to let them know that he was not disturbed by all their threats, that he had sent back all his men, except fifty Frenchmen; that he had three hundred musket-shots to fire, and enough ammunition with which to receive them; that if he should by chance encounter any one of their tribe, he could not answer for the consequences;

to Canada, the name was applied more especially to the Penobscot tribe." The Sokoki were one of the tribes in this confederacy. In 1903 the Abnaki of Canada (which include remnants of other New England tribes) numbered 395; and the Penobscot of Maine say that their present population is between 300 and 400. — JAMES MOONEY and CYRUS THOMAS, in *Handbook Amer. Indians.*

and that it would be useless for them to ask him to land
at their village.

The Puan chief returned to the bay, where he exaggerated still further what Perrot had said to him.
The Renard chief visited him expressly to ascertain the
truth of the matter, and dared not wait for Perrot. He
departed with eighty of his warriors to march against
the Nadouaissioux, after he had given orders to the
people of his village to assure Perrot in his behalf that
he loved him, and to take great pains to entertain him
well. He proceeded to the post of the Frenchmen who
were sojourning in the country of the Nadouaissioux;
as they were afraid of him, they gave him presents – a
gun, a shirt, a kettle, and various munitions of war; and
he told them that Le Petit Bled d'Inde had resolved to
recall them to the bay. This news, which was not very
agreeable to them, induced them to quit that establishment; and they retired to a place eighty leagues farther
inland, where they engaged the Nadouaissioux to go
hunting, and to return to them in the winter. The
Outagamis profited by this opportunity to attack the
Nadouaissioux, of whom they slew many, and took several captives. The alarm was immediately given among
the villages; the warriors fell upon them, and likewise
slew many of the Outagamis, and took some captives.
The chief fought on the retreat with extraordinary courage, and would have lost many more of his people if he
himself had not made so firm a stand at the head of his
band.

Chapter XVIII

The Miamis, who had heard the report that Perrot
would soon arrive at the bay, set out to visit him, to the
number of forty, loaded with beaver-skins; when they

came near the house of the Jesuits,[21] canoes were sent to them that they might cross a little stream. The chief sent his young warriors to erect some cabins; when these had been made, they all resorted thither, in order to consult about the interview that they expected to hold with Sieur Perrot. An accident happened to a Saki who was at the time in his cabin; while he was sitting in the floor, a kettle which hung over the fire fell over him, and part of his body was burned, as he wore only an old raccoon-skin. He uttered a yell, with contortions that made those who were present laugh, despite the compassion which they could not help feeling for him. A Frenchman said to him, jestingly, that a man as courageous as he was ought not to fear the fire; that it was the proper thing for a warrior such as he to sing; but that, to show him that he felt grieved at the accident, he would lay over the scalded part a plaster, consisting of a brasse of tobacco. The Saki replied that such an act showed good sense; and that the tobacco had entirely healed him. The Miamis sent to beg Perrot to visit them in their cabins, that he might point out to them a place where he desired them to assemble. The place of rendezvous was at the house of the Jesuits, to which they brought one hundred and sixty beaver-skins, which they piled in two heaps. The Miami chief, standing by one of them,

[21] In this connection may be mentioned a most interesting relic owned by the Roman Catholic diocese of Green Bay, and deposited in the State Historical Museum at Madison, Wis. It is an ostensorium or monstrance of silver, fifteen inches high, of elaborate workmanship. Around the rim of its oval base is an inscription in French, somewhat rudely cut on the metal, which translated reads: "This monstrance [French, *soleil*, referring to its shape] was given by Mr. Nicolas Perrot to the mission of St. François Xavier at the Bay of Puants [i.e., Green Bay], 1686." This is, so far, the oldest relic existing of French occupancy in Wisconsin. For description and illustration of this ostensorium, see *Wis. Hist. Colls.*, vol. viii, 199-206; and *Jesuit Relations*, vol. lxvi, 347. The Jesuit Mission was located a little above the mouth of Fox River, at the present Depere. — ED.

spoke after this fashion: "My father, I come to tell thee
that thy dead men and mine are in the same grave; and
that the Maskoutechs have killed us, and have made us
eat our own flesh. My three sisters, who were made
prisoners in the year of the battle with the Tsonnontouans, seeing that the Iroquois were routed by Onontio
[footnote, 'The Marquis de Denonville'], escaped
from their hands. Some Maskoutechs, whom they encountered at the river of Chikagon, found on their way
two Frenchmen who were returning from the Islinois,
and assassinated them. Their dread that the women
would make known this murder led the assassins to break
their heads; but they carried away the scalps, which
they have given us to eat, saying that they were those of
some Iroquois. The Spirit has punished those assassins
by a malady which has caused them and all their children to die; at last one of them confessed his crime
when he was dying. Those beaver-skins which thou
seest on the other side tell thee that we have no will but
thine; that, if thou tellest us to weep in silence, we will
not make any move [against the Maskoutechs]."

Perrot made them several presents, and spoke to them
in nearly the following words: "My brothers, I delight
in your speech, and war is odious when you fight against
the Maskoutech; he is brave, and will slay your young
men. I do not doubt that you could destroy him, for
you are more numerous and more warlike than he; but
desperation will drive him to extremity, and he has
arrows and war-clubs, which he can handle with skill.
Besides, the war-fire has been lighted against the Iroquois, and will be extinguished only when he ceases to
exist. War was declared on your account when he
swept away your families at Chikagon; those dead persons are seen no longer, for they are covered by those of

the Frenchmen whom the Iroquois have betrayed through the agency of the Englishman – who was our ally, and upon whom we have undertaken to avenge ourselves for his treacherous conduct. We have also for an enemy the Loup, who is his son. Accordingly, we shall not be able to assist you if you undertake war against the Maskoutechs."

After he had delivered this speech to them he also made two heaps of merchandise; and, displaying these, continued thus: "I place a mat under your dead and ours, that they may sleep in peace; and this other present is to cover them with a piece of bark, in order that bad weather and rain may not disturb them. Onontio, to whom I will make known this assassination, will consider and decide what is best to do." The Miamis, then, had reason to be satisfied; since they begged him to locate his establishment upon the Missisipi, near Ouiskensing [Wisconsin], so that they could trade with him for their peltries. The chief made him a present of a piece of ore which came from a very rich lead mine, which he had found on the bank of a stream which empties into the Missisipi;[22] and Perrot promised them that he

[22] This was probably the Galena River. It is not probable that the Indians of early days worked these mines along the upper Mississippi that now yield so great a supply of lead; but after they learned from the French the use of firearms they began to place much value on this metal, and probably obtained supplies of it in some crude fashion from outcropping ores. From them the French early learned the location of lead deposits, and during the eighteenth century worked mines here and there along the Mississippi, often employing Indians to do the work under their direction. The most noted of these mine-owners was Julien Dubuque, who obtained from the Sacs and Foxes (1788) permission to work mines on their lands, and from the Spanish authorities (1796) the grant of a large tract of land on the west side of the Mississippi, by means of which he acquired great wealth. See Thwaites's "Notes on Early Lead Mining," in Wis. Hist. Colls., vol. xiii, 271-292, and succeeding articles by O. G. Libby on "Lead and Shot Trade in early Wisconsin History." Cf. Meeker's "Early History of the Lead Region," id., vol. vi, 271-296.

would within twenty days establish a post below the Ouiskonche [Wisconsin] River. The chief then returned to his village.

All the Saki chiefs and the Pouteouatemis assembled near the Jesuit house. Perrot gave them presents of guns, tobacco, and ammunition, and encouraged them to deal harder blows than ever at the Iroquois, to whom no one was a friend; and he told them how utterly knavish the Iroquois were. He said that the allies should distrust their artful words and their fine collars, which were only so many baits to lure them into their nets; and that, if they should unfortunately fall into those snares, Onontio could not any longer draw them out. He told them that they had cause to be glad that they had continued in their fidelity notwithstanding all the foolish proceedings of the Outaouaks, who had tried to induce the allies to espouse their interests instead of his. He repeated to them the details of all that he had said to the tribes on Lake Huron; and also made them understand that, if they undertook to declare themselves in favor of the Iroquois, they could go to live among them, since we would not suffer them to remain upon our lands. They protested that they would never stray from their duty; and that, although the Outaouaks had always been their friends, they were resolved to perish rather than to abandon the cause of the French.

When Perrot had reached a small Puan village which was near the Outagamis, the chief of the Maskoutechs and two of his lieutenants arrived there. They entered Perrot's cabin, excusing themselves for not having brought any present by which they could talk to him, as their village was upon his route; the chief entreated him to sojourn there, as he had something of importance to communicate to him. Although we were greatly of-

fended with both them and the Outagamis, who had
sworn the ruin of the French who were among the
Nadouaissioux, Perrot promised to stop at their village
in order to forget the resentment that he felt toward
them and to pardon them their error, which had been
made only through the fault of the Renards.

The Sakis returned by way of the Outagamis, to
whom they reported all that had been said to them.
Perrot encountered two Outagami chiefs, who came to
meet him; they approached him trembling, and begged
him, in the most submissive terms, to land, in order to
hear them for a little while. After he had landed, they
lit a fire, and laid on the ground a beaver robe to serve
him as a carpet, on which he seated himself; they were
so beside themselves that for a time they could not speak.
Finally one of them began to talk, saying: "The Outagamis have done wrong not to remember what thou didst
formerly tell them. Since they became acquainted with
thee thou hast never deceived them; and when they do
not see thee they let themselves be carried away by the
solicitations of the Outaouaks and others who try to induce them to abandon the French. I have tried to prevent our people from undertaking anything against thy
young men; but they would not believe me, and I have
been alone in my opinion. When they learned that thou
wert coming, they were afraid of thee, and have begged
me to tell thee on their behalf that they wish to see thee
in their village, in order to reunite themselves to thy
person—which they have not altogether abandoned,
since if they had carried out the scheme with which the
Outaouaks inspired them against the French, they would
have taken care of thy children. As for me, I have taken
no part in their conspiracy; and on that account I have
come to meet thee, to entreat that, if thou wilt not grant

me anything for them, thou wilt at least not refuse to
come and listen to them, out of consideration for me."

It was very difficult to obtain from those peoples all
the satisfaction which we had desired. Their great distance from us prevents us from reducing them to obedience; and the blustering manner which must be
assumed with them was the best policy that could be
adopted to make them fear us. Perrot, who understood
their character, yielded the point out of consideration
for this chief, and promised to remain with them half a
day, in order to listen to their words. The chief went
away to console his people; he came back alone to meet
Perrot, to ask him that he would land at the village.
Another chief, seeing that the French did not leave their
canoes, said that they were afraid. Our men answered
that we did not fear them, and that the weapons of the
French were able to make them repent, if they had the
temerity to offer us any affront. The first-named chief
was greatly incensed against this one, and said to his
countrymen: "O Outagamis, will you always be fools?
You will make the Frenchman embark, and he will
abandon us. What will become of us? can we plant our
fields if he will not allow it?" Throughout the village
there were endless harangues, to quiet those who were
seditious, and to induce the others to give Sieur Perrot
a good reception. The head chief conducted him to his
own cabin, where were present the most influential men
of the tribe, who said to him "Welcome!" while offering
him every token of kind feeling. Two young men entirely naked, armed as warriors, laid at his feet two packages of beaver-skins; and, sitting down, cried out to
him, "We submit to thy wishes, and entreat thee by this
beaver to remember no more our foolish acts. If thou
art not content with this atonement, strike us down; we

will suffer death, for we are willing to atone with our
blood for the fault that our nation has committed."
All these acts of submission had no other object than to
procure ammunition and weapons for the peltries, foreseeing that he would refuse these supplies to them. Perrot made them understand that he had come to their village only to hear them; that, if they repented of their
inconsiderate demands, he would pardon them; that, although they might escape from one hand, he would hold
them tightly with the other; that he was holding them
by no more than one finger, but that, if they would bestir
themselves a little, he would take them by the arms and
gradually bring them into a safe place where they could
dwell in peace.

All the chiefs begged him, one after another, to receive them under his protection, imploring him to give
them ammunition for their peltries so that they could
kill game to make soup for their children. He would
not grant them more than a small amount [après-dîné].
A war-chief, who carried in his hand a dagger, thought
that Perrot's clerk had not given him enough powder,
and spoke so fiercely to him that the clerk yielded all
he asked. Perrot was greatly irritated against them,
and gave orders to have everything taken back to the canoes; but after some explanation he recognized that the
chief had no bad intention. Those peoples are so brutal
that persons who do not understand them suppose that
they are always full of anger when they are speaking.

Chapter XIX

Their trading being ended, the Frenchmen reëmbarked; they did so very opportunely, for the desperate
frame of mind in which the Outagamis found themselves the next day, at tidings of the defeat of their peo-

ple by the Nadouaissioux, would have made them forget the alliance which they had just renewed; in the sequel, they made that feeling sufficiently evident. The French arrived at a place a little below the village of the Maskoutechs, where they encamped. The chiefs, accompanied by their families, came to receive Perrot on the bank of their river; they entreated him to enter a cabin; and by a package of beaver-skins they told him that they covered the dead whom their people had assassinated, including three Miami slaves who had escaped from the Iroquois. By another present, they begged that he would allow them to establish their village at the same place where the French were going to settle, saying that they would demonstrate to him their fidelity, and would trade with him for their peltries. Perrot told them that they had a right to settle wherever they pleased; but that, if he permitted them to come near the French, they must turn their war-clubs against the Iroquois only; that they must hang up the hatchet against the Nadouaissioux until the fire of the Iroquois should be wholly extinguished. He told them that since Onontio had undertaken war against the Iroquois (who was [formerly] his son) – on account of the Miamis who had been slain at Chikagon, and of the Maskoutechs themselves, who had lost their families – he could chastise the Nadouaissioux more easily than they were aware, when he saw that all his children were uniting their forces with his to destroy the common foe. On the next day they presented to the Frenchmen a buffalo and some Indian corn, and fire, [23] which were of great assistance to them during the rest of their journey. He disclosed to

---

[23] Thus in original (*feu*); it may be a misprint for some other word, or it may mean a box containing smouldering tinder (for which "punk," or decaying wood, was often used) – which would be a convenience to the French on their river voyage, even though they carried with them their own fire-steels. – ED.

them the project formed by all the tribes – the Miamis, the Outagamis, the Kikabous, and many of the Islinois. All these tribes were to assemble at the Missisipi, to march against the Nadouaissioux. The Miamis were to command the army; the Maskoutechs also were under obligation to join them, in order to avenge the assassination of the Miami slaves. At that moment some Outagamis brought the news of the defeat of their people by the Nadouaissioux; and they secretly tried to induce the Maskoutechs to unite with them against the French, who had furnished weapons to their enemies. The Maskoutechs were careful not to embroil themselves with the French; and the difficulty which they had already experienced in reinstating themselves in the good graces of the latter hindered them from undertaking any enterprise which would displease the French. These Outagamis, who had got wind of Perrot's sending to the bay a canoe loaded with peltries, went to inform their chief of it; he sent out some men to carry it away. The Frenchmen in the canoe, hearing at night the noise of paddles, and suspecting that the savages were going to capture them, hastily slipped among the tall reeds, which they traversed without being perceived.

Perrot reëmbarked, with all his men, in good order; he encountered at the [Fox-Wisconsin] portage a canoe of Frenchmen who were coming from the country of the Nadouaissioux. He warned them not to trust the Maskoutechs, who would plunder them; but his warning was in vain. Some of that tribe, discovering them, bestowed upon them every kindness, entreating them to stop and rest themselves, on their way, at their village; but the Frenchmen had no sooner arrived there than they were pillaged. The other Frenchmen reached the Missisipi; Perrot sent out ten men to warn, in behalf of

Monsieur de Frontenac, the Frenchmen who were
among the Nadouaissioux to proceed to Michilimakinak. Perrot's establishment was located below the Ouiskonche, in a place very advantageously situated for
security from attacks by the neighboring tribes. [24] The
great chief of the Miamis, having learned that Perrot
was there, sent to him a war-chief and ten young warriors, to tell him that, as his village was four leagues
farther down, he was anxious to sit down with Perrot at
the latter's fire. That chief proceeded thither two days
later, accompanied by twenty men and his women, and
presented to the Frenchman a piece of ore from a lead
mine. Perrot pretended not to be aware of the useful-
ness of that mineral; he even reproached the Miami for
a similar present by which he pretended to cover the
death of the two Frenchmen whom the Maskoutechs had
assassinated with the three Miami women who had escaped from an Iroquois village. The chief was utterly
astonished at such discourse, imagining that Perrot was
ignorant of their deed; and told him that, since he knew
of that affair, he would do whatever Perrot wished in
the matter. The chief also assured him that, when the
allies were assembled, he would make them turn the
hatchet against the Iroquois; but that until they came
to the general rendezvous it was necessary that he himself should be ignorant of their design, in order that he
might be there with his tribe and be able to raise a large
troop against the Iroquois. The ice was now strong
enough to support a man; and the Maskoutech chiefs
had sent to him a warrior to inform him that the Outagamis were far advanced into the country of the Nadou-

---

[24] Although the exact location of this post is unknown, it probably was not
far from the present Dubuque, Iowa — where, and at Galena on the Illinois
side, were located the lead mines often mentioned by La Potherie; and later, by
Charlevoix, as "Perrot's mines." See Wis. *Hist. Colls.*, vol. x, 301. — ED.

aissioux, and prayed the Miamis to hasten to join them; but the latter had replied that they would do nothing without the Frenchman's consent.

The Tchidüakoüingoües, the Oüaoüiartanons, the Pepikokis, the Mangakekis, the Poüankikias, and the Kilataks, all Miami tribes,[25] coming from all directions, marched by long stages to reach that rendezvous. The first five of these tribes were the first to arrive, with their families, at the French post; if the Tchidüakoüingoües had not been at hand with a good supply of provisions, the other bands would have perished from hunger. Perrot made them many presents, to induce them to turn their war-club against the Iroquois, the common enemy. They excused themselves from a general advance, asserting, nevertheless, that all their young men would go in various detachments to harass the Iroquois youth and carry away some of their heads. But, far from keeping their promise, they amused themselves for an entire month with hunting cattle; meanwhile, all the warriors who had joined the Outagamis and Maskoutechs were intending to march against the Nadoüaissioux, while the old men, women, and children would remain with the French.

The savage's mind is difficult to understand; he speaks in one way and thinks in another. If his friend's interests accord with his own, he is ready to render him a service; if not, he always takes the path by which he can most easily attain his own ends; and he makes all his courage consist in deceiving the enemy by a thousand artifices and knaveries. The French were warned of all

---

[25] For account of the Miami tribes, see vol. i, note 212; cf. note 190 also. The Ouiatanon were generally called Wea by the English, which name is still applied to the present remnant of the tribe. The Piankashaw (Poüankikias) also are not quite extinct; but the other tribes named in the text are no longer known. — ED.

the savages' intrigues by a Miami woman; all these
hostile actions would have greatly injured Perrot's
scheme that they should turn their weapons against the
Iroquois—who, moreover, were delighted that these
peoples should be thus divided among themselves, for
whatever discord could be aroused among them was the
only way by which their plans could be made to fail.
Perrot sent for the chief of the Miamis; he made him
believe that he had just received a letter which informed
him that the Maskoutechs – jealous at seeing themselves
obliged, by way of satisfaction, to join their war-club to
that of their allies – had won over the Outagamis, and
that they would by common consent attack the Miamis
while on the general march against the Nadouaissioux.
The chief, believing Perrot's statement, did not fail to
break up the band of his warriors, and sent them the
next day to hunt buffalo; they also held a war-feast, at
which they swore the ruin of the Maskoutechs. The
Outagamis, who had displayed more steadfast courage
than did the other allies, finding that they were advanced
into the enemy's country, consulted the medicine-men to
ascertain whether they were secure. Those jugglers delivered their oracles, which were that the spirits had
showed them that the Sauteurs and the Nadouaissioux
were assembling to march against them. [26] Whether the

[26] "Mediators between the world of spirits and the world of men may be
divided into two classes: the shamans, whose authority was entirely dependent
on their individual ability; and priests, who acted in some measure for the
tribe or nation, or at least for some society. 'Shaman' is explained variously
as a Persian word meaning 'pagan,' or, with more likelihood, as the Tungus
equivalent for 'medicine-man,' and was originally applied to the medicine-
men or exorcists in Siberian tribes, from which it was extended to similar individuals among the tribes of America." Often the shaman performed practically
all religious functions, and sometimes was also a chief, thus obtaining also
civil authority; his office was sometimes inherited, sometimes acquired by
natural fitness; and as a preliminary to its exercise he would enter into a
condition of trance for a certain period, or gain the proper psychic state through

devil had really spoken to these men (as is believed in all Canada), or the Outagamis were seized with fear at finding themselves alone, without assistance – however that might be, they built a fort, and sent their chiefs and two warriors to Perrot, begging that he would go among the Nadoüaissioux to check their advance, and thus enable the Outagamis, with their families, to take refuge in their own village.

The Miamis would actually have engaged in battle with the Maskoutechs, if the Frenchman had not dissuaded their chief from doing so. They received the Outagami chief with all possible honors; he told them that their people were dead. Perrot asked him how many the dead were. He replied: "I do not know anything positively; but I believe that they all are dead, for our diviners saw the Nadouaissioux assemble together

the sweat-bath – or sometimes as the result of a narrow escape from death. In treating the sick or in other functions of their office, shamans were among many tribes supposed to be actually possessed by spirits, but among the Iroquois they controlled their spirits objectively. "Hoffman enumerates three classes of shamans among the Chippewa, in addition to the herbalist or doctor, properly so considered. These were the *Wâbĕnō'*, who practiced medical magic; the *Jĕs'sakkī'd*, who were seers and prophets deriving their power from the thunder god; and the *Midē'*, who were concerned with the sacred society of the *Midē'wiwin*, and should rather be regarded as priests. . . As distinguished from the calling of a shaman, that of a priest was, as has been said, national or tribal rather than individual, and if there were considerable ritual his function might be more that of a leader in the ceremonies and keeper of the sacred myths than direct mediator between spirits and men. . . Even where shamanism flourished most there was a tendency for certain priestly functions to center around the town or tribal chief. . . Most of the tribes of the eastern plains contained two classes of men that may be placed in this category. One of these classes consisted of societies which concerned themselves with healing and applied definite remedies, though at the same time invoking superior powers, and to be admitted to which a man was obliged to pass through a period of instruction. The other was made up of the one or few men who acted as superior officers in the conduct of national rituals, and who transmitted their knowledge to an equally limited number of successors. Similar to these perhaps were the priests of the Midē'wiwin ceremony among the Chippewa, Menominee, and other Algonquian tribes. – JOHN R. SWANTON, in *Handbook Amer. Indians*, art. "Shamans and priests."

in order to come against us; they are very numerous, and
we are greatly troubled on account of our women and
children, who are with us. The old men have sent me to
thee, to beg thee to deliver us from the danger into
which we have too blindly rushed; they hope that thou
wilt go among the Nadouaissioux to stop their advance."
Perrot told him that they ought not to place any confidence in their jugglers, who are liars; and that it was
only the Spirit who could see so far. "Not at all," replied the Outagami; "the Spirit has enabled them to see
what they have divined, and that is sure to happen."
The Miamis were strongly in favor of advancing. The
Frenchman, who felt obliged by the orders that he had
received from Monsieur de Frontenac to keep everything quiet among the allies, concluded that it would be
best to avert an attack so fatal to the Outagamis; their
destruction would have been very detrimental to the
Frenchmen who happened to be in those regions, because
the savages, who are naturally unruly, would have taken
the opportunity to vent their resentment against them.
He made them understand, however, that since the safety
of a band of their tribe was concerned, he would go to
make some attempt at ameliorating their situation. He
encountered on the voyage five cabins of Maskoutechs,
a village which was preparing to go to the French establishment to trade there for ammunition. He told
them the reason for his departure, and warned them not
to trust themselves with the Nadouaissioux.

Perrot finally arrived at the French fort,[27] where he
learned that the Nadouaissioux were forming a large
war-party to seek out the Outagamis or some of their
allies. As he was then in a place under his own author-

<hr>

[27] This fort may have been Perrot's supposed winter-quarters (1685-1686;
see note 172) near Trempealeau, Wis., or else one of the forts he had built on
Lake Pepin. — ED.

ity, he made known his arrival to the Nadouaissioux, whom he found, to the number of four hundred, ranging along the Missisipi in order to carry on some warlike enterprise. They would not allow his men to return to him, and themselves came to the fort, to which they flocked from all sides in order to pillage it. The commandant demanded why their young men appeared so frightened at the very time when he came to visit his brothers in order to give them life. A chief, arising, made the warriors retire, and ordered them to encamp. When their camp was made, Perrot summoned their leading men, and told them that he had come to inform them that the Miamis, the Outagamis, the Islinois, the Maskoutechs, and the Kikabous had formed an army of four thousand men to fight with them; that they were to march in three parties—one along the Missisipi, another at a day's journey farther inland, but following the river, and a third at a similar distance from the second. He told them that he had stayed this torrent that was going to carry them away; but finding them by chance in this locality, he exhorted them to return to their families and hunt beavers. They replied with much haughtiness that they had left home in order to seek death; and, since there were men, they were going to fight against them, and would not have to go far to find them. They exchanged some peltries; when that was done, they sent to ask Perrot to visit their camp, and there manifested to him the joy that they felt at his saying that they would find their enemies, entreating him to allow them to continue their route. He tried all sorts of means to dissuade them from this purpose; but they still replied that they had gone away to die; that the Spirit had given them men to eat, at three days' journey from the French; and that Perrot had invented a falsehood to them, since

their jugglers had seen great fires far away. They even
pointed out the places where these fires were: one was
on this side, and at some distance inland; another at some
distance, and farther inland; and a third, which they believed to be the fire of the Outagamis. All these statements were true, for the five cabins of the Maskoutechs
were at three days' journey from the French establishment; their village was on one side, the fort of the Outagamis opposite, and the Miamis and Islinois at a considerable distance farther. It is believed that the demon
often speaks to the savages; our missionaries even claim
to have recognized him on several occasions. There was
much truth in what the evil spirit had communicated to
their jugglers. Other expedients must be employed to
stop them; to gain their attention, Perrot gave them two
kettles and some other wares, saying to them with these:
"I desire you to live; but I am sure that you will be defeated, for your devil has deceived you. What I have
told you is true, for I really have kept back the tribes,
who have obeyed me. But you are now intending to
advance against them; the road that you would take I
close to you, my brothers, for I am not willing that it
should be stained with blood. If you kill the Outagamis
or their allies, you cannot do so without first striking me;
if they slay you, they likewise slay me; for I hold them
under one of my arms, and you under the other. Can
you then do them any wrong without doing it to me?"
He was holding the same calumet which they had sung
to him when he first made discovery of their tribe; he
presented it to them to smoke, but they refused it. The
insult which they thus offered was so great that he flung
the calumet at their feet, saying to them: "It must be
that I have accepted a calumet which dogs have sung
to me, and that they no longer remember what they said
to me. In singing it to me, they chose me as their chief,

and promised me that they would never make any advance against their enemies when I presented it to them;
and yet today they are trying to kill me." Immediately
a war-chief arose, and told Perrot that he was in the
right; he then extended it toward the sun, uttering invocations, and tried to return it to Perrot's hands. The
latter replied that he would not receive it unless they
assured him that they would lay down their weapons.
The chief hung it on a pole in the open place within the
fort, turning it toward the sun; then he assembled all the
leading men in his tent, and obtained their consent that
no hostile advance should be made. He then called Perrot thither, and sent for the calumet; he placed it before him, one end in the earth and the other held upright
by a small forked stick. He drew from his war-pouch a
pair of moccasins, beautifully made; then he took off
Perrot's shoes, and with his own hands put the moccasins
on the Frenchman's feet. Finally he presented to him
a dish of dried grapes, and three times put some of the
fruit in Perrot's mouth. After he had eaten these, the
chief took the calumet and said to him: "I remember
all that these men promised to thee when they presented
to thee this calumet; and now we listen to thee. Thou
art depriving us of the prey that the Spirit had given
us, and thou art giving life to our enemies. Now do for
us what thou hast done for them, and prevent them from
slaying us when we are dispersed to hunt for beaver,
which we are going to do. The sun is our witness that
we obey thee."

Chapter XX

Quiet was restored by the good management of Sieur
Perrot, who returned to his establishment. He related
to the Maskoutechs, who came to meet him, all that he
had accomplished among the Nadouaissioux in favor of

them and their allies; and compelled them to settle, with
the Kikabous, at a place two days' journey from him
near a Miami village—in order that, if the Nadouaissioux should happen to break their promise, these tribes
might be able to resist them. They sent a band of forty
warriors against the Iroquois, and brought back twelve
of their scalps.

The French discovered the mine of lead, which they
found in great abundance; but it was difficult to obtain
the ore, since the mine lies between two masses of rock—
which can, however, be cut away. The ore is almost free
from impurities, and melts easily; it diminishes by a
half, when placed over the fire, but, if put into a furnace,
the slag would be only one-fourth.

The Outaouaks, seeing that all was quiet among the
tribes of the south, rightly judged that now they could
easily carry fire and sword among those peoples. The
alliance which they desired to contract with the Iroquois
continually possessed their minds; and however great
the ascendancy that the Jesuits had gained over them, or
the skill with which Monsieur de Louvigni managed
them, in order to keep them in submission to Monsieur
de Frontenac's orders, nothing could prevail over their
caprice. They left Michilimakinak, to the number of
three hundred, and formed two war-parties; one was to
join the Islinois against the Ozages and the Kanças, and
the other was to disperse into the country of the Nadouaissioux. Their course of conduct could only be very
detrimental to the interests of the French colony, which
would thus be prevented from receiving general aid
from all the southern tribes against the Iroquois. When
they had arrived at the Bay des Puans, they could not
refrain from shouting that they found in their road a
very precipitous place, which they did not believe they

could scale or overturn. "There is Metaminens," they said, "who is going to stretch out legs of iron, and will compel us to retrace our steps; but let us make an effort, and perhaps we shall get over them." They remembered that he had restrained them at Michilimakinak when they, after the raid of the Iroquois upon the island of Montreal, declared themselves against the French. Their fear that he would exasperate the minds of certain tribes in that region made them speak thus. Monsieur de Louvigni had taken the precaution to inform them that Perrot had pledged the Outagamis to our cause, and knew that he could accomplish a great deal in circumstances of such importance. Perrot was prudent enough to say nothing to the Outaouaks about their enterprise; he only inquired from some of the war-chiefs if they had not some letters from Michilimakinak to give him. They told him that they had none, and that they were going to seek for the bones of their dead among the Nadouaissioux, hoping that he would consent to their project, as the Jesuit fathers and Monsieur de Louvigni had done. He treated them very affably, and had them smoke a pipe, without saying anything to them of other matters. Some one privately gave him the name of the chief who had hidden one of his letters; Perrot went to see this chief at night, and demanded why he had not given him the letter. "Dost thou not suppose," he said to him, "that the Spirit who has made writing will be angry with thee for having robbed me? Thou art going to war; art thou immortal?" The chief was, of course, somewhat surprised, imagining that the other had had some revelation in regard to the letter; he restored it to Perrot, and on the next day asked him to tell what he had read therein. The substance of it was, that he positively must restrain the Outaouaks; or, if he could not do that, he must render them objects of suspicion to the Outagamis. The chief of the Puans was extremely friendly to the French, to whom he offered any service that he could render; he was thoroughly convinced that, if the Outaouaks should advance, all the other nations would undoubtedly follow them, and that an army of two thousand warriors would be formed. All the prominent men of that tribe desired to hear the speech that Perrot was going to deliver to them; and it was in the following manner that he addressed them, holding his calumet in his hand, and having at his feet twelve brasses of tobacco: "Cinagots, Outaouaks, and you other warriors, I am astonished that, after having promised me last year that you would have no other will than Onontio's, you should tarnish his glory by depriving him of the forces that I have with much labor obtained for him. How is this? you who are his children are the first to revolt against him. I come from a country where I have hung up a bright sun, to give light to all the tribes that I have seen – who now leave their families in quiet, without fearing any storms, while warriors are seeking to avenge the bones of their dead among the Iroquois; but you are trying to raise clouds there which will give birth to thunderbolts and lightnings, in order to strike them, and perhaps to destroy even us. I love peace in my country; I have discovered this land, and Onontio has given the charge of it to me; and he has promised me all his young men to punish those who undertake to stain it with blood. You are my brothers; I ask from you repose. If you are going to war against the Nadouaissioux, go by way of Chagouamigon,[28] on Lake Superior, where you have al-

---

[28] Shaugawaumikong, one of the most ancient Chippewa villages, situated on Long Island (formerly known as Chequamegon peninsula), in Ashland County, Wis. On account of the inroads of the Sioux it was at one time re-

ready begun war with them. What will Onontio say
when he learns of the measures that you are taking to
deprive him of the aid that he is expecting from you,
and from his other children, whom you are trying to
seduce? You have forgotten that your ancestors in
former days used earthen pots, stone hatchets and knives,
and bows; and you will be obliged to use them again, if
Onontio abandons you. What will become of you if he
becomes angry? He has undertaken war to avenge you,
and he has maintained it against nations far stronger
than you. Know that he is the master of peace, when he
so wills; the Iroquois are asking it from him, and it
would be made if he did not fear that you would be
made its victims, and that the enemy would pour out
upon you his vengeance, to satisfy the shades of the many
families that he has sacrificed on your account. With
what excuses will you defend yourselves before him
from all the charges that will be made against you?
Cease this hostile advance which he forbids to you. I
do not wash the blackened countenances of your warriors; I do not take away the war-club or the bow that I
gave you on Onontio's behalf; but I recommend to you
to employ them against the Iroquois, and not against
other peoples. If you transgress his orders, you may be
sure that the Spirit who made all, who is master of life
and of death, is for him; and that he knows well how to
punish your disobedience if you do not agree to my demands." He lighted his calumet, and, throwing to them
the twelve brasses of tobacco, continued: "Let us smoke
together; if you wish to be children of Onontio, here is

moved to Madeleine Island, on the site of the modern La Pointe; and in later
years was located on the mainland, near Bayfield. It was on Long Island
(which stretches across the entrance of Chequamegon Bay) that the Jesuits
established in 1655 the mission of La Pointe du Saint Esprit; it became large
and prosperous, but was broken up in 1670 by the Sioux. — JAMES MOONEY, in
Handbook Amer. Indians.

his calumet. I shall not fail to inform him of those who
choose to set him at naught."

He presented it to them, but there was one war-chief
who refused it; the result, however, was more propitious
than Perrot had expected. The Puans, seeing that the
only question now at issue was to appease this man, offered to him the calumet, and made him a present of
six kettles, with two porcelain collars. The next day,
they made a solemn feast for the Outaouaks, and sang
the calumet to them. At the time when these three hundred warriors set out to return to Michilimakinak, a
young warrior, with several of his comrades, left the
troop, in order to continue their march against the
Nadouaissioux. The Outaouaks, who had fully decided
to forget all their resentment, were so offended at this
proceeding that they threw all the baggage of these men
into the river, and dragged their canoe more than a
hundred paces up on the land.

Chapter XXI

The only tribes who defended the interests of the colony in the midst of this great revolution were the Nepiciriniens and the Kikabous; they marched against the
Iroquois, and brought back some scalps of the latter,
which they presented to the commandants at Michillimakinak. A few days later was seen the arrival of other
canoes, who had carried away an Iroquois; he was released before they came ashore, which was contrary to
the laws of war–which require that a general council
be held in order to deliberate on the death or the life of
a prisoner. It was known that the Outaouaks were responsible for this proceeding; they had maliciously
informed this freedman of several grievances which they

had invented against the French people. He said that his people had fought a battle in the vicinity of Montreal, in which four hundred Frenchmen had been slain, and that Onontio had not dared to go outside the town. As this tale, mingled with insulting language, made evident the evil intentions of those peoples, it was [considered] proper to come to an understanding [with them] in regard to the many insolent utterances which were heard on every side. The more prominent chiefs tried to justify themselves, and in truth there were some of them who had taken no part in this dissension; the author of it was the man who seemed least opposed to our interests, but he nevertheless caused all these disorders. He assembled a general council, to which all the Nepiciriniens were summoned. They came to see the French, with five collars, and asked them by the first, to forget their error; by the second, they assured us that they had united themselves to the body of their father, never to be detached from him. By the third, that he would know them in the following spring, by the war-parties that they would send against the Iroquois; by the fourth, that they submitted to Onontio; and by the fifth, that they renounced the English and their trade.

Reply was made, by five presents, to all that they had said; and it was represented to them that the trade with the English, which they so eagerly sought to obtain, would deliver them into the hands of the Iroquois, whose only endeavor was to deceive them.

The long stay made at Montreal by four canoes which had been sent thither to learn news of the colony made the savages suspect that [our] affairs were going ill; they made a feast in the village, which was attended by the chiefs only. A Frenchman who passed that way was

invited to it, and the most distinguished among the
chiefs said to him: "Thou who meddlest in thwarting
us, cast a spell to learn what has become of our men
whom thy chief sent into thy country to be eaten there."
This savage had had secret connections with the English, in order to secure for them entrance into the beaver-
trade; and he made them a present of ten packets of
pelts, as a pledge for the promise that he had given them.
All the allied tribes acted only by his order; he was the
originator of all that was done among those peoples;
and he had rendered himself so influential that whatever he required was blindly followed. In his childhood he had been carried away [from his home] as a
slave. This Frenchman whom he told to play the juggler replied that "The Frenchmen were not in the habit
of eating men; that if this man were a chief he would
answer him, but he was a slave; and that it was not a
dog like him with whom the Frenchman compared, he
who bore the message of one of the greatest captains
who had ever been heard of." This savage replied [to
the other savages]: "You who are here behold the insults which I meet in your village from this man who
is troubling our peace, when I am trying to maintain
our common interest." All the guests began to show
their discontent, and matters would perhaps have turned
to the disadvantage of the Frenchman if he had not instantly found some expedient for rendering this very
chief odious to them. He had been a slave of a man
named Jason [sc. Talon] (of whom I have already
spoken), who had been the first to go from the north to
Three Rivers, the second government district in Canada, and who for all the services which he had rendered
to the tribe had been chosen its head chief. At his death
he left several children, who could not maintain that

high position because this slave, who was freed, had by
his ability acquired the general esteem of all those peoples. This Frenchman, I say, began to call out in the
middle of the feast: "Where art thou, Talon? where
art thou, Brochet?" (another head chief) ; "it was you
two who ruled over all this country; but your slave has
usurped your authority and is making your children his
slaves, although they ought to be the real masters. But
I will sacrifice everything to maintain their rights, and
Onontio will favor us; he will know how to restore them
to the rank that they ought to occupy." Hardly had he
spoken when the sons and relatives of those two chiefs
arose, and took the Frenchman's part, uttering threats
against this seditious man; and it lacked little of their
reaching the utmost violence of conduct. Those young
chiefs, remembering what their ancestors had been,
compelled this old man to render satisfaction to the
Frenchman; and the fear which they also felt of being
exposed to unpleasant results constrained them to entreat the missionary fathers to adjust all these matters.

The French themselves did not know what to think
of the delay of those canoes; at last they arrived, after
a three months' wait. They reported that a battle had
been fought at the Prairie de la Madeleine, three
leagues from and opposite Montreal, against the Iroquois and the English, in which we had gained all the
advantage – it might be said that the enemy had suffered extreme injury.

This news made some impression on the minds of
the Outaouaks, but the Miamis of the Saint Joseph
River easily forgot what they had promised to execute
against the Iroquois; they no longer thought of anything
except of opening the way to the Loups, who had
opened a commerce with the English. Those of Mara-

mek were somewhat unsettled; they were reminded that
the bow and war-club of Onontio had been delivered to
them in order to attack the Iroquois and avenge their
own dead. The story of the battle at the Prairie, and of
the raising of the siege of Quebec [1690] by the English
(who had come thither with all the forces of New England), was related to them. "Your father," it was said
to them, "does not cease to labor for your peace; but you
have always remained inactive since he undertook war
against the Iroquois. The Spirit favors his arms; his
enemies fear him, but he does not heed them." They
were counseled to avail themselves of his aid while he
was willing to favor them; and they were told that there
was reason to complain of their indifference while he
was sacrificing his young men. They promised to send
out three hundred warriors, who would not spare either
the Loups or the English. The Maskoutechs, who had
seemed to have our interests so strongly at heart, gave
very unsatisfactory evidence of their fidelity; they
amused themselves with making raids into the lands of
the Nadouaissioux, where they carried away captive
some Puans and some Ayoës who had made a settlement
there, without troubling themselves whether those two
tribes were their allies. The jealousy which they felt
because some Frenchmen had promised to barter merchandise among the Miamis in preference to them inspired them to send to that people ten large kettles, to
warn them to distrust the Frenchmen, who were going
to form a large band of Abenaquis and their [other]
allies to deal a blow on the families of the Miamis after
their men had set out on the march against the Iroquois.
This present put an end to all their war-parties, excepting only their chief, who went away with eighty warriors. The Outagamis, who had been very quiet, not-

withstanding the promise that they had given to join
with that tribe against the common enemy, promised to
do so when the Sakis, the Puans, and the Pouteouatemis
should take the war-path.   For this purpose an Iroquois
scalp and a gun were given to them, and this speech was
made to them: "Here is an Iroquois who is given to
you to eat; this scalp is his head, and this gun is his body.
We wish to know whether you are French or Iroquois,
in order to send word to Onontio; if you go to war we
shall believe that you are French, if you do not go we
shall declare you an enemy."

Chapter XXII

The great distance which lay between us and all these
allies was a hindrance in causing them to show all the
activity that we could have desired.   The French who
went among them, either to facilitate their trading or to
maintain them in entire harmony, were even exposed to
many dangers.   Perrot was on the point of being burned
by the Maskoutechs, who had received from him so
many benefits.   That tribe, insatiable for all that they
saw, sent to ask him to come to their village, to trade for
beaver-skins; and a chief of the Pouteouatemis accompanied him.   Hardly had he reached their village, with
six Frenchmen, when the savages seized all their merchandise; and they displayed more inhumanity to him
than to the meanest of their slaves.   It is a rule among
all the tribes to give to the captives the first morsels of
what food may be eaten; but these savages would not
give him any food.   One of their chiefs could not refrain from complaining that he would not have the
strength to endure the fire, if they did not take better
care of him; they intended to sacrifice him to the shades

of many of their men who had been killed in various
fights, and they said that Perrot was the cause of their
death. A warrior who came to him to pronounce his
sentence told him that they had intended to burn him in
the village, but that part of them would not be witnesses of this execution. He said to Perrot: "Thou
wilt set out at sunrise, and wilt be closely followed, and
at noon thou wilt be burnt on the plain. Thou art a sor-
cerer, who hast caused the deaths of more than fifty of
our men, in order to pacify the shades of two Frenchmen
whom we killed at Chikagon. If thou hadst taken revenge for those two alone we would not have said anything, for blood must be paid for with blood; but thou
art too cruel, and therefore thou art going to be the
victim who is to be sacrificed to them." Great stead-
fastness was necessary in so terrible an emergency. The
Pouteouatemi chief also sang his death-song, on the eve
of his departure, and they made him and Perrot set out
the next morning from the village, with the other
Frenchmen, who were lamenting their wretched fate.
While the people in the village were amusing themselves with dividing all the property of the Frenchmen,
the latter went forward a little distance on a beaten path,
and then they bethought themselves to take several wrong
directions without losing sight of one another. Some
warriors were sent after them, who could not find their
tracks; but the French do not know whether these men
really could not discover them, or only pretended not to
find them. However that may be, a Miami who had
married a Maskoutech woman saw these warriors start,
and immediately gave notice of it to his tribe, telling
them that Perrot had been plundered and burned by the
Maskoutechs. The chief of the Miamis was at that time
at war with the Iroquois; and the Miamis were only
waiting the moment of his arrival, in order to avenge

this death. The tribes of the bay were also notified of it, and desired to seize the war-club for the chastisement of those peoples.   Perrot arrived safely among the Puans, where they immediately hung up some war-kettles, as if to go in search of what had been taken from him, and to kill some Maskoutechs; but as it was a question of holding together all those tribes in their desire to form a connection with the common enemy, he obliged them to suspend their anger, for the sake of the French nation.

On all sides hostilities were begun in earnest against the Iroquois. The Outaouaks sent out war-parties against them from all quarters, and during the summer killed or captured more than fifty of them. The Miamis of Muramik [sc. Maramek] [29] carried off eight Loups, to whom the English had given many presents; four of these captives they gave to the commandant on the Saint Joseph River, and reserved the others for Frenchmen, friends of theirs who had rendered them many services. Monsieur de Louvigny sent thirty-eight men to go in quest of these, with orders to induce the Miamis to put them in the kettle if they could not be taken to Michillimakinak; but those of Saint Joseph had carried them away. The tribe of Loups was entirely devoted to the interests of the English, who were trying to make use of them in order to gain entrance among our allies; and the Iroquois profited by this union. Too many precautions, therefore, could not be taken to keep back the former from the beaver trade, and to obtain the advantage from acts of hostility against the latter. A present of fifty pounds of gunpowder was given to the Miamis of Maramek, to unite them to our interests; and they took the war-path to the number of two hundred – who

---

[29] Marameg (Maramek) was the early name of Kalamazoo River, Mich. — Ed.

separated into four bands, after having divided the powder among them. On the next day after their departure a solemn feast was made by order of Ouagikougaïganea, the great chief, to obtain from the Spirit a safe return. They erected an altar, on which they placed bear-skins arranged to represent an idol; they had smeared the heads of these with a green clay, as they passed in front of these skins, kneeling down before them; and every one was obliged to assist at this ceremony.[30] The jugglers, the medicine-men, and those who were called sorcerers occupied the first row, and held in their hands their pouches for medicines and for jugglery; they cast the spell, they said, upon those whose deaths they wished to cause, and who feigned to fall dead. The medicine-men placed some drugs in the mouths of these, and seemed to resuscitate them immediately by rudely shaking them; the one who made the most grotesque appearance attracted the most admira-

---

[30] The term "ceremony" means, in the strict sense, "a religious performance of at least one day's duration. These ceremonies generally refer to one or the other of the solstices, to the germination or ripening of a crop, or to the most important food supply. There are ceremonies of less importance that are connected with the practices of medicine-men or are the property of cult societies. Ceremonies may be divided into those in which the whole tribe participates and those which are the exclusive property of a society, generally a secret one, or of a group of men of special rank, such as chiefs or medicine-men, or of an individual. Practically all ceremonies of extended duration contain many rites in common. An examination of these rites, as they are successively performed, reveals the fact that they follow one another in prescribed order, as do the events or episodes of the ritual." Among some tribes the ritual predominates, among others it is subordinated to the drama. The rites are partly secret (and proprietary), and partly public (constituting the actual play or drama); there are also semi-public performances, but conducted by priests only. There is much symbolism connected with most of these elaborate ceremonials. "Inasmuch as ceremonies form intrinsic features and may be regarded as only phases of culture, their special character depends on the state of culture of the people by which they are performed; hence there are at least as many kinds of ceremonies as there are phases of culture in North America. . . In those tribes or in those areas extended forms abound where there exists a sessile population or a strong form of tribal government."
— GEORGE A. DORSEY, in *Handbook Amer. Indians*.

tion. They danced to the sound of drums and gourds; they formed, as it were, two hostile parties, who attacked and defended in a battle. They had for weapons the skins of serpents and otters, which, they said, brought death to those on whom they cast the spell, and restored life to those whom they wished [to live]. The director of the ceremony, accompanied by two old men and two women at his side, walked with serious manner, going into all the cabins of the village to give notice that the ceremony was to begin soon. They practiced the imposition of hands on all persons whom they met, who, by way of thanks, embraced their legs. Everywhere were seen dances, and one heard only the howls of the dogs which they were killing in order to offer the sacrifices. The bones of those which were eaten were afterward burned, as in a holocaust. The persons who had been killed, and whom the medicine-men brought back to life by the spell, danced separately, while the others remained as if dead. Men, women, girls, and boys of twelve years old, fell dead or were restored to life, as were even the jugglers, the medicine-men, and the sorcerers. Every one had offered the handsomest ornaments that he could. Some persons thrust down their throats sticks a foot and a half long, and as large as one's thumb, and feigned to lie dead; then they were carried to the medicine-men, who brought them back to life and sent them away to dance. Others swallowed feathers of the swan or eagle, then drew these out, and fell down, as if dead; and these also were resuscitated. In short, one recognized in their antics only diabolical contrivances.

The best thing in this festival was, that all the riches of the village were destined for the jugglers. The ceremonies lasted during five days, both day and night; at the latter time they were within the cabins, and by day in the public place – where they approached from all sides, marching as if in procession. It was useless to represent to them that all this that they were doing was criminal before God; they answered that this was the right way to secure his favor, to the end that he should give some enemies to be eaten by their young men, who would die without that if they did not observe this solemnity. One of their war-parties arrived at the end of thirty days; they had killed many Iroquois, without losing one of their own men, and they said to the French: "Believe us, our sort of ceremony has made the Spirit listen to us." The other bands came back some time afterward, with a number of prisoners, and the Loups whom the men of Saint Joseph had made to turn aside.

While the Miamis were giving to Monsieur de Frontenac proofs of their fidelity, the Maskoutechs had openly declared hostilities against their allies the Ayoës, and had cut to pieces all the inhabitants of the Ayoës's main village. Some of them came to the Miamis and tried to induce Perrot to go among them, assuring him that they would make reparation for the pillage of his merchandise; but the Miamis, who knew that the Maskoutechs intended to eat him, sharply asked them if they thought that he was a dog, whom they could drive away when he disturbed them, and then bring him back at the first caress which they offered him. The Maskoutechs learned that all the peoples of the bay, with the Miamis and several other tribes, had intended to avenge the injury which the former had inflicted on Perrot; and they sent him two deputies to ask that he would not go away from Maramek, where they wished to confer with him. Their chief came in person, with a number of warriors, and entered the cabin of the Miami chief, where a meeting was called of the more prominent men of the tribe, and of the Kikabous. The Maskoutechs had carried away some Ayoës slaves, a woman and three children, whom they seated before Perrot, and said to him: "We have borrowed thy guns; they have thundered upon a village, which they have made us eat. See the effect which they produced, and which we bring to thee," at the same time displaying these slaves. They placed forty beaver robes before him, and continued their speech thus: "We have taken from thee a garment to dazzle the sight of our enemies and make ourselves feared by them, and we pay thee for it by this beaver; we do not pay thee for thy guns and merchandise. If thou art willing to receive us with forgiveness, we know where are some beavers, for we saw them on our road [to this place]. If we live a few years, thou shalt be satisfied; for we did not intend to plunder thee, and we have only placed thy merchandise to thy credit."

This chief was told that in order to appease the wrath of Onontio it was necessary to destroy a village of Iroquois; and that they must not attack people who had not made war on them; that they were easily forgetting their own dead [killed by the Iroquois], whom the French were continually avenging; that they would do well to send to Montreal one of their chiefs, in order to appease Onontio; that his fire was lighted, to receive all those who desired to warm themselves at it – and even the Iroquois, although they were his enemies; and that they might be sure that we would have taken vengeance on their tribe, if we had not caused all the others to hang up their hatchets. A chief resolved to accompany that Frenchman [i.e., Perrot] to Montreal, in order to turn aside the resentment of Monsieur de Frontenac; and forty Miamis escorted him as far as the bay. When they arrived among the Outagamis, the latter dissuaded

the Maskoutech from going farther; because they told
him that the rule of the French was to hang thieves,
without any pardon, and that he would for love of his
people certainly suffer the same fate—which caused him
to return home.

The English, who had until then made all sorts of
attempts to insinuate themselves among the Outaouaks,
found the finest opportunity in the world for succeeding
in this. As soon as they learned that the Iroquois had
granted life to the son of a Sauteur chief, they procured
his freedom; they had thought that, as his father was
dead, he might succeed the latter, and that the ascendency which he possessed over the minds of his people
would be an effectual means to facilitate to them some
further entrance among the neighbors of the Sauteurs.
The gratitude that this freedman felt (as they believed
beyond doubt) for so great a benefaction must induce
him to engage in any undertaking in favor of his libera-
tors. Moreover, the Iroquois were planning also to
obtain some advantage from this matter; and on both
sides they gave the Sauteur collars and presents in order
to persuade our allies to take sides and carry on trade
with them. He met the Outaouaks out hunting, in the
midst of the winter; they met together to hear the explanation of those collars, and at the same time concluded
to keep the affair secret. They secretly sent, "under
ground," many presents to the Sakis and to the peoples
at the bay, to constrain them to withdraw from the war
against the Iroquois; among those tribes many visits
were made [by the Outaouak envoys], but they replied
that all those solicitations were useless, and that they
would die rather than abandon the interests of the
French. The Sauteurs, who were beginning to realize
that the Iroquois had spared their lives, declared them-

selves against our allies if they intended to continue war against the Iroquois. Nothing could make them go back from their decision; they said that they were men, capable of resisting whomsoever undertook to thwart them in what they had resolved. The commandant at Michillimakinak, when he heard of the friendship of the Sakis, sent word to them that he and his Frenchmen would die [for them] if they were attacked, even offering them his fort as a refuge. The Cinago Outaouaks, who had declared in favor of the Sauteurs, fearing that the Sakis would carry far the resentment which they had displayed against the latter, on the one hand undertook to reconcile them with the Sakis, and on the other did everything in their power to turn them aside from the Iroquois War. They made presents to the Sauteurs, and gave them a calumet which said that their dead lay together among the Nadouaissioux, and that, since they were relatives, they ought to hang up their hatchets this year – but assuring them of no interference another year, if they wished to resume the war.

The Outaouaks faithfully kept the secret of the collar which the Iroquois had given to the Sauteurs, and, in order not to cause suspicion in the French, they asserted to Monsieur de Louvigny that they had received it for the sake of peace, and that they had been urged to become mediators with Onontio for that end. They tried to persuade that officer to accept this collar himself, since he was commandant at Michillimakinak; but he excused himself, and informed them that they must go to present it to Onontio. They did not hesitate to send envoys to him, who took advantage of the departure of the Sakis.

We may say that the Hurons and the Outaouaks were in extreme blindness about all that concerned the Iroquois, whom they believed to be really their friends; for while they did whatever the latter wished, in order to give them substantial proofs of their friendship, the Iroquois sought, underhand, for occasions to take the others by surprise. After the departure of those envoys the Hurons captured two Iroquois, whom they sent back to their homes with many presents, as a pledge to their nation that the Outaouak people had no greater desire than alliance with them – at the same time congratulating them on having spared the lives of the Sauteurs; but the Iroquois did not act in so good faith.

Dabeau, a Frenchman who had been a slave among them for several years, was with a band of warriors who went out to attack whomsoever they should encounter; being left alone with eight of their men and two women, he killed them all while they were asleep, and took the women to the first village of our allies that he could light on, when he found two Hurons hunting beavers. His fear of being himself slain by men who could have appropriated to themselves the exploit which he had performed constrained him to make them a present of the two slaves, and of the scalps which he had brought with him. He embarked with them for Michillimakinak. The arrival of these two women threw much light [on the designs of the Iroquois], and the [Huron] people felt indignation at finding themselves thus deceived. Immediately a war-party was sent out, who laid violent hands on thirteen Iroquois who were coming to make war on them; they killed five and captured seven of these, and only one escaped. As it was known that an agreement had been made between the Hurons and the Iroquois that they would on both sides spare the lives of captives whom they might take, our people observed that the Hurons were planning to act thus by these Iroquois. Some Frenchmen, seeing them come ashore, killed two of the captives with their knives; the Hurons rescued the other five and took them into their village, and seized their weapons. General disorder arose; the Outaouaks remained neutral, and stepped aside to be spectators of the fracas. Nansouakouet, the only friend of the French, called his warriors together, in order to support the French in case fighting arose. The Hurons, who knew the generous nature of the French, incapable of doing harm to those who were in their power, hastened to our fort, in order to find an asylum there. The Hurons did not push their violent acts further; the old men entreated the commandant not to pay attention to the insolence of their young men, and brought to him the chief of the Iroquois band, to dispose of him as he should think best. Although the character of the French is opposed to inhumanity, it was impossible to avoid giving a public example of it [in this case]. The continual favors which were bestowed on the captives by our allies–who at heart were more our enemies than were even the Iroquois–only secured the continuance on both sides of the secret arrangements which existed between them; and, in order to exasperate at least the Iroquois, it was considered best to sacrifice this chief. For this purpose all the Outaouaks were invited "to drink the broth of this Iroquois," to express myself after their manner of speech. A stake was planted, to which he was attached by his hands and feet, leaving him only enough freedom to move around it; and a large fire was kindled near him, in which iron implements, gun-barrels, and frying-pans were made red-hot, while he sang his death-song. All being ready, a Frenchman began to pass a gun-barrel over his feet; an Outaouak seized another instrument of torture, and one after an-

other they broiled him as far as the knees, while he continued to sing tranquilly. But he could not refrain from
uttering loud cries when they rubbed his thighs with
red-hot frying-pans, and he exclaimed that the fire was
stronger than he. At once all the crowd of savages derided him with yells, saying to him, "Thou art a war-
chief, and afraid of fire; thou art not a man!" He was
kept in these torments during two hours, without giving
him any respite; the more he gave way to despair and
struck his head against the stake, the more they flung
jests at him. An Outaouak undertook to refine on this
sort of torture; he cut a gash along the captive's body,
from the shoulder to the thigh, put gunpowder along
the edges of the wound, and set fire to it. This caused
the captive even more intense pain than had the other
torments, and, as he became extremely weak, they gave
him something to drink – but not so much to quench his
thirst as to prolong his torture. When they saw that his
strength began to be exhausted, they cut away his scalp,
and left it hanging behind his back; they lined a large
dish with hot sand and red-hot coals, and covered his
head with it; and then they unbound him, and said to
him, "Thou art granted life." He began to run, falling
and again rising, like a drunken man; they made him
go in the direction of the setting sun (the country of
souls), shutting him out from the path to the east; and
they allowed him to walk only so far as they were willing
he should go. He nevertheless had still enough strength
to fling stones at random; finally they stoned him, and
every one carried away [a piece of] his broiled flesh.

Those savages who were most incensed quieted down
after the departure of the deputies who carried to Monsieur de Frontenac the Sauteur's collar; and our people
made various attempts to ascertain its real meaning, and

what reply the Outaouaks and the other tribes made to
the English and the Iroquois. At Michilimakinak there
was a Frenchman who was an intimate friend of one of
the principal council chiefs among our allies; he assured
this chief of entire protection from Onontio. As man
readily discloses his thought in the midst of joy, the
chief, after being warmed by a little brandy, promised
the Frenchman to meet him next day in the woods,
where he would tell him in confidence the entire condition of affairs; and the two went to the appointed place.
The Outaouak assured him that the English had sent
to the tribes four collars. By the first they sent word
that they would establish a post on Lake Herier, where
they would come to trade; the second took the savages
under their protection. By the third, the English ceased
to remember the pillage, by the savages together with
the French, from their warriors who were going to
Michilimakinak; and by the fourth they promised to
furnish their merchandise at lower prices than those
asked by Onontio – who was avaricious and robbed them.

As for the Iroquois, they had sent to these tribes eight
collars. By the first, they said that they remembered the
peace that they had made with La Petite Racine, and
that they had not desired to break it, even though their
brothers the Outaouaks should kill them every day; by
the second, they buried all the dead whom their brothers
had slain. The third hung up a sun at the strait between
Lake Herier and Lake Huron, which should mark the
boundaries between the two peoples, and this sun should
give them light when they were hunting. By the fourth,
they threw into the lake, and into the depths of the earth,
the blood that had been shed, in order that nothing
might be tainted with it. By the fifth, they sent "their
own bowl," so that they might have but one dish from

which to eat and drink. By the sixth, they promised to eat the "wild beasts" around them which should be common [enemies] to both. The seventh was to make them "eat together of the buffalo," meaning that they would unite to make war on the Miamis, the Islinois, and other tribes. By the eighth, they were to eat "the white meat," meaning the flesh of the French.

This chief told the Frenchman the replies of the Outaouaks, who consented to all these demands and sent return messages by means of collars, red-stone calumets,[31] and bales of beaver-skins; and he was secretly engaged to go down to Montreal and talk with Onontio, who would not fail to question closely the Sauteurs who had gone away with the Outaouak deputies.

[31] Among the Indians a favorite material for their pipes was "the red claystone called catlinite, obtained from a quarry in southwestern Minnesota, and so named because it was first brought to the attention of mineralogists by George Catlin, the noted traveler and painter of Indians. . . When freshly quarried it is so soft as to be readily carved with stone knives and drilled with primitive hand drills." The deposit of catlinite occurs in a valley near Pipestone, Minn.; the stratum of pipestone varies from ten to twenty inches in thickness, the fine, pure-grained stone available for the manufacture of pipes being, however, only three or four inches thick. The aboriginal excavations were quite shallow, and extended nearly a mile in length; but since the entrance of the whites into that region the Indians have carried on much more extensive operations, with the aid of iron implements obtained from the whites. "This quarry is usually referred to as the sacred pipestone quarry. According to statements by Catlin and others, the site was held in much superstitious regard by the aborigines;" and there is reason to believe that it was held and owned in common, and as neutral ground, by tribes elsewhere hostile to one another. "Since the earliest visits of the white man to the Côteau des Prairies, however, the site has been occupied exclusively by the Sioux, and Catlin met with strong opposition from them when he attempted to visit the quarry about 1837." In 1851 these lands were relinquished to the Federal government, and by a treaty in 1858 the privilege of freely mining and using the red stone was guaranteed to the Sioux; accordingly those people annually obtain from the quarry so much of the stone as they desire to use. They manufacture pipes and various trinkets from it, and sell much of the stone to the whites, who in turn manufacture and sell similar articles, using lathes in making them; in consequence, the genuine Indian products are crowded out of the market, and are seldom found. — W. H. HOLMES, in *Handbook Amer. Indians.*

Chapter XXIII

The Miamis, continually occupied against the Iroquois, levied a force of three hundred warriors. Some Frenchmen who were in that quarter, looking only at their own interests, made the savages believe that Onontio desired them to hunt beavers for one winter, to trade these for ammunition, in order to undertake in the following spring an expedition against the common enemy; but this advice did not hinder them from sending out a war-party, who captured and tomahawked twelve Iroquois. Finding themselves pursued by a great number, in another encounter they killed sixteen of the enemy. The Sakis and their allies also displayed their fidelity to Onontio; and it was only the Outagamis and the Maskoutechs who broke all their promises. They were implacable against only the Nadouaissioux, whatever the peace which they had made together, and whatever the difficulty in which they had found themselves, from which they were only extricated through the mediation of the French. This passion for vengeance which dominated them could never be effaced from their minds, and they set out on the war-path, with all their families. They destroyed [a village of] eighty cabins of Nadouaissioux, and cut to pieces all who offered resistance; and they practiced unheard-of cruelties on their captives. In this fight they lost fifteen men, and in revenge for this they burned two hundred women and children. Six Frenchmen went among them in order to redeem some of these slaves, and themselves narrowly escaped being consigned to the flames. The Miamis were deeply moved by all these disturbances of the peace; and they feared that the Nadouaissioux, desiring to take revenge, would attack them on their journey. As they had not

been at all implicated with the Maskoutechs, they engaged Perrot to go to the Nadouaissioux, to assure them
of the sympathy felt for them by the Miamis. Perrot
encountered a band of Nadouaissioux who were coming
as scouts against the Maskoutechs, who told him that
at eight leagues above he would find sixty of their men,
who formed an advance-guard to watch lest their enemies should return to the attack. He had no sooner
reached that place than those men approached him, all
bathed in tears, and uttering cries which would touch
even the most unfeeling. After they had wept about
half an hour, they placed him on a bear-skin and carried
him to the summit of a mountain, on which they had
encamped; this was done at the moment when he appeared deeply affected by their disaster. He asked them
to make his arrival known at the French fort; and a few
days later six Nadouaissioux set out with him, to go
thither. He passed through the village, which was entirely ruined, and where nothing could be seen except
melancholy remains from the fury of their enemies; the
laments of those who had escaped from their cruelty
were heard on every side. A Frenchman was there at
this time who called himself a great captain; he had
persuaded the savages, while displaying many pieces of
cloth, that he was unfolding these in order to bring
death on those who had devoured their families – a deception which only served him to get rid of his merchandise more quickly. But when the Nadouaissioux
learned that Perrot had arrived they came to find him at
this village and conducted him to his fort; and he took
advantage of so favorable an opportunity to present to
them the calumet on behalf of the Miamis. It was in
this manner that he delivered his message:

"Chiefs, I weep for the death of your children, whom

the Outagamis and the Maskoutechs have snatched
from you, while they told lies to me; Heaven has seen
their cruelties, and will punish them for it. This blood
is still too fresh to undertake vengeance for it at once.
God allows you to weep, in order to incline him toward
you; but he declares against you and will not aid you if
you set out on the war-path this summer. I have heard
that you are assembling together to seek your enemies;
they form but one body, and are resolutely awaiting you.
They have entrenched themselves in a strong fort; the
Outagamis have with them the greater part of their prey,
and will certainly massacre those captives if you make
your appearance. I cover your dead, by placing over
them two kettles. I do not bury them deep in the
ground, and intend only to protect them from the bad
weather until Onontio has heard of your loss; he will
deliberate on what he can do for you. I will go to see
him, and will try to obtain from him that he should
cause the restoration of your children who are slaves
among your enemies; it is not possible that he should
not be moved by compassion. The Miamis, who are his
children, obeyed him when I told them in his behalf to
put a stop to the war which they were waging against
you; they have heard of your affliction, and they weep
for your calamity. See their calumet which they have
sent you; they send you word that they disapprove the
actions of the Maskoutechs and the Outagamis. They
ask you to renew this alliance which exists between them
and you; and, if you send out war-parties to go to find
your bones, do not make a mistake by perhaps attacking
their families on your way."

This discourse was followed by many bitter lamentations; only cries and songs of death were heard. They
seized burning brands, with which they burned their

own bodies, without making any display of pain, repeat-
ing many times this expression of despair, *Kabato! Kabato!* and they scorched their flesh, with wonderful fortitude.

Perrot, having allowed them time to yield to the
natural emotions all that a just resentment could inspire
in them, placed before them several brasses of tobacco,
and said: "Smoke, chiefs! smoke, warriors! and smoke
peacefully, in the expectation that I will send back to
you some of your women and children, whom I will
draw out from the mouths of your enemies. Place all
your confidence in Onontio ["Monsieur de Frontenac" – La Potherie], who is the master of the land, and
from whom you will receive all sorts of satisfaction."
Then he gave them five or six packages of knives, and
again spoke to them: "These knives are for skinning
beavers, and not for lifting the scalps of men; use them
until you have tidings from Onontio."

The Frenchmen who had detained them to trade for
their peltries were obliged to come to the fort to sell
their merchandise. He whom they had regarded as a
great captain having arrived there, the savages went to
find him, and told him that, since the goods which he
had displayed to them would cause the deaths of the
Outagamis and the Maskoutechs, they desired to sing
to him and Perrot some "funeral calumets," in order
that these might aid them in their enterprises. They
said: "We have resolved not to leave our dead until
we have carried away [the people of] a village, whom
we intend to sacrifice to their shades. We recognize the
Miamis as our brothers, and we are going to send deputies to make peace with them. We do not bear much
ill-will to the Outagamis for their having carried away
our women, for they have spared their lives, and did not

pursue them when they ran away from them. Ten of
the women have arrived here, who report to us that the
Outagamis have good hearts, and that they take it ill
that the Maskoutechs have eaten all their slaves. Here
are three young men who have just arrived, who report
that for one Maskoutech who was killed in the battle
they have burned and put to death twenty of our wives
and children; and that in their retreat their only food
was our flesh."

This Frenchman said that he was ready to receive the
calumet, if Perrot was willing to accept the other. The
Nadouaissioux assembled in the cabin of the war-chief,
where they went through the ceremonies connected with
calumets of war; they made the two Frenchmen smoke
these, and placed the ashes of the tobacco in the ground,
invoking the [Great] Spirit, the sun, the stars, and all
the other spirits. With difficulty Perrot refused this
calumet, excusing himself as being only a child, who
could not do anything without the consent of his father.
He said that he had come to weep for their dead, and to
bring them the calumet for the Miamis, who had had
no share in the barbarous act of their enemies; and that
if they would give him a calumet as a response to the
Miamis he would carry it to them. But he could not
declare against the Maskoutechs, who would distrust
him because they would not fail to hear that the "funeral calumets" had been sung to him. He said that he had
very strong reason to complain of them, since he had run
the risk of being himself burned among them; but that
everything must be referred to Onontio. The Nadouaissioux admitted that he was right, and said that they
would hang up the war-club until they should have informed Monsieur de Frontenac of all that had occurred.
The Outagamis would have been glad if the Frenchmen

had conducted some Nadouaissioux to them to arrange for peace; they were much encumbered with their prisoners, and they were not ignorant that their proceedings had been contrary to the law of nations. The Nadouaissioux did not think it best to expose their deputies, alone [to danger], and to the number of thirty they set out for the Miami village; and they spent some time on the bank of the Missisipi, at a French post opposite the lead mine. Notice was given to the Miamis of the arrival of envoys from the Nadouaissioux, and forty of them set out to join the latter. The conference that took place between these two tribes was occupied with offers of service from one, and lamentations on the part of the other. The Nadouaissioux (according to their custom) poured many tears on the heads of the Miamis, who made them a present of a young girl and a little boy whom they had rescued from the hands of the Maskoutechs. They covered the dead of the Nadoüaissioux by giving them eight kettles, assuring them of their friendship, and made the chiefs smoke – promising them that they would obtain as many as they could of their [captive] women and children. They held secret conferences (unknown to the French) during one night, and the Miamis swore the entire destruction of the Maskoutechs. Our people sent word to a village of Miamis, established on the other side of the Missisipi, that we had something to communicate to them from Onontio; and they came, to the number of twenty-five. They were told that in the post where they were settled they were of no use for supporting Onontio in the Iroquois War; that they would obtain no more supplies for war unless they turned the war-club against the Iroquois; and that they ought to fear that the Nadouaissioux would fall upon them when that people should go to take vengeance for their dead upon the Maskoutechs. They promised to locate their fires at Maramek. They would have done so at the Saint Joseph River, at the solicitation of the chief of that district; but his refusal to furnish them gunpowder and balls gave them too unfavorable an opinion of his avarice to attract them to a union with him. The Maskoutechs got wind of the meeting between the Nadouaissioux and the Miamis that was brought about by Perrot; and they imagined that this could only be the result of his remembering the injuries that they had done him. [Accordingly] they immediately swore his ruin, and flattered themselves that, by plundering all the property of Perrot and the Frenchmen who were with him, they would have the means for taking flight more easily to the Iroquois country if they had to give way under the power of the [other] tribes. One night they tried to take him by surprise, but some dogs – who have a very strong antipathy for the savages, who commonly eat them – caused them to be discovered; and this obliged Perrot to put himself in an attitude of defense. The Maskoutechs, whose attack had miscarried, retreated without making any further effort; and their fear lest the French and the Miamis might form a league with the Nadouaissioux against them induced them to send one of their chiefs to Maramek, to sound the Miamis adroitly. He there encountered Perrot, with whom he had a private conversation. The savage is ordinarily politic and very pliant in behavior; this man said to Perrot with a smile, "Thou rememberest what I did to thee; thou art seeking to revenge thyself," and told him that he was sure that the tribes felt much resentment against the Nadouaissioux, who knew well that they were surrounded on all sides by their enemies; but that what was causing the Mas-

koutechs most regret was the seizure that they had made
of all his merchandise – for which, it would appear, he
sought an opportunity to take revenge. It was a matter
of prudence not to exasperate this chief too much, and
unreasonable acts often cause ruinous results; and it
might be that, if he were told that the French would
find means to put a stop to all the annoyances to which
they were continually exposed, the Maskoutechs would
come and attack the Miamis, as people who no longer
placed bounds to their conduct with any one whatever.
Perrot contented himself with very concisely upbraid-
ing the Maskoutech for all his tribe's acts of perfidy, in
regard to not only the French but the Nadouaissioux.
Meanwhile some young Maskoutech warriors came into
their cabin, who told this chief that he was required at
the village, and that their men had discovered the army
of the Nadouaissioux at the lead mine. He was very
ready to break off the conversation, and ran precipitately into the village, where he uttered shouts to notify his
men, who were dispersed, that they must retreat to their
own village in order to build a fort as quickly as possible.

The principal chiefs of the Miamis took advantage
of the departure of the French, who were going back to
Montreal, and nearly all the village escorted them as
far as the Bay of Puans. The Sakis and the Pouteouatemis wished to be also of this party; and on all sides
were heard many expressions of eagerness to go to hear
the voice of Monsieur de Frontenac. The Frenchmen
devoted themselves, while waiting for their embarca-
tion, to the deliverance of the Nadouaissioux prisoners
who were among the Outagamis. The latter had received as a present two Iroquois from the Miamis of
Chikagon; and policy restrained them from burning

these captives, because they hoped that, in case the Nadouaissioux came to attack their village, they could immediately retire with their families among the Iroquois, who would protect them from their enemies. They were persuaded [by the French] that all the peoples of these quarters desired their complete ruin; the Sauteurs had been plundered, the French treated in a brutal manner, and all their allies insulted. They had intended to send to the Iroquois one of their chiefs, with these two liberated captives, in order to invite that nation to join them on the confines of Saint Joseph River, and were inclined to ask the Maskoutechs to unite with them – which would have enabled them to collect a body of nine hundred warriors, in order to attack first the Miamis and the Islinois. The son of the great chief of the Outagamis came to the bay, where he had a secret conversation with one of the most distinguished Frenchmen. It was no sooner learned that he had resolved to go down to Montreal than some men of his tribe did all that they could to hinder him from this; but he told them that he was very glad to visit the French colony. The French departed as soon as they had sent some Nadouaissioux, whom they had redeemed, back to their own country.

Chapter XXIV

The Outaouaks at Michilimakinak conceived jealousy at the arrival of these newcomers, and did what they could to make them return each to his own country; it was suspected that they were still plotting something against the French nation. An Outaouak was adroitly sounded, in order to find out [if there were] new intrigues, and many presents were promised to him. He asked for a drink of brandy, intending to feign intoxication, so that he could make one of his companions talk who was actually in that condition; he told the latter, very angrily, that he would prevent the scheme of the Michilimakinak people from succeeding. The other replied that he was not able to prevent it; and there was much disputing on both sides. The Outaouak acknowledged, privately, that the Hurons had gone to the Iroquois, with a calumet ornamented with plumes, and several collars, in order to carry the message of the Outaouaks; the latter asked for full union with the Iroquois, and desired to abandon the side of the French, in order to place themselves under the protection of the English. Our people attempted to gain further and more thorough information by means of another Outaouak, who was the most influential man in that tribe; and he was regarded as the most faithful friend of the French. He said only this, that the Hurons, pretending to go to Sakinan in search of medicinal herbs, had really gone to the Iroquois country. Soon afterward it was learned that the Hurons were to bring some of the Iroquois with them to make arrangements, during the coming winter, for the place of rendezvous; but they did not fail to send chiefs to Montreal to beguile Monsieur de Frontenac. The Outagamis were very undecided over the conduct that they should observe in regard to the Iroquois, since the son of their chief had gone to visit our governor; whatever inclination they may have felt for the Iroquois, they concluded to await his return. The Hurons and the Outaouaks practiced all their tricks, as they had planned. Monsieur de Frontenac gave them several public audiences, at which they presented to him collars which assured him of their unshakable attachment. They returned home well pleased, and kept on the defensive in the river of the Outaouaks, not daring even to travel in the daytime for fear of the Iroquois – who on the voyage down the river had killed one of their men, and wounded a Frenchman and the Huron chief Le Baron. We can say that all those peoples were strangely blind as to their own interests. There was [among them] only eagerness to become attached to the Iroquois, whom they believed to be their friends – who, however, did not spare them when they could find an opportunity [to attack them]; but when it was a question of declaring in our favor they did so in the most indifferent possible manner.

Soon after their departure from Montreal, a rumor circulated that six hundred Iroquois were coming to ravage all our coasts; Monsieur de Frontenac made a general review of all his troops, and detached ten or twelve hundred men to resist the enemy at the start. The Pouteouatemis, the Sakis, the Malhominis, and that son of the great chief of the Outagamis undertook to go out themselves scouting as far as Lake Frontenac. The zeal that they displayed in this emergency deeply touched the governor, and he made them many presents on their return; and he assured the Outagami that, although his tribe had always been hostile to us, by plundering and insulting the French, they would be numbered with our allies.

Meanwhile the fleet of the French and the allies who were bringing their peltries arrived at Montreal; they informed us of the death of the famous Outaouak chief *Nansoaskoüet*, who had been slain among the Osages. [32]

---

[32] The Osage (a name corrupted by French traders from *Wazhazhe*, their own name) are the most important southern Siouan tribe of the western division. Dorsey classed them "in one group with the Omaha, Ponca, Kansa, and Quapaw, with whom they are supposed to have originally constituted a single body living along the lower course of the Ohio River. . . The first historical notice of the Osage appears to be on Marquette's autograph map of 1673, which locates them apparently on Osage River, and there they are placed

He was the supporter of the French in his own country,
and had been an opponent of the English, in spite of his
tribe. He had gone to the Islinois the preceding
autumn, at the solicitation of his warriors, who for a
long time tried to deprive us of the succor which the
tribes of the south were giving us in the Iroquois War.
He had, I say, gone to the Islinois, to avenge the death
of the son of Talon (who had died from sickness in the
war which he had undertaken to wage on the Kanças
and the Osages), and had induced all the Islinois to
join his expedition. In the attack on a village they encountered sturdy resistance; Nansoaskoüet, who tried
to storm it, pushed too far in advance [of his men]
and was surrounded, and they pierced him with arrows,
which caused his death. The Outaouaks who had come
down in this fleet brought some presents and an Osage
slave, by way of announcing to Monsieur de Frontenac
the death of this great chief; he made answer to them
that they ought first to take revenge against the Iroquois,
who had slain his nephew (meaning Nansoaskoüet's),
and that he would send his warriors against the Osages

by all subsequent writers until their removal westward in the nineteenth century. . . In 1714 they assisted the French in defeating the Foxes at Detroit.
Although visits of traders were evidently quite common before 1719, the first
official French visit appears to have been in that year by Du Tisné, who learned
that their village on Osage River then contained 100 cabins and 200 warriors.
The village of the Missouri was higher up. "Then, as always, the tribe was
at war with most of the surrounding peoples." By a treaty of Nov. 10, 1808,
the Osage ceded a large part of their lands to the United States, and still
more by later agreements. "The limits of their present reservation were established by act of Congress of July 15, 1870. This consists (1906) of
1,470,058 acres, and in addition the tribe possessed funds in the Treasury of
the United States amounting to $8,562,690, including a school fund of $119,911,
the whole yielding an annual income of $428,134. Their income from pas-
turage leases amounted to $98,376 in the same year, and their total annual
income was therefore about $265 per capita, making this tribe the richest in
the entire United States. By act of June 28, 1906, an equal division of the
lands and funds of the Osage was provided for." Their population in the
last-named year was 1,994, having dwindled to that figure from some 5,000
a century ago. — JOHN R. SWANTON, in Handbook Amer. Indians.

and the Kancas. This response pleased them little, because, as the savages are very capricious, they do not allow themselves to be easily influenced by mere promises. They went back, however, to Michilimakinak, as did all our allies, with the wife of the chief of the Nadouaissioux, who had been one of the prisoners whom the Outagamis had taken; she was sold to an Outaouak, and ransomed by a Frenchman who brought her to Montreal. There remained only one Nadouaissioux, who was kept there some time; our people were very glad to let him see the colony, in order that he might give his own people some idea of the power of the French. He had come expressly to arouse in Monsieur de Frontenac some compassion for their calamity.

Chapter XXV

Monsieur the Count de Frontenac had reason to believe that the Hurons and the Outaouaks had spoken to him with open heart in the audiences that he had given them; but he was much surprised to learn that the Hurons had sent ambassadors to the Iroquois, and the Iroquois to the Hurons. The French commandant at Michilimakinak did not doubt that the presence of these latter would cause a great disturbance, and tried to make the Outaouaks tomahawk them. Great disorder prevailed, and the savages generally took up arms against him; they were, however, obliged to send the envoys back to their homes, for fear of some accident. The Outaouaks departed, the following winter, in order to hunt game at the rendezvous that they had appointed, where they were to conclude a full and substantial peace. They had taken the precaution to leave at Michilimakinak a chief to keep up friendly intercourse with the French, and as a pledge of their fidelity to Onontio, without letting it be known that they had any premeditated design – even asserting that, if they saw any Iroquois, they would gradually lure them on, in order to "put them into the kettle." The French affected not to distrust their fidelity, but sent an envoy to the Bay of Puans to induce our allies to send out meantime some bands who could hinder this [proposed] interview. At the bay were found only the old men – as at that time all the young men were out hunting except those who had gone down to Montreal, who had [not yet?] returned home – and one chief, who was told that a favorable opportunity now offered itself which might secure for him recommendation to Onontio, from whom he would receive all possible advantages if he would go to persuade his people to fight the Iroquois at the rendezvous which the latter had granted to the Outaouaks. He promised that he would go gladly, for love of Onontio, and immediately set out without attempting to make a war-feast beforehand. The Outagamis were weaned from the ardor that they had had for going with their families to join the Iroquois. The son of their chief, who had returned from Montreal, made a deep impression on their minds by the account which he gave of the power of the French. The Sakis had always supported our interests during that time; they lost some men and various captives were taken from them, for they found themselves surrounded by six hundred Iroquois who were going to Montreal for war. It was this army (who had been discovered by our Iroquois of the Saut), whom the Outagami chief's son and our other allies had gone to reconnoiter at Lake Frontenac. These Sakis were taken to Onnontagué, where the ambassadors of the Hurons had arrived; and the Onnontaguais[33] censured the

33 Onondaga (or Onontagués), one of the Iroquois Five Nations, formerly living on Onondaga Lake, N.Y., and extending northward to Lake Ontario,

Hurons for coming to treat of peace while their allies the Sakis were killing the Iroquois. The Hurons replied that they did not regard the Sakis as friends or as allies; and for the purpose of confirming this assertion they immediately burned the hands and cut off the finger ends of the Saki prisoners. The Outagamis and the Sakis made every possible effort to form a peace with the Nadouaissioux. They promised the French that they would, if the latter would prevent the incursions of the Nadouaissioux, take the war-path against the Iroquois to the number of twelve or fifteen hundred men; and even that, if the Outaouaks made peace with that nation, they would strike higher up – "in order to clear the road," they said, "which the Outaouaks would proceed to close against the French who should come to trade at the bay and with the southern tribes." All the Frenchmen who were in those quarters were called together; and it was decided that an attempt must be made to restrain the Nadouaissioux, to the end that the Outagamis might place in the field an expedition that would without fail be successful. The French bought six boys and six girls, the children of chiefs, besides the great chief's wife whom they already had; and they set out across the country to conduct these captives to the Nadouaissioux. Perrot was selected to transact this business; he also held special orders from Monsieur de

and southward to perhaps the Susquehanna. Their principal village, Onondaga, was also the capital of the confederation; and their present reserve is in the valley of Onondaga Creek. "Many of the Onondaga joined the Catholic Iroquois colonies on the St. Lawrence, and in 1751 about half of the tribe was said to be living in Canada." In 1775 most of the Iroquois took sides with the British, who at the close of the war granted them lands on Grand River, Ont., where a part of them still reside. "The rest are still in New York, the greater number being on the Onondaga reservation, and the others with the Seneca and Tuscarora on their several reservations. . . In 1906 the Onondaga in New York numbered 553, the rest of the tribe being with the Six Nations in Canada." – J. N. B. HEWITT, in *Handbook Amer. Indians.*

Frontenac for other enterprises. He arrived in the country of the Miamis, who sent people to meet him and point out to him their village, having learned from some one of their people who had come from Montreal that he was coming to see them again. On his arrival he announced to them that Onontio gave positive orders that they should quit their [present] fires, and light them at the Saint Joseph River; for the execution of this order they gave him, on their part, five collars. He told them that he was going to make efforts to restrain the Nadouaissioux, and to return to them some slaves whom he had rescued from their enemies; and he admonished them all to be present in their village on his return thither. The Nadouaissioux had sent to the Miamis seven of their women, whom they had rescued from the hands of the Maskoutechs; and the Miamis made them presents of eight kettles, a quantity of Indian corn, and tobacco.

Chapter XXVI

Twelve hundred Nadouaissioux, Sauteurs, Ayoës, and even some Outaouaks were then on the march against the Outagamis and the Maskoutechs, and likewise were not to spare the Miamis. They had resolved to take revenge on the French, if they did not encounter their enemies. These warriors were only three days' journey distant from the Miami village from which Perrot had departed; they learned that he was coming among them with their women and children and the wife of the great chief. This was enough to make them lay down their arms and suspend war until they had heard what he had to say to them. He reached his fort, where he learned these circumstances; he was also told that it was believed that the Miamis were already routed. As he did not know that the Nadouaissioux had the news that

he was coming, he sent to them two Frenchmen, who
came back the next day with their great chief. I cannot
express the joy that they displayed when they saw their
women. The remembrance of the loss of the other captives caused at the same time so much grief that it was
necessary to allow a day's time to their tears and all the
lamentations that they uttered. According to them,
Perrot was a chief whose "feet were on the ground and
his head in the sky;" he was also the "master of the
whole earth," and they heaped on him expressions of
joy and endearment, regarding him as a divinity. They
were so busy in weeping hot tears on his head and on the
captives, and in gazing on the sun with many exclamations, that he could not obtain from them any satisfaction. On the next day they told him that when "the
men" arrived they would render him thanks; it is thus
that all the savages are designated among themselves,
while they call the French "French," and the [other]
people from Europe by the names of their respective
nations. They are persuaded that in all the world they
are the only real men; and the greatest praise that they
can bestow on a Frenchman whose worth they recognize is when they say to him, "Thou art a man." When
they wish to show him that they have contempt for him,
they tell him that he is not a man. The chief desired to
bring up all his men near the fort, but the Sauteurs, the
Ayoës, and several villages of the Nadouaissioux had
made their arrangements for hunting beaver, and there
were only two villages, of about fifty cabins each, who
came to the fort. After the Nadouaissioux had encamped, this chief sent to ask Perrot to come to his
cabin, with all the men who had accompanied him. His
brother, seeing a Saki, exclaimed that he was an Outagami, saying, "Behold the man who has eaten me!"
This Saki, knowing well that he was not safe, offered

him his calumet, which the Nadouaissioux refused. A Miami, who also was with the French, took his own calumet and offered it, which he accepted. Perrot gave his own calumet to the Saki, and told him to offer it; the Nadouaissioux did not dare to refuse, and took and smoked it – but with the cries and tears of an angry man, calling the Great Spirit, the Sky, the Earth, and all the spirits to witness that he asked to be pardoned if he received the calumet which his enemy offered him, which he dared not refuse because it belonged to a captain whom he esteemed. There was no one save a woman whom this very Saki had rescued from slavery who could prove who he was. He was so frightened that, if he had not felt some confidence in the outcome, he would have longed to be far away. During several days feasts were made, and the result of this conference was, that the Nadouaissioux were very willing to make peace with the Outagamis if the latter would restore the rest of their people; but in regard to the Maskoutechs they had, together with the Miamis, sworn to ruin them; and they parted, each according to his own side. The Miamis were advised not to rely on the Nadouaissioux, and they were more than ever attracted to the idea of abandoning Maramek in order to settle on Saint Joseph River, as Onontio had commanded them. They were given two hundred pounds of gunpowder in order to procure subsistence for their families while on the journey, and to kill any Iroquois whom they might meet. The Saki who had been so frightened in the cabin of the Nadouaissioux chief took to flight, and filled the Outagamis with such alarm that even the women and children worked, day and night, to build a fort in which they could make themselves safe. The arrival of one of their men, who was out hunting beaver, increased their ter-

ror. He had indeed seen the camp of the Nadouaissioux
army, but had not been able to consider whether it was
recently made. The alarm therefore broke out more
wildly than ever; they made many harangues to encourage all the warriors to make a stout defense; and
each vied with the others in showing the best way of
ordering the combat. Word was sent to the bay to inform the tribes of the march of the Nadouaissioux, and
at the same time to ask them to furnish aid to that people. Scouts went out in all directions; some reported
that they had seen the fires of the army and some freshly-
killed animals, at two days' distance; and others, who
arrived the next day, said that the army was only one
day's march from there. Finally, people came in great
haste to say that the river was all covered with canoes,
and that, from all appearances the general attack was to
be made at night; nothing, however, was visible. Perrot, who was then among them, wished to go in person
to reconnoiter; but they prevented him from this, in the
fear which they felt, [imagining that] by detaining him
the enemy would not come to surprise them. Some
hunters, who had been bolder than the others, reported
that the [alleged] camp had been made the preceding
winter. Their minds began to regain confidence, and
they no longer sought for anything save the means for
sending back their prisoners in order to secure peace,
and for making ready after that to march against the
Iroquois; and they again entreated Perrot to be their
mediator for peace. He went among them and proposed to them the above arrangement, which they accepted; and promised to conduct their people [to the
Nadouaissioux country] in the moon when the [wild]
bulls would be rutting. The savages divide the year
into twelve moons, to which they give the names of ani-

mals, but which are similar to our months. Thus, January and February are the first and second m ∩ns, when the bears bring forth their young; March is th. moon of the carp, and April that of the crane; May is the moon of the Indian corn; June, the moon when the wild geese shed their feathers; July, that when the bear is in rut; August, the rut of the bulls; September, that of the elk; October, the rut of the moose; November, that of the deer; December, the moon when the horns of the deer fall off.   The tribes who dwell about the [Great] Lakes call September the moon when the trout milt; October, that of the whitefish; and November, that of the herring; to the other months they give the same names as do those who live inland. [34]   Perrot then assured them that at the

[34] "Although the methods of computing time had been carried to an advanced stage among the cultured tribes of Mexico and Central America, the Indians north of Mexico had not brought them beyond the simplest stage. The alternation of day and night and the changes of the moon and the seasons formed the bases of their systems. The budding, blooming, leafing, and fruiting of vegetation, the springing forth, growth, and decay of annuals, and the molting, migration, pairing, etc., of animals and birds, were used to denote the progress of the seasons. The divisions of the day differed, many tribes recognizing four diurnal periods — the rising and setting of the sun, noon, and midnight — while full days were usually counted as so many nights or sleeps. The years were generally reckoned, especially in the far north, as so many winters or so many snows; but in the Gulf States, where snow is rare and the heat of summer the dominant feature, the term for year had some reference to this season or to the heat of the sun. As a rule the four seasons — spring, summer, autumn, and winter — were recognized and specific names applied to them; but the natural phenomena by which they were determined, and from which their names were derived, varied according to latitude and environment, and as to whether the tribe was in the agricultural or the hunter state. . . The most important time division to the Indians north of Mexico was the moon, or month, their count of this period beginning with the new moon." Some tribes counted twelve moons to the year, and some thirteen. "There appears to have been an attempt on the part of some tribes to compensate for the surplus days in the solar year. Carver (*Travels*, ed. 1796, 160), speaking of the Sioux or the Chippewa, says that when thirty moons have waned they add a supernumerary one, which they term the lost moon. . . The Indians generally calculated their ages by some remarkable event or phenomenon which had taken place within their remembrance; but few Indians of mature years could possibly tell their age before learning the white man's way of counting time. Sticks were sometimes notched by the Indians as an aid in time

time of the bulls' rutting he would be present at the mouth of the Ouisconk [i.e., the Wisconsin River], where the peace was to be concluded. He sent word to the Outagamis to have the Nadouaissioux slaves all ready; the chiefs met together for that purpose, and placed all the slaves in one cabin. Then they suddenly heard death-cries from the other side of their river; they believed that the Nadouaissioux had defeated the Miamis, and immediately sent messengers to find out how affairs stood; and these reported that the Nadouaissioux had destroyed forty of the Miami cabins, in which all the women and children and fifty-five men had been killed. This act of hostility against people whom they regarded as friends made them suspect that the Nadouaissioux would not spare them [even] after they had sent back the people of the latter. Twelve Frenchmen immediately set out with Perrot in order to try to overtake the Nadouaissioux, and to induce them to give back the slaves whom they had just taken. They reached the French fort which is in the country of those peoples, and there they obtained information of everything. The French undertook to join the Nadouaissioux, in a village which was inaccessible on account of numberless swamps, from which they could not extricate themselves; and they traveled through the bogs, without food for four days. All these Frenchmen took refuge on a little island, except two who, still trying to find some exit, encountered two hunters, who conducted them to their village. The Nadouaissioux were unwilling to send for the other Frenchmen, not daring to let them enter [their village] on account of their fear lest the French

counts. . . Some of the northern tribes kept records of events by means of symbolic figures or pictographs;" some of these are described in the 10th and 17th annual *Reports* of the Bureau of Ethnology. — CYRUS THOMAS, in *Handbook Amer. Indians*.

would kill them in order to avenge the Miamis. The latter sent presents to the Outagamis, with entreaties to furnish them assistance and with them avenge their dead, by a general march [against the Nadouaissioux], which they would make in the approaching winter. The commandant of Michilimakinak, when he heard of the treachery of the Nadouaissioux, wrote to Perrot to make the Miamis hang up the war-club, so that he could go to the Nadouaissioux country and bring away all the Frenchmen, as he did not wish them to become the victims of this new war; and he had even resolved to destroy that people who had so injured our best friends. The Miamis, who had abandoned everything to escape from that furious attack, were destitute of ammunition and of many articles which they obtained only from the French, who exchanged these for peltries. The Outagamis were resolved to give their lives for the cause of the Miamis, in case the French would consent to this; the Kikabous also asked for nothing better. A general expedition was formed to go to join the Miamis, their women and children also going with them. Perrot met on the way four Miamis, whom the chief had sent to ask that he would come to their camp; and he left all that procession, to go thither. The allies, being in sight of the camp, fired some gunshots as a signal of his arrival; and all the Miami young men stood in rows, and watched him pass them. He heard a voice saying *Pakumiko*! which signifies in their language, "Tomahawk him!" and he rightly judged that there was some decree of death against him; but he feigned to take no notice of this speech, and continued his walk to the chief's cabin, where he called together the most prominent men among them. He set forth to them that, as he had not been able to secure a more favorable opportunity for giving them proofs of the interest which he took in the matters which concerned their tribe, he had engaged the Outagamis and Kikabous who were following him to take up arms to avenge the Miami dead against the Nadouaissioux. These words turned aside the evil design which they had formed against him, and they regaled him. At the same time there arrived a young man, who brought the news that the Frenchmen who were living in the Nadouaissioux country were at the portage. The chief assigned fifty women to transport their bales of peltries; but the young men, who had received a private order to plunder these, carried off everything that they could into the woods, and hid themselves there. The chief, being informed of this act, pretended to make a great commotion in the village, to the end that they should bring back what had been stolen; but there was one of the people who objected that this pillage had been made with the chief's consent, since he had even ordered them to kill the French; and very few of the peltries were brought back. A great tumult arose among the chiefs, who quarreled together, some taking the side of the French, and others that of the tribe. In that place were three different tribes: the Pepikokis, the Mangakokis, and the Peouanguichias [35] (who had conspired against the French). One of their chiefs said that he knew how to plunder merchandise and slay men,

---

[35] The Piankashaw were formerly a subtribe of the Miami, but later a separate people. La Salle induced some of them to come to his fort in Illinois; Cadillac mentions them (1695) as being "west of the Miami village on St. Joseph's River, Mich., with the Mascoutens, Kickapoo, and other tribes;" and a little later they had a village on Kankakee River. Their ancient village was on the Wabash, at the junction of the Vermillion; later they formed another village, at the present site of Vincennes, Ind. In the beginning of the nineteenth century they and the Wea began to remove to Missouri, and in 1832 both tribes sold their lands to the government and went to a reservation in Kansas, in 1867 again removing to Oklahoma with the Peoria (with whom they had united about 1854). "The Piankashaw probably never numbered

and that, since his children had been eaten by the Sioux (who had formerly been his enemies), on whom the French had taken pity, obliging the Miamis to make peace with them, he would now avenge himself on the French. Four of his warriors immediately sang [their war-song], to invite their comrades to join all together in an attack on the French. Two other tribes, who had always had much intercourse with us, at the same time took up arms; they obliged the others to cross the river the next day, after reproaching them with having robbed themselves in pillaging the Frenchmen, who were coming to succor them. "It is we," they said, "who have been ill-treated by the Nadouaissioux, whom we regarded as our allies; why stir up an unseasonable quarrel with the French, with whom you ought not to have any strife?" Those who had been so well-intentioned requested from the French only four men to accompany them to the Nadouaissioux country, in order that, in case the enemy should be entrenched there, the Frenchmen might show them how to undermine the fort. They would not depend at all upon the rest of the Frenchmen,

---

many more than 1,000 souls. . . In 1825 there were only 234 remaining, and in 1906 all the tribes consolidated under the name of Peoria numbered but 192, none of whom was of pure blood."

The Pepikokia are "an Algonquian tribe or band mentioned in the latter part of the seventeenth century as a division of the Miami. In 1718 both they and the Piankashaw were mentioned as villages of the Wea. That the relation between these three groups was intimate is evident. They were located on the Wabash by Chauvignerie (1736) and other writers of the period. They are spoken of in 1695 as Miamis of Maramek River, that is, the Kalamazoo. A letter dated 1701 (Margry, *Découvertes*, vol. iv, 592) indicates that they were at that time in Wisconsin. Chauvignerie says that Wea, Piankashaw, and Pepikokia 'are the same nation, though in different villages,' and that 'the devices of these Indians are the Serpent, the Deer, and the Small Acorn.' They were sometimes called Nation de la Grue, as though the crane was their totem. They disappear from history before the middle of the eighteenth century and may have become incorporated in the Piankashaw, whose principal village was on the Wabash at the junction of the Vermillion. — JAMES MOONEY, in *Handbook Amer. Indians*.

whom they even entreated to return to the bay. Orders were given to these four men to desert when they should come within a day's journey from the French fort, in order to give warning there to keep on their guard, and to inform the Sauteurs of the plans of the Miamis, who intended to slaughter them. The Miamis began their march, and crossed the river; only a few chiefs were left, who spent the night with the Frenchmen. At nine o'clock in the evening the moon was eclipsed; and they heard at the camp a volley of three hundred gunshots, and yells as if they were being attacked; these sounds were repeated. These chiefs asked the Frenchmen what they saw in the sky; the latter answered that the Moon was sad on account of the pillage that they had suffered. The chiefs answered, gazing at the moon: "This is the reason for all the gunshots and cries that you hear. Our old men have taught us that when the Moon is sick it is necessary to assist her by discharging arrows and making a great deal of noise, in order to cause terror in the spirits who are trying to cause her death; then she regains her strength, and returns to her former condition. If men did not aid her she would die, and we would no longer see clearly at night; and thus we could no longer separate the twelve months of the year."

The Miamis continued to fire their guns, and only ceased when the eclipse was ended; on this occasion they did not spare the gunpowder that they had taken from us. It would have been very easy for the French to bind these chiefs and sacrifice them to the Nadouais-sioux, but the Miamis could have taken vengeance for this on our missionaries, on our Frenchmen at the Saint Joseph River, and on those at Chikagon; and our men took the road to the bay. They met three cabins of Outa-gamis, who were surprised at their return, and at seeing

their canoes; they concluded that the Miamis had stolen
these, but the latter were exonerated [by the French]
from an act in which they had been suspected of taking
part.

When these Frenchmen arrived at the bay they found
one hundred and fifty Outaouaks, sixty Sakis, and
twenty-five Pouteouatemis, who were going to hunt
beavers toward the frontiers of the Nadouaissioux; these
savages held a council, to ascertain the decision of the
leading Frenchmen regarding their voyage from Michilimakinak. The Miamis of Saint Joseph River had
informed the commandant of Michilimakinak of the
hostile acts which the Nadouaissioux had committed on
them, and demanded his protection. This commandant
sent out despatches prohibiting the French in all those
regions to go up to the Nadouaissioux country; and
ordering those who had come thence to ask the Miamis
to hang up the war-club until spring, as he was going to
avenge them, with all the French who should be at
Michilimakinak. The aspect of affairs had necessarily
changed since the Miamis had pillaged the Frenchmen;
the Outaouaks therefore held a council, to learn the
final resolution of the latter. They set forth that they
found no one at Michilimakinak, and that, if these
Frenchmen did not choose to join them, they could prevent the ruin of the Sauteurs through the agency of the
Outagamis; and the Frenchmen themselves were running a risk, in case they were not backed up, since the
Outagamis had been displeased at the intercourse which
the former had held with the Nadouaissioux in the past.
These arguments were sufficiently strong to induce the
greater number of the French to join the Outaouaks.
They set out on the march across the country, and a few
days later two Sakis were sent to notify the Outagamis

of it, and to ask them not to go to Ouiskonch until this
army had reached their village; they were also requested
to inform the Miamis that Perrot was going to find
them, without positively telling the latter, however, that
he was coming to furnish them assistance in their war.
These two Sakis reported that the Outagamis and Kikabous, having heard of the plunder of the French by the
Miamis, were all dispersed through the country in
search of means for subsistence – having been unwilling,
since that news, to take up the cause of these tribes
against the Nadouaissioux; that they were grieved because Sieur Perrot had not gone to find them after that
pillage, since they would have sacrificed themselves in
order to secure the restitution of his goods; that they
were going to send for all their people, so as to receive
them on the shore of Ouiskonche, which they would not
cross until everybody should arrive there. They said
also that they had found the chief of the Miamis, with
two of those Frenchmen who were to accompany them
to the Nadouaissioux; this chief was urgently soliciting
the Outagamis to march with the Miamis as they had
promised, but the latter had replied that the Miamis
could continue their course if they would not wait for
the arrival of the French and the Outaouaks. The bad
roads and the lack of provisions obliged the Outaouaks
to remain [on the way] for some time; finally they
reached the nearest cabins of the Outagamis, among
whom they were well entertained. The chiefs of twenty-
five [Outagami] cabins, and fifteen of the Kikabou
cabins, becoming impatient because the Outaouaks did
not arrive, had gone a little too far ahead, in order to
gain Ouiskonch; the Miamis who met them constrained
them to go to their camp, where they displayed little
consideration for the newcomers. The latter sent in

haste a Saki and a Frenchman to urge the Outaouaks to hasten their arrival as soon as possible, saying that meanwhile they would try to divert the Miamis and prevent them from beginning the march.

Two or three Frenchmen set out at once, and at night reached the cabin of the Outagami chief, who immediately had their arrival made public. The Miamis promptly made their appearance there, and demanded, "Where are the other warriors?" On both sides deputies were sent to fix the place for the general rendezvous, which was at the entrance of a little river. The Miamis, who numbered five villages, desiring to break camp, sent out some men from each group to kindle fires, which was the signal of departure; they built five of these, abreast, the Outagamis two, and the Kikabous one. When these fires were kindled the call to break camp was uttered; all the women folded up the baggage, and gathered at the fires of their respective tribes, at which the men also assembled. All the people being ready, the war-chiefs (with their bags on their backs) began to march at the head, singing, making their invocations, and gesticulating; the warriors, who were on the wings, marched in battle array, abreast, and forming many ranks; the convoy for the women composed the main body, and a battalion of warriors formed the rear-guard. This march was made with order; some Frenchmen were detailed to go to meet the Outaouaks. The latter, having arrived in sight of the Miami camp, began to defile, and fired a volley of musketry. The Outagamis refused to return the salute to them; on the contrary, they sent word to the Miami camp to make no commotion, for fear of frightening their brothers, the Outaouaks – because the Outagamis feared lest the Miamis, already entertaining evil thoughts, might lay violent hands on them, under pretext of receiving them as friends. The Outaouaks having made their camp, their chiefs entered the cabin of the chief of the Outagamis, with two guns, twelve kettles, and two collars made of round and long porcelain beads; but they sent to call the Miamis, without making them any present. They asked from the Outagamis permission to hunt on their lands, intending to devote themselves only to the beavers and [other] quadrupeds, as they had come under the protection of the French. The Outagamis divided their presents into three lots; they gave the largest to the Miamis, the second to the Kikabous, and reserved the smallest for themselves.

The Miamis did not show to the Outaouaks the resentment which they felt at the affront which they had just received. They assembled about three hundred warriors to perform their war-dances, and in these they chanted the funeral songs, in which they named the persons who had been slain by the Nadouaissioux. They should, according to the custom in war, make the round of the camp while singing and dancing; it was their design [while doing so] to kill at the same time all the dogs belonging to the Outaouaks, in order to make a war-feast with them. The Outagamis, fearing that they would go to this extreme, came to meet them, so as to prevent the Miamis from acting toward the Outaouaks as they had done in regard to the Outagami dogs. The Outaouaks had already placed themselves on the defensive; however, everything went off without a disturbance.

After this last people had ended their council, the Miamis assembled at night with the Fox Outagamis; they imagined that the French – [especially] two among them – had come only to prevent the Outagamis from

uniting with them. A war-chief, desiring to irritate his
tribe against the Frenchmen, was urging his people to
burn them; the report of this ran through the camp.
An Outagami, hearing the discourse of this chief, went
out and told the Miamis that after having eaten the
Outagamis they would probably eat these two Frenchmen; he gave the alarm to the men of his tribe, who
placed themselves under arms. Another Miami, addressing his people, said that it was absolutely necessary
to burn them. All the night there was nothing but com-
motions on the part of the Miamis, who only longed for
the moment to attack the Outaouaks – whom they called
friends of the Sioux and the Iroquois who had eaten
them. The Outagamis did not pay much attention to
all these incivilities; their only endeavor was to follow
the wishes of the Frenchmen. When the day had come,
the Miamis beat the salute, and defiled in battle array,
the Outagamis and the Kikabous remaining stock-still.
The decision which the French advised the Outagamis
to make was, to join their forces with the Miamis, saying: "Go with them; they mean to slay the Frenchmen
who are in the country of the Nadouaissioux, without
sparing the Sauteurs. Even though the latter may be
your enemies, spare their lives; and prevent the Miamis
from attacking them or insulting the French. Go, then,
to assist them, rather than to wage war against the
Nadouaissioux. If they engage in fighting, remain in
the reserve force, and quit it only when the enemy shall
take to flight." The old men of the Miamis had remained at the camp in order to know the final decision
of the Outagamis; they came into the council cabin,
where these Frenchmen were present. The eldest of
them offered his calumet to one of the latter, who
smoked it, and told the other that he had heard the

clamor of their speech-maker, who was inciting all the
Miamis to burn his body so as to put it into the kettle;
and had heard this man's brother, who said that it was
necessary to lay violent hands on the Outaouaks whom
the French had brought, although they had come to
avenge the dead of the Miamis. He said that, since he
found in them so little good sense and was aware of
their misconduct, the French would abandon their enterprise, and would join the four other Frenchmen who
had been furnished to accompany them into the Nadouaissioux country. "Eat," said this Frenchman to the old
man, "eat the French who are among the Nadouaissioux, but thou wilt no sooner take them in thy teeth than
we will make thee disgorge them." Then every one
arose; and all the Outagamis and the Kikabous had their
bundles tied up by the women, so as to go to join the
Miamis in their camp – excepting the old men, and some
people who were not very alert.

The first news that came after their departure was,
that the Miamis had been defeated; that the Outagamis
and the Kikabous had lost no men; and that the Outagamis had saved the Sauteurs and the French. Four
of the Outagami youth arrived some days later, sent by
the chiefs to give information of all that had occurred
since the departure of the army. At the outset, they
were heard to utter eight death-cries, but without saying
whether they were Miamis or of some other tribe. A
kettle was promptly set over the fire for them, and even
before the meat was cooked they were set to eating.
After they had satisfied their hunger, one of them spoke
before the old men and some Frenchmen. He said:

"A chief of the Chikagons having died from sickness,
the Miamis made no present to his body; but our chiefs,
touched by this lack of feeling, brought some kettles to

cover it. The Miamis of Chikagon were so grateful for this that they told our chiefs that they would unite with them, to the prejudice of their allies – who paid them no attention when they were dying, even though they had come to avenge them. A Piouanguichias also died, a little farther on; we went to bury him, and made him presents; but the Miamis again did nothing. I tell you, old men, that these two tribes would have turned the war-clubs of the Miamis against us if we had undertaken to do the same by them. When we arrived at one of the arms of the Missisipi, eight Miamis who had gone out as scouts brought to the camp two Frenchmen who were coming from the Sauteur country; it was planned to burn them, but our warriors opposed this, loudly declaring that we had set out to wage war on the Nadouaissioux. They kept one of the prisoners, and sent back the other, with some Miamis, to the Sauteurs, who received them well. This Frenchman remained there only one day; on the next day ten Sauteurs and Outaouaks accompanied him to come after the Miamis, to whom they made a present of twelve kettles. Our people were displeased that the Sauteurs were not divided between them and us in the cabins, and that they had presented to the Miamis seven kettles, while the Kikabous and we received only five; but what we considered extraordinary was, that at night the Miamis came to find our chiefs with the kettles of the Sauteurs, and other goods which they had added to these, to invite us to eat these ambassadors with them. It is true that our chief immediately drew out a collar which a Frenchman had given to him, without our knowledge, by which he asked our chief not to attack his people who were among the Nadouaissioux, or the Sauteurs, or any of the allies of Onontio. This collar, I say, restrained us all. Then they allowed the Sauteurs to go away; the latter pointed out the village of the Nadouaissioux, who had built a strong fort in order to take refuge in it in case of need. A part of the Miamis resolved to carry them away from it; but we also followed, so as to hold them back. The Oüaouyartanons and the Peoüanguichias, remembering the obligations which they were under to us for the care which we had taken of their dead, broke their camp, in order to thwart the designs of their allies. While they were making up their bundles, a young Sauteur arrived who had had some dispute with a Nadouaissioux; he said that he came to join our party; but a Miami immediately tomahawked him and cut off his scalp. This proceeding obliged us to pack our baggage and follow the Oüaouyartanons and the Peoüanguichias. The Miamis, seeing that they were not strong enough to attack the Nadouaissioux, broke camp as we had done, and followed us. At evening they concluded that it was necessary to go toward the Missisipi, where they would find more game than upon the road which they had so far taken. They sent forty of their warriors to the French fort, and imagined that they could enter it as they would one of our cabins. The dogs of the fort, discovering them, barked at them. The French, seeing men who were marching with hostile aspect, seized their arms and told them to advance no farther; the Miamis derided them, but the French fired over their heads and made them retire. The Miamis who had broken camp on the day after this detachment had set out took the same route as the latter. When we saw that they were going toward the French post we followed them, fearing lest they would go to make trouble for the French; the Oüaoüyartanons and the Peoüanguichias refused to abandon us. We saw the arrival of the above-mentioned

[Miami] detachment, who as they came cried out that
the French had fired on them; and by that we knew that
they had attempted to take the French fort by surprise.
This was enough to make our chiefs reproach the Miamis for trying to ruin the land and redden it with the
blood of the French. The Oüaoüyartanons stoutly supported us; we declared to them that we would go to
visit the French, and that we felt sure we would be well
received. At the same time our young chief set out with
forty warriors; on arriving at the fort, they called out
to the Frenchmen, and the chief had no sooner told his
name than three of those who had been plundered with
Metaminens recognized him. Immediately they made
our people enter, who had a hearty meal, and whom the
French loaded with Indian corn and meat – also warning
them to beware of the Miamis, who were planning
treachery toward them. After they had eaten they came
to join us at the camp, where they related the friendly
reception which the French had given them; but when
the Miamis saw that their design had been unmasked
they acknowledged that they could no longer hope for
any success – that Metaminens was against them, and
that Heaven seconded him. They gave up, therefore,
their design of going to attack the French, but that did
not prevent them from going afterward to encamp in
the vicinity of the fort; the French defended its approaches from them by volleys of musketry, and even
defied them to come on to the attack, asking us to remain neutral. The chief of the Miamis, however, asked
them to [let him] enter the fort alone, which was
granted. He asked the French to inform the Nadouaissioux that the Miamis were going to hunt, in order to
make amends for the theft of merchandise which they
had committed on the French; and to accompany them

to the Nadouaissioux village, in order to obtain their women and children whom the latter were holding as slaves. What happened? the French were simple enough to send this message, believing that this chief had spoken in good faith. The Miamis encamped meanwhile at a place two leagues below the fort, and sent three hundred warriors, with forty of our men, to go among the Nadouaissioux. The French, who had done their errands, heard on their return many gunshots; they saw plainly that they had been deceived, and immediately suspected that the Miamis were under the guidance of a slave who had recently escaped. The French hastened to find again the Nadouaissioux, who were abandoning their fort for lack of provisions. When they knew of the Miami expedition, they went back into the fort, and on the morrow at daybreak they were attacked; a Nadouaissioux went out with the calumet, in order to hold a parley, but a Miami shot him dead, and his men brought him back to the fort. The Miamis came against the fort to cut it away, with great intrepidity; but they were charged at so vigorously that they were compelled to abandon the attack with much loss of men. We all withdrew from the siege, and after making a general retreat we separated, five days later. Our chiefs have sent us ahead, to give you the detailed account of all that I have just related to you; they have remained to set the young men at hunting, and will arrive in a little while."

The conduct of the Outagamis on this occasion was altogether discreet: for the Outaouaks who were in those regions were not attacked by the Miamis (who were seeking a quarrel with them), the Sauteurs escaped falling into the hands of their enemies, the French profited by the warning that was given them to be on their guard,

and the Nadouaissioux were not worsted [in the fight].
The tribe, certain that Monsieur de Frontenac would be
pleased at the services which they had just rendered
him, sent him several chiefs, to whom he gave a most
friendly reception. The Outaouaks, who were then at
Michilimakinak, kept them there a fortnight, in order
to entertain them. Everything seemed to turn to the advantage of the Colony, when an event occurred which
was of infinite benefit to it; this was a great quarrel between the Iroquois and the Outaouaks, which resulted
in overthrowing all the schemes of the former. After
I have given an account of a battle that was fought on
Lake Herier between these two peoples, I will also
finish describing the disturbances which occurred among
all those tribes.

Chapter XXVII

Among the Outaouaks of Michilimakinak, who always joined with the Hurons in favor of the Iroquois,
there were some chiefs who did not fail to support our
cause manfully. One day, loud reproaches passed between the Hurons and our partisans, who told the former
that Le Baron was, with impunity, deceiving Onontio
with the protestations of friendship and alliance that he
was again making to the governor, even while he was
employing all sorts of stratagems to injure our allies;
and that it was very well known that the Hurons intended to go with the Iroquois to Saint Joseph River to
destroy the Miamis. On both sides there were long explanations. The Hurons acknowledged their design;
but, as they felt piqued, they told the Outaoüaks that if
they would accompany them they would together attack
the Iroquois, for whom they cared very little to show
any consideration. They also said that, in order that the
Outaoüaks might not think that they intended to sacri-

fice them, they would give up their women and children
to them, and the Outaoüaks should be masters of these
in case there were any treachery; they departed, accordingly, in equal numbers. In the middle of Lake Herier
they found three canoes of Sakis, who were seeking
refuge from a defeat which they had suffered from the
Iroquois – who had slain their chief, with two of his
brothers and one of his cousins, while the Iroquois had
lost on their side eight men. The Sakis joined the Hurons and Outaoüaks; they fired several gunshots, in
order to notify the Iroquois [of their coming]; and, having descried a great cloud of smoke, they sent four men
to reconnoiter, who marched through the woods. When
they were on the shore, nearly where they could catch a
glimpse of any one, they saw four men who were walking on the edge of the lake; they went back into the
woods, from which they fired a volley at these Iroquois,
and then immediately gained their own canoes. The
Iroquois, who were at work making canoes of elm-bark
(of which they had at the time only five made), numbered three hundred; they rushed into these, to attack
the Outaouaks, with such headlong haste that they broke
asunder two of the canoes, and then went in pursuit with
the three others; the first contained thirty men, the second twenty-five, and the third sixteen. The Hurons,
the Sakis, and the Outaoüaks, who had a like number of
men, saw that they were on the point of being captured,
but rallied, and resolved to endure the first fire of their
enemies. The war-chief of the Outaouaks and a Huron
were killed at the outset, but the others steadily advanced until they were close up to the Iroquois; then
they fired their volley at the canoe of thirty men, of
whom so many were killed that the dead bodies caused
it to capsize, so that all the thirty perished – some by
drowning, some by the war-club, some by arrows. The

canoe of twenty[-five] met the same fate, but five of
the braves were made prisoners. The great chief of the
Tsonnontouans was mortally wounded in this encounter;
they tomahawked him, and carried away his scalp. At
last these prisoners arrived at Michilimakinak, and they
appeared deeply hurt because their people had been
duped by the Hurons, whom they were regarding as
their best friends; see in what manner they complained
of it:

"The Hurons have killed us. Last autumn they invited us by collars to be on hand near the Saint Joseph
River, where they were to assemble. They had promised to give us the village of the Miamis there to eat;
and after this expedition they were to take us to Michilimakinak to deliver to us the Outaouaks, and even their
own people who might be there. For this purpose our
chiefs raised the war-party that you have seen; but the
Hurons have betrayed us. Believe us, we are among
your friends. We know well that it is the Pouteouatemis who have drawn you in with them to attack us, when
you have defeated us, ten cabins in all. We do not blame
you, but them; and we have never plotted against you."
This defeat of the Iroquois confirmed the Hurons and
all our allies on our side. [End of volume II.]

[Volume iv[36] contains four letters, which are occu-

---

[36] La Potherie, before publishing his *Histoire*, desired for it the approval
of Jacques Raudot, intendant of New France during 1705-1711; the latter requested one Father Bobé — a secular priest, who was greatly interested in the
Canadian colony, and wrote various memoirs regarding its affairs — to read
the manuscript and give him an opinion as to its quality and merit. At the
end of vol. iv of the *Histoire* appears a letter from Bobé to Raudot, making
the desired report on the book, which this priest warmly commends. The following passages in the letter are of special interest, as indicating La Potherie's
methods, and his sources of information:

"Having read it very attentively, I have been surprised that it has so well
fulfilled a project which, as it seemed to me, was very difficult to carry out
successfully. He certainly must have taken much pains to inform himself of
all that was necessary to disentangle the numerous intrigues of so many savage

pied with the relations existing between the French and
Iroquois – and, more or less, those of the western tribes

peoples, in relation to both their own interests and those of the French. He
has assured me that after he had personally obtained a knowledge of the
government of Canada in detail – of which he has written a history, which he
has had the honor of dedicating to his royal Highness Monseigneur the Duc
d'Orleans – he had intended to penetrate [the wilderness] to a distance six
hundred leagues beyond; but as his health and his occupations had not permitted him to go through that vast extent of territory, he had contented himself
with forming friendships with most of the prominent chiefs of the peoples
allied with New France who came down to Montreal every year to conduct
their trade in peltries. At the outset, he had made a plan of the present
history; he has therefore had no trouble, in all the conversations that he has
held with them, in gaining a knowledge of their manners, their laws, their
customs, their maxims, and of all the events of special importance which have
occurred among them.

"Sieur Joliet has contributed not a little to this end; for during the lessons
in geometry which he gave to the author he informed him of all that he had
seen and known among those peoples. The Jesuit fathers, who were excellent friends of his, have been very helpful to him. Sieur Perrot, who is the
principal actor in all that has occurred among those peoples during more than
forty years, has given the author the fullest information, and with the utmost
exactness, regarding all that he narrates. Monsieur de la Potherie, to whom
I expressed my surprise that he had been able to obtain so clear a knowledge
of so great a number of facts, and reduce to order so many matters that were
so entangled, avowed to me that all these persons had been of the utmost
assistance to him. He said that he questioned them in order [of events], in
accordance with his plan [for the book], and that he immediately set down in
writing what the savages had told him, and then he read to them these notes
in order to make proper corrections therein; and that it was by these careful
means that he escaped from the labyrinth.

"I assure you, Monsieur, that I have read this manuscript with pleasure;
and that I have learned from it things which I had not found in Lahontan, in
Father Hennepin, or in all the others who have written about New France.
I believe that every one will read it with the same satisfaction. . . In it
we shall see the attachment of all those peoples for the French nation; and
we shall admire the prudence and adroitness of the French in managing the
minds of those savages, and retaining them in alliance with us despite all the
intrigues of the English, and of their emissaries the Iroquois – who exerted
every effort to render them our enemies – or in persuading them to wage war
against those nations, and by that means to secure them in their own interests.
We shall be surprised at the boldness and intrepidity of the French who lived
among those barbarians, who were continually threatening to burn them at the
stake or to murder them. We shall recognize that those peoples whom we
treat as savages are very brave, capable leaders, good soldiers, very discreet
and subtle politicians, shrewd, given to dissimulation, understanding perfectly
their own interests, and knowing well how to carry out their purposes. In

with both peoples – during the years 1695-1701. The record is mainly one of hostilities with the Iroquois (who are, as usual, fierce and treacherous), varied by negotiations for peace, which is finally concluded in the summer of 1701. Much space is given to detailed reports of the various conferences held by Frontenac and his successor Callières with the deputations of Indians who come to Quebec to settle their affairs with the governor; and the speeches on both sides are given *in extenso*. At one of these (in 1695) a Sioux chief named Tioskatin participated; he was the first of his tribe to visit Canada, conducted thither by Pierre C. La Sueur, who afterward made explorations on the Upper Mississippi. At the great conference of all the tribes held at Montreal, beginning July 25, 1701, the most noted of their chiefs were present and made speeches – including the Ottawa Outoutaga (also known as Le Talon, and as Jean le Blanc); Chingouessi, another Ottawa; the Huron Le Rat; Ounanguicé, a Potawatomi, who spoke for all the Wisconsin tribes; Quarante-Sols, a Huron; Chichikatalo, a Miami; Noro (or "the Porcupine"), of the Outagamis; Ouabangué, head of the Chippewas of the Sault; Tekaneot, Tahartakout, and Aouenano, from the various Iroquois tribes. A general peace was concluded, after long discussion and much giving of presents, on August 7 – an event which crowned the long efforts of Frontenac to end the Iroquois Wars, which had so long wasted the resources and population of the French settlements, paralyzed their industries, and interrupted the trade with the Indians on which almost their life depended. This peace was negotiated by Callières, Frontenac having died on Nov. 28, 1698. – ED.]

---

short, the French and the English have need of all their cleverness and intellect to deal with the savages."

MEMOIRS RELATING TO THE SAUK AND FOXES

Letter to Reverend Dr. Jedidiah Morse, by Major Morrell Marston, U.S.A., commanding at Fort Armstrong, Ill.; November, 1820.

From original manuscript in the library of the Wisconsin Historical Society.

"Account of the Manners and Customs of the Sauk and Fox nations of Indians Traditions." A report on this subject, sent to General William Clark, Superintendent of Indian Affairs, by Thomas Forsyth, Indian agent for the U.S. Government; St. Louis, January 15, 1827.

From the original and hitherto unpublished manuscript in the library of the Wisconsin Historical Society.

Letter of Major Marston to Reverend Doctor Morse

Fort Armstrong, November, 1820.

SIR: Your letter dated "Mackinaw, June 20, 1820," requesting me to give you the *names* of the Indian tribes around me within as large a circle as my information can be extended with convenience and accuracy – the extent of the territories they respectively occupy, with the nature of their soil and climate – their mode of life, customs, laws and political institutions – the talents and character of their chiefs and other principal and influential men, and their disposition in respect to the introduction and promotion among them, of education and civilisation; what improvements in the present system of Indian trade could in my opinion be made, which would render this commercial intercourse with them more conducive to the promotion of peace between them and us, and contribute more efficiently to the improvement of their moral condition; together with a number of particular questions to be put to the Indians for their answers or to be otherwise answered according to circumstances, came to hand in due time and would have been answered immediately, had it been in my power to have done so as fully as I wished. [37]

[37] Early in 1820 Rev. Jedidiah Morse, D.D., held commissions from the Society in Scotland for Propagating Christian Knowledge, and from the Northern Missionary Society of New York, to visit the Indian tribes of the United States and ascertain their condition, and devise measures for their benefit and advancement. He suggested to the United States government the desirability of its coöperation in this undertaking, and was authorized to carry it out as an accredited agent of the government, which paid his expenses and

Soon after the receipt of your communication, I invited four of the principal chiefs of the Sauk and Fox nations to my quarters, with a view of gaining all the information wished or expected from them, three of whom accordingly attended, when I made known to them that you as an agent of the President had requested certain information relating to their two nations, which I hoped they would freely communicate to the best of their knowledge and belief, as their great father the President was anxious to be made acquainted with their situation in order to be enabled to relieve their wants and give them such advice from time to time as they might need. They replied, that they were willing and ready to communicate all the information in their power to give relative to their two nations; but I soon found that when the questions were put to them they became suspicious and unwilling to answer to them, and that

directed him to make a report of his work in this field; this appears from the letter written to him by the then secretary of war, J. C. Calhoun, dated Feb. 7, 1820. He left New Haven on May 10 following, and returned home on August 30, this period having been devoted to visiting the Indian tribes as far west as Detroit, Mackinaw, and Green Bay. His report to the war department, dated November, 1821, was published at New Haven in 1822, under the title "A Report to the Secretary of War of the United States, on Indian Affairs, comprising a narrative of a tour performed in the summer of 1820, under a commission from the President of the United States, for the purpose of ascertaining, for the use of the Government, the actual state of the Indian Tribes in our country." The greater part of this book is in the form of appendices, in which Dr. Morse incorporated a vast mass of information regarding the Indian tribes at that time, including reports, interviews, etc., from Indian agents, missionaries, army officers, traders, Indian chiefs, and others. He also gives statistical tables of the tribes and their population, residence, etc.; the annuities paid to them by the government; the lands purchased from them; and schools established among them. At the end of the report proper, Dr. Morse presents his views as to the policy which the government should adopt in dealing with the Indians, with plans for civilizing and educating them, and for the conduct of the Indian trade. The report by Major Marston (which the present editor has reproduced from that officer's original manuscript) was printed in Dr. Morse's report (pages 120-140), with some slight editorial changes intended to give it better form for publication – mainly in spelling, the correct form of sentences, etc. – ED.

many of their answers were evasive and foreign to the questions.[38]   Such information, however, I was able to obtain, by putting your questions to them follows:

Question to Mas-co, a Sauk chief – What is the name of your nation? *Answer* – Since we can remember we have never had any other name than Saukie or Saukie-uck.[39]

Question to Mas-co – What its original name? *Answer* – Since the Great Spirit made us we have had that name and no other.

Question to Mas-co – What the names by which it has been known among Europeans? *Answer* – The French called us by that name; they were the first white people

[38] Gov. Ninian Edwards of Illinois wrote to Thomas Forsyth (from Kaskaskia, Jan. 28, 1813): "The truth is that all the different tribes of Indians view our increase of population and approximation to their villages and hunting grounds with a jealous eye, are predisposed to hostility and are restrained only by fear from committing aggressions. I make no calculations upon their friendship, nor upon anything else but the terror with which our measures may inspire them and therefore I am now and long have been opposed to temporizing with them. I am very glad you contradicted the report of my having sent a Pipe, etc., to the Pottowattomies, for nothing can be more false than that report. There is in my opinion only one of two courses that ought to be pursued with the Sacs. If there be just grounds to believe that a part of them are friendly they should be brought into the interior of the country, furnished with provisions, and some ground to make their sweet corn, etc., which they would want when they should retire to their own country. This proposition w^d test their sincerity – if they accepted it, it would be advantageous to us by withdrawing so much force from the hostile confederacy whilst we are waging war against it – if they refused I w^d consider them all as enemies and treat them accordingly, making the whole tribe responsible for the conduct of all its members. No other plan of separating the hostile from the friendly part or discriminating between them can succeed. . . The Kickapoos are among the Sacs – and most certainly if they wish to harbor our enemies they can not be considered nor ought they to be treated as our friends – under the circumstances the only line I shall prescribe to them will be to keep out of the way of my rangers. I should however be glad to send them a talk first requiring them to drive the Kickapoos from among them – and I wish to procure some person to go on this business." (*Forsyth Papers*, vol. i, doc. 13.) – Ed.

[39] Saukie is the singular and Saukieuck the plural: the plural number of most names in the Sauk and Fox language is formed by the addition of the syllable *uck*. – Marston.

we had ever seen; since, the white people call us Sauks.

Question to Wah-bal-lo [40] the principal chief of the Fox nation – What is the name of your nation? *Answer* – Mus-quak-kie or Mus-quak-kie-uck.

Question to Wah-bal-lo – What its original name? *Answer* – Since the Great Spirit made us we have had that name and no other.

Question to Wah-bal-lo – What the names by which it has been known among Europeans? *Answer* – The French called us Renards, and since, the white people have called us Foxes.

Question – Are any portion of your tribes scattered in other parts? *Answer* – Yes.

Question – Where? *Answer* – There are some of our people on the Miſsouri, some near Fort Edwards [41] and some among the Pottawattanies.

Question – To what nations are you related by language? *Answer* – The Sauk, Fox and Kickapoo nations are related by language.

Question – Manners and customs? *Answer* – The Sauk, Fox and Kickapoo's manners and customs are alike except those who have had intercourse with the whites.

One of the chiefs added that the Shawnees descended from the Sauk nation: that at a bears-feast a chief took the feet of the animal for his portion who was not entitled to them (which were esteemed the greatest luxury) and that a quarrel ensued, in consequence of which he

[40] Waa-pa-laa, Wah-bal-lo, Wapello, Waupella, are all variants of the same name, which means "He who is painted white." This chief was a signer of four treaties (1822 to 1836); he took no part in the Black Hawk War, but seems to have been a prisoner with Black Hawk in 1832. See Wis. *Hist. Colls.*, vol. v, 305, and vol. x, 154, 217. – ED.

[41] Fort Edwards was on the east side of the Mississippi (a little above the mouth of Des Moines River), fifty miles above Quincy, Ill. In 1822 Marston was in command of this fort. See Wis. *Hist. Colls.*, vol. vi, 190, 273-279. – ED.

WAA-PA-LAA (Fox)

and his band withdrew and have ever since been called the Shawnee nation.

They acknowledge that the Sauks, Foxes, Kickapoos and Iowas are in close alliance, but observed that the reason for being in alliance with the Iowas was, because they were a bad people, and therefore it was better to have their friendship than enmity.

Question—With what tribes can you converse, and what is the common language in which you converse with them? *Answer*—There are only three nations with which we can [talk,] the Sauk, Fox and Kickapoo nations, by being with [any] other nation we might learn their language, but if we [don't] see them how can we speak to them or they to us? Is [it] not the same with you white people?

Question—What tribe do you call Grandfather? *Answer*—The Delawares call us and all other Indians Grandchildren, and we in return call them Grandfather; but we know of no relationship subsisting between them and us.

Question—What tribes are Grandchildren? *Answer*—There are no tribes or other nations we call grandchildren.

Question—Where is the great council fire for all the tribes connected with your own tribes? *Answer*—We have no particular place, when we have any busineſs to transact it is done at some one of our villages.

Question—Do you believe that the soul lives after the body is dead? *Answer*—How should we know, none of our people who have died, have ever returned to inform us.

No other questions were put to the chiefs as they appeared to be determined to give no further information. In conversation with one of them afterwards upon the

subject, they give as a reason for declining to answer the
remainder of the questions, that Gov' Clark[42] had not
treated them with that attention they were entitled to
when last at S' Louis. This plea however, was probably without foundation. It is the character of these
people to conceal as much as possible their history, religion and customs from the whites, it is only when they
are off their guard that any thing upon these subjects
can be obtained from them.

I have since been informed by some of the old men
of the two nations that the Sauk and Fox nations emi-
grated from a great distance below Detroit and established themselves at a place called Saganaw[43] in
Michigan Territory, that they have since built villages
and lived on the Fox River of the Illenois, at Mil-wah-
kee[44] near Lake Michigan, on the Fox River of Green
Bay and on the Ouesconsen: that about fifty years since
they removed to this vicinity, where they lived for some
time, and then went down to the Iowa River and built
large villages; that the principal part of both nations

---

[42] Referring to Gen. William Clark, companion of Meriwether Lewis in
their famous exploring expedition to the Pacific coast in 1803-1806. He was
born on Aug. 1, 1770, near Charlottesville, Va.; and in 1784 his family removed
to the vicinity of Louisville, Ky. From his nineteenth year until 1796, Clark
was in the United States military service, and became a brave and able officer.
During the period from July, 1803, to September, 1806, Clark was engaged in
the famous expedition to the Pacific coast under direction of Meriwether Lewis
and himself. Soon after his return (March, 1807) Clark was made superintendent of Indian affairs and brigadier-general of militia. From 1813 to 1820
he was governor of Missouri, and during the next two years was again
superintendent of Indian affairs. In 1822 he was appointed surveyor-general
for Illinois, Missouri, and Arkansas Territory. Clark died at St. Louis,
Sept. 1, 1838, aged sixty-nine. He was twice married, and left six children.
See detailed account of his life in Thwaites's *Original Journals of the Lewis
and Clark Expedition* (N.Y., 1904), vol. i, pp. xxvii-xxxiii, liv. — ED.

[43] *Saganaw* is probably derived from *Sau-kie-nock* (Saukie-town).
— MARSTON.

[44] *Milwahkee* is said to be derived from *Man-na-wah-kee* (good land).
— MARSTON.

remained on this river until about sixteen years ago, when they returned to their present situation. This is all the information I have been able to collect from themselves relating to the rise and progress of their two nations. At present their villages are situated on a point of land formed by the junction of the Rock and Miſsiſsippi Rivers, which they call *Sen-i-se-po Ke-be-sau-kee* (Rock River Peninsula) this land as well as all they ever claimed on the east side of the Miſsiſsippi was sold by them to our government in 1805. The agents of government have been very desirious for some time to effect their removal, but they appear unwilling to leave it.

I recently spoke of one of the principal Fox chiefs upon this subject and he replied that their people were not willing to leave Ke-be-sau-kee in consequence of a great number of their chiefs and friends being buryed there, but that *he* wished them to remove, as they would do much better to be farther from the Miſsiſsippi where they would have leſs intercourse with the whites. They claim a large tract of country on the west of the Miſsiſsippi: it commences at the mouth of the upper Iowa River, which is above Prairie du Chien and follows the Miſsiſsippi down as far as Des Moine River and extending back towards the Miſsouri as far as the dividing ridge, and some of them say quite to that River – a large proportion of this tract is said to be high prairie; that part of it which lies in the vicinity of the Iowa and Des Moine Rivers is said to be valuable; their hunting grounds are on the head waters of these rivers, and are considered the best in any part of the Miſsiſsippi country. I have not been able to ascertain the extent of Territory claimed by any other nations.

The Sauk village is situated on the bank of the Rock

River and about two miles from its mouth, and contains
[blank in Ms.] lodges, the principal Fox village is on
the bank of the Miſsiſsippi opposite Fort Armstrong, it
contains thirty five permanent lodges. There is also a
small Sauk village of five or six lodges on the left bank
of the Miſsiſsippi near the mouth of des Moine and below Fort Edwards, and a Fox village near the lead
mines (about hundred miles above this place) of about
twenty lodges, and another near the mouth of the Wapsipinica [River] [45] of about ten lodges. The Sauk and
Fox nations according to their own account, which I
believe to be nearly correct, can muster eight hundred
warriors, and including their old men, women and children, I think they do not fall short of five thousand souls;
of this number about two fifths are Foxes, but they are
so much mixed by intermarries and living at each others
villages, it would be difficult to ascertain the proportion
of each with any great precision. These two nations
have the reputation of being better hunters than any
other that are to be found inhabiting the borders of
either the Miſsouri or Miſsiſsippi.

They leave their villages as soon as their corn, beans,
etc., is ripe and taken care of, and their traders arrive
and give out their credits (or their outfits on credit—
Morse) and go to their wintering grounds; it being
previously determined on in council what particular
ground each party shall hunt on. The old men, women,

[45] *Wap-si-pin-i-ca.* So called from a root of that name which is found in
great plenty on its shores and which they use as a substitute for bread.
— MARSTON.

Wapsipinica (the same as *wâpisipinik*, plural of *wâpisipin*, meaning "swan-
root") is the tuber of the arrowhead (*Sagittaria variabilis*). The tubers are
generally as large as hens' eggs, and are greatly relished when raw; but they
have a bitter milky juice, not agreeable to the palates of civilized men. This,
however, is destroyed by boiling, and the roots are thus rendered sweet and
palatable. They afford nourishment to the swans and other aquatic birds that
congregate in great numbers about the lakes of the northwest. — WM. R. GERARD.

and children embark in canoes, the young men go by
land with their horses; on their arrival they immediately
commence their winter's hunt, which last about three
months. Their traders follow them and establish themselves at convenient places in order to collect their dues
and supply them with such goods as they need. In a
favorable season most of these Indians are able not only
to pay their traders, and will supply themselves and families with blankets, [46] strouding, amunition, etc., during

---

[46] "In the popular mind the North American Indian is everywhere associated with the robe or the blanket. The former was the whole hide of a
large mammal made soft and pliable by much dressing; or pelts of foxes,
wolves, and such creatures were sewed together; or bird, rabbit, or other
tender skins were cut into ribbons, which were twisted or woven. The latter
were manufactured by basketry processes from wool, hair, fur, feathers, down,
bark, cotton, etc., and had many and various functions. They were worn like
a toga as protection from the weather, and, in the best examples, were conspicuous in wedding and other ceremonies; in the night they were both bed
and covering; for the home they served for hangings, partitions, doors, awn-
ings, or sunshades; the women dried fruit on them, made vehicles and cradles
of them for their babies, and receptacles for a thousand things and burdens;
they even then exhausted their patience and skill on them, producing their
finest art work in weaving and embroidery; finally, the blanket became a
standard of value and a primitive mechanism of commerce. . . After the
advent of the whites the blanket leaped into sudden prominence with tribes
that had no weaving and had previously worn robes, the preparation of which
was most exhausting. The European was not slow in observing a widespread
want and in supplying the demand. When furs became scarcer blankets were
in greater demand everywhere as articles of trade and standards of value.
Indeed, in 1831 a home plant was established in Buffalo for the manufacture
of what was called the Mackinaw blanket. . . In our system of educating
them, those tribes that were unwilling to adopt modern dress were called
'blanket Indians.' " The manufacture of blankets still continues among some
of the southwestern tribes, and many of their products are highly valued by
white people. — OTIS T. MASON and WALTER HOUGH, in Handbook Amer.
Indians.

R. R. Elliott says (U.S. Cath. Hist. Mag., vol. iv, 312): "Blankets marked
with 'points' were formerly manufactured in Europe especially for the northwestern American trade, and during the present century were distinguished
commercially as 'Mackinac blankets.' They were made of good, honest wool,
half-inch thick, with two black stripes at each end. The size was marked by
a black line four inches long and about half an inch wide, woven in a corner
of the blanket." Strouding is defined by the Standard Dictionary as "a coarse,
warm cloth or blanketing, formerly used in the Indian trade." A blanket made

the winter, but to leave considerable of the proceeds of their hunt on hand; the surplus which generally consists of the most valuable peltries, such as beaver, otter, etc., they take home with them to their Villages, and dispose of for such articles as they may find necessary. In the winter of 1819-1820 these two nations had five traders. This number of traders employed nine clerks and interpreters, with annual salaries of from two hundred to twelve hundred dollars each (the average about four hundred dollars), and forty-three labourers whose pay was from one hundred to two hundred dollars each p^r annum. These traders including the peltries received at the United States factory [47] near Fort Edwards, col-

of this goods was called a "stroud." The name is said to be derived from a place in Gloucestershire, Eng., named Stroud. — ED.

[47] During the eighteenth century "trade was mostly by barter or in the currency of the colonies or the government. The employment of liquor to stimulate trade began with the earliest venture and was more and more used as trade increased. The earnest protests of Indian chiefs and leaders and of philanthropic persons of the white race were of no avail, and not until the United States government prohibited the sale of intoxicants was there any stay to the demoralizing custom. Smuggling of alcohol was resorted to, for the companies declared that 'without liquor we cannot compete in trade.' To protect the Indians from the evil effects of intoxicants and to insure them a fair return for their pelts, at the suggestion of President Washington the act of April 18, 1796, authorized the establishment of trading houses under the immediate direction of the president. In 1806 the office of Superintendent of Indian Trade was created, with headquarters at Georgetown, D.C." In 1810 there were fourteen of these trading establishments, among them the following: At Ft. Wayne, on the Miami of the Lakes, Indiana T.; at Detroit, Michigan T.; at Belle Fontaine, mouth of the Missouri, Louisiana T.; at Chicago, on L. Michigan, Indiana T.; at Sandusky, L. Erie, Ohio; at the island of Michilimackinac, L. Huron, Michigan T.; at Ft. Osage, on the Missouri, Louisiana T.; at Ft. Madison, on the upper Mississippi, Louisiana T. "At that time there were few factories in the country where goods required for the Indian trade could be made, and, as the government houses were restricted to articles of domestic manufacture, their trade was at a disadvantage, notwithstanding their goods were offered at about cost price, for the Indian preferred the better quality of English cloth and the surreptitiously supplied liquor. Finally the opposition of private traders secured the passage of the act of May 6, 1822, abolishing the government trading houses, and thus 'a system fraught with possibilities of great good to the Indian' came to an end. The official records

lected of the Sauk and Fox Indians during this season
nine hundred and eighty packs.

They consisted of 2760 beaver skins; 922 Otter;
13,440 Raccoon; 12,900 Musk Rat skins; 500 Mink;
200 Wildcat; 680 Bear skins; 28,680 Deer; whole number—60,082. The estimated value of which is fifty eight
thousand and eight hundred dollars.

The quantity of tallow presumed to be collected from
the Deer is 286,800 pounds. The traders also collected
during the same time from these savages at least: 3,000
lbs. of feathers; 1,000 lbs. of bees wax.

They return to their villages in the month of April
and after putting their lodges in order, commence preparing the ground to receive the seed. The number of
acres cultivated by that part of the two nations who reside at their villages in this vicinity is supposed to be
upwards of three hundred. They usually raise from
seven to eight thousand bushels of corn, besides beans,
pumpkins, melons, etc. About one thousand bushels of
the corn they annually sell to traders and others. The
remainder (except about five bushels for each family,
which is taken along with them) they put into bags, and
bury in holes dug in the ground for their use in the
Spring and Summer.

The labor of agriculture is confined principally to
the women, and this is done altogether with the hoe.[48]

show that until near the close of its career, in spite of the obstacles it had to
contend with and the losses growing out of the War of 1812, the government
trade was self-sustaining." — ALICE C. FLETCHER, in *Handbook Amer. Indians.*

See Draper's "Fur Trade and Factory System at Green Bay, 1816-21,"
with sketch of the factory there, Matthew Irwin, in Wis. *Hist. Colls.*, vol. vii,
269-288; F. J. Turner's "Character and Influence of the Indian Trade in
Wisconsin," in Johns Hopkins University *Studies*, vol. ix (1891), 543-615; H. M.
Chittenden's *American Fur Trade of the Far West* (N.Y., 1902); C. Larpenteur's *Fur Trade on the Upper Missouri*, 1833-1872 (N.Y., 1898). — ED.

[48] There has been a widely prevalent popular notion that before and after
the coming of Europeans to America nearly all the Indians north of Mexico

In June the greatest part of the young men go out on a summer hunt, and return in August. While they are absent the old men and women are collecting rushes for mats, and bark to make into bags for their corn, etc. The women usually make about three hundred floor

were virtually nomads, and hence practiced agriculture to a very limited extent. But this is certainly a misconception regarding most of the tribes in the temperate regions; for the earlier writers "almost without exception notice the fact that the Indians were generally found, from the border of the western plains to the Atlantic, dwelling in settled villages and cultivating the soil." Moreover, the early white colonists in all the European settlements "depended at first very largely for subsistence on the products of Indian cultivation." Of these, Indian corn was the chief and universal staple, and according to Brinton (*Myths of the New World*, 22) "was found in cultivation from the southern extremity of Chile to the 50th parallel of north latitude." The amount of corn destroyed by Denonville in his expedition of 1687 against the Iroquois was estimated at 1,000,000 bushels. "If we are indebted to Indians for the maize, without which the peopling of America would probably have been delayed for a century, it is also from them that the whites learned the methods of planting, storing, and using it. . . Beans, squashes, pumpkins, sweet potatoes, tobacco, gourds, and the sunflower were also cultivated to some extent, especially in what are now the Southern States," and Coronado even found the Indians of New Mexico cultivating cotton. Among those southwestern tribes irrigation was practiced by the natives before white men came to America; and some of the eastern tribes used fertilizers on their land. Primitive tools for cultivating the soil were made of stone or wood, and sometimes sharp shells or flat bones were fastened into wooden handles for this purpose. "It was a general custom to burn over the ground before planting, in order to free it from weeds and rubbish. In the forest region patches were cleared by girdling the trees, thus causing them to die, and afterward burning them down." As a rule, the field work was done by the women; later, as the tribes became more or less civilized, this work was shared by the men. "Though the Indians as a rule have been somewhat slow in adopting the plants and methods introduced by the whites, this has not been wholly because of their dislike of labor, but in some cases has been due largely to their removals by the government and to the unproductiveness of the soil of many of the reservations assigned them. Where tribes or portions of tribes, as parts of the Cherokee and Iroquois, were allowed to remain in their original territory, they were not slow in bringing into use the introduced plants and farming methods of the whites, the fruit trees, live stock, plows, etc."
— CYRUS THOMAS, in *Handbook Amer. Indians*.

See B. H. Hibbard's "Indian Agriculture in Southern Wisconsin," in *Proceedings* of Wisconsin Historical Society, 1904, pp. 145-155; and C. E. Brown's "Wisconsin Garden Beds," in *Wis. Archeologist*, vol. viii, no. 3, 97-105. See references to Wis. *Hist. Colls.* in note 254 to this book, for mention of lead mining by Indians. — ED.

mats every summer; these mats are as handsome and as durable as those made abroad. The twine which connects the rushes together is made either of baſswood bark after being boiled and hammered, or the bark of the nettle; the women twist or spin it by rolling it on the leg with the hand. Those of the able bodied men who do not go out to hunt are employed in digging and smelting lead at the mines on the Miſsiſsippi: in this buſineſs a part of the women are also employed, from four to five hundred thousand weight of this mineral is dug by them during a season: the loſs in smelting of which is about 25 p^r cent; most of it however is disposed of by them in the state that it is dug out of the mine, at about two dollars p^r hundred.

I now proceed to give such further information as a year's residence in the vicinity of the Sauk, Fox, and a part of the Kickapoo nations (about two hundred souls of which built a village last season near the mouth of Rock River) and considerable intercourse with several other nations has enabled me to collect.

In the first place it is no more than justice for me to acknowledge that I am greatly indebted for much of the information contained in this letter to Thomas Forsyth Esqr Indian Agent, Mr. George Davenport, and Dr. Muir[49] Indian traders; from the first mentioned gentleman I am principally indebted for an account of the

---

[49] Dr. Muir was a physician, a Scotchman, educated at Edinburgh; he came to this country, and in 1814-1815 was connected with the U.S. army. At this time some Indians conspired to kill him, but his life was saved by a young Sauk girl. In gratitude for this he took her as his wife, and settled in Galena, where he had several children by her. Afterward, he was one of the first settlers of Keokuk, Ia., where he engaged in the Indian trade. After his death, his family joined the Indians. — L. C. DRAPER, in Wis. *Hist. Colls.*, vol. ii, 224.

The Blondeau here mentioned was evidently Maurice, son of Nicholas Blondeau and a Fox woman; they resided at Portage des Sioux. Maurice was born about 1780, and died probably near 1830; he married a Sauk half-breed woman and had two children. — ED.

manners and customs of the Chippewa, Ottawa, and Pottawattamie nations, which are similar, if not the same as those of the Sauks, Foxes, and Kickapoos. In addition to the information furnished by these gentlemen, I have long been in expectation of receiving from Mr. Blondeau late a Sub. I. Agent and a man of intelligence in the religion, manners, and customs of the Sauk and Fox nations; he was born with the Sauks, his mother being a woman of that nation, and is probably more competent to give a correct account of them than any other man; this however, I have been disappointed as yet in receiving; the expectation of receiving this document has been the principal cause of delay in answering your communication.

Among your queries are the following. – What are your terms for father, mother, Heaven, Earth; the pronouns *I, thou, he?* In what manner do you form the genitive case and plural number? How do you distinguish present, past and future time?

In the Sauk tongue: *No-sah*, is my father; *Co-sah*, your father; *Oz-son*, his father; *Na-ke-ah*, is my mother; *Ke-ke-ah*, your mother; *O-chan-en-e*, his mother; Heaven is *che-pah-nock*; Earth, *Ar-kee*; I is *Neen*; thou, *keen*; you (in the plural), *Keen-a-wa*; he, *Ween*; us, *Ne-non*; they, *We-ne-wa*. I have not been able to afcertain the manner they form the genitive case. The plural number of most nouns is formed by the addition of the syllable *uck* as *Sau-kie, Sau-kie-uck*. The plural of personal pronouns is generally formed by the addition of the syllable *wah*.

The name of the principal chief of the Sauks is *Nan-nah-que*, he is about forty years of age, rather small in stature, unassuming in his deportment, and disposed to cultivate the friendship of the whites; but he does not appear to poſseſs any extraordinary capacity. The two next chiefs in rank are *Mus-ke-ta-bah* (red head) and *Mas-co*; the latter is a man of considerable intelligence but rather old, and too fond of whiskey to have much influence with his nation. These chiefs are all decidedly opposed to a change of their condition. About a year since this nation met with a heavy loſs in the death of *Mo-ne-to-mack*, the greatest chief that they have had for many years. Among other things which he contemplated accomplishing for the good of his people, was to have their lands surveyed and laid off into tracts for each family or tribe. He has left a son, but as yet he is too young to aſsume any authority.

The principal chief of the Fox nation is Wah-bal-lo; he appears to be about thirty. He is a man of considerable capacity and very independent in his feelings, but rather unambitious and indolent. The second chief of this nation is *Ty-ee-ma* (Strawberry) ; he is about forty. This man seems to be more intelligent than any other to be found either among the Foxes or Sauks, but he is extremely unwilling to communicate any thing relative to the history, manners and customs of his people. He has a variety of maps of different parts of the world and appears to be desirous of gaining geographical information; but is greatly attached to the savage state. I have frequently endeavored to draw from him his opinion with regard to a change of their condition from the savage to the civilised state. He one day informed me when conversing upon this subject, that the Great Spirit had put Indians on the earth to hunt and gain a living in the wilderneſs; that he always found that when any of their people departed from this mode of life, by attempting to learn to read, write and live as white people do, the Great Spirit was displeased, and they soon died; he concluded by observing that when the Great Spirit made them he gave them their *medicine bag* and they intended to keep it.

I have not had an opportunity of becoming much acquainted with that part of the Kickapoo nation living in this vicinity. There are two principal chiefs among them, *Pah-moi-tah-mah* (the swan that cries) and *Pecan* (the Nut) the former is an old man; the latter appears to be about forty; this nation has had considerable intercourse with the whites, but they do not appear to have profited much from it. They appear to be more apt to learn and practice their vices, than their virtues.

The males of each nation of the Sauks and Foxes are divided into two grand divisions, called *kish-co-qua* and *osh-kosh*: to each there is a head called, *war chief*. As soon as the first male child of a family is born he is arranged to the first band, and when a second is born to the second band, and so on. [50]

The name of the Chief of the first band of Sauks, is

---

[50] "There is abundant evidence that the military code was as carefully developed as the social system among most of the tribes north of Mexico. . . East of the Mississippi, where the clan system was dominant, the chief military functions of leadership, declaration, and perhaps conclusion of war, seem to have been hereditary in certain clans, as the Bear clan of the Mohawk and Chippewa, and the Wolf or Munsee division of the Delawares. It is probable that if their history were known it would be found that most of the Indian leaders in the colonial and other early Indian wars were actually the chiefs of the war clans or military societies of their respective tribes. . . Among the confederated Sauk and Foxes, according to McKenney and Hall, nearly all the men of the two tribes were organized into two war societies which contested against each other in all races or friendly athletic games and were distinguished by different cut of hair, costume, and dances. . . Throughout the plains from north to south there existed a military organization so similar among the various tribes as to suggest a common origin, although with patriotic pride each tribe claimed it as its own." In these societies (four to twelve in each tribe) were enrolled practically all the males from boys of ten years old to the old men retired from active service. "Each society had its own dance, songs, ceremonial costume, and insignia, besides special tabus and obligations. . . At all tribal assemblies, ceremonial hunts, and on great war expeditions, the various societies took charge of the routine details and

Ke-o-kuck; when they go to war and on all public occasions, his band is always painted white, with pipe clay. The name of the second war chief is *Na-cal-a-quoik*: his band is painted black. Each of these chiefs is entitled to one or two aid-de-camps, selected by themselves from among the braves of their nation, who generally accompany them on all public occasions and whenever they go abroad. These two chiefs were raised to their present rank in consequence of their succeſs in opposing the wishes of the majority of the nation to flee from their village on the approach of a body of American troops during the late war; they finally persuaded their nation to remain on the condition of their engaging to take the command and sustain their position. Our troops from some cause or other did not attack them, and they of course remained unmolested. In addition to these, there are a great number of petty war chiefs or partizans, who frequently head small parties of volunteers and go against their enemies; they are generally those who have lost some near relative by the enemy. An Indian intending to go to war will commence by blacking his face, permitting his hair to grow long, and neglecting his personal appearance, and also, by frequent fastings, some times for two or three days together, and refrain-

acted both as performers and police." — JAMES MOONEY, in *Handbook Amer. Indians.*

The term Oshkushi "is the animate form of an inanimate word referring to 'hoof,' 'claw,' 'nail;' applied to a member of the social divisions of the Sauk, Foxes, and Kickapoo. The division is irrespective of clan and is the cause of intense rivalry in sport. Their ceremonial color is black."

— WILLIAM JONES, in *Handbook Amer. Indians.*

The name Oshkosh was borne by a chief of the Menominee, born in 1795, died Aug. 31, 1850. He, with a hundred of his tribesmen, fought under the British in the capture of Ft. Mackinaw from the Americans in July, 1812. At the treaty of Butte des Morts (Aug. 11, 1827) he represented his tribe, being named chief at that time for this purpose. A portrait of him, painted by Samuel M. Brookes, is in the possession of the Wisconsin State Historical Society. The city of Oshkosh, in Wisconsin, bears his name. — ED.

ing from all intercourse with the other sex; if his dreams
are favorable he thinks that the Great Spirit will give
him succefs; he then makes a feast, generally of dog's
meat (it being the greatest sacrifice that he can make to
part with a favorite dog) ; when all those who feel inclined to join him will attend the feast; after this is concluded they immediately set off on their expedition. It
frequently happens that in consequence of unfavorable
dreams or some trifling accident the whole party will
return without meeting with the enemy. When they are
succefsful in taking prisoners or scalps, they return to
their villages with great pomp and ceremony. The party
will halt several miles from a village and send a mefsen-
ger to inform the nation of their succefs, and of the time
that they intend to enter the village; when all the female
friends of the party will drefs themselves in their best
attire and go out to meet them; on their arrival it is the
privilege of these women to take from them all their
blankets, trinkets, etc., that they may pofsefs; the whole
party then paint themselves and approach the village
with the scalps stretched on small hoops and suspended
to long poles or sticks, dancing, singing, and beating the
drum, in this manner they enter the village. The chiefs
in council will then determine whether they shall dance
the scalps (as they term it) or not, if this is permitted,
the time is fixed by them, when the ceremony shall commence, and when it shall end. In these dances[51] the
women join the succefsful warriors. I have seen myself

[51] "The dance of the older time was fraught with symbolism and mystic
meaning which it has lost in civilization and enlightenment. It is confined
to no one country of the world, to no period of ancient or modern time, and to
no plane of human culture. Strictly interpreted, therefore, the dance seems
to constitute an important adjunct rather than the basis of the social, military,
religious, and other activities designed to avoid evil and to secure welfare. . . The dance is only an element, not the basis, of the several festivals, rites, and ceremonies performed in accordance with well-defined rules

KEOKUCK (Sauk)

more than a hundred of them dancing at once, all painted, and clad in their most gaudy attire. The foregoing manner of raising a war party, etc., is peculiar to the Sauks, Foxes and Kickapoos; with the Chippewas, Ottawas, and Pottawattamies it is some what different. A warrior of these nations wishing to go against his enemies, after blacking his face, fasting, etc., prepares a temporary lodge out of the village in which he seats himself and smokes his pipe; in the middle of his lodge hangs a belt of wampum or piece of scarlet cloth, ornamented; a young Indian wishing to accompany him goes into the lodge and draws the belt of wampum or piece of cloth thro' his left hand and sits down and smokes of the tobacco already prepared by the partizan. After a sufficient number is collected in this manner, the whole begin to compare their dreams daily together; if their dreams are favorable, they are anxious to march immediately; otherwise they will give up the expedition for the present saying, that it will not please the Great Spir-

and usages, of which it has become a part. The dance was a powerful impulse to their performance, not the motive of their observance. . . The word or logos of the song or chant in savage and barbaric planes of thought and culture expressed the action of the orenda, or esoteric magic power, regarded as immanent in the rite or ceremony of which the dance was a dominant adjunct and impulse. In the lower planes of thought the dance was inseparable from the song or chant, which not only started and accompanied but also embodied it. . . There are personal, fraternal, clan or gentile, tribal, and inter-tribal dances; there are also social, erotic, comic, mimic, patriotic, military or warlike, invocative, offertory, and mourning dances, as well as those expressive of gratitude and thanksgiving. Morgan (*League of the Iroquois*, 1904, vol. i, 278) gives a list of thirty-two leading dances of the Seneca Iroquois, of which six are costume dances, fourteen are for both men and women, eleven for men only, and seven for women only. Three of the costume dances occur in those exclusively for men, and the other three in those for both men and women. . . The ghost dance, the snake dance, the sun dance, the scalp dance, and the calumet dance, each performed for one or more purposes, are not developments from the dance, but rather the dance has become only a part of the ritual of each of these important observances, which by metonymy have been called by the name of only a small but conspicuous part or element of the entire ceremony." — J. N. B. HEWITT, in *Handbook Amer. Indians.*

it for them to go, or that their medicine is not good or, that their partizan has cohabited with his wife. If every thing goes right the whole will meet at their leader's lodge, where they will beat the drums and pray the Great Spirit to make them succeſsful over their enemies. When the party consists of twenty or upwards, its leader will appoint a confidential man, to carry the great medicine bag. After they are aſsembled at the place of rendezvous and in readineſs to march, the partizan will make a speech in which he will inform them that they are now about to go to war; that when they meet their enemies he hopes they will behave like men, and not fear death; that the Great Spirit will deliver their enemies into their hands, and that they shall have liberty to do as they please with them; but at the same time if there are any among them who are fearful of anything whatever, such had better remain at home and not set out on such a hazardous expedition.

Among the Ottawas the partizan leads when they march out but the warrior who first delivers him a scalp or prisoner leads the party homeward and receives the belt of wampum. On the arrival of the party at the village, they distribute the prisoners to those who have lost relations by the enemy; or if the prisoners are to be killed, their spirits are delivered over to some particular person's relations who have died and are now in the other world.

Among the Pottawattamies it is different; all prisoners or scalps belong to the partizan, and he disposes of them as he may think proper: he will some times give a prisoner to a family who has lost a son and the prisoner will be adopted by the family and considered the same as though he was actually the person whose place he fills. This latter practice is also observed among the Sauks and Foxes.

In addition to the grand divisions of the males, each nation is subdivided into a great number of families or tribes. Among the Sauks there are no less than fourteen tribes; each of them being distinguished by a particular name (generally by the name of some animal) some of which are as follows – The bear tribe, wolf tribe, dog tribe, elk tribe, eagle tribe, partridge tribe, sturgeon tribe, sucker tribe, and the thunder tribe. Except in particular cases all the Indian nations mentioned in the foregoing are governed almost altogether by the advice of their chiefs and the fear of punishment from the evil spirit not only in this, but in the other world. The only instances wherein I have ever known any laws enforced or penalties exacted for a disobedience of them by the Sauks and Foxes, are when they are returning in the spring from their hunting grounds to their village. The village chiefs then advise the war chiefs to declare the martial law to be in force, which is soon proclaimed and the whole authority placed in the hands of the war chiefs. [52] Their principal object in so doing appears to

[52] "Among the North American Indians a chief may be generally defined as a political officer whose distinctive functions are to execute the ascertained will of a definite group of persons united by the possession of a common territory or range and of certain exclusive rights, immunities, and obligations, and to conserve their customs, traditions, and religion. He exercises legislative, judicative, and executive powers delegated to him in accordance with custom for the conservation and promotion of the public weal. The wandering band of men with their women and children contains the simplest type of chieftaincy found among the American Indians, for such a group has no permanently fixed territorial limits, and no definite social and political relations exist between it and any other body of persons. The clan or gens embraces several such chieftaincies, and has a more highly developed internal political structure with definite land boundaries. The tribe is constituted of several clans or gentes and the confederation of several tribes." In the course of social progress and the advance of political organization, multiplied and diversified functions also required various kinds and grades of officials, or chiefs; there were civil and war chiefs, and the latter might be permanent or temporary, the former existing where the civil structure was permanent, as among the Iroquois. "Where the civil organization was of the simplest character the authority of the chiefs was most nearly despotic; even in some instances where

be to prevent one family from returning before another whereby it might be exposed to an enemy; or by arriving at the village before the others, dig up its neighbours' corn. It is the businefs of the war chiefs in these cases to keep all the canoes together; and on land to regulate the march of those who are mounted or on foot. One of the chiefs goes ahead to pitch upon the encamping ground for each night, where he will set up a painted pole or stake as a signal for them to halt; any Indian going beyond this is punished, by having his canoe, and whatever else he may have along with him, destroyed. On their arrival at their respective villages, sentinels are posted, and no one is allowed to leave his village until every thing is put in order; when this is accomplished the martial law ceases to be in force. A great deal of pains appears to be taken by the chiefs and principal men to imprefs upon the minds of the younger part of their respective nations what they conceive to be their duty to themselves and to each other. As soon as day light appears it is a practice among the Sauks and Foxes for a chief or principal man to go through their respective villages, exhorting and advising them, in a very loud voice, what to do, and how to conduct themselves. Their families in general appear to be well regulated, all the laborious duties of the lodge, and of the field, however, are put upon the women, except what little afsistance the old men are able to afford. The children appear to be particularly under the charge of their mother; the boys until they are of a suitable age to handle the bow or gun.

the civil structure was complex, as among the Natchez, the rule of the chiefs at times became in a measure tyrannical, but this was due largely to the recognition of social castes and the domination of certain religious beliefs and considerations. The chieftainship was usually hereditary in certain families of the community, although in some communities any person by virtue of the acquisition of wealth could proclaim himself a chief. Descent of blood, property, and official titles were generally traced through the mother."

— J. N. B. HEWITT, in Handbook Amer. Indians.

Corporal punishment is seldom resorted to for their correction; if they commit any fault, it is common for their mother to black their faces, and send them out of the lodge, when this is done they are not allowed to eat until it is washed off; sometimes they are kept a whole day in this situation as a punishment for their misconduct.

When the boys are six or seven years of age a small bow is put into their hands and they are sent out to hunt birds about the lodge or village; this they continue to do for five or six years, when their father purchases them shot guns, and they begin to hunt ducks, geese, etc. Their father (particularly in winter evenings) will relate to them the manner of approaching a Deer, Elk, or Buffaloe, also the manner of setting a trap, and when able, he will take them a hunting with him, and show them the tracks of different animals, all of which the boy pays the greatest attention to.

The girls as a matter of course are under the direction of their mother, and she will show them how to make moggazins, leggins, mats, etc. She is very particular to keep them continually employed, so that they may have the reputation of being industrious girls, and therefore the more acceptable or more sought after by the young men.

Most of the Indians marry early in life, the men from sixteen to twenty generally, and the girls from fourteen to eighteen. There appears to be but little difficulty in a young Indians procuring himself a wife, particularly if he is a good hunter, or has distinguished himself in battle. There are several ways for a young Indian to get himself a wife; sometimes the match is made by the parents of the young man and girl without his knowledge, but the most common mode of procuring a wife is as follows:

A young man will see a young woman that he takes a

fancy to; he will commence by making a friend of some young man, a relation of hers (perhaps her brother); after this is done he will disclose his intentions to his friend, saying, that he is a good hunter and has been several times to war, etc., appealing to him for the truth of his assertions, and conclude by saying, if your parents will let me have your sister for a wife I will serve them faithfully, that is to say, according to custom, which is until she has a child; after which he can take her away to his own relations or live with his wife's. During the servitude of a young Indian neither he nor his wife has any thing at their disposal, he is to hunt, and that in the most industrious manner, his wife is continually at work, dressing skins,[53] making mats, planting corn, etc. The foregoing modes of procuring

---

[53] "In the domestic economy of the Indian skins were his most valued and useful property, as they became later his principal trading asset; and a mere list of the articles made of this material would embrace nearly half his earthly possessions. Every kind of skin large enough to be stripped from the carcass of beast, bird, or fish was used in some tribe or other, but those in most general use were those of the buffalo, elk, deer, antelope, beaver" [in the region covered in the present book]. Among the chief articles made from skins were tipis, boxes, bed-covers, pouches, and bags, blankets, harness for animals, the boats used by the upper Missouri tribes, clothing of all kinds, shields, cradles, fishing lines and nets. "The methods employed for dressing skins were very much the same everywhere north of Mexico, the difference being chiefly in the chemicals used and the amount of labor given to the task. Among the plains tribes, with which the art is still in constant practice nearly according to the ancient method, the process consists of six principal stages, viz, fleshing, scraping, braining [anointing the skin with a mixture of cooked brains, etc.], stripping, graining, and working, for each of which a different tool is required. . . According to Schoolcraft (*Narr. Jour.*, 323; 1821) the eastern Sioux dressed their buffalo skins with a decoction of oak bark, which he surmises may have been an idea borrowed from the whites." Various kinds of skins, and those for special purposes, receive special kinds of treatment, according to varying circumstances. "It is doubtful if skin dyeing was commonly practiced in former times, although every tribe had some method of skin painting. The process as described in practice by the plains tribes refers more particularly to the northern and western tribes of the United States; those dwelling south of the Algonquian tribes, from the Mississippi to the Atlantic, had a somewhat different method. This is described, as seen among the Choctaw." — JAMES MOONEY, in *Handbook Amer. Indians.*

a wife apply particularly to the Sauk, Fox, and Kickapoo nations; with the Chippewas, Ottawas, and Pottawattamies, a wife is sometimes purchased by the parents of the young man, when she becomes at once his own property; but the most common mode of procuring a wife in all these nations is by servitude. It frequently happens that when an Indians servitude for one wife has expired he will take another (his wife's sister perhaps) and again serve her parents according to custom. Many of these Indians have two or three wives, the greatest number that I have known any man to have at one time was five. When an Indian wants more than one wife, he generally prefers that they should be sisters, as they are more likely to agree and live together peaceable. An old man of fifty or sixty will frequently marry a girl of sixteen and who already has two or three wives. It seldom happens that a man separates from his wife, it sometimes does however happen, and then she is at liberty to marry again. The crime of adultery is generally punished by the Pottawattamies, by the husband's biting off the woman's nose and afterwards separating from her.

There appears to be no marriage ceremony among these Indians at the present day.

The Pottawattamies have a ceremony in naming their children;[54] which is generally performed when they are about a month old; it is as follows. The parents of the

[54] "Among the Indians personal names were given and changed at the critical epochs of life, such as birth, puberty, the first war expedition, some notable feat, elevation to chieftainship, and, finally, retirement from active life was marked by the adoption of the name of one's son. In general, names may be divided into two classes: (1) True names, corresponding to our personal names; and (2) names which answer rather to our titles and honorary appellations. The former define or indicate the social group into which a man is born, whatever honor they entail being due to the accomplishments of ancestors, while the latter mark what the individual has done himself. There are characteristic tribal differences in names, and where a clan system existed each

child invite some old and respectable man to their lodge in the evening, and inform him, that they wish him to name their child the day following. The old man then engages two or more young men to come to the lodge early in the next morning to cook a feast; this feast must be cooked by young men in a lodge by themselves, no other person is permitted to enter until it is ready for the guests who are then and not before invited. After the feast is over the old man then rises and informs the company the object of their being together, and gives the child its name, and then goes on to make a long speech, by saying, that he hopes the Great Spirit will preserve the life of the child, make a good hunter and a succefsful warrior, etc. With the Sauks, Foxes, and Kickapoos this ceremony is not always attended to; they however, in common with the Chippewas, Ottawas, and Pottawattamies, have a great number of feasts. They all make a feast of the first Dear, Bear, Elk, Buffaloe,

---

clan had its own set of names, distinct from those of all other clans, and, in the majority of cases, referring to the totem animal, plant, or object. At the same time there were tribes in which names apparently had nothing to do with totems, and some such names are apt to occur in clans having totemic names. . . Names of men and women were usually, though not always, different. When not taken from the totem animal, they were often grandilo-quent terms referring to the greatness and wealth of the bearer, or they might commemorate some special triumph of the family, while, as among the Navaho, nicknames referring to a personal characteristic were often used. . . Often names were ironical, and had to be interpreted in a manner directly opposite to the apparent sense. . . Names could often be loaned, pawned, or even given or thrown away outright; on the other hand, they might be adopted out of revenge without the consent of the owner. The possession of a name was everywhere jealously guarded, and it was considered discourteous or even in-sulting to address one directly by it. This reticence, on the part of some Indians at least, appears to have been due to the fact that every man, and every thing as well, was supposed to have a real name which so perfectly expressed his inmost nature as to be practically identical with him. This name might long remain unknown to all, even to its owner, but at some critical period in life it was confidentially revealed to him. . . In recent years the Office of Indian Affairs has made an effort to systematize the names of some of the Indians for the purpose of facilitating land allotments, etc."

— JOHN R. SWANTON, in *Handbook Amer. Indians.*

etc., a young man kills; even the first small bird, that a boy kills, is preserved and makes a part of the next feast. There appears to be a great deal of secrecy and ceremony in preparing these feasts.

Other feasts to the Great Spirit are frequently made by these Indians, sometimes by one person alone; but it is oftener the case, that several join in making them. They repair to the lodge where the feast is to be made, shut themselves up, and commence beating the drum, shaking the *che-che-quon* (a gourd shell with a handful of corn in it),[55] singing and smoking; this is alternately continued during the whole time that the feast is preparing, which generally continues from twelve to eighteen hours. When everything is in readinefs the guests are invited by sending to each a small stick or reed; as soon as they arrive, they seat themselves in a circle on the ground in the middle of the lodge, when one of the guests places before each person a wooden bowl with his proportion of the feast, and they imme-

---

[55] The rattle is "an instrument for producing rhythmic sound, used by all Indian tribes except the Eskimo. It was generally regarded as a sacred object, not to be brought forth on ordinary occasions, but confined to rituals, religious feasts, shamanistic performances, etc. This character is emphasized in the sign language of the plains, where the sign for rattle is the basis of all signs indicating that which is sacred. Early in the 16th century Estevan, the negro companion of Cabeza de Vaca, traversed with perfect immunity great stretches of country occupied by numerous different tribes, bearing a cross in one hand, and a gourd rattle in the other. . . Rattles may be divided into two general classes, those in which objects of approximately equal size are struck together, and those in which small objects, such as pebbles, quartz crystals, or seeds, are inclosed in a hollow receptacle. The first embraces rattles made of animal hoofs or dewclaws, bird beaks, shells, pods, etc. These were held in the hand, fastened to blankets, belts, or leggings, or made into necklaces or anklets so as to make a noise when the wearer moved. . . The second type of rattle was made of a gourd, of the entire shell of a tortoise, of pieces of rawhide sewed together, or, as on the N.W. coast, of wood. It was usually decorated with paintings, carvings, or feathers and pendants, very often having a symbolic meaning. The performer, besides shaking these rattles with the hand, sometimes struck them against an object." — JOHN R. SWANTON, in *Handbook Amer. Indians.*

diately commence eating. When each man's proportion is eaten, the bones are all collected and put into a bowl and afterwards thrown into the river or burnt.[56] The whole of the feast must be eaten; in case a man can not eat his part of it he paſses his dish with a piece of tobacco to his neighbor and he eats it and the guests then retire. Those who make a feast never eat any part of it themselves, they say, they give their part of it to the Great Spirit, they always have some consecrated tobacco, which they afterwards bury, and then the feast is concluded. The women of these nations are very particular to remove from their lodges, to one erected for that particular purpose, when their menstrual term approaches;[57] no article of furniture that is used in this

[56] Cf. allusions to the superstitious burning of bones, in *Jesuit Relations*, vol. ix, 299, vol. xx, 199, vol. xli, 301, 303 (and others, for which see Index, vol. lxxii, 323). This belief is thus explained by Brinton (*Myths of New World*, first edition, 257-261): "The opinion underlying all these [burial] customs was, that a part of the soul, or one of the souls, dwelt in the bones; that these were the seeds, which, planted in the earth, or preserved unbroken in safe places, would in time put on once again a garb of flesh, and germinate into living human beings. . . Even the lower animals were supposed to follow the same law. Hardly any of the hunting tribes, before their original manners were vitiated by foreign influence, permitted the bones of game slain in the chase to be broken, or left carelessly about the encampment. They were collected in heaps, or thrown into the water." Also (144, 145): "As the path to a higher life hereafter, the burning of the dead was first instituted. . . Those of Nicaragua seemed to think it the sole path to immortality, holding that only such as offered themselves on the pyre of their chieftain would escape annihilation at death; and the tribes of upper California were persuaded that such as were not burned to death were liable to be transformed into the lower orders of brutes." See also Long's *Expedition* (Phila., 1823), vol. i, 278. — ED.

[57] For this clause is substituted in Morse's *Report*, obviously by that learned doctor, the following words, "at such seasons as were customarily observed by Jewish women, according to the law of Moses." For further mention of this seclusion of women, and superstitions connected with it, see *Jesuit Relations*, vol. iii, 105, vol. ix, 123, 308, 309, vol. xiii, 261; also *Report* of Bureau of Amer. Ethnology, 1881-1882, 263, 267, and 1892-1893, 175. The same custom was connected with childbirth; see *Report* of 1883-1884, 497; of 1884-1885, 610; and 1887-1888, 415. — ED.

This was a form of taboo, "a Polynesian term (*tabu*) applied to a sacred interdiction proper to or laid upon a person, place, day, name, or any conceiv-

lodge is ever used in any other, not even the steel and
flint with which they strike fire.   No Indian ever approaches this lodge while a woman occupies it, and

able thing which is thereby rendered sacred and communication with it except
to a few people or under certain circumstances forbidden. It was formerly
such a striking institution, and was in consequence so frequently mentioned by
explorers and travelers, that the word has been adopted into English both as
applying to similar customs among other races and in a colloquial sense. Its
negative side, being the more conspicuous, became that attached to the adopted
term; but religious prohibitions among primitive races being closely bound up
with others of a positive character, it is often applied to the latter as well; and
writers frequently speak of the taboos connected with the killing of a bear or
a bison, or the taking of a salmon, meaning thereby the ceremonies then performed, both positive and negative. In colloquial English usage, it has
ceased to have any religious significance. Whether considered in its negative
or in its positive aspect this term may be applied in North America to a number of regulations observed at definite periods of life, in connection with important undertakings, and either by individuals or by considerable numbers of
persons. Such were the regulations observed by boys and girls at puberty; by
parents before the birth of a child; by relatives after the decease of a relative;
by hunters and fishermen in the pursuit of their occupations; by boys desiring
guardian spirits or wishing to become shamans; by shamans and chiefs desiring
more power, or when curing the sick, prophesying, endeavoring to procure food
by supernatural means, or 'showing their power' in any manner; by novitiates
into secret societies, and by leaders in society or tribal dances in preparation
for them. . . In tribes divided into totemic clans or gentes each individual
was often called upon to observe certain regulations in regard to his totem
animal," which sometimes took the form of an absolute prohibition against
killing that animal; "but at other times it merely involved an apology to the
animal or abstinence from eating certain parts of it. The negative prohibitions, those which may be called the taboos proper, consisted in abstinence
from hunting, fishing, war, women, sleep, certain kinds of work, etc., but
above all abstinence from eating; while among positive accompaniments may
be mentioned washing, sweat-bathing, flagellation, and the taking of emetics
and other medicines. In the majority of American tribes, the name of a dead
man was not uttered — unless in some altered form — for a considerable period
after his demise; and sometimes, as among the Kiowa, the custom was carried
so far that names of common animals or other terms in current use were entirely dropped from the language because of the death of a person bearing such
a name. Frequently it was considered improper for a man to mention his own
name, and the mention of the personal name was avoided by wives and husbands in addressing each other, and sometimes by other relatives as well. But
the most common regulation of this kind was that which decreed that a man
should not address his mother-in-law directly, or vice versa; and the prohibition of intercourse often applied to fathers-in-law and daughters-in-law
also." Anything desired or feared by man might occasion these prohibitions or

should a white man approach it and wish to light his pipe by the fire of a woman while in this situation, she will not allow him by any means to do so, saying, that it will make his nose bleed and his head ache; that it will make him sick.

When an Indian dies, his relations put on him his best

regulations; misfortunes might result from their non-fulfilment, or they might bring good fortune — more or less as the regulation was more or less strictly observed. The taboo "is one aspect of religious phenomena known by many other names; and, at least among the lower races, is almost as broad as religion itself.

"The significance of a girl's entrance into womanhood was not only appreciated by all American tribes, but its importance was much exaggerated. It was believed that whatever she did or experienced then was bound to affect her entire subsequent life, and that she had exceptional power over all persons or things that came near her at that period. For this reason she was usually carefully set apart from other people in a small lodge in the woods, in a separate room, or behind some screen. There she remained for a period varying from a few days, preferably four, to a year or even longer — the longer isolation being endured by girls of wealthy or aristocratic families — and prepared her own food or had it brought to her by her mother or some old woman, the only person with whom she had anything to do. Her dishes, spoons, and other articles were kept separate from all others, and had to be washed thoroughly before they could be used again, or, as with the Iroquois, an entirely new set was provided for her. For a long period she ate sparingly and took but little water, while she bathed often. Salt especially was tabooed by the girl at this period." Many other taboos were in vogue, among the different tribes, and the girl was made the subject of various ceremonies peculiar to this period of her life; and many superstitions regarding her and her condition were current among the savages. "The whole period of isolation and fast usually ended with a feast and public ceremonies as a sign that the girl was now marriageable and that the family was now open to offers for her hand. . . Although not so definitely connected with the puberty, certain ordeals were undergone by a boy at about that period which were supposed to have a deep influence on his future career. Among these are especially to be noted isolation and fasts among the mountains and woods, sweat bathing and plunging into cold water, abstinence from animal food, the swallowing of medicines sometimes of intoxicating quality, and the rubbing of the body with fish spines and with herbs. As in the case of the girl, numbers of regulations were observed which were supposed to affect the boy's future health, happiness, and success in hunting, fishing, and war. . . The regulations of a boy were frequently undergone in connection with ceremonies introducing him into the mysteries of the tribe or of some secret society. They were not as widespread in North America as the regulations imposed upon girls, and varied more from tribe to tribe. It has also been noticed that they break down sooner before contact with whites." — JOHN R. SWANTON, in *Handbook Amer. Indians.*

clothes, and either bury him in the ground or put him on a scaffold; but the former is the most common mode of disposing of the dead. As soon as an Indian dies his relations engage three or four persons to bury the body; they usually make a rough coffin of a piece of a canoe or some bark, the body is then taken to the grave in a blanket or buffaloe skin, and placed in the coffin, together with a hatchet, knife, etc., and then covered over with earth. Some of the near relations usually follow the corps; the women on these occasions appear to be much affected. If the deceased was a warrior, a post is usually erected at his head, on which is painted red crofses of different sizes, to denote the number of men, women, and children he has killed of the enemy during his life time, and which they say he will claim as his slaves now that he has gone to the other world. It is frequently the case that some of his friends will strike a post, or tree, and say I will speak; he then in a loud voice will say at such a place I killed an enemy, I give his spirit to our departed friend; and sometimes he may give a greater number in the same manner. The friends of the deceased will afterwards frequently take victuals, tobacco, etc., to his grave and there leave it, believing that whatever they present to him in this manner, he will have in the other world.

An Indian always mourns for the lofs of near relations from six to twelve months, by neglecting his personal appearance, blacking his face, etc. A woman will mourn for the lofs of a husband, at least twelve months, during which time she appears to be very solitary and sad, never speaking to any one unlefs necefsary, and always wishing to be alone; at the expiration of their mourning she will paint and drefs as formerly, and endeaver to get another husband.

The belief of these Indians relative to their creation

is not very dissimilar to our own. Masco, one of the chiefs of the Sauks informed me that they believed, that the Great Spirit in the first place created from the dirt of the earth two men; but finding that these alone would not answer his purpose, he took from each man a rib and made two women, from these four he says sprang all red men; that the place where they were created was Mo-ne-ac (Montreal). That they were all one nation until they behaved so badly that the Great Spirit came among them, and talked different languages to them, which caused them to separate, and form different nations: he said that it was at this place that Indians first saw white men, that they then thought they were spirits. I asked him how they supposed white men were made; he replyed that Indians supposed the Great Spirit made them of the fine dust of the earth as they knew more than they did. They appear to entertain a variety of opinions with regard to a future state; a Fox Indian told me that their people generally believed that as soon as an Indian left this world, he commenced his journey for the habitation provided for him by the Great Spirit in the other world; that those who had conducted themselves well in this life, met with but little difficulty in finding the road which leads to it; but that those who had behaved badly always got into the wrong road, which was very crooked and very difficult to travel in; that they frequently met with broad rivers which they had to ford or swim; and in this manner they were punished, until the Great Spirit thought proper to put them into the good road, and then they soon reached their friends, and the country of their future residence, where all kinds of game was plenty, and where they had but little to do, but to dance by night, and sleep by day; he further observed that when young children died they did not at first fare so well. That originally there were two Great Spirits who were brothers, and equally good, that one of them died and went to another world and has ever since been called Mach-i-Man-i-to (the Evil Spirit) that this Spirit has a son who makes prisoners of all the children that die too young to find the good path, and takes them to his own town, where they were formerly deprived by him of their brains, in order that when they grew up they might not have sense enough to leave him. That the Good Spirit seeing this, sent an eagle to peck a hole in the head of every young child as soon as it dies and makes its appearance in the other world, and to deprive it of its brain and conceal the same in the ground; that the child is always immediately after taken as a prisoner by the Evil Spirit and kept until of a suitable age to travel, when the eagle returns its brain; and then, it having sense enough, immediately leaves the Bad Spirit and finds the good road.

Most of these Indians say that their deceased friends appear occasionally to them in the shape of birds and different kinds of beasts. A Fox Indian observed one morning last summer that the spirit of a certain Indian (who was buryed the day before) appeared last night near his grave in the shape of a Turkey, and that he heard the noise of him almost all night. I enquired of another Indian (quite an old man) if any of their people had ever returned from the dead, he replyed, that he had heard of only one or two instances of the kind; but that he believed they knew what they were about in this world.

I do not at the present time think of anything further relative to the history, manners, religion and customs of the Indians worthy of notice. No part of what I have written is taken from books, but almost every thing has been drawn from either the Indians themselves or from persons acquainted with their language, manners, customs, etc., on this account I presume that it will be the more acceptable.

I will now proceed agreeably to your request to give you my ideas relative to the Indian trade, etc.[58]

In the first place I have to observe, that the Factory System for supplying the Indians with such articles as they may need, does not appear to me to be productive of any great advantage, either to the savages, themselves, or to the government. But very few, if any of the Indians have sufficient forecast to save enough of the proceeds of their last hunt to equip themselves for the next; the consequence is, that when the hunting season approaches they must be dependant upon some one for a credit. An Indian family generally consists of from five to ten persons, his wife, children, children-in-law, and grandchildren, all of whom look to its head for their supplies; and the whole of the proceeds of the hunt goes into one common stock, which is disposed of by him for the benefit of the whole. When cold weather approaches they are generally destitute of many articles, which are necefsary for their comfort and convenience; besides guns, traps, and ammunition; some kettles, blankets, strouding, etc., are always wanting; for these articles they have no one to look to but the private trader; as it is well known that the United States Factors give no credit; but even if they did, the number of these establishments is too limited to accommodate any considerable number of Indians, as but few of them will travel far to get their supplies if it can be avoided: and farther, the Indians (who are good judges of the quality of the articles they are in want of) are of the opinion

---

[58] The rest of Marston's letter (except the last two paragraphs) was printed by Morse on pages 56-59 of the *Report.* — ED.

that the Factor's goods are not so cheap, taking into consideration their quality, as their private trader's; in this I feel pretty well convinced, from my own observation, and the acknowledgment of one of the most respectable Factors of our government, Judge Johnson, of Prairie du Chien, that they are correct; this gentleman informed me but a few months ago that the goods received for his establishment were charged at least 25 pc^t higher than their current prices, and that he had received many articles of an inferior and unsuitable quality for Indian trade.[59] If you speak to an Indian upon the subject of their great father, the President, supplying them with goods from his factories, he will say at once you are a *pash-i-pash-i-to* (a fool), our great father is certainly no trader, he has sent these goods to be given to us as presents, but his agents are endeavoring to cheat us by selling them for our peltries.

The amount of goods actually disposed of by the United States Factors at Green Bay, Chicago, Prairie du Chien, and Fort Edwards, if I am rightly informed is very inconsiderable. The practice of selling goods to the whites and of furnishing outfits to Indian traders,

[59] "A similar complaint was made by the Six Nations at Buffalo the last August, when I was present. A member of Congress, I was told, had been invited to inspect the goods and to witness the fact of their inferiority. It was asserted to me that much better goods, and at a less price than those which were distributed at this time (an annuity payment) by the Indian agent, could have been purchased at New York. Had the amount due these Indians been judiciously expended in that city, the Indians, it was said, might have been benefited by it, in the quality of their goods, several hundred dollars. It was added, that the Indians are good judges of the quality of goods, and know when they were well or ill treated. But they had, in this case, no means of redress." — Rev. J. Morse.

"John W. Johnson, a native of Maryland, was United States factor at Prairie du Chien, in 1816, and afterwards. In his manners, he was a real gentleman, and a very worthy man; but unfortunately, he was quite deaf. He married a Sauk woman, and raised several children, and educated them; and finally retired to St. Louis, wealthy, where he resided the last I heard of him." — John Shaw, in Wis. *Hist. Colls.*, vol. x, 222.

are the principal causes of their sales being so great as they actually are.

In my opinion the best plan of supplying the natives is by private American traders of good character, if they could be placed under proper restrictions.

In the first place it is for their interest to please the Indians and prevent their having whiskey (particularly when they are on their hunting grounds) and to give them good advice.

Secondly. They always give them a credit sufficient to enable them to commence hunting.

Thirdly. They winter near their hunting grounds and agreeably to the suggestion of a late secretary of war, take to themselves "help mates" from the daughters of the forest, and thereby do much towards civilizing them.

Fourthly. They always have comfortable quarters for the Indians when they visit them, and by the frequent intercourse which subsists between them become acquainted with us and imperceptibly imbibe many of our ideas, manners, and customs.

Fifthly. From interested motives, if from no other, traders will always advise the Indians to keep at peace among themselves and with the whites.

There are some changes which I think might be made to advantage in the regulations for Indian traders. In the first place with a view to do away the imprefsion which almost universally prevails in the minds of the Indians in this part of the country, that the traders, clerks, interpreters, boatmen, and laborers, and also their goods are almost all British (which unfortunately happens to be nearly the truth, for their is scarcely a single boatman or laborer employed by the traders who is not a British subject, their goods it is well known are almost altogether of British manufacture), I would recommend, that no clerk, interpreter, boatman or laborer be employed by them who is not a citizen of the United States; and further, that every trader be obliged to display the American flag on his boat when travelling, and at his tent or hut when encamped.

The best and most succefsful means which could be employed by government to civilize the Indians or render them lefs savage than they now are, in my opinion would be for the agent of each nation to reside at or near one of their principal villages, there to have a comfortable habitation and a council room sufficiently large to accommodate all who might wish to attend his councils. To employ a blacksmith and a carpenter, and of course have shops and suitable tools for them; every nation has a great deal for a blacksmith to do; there would probably be lefs for a carpenter to attend to, but he might be advantageously employed in making agricultural implements, etc. For him to cultivate in the vicinity of the village, with the consent of the nation a small farm and to keep a small stock of horses, oxen and cows. It should be understood among the Indians that the farming establishment is solely for the benefit of the agent, should it be known among them that the object was to learn them to cultivate the soil as the whites do, they would most certainly object to it; but if this is not known, they will soon see the advantages of employing the plough, harrow, etc., and be induced to imitate our examples; and thus get on the road which leads to civilization before they are aware of it.

If an agent of government should go among them, as has sometimes been the case, and inform them that he had been sent by their great father, the president, to learn them how to cultivate the soil, spin, weave cloth and live like white people, they would be sure to set their faces against him and his advice, and say that he is a fool; that Indians are not like white people, the Great Spirit has not made them of the same color, neither has he made them for the same occupations.

The next step towards their civilization would probably be, that some of their old people would remain at their respective villages, if [they] could be afsured of their being secure from their enemies, while the others are on their hunting grounds: thus they would go on from step to step until they would become not only civilized beings, but Christians.

I consider it important that government should exchange as soon as practicable all British flags and medals which the Indians may have in their pofsefsion for American ones.[60] The Sauk and Fox Indians have no American flags at present and but few American medals; if you speak to them of the impropriety of their displaying British flags and wearing British medals,

[60] Presents of various kinds were made by European governments, and later by that of the United States, to Indian chiefs as rewards for loyalty. These were often military weapons, especially brass tomahawks; also were given hat-bands, gorgets, and belt-buckles of silver, often engraved with the royal arms, or with emblems of peace. "The potency of the medal was soon appreciated as a means of retaining the Indian's allegiance, in which it played a most important part. While gratifying the vanity of the recipient, it appealed to him as an emblem of fealty or of chieftainship, and in time had a place in the legends of the tribe. The earlier medals issued for presentation to the Indians of North America have become extremely rare from various causes, chief among which was the change of government under which the Indian may have been living, as each government was extremely zealous in searching out all medals conferred by a previous one and substituting medals of its own. Another cause has been that within recent years Indians took their medals to the nearest silversmith to have them converted into gorgets and amulets. After the Revolution the United States replaced the English medals with its own, which led to the establishment of a regular series of Indian peace medals. Many of the medals presented to the North American Indians were not dated, and in many instances were struck for other purposes. Medals were also given to the Indians by the fur companies, and by missionaries (these

they will reply, we have no others, give us American flags and medals and you then will see them only. The flags given to them ought to be made of silk, their British flags being made of that material, and besides they are more durable as well as more portable than the worsted ones. One of each nation should be of a large size, for them to display at their villages on public occasions: they have at present British flags considerably larger than the American Army standards. The practice of painting these flags causes them to break and soon wear out, they should be made in the same manner that navy flags are.

The annuities paid by government to the Sauk and Fox nations [61] appears to be a cause of dissatisfaction

latter usually religious in character). — PAUL E. BECKWITH, in *Handbook Amer. Indians.*

The article here cited contains a description, with several illustrations, of the known Spanish, French, British, and United States medals given to Indians. — ED.

[61] In Morse's *Report* is a table, occupying pages 376-382, 391, showing the annuities paid (1820-1821) to every tribe in the United States. Some of these were limited, but most of them were permanent; a few were granted to individual chiefs. The total annual amount of these payments was $154,575, representing a total capital of $2,876,250. Among the tribes receiving them are the following: Piankeshaws, $500; Kaskaskias, $500; Six Nations (Iroquois), $4,500; Sauks, $600; Foxes, $400; Ottawas, $4,300; Chippewas, $3,800; Miamis, $17,300; and to those on Eel River $1,100 more; Pottawatamies, $57,666,66⅔; Weas, $3,000; Kickapoos, $4,000; Ottawas, Chippewas, and Pottawatamies residing on the Illinois and Melwakee Rivers, etc., $1,000; the remnant of the Illinois (five tribes), $300; Wyandots, $5,900, besides $825 paid to them and to eastern tribes living with them. Besides these, a permanent annuity of salt was paid to a number of western tribes. Another table (pages 383-390) gives an "estimate of the quantity of land that has been purchased from the Indians," showing the amount sold by each tribe, with place and date of treaty therefor, and remarks on these. The total amount of lands thus acquired (1784-1821) is 191,998,776 acres, besides several tracts of "unknown" extent. In vol. ix of the Forsyth Mss. is an account by Forsyth of the original causes of the Black Hawk War, in which he relates the circumstances of the alleged cession by the Sauk and Foxes of their lands by the treaty of 1804 at St. Louis (an agreement which he pronounces worthless, as well as most unjust); he thus mentions the annuities given them on account of it: "When the annuities were delivered to the Sauk and Fox nations of Indians according

among them, in consequence of their not being able to divide and subdivide the articles received so as to give every one a part. I believe that powder, flints, and tobacco would be much more acceptable to them than the blankets, strouding, etc., which they have been in the habit of receiving.

I enclose a list of ten nations of Indians who inhabit the upper Miſsiſsippi [and] the borders of the great lakes, showing the names given them by Europeans and by each other. The latter information I have obtained principally from the Indians themselves. [62]

I have the honor to remain with great respect your Obᵗ Serᵗ   M. MARSTON, Bᵗ Maj. 5 Infʸ, Command'g. To the REV. Dʳ MORSE, New Haven, Connecticut.

---

to the treaty (amounting to $1,000 per annum) the Indians always thought that they were presents (as the annuities of the first twenty years were always paid in goods, sent on from George Town District of Columbia and poor sort of merchandise they were [see note 289], very often damaged, and not suitable for Indians) until I as their agent convinced them to the contrary in the summer of 1818. When the Indians heard that the goods were delivered to them as annuities, for lands sold by them to the United States, they were astonished, and refused to accept the goods, denying that they ever sold the land as stated by me." — ED.

[62] This list is found in vol. ii of the Forsyth Papers in the Draper Collection (pressmark "2,T"); by some oversight in arranging the documents for binding, it was separated from Marston's letter to Morse, which is found in vol. i. The list of tribes is printed in the *Report*, 397. — ED.

An account of the Manners and Customs of the Sauk and Fox Nations of Indians Tradition

The original and present name of the Sauk Indians, proceeds from the compound word Sakie alias, A-saw-we-kee literally Yellow Earth.

The Fox Indians call themselves Meſs-qua-kee alias Meſs-qua-we-kee literally Red Earth, thus it is natural to suppose, that those two nations of Indians were once one people, or part of some great nation of Indians, and were called after some place or places where they then resided, as yellow banks, and red banks, etc. Both the Sauk and Fox Indians acknowledge, that they were once Chipeways, but intestine quarrels, and wars which ensued separated one band or party from another, and all became different in manners, customs and language. The Sauk Indians, are more immediately related to the Fox Indians than any other nation of Indians, whose language bears an affinity to theirs, such as the Kicapoos and Shawanoes to whom they (the Sauks˜ and Foxes) claim a relationship by adoption. The Kicapoos and Shawanoes call the Sauk and Fox Indians their Younger Brothers, the Sauks call the Foxes (and the Foxes call them) their kindred.

The earliest tradition of a particular nature among them, is the landing of the whites on the shores of the Atlantic, somewheres about the Gulf of St. Lawrence. The Sauk and Fox Indians have been at war formerly

with the Iroquois, and Wyandotts,[63] who drove the
Sauks up the St. Lawrence to the lakes, and the Foxes
up the Grand River, and at Green Bay they formed a
coalition and renewed their former relations to each
other, since then (in alliance with the Chipeways, Ottawas, and Pottawatimies), they have been engaged in a
war with the Illinois Indians, which ended in their
final extermination: afterwards the Sauks and Foxes in
alliance with other nations of Indians, made war against
the Oſsage Indians, and on settlement of their differences they allied themselves to the Oſsage Indians,
against the Pawnee Indians, with whom in alliance with
the Oſsages they had a severe fight in 1814 on the head
waters of the Arkansas River, where the Sauks lost the
Blue Chief who was then celebrated among them. Thro
the interference of the government that war was
quashed.

The Sauk and Fox Indians repeatedly told me that
from depredations continually committed on them by
the Sioux Indians of the interriour (the Yanctons and
Sciſsitons [i.e., Sisseton] bands) they (the Sauk and
Fox Indians) thro the solicitations of their young men,
they commenced a war against the above mentioned
Sioux Indians in the Spring of the year 1822, but the
General Council held at Pirarie du Chiens in August
1825 put a final stop to that war, otherwise, not a Sioux
Indian would have been seen south of St. Peters River,

---

[63] Up to 1650 the tribe called Tionontati (or by the French, *Nation du
Petun*, "Tobacco Nation," from their cultivation of and trade in tobacco) were
living in the mountains south of Nottawasaga Bay, on the eastern coast of
Lake Huron; but they were then forced to abandon their country, by a sudden
murderous incursion of the Iroquois, and they fled to the region southwest of
Lake Superior. Eight years later they were with the Potawatomi near Green
Bay; soon afterward they joined the Hurons who also had been driven westward by the Iroquois, and about 1670 both tribes were at Mackinaw, and
later in the vicinity of Detroit. From that time they were practically the same
people, and, thus blended, became known by the modernized name of Wyandot. — JAMES MOONEY, in *Handbook Amer. Indians.*

in twelve months after the termination of that council.

Belts, Alliances, etc.

The wampum belts are woven together by thread
made of the deer's sinews, [64] the thread is pafsed through
each grain of wampum and the grains lay in the belt
parallel to each other, the Belts are of various sizes,
some more than two y^{ds} in length, if for peace or friendship the Belts are composed solely of white grained
wampum, if for war, they are made of the blue grained
wampum painted red with vermillion, the greater the
size of the Belt, the more force of exprefsion is meant
by it to convey.   In forming alliances other Belts are
made of white wampum interspersed with diamond like
figures of blue wampum, representing the various nations with whom they are in alliance or friendship. [65]

[64] "Sinew is the popular term for the tendonous animal fiber used by the
Indians as thread for sewing purposes" — not, as is commonly supposed, the
tendon from the legs, but the large tendon, about two feet in length, lying along
each side of the backbone of the buffalo, etc., just back of the neck joint.
"The tendons were stripped out and dried, and when thread was needed were
hammered to soften them and then shredded with an awl or a piece of flint.
Sometimes the tendon was stripped of long fibers as needed, and often the
tendons were shredded fine and twisted. . . Practically all the sewing of
skins for costume, bags, pouches, tents, boats, etc., was done with sinew, as
was embroidery with beads and quills." It was also used for bowstrings, and
to render the bow itself more elastic; also in feathering and pointing arrows,
and in making fishing lines, cords, etc. — WALTER HOUGH, in Handbook Amer.
Indians.

[65] The early white explorers found everywhere among the natives shells,
or beads made from them, in use as currency, and for personal adornment;
and the English colonists adopted the name for this article that was current
among the New England Indians, "wampum." This term was afterward
extended to the glass or porcelain beads brought from Europe by traders. The
beads were strung upon cords or sinews, and when woven into plaits about as
broad as the hand formed "wampum belts;" these constituted practically the
official form of presents sent by one tribe or one village to another, and were
used in negotiating and in recording treaties. Wampum also was the mark
of a chief's authority, and was sent with an envoy as his credentials. See
Holmes's account of beads, wampum, etc., in Report of Bureau of Amer. Ethnology, 1880-1881, 230-254; R. E. C. Stearns's "Ethno-Conchology," in Report

Government

The Sauk and Fox nations of Indians are governed
by hereditary chiefs, their power descending to the oldest male of the family, which on refusal extends to the
brothers or nephews of the chief and so on thro the male
relations of the family. They have no war chiefs, any
individual of their nations may lead a party to war, if
he has enfluence to raise a party to redreſs any real or
supposed grievance.

The chiefs interfere and have the sole management in
all their national affairs, but they are enfluenced in a
great measure by their braves or principal men in matters of peace or war. The province of the chief is to
direct, the braves or warriors to act. The authority of
the chiefs is always supreme in peace or war. There are
no female chiefs among the Sauk and Fox nations of
Indians, a boy (if a chief) is introduced into the councils of the nation, accompanied by some older branch of
the family capable of giving him instructions. When
the chiefs direct the head or principal brave of the nation to plant centinels for any particular purpose, if
they neglect their duty or fail to effect the purpose, they
are flogged with rods by the women publicly. There is
no such thing as a summary mode of coercing the payment of debts, all contracts are made on honor, for redreſs of civil injuries an appeal is made to the old people
of both parties and their determination is generally ac-
ceded to. In case of murder, it is determined by the
relations of the deceased, they say, that by killing the
murderer, it will not bring the dead to life, and it is
better to receive the presents offered by the relations of
the murderer than want them. Horses, merchandise

of U.S. Natl. Museum, 1887, 297-334; Ingersoll's "Wampum and its History," in *Amer. Naturalist*, vol. xvii (1883), 467-479; *Jesuit Relations*, vol. viii, 312-314. — ED.

and silver works sometimes to a very large amount are given to the relations of a murdered person, and indeed in some instances the murderer will marry or take to wife the widow of the person whom he has killed.

Sometimes it may happen, that the relations of the deceased will refuse to receive any thing for the lofs of a murdered relation, the chiefs then interfere, who never fail to settle the businefs. There is nothing that I know of that an Indian may be guilty what is considered a national offence, except aiding and afsisting their enemies, such a person if taken in war is cut to pieces, such things rarely happen.

The Sauk and Fox Indians are not thievish, they seldom steal any thing from their traders, they sometimes steal a few horses from a neighboring nation of Indians, and formerly they used to steal many from the white settlements and their excuse is always that they were in want of a horse, and did not take all they seen. Stealing horses from their enemies is accounted honorable, the women will sometimes steal trifling articles of drefs or ornament, the men very seldom. The traders feel perfectly safe among them, so much so, that they seldom or ever close their doors at night, but give them free accefs to come in and go out at all hours day and night. All questions relating to the nations are settled in council by the Chiefs, and when it is necefsary that the council must be a secret one, [66] the chiefs apply to the principal brave for centinels, who must do their duty, or they are punished by the women by stripes on their bare backs. In all Indian Councils that I have seen and heard of, the whole number of chiefs present must be of the same opinion otherwise nothing is done.

[66] "I never was at more than one secret council all the time I were among the Indians, and it was strictly a secret council to all intents and purposes."
— T. FORSYTH.

Council Fire at Brownstown in Michigan Territory

It is hard for me to say at this late day where and when the council fire originated, but I believe it to have originated immediately after the reduction of Canada by the British. A similar one is supposed to have existed on the Mohawk River at Sir William Johnston's place of residence previous to our Revolution. The first knowledge I have of it, is when it existed at old Chilicothe in the State of Ohios, and from the Indian war that took place subsequently to the peace of 1783 the council fire was by unanimous consent removed to Fort Wayne thence afterwards to the foot of the rapids of the Miamie River of the Lakes, where it remained until 1796 when it was removed to Brownstown where it now is. The British in confederacy with the Shawanoes, Delawars, Mingoes, Wyandots, Miamies, Chipeways, Ottawas and Pottawatimies offensive and defensive are the members of the council fire. The first nation of Indians who joined were the Shawanoes and Delawars and the other nations fell in or joined afterwards.

The British as head of the confederacy have a large belt of white wampum of about six or eight inches wide at the head of which is wrought in with blue grains of a diamond shape, which means the British Nation: the next diamond in the belt is the first Indian Nation who joined in alliance with the British by drawing the belt thro their hands at the council fire and so on, each nation of the confederacy have their diamond in the belt, those diamonds are all of the same size and are placed in the belt at equal distances from each other. When any businefs is to be done that concerns the confederacy it must be done at this council fire where are afsembled as many chiefs as can be conveniently collected. At any meeting at this council fire, [67] the British government is always represented by their Indian Agent, and most generally accompanied by a military officer, to represent the soldiers or braves.   By consent of the confederacy,

[67] "In a conversation I had with General Clark previous to my giving him a copy of this production, I told him about this council fire at Brownstown in Michigan Territory: he observed 'no other agent but yourself knows anything about this Council fire.'   There is more besides that, that the Indian agents do not know said I to him, and if I had included himself I would have done right, for in Indian affairs he is a perfect ignoramus.   But he is superintendant and can do no wrong." — T. FORSYTH.

Early in the eighteenth century an alliance was formed by the Wyandotts, Chippewa, Ottawas, and Potawatamies for their mutual protection against the incursions of hostile western tribes; the French made a fifth party to this alliance — which before many years fell through.   About 1720 those four tribes made an arrangement as to the respective territories which they were to occupy — each tribe, however, to have the privilege of hunting in the territory of the others.   The Wyandotts were made the keepers of the international council-fire (a figurative expression, meaning their international archives), and arbiters, in their general council, of important questions that concerned the welfare of all the four tribes.   "From that period might be dated the first introduction of the wampum belt system, representing an agreement among the four nations.   The belt was left with the keepers of the council-fire.   From that time forward until the year 1812 (when the council-fire was removed from Michigan to Canada) every wampum belt representing some international compact was placed in the archives of the Wyandott nation.   Each belt bore some mark, denoting the nature of a covenant or contract entered into between the parties, and the hidden contents of which was kept in the memory of the chiefs."   About 1842 part of the Wyandotts left Canada, to join their tribesmen in Ohio, and with them remove to Kansas, to which territory they sent (1843) their archives; but when these were desired (about 1864) by the eastern Wyandotts it was found that most of the belts and documents were dispersed and lost.   The last general council of those tribes, at which the belts were displayed and their contents recited, was held in Kansas in 1846. Brownstown (later called by the whites Gibraltar) was thus named for a noted chief of the Wyandotts, Adam Brown, who was captured in Virginia by one of their scouting parties about 1755, and taken to their village near Detroit; he was an English boy, then about eight years old.   He was adopted by a Wyandott family belonging to one of the ruling clans, and afterward married a Wyandott woman; he was finally made a chief, and was greatly esteemed by that tribe, and died after the War of 1812.   He was a compassionate and honorable man, and never approved the attacks made by Indian parties on the whites in their homes.   See *Origin and Traditional History of the Wyandotts* (Toronto, 1870), by Peter D. Clarke, himself a grandson of Adam Brown. — ED.

the Shawanoe nation were formerly the leading nation, that is to say, the Shawanoes had the direction of the wars that the parties might be engaged in, the power of convening the allies, etc. Since the late war, the Chipeways are at the head of those affairs and no doubt receive occasional leſsons from their British father. All Indians in forming alliances with each other, select a central spot to meet every two or three years, to commemorate and perpetuate, their alliances. It is very well known that for many years an alliance has existed between the Chipeways, Ottawas and Pottawatimies, and their chiefs encourage intermarriages with each other, for the purpose of linking themselves strongly together, and at a future period to become one people. These alliances are strictly attended to by all the parties concerned, and should there be any neglect to visit the council fire (by deputies or otherwise), to commemorate their alliances, it is considered as trifling with their allies. In 1806 or 7, the Chipeway, and Ottawa chiefs sent a speech to the Pottawattimies Indians, saying that for many years they had not sent deputies to the Island of Mackinac to the council fire according to custom, and if they declined sending deputies the ensuing summer, their part of the council fire would be extinguished: the Pottawatimies fearful of the consequences sent deputies the following year to Mackinac which satisfied all parties.

Names and Number of Tribes [i.e., clans] among the Sauk Nation[68] *of Indians*

1	Na-ma-wuck	or	Sturgeon Tribe
2	Muc-kis-sou	"	Bald Eagle
3	Puc-ca-hum-mo-wuck	"	Ringed Perch

[68] The Sauk were a canoe people while they lived near the Great Lakes; they practised agriculture on an extensive scale. "Despite their fixed abode

4	Mac-co. Pen-ny-ack	or	Bear Potatoe
5	Kiche Cumme	"	Great Lake
6	Pay-shake-is-se-wuck	"	Deer
7	Pe-she-pe-she-wuck	"	Panther
8	Way-me-co-uck	"	Thunder
9	Muck-wuck	"	Bear
10	Me-se-co	"	Black Bafs
11	A-ha-wuck	"	Swan
12	Muh-wha-wuck	"	Wolf

and villages they did not live a sedentary life altogether, for much of the time they devoted to the chase, fishing, and hunting game almost the whole year round. They were acquainted with wild rice, and hunted the buffalo; they did not get into possession of the horse very much earlier than after the Black Hawk War in 1832. . . Their abode was the bark house in warm weather, and the oval flag-reed lodge in winter; the bark house was characteristic of the village. Every gens had one large bark house wherein were celebrated the festivals of the gens. In this lodge hung the sacred bundles of the gens, and here dwelt the priests that watched over their keeping. It is said that some of these lodges were the length of five fires. The ordinary bark dwelling had but a single fire, which was at the center."

"In the days when the tribe was much larger there were numerous gentes. It may be that as many as fourteen gentes are yet in existence. These are: Trout, Sturgeon, Bass, Great Lynx or Water monster, Sea, Fox, Wolf, Bear, Bear-Potato, Elk, Swan, Grouse, Eagle, and Thunder. It seems that at one time there was a more rigid order of rank both socially and politically than at present. For example, chiefs came from the Trout and Sturgeon gentes, and war chiefs from the Fox gens; and there were certain relationships of courtesy between one gens and another, as when one acted the rôle of servants to another, seen especially on the occasion of a gens ceremony."

These were two great social groups: Kīshkōᵃ and Oshkashᵃ. "A person entered into a group at birth, sometimes the father, sometimes the mother determining the group into which the child was to enter. The division was for emulation in all manner of contests, especially in athletics. The Sauk never developed a soldier society with the same degree of success as did the Foxes, but they did have a buffalo society; it is said that the first was due to contact with the Sioux, and it is reasonable to suppose that the second was due to influence also from the plains. There was a chief and a council. The chiefs came from the Trout and Sturgeon gentes, and the council was an assembly of all the warriors. Politically the chief was nothing more than figurehead, but socially he occupied first place in the tribe. Furthermore, his person was held sacred, and for that reason he was given royal homage." — WILLIAM JONES, in *Handbook Amer. Indians.*

The sixth in Forsyth's list of Fox clans is called by Morgan Nă-nă-má-kew-uk (*Ancient Society*, 170). He also mentions the buffalo clan, Na-nus-sus-so-uk, as among the Sauk and Foxes. — ED.

Names and Number of Tribes among the Fox Nation of Indians

1	Wah-go	or	Fox Tribe
2	Muc-qua	"	Bear
3	Mow-whay	"	Wolf
4	A-ha-wuck	"	Swan
5	Puck-kee	"	Partridge (drumming)
6	Ne-nee-me-kee	"	Thunder
7	Me-sha-way	"	Elk
8	As-she-gun-uck	"	Black Baſs

War and its Incidents

The warriours[69] of the Sauk Nation of Indians are divided into two bands or parties, one band or party is called Kees-ko-qui or long hairs, the other is called Osh-cush which means brave the former being considered something more than brave, and in 1819 each party could number 400 men, now (1826) perhaps they

[69] Among the aborigines there was no paid war force, organized police, or body of men set aside for warfare; but all these duties rested in the tribe on every able-bodied man, who from his youth had been trained in the use of arms and taught to be always ready for the defense of home and the protection of the women and children. "The methods of fighting were handed down by tradition, and boys and young men gained their first knowledge of the warrior's tactics chiefly from experiences related about the winter fire." In the lodge the young men were placed near the door where they would be first to meet an attack by enemies. "There was however a class of men, warriors of approved valor [called 'soldiers' by some writers], to whom were assigned special duties, as that of keeping the tribe in order during the annual hunt or at any great ceremonial where order was strictly to be enforced. . . In many tribes warriors were members of a society in which there were orders and degrees. The youth entered the lowest, and gradually won promotion by his acts. Each degree or order had its insignia, and there were certain public duties to which it could be assigned. Every duty was performed without compensation; honor was the only pay received. These societies were under the control of war chiefs and exercised much influence in tribal affairs. In other tribes war honors were won through the accomplishment of acts, all of which were graded, each honor having its peculiar mark or ornament which the man could wear after the right had been publicly accorded him. There were generally six grades of honors. It was from the highest grade that the 'soldier' spoken of above was taken." — ALICE C. FLETCHER, in Handbook Amer. Indians, art. "Soldier."

can number 500 men each. The Kees-ko-quis or long hairs are commanded by the hereditary brave of the Sauk Nation named Keeocuck[70] and whose standard is red. The head man of the Osh-cushes is named Waa-cal-la-qua-uc and his standard is blue: him and his party are considered inferiour in rank to the other party. Among the Sauk Indians every male child is clafsed in one of the two parties abovementioned in the following manner. The first male child born to a Kees-ko-qui, is and belongs to the band or party of Kees-ko-quis. The second male child (by the same father) is an Osh-cush,

[70] Keeocuck is a sterling Indian and he is the hinge on which all the affairs of the Sauk and Fox Indians turn on, he is a very smart man, his manners are very prepossessing, his mother was a half breed, and much attached to white people. Keeocuck is about 46 years old now in 1832. — T. FORSYTH.

Keokuk, the noted Sauk leader, was born on Rock River, Ill., about 1780. "He was not a chief by birth, but rose to the command of his people through marked ability, force of character, and oratorical power. His mother is said to have been half French." He was ambitious to become the foremost man in his tribe, and by affability and diplomacy gradually attained great popularity among them; he lost much of this prestige, however, by his passive attitude regarding the St. Louis treaty of 1804, by which a small band of Sauk who wintered near that post agreed to cede the Rock River country to the U.S. government. The rest of the tribe refused to confirm this agreement, and part of them decided to take up arms against its enforcement. Not finding Keokuk favorable to this action, they turned to Black Hawk as their leader; and he was forced to begin hostilities with a much smaller force than he had expected, as Keokuk with his adherents joined the Foxes — whose union with the Sauk had been already broken, largely through the intrigues of Keokuk. After the war was over, Keokuk was made chief of the Sauk, an act which "has always been regarded with ridicule by both the Sauk and the Foxes, for the reason that he was not of the ruling clan. But the one great occasion for which both the Sauk and the Foxes honor Keokuk was when, in the city of Washington, in debate with the representatives of the Sioux and other tribes before government officials, he established the claim of the Sauk and Foxes to the territory comprised in what is now the state of Iowa. He based this claim primarily on conquest." Keokuk died in 1848, in Kansas, after residing there three years; in 1883 his remains were removed to Keokuk, Iowa, and a monument was erected over his grave by the citizens of that town. His authority as chief passed to his son, Moses Keokuk — a man of great ability, intellectual force, eloquence, and strong character, who won high esteem from his tribe. He was converted to the Christian faith, late in life; and died near Horton, Kans., in 1903. — WILLIAM JONES, in Handbook Amer. Indians.

the third a Kees-ko-qui and so on. The first male child
of an Osh-cush is also an Osh-cush the second is a Kees-
ko-qui and so on as among the Kees-ko-qui's. When
the two bands or parties turn out to perform sham battles, ball playing, or any other diversion the Kees-ko-
quis paint or daub themselves all over their bodies with
white clay. The Osh-cushes black their bodies on same
occasions with charcoal. The Sauk and Fox Indians
have no mode of declaring war, if injured by another
nation they wait patiently for a deputation from the
nation who committed the injury, to come forward and
settle the businefs, as a Fox Chief told me some years
ago, "the Sioux Indians have killed of[f] our people
four different times, and according to our custom, it is
time for us to prepare for war, and we will do so, as we
see the Sioux chiefs will not come forward to settle
matters." Sometimes a nation of Indians may be at
peace with all others when they are invited by a neigh-
bouring nation to afsist them in a war, by promising
them a portion of the enemy's country they may conquer.
Young Indians are always fond of war, they hear the
old warriours boasting of their war exploits and it may
be said, that the principle of war is instilled into them
from their cradles, they therefore embrace the first opportunity to go to war even in company with strange
nations so that they may be able to proclaim at the
dance, I have killed such a person, etc. One or more
Indians of the same nation and village may at same time
fast, pray, consult their Munitos or Supernatural Agents
about going to war. The dreams they may have during
their fasting, praying, etc., determine every thing, as
they always relate in public the purport of their lucky
dreams to encourage the young Indians to join them.
Those Indians who prepare for war by dreams, etc.,
may be any common Indian in the nation, and if the

warriours believe in his dreams, etc., he is never at a loſs for followers, that is to say, after a partizan is done fasting, and praying to the great Spirit, and that he continues to have lucky dreams, he makes himself a lodge detached from the village, where he has tobacco prepared, and in this lodge a belt of blue wampum painted red with vermillion, or a stripe of scarlet cloth hanging up in his lodge, and each warriour who enters the lodge smokes of the partizan's tobacco and draws the wampum or scarlet cloth thro his hands, as much as to say, he is enlisted in his service. If a nation of Indians or a village are likely to be attacked, every one turns out for the general defence.

Two or more partizans may join their parties together, and may or may not divide when near the enemies' country. The busineſs of the partizan is to shew his followers the enemy, and they are to act, the partizan may if he pleases go into the fight. In going to war, the Indians always travel slowly, and stop to hunt occasionally, where they deposit their jerked meat for their return, in going off the partizan leads the party, carrying his Mee-shome or medicine sack on his back, and on leaving the village sings the She-go-dem or war song, i.e. the partizan takes up his medicine sack and sings words to the following effect: "We are going to war, we must be brave, as the Great Spirit is with us." The warriours respond by singing heugh! heugh! heugh! in quick time dancing round the partizan. Sometimes a certain place distant from the villages is appointed for the party to rendevous at, in this case, every one as he departs from his residence sings his war song, and on the departure of the whole from the general rendevous, they sing the She-go-dem or general war song as described above.

The form of a war encampment is this, small forks

the size of a mans arm are planted in two rows about
five or six feet a part and about four feet out of the
ground, on which are laid small poles, these rows extend in length proportionate to the number of warriours, and the rows are about fifteen feet apart, thro the
center are other forks set up on which other poles are
placed, these forks are about six feet out of the ground,
and them with the poles are stoughter then the side forks
and poles. The warriours lay side by side with their
guns laying against the side poles if the weather is fair,
if wet they place them under their blankets.

The Indian who carries the kettle is the cook for the
party and when encamped the warriours must bring him
wood and water, furnish meat, etc., the cook divides the
vituals, and has the priviledge of keeping the best morsel
for himself. The partizan and warriours when preparing for war, are very abstemious, never eating while the
sun is to be seen, and also abstemious from the company
of women, after having accepted the wampum or scarlet
cloth before spoken of the[y] cease to cohabit with their
wives, and they consider the contrary a sacrilidge. A
woman may go to war with her husband, but must cease
during the period to have any connection. Before making an attack they send forward some of their smartest
young men as spies, the attack is generally made a little
before day light, the great object is to surprise, if defeated, every one makes the best of his way home stopping and taking some of the meat jerked and burried on
the way out. If a party is victorious the person who
killed the first of the enemy heads the party back, by
marching in front, the prisoners in the center and the
partizan in the rear. On the arrival of a victorious
party of Indians at their village they dance round their
prisoners by way of triumph after which the prisoners

are disposed of: elderly prisoners are generally killed
on the way home, and their spirits sent as an atonement
to that of their deceased friends. Young persons taken
in war are generally adopted by the father or nearest
relation of any deceased warriour who fell in the battle
or child who died a natural death and when so adopted,
are considered the representatives of the dead, prisoners who are slaves are bought and sold as such. When
they grow up the males are encouraged by the young
men of the nation they live with, to go to war, if they
consent and kill one of the enemy the slave changes his
name and becomes a freeman to all intents and purposes.
The female slaves are generally taken as concubines to
their owners and their offspring if any are considered
legal.

Sometimes an owner will marry his female slave, in
that case, she becomes a freewoman, but whether a slave
or free, the Sauks and Fox Indians treat their prisoners
with greatest humanity, if they have the luck to get to
the village alive, they are safe and their persons are considered sacred. I never heard except in the war with
the Ninneways[71] of the Sauk or Fox Indians burning
any of their prisoners, and they say, that the Ninneways
commenced first, I remember to have heard sometime
since of a Sauk Indian dying and leaving behind him a
favorite male slave, the relations of the deceased killed
the slave so that his spirit might serve on the spirit of his
deceased master in the other world. The young Sauk
and Fox Indians generally go to war about the age of
from 16 to 18 and some few instances as young as 15
and by the time they are 40 or 45 they become stiff from
the hardships they have encountered in hunting and

[71] Ninneways so called by the Sauk, Fox, Chipeway, Ottawa, and Pottawatimie Indians: but they called themselves Linneway, i.e., men from which
comes the word Illinois. — T. FORSYTH.

war, they are apt at that age to have young men sons or
sons-in-law to provide for them: they pafs the latter
part of their days in peace (except the village is attacked). A good hunter and warriour will meet with
no difficulty in procuring a wife in one of the first families in the nation. I know a half-breed now living
among the Sauk Indians who had the three sisters for
wives, they were the daughters of the principal chief of
the Nation. I have always observed that the half-breeds
raised among the Indians are generally resolute, remarkably brave and respectable in the nation.[72] The
case that leads to war are many: the want of territory
to hunt, depredations committed by one nation against
another, and also the young Indians to raise their names,
will make war against their neighbors without any cause
whatever. The Sauk and Fox Indians have for many
years back wished much for a war with the Pawnees
who reside on the heads of the River Platte, they know
that country is full of game and they don't fear the other

---

[72] "It has long been an adage that the mixed-blood is a moral degenerate,
exhibiting few or none of the virtues of either, but all the vices of both of the
parent stocks. In various parts of the country there are many mixed-bloods
of undoubted ability and of high moral standing, and there is no evidence to
prove that the low moral status of the average mixed-blood of the frontier is
a necessary result of mixture of blood, but there is much to indicate that it
arises chiefly from his unfortunate environment. The mixed-blood often finds
little favor with either race, while his superior education and advantages, derived from association with the whites, enable him to outstrip his Indian
brother in the pursuit of either good or evil. Absorption into the dominant race
is likely to be the fate of the Indian, and there is no reason to fear that when
freed from his environment the mixed-blood will not win an honorable social,
industrial, and political place in the national life. — HENRY W. HENSHAW,
in *Handbook Amer. Indians*, art. "Popular fallacies."

In the Forsyth Mss., vol. ii, doc. 7 (pressmark "2T7") is a list of the Sauk
and Fox half-breeds claiming land according to the treaty made at Washington,
Aug. 4, 1824. It contains thirty-eight names. Another and similar list (doc. 8)
gives thirty-one names, and fourteen others which are considered doubtful.
Among the (presumably) rightful claimants appears Maurice Blondeau, mentioned in note 49. — ED.

nations who live in the way such as the Ottos, [73] Mahas, and Kansez, they don't consider them formidable. The Sauk and Fox Indians would long ago have made war against the Pawnees if they thought the United States government would allow them, they are well acquainted with the geography of the country west as far as the mountains, also the country south of the Mifsouri River as far as Red River which falls into the Mifsifsippi River down below. [74] More than a century ago all the country commencing above Rocky River and running down the Mifsifsippi to the mouth of Ohio up that river to the mouth of the Wabash, thence to Fort Wayne

---

[73] The traditions of the Siouan tribe called Oto — who resided on the Missouri and Platte Rivers successively, and went to Indian Territory in 1880-1882 — relate that before the arrival of the white people they dwelt about the Great Lakes, under the name of Hotonga ("fish-eaters"); migrating to the southwest, in pursuit of buffalo, they reached Green Bay, where they divided. A part of them remained there, and were called by the whites Winnebago; another band halted at the mouth of Iowa River, and formed the Iowa tribe; and the rest traveled to the Missouri River, at the mouth of the Grand, afterward moving farther up the Missouri, in two bands, called respectively Missouri and Oto. Information to this effect was given to Major Long and to Prince Maximilian when they visited these people. In 1880-1882, they removed to Indian Territory. — Handbook Amer. Indians.

[74] The Arctic peoples, and the Algonquian tribes of northern Canada were able to travel rapidly and for long distances on account of their using dogs and sleds for this purpose; but the tribes south of them were obliged to travel on foot until the Spaniards introduced the horse. These peoples, however, accomplished long and remote journeys, often in the midst of great hardships, in which they often showed phenomenal speed and endurance. It is probable that they first made their trails in the search for food, for which purpose they needed only to follow those already made by the wild animals, especially the buffalo. "The portages across country between the watersheds of the different rivers became beaten paths. The Athapascan Indians were noted travelers; so also were the Siouan and other tribes of the great plains, and to a smaller degree the Muskhogean; while the Algonquian tribes journeyed from the extreme east of the United States to Idaho and Montana in the west, and from the headwaters of the Saskatchewan almost to New Orleans. Evidences of such movements are found in the ancient graves, as copper from Lake Michigan, shells from the Atlantic Ocean and the Gulf of Mexico, and stone implements from various quarters. Pipes of catlinite are widely distributed in the graves and mounds. These articles show that active trade was going on over

on the Miamie River, of the lakes down that river some
distance, thence north to St. Joseph and Chicago also
all the country lying south of River de Moine down
(perhaps) to Mifsouri River was inhabited by a numerous nation of Indians who called themselves Linneway and called by other Indians, Ninneway (literally
men) this great nation of Indians were divided into
several bands and inhabited different parts of an extensive country as follows. The Michigamians, the country south of River de Moine; the Cahokians, the country
east of the present Cahokia in the state of Illinois; the
Kaskaskias, east of the present Kaskaskia; the Tamorois
had their village near St. Phillip, nearly central be-

a wide region. There is good evidence that the men engaged in this trade
had certain immunities and privileges. They were free from attack, and were
allowed to go from one tribe to another unimpeded." – O. T. MASON, in *Handbook Amer. Indians.*

There is much evidence that from far prehistoric times the Indians were
familiar with vast regions of territory besides these of their own abode, and
made long journeys over well-defined routes of travel. The great river-systems
of the continent, whose headwaters often interlocked together, and their numerous tributaries furnished the easiest routes in the extensive forest regions
of the north and east, which were penetrated by canoes or dugouts; on the
plains and prairies well-worn trails still remain to indicate the lines of aboriginal travel and trade. These paths also existed along or between the river
routes, many of them originally made by the tracks of deer or buffalo in their
seasonal migrations or in search of water or salt. These same early trails
(which generally followed the lines of least natural resistance) have since been
utilized in many cases by the whites as lines for highways and railroads.
"The white man, whether hunter, trader, or settler, blazed the trees along the
Indian trails in order that seasonal changes might not mislead him should he
return." – J. D. McGUIRE, in *Handbook Amer. Indians.*

It is remarkable how the old plainsmen who laid out the Santa Fe trail
across the State of Kansas and on into New Mexico, were able to follow the
grades so well and get such a straight road. They simply used their eyes, for
in those days there were no engineers on the western plains. "We tried to best
it with our own engineering," W. B. Strang said, "but we finally ended by
following the old trail made by the wheels of the wagon trains. Eleven times
our engineers surveyed other lines, but they finally concluded that the grades
made by the men without the knowledge of mathematics fifty years ago were
the most practical, and hence we are keeping very near the old Santa Fe trail
in the building of our line to the west from Kansas City." – Chicago *Record-
Herald*, Jan. 2, 1910.

tween Cahokia and Kaskaskia; the Piankishaws, near Vincennes; the Weahs up the Wabash; the Miamies, on the head waters of the Wabash and Miamie of the lakes, on St. Joseph River and also at Chicago; the Piankishaws, Weah, and Miamies must have hunted in those days south towards and on the banks of the Ohio River. The Peorias (being another band of the same nation) lived and hunted on Illinois River: also the Masco or Mascotins called by the French *Gens des Pirarie* lived and hunted in the great Pirraries lying between the Illinois River and the Wabash. All those different bands of the Ninneway Nation spoke the language of the present Miamies, and the whole considered themselves as one and the same people, yet from the local situation of the different bands and having no standard to go by, their language aſsumed different dialects, as at present exists among the different bands of the Sioux and Chipeway Indians. Those Indians (the Ninneways) were attacked by a general confederacy of other nations of Indians such as the Sauks and Foxes who then resided at or near Green Bay and on Ouisconsin River, the Sioux Indians whose frontiers extended south and on the River des Moine, the Chipeways and Ottawas from the lakes and the Pottawatimies from Detroit as also the Cherrokees, Chickashaws and Chactaws from the south. This war continued for a great many years, until that great nation (the Ninneways) were destroyed except a few Miamies and Weahs on the Wabash and a few who are now s[c]attered among strangers. Of the Kaskaskia Indians from their wars, their great fondneſs for spirituous liquor and frequent killing each other in drunken frolics, there remains but a few of them say 30 or 40 souls, of the Peorias near St. Geneveve about 10 or 15 souls, of the Piankishaws 40 or 50 souls. The Miamies are the most numerous band. They did a few years ago consist of about 400 souls, they don't exceed in my opinion at the present day more than 500 souls of the once great Ninneway Nation of Indians. Those Indians (the Ninneways) were said to be very cruel to their prisoners, they used to burn them, and I have heard of a certain family among the Miamies who were called man eaters [75] as they always made a feast of human flesh when a prisoner was killed, that being part of their duty so to do.

From enormities, the Sauk and Fox Indians, when they took any of the Ninneways, they give them up to the women to be buffeted to death. They speak of the Mascota or Mascotins at this day with abhorance for their cruelties. In the history of the Sauks and Foxes, they speak of a severe battle having been fought opposite the mouth of Ihowai River, about 50 or 60 miles below the mouth of Rocky River.

The Sauk and Fox Indians descended the Miſsiſsippi River in canoes, from their villages on Ouisconsin River, and landed at the place abovementioned, and started east towards the enemy's country, they had not gone far, before, they were attacked by a party of Mascota or Mascotins, the battle continued nearly all day, the Sauks and Foxes gave way for want of amunition, and fled to their canoes. The Mascotins pursued, fought desperately and left but few of the Sauks and Foxes to return home to tell the story. The Sauk Indians at-

---

[75] Cf. this interesting allusion to cannibalism among the Malays in early times, referring to the islands of Samar and Leyte in the Philippines (cited in Blair and Robertson's *Philippine Islands*, vol. lii, 331): "In almost every large village there are one or more families of Asuáns, who are universally feared and avoided, and treated as outcasts, and who can marry only among their own number; they have the reputation of being cannibals. Are they perhaps descended from men-eaters? The belief is very general and deeply rooted. When questioned about this, old and intelligent Indians answered that certainly they did not believe that the Asuáns now ate human flesh, but that their forefathers had without doubt done this." — Ed.

tacked a small village of Peorias about 40 or 50 years ago, this village was about a mile below S\u1d57 Louis, and has been said by the Sauks themselves that they were defeated in that affair. At a place on the Illinois River called the Little Rock there were killed by the Chipeways and Ottowas a great number of men, women and children of the Ninneway Indians. In 1800 the Kickapoos made a great slaughter among the Kaskaskia Indians. The celebrated Main Poque[76] the Pottawatimie jugler in 1801 killed a great many of the Piankishaws on the Wabash. It does not appear that the Kicapoos entered into the war against the Ninneway Indians

[76] In vol. iv of the *Forsyth Papers* ("Letter-book, 1814-1827") is a sketch (evidently composed by Forsyth) of the Potawatomi chief Main Poque — a name, probably the French translation of his Indian name, meaning "swelled hand," doubtless in allusion to his left hand, which at his birth was destitute of fingers and thumb. "He used much to impose on the Indians by telling them that it was a mark set on him by the Great Spirit, to know him from other Indians when they met." He was a great orator, few surpassing him in eloquence. His father's standing as head military chief in the tribe gave prestige to the son, who added to this his own renown as a warrior. Thus Main Poque gained great influence among not only his own tribe, but the Sauk, Foxes, and others. He was in the habit of retiring alone into the woods for several days at a time, on his return home professing to have held conversations with the Great Spirit, on certain plans which he would propose to the tribe. It was rumored that this man had obtained arsenic from the whites, and had used it to cause the deaths of some persons in his tribe; and "at one time the Indians dreaded him as if he was a real deity, and thought his word was sufficient to destroy any or the whole of them. Indians have told me that the Main Poque was not born of a woman, that he was got by the Great Spirit and sprung out of the ground, and that the Great Spirit marked him in consequence" (alluding to his hand). They thought he was invulnerable to all weapons; and when he was wounded in a fight with the Osages (1810) his people said that it was done by "a gun that must have been made by some great Munito," and regarded the weapon with superstitious reverence. Main Poque was immoderately fond of spirituous liquor, and a confirmed drunkard, also very licentious; he always had three wives, and at one time had six. "He died last summer (1816) at a place called the Manesti [Manistique?] on Lake Michigan." He left two sons and three daughters, and five or six grandchildren. "His youngest son is a perfect Ideot, and his oldest son may redily be called a thick headed fool. . . The Main Poque may be considered as having been a bad Indian and it is of service to the whites and Indians that he is out of the way." — ED.

untill after they (the Kicapoo Indians) left the Wabash
River which is now about 50 or 60 years ago and made
war against the band of Kaskaskias. I do not mean to
say that all the Kicapoos left the Wabash at the same
time above mentioned as Joseph L'Reynard and a few
followers never would consent to leave the Wabash, and
go into the Piraries, and it is well known that he directed
that after his death that his body must be burried in a
Coal Bank on the Wabash, so that if the Kicapoos sold
the lands after his death, they would also sell his body,
and their flesh, such was his antipathy to sell any land.

Peace

I never heard of any peace having been made between
two nations of Indians (when war had properly commenced) except when the government of the United
States interfered, and that the Indians were within
reach of the power of the United States to compel them
to keep quiet, for when war once commenced, it alwavs
led to the final extermination of one or the other of the
parties.

Some years ago a war commenced between the Sauk
and Fox Indians against the Ofsage Indians. The Sauks
and Foxes being a very politic and cunning people,
managed matters so well, that they procured the afsistance of the Ihowais, Kicapoos, and Pottawatimies
headed by the celebrated Main Poque, and in pafsing
by the Sauk village on Rocky River in one of his war
expeditions he was joined by upwards of one hundred
Sauk Indians, this happened in 1810, the government
interfering, put a final stop to the war, otherwise before
this there can be no doubt the whole of the Ofsages
would have been driven beyond reach, as some of the
Chipeways and Ottawa Indians accompanied the Main

Poque. This confederacy, would have gained strength daily. It is true we hear of belts of wampum and pipes accompanied with presents in merchandise as peace offerings sent with conciliatory talks to make peace, but such a peace is seldom or never better than an armistice, witneſs the Sioux and Chipeway Indians, they have been at war for the last 60 or 80 years, the British government thro their agents, General Pike [77] when he traveled to the heads of the Miſsiſsippi River and last year (1825) the United States Commiſsioners at Pirarie des Chiens made peace (apparently) between the Sioux and Chipeway Indians but the war is going on as usual, the reason is because those nations are out of reach of the power of the United States. The Ihowai Indians, sent a deputation of their people some years ago, to the Sioux Indians, to ask for peace, the Meſsengers were all killed and the war continued untill a general peace took place at Pirarie des Chiens last year (1825). In the summer of 1821 I advised the Sauk and Fox Indians to make peace with the Otto and Maha Indians living on the Miſsouri River, they took my advise and the winter following they sent Meſsengers to the Council Bluffs with a letter from me to the Indian Agent at that post, the Sauk and Fox Meſsengers proceeded on to the Otto and Maha villages where they made peace and mutual presents took place among them to the satisfaction of all parties. I know of no armorial bearings among the Sauk and Fox Indians, except Standards of White and Red feathers, they have flags American and British which they display at certain ceremonies.

[77] Referring to Zebulon M. Pike who made in 1805-1806 an expedition to the headwaters of the Mississippi. In September, 1805, he made a treaty of peace between the Sioux and the Chippewa tribes. He published (Phila., 1810), a narrative of that expedition. — ED.

Death and its Incidents

When an Indian is sick and finds he is going to die, he may direct the place and manner of his interment, his request is religeously performed. The Sauk and Fox Indians bury their dead in the ground and sometimes have them transported many miles to a particular place of interment. The grave is dug similar to that of white people, but not so deep, and a little bark answers for a coffin, the body, is generally carried to the grave by old women, howling at intervals most pitiously. Previous to closing the grave one or more Indians who attend the funeral will make a motion with a stick or war-club called by the Indians Puc-ca-maw-gun speaking in an audible voice, "'I have killed so many men in war, I give their spirits to my deceased friend who lies there (pointing to the body) to serve him as slaves in the other world." After which the grave is filled up with earth, and in a day or two afterwards a kind of cabin is made over the grave with split boards something like the roof of a house, if the deceased was a brave a post is planted at the head of the grave, on which is painted with vermillion the number of scalps and prisoners he had taken in war, distinguishing the sexes in a rude manner of painting peculiar to themselves. The Indians bury their dead as soon as the body becomes cold, after the death of an adult all the property[78] of the deceased is given

[78] "Broadly speaking, Indian property was personal. Clothing was owned by the wearer, whether man, woman, or child. Weapons and ceremonial paraphernalia belonged to the man; the implements used in cultivating the soil, in preparing food, dressing skins, and making garments and tent covers, and among the Eskimo the lamp, belonged to the women. In many tribes all raw materials, as meat, corn, and, before the advent of traders, pelts, were also her property. . . Communal dwellings were the property of the kinship group, but individual houses were built and owned by the woman. While the land claimed by a tribe, often covering a wide area, was common to all its members and the entire territory was defended against intruders, yet individual occupancy of garden patches was respected. . . The right of a family to gather

away to the relations of the deceased and the widow or
widower returns to his or her nearest relations, if a
widow is not too old, after she is done mourning, she is
compelled to become the wife of her deceased husband's
brother, if he wishes. Sometimes an Indian will take
the wife of his deceased brother, and dismiſs his other
wife or wives from all obligations to him, or he may
keep them all. Many may mourn for the loſs of a rela-

<hr>

spontaneous growth from a certain locality was recognized, and the harvest
became the personal property of the gatherers. For instance, among the Menominee a family would mark off a section by twisting in a peculiar knot the
stalks of wild rice growing along the edge of the section chosen; this knotted
mark would be respected by all members of the tribe, and the family could
take its own time for gathering the crop. . . Names were sometimes the
property of clans. Those bestowed on the individual members, and, as on the
N.W. coast, those given to canoes and houses, were owned by 'families.' Property marks were placed upon weapons and implements by the Eskimo and by
the Indian tribes. A hunter established his claim to an animal by his personal mark upon the arrow which inflicted the fatal wound. Among both the
Indians and the Eskimo it was customary to bury with the dead those articles
which were the personal property of the deceased, either man or woman. In
some of the tribes the distribution of all the property of the dead, including the
dwelling, formed part of the funeral ceremonies. There was another class of
property, composed of arts, trades, cults, rituals, and ritual songs, in which
ownership was as well defined as in the more material things. For instance,
the right to practise tattooing belonged to certain men in the tribe; the right
to say or sing rituals and ritual songs had to be purchased from their owner
or keeper. . . The shrine and sacred articles of the clan were usually in
charge of hereditary keepers, and were the property of the clan. . . The
accumulation of property in robes, garments, regalia, vessels, utensils, ponies,
and the like, was important to one who aimed at leadership. To acquire
property a man must be a skilful hunter and an industrious worker, and must
have an able following of relatives, men and women, to make the required
articles. All ceremonies, tribal festivities, public functions, and entertainment
of visitors necessitated large contributions of food and gifts, and the men who
could meet these demands became the recipients of tribal honors. Property
rights in harvest fields obtained among the tribes subsisting mainly on maize
or on wild rice. Among the Chippewa the right in wild rice lands was not
based on tribal allotment, but on occupancy. Certain harvest fields were
habitually visited by families that eventually took up their temporary or permanent abode at or near the fields; no one disputed their ownership, unless an
enemy from another tribe, in which case might established right. Among the
Potawatomi, according to Jenks, the people 'always divide everything when
want comes to the door.'"—ALICE C. FLETCHER, in Handbook Amer. Indians.

tion but the widows are always the principal mourners, they are really sincere, they are to be seen all in rags, their hair disheveled, and a spot of black made with charcoal on the cheeks, their countenance dejected, never seen to smile but appears always pensive, seldom give loose to their tears unleſs it is alone in the woods, where they are out of the hearing of any person, there they retire at intervals and cry very loud for about fifteen minutes, they return to their lodges quite composed. When the[y] cease from mourning which is generally at the suggestion of their friends, they wash themselves put on their best clothes and ornaments, and paint red. I have heard Indians say, that, the spirit of a deceased person, hovers about the village or lodge for a few days, then takes its flight to the land of repose.[79]

---

[79] The aboriginal ideas relating to the soul are based on various mental processes: concepts of life and the power of action; the phenomena of the will: the power of imagery, which produces impressions both subjective and objective, as in memory images, the conceptions of fancy, dreams, and hallucinations. All these "lead to the belief in souls separate from the body, often in human form, and continuing to exist after death. The lack of tangibility of the soul has led everywhere among Indians to the belief that it is visible to shamans only, or at least that it is like a shadow (Algonquian), like an unsubstantial image (Eskimo)," etc. Almost everywhere the soul of the dead is identified with the owl. "The beliefs relating to the soul's existence after death are very uniform, not only in North America but all over the world. The souls live in the land of the dead in the form that they had in life and continue their former occupations. Detailed descriptions of the land of the dead are found among almost all American tribes. . . The most common notion is that of the world of the ghosts lying in the distant west beyond a river which must be crossed by canoe. This notion is found on the western plateaus and on the plains. The Algonquians believe that the brother of the Culture Hero lives with the souls of the dead. Visits to the world of the dead by people who have been in a trance are one of the common elements of American folk-lore. They have been reported from almost all over the continent." — FRANZ BOAS, in *Handbook Amer. Indians.*

The Indians certainly believe in a future life, but their ideas of its nature and location were vague and undefined. "Nor does it appear that belief in a future life had any marked influence on the daily life and conduct of the individual. The American Indian seems not to have evolved the idea of hell and future punishment." — HENRY W. HENSHAW, in *Handbook Amer. Indians,* art. "Popular fallacies."

The spirit on its way arrives at a very extensive Pirarie, over which they see the woods at a great distance appearing like a blue cloud, the spirit must travel over the Pirarie and when arrived at the further border, the Pirarie and woodland are separated by a deep and rapid stream of water, acrofs this stream is a pole which is continually in motion by the rapidity of the water, the spirit must attempt to crofs on the pole, if he or she has been a good person in this world, the spirit will get safe over and will find all of his or her good relations who died formerly. In those woods are all kinds of game in plenty, and there the spirits of the good live in everlasting happinefs, if on the contrary, the person has done bad in this life, his or her spirit will fall off the pole into the water, the current of which will carry the spirit to the residence of the evil spirit, where it will remain for ever in indigence and extreame mifsery. If convenient, the graves of deceased Indians are often visited, they hoe away the grafs all about and sweep it clean, and place a little vituals occasionally with some tobacco near the grave. All Indians are very fond of their children and a sick Indian is loth to leave this world if his children are young, but if grown up and married they know they are a burden to their children and don't care how soon they die. An Indian taken prisoner in war, or so surrounded by his enemies that he cannot escape, or that he is to suffer for murder, he will smile in the face of death, and if an opportunity offers he will sell his life dear. In burying Indians they place all their ornaments of the deceased, sometimes his gun and other implements for hunting, also some tobacco in his grave, paint and drefs the dead body as well as pofsible previous to interment.

Birth and its Incidents

A couple marrying the offspring belong to the tribe
of the father, therefore are named from some particular
thing or incident that has relation to the name of the
tribe: for example, if the man belongs to the Bear Tribe,
he takes the name of the child from some part of the
bear, or the bear itself. A few days after a child is born
and some of the old relations of the father or mother's
side are near, the mother of the child gives a feast and
inviting a few of her or her husband's oldest relations,
she having previously hinted to some or all of them the
nature of the feast, one of the oldest relations gets up
while the others are sitting on the ground in a ring with
a dish containing some vituals before each person (the
mother and child being present but do not taste of the
feast) and makes a speech to the following purport.
"We have gathered together here to day in the sight of
the Great Spirit, to give that child a name; we hope the
Great Spirit will take pity on our young relation (if a
male) make him a good hunter and warriour and a man
of good cense, etc. (if a female) that she may make an
industrious woman, etc., and we name him or her."

This name cannot be changed untill he goes to war,
when an Indian commonly changes his name from some
fete [i.e., feat] in war, which has no analogy to the
tribe he belongs to. A female after marriage may
change her name, perhaps a dream may occasion a
woman to change her name or some incident that has
happened may do so. An Indian may change his name
half a dozen times without being to war more than once,
an Indian who has been to war and returns home after
travelling towards the enemy's country for a few days,
may change his name, and very often in changing their
names, take the name of one of their ancestors so that

those names may be handed down to posterity. I know
a Fox Indian whose name is Muc-co-pawm which is in
English language Bear's Thigh or ham, he belongs to
the Bear Tribe. A Sauk Indian named Muc-it-tay
Mish-she-ka-kake in English the Black Hawk, [80] he
belongs to the Eagle Tribe. Wab-be-we-sian or White
hair (of an animal) belongs to the Deer Tribe.

[80] Black Hawk was a subordinate chief in the Sauk tribe, and noted as the
leader in the war of 1832 which is named for him; was born in 1767, in the
Sauk village at the mouth of Rock River, Ill. This name is the English translation of his Sauk name, Ma'katawimeshekä'käª. From the age of fifteen years
he was distinguished as a warrior; and while still a young man he led expeditions against the Osage and Cherokee tribes, usually successful. In the War
of 1812 he fought for the British, and after that war he was the leader of those
among his tribesmen who preferred British to American affiliations. When
the tide of American migration pushed into the old territory of the Sauk and
Foxes (which had been surrendered to the Federal government by the treaty
of 1804) part of those tribes, under the chief Keokuk, moved across the Mississippi into Iowa; but Black Hawk refused to leave, saying that he had been
deceived in signing that treaty. "At the same time he entered into negotiations
with the Winnebago, Potawatomi, and Kickapoo to enlist them in concerted
opposition to the aggressions of the whites." Open hostilities ensued, lasting
from April to August, 1832, being ended by the capture of Black Hawk; he
was confined for a time at Fortress Monroe, and finally settled on the Des
Moines River, where he died on October 8, 1838. — JOHN R. SWANTON, in Handbook Amer. Indians.

For particulars of his life and of the "Black Hawk War" see Wis. Hist.
Colls., vols. i, iv, v, x, xii; also Forsyth's own account (Forsyth Mss., vol. ix),
"Original causes of the troubles with a party of Sauk and Fox Indians under
the direction or command of the Black Hawk who is no chief." He says that
the treaty of 1804 was signed only by two Sauk chiefs, one Fox chief, and one
warrior; and that those tribes were not consulted and knew nothing about it
(see note 291). Squatters came upon their lands, and robbed and abused the
Indians, besides selling them whisky, regardless of the objections made to this
by the chiefs, especially Black Hawk. They were not allowed to hunt on the
lands alleged to have been ceded by them to the government, although this
privilege was granted to them by the treaty of 1804. In 1830 they decided to
remove to their lands in Iowa, and Forsyth (at their own request) asked for
certain action on this by Gen. Clark, who paid no attention to the matter —
neglect which Forsyth blames as causing the later hostilities with Black Hawk.
He praises that leader as always a friend to the whites, and says that when he
came back to Illinois in 1832 with his people he had no intention of fighting,
and did so only because they were first attacked by the whites and naturally
undertook to defend themselves. — ED.

The Eagle Tribe have a peculiar monumental way of designating their dead from others by placing the trunk of a fallen tree at the head of their graves, with the roots upwards. The other tribes have also a peculiar way of marking their graves but I am not acquainted in what manner. All Indians that I am acquainted with are always unwilling to tell their names except when immediate necefsity require it before many people, if you ask an Indian what his name is, he will not answer you, some other Indian present will generally answer for him: it is considered impolite to ask an Indian his name promptly: in speaking of an Indian not present, his name is mentioned, but if present the Indians will say, him, that man. If a few old acquaintances meet, they call one another comrade, uncle, nephew, brave, etc. Children while young are altogether under the guidance of their mothers, they seldom or ever whip their children particularly the boys. The mother reports to their children all the information she pofsefses relating to any great event that she recollects or has heard of. When a boy grows up to be able to hunt they follow their father a hunting, he shews them the different tracks of animals, and the art of hunting different animals, and the mode of preparing the medicine for the Beaver Traps and how to apply it, etc.

A female always keeps close to her mother until she gets married who teaches her how to make mocosins, drefs skins, make or construct a lodge, etc. Males after marriage or being once to war are considered men, yet if a young Indian has to serve for a wife, he has nothing to say in the disposial of his hunt until after the birth of the first child, after which he considers himself his own master, and master of his wife. In delivering to the Indians annuities or presents for the whole it is divided among the poorer clafs of the Indians, the chief and braves seldom keep any of the annuities or presents for themselves. Old people are a very great incumbrance to their relations except the[y] live exclusively on the bank of rivers or creeks, where they may be easily transported in canoes. A great many of the old people of the Sauk and Fox Indians may be seen pafsing the winter on the banks of the Mifsifsippi, they live on corn, pumpkins and such other provision as a boy or two can procure such as wild fowl, raccoons, etc. They are very indigent in the absence of their relations in the interiour of the country yet never complain. All adopted children are treated as real children and considered in same light, it is often the case, a man may adopt his nephew whom he calls his son, and the nephew calls the uncle father. All young Indian children are tied up in an Indian cradle, I know of no difference made between the children untill the boys begin to hunt, then the mother shews a preference to the best hunter or the oldest (as it generally happens that they are all hunters in time) in giving them good leggins, mocosins, etc. The young females are also very industrious in attending on their brothers, as they well know the hardships their brothers endure in hunting. When young Indians grow up to seventeen or eighteen and their fathers are hard to them, they leave their parents, but when the young Indian begins to kill deer, they are seldom spoken harsh to, on the contrary, they are flattered with silver works, wampum, vermillion and other ornaments.

In the event of an Indian dying and leaving a family of children, the relations take care of them untill they are married, if the orphan children have no relations their situation is bad, but it is almost impofsible for a child or children in the Sauk and Fox nations not to have relations. The mother always takes care of her children, legitimate or illegitimate. It seldom happens that Indian women have more than one child at a birth, and I never heard of any Indian woman having more than two.

Marriages

An Indian girl may become loose, and if she happens to be taken off by a young Indian in a summer hunting excursion (as it frequently happens) on his return he will give her parents part of his hunt, probably a horse, or some goods and a little whiskey, telling them that he means to keep their daughter as his wife: if the old people accept of the presents, the young couple live peaceably together with his or her relations, and so end that ceremony. A young Indian may see a girl whom he wishes for a wife, he watches opportunities to speak to her, if well received, he acquaints his parents: his parents not wishing to part with their son if he is a good hunter, the old people make an offer of goods or horses for the girl, and if they succeed they take home their daughter-in-law. On the contrary if the parents of the girl will not agree to receive property but insist on servitude, the young Indian must come to hunt for his wife's parents for same one, two, or three years as may be agreed on before the parents will relinquish their right to their daughter. I do not know of any marriage ceremony except the contract between the parties. An Indian may have two, three or more wives, but always prefer sisters as they agree better together in the same lodge, the eldest has generally the disposal of the hunt, purchase all the goods and regulate all the domestic affairs. Adultery among the Sauk and Fox Indians is punished by cutting off the ears, or cutting or biting off the nose of the woman, the punishment is generally per-

formed by the husband on the wife, however this seldom
happens, and altho there are many loose girls among
them, the married women are generally very constant.
An Indian will not be blamed for committing the act,
if he has not made use of force, the old women will say,
he is a Kit-che-Waw-wan-ish-caw, i.e. a very worthleſs
rake, however the injured husband might in a fit of
jealousy kill both of them.

An Indian's wife is his property, and has it in his
power to kill her if she acts badly without fear of revenge from her relations. There is no such thing as
divorces, the Indians turn off their wives, and the wives
leave their husbands when they become discontented,
yet the husband can oblidge his wife to return if he
pleases. Women seldom leave their husbands and the
Sauk and Fox Indians as seldom beat or maltreat their
wives. An Indian will listen to a woman scold all day,
and feel no way affected at what she may say. Barreneſs
is generally the cause of separation among the Indians.

The Indian women never have more than one husband at a time, nor does an Indian ever marry the mother
and daughter, they look with contempt on any man that
would have connection with a mother and her daughter,
he would be called a worthleſs dog. The relationship
among Indians is drawn much closer than among us, for
instance, brother's children consider themselves and call
one another brothers and sisters and if the least relationship exists between an Indian and a girl it will prevent
them from being married. An old Sauk chief who died
a few years ago named Masco, told me that he was then
upwards of ninety years of age, I hesitated to believe
him, but he insisted on what he said to be true, he spoke
of the taking of Canada by the British also about the
French fort at Green Bay on Lake Michigan, mentioned

the French commandant's name Monsieur Marrin[81] which left no doubt with me of his being a very old man. There are now many very old people among the Sauk and Fox Indians but as all Indians are ignorant of their exact age, it is impofsible to find out the age of any of the old people. It is very uncommon for unmarried women to have children, except it be those who live with whitemen for sometime, in that case, when they return to live with their nation, necefsity compels them to accept the first offer that is made to them and they generally get some poor, lazy, worthlefs fellow who cannot procure a wife in the usual way.

There are few women among the Sauk and Fox Indians who are sterile: the proportion of sterile women to them who bear children, are about one to 500, it will not be too much to say, that each married woman on an average have three children. Girls seldom arrive at the age of sixteen without being married, fourteen is the usual age of getting married for the young girls, and we often see a girl of fourteen with her first child on her back, Indian women generally have a child the first year after marriage, and one every two years subsequent, they allow their children to suck at least twice as long as a whitewoman do, they generally leave off child bearing about the age of thirty.

Family Government, etc.

The duties of an Indian is to hunt, to feed and clothe his wife and children, to purchase arms and amunition for himself and sons, purchase kettles, axes, hoes, etc., to make canoes, paddles, poles, and saddles, to afsist in

---

[81] There were two French officers named Marin in the northwestern Indian country, and their identity has been sometimes confused. Pierre Paul, sieur Marin was born in 1692, and was for a long time a trader among the Sioux and the Wisconsin Indians. From 1745 until his death in 1753, he held commands in the French-Canadian troops. His son Joseph followed also a military

working the canoes also in hunting, saddling and driving the horses.

The duties of the women [82] is to skin the animals when brot home, to stretch the skins and prepare them for market, to cook, to make the camp, to cut and carry wood, to make fires, to dreſs leather, make mocosins and leggins, to plant, hoe and gather in the corn, beans, etc.,

career, from 1748 until the fall of Quebec (1763), when he returned to France. The man named Marin (or Morand) reported as living in Wisconsin after 1763 was probably a half-breed. — Wis. *Hist. Colls.*, vol. xvii, 315. [Cf. also many references in indexes, vols. v, viii, xvi, xvii. — ED.]

[82] The position of woman in Indian society, especially as regards the division of labor has been misunderstood. In the idea that she was a mere drudge and slave, and her husband only indolent, there was some truth, but it was much overdrawn, "chiefly because the observations which suggest it were made about the camp and village, in which and in the neighboring fields lay the peculiar province of woman's activity." Her field of labor was naturally the home and household industries, and the rearing of the children, and among agricultural tribes generally tillage of the fields was largely woman's work; but she had some leisure time for amusement and social intercourse. "In an Indian community, where the food question is always a serious one, there can be no idle hands. The women were aided in their round of tasks by the children and old men. Where slavery existed their toil was further lightened by the aid of slaves, and in other tribes captives were often compelled to aid in the women's work.

"The men did all the hunting, fishing, and trapping, which in savagery are always toilsome, frequently dangerous, and not rarely fatal, especially in winter. The man alone bore arms, and to him belonged the chances and dangers of war." It was men also who attended to the making and administration of laws, the conduct of treaties, and the general regulation of tribal affairs, "though in these fields, women also had important prerogatives;" and important ceremonies and religious rites, and the memorizing of tribal records, and of treaties and rituals, were intrusted to the men. "The chief manual labor of the men was the manufacture of hunting and war implements, an important occupation that took much time." They also made the canoes, and often dressed the skins of animals, and sometimes even made the clothing for their wives. "Thus, in Indian society, the position of woman was usually subordinate, and the lines of demarcation between the duties of the sexes were everywhere sharply drawn. Nevertheless, the division of labor was not so unequal as it might seem to the casual observer, and it is difficult to understand how the line could have been more fairly drawn in a state of society where the military spirit was so dominant. Indian communities lived in constant danger of attack, and their men, whether in camp or on the march, must ever be ready at a moment's warning to seize their arms and defend their homes and families."
— HENRY W. HENSHAW, in *Handbook Amer. Indians.*

and to do all the drudgery. They will scold their husbands for getting drunk or parting with a favorite horse or wasting any property to purchase spiritous liquor, will scold their children for wasting or destroying any property. It is a maxim among the Indians that every thing belong to the woman or women except the Indian's hunting and war implements, even the game, the Indians bring home on his back. As soon as it enters the lodge, the man ceases to have anything to say in its disposal, properly speaking, the husband is master, the wife the slave, but it is in most cases voluntary slavery as the Indians seldom make their wives feel their authority, by words or deeds, they generally live very happy together, they on both sides make due allowances.

Medicines

The Sauk and Fox Indians are much troubled with the pleuricy and sore eyes, one proceeds from their fatigue and exposure in hunting and war, the other I suppose from smoke in their lodges. They understand the use of medicine [83] necefsary for the cure of the most

---

[83] "Many erroneous ideas of the practice of medicine among the Indians are current, often fostered by quacks who claim to have received herbs and methods of practice from noted Indian doctors. The medical art among all Indians was rooted in sorcery; and the prevailing idea that diseases were caused by the presence or acts of evil spirits, which could be removed only by sorcery and incantation, controlled diagnosis and treatment. This conception gave rise to both priest and physician. Combined with it there grew up a certain knowledge of and dependence upon simples, one important development of which was what we know as the doctrine of signatures, according to which, in some cases, the color, shape, and markings of plants are supposed to indicate the organs for which in disease they are supposed to be specifics. There was current in many tribes, especially among the old women, a rude knowledge of the therapeutic use of a considerable number of plants and roots, and of the sweating process, which was employed with little discrimination."
— Henry W. Henshaw, in *Handbook Amer. Indians.*
Many of the medicinal roots of eastern and southern United States were adopted by the whites from the Indian pharmacopeia; some of these are still known by their native names, and about forty are quoted in current price lists of crude drugs. Indians formerly gathered medicinal roots to supply the trade

complaints, they are subject to, they make the use of purgatives and emetics, some of them operate promptly,
some of the Indians understand the art of bleeding, and
make use of the lancet or penknife for that purpose, they
make use of decoctions of roots, and there are few die
for want of medicines, probably some die from taking
to much.

Anatomy

I am informed that the Indians in general are much
better acquainted with the anatomy of the human body,
than the commonalty of white people, and in many instances, making surprising cures, they are very succefsful
in the treatment of wounds: I have known many to have
been cured after having been shot in the body with ball
and arrows, they are rather rough in their surgical
operations, they cut away with a small knife, and I
have seen them make use of a pair of old scifsors, to extract an arrow point stuck in the thigh bone, and succeeded after much carving to get at it.   Every Indian
is acquainted either more or lefs with the use of common
medicines, in extreame cures [sc. cases], they apply to
some of their most celebrated jugglers, they in addition
to their medicine make use of superstitious ceremonies,
to imprefs on the minds of the sick, or the persons
present, that he makes use of supernatural means for the
recovery of the person sick: also that the sick persons is
bewitched and will work away making use of the most
ludicrous experiments all of which is swallowed by the
credulous Indians.   The conjuror or Manatoo-Caw-So

that arose after the coming of the whites.   Many roots were exported, especially ginseng, in which there was an extensive commerce with China; and,
curiously enough, the Iroquois name for the plant has the same meaning as the
Chinese name." — WALTER HOUGH, in *Handbook Amer. Indians.*

See the list of trees and plants used for medicinal purposes by the Chippewa
in Minnesota, in Hoffman's "Midē'wiwin of the Ojibwa," in *Seventh annual
Report* of the Bureau of Amer. Ethnology, 198-201. — ED.

or doctor are feared by the bulk of the Indians, and never dare to do any thing to displease them.

Astronomy

The general opinion of all Indians is, that the earth is flat, and [they] appear to be acquainted with several stars, they know all the fixed stars, and have names for them all, also for others that apparently change their position, the[y] regulate their seasons as well by the stars as by the moon. The year the[y] divide into four seasons, as we do. Spring – Man-no-cum-ink. Summer – Pen-a-wick. Autumn – Tuc-quock. Winter – Pap-po-en. Also into twelve moons as follows:

Tuc-wot-thu	Keeshis	First frosty moon commencing in Sept.	
Amulo	"	Rutting "	October
Puccume	"	Freezing "	November
Kiche Muqua	"	Big Bear "	December
Chuckee Muqua	"	Little Bear "	January
Tuc-wun-nee	"	Cold "	February
Pa-puc-qua	"	Sap "	March
A-paw-in-eck-kee	"	Fish "	April
Uc-kee-kay	"	Planting "	May
Pa-la-nee	"	First summer or flowering moon	June
Na-pen-nee	"	Midsummer moon	July
Mish-a-way	"	Elk "	August

Their year is quoted as the[y] are placed in the above list of moons, commencing with the moon that changes in September, being the time the[y] usually leave their villages (after saving their corn) to go westward to make their fall and winter's hunt. The Sauk and Fox Indians say that the Great Spirit made every thing, the earth, moon, sun, stars, etc., all kinds of birds, beasts, and fishes, and all for the use of the Indians. As a proof they say, that it is only in their country that the buffaloe, elk, deer, bear, etc., are to be found, therefore they were specially intended for the Indians. To the white people the Great Spirit gave the book, and taught them the use of it, which the Great Spirit thought was absolutely necefsary for them to guide them through life: he also shewed them how to make blankets, guns, and gunpowder, all of which were special gifts to the whites. The use of letters particularly astonish them, and the[y] hold writing of any sort in great esteem, they have many papers among them of sixty and seventy years old in the French and Spanish languages, they take care of all old papers, without knowing any thing of the purport of them: the old papers are generally recommendations formerly written by French and Spanish commandants, commonly called patents by the French and Spaniards.

The Indians do not like to see eclipses of the sun or moon, they say that some bad munitoo is about to hide and devour the sun or moon, the Indians always fire at the eclipse to drive away the munitoo, which they think they succeed in when the eclipse is over. The Indians also fire ball at any comet, or bright star, which they think are munitoos.

All Indians can count as far as 1,000, which they call a big hundred, a great many can count to 10,000. They know as much of arithmetic as is sufficient to do their own businefs, altho they have no particular mark to represent numbers. The method the Indians describe north, east, south, and west, is as follows. They point to the north (or at night to the north star which they call the immoveable star) which they call the cold country: south the warm country, east the rising sun, west the setting sun. The Indians are excellent judges of the weather, and I have known them prepare for rain, when I could observe no signs whatever. Met[e]ors they cannot comprehend, they call them munitoos. In making calculations for the appearance of the new moon, they say, in so many days the present moon will die, and in so many more days, the next moon will hang in the firmament (or the moon will be visible).

Few of the Indians know any thing of Europe, or the ocean, the little they know, they have learned it from the traders.

Music

The only musical instruments the Sauk and Fox Indians make use of, is the flute, made of a piece of cane of two pieces of soft wood hallowed out and tied together with leather thongs, also a drum, which they beat with a stick, the flute they blow at one end, and except the key it is something like a flagelet. They beat the drum at all kinds of feasts, dances, and games, they dance keeping time with the tap of the drum, their tunes are generally melancholly, they are always on a flat key, and contain many variations, they have a peculiar mode of telling stories, elegantly illustrated with metaphor and similie, in telling their stories they always retain something to the last, which is necefsary to explain the whole.

Religion

The Sauk and Fox Indians believe in one great and good Spirit,[84] who superintends and commands all things, and that there are many supernatural agents or

[84] "Among the many erroneous conceptions regarding the Indian none has taken deeper root than the one which ascribes to him belief in an overruling deity, the 'Great Spirit.' Very far removed from this tremendous conception of one all-powerful deity was the Indian belief in a multitude of spirits that dwelt in animate and inanimate objects, to propitiate which was the chief object of his supplications and sacrifices. To none of his deities did the Indian ascribe moral good or evil. His religion was practical. The spirits were the source of good or bad fortune, whether on the hunting path or the war trail, in the pursuit of a wife or in a ball game. If successful he adored, offered sacrifices, and made valuable presents. If unsuccessful he cast his manito away and offered his faith to more powerful or more friendly deities. In this world

munitoos permitted by the Great Spirit to interfere in the concerns of the Indians.

They believe the thunder presides over the destinies of war, also Mache-muntitoo or bad Spirit is subordinate to Kee-shay-Munitoo or the Great Spirit, but that the bad Spirit is permitted (occasionally) to revenge himself on mankind thro the agency of bad medicine, poisonous reptiles, killing horses, sinking canoes, etc., every accident that befalls them, they impute to the bad Spirit's machinations, but at same time, conceive it is allowed to be so, in atonement for some part of their misdeeds. All Indians believe in ghosts, and when they imagine they have seen a ghost, the friends of the deceased immediately give a feast and hang up some clothing as an offering to pacify the troubled spirit of the deceased; they pray by singing over certain words before they lay down at night, they hum over a prayer also about sunrise in the morning. The Sauk and Fox Indians are very religious so far as ceremony is concerned, and even in paſsing any extraordinary cave, rock, hill, etc., they leave behind them a little tobacco for the munitoo, who they suppose lives there. There is a particular society among the Sauk and Fox Indians (and I believe among some other nations of Indians), the particulars of which, I understand is never divulged by any of the society. They hold their meetings in secret, and what ever paſses among them at their meetings, is never spoken of by any of them elsewhere, this society is composed of some of the best and most sencible men in the two nations.[85]   I have given myself

of spirits the Indian dwelt in perpetual fear. He feared to offend the spirits of the mountains, of the dark wood, of the lake, of the prairie."
— HENRY W. HENSHAW, in *Handbook Amer. Indians.*

[85] "Societies or brotherhoods of a secret and usually sacred character existed among very many American tribes, among many more, doubtless, than those from which there is definite information. On the plains the larger number of

much trouble to find out the particulars of this society,
but have been able to succeed in a very small part only.
The Indians of this society are called the Great Medicine men, and when a young Indian wish to become
one of the society, he applies to one of the members to
intercede for him, saying "you can vouch for me as

these were war societies, and they were graded in accordance with the age and
attainments of the members. The Buffalo Society was a very important body
devoted to healing disease. The Omaha and Pawnee seem to have had a great
number of societies, organized for all sorts of purposes. There were societies
concerned with the religious mysteries, with the keeping of records, and with
the dramatization of myths, ethical societies, and societies of mirth-makers, who
strove in their performances to reverse the natural order of things. We find
also a society considered able to will people to death, a society of 'big-bellied
men,' and among the Cheyenne a society of fire-walkers, who trod upon fires
with their bare feet until the flames were extinguished." Hoffman describes
the Grand Medicine society, or Midē'wiwin, and its four degrees; "as a result
of these initiations the spiritual insight and power, especially the power to
cure disease, was successively increased, while on the purely material side the
novitiate received instruction regarding the medicinal virtues of many plants.
The name of this society in the form *medeu* occurs in Delaware, where it was
applied to a class of healers." — JOHN R. SWANTON, in *Handbook Amer. Indians*, art. "Secret societies."

W. J. Hoffman says in his paper on the above-named "Grand Medicine
Society" of the Chippewa (or Ojibwa) — which was published in the *Seventh
annual Report* of the Bureau of American Ethnology (1885-1886), 143-299 — in
speaking of the opposition made by the medicine-men (often called sorcerers),
from the outset, to the introduction of Christianity: "In the light of recent
investigation the cause of this antagonism is seen to lie in the fact that the traditions of Indian genesis and cosmogony and the ritual of initiation into the
Society of the Midē' constitute what is to them a religion, even more powerful
and impressive than the Christian religion is to the average civilized man.
This opposition still exists among the leading classes of a number of the Algonkian tribes, and especially among the Ojibwa, many bands of whom have been
more or less isolated and beyond convenient reach of the church. The purposes
of the society are twofold: first, to preserve the traditions just mentioned, and,
second, to give a certain class of ambitious men and women sufficient influence
through their acknowledged power of exorcism and necromancy to lead a comfortable life at the expense of the credulous. The persons admitted into the
society are firmly believed to possess the power of communing with various
supernatural beings — manidos — and in order that certain desires may be
realized they are sought after and consulted" (page 151). Hoffman made
personal investigations among the Ojibwa during the years 1887-1889, at
Leech Lake, Minn., to obtain data for this paper, and much of his information
was furnished directly by the shamans ("medicine-men") themselves. — ED.

being a good Indian, etc.," the friend of the applicant mentions the circumstance to the headman of the society, who gives an answer in a few days after consulting others of the society, if the applicant is admitted, his friend is directed to prepare him accordingly, but what the preparation, etc., is, I never could find out, but no Indian can be admitted untill the expiration of one year, after application is made. This society or Great Medicine consists of four roads (or as we would call them, degrees) and it requires to do something to gain the first road, and so on to the second, third, fourth roads or degrees. It costs an Indian from forty to fifty dollars in goods, or other articles to be initiated or admitted into this society, and am told there are but few of them who can gain the end of the fourth road. A trader once, offered fifty dollars in goods to a particular Indian friend of his, who is the head or principal man of this society among the Sauk and Fox Indians, to be allowed to be present at one of their meetings, but was refused. Age has nothing to do with an applicant who wishes to become a member of this society, as I have been told the Minnominnie Indians admit boys of fourteen and fifteen years of age, but the Sauk and Fox Indians will not admit any so young. The Sauk and Fox Indians believe in wizards and witches and none but their jugglers have power to allay them.

General Manners and Customs

The Sauk and Fox Indians (like all other Indians) did formerly eat human flesh, and in their war excursions would always bring home pieces of the flesh of some of their enemies killed in battle, which they would eat, but for the last forty or fifty years they have abandoned that vile practice, and sometimes will yet bring home a small piece of human flesh of their enemies for their little children to gnaw, to render them brave as they say. The Sauk and Fox and all other Indians that I am acquainted with have no particular salutation in meeting or parting from each other, with the whiteman they will shake hands in deference to our custom. The Sauk Indians pay great respect to their chiefs when aſsembled in council, but the Fox Indians are quite to the contrary, they pay no respect to their chiefs at any time, except necefsity compels them, but as there are so much equality among all Indians, the chiefs seldom dare insult a private individual.[86] The Indians have no language like our profane cursing and swearing, they on emergencies appeal to the deity to witnefs the truth of their statements. They will say such a man is a worthlefs dog, a bad Indian, etc. Friendship between two Indians as comrades has no cold medium to it, an Indian in love is a silly looking mortal, he cannot eat, drink, or sleep, he appears to be deranged and with all the pains he takes to conceal his passion, yet it is so vifsible that all his friends know what is the matter with

[86] "Equality and independence were the cardinal principles of Indian society. In some tribes, as the Iroquois, certain of the highest chieftaincies were confined to certain clans, and these may be said in a modified sense to have been hereditary; and there were also hereditary chieftaincies among the Apache, Chippewa, Sioux, and other tribes. Practically, however, the offices within the limits of the tribal government were purely elective. The ability of the candidates, their courage, eloquence, previous services, above all, their personal popularity, formed the basis for election to any and all offices. Except among the Natchez and a few other tribes of the lower Mississippi, no power in any wise analogous to that of the despot, no rank savoring of inheritance, as we understand the term, existed among our Indians. Even military service was not compulsory, but he who would might organize a war party, and the courage and known prowess in war of the leader chiefly determined the number of his followers. So loose were the ties of authority on the war-path that a bad dream or an unlucky presage was enough to diminish the number of the war party at any time, or even to break it up entirely. . . The fact is that social and political organization was of the lowest kind; the very name of tribe, with implication of a body bound together by social ties and under some central authority, is of very uncertain application." — HENRY W. HENSHAW, in *Handbook Amer. Indians*, art. "Popular fallacies."

him. They never laugh at him but rather pity him. After an Indian returns home from hunting he will throw his game at the door of the lodge, enter in, put away his gun, undrefs his leggins and mocosins, and sit down without speaking a word with his head between his knees: immediately some thing to eat is placed before him, after eating heartily he looks at his wife or friends, smiles, and enters into conversation with them about what he has seen extraordinary during the day a hunting. Their power of recollection don't seem to be as strong as ours, many circumstances that have occurred within my recollection they have totally forgot. The Indians have only one way of building their bark huts or summer residences, they are built in the form of an oblong, a bench on each of the long sides about three feet high and four feet wide, paralel to each other, a door at each end, and a pafsage thro the center of about six feet wide, some of those huts, are fifty or sixty feet long and capable of lodging fifty or sixty persons. Their winter lodges are made by driving long poles in the ground in two rows nearly at equal distances from each other, bending the tops so as to overlap each other, then covering them with mats made of what they call puc-wy [87] a kind of rushes or flags, a Bearskin generally serves for a door, which is suspended at the top and hangs down, when finished it is not unlike an oven with the fire in the

[87] *Puc-wy*: a corruption of Ojibwa *apakweiashk*, meaning "roof-mat grass;" the "cat-tail flag" (*Typha latifolia*) the leaves of which are used for making mats for covering wigwams (*apakweiak*, plural of *apakwei*, from a root meaning "to roof"). The rush used for making floor-mats (*anâkanak*, from a root meaning "to spread out upon the ground") is the widely-distributed bulrush (*Scirpus lacustris*), called by the Ojibwa *anâkanashk*, or "floor-mat grass." The root of this rush, in California called "tule" (from Mexican *tolin*) is much eaten by some Indians; it affords a white, sweet, and very nutritious flour.
— WM. R. GERARD.
   Lake Puckaway, in Green Lake County, Wis., is evidently named for this plant. — ED.

center and the smoke omits thro the top. The Indians are acquainted with the various ways in which different nations of Indians encamp, and when they happen to come to an old encampment they can tell by the signs, the peculiar mode of making spits to roast their meat on, etc., whether it was their own people or whom and how many days old the encampment was, also which way they came and which way they went. The reasons that the Indians spare the lives of snakes is thro fear of offending them, they wish to be friendly with the whole family of snakes particularly the venemous kinds, they frequently throw them tobacco and to the dead ones they lay a few scraps of tobacco close to their heads.

Food, Mode of Living, Cooking Meals, etc.

There are few animals a hungry Indian will not eat, but the preference is always given to venison or bear's meat, and are the chief kinds of meat they eat, they feel always at a lofs without corn, even in the midst of meat. Corn with beans and dryed pumpkins well prepared, and sweet corn boiled with fat venison, ducks, or turkies, are delicious in the extreme. The Sauk and Fox Indians eat but few roasts, as they raise an immensity of corn, they sometimes make use of the wild potatoe a-pin, and the bear potatoe or Muco-co-pin also wah-co-pin or crooked root, Wab-bis-see-pin or Swan root.[88]   They

---

[88] "The Indians put the roots and other valuable parts of plants to a greater variety of uses than they did animal or mineral substances, even in the arid region, though plants with edible roots are limited mainly to the areas having abundant rainfall. The more important uses of roots were for food, for medicine, and for dyes, but there were many other uses, as for basketry, cordage, fire-sticks, cement, etc., and for chewing, making salt, and flavoring. Plants of the lily family furnished the most abundant and useful root food of the Indians throughout the United States. . . The tubers of the arrowhead plant (*Sagittaria arifolia* and *S. latifolia*), wappatoo in Algonquian, were widely used in the northwest for food. . . The Chippewa and Atlantic coast Indians also made use of them. . . The Sioux varied their diet with roots of the Indian turnip, two kinds of water-lily, the water grass, and the

do not make much use of wild rice, because they have little or none in their country, except when they procure some from the Winnebagoes or Minnominnie Indians. They most generally boil every thing into soup. I never knew them to eat raw meat, and meat seems to disgust them when it is not done thoroughly. They use fish only when they are scarce of tallow in summer, then they go and spear fish both by night and day, but it appears they only eat fish from necefsity. The old women set the kettle a boiling in the night, and about day break all eat whatever they have got, they eat in the course of the day as often as they are hungry, the kettle is on the fire constantly suspended from the roof of the lodge, every one has his wooden dish or bowl and wooden spoon [89] or as they call it Me-quen which they carry

modo of the Sioux, called by the French *pomme de terre*, the ground-nut (*Apios apios*). To these may be added the tuber of milkweed (*Asclepias tuberosa*), valued by the Sioux of the upper Platte, and the root of the Jerusalem artichoke (*Helianthus tuberosa*), eaten by the Dakota of St. Croix River. . . The Miami, Shawnee, and other tribes of the middle west ate the 'man of the earth' (*Ipomœa pandurata*) and Jerusalem artichoke (*Helianthus tuberosa*). . . The Hopi, Zūni, and other tribes eat the tubers of the wild potato (*Solanum jamesii*). The southern and eastern tribes also made use of the potato. Though this acrid tuber is unpalatable and requires much preparation to render it suitable for food, many tribes recognized its value. The Navaho, especially, dug and consumed large quantities of it, and, on account of the griping caused by eating it, they ate clay with it as a palliative. . . Hariot mentions (*Briefs and True Report*, 1590) six plants the roots of which were valued as food by the Virginia Indians, giving the native name, appearance, occurrence, and method of preparation. . . Although the use of edible roots by the Indians was general, they nowhere practiced root cultivation, even in its incipient stages. In the United States the higher agriculture, represented by maize cultivation, seems to have been directly adopted by tribes which had not advanced to the stages of root cultivation." — WALTER HOUGH, in *Handbook Amer. Indians*.

[89] "With the Indian the bowl serves a multitude of purposes; it is associated with the supply of his simplest needs as well as with his religion. The materials employed in making bowls are stone (especially soapstone), horn, bone, shell, skin, wood, and bark. Bowls are often adapted to natural forms, as shells, gourds, and concretions, either unmodified or more or less fully remodeled, and basket bowls are used by many tribes." They were used in preparing and serving food, for the drying, gathering, etc. of seeds in games of chance and divination, and in religious ceremonies; and "the most ancient

along with them when they are invited to feasts. Their cooking are not very clean, they seldom wash their kettles, dishes or meat, the old women will sometimes by way of cleanlinefs wipe the dish with her fingers.

Games, Dances, etc.

The Sauk and Fox Indians have many games, such as the mocosin, the platter, etc. Their most active game is what they call Puc-a-haw-thaw-waw, it is not unlike what we call shinny or bandy, they make use of a yarn ball covered with leather, the women also play this game, also the platter which is exclusively theirs. Runing foot races and horses they are very fond of. The Sauk and Fox nations have dances peculiar to themselves, also others they have adopted from other nations. The[y] dance the buffallow-dance and the otter dance, in dancing the buffallow-dance, they are drefsed with the pate of a buffallow skin with the horns, they imitate the buffallow by throwing themselves into different postures, also by mimicing his groans, attempting to horn each other, keeping exact time with the drum, the women often join in these dances, but remain nearly in the same spot (while dancing) and singing in a shrill voice above the men. The medicine dance or Mit-tee-wee, all those who belong to that fraternity, are made

permanent cooking utensil of the plains tribes was a bowl made by hollowing out a stone." — *Handbook Amer. Indians.*

Spoons and ladles were used among all tribes of the United States; they were made of a great variety of materials — stone, shell, bone, horn, wood, gourd, pottery, etc. — and in size were larger than European utensils of this sort. Wood was the most usual material for these articles; and some of the tribes on the northwest coast made them of highly artistic form and decoration. Among the eastern and southern Indians from New York to Florida they were made with the pointed bowl, a form which occurs in no other part of the United States. "Gourds were extensively used and their forms were often repeated in pottery." Spoons of shell were common where shells were available, and artistically wrought specimens have been found in the mounds.

— WALTER HOUGH, in *Handbook Amer. Indians.*

acquainted by some of the head persons, that on a certain day, the whole will afsemble at a particular place;
on the day appointed they make a shade, both males and
females make their best appearance, they have two
drums on the occasion, the businefs is opened with a
prayer from one of the members, after which the drum-
mers sing a doleful ditty, beating at same time on their
drums, each person male and female are provided with
a sac or pouch of the whole skin of some animal as the
raccoon, mink, marten, fisher, and otter, but generally
of the last mentioned: one of the elders get up and commence dancing round the inside of the lodge, another
follows, and so on untill they are all in motion, as they
pafs by each other, they point the nose of the sacs or
pouches at each other blowing a whiff at the same time,
the person so pointed at, will fall down on the ground
apparently in pain, and immediately get up again and
touch some other one in turn, who will do the same in
succefsion, etc. The Sauk and Fox Indians play at
cards, and frequently play high, they bet horses, wampum, silver works, etc. They frequently in the summer
season have sham battles, a party of footmen undertake
to conduct to their village some friends, they on their
journey are attacked by a party of horsemen who rush
on them from the woods and surround them, the footmen throw themselves into the form of a hollow square,
the horsemen are armed with pistols, the footmen receive them with a volley, and beat them off, and are
again attacked from another quarter and so on alternately untill they succeed in bringing their friends safe
to their village. In those encounters many get thrown
from their horses and sometimes, the footmen get
trampled on by the horses, but during the whole of the
transaction nothing like anger makes its appearance,

they all retire on the best terms with each other, and it would be considered as shameful and to much like a woman for a man to become angry in play. [90]

International Law of Relations

The Sauk and Fox Nations of Indians are in very strict alliance with each other, indeed their affinity are

---

[90] "When not bound down by stern necessity, the Indian at home was occupied much of the time with dancing, feasting, gaming, and story-telling. Though most of the dances were religious or otherwise ceremonial in character, there were some which had no other purpose than that of social pleasure. They might take place in the day or the night, be general or confined to particular societies, and usually were accompanied with the drum or other musical instrument to accentuate the song. The rattle was perhaps invariably used only in ceremonial dances. Many dances were of pantomimic or dramatic character, and the Eskimo had regular pantomime plays, though evidently due to Indian influence. The giving of presents was often a feature of the dance, as was betting of all athletic contests and ordinary games. . . From Hudson Bay to the Gulf of Mexico, and from the Atlantic to the border of the plains, the great athletic game was the ball play, now adopted among civilized games under the name of 'lacrosse.' In the north it was played with one racket, and in the south with two. Athletes were regularly trained for this game, and competitions were frequently intertribal. The wheel-and-stick game in one form or another was well-nigh universal. . . Like most Indian institutions, the game often had a symbolic significance in connection with a sun myth. . . Target practice with arrows, knives, or hatchets, thrown from the hand, as well as with the bow or rifle, was also universal among the warriors and boys of the various tribes. The gaming arrows were of special design and ornamentation, and the game itself often had a symbolic purpose. . . Games resembling dice and hunt-the-button were found everywhere and were played by both sexes alike, particularly in the tipi or the wigwam during the long winter nights. . . Investigations by Culin show a close correspondence between these Indian games and those of China, Japan, Korea, and northern Asia. Special women's games were shinny, football, and the deer-foot game, besides the awl game already noted. . . Among the children there were target shooting, stilts, slings, and tops for the boys, and buckskin dolls and playing-house for the girls, with 'wolf' or 'catcher,' and various forfeit plays, including a breath-holding test. Cats'-cradles, or string figures, as well as shuttlecocks and buzzes, were common. As among civilized nations, the children found the greatest delight in imitating the occupations of the elders. Numerous references to amusements among the various tribes may be found throughout the annual reports of the Bureau of American Ethnology. Consult especially 'Games of the American Indians,' by Stewart Culin, in the 24th *Report*, 1905." — JAMES MOONEY, in *Handbook Amer. Indians*, art. "Amusements."

doubly rivited by intermarriages, similarity of manners and customs as also in the similarity of language. I have never heard where their council fire is but believe it to be at the Sauk Village on the Rocky River, it may be elsewhere. The alliance between the Sauk and Fox Indians and the Ofsages was made at the Ofsage village on the Ofsage River which falls into the Mifsouri River. The alliance between the Sauk and Fox Nations and the Kicapoo Nation of Indians, was formed at the Sauk Village as above described. All those Nations of Indians except the Ofsages have long since joined the General Confederacy at Browns Town in Michigan Territory, and it still exists. The Sauk and Fox Indians have no national badge that I know, they call the Shawanoes and Kicapoos their elder brothers. Every nation of Indians think themselves as great as any other, and I never heard of any relative rank among the different nations of Indians, except what has been said about the council fire at Brownstown.

Hunting

About the middle of September (some years later) the Sauk and Fox Indians all begin to move from their villages to go towards the country the[y] mean to hunt during the ensuing winter, they generally go westwards in the interiour on the head waters of Ihoway and Demoine Rivers and some go beyond those rivers quite in the interiour of the country. There are some who have no horses as also many old people who descend the Mifsifsippi River in canoes as far as the Ihoway, Scunk and other rivers and ascend those rivers to the different places where they mean to pafs the winter a hunting. Those Indians who have a sufficiency of horses to transport their families and baggage go as far westward in their hunting excursions as the Mifsouri River and sometimes are invited by the Kansez and other Indians to crofs the Mifsouri River and hunt in this country as far westward on small streams that fall into Arkansaw. River. They generally stop hunting deer when the winter begins to be severe and forms themselves into grand encampments to pafs the remainder of the winter or severe weather. They at this time are visited by their traders who go and receive their credits and also trade with them.[91] On opening of the spring those that have traps go to beaver hunting others to hunt bear and they generally finish their hunt about the 10th of April. They formerly had general hunting parties or excursions before the buffaloe removed so far westward. It is customary to make a feast of the first animal killed by each party, the whole are invited with some ceremony. In case of sicknefs they feast on dog's meat and sacrifice dogs by killing them with an axe, tying them to a sapling with their noses pointed east or west and painted with vermillion. When strangers of another nation visit their villages, the crier makes a long harangue thro the village in a loud voice, to use the strangers well, while they stay, etc. The strangers may be invited to several feasts in the course of the same day, while the[y] remain at the village; however particular Indians give feasts to particular individuals, their particular friends and relations, and the custom of feasting strangers is not so common now among the Sauk and Fox Indians as formerly, or as is at present among the Indians of Mifsouri.

The Sauk and Fox Indians will on great emergencies hold a general feast throughout their nations, to avert

---

[91] In the *Forsyth Mss.* (vol. iii, doc. 1) is a list of the licenses to traders granted by Forsyth at the Rock River agency, 1822-1827. Twenty-six licenses, sometimes more than one to the same person, are described, all issued for one year. The number of clerks for each varied from one to six; and the capital employed, from $518.16 to $6,814.71. — ED.

some expected general calamity, while the magicians are praying to the Great Spirit and making use of numerous ceremonies.

It is a very mistaken idea among many of the white people to suppose, that the Indians have not hair on every part of their body, that they have both males and females: they pull it out with an instrument made of braſs wire in the form of a gun worm. They consider it indecent to let it grow.

The Sauk and Fox Indians shave their heads except a small patch on the crown, which they are very fond of dreſsing and plaiting, the[y] suspend several ornaments to it of horse or deer's hair died red as also silver ornaments, feathers of birds, etc., they paint their faces red with vermillion, green with verdigrease and black with charcoal, their prevailing colour is red, except before or after coming from war, after returning from war they divest themselves of all their ornaments, wear dirt on their heads, and refrain from using vermillion for one year. The women tye their hair in a club with some worsted binding, red, blue, or green but the former is prefered leaving two ends to hang down their backs. [92]

[92] "The motive of personal adornment, aside from the desire to appear attractive, seems to have been to mark individual, tribal, or ceremonial distinction. The use of paint on the face, hair, and body, both in color and design, generally had reference to individual or clan beliefs, or it indicated relationship or personal bereavement, or was an act of courtesy. It was always employed in ceremonies, religious and secular, and was an accompaniment of gala dress donned to honor a guest or to celebrate an occasion. The face of the dead was frequently painted in accordance with tribal or religious symbolism. The practice of painting was widespread and was observed by both sexes. Paint was also put on the faces of adults and children as a protection against wind and sun." Other forms of adornment consisted in plucking out the hairs on the face and body, head-flattening, tattooing, the use of fat, and that of perfumes; and the wearing of earrings, labrets, and nose-rings. Garments were often elaborately ornamented — among the inland tribes largely with porcupine and feather quills, which were later replaced by beads of European manufacture — and sometimes were painted. Such work was not only decorative, but often symbolic, ceremonial, or even historical. — ALICE C. FLETCHER, in *Handbook Amer. Indians.*

The Indians admire our manufactories but more particularly guns and gunpowder, but many old Indians say they were more happy before they knew the use of fire arms, because, they then could kill as much game as they wanted, not being then compelled to destroy game to purchase our merchandise as they are now oblidged to do.

They say that the white people's thirst after land is so great that they are never contented untill they have a belly full of it, the Indians compare a white settlement in their neighbourhood to a drop of raccoon's grease falling on a new blanket the drop at first is scarcely perceptible, but in time covers almost the whole blanket. The Sauk and Fox Indians do almost all their carrying on horseback and in canoes, if any carrying is oblidged to be done for want of horses, the women have to shoulder it. Among the Sauk and Fox Indians the young men are most generally handsome, well made, and extreamely modest.

The young men and women, when they begin to think of marrying use vermillion. I have observed in the course of my life, that Indians are not now so stout and robust as formerly, in general they are very atheletic with good constitutions, yet whatever may be the cause, they have not the strength we have. Their general heighth is about five feet, eight inches, a great many of the old people are much taller, however they are not in my opinion degenerating. It is impofsible to ascertain the proportion of births to the deaths but it is well known they are on the increase. [93] In a conversation I had with Keeocuck the most intelligent Indian among

[93] "It has been supposed that, in his physiologic functions the Indian differs considerably from the white man, but the greater our knowledge in this direction the fewer the differences appear; there is, however, a certain lack of uniformity in this respect between the two races." The development and life of

the Sauk and Fox Indians (and a Sauk by birth) last summer (1826) he told me the Sauk Nation could furnish twelve hundred warriours, three fourths of which were well armed with good rifles and remainder with shot guns and some few with bows and arrows. The Sauk and Fox Indians encourage polygamy and the adoption of other Indians in their nations, which serves to augment their nations rapidly. All belts of wampum are presented in council (after speaking) by the prin-

the Indian infant are quite similar to those of the white child. The period of puberty is notably alike in the two races. Marriage takes place earlier among the Indians than among the whites; "only few girls of more than eighteen years, and few young men of more than twenty-two years, are unmarried," and sometimes girls marry at thirteen to fifteen years. "Indian women bear children early, and the infants of even the youngest mothers seem in no way defective. The birth rate is generally high, from six to nine births in a family being usual. . . The adult life of the Indian offers nothing radically different from that of ordinary whites. The supposed early aging of Indian women is by no means general and is not characteristic of the race; when it occurs, it is due to the conditions surrounding the life of the individual. . . But few of them know their actual age. . . The longevity of the Indian is very much like that of a healthy white man. There are individuals who reach the age of one hundred years and more, but they are exceptional. Among aged Indians there is usually little decrepitude. Aged women predominate somewhat in numbers over aged men."

"Among the more primitive tribes, who often pass through periods of want, capacity for food is larger than in the average whites. Real excesses in eating are witnessed among such tribes, but principally at feasts. On the reservations, and under ordinary circumstances, the consumption of food by the Indian is usually moderate. All Indians readily develop a strong inclination for and are easily affected by alcoholic drinks. The average Indian ordinarily passes somewhat more time in sleep than the civilized white man; on the other hand, he manifests considerable capacity for enduring its loss."

"Dreams are frequent and variable. Illusions or hallucinations in healthy individuals and under ordinary conditions have not been observed. . . The sight, hearing, smell, and taste of the Indian, so far as can be judged from unaided but extended observation, are in no way peculiar. . . The physical endurance of Indians on general occasions probably exceeds that of the whites. The Indian easily sustains long walking or running, hunger and thirst, severe sweating, etc.; but he often tires readily when subjected to steady work. His mental endurance, however, except when he may be engaged in ceremonies or games, or on other occasions which produce special mental excitement, is but moderate; an hour of questioning almost invariably produces mental fatigue."

—*Handbook Amer. Indians.*

cipal chiefs, the principal brave or chief of the soldiers
also delivers his speech and wampum in public council
when it is a national affair or that they wish to do any
thing permanent. They make use of no heiroglyphicks
except painting on a tree or rock or on a post at the head
of graves, [94] the representation of the tribe the person
belong to, the number of scalps and prisoners taken from
the enemy, etc. Strings or belts of white wampum are
occasionally sent with a piece of tobacco tied to the end

[94] "Pictography may be defined as that form of thought-writing which
seeks to convey ideas by means of picture-signs or marks more or less sug-
gestive or imitative of the object or idea in mind. Significance, therefore, is
an essential element of pictographs, which are alike in that they all express
thought, register a fact, or convey a message. Pictographs, on the one hand,
are more or less closely connected with sign language, by which they may have
been preceded in point of time;" and, on the other hand, "with every varying
form of script and print, past and present, the latter being, in fact, derived
directly or indirectly from them." Picture-signs have been employed by all
uncivilized peoples, but "it is chiefly to the American Indian we must look for
a comprehensive knowledge of their use and purpose, since among them alone
were both pictographs and sign language found in full and significant employ. Pictographs have been made upon a great variety of objects, a favorite
being the human body. Among other natural substances, recourse by the picto-
grapher has been had to stone, bone, skins, feathers and quills, gourds, shells,
earth and sand, copper, and wood, while textile and fictile fabrics figure
prominently in the list. . .
"From the earliest form of picture-writing, the imitative, the Indian had
progressed so far as to frame his conceptions ideographically, and even to
express abstract ideas. Later, as skill was acquired, his figures became more
and more conventionalized till in many cases all semblance of the original was
lost, and the ideograph became a mere symbol. While the great body of Indian glyphs remained pure ideographs, symbols were by no means uncommonly
employed, especially to express religious subjects, and a rich color symbolism likewise was developed, notably in the southwest." Usually the Indian glyphs "are
of individual origin, are obscured by conventionalism, and require for their
interpretation a knowledge of their makers and of the customs and events of the
times, which usually are wanting" — hence the need of great caution, and frequent failure, in trying to explain them. Nevertheless, "their study is important. These pictures on skin, bark, and stone, crude in execution as they
often are, yet represent the first artistic records of ancient, though probably not
of primitive man. In them lies the germ of achievement which time and effort
have developed into the masterpieces of modern eras. Nor is the study of
pictographs less important as affording a glimpse into the psychological work-
ings of the mind of early man in his struggles upward." — HENRY W. HENSHAW,
in *Handbook Amer. Indians.*

of it as a friendly mefsage or invitation from one nation to another for the purpose of opening the way to an adjustment of differences or any other subject of importance. Blue wampum painted red, with tobacco in the same manner denotes hostility or a solicitation to join in hostility against some other power. Those strings or belts of wampum are accompanied by speeches to be repeated verbatim or presenting them to the person or persons to whom they are sent, should the terms offered or the purport of the mefsage be acceeded to the parties accepting the wampum smoke of the tobacco thus tied to it and return their answer in a similar way. A belt of wampum sent to a neighboring nation for afsistance in war, is made of blue wampum, at one end is wrought in with white grains the figure of a tomyhawk, presented towards a dimond of white grains also both painted red with vermillion. Should the nation accept the mefsage, they work their dimond of white grains of wampum in the same way.

Language

The Sauk and Fox languages are guttural and nosal the following letters are made use in their language as well as other sounds that cannot be represented by any letters in an alphabet – A, B, C, H, I, K, L, M, N, O, P, Q, S, T, U, W, Y, Z, are letters of our alp[h]abet that are sounded in their language: the accent is generally placed on the second syllable and often on the first. They place a very strong emp[h]asis on the superlative degree of their ajectives also their adverbs of quality and interjections. They designate the genders thus –

MASCULINE	FEMININE
Man, Ninny	Woman, Hequa
Men, Ninnywuck	Women, Hequa-wuck
Buck, Iawpe	Doe, A-co
Deer [plural?], Pay-shakes-see	

The genders of all other animals are formed by placing the word [for] male or female before them. The plurals of substantives are formed by the termination of *uck* or *wuck*

SINGULAR	PLURAL
Child, A-pen-no	Children, A-pen-no-wuck
Chief, O-ke-maw	Chiefs, O-ke-maw-wuck
Indian, Me-thu-say-nin-ny	Indians, Me-thu-say-nin-ny-wuck

also the termination of y or wy to the name of an animal is the proper name of its Skin.

SINGULAR	PLURAL
Buckskin, I-aw-pe-wy	Buckskins, I-aw-pe-wy-uck
Muskrat [skin], Shusk-wy	Muskratskins, Shusk-wy-uck

[*Vocabulary*]

American,[95] Muc-a-mon	Englishman, Sog-o-nosh
French, Mith-o-cosh	Blanket, Mi-co-say

---

[95] Derivation of the Indian names for American, English and French people — It is very well known, that the first white people the Indians saw in North America, were the French, who landed in Canada at an early day. The Indians say, that the French wore long beards in those days, from which circumstance, the Indians called them Wa-bay-mish-e-tome, i.e., white people with beards, and Wem-ty-goush is an abbreviation of the former Indian words of Wa-bay-mish-e-tome.

Sog-o-nosh, appears to be derived from the gallic word Sasenaugh, which as I am well informed, means Saxon. The manner in which the Indians became acquainted with this word is as follows. At an early period, perhaps, in the latter part of the seventeenth, or the beginning of the eighteenth century, the British were about to make an attack on Quebeck; some Scotchmen who were officers in the French army, at that place, told the Indians to be strong, and they, combined with the French, would kill all those bad Sasenaghs (meaning the British Army) who dared come against them. The Indians took the word, and pronounced it as now spoken, Sog-o-nosh. Both words as Wem-ty-goush and Sog-o-nosh originated with the lake Indians.

Kit-chi-mo-co-maun or Big Knife is of a more recent origin, than the two former names. In some one of the many battles between the settlers of the then province (now State) of Virginia, the Indians were attacked by a party of white men on horseback, with long knives (swords), and were ever after called Big Knives by the Indians in that quarter, which name reached the more northern Indians, and the name of Big Knife has ever since been given by the Indians to every American. The Indians in Lower Canada used to call the New England people Pos-to-ney which I presume was borrowed from the French Bostoné, but at the present day and for many years back, all Indians

Powder (gun), Muck-i-tha

Flint, Sog-o-cawn

Whiskey or rum, Scho-ta-wa-bo

Cow, Na-no-ee

Cat, Caw-shu

Cat (wild), Pis-shew

Fowls, Puck-a-ha-qua

Looking glaſs, Wa-ba-moan

Silver, Shoo-ne-aw

Knife, Mau-thiſs

Dog, A-lem-mo

Saddle, Tho-me-a-cul

Bridle, So-ke-the-na-pe-chu-cun

Canoe, It-che-maun

Paddle, Up-we

Water, Neppe

Sun, Keeshis

Otter, Cuth-eth-tha

Beaver, Amic-qua

Elk, Mesh-shay-way

Bear, Muc-qua

Wild goose, Alick-qua

Duck, She-sheeb

Eagle, Mick-is-seou

Owl, We-thuc-co

Swan, A-ha-wa

Pidgeon, Mee-mee

Eye, Os-keesh-oc-qua

Hand, Neek

Mouth, Thole

Nose, co-mouth

Teeth, Wee-pee-thul

call all Americans, Kit-chi-mo-co-maun, i.e., Big Knives. — T. FORSYTH (among memoranda following his memoir).

Many curious names were given by the aboriginal peoples to the white men, "appellations referring to their personal appearance, arrival in ships, arms, dress, and other accouterments, activities, merchandise and articles brought with them, as iron, and fancied correspondence to figures of aboriginal myth and legend." In some cases the term for men of one nation was afterward extended to include all white men whom they met. Thus, "the Chippewa term for 'Englishman,' *shāganāsh* (which probably is connected with 'spearman,' or the 'contemptible spearman.' — WM. JONES, 1906) has been extended to mean 'white man.'" The Americans (i.e., the inhabitants of the English colonies which are now part of the United States) were called, in and after the Revolutionary period, various names by the Indians to distinguish them from the British and French. "Probably from the swords of the soldiery several tribes designated the Americans as 'big knives,' or 'long knives.' This is the signification of the Chippewa and Nipissing *chĭmo'koman*. . . The prominence of Boston in the early history of the United States led to its name being used for 'American' on both the Atlantic and the Pacific coast. Another Algonquian term for Frenchman is the Cree *wemistikojiw*, Chippewa *wemĭtĭgoshĭ*, probably akin to the Fox *wämē'tĕgowisĭta*, one who is identified with something wooden, probably referring to something about clothing and implements. The Fox name for a Frenchman is *wämē'tĕgoshĭa* (WM. JONES, 1906); Menominee, *wameqtikosiu*; Missisauga, *wamitigushi*, etc. The etymology of this name is uncertain." — A. F. CHAMBERLAIN, in *Handbook Amer. Indians*, art. "Race names."

In a letter to the editor, Dr. F. W. Hodge says: "Forsyth's *Wem-ty-goush* is from the Chippewa *wemĭtĭgoshĭ*, meaning 'people of the wooden canoes.'"

— ED.

Legs, Cau-then

Arms, Nitch

Head, Weesh

Foot, Couth

Hair (of the head), We-ne-sis

Hair (of animals), We-se-an

Corn, Thaw-meen

Tree, Ma-thic-quai

Moon, Kee-shis

Stars, A-law-queek

Day, Keesh-o-co

Night, Tip-pic-quoc

Father, Oce

Mother, Kea

Sister, Ni-thuc-quame

Brother (elder), Si-say

Brother (younger), Se-ma

Sister (elder), Ne-mis-sa

Sister (younger), Chu-me-is-sum

Son, Quis

Daughter, Thaunis

Grandfather, Mish-o-mifs

Grandmother, Co-mifs

Friend, Cawn

Yesterday, O-naw-co

To-day, He-noke

Tomorrow, wa-buck

Warriour, Wa-taw-say

Spring, Man-no-cum-me

Rock, As-sen

Sand, Na-kow

Wood, Ma-thi-a-cole

Mifsifsippi, Mes-is-se-po

Wind, No-then

Snow, Ac-coen

Rain, Kee-me-a

Thunder, An-a-mee-kee

Dance, Ne-mee

Path, Me-ow

God, Man-nit-too

Devil, Mache-man-nit-too

Fire, Scho-tha

Boy, Qui-es-ea

Girl, Squa-cy

Tobacco, Say-maw

Sail, Caw-tha-sum

Thought, Es-she-thai

Courage, A-e-qua-me

Hatred, Es-*kin*-a-wa

Fear, Co-suc-kea

Love, Tip-pawn-nan

Eternity, Caw-keek

Happinefs, Men-we-pem-au-this-see

Strength, We-shic-is-see

Beauty, Wa-wan-is-see

Insanity, Waw-wen-au-this-se-ow

Revenge, Ash-e-tho-a-caw-no

Cowardice, Keesh-kee-tha-hum

Hunger, Wee-shaw-pel

Round, *Wa*-we-i-au

White, Wa-bes-kiou

Black, Muck-et-tha-wa

Yellow, As-saow

Green, Ski-buc-ki-a

Red, Mus-quaou

Blue, We-pec-qua

Song, Nuc-a-moan

Feast, Kay-kay-noo

Salt, See-wee-thaw-gun

Sugar, Sis-sa-bac-quat

White Oak, Mec-she-mish

Red Oak, Ma-thic-wa-mish

Cedar, Mus-qua-aw-quck

Pine, Shin-qua-quck

Cottonwood, Me-thew-wuck

Sycamore, Keesh-a-wock-quai

Grafs, Mus-kis-kee

Hill, Mes-is-sauk

Island, Men-nefs

River, Seepo
Flat, Puc-puc-kis-kia
Alive, Pematiſs
Dead, Nippo
Sick, Oc-co-muth
Well, Nes-say
Tired, je-qua
Lazy, Naw-nee-kee-tho
Early, Maw-my
Late, A-maw-quas
Handsome, Waw-won-niſs-see
Ugly, Me-aw-niſs-see
Rich, O-thai-wiſs-see

Poor, Kitch-a-moc-is-see
Good, Wa-wun-nitt
Better, Na-kai-may-wa-won-nitt
Best, One-wak-men-we-wa-won-
    nitt
Bad, Me-aw-nith
Worse, A-ne-kai-may-me-aw-nith
Worst, A-me-kaw-she-me-aw-
    nith [96]

Boat, Mis-se-gock-it-che-man
Flute, Paw-pe-guen
Boards, Miſs-see-gock

PERSONAL PRONOUNS

Singular	*Plural*
I, Neen	We, Neenwaw
Thou or you, Keene	Ye, Keenwaw
He, she, or it, Weene	They, Weenwaw

Poſseſsion

Singular	*Plural*
Mine or my, Nichi Enim [97]	Ours, Neen-ane-i-thi-enim
Thy or thine, Kiche Enim	Yours, Keen-ane-othi-enim
His or hers, O-thi-Enim	Theirs, Ween-waw-othi-enim

CONJUGATION VERB TO LOVE

Singular	*Plural*
I love, ne-neen-wen-a-maw	We love, Neen-wa-ke-men-a-kia
Thou lovest, Ke-men-wen-a-maw-kia	Ye or you love, Keen-wa, etc.
He loved, O-men-wen-a-maw-kia	They love, Ween-wa, etc.
	Loved, Men-a-wa-kia-pie

Loving, Men-wen-a-meen

[NUMBERS]

One, Necouth	Four, Ne-a-we
Two, Neesh	Five, Nee-aw-neen
Three, Neſs	Six, Ne-coth-wa-sick

[96] These comparisons of "bad," as also the specimens of plural formation for substantives (page 240) have been transposed to their present and logical position because in the Ms. they were evidently misplaced by some forgetfulness or oversight of Forsyth's. — ED.

[97] The termination *enim* has reference to things. — T. FORSYTH (in marginal note.)

Seven, No-wuck	12, Mittausway Neshway niſsee
Eight, Nip-wash-ick	13, Mittausway Neſs-way Niſsee
Nine, Shauck	20, Neesh Wap-pe-tuck
Ten, Mit-taus	30, Neſs Wap-pe-tuck
11, Mittausway Necouth a niſsee	100, Necouth-wock-qua

1,000, Mittaus wock-qua or necouth kichi wock
10,000, Mit-taus Kichi wock or ten great hundreds

The Sauk and Fox and I believe all other Indians count decimally.

PREPOSITIONS

Come with me	Ke-we-thay-me
Go to him	E-na-ke-haw-loo
I will fight for you	Ke-me-caw-thu-it-thum-one
Come in with me	Pen-the-kay-thaun
Let us wade thro the water	Pee-than-see-e-thawn

ADVERBS

He shoots badly	Me-awn-os-show-whai
He eats much	Kichu-o-we-sen-ne
The River rises rapidly	Kichu-mos-on-hum-o-see-po
Come here	Pe-a-loo
Go there	E-tip-pe-haw-loo
Behave well	Muc-quache-how-e-wa
Not you but me	A-qua-kun-neen
Neither you nor I	A-qua-necoth I-O

The above is submitted to your better Judgment of Indian Manners and Customs by your obedient servant
THOMAS FORSYTH.[98]

St. Louis, 15th January, 1827

[Addressed:] GENERAL WILLIAM CLARK,[99] Sup[td] of In. affs, St. Louis..

---

[98] Thomas Forsyth was of Scotch-Irish origin, his father, William Forsyth, coming to America in 1750, and entering military service here; after the French and Indian War he was stationed at Detroit, where Thomas was born, Dec. 5, 1771. When but a youth, Thomas entered the Indian trade; he spent several winters at Saginaw Bay, and as early as 1798 spent a winter on an island in the Mississippi River, near Quincy, Ill. About 1802 he, with Robert Forsyth and John Kinzie, established a trading-post at Chicago, and later settled as a trader at Peoria. April 1, 1812, he was appointed a sub-agent of Indian affairs (with a salary of $600 a year, and three rations a day), under Gen. William

Clark, and for many years (until a short time before the Black Hawk War) was agent at first for the Illinois district, and then among the Sauk and Fox tribes. He died at St. Louis, Oct. 29, 1833, leaving four children. Forsyth's letter-books, covering the period from 1812 to his death, with many letters received by him from prominent men of his time, copies of his official accounts rendered to the government, and several memoirs on the Indians — forming a collection of original documents of great value and interest for western and Indian history of that period — are in the possession of the Wisconsin Historical Society. Forsyth was a man of great ability, and was generally considered one of the most competent among the early Indian agents; he had much influence with the Indians, and did much to retain them on the side of the Americans in the war of 1812-1815. See biographical and other information regarding him in Wis. *Hist. Colls.*, vol. vi, 188, and vol. xi, 316. — ED.

[99] General Clark was heard to say that this account of the manners and customs of the Sauk and Fox Indians was "tolerable." It was so tolerable that he nor any of his satelites could equal it, and I should be glad to see some of their productions on this head. — T. FORSYTH (marginal note).

APPENDICES

A. Biographical sketch of Nicolas Perrot; condensed from the notes of Father Tailhan.

B. Notes on Indian social organization, mental and moral traits, and religious beliefs; and accounts of three remarkably religious movements among Indians in modern times. Mainly from writings of prominent ethnologists; the remainder by Thomas Forsyth and Thomas R. Roddy.

C. Various letters, etc., describing the character and present condition of the Sioux, Potawatomi, and Winnebago tribes; written for this work by missionaries and others who know these peoples well.

APPENDIX A

[The following sketch of Perrot's life is condensed from Tailhan's notes on the explorer's narrative, pages 257-279, 301-308 (see present work, volume i, note 171), and 319-336, of the original publication. This account is given as far as possible in Tailhan's own language, and includes all his statements of facts; but his long citations from La Potherie and others are omitted, as also various unimportant comments and details.]

"We would know [from his memoirs] absolutely nothing about the family of our author, the year and the place of his birth, his youth, and his first expeditions among the savages of the west, if Charlevoix and La Potherie had not, at least in part, made amends for his silence. In this note I have brought together the somewhat scanty records for which we are indebted to them, and of which they too often leave us in ignorance of the exact date. Nicolas Perrot, born in 1644, came (I know not in what year) to New France. He belonged to a respectable but not wealthy family; accordingly, after he had obtained some smattering of knowledge he found that he must break off his studies, in order to enter the service of the missionaries. The Jesuits, at that time dispersed afar among the savage peoples whom war and famine vied in destroying, had soon realized that they could not without rashness place themselves, as regards their subsistence, at the mercy of the poor Indians in the midst of whom they were living. It was therefore necessary for them, as well as for their neophytes, to seek their daily food from hunting, fishing, and agriculture. These toils, to which their earlier education had left them strangers, were besides incompatible with the functions of their ministry. The few European coadjutor brethren who were included in their number being almost as unskilled in these pursuits as were the missionaries themselves, the latter took as associates some young men of the country, who, either gratuitously or for a salary, consented to share their dangers, fatigues, and privations, and made provision for their needs. Fathers Mesnard (*Relation* of 1663, chap. viii), Allouez (*id.* of 1667, chap. xvi), Marquette (*Récit*, chap. i), and many others before or after them, had for companions of their apostolic journeys a certain number of these *donnés* or *engagés*. It is among these latter that Perrot was enrolled, which gave him the opportunity to visit most of the indigenous tribes and to learn their languages (Charlevoix, *Histoire*, vol. i, 437). What was the exact duration of this sort of apprenticeship? I do not know, but it could not have lasted very long. We know, indeed, through La Potherie (*Histoire*, vol. ii, 88, 89) that Perrot was the first to visit the Poutéouatamis, in order to trade with them in 'iron' – that is, in arms and munitions of war. At that time, therefore, he had already quitted the service of the missionaries. But this voyage could not have been made later than 1665; since, on the one hand, Perrot went from the Poutéouatamis and arrived among the Outagamis in the very year following the settlement of this latter tribe in the neighborhood of the Sakis and the Bay (La Potherie, *Histoire*, vol. ii, 99), and, on the other, this migration of the Outagamis was accomplished by the year 1665 (*Relation* of 1667, chap. x). We are then necessarily led to assign to Perrot's engagement a length of only four or five years at most (from 1660 to 1664 or 1665); for we can hardly suppose that Perrot became companion to the missionaries before his sixteenth year." The statement that he was the first Frenchman to visit the Poutéouatamis (who had been settled at the entrance to Green Bay since 1638) seems to conflict with the other one (*Relation* of 1660, chap. iii) that they had been visited by two Frenchmen in 1654; but La Potherie may refer to only one of the villages of that tribe, the one farthest up the bay. But, however that may be, "it is certain that before 1670 Perrot made several journeys among the various tribes of the Bay of Puans and of Wisconsin. . . Perrot was not a common trader, occupied solely with his own interests and those of his employers. From the beginning of his career he realized how important it was to the Colony and to France to see all the peoples of the west united together against their common enemy, the Iroquois. Accordingly, having learned on his arrival among the Poutéouatamis that hostilities had already broken out between those Indians and their neighbors the Maloumines or wild-rice people, from whom his hosts feared an attack – all the more to be dreaded just then because all their warriors were at Montréal trading – he offered to go in person to negotiate peace with their enemies. This proposition was welcomed with gratitude by the old men of the tribe, and Perrot immediately set out to execute his mission." (See La Potherie's *His-*

toire, vol. ii, 90-98, for account of this embassy and its success, and
Perrot's welcome by the grateful Poutéouatamis.) "These attentions,
these marks of honor, and these enthusiastic demonstrations were not
as disinterested as might be supposed. Perrot somewhere observes
that in their traffic with Europeans the savages are such only in
name, and can employ more skilfully than they the means most certain for securing their own ends. The object which in this case they
proposed to attain was to gain the confidence of Perrot and the
merchants of the colony, to bring the French among themselves to
the exclusion of other peoples, and thus to become the necessary
middlemen for the commerce of New France with all the Indians of
the west. It was with this purpose that they sought to prevent, as
far as possible, the establishment of direct relations between Perrot
and the more remote tribes, by hastening to send deputies to those
tribes, commissioned to inform them of the alliance of the Poutéouatamis with the French, the voyage of the former to Montreal, and
their return with a great quantity of merchandise – for which they
invited those distant peoples to come and exchange their furs. But
if they had an object Perrot had also his own, from which he did not
allow himself to turn aside. His patriotism and his adventurous
spirit urged him on to visit for himself the various tribes of the Bay
and of adjoining regions; and in dealing with them personally he
endeavored to attach them to himself and to France, and he accomplished this in the course of the following years.

"The Outagamis or Renards, driven from their ancient abodes by
fear of the Iroquois, had taken refuge at a place called Ouestatinong,
twenty-five or thirty leagues from the Bay of Puans, toward the
southwest (*Relation* of 1670, chap. xii). The exact time of this
migration is not known to us. What is certain is, that (1) it took
place after 1658, since the Outagamis do not figure in the enumeration of the peoples of the Bay and of Méchingan given in the *Relation*
of that year (chap. v); and (2) that it was already made at the end
of 1665 (cf. *supra*). This tribe, of Algonquin race, were relatives
and allies of the Sakis, whose language they spoke (*Relation* of 1667,
chap. x; *id.* of 1670, chap. xii; Perrot, 154). This is why they sent,
in the spring of the year which followed their new settlement, deputies commissioned to announce to the latter tribe their arrival. The
Sakis, in their turn, resolved to despatch some chiefs as ambassadors
to congratulate the Outagamis on their coming to that region, and to
entreat them not to move any farther. Perrot did not let slip this

opportunity to visit a tribe which until then had had no intercourse
with the French (La Potherie, *Histoire*, vol. ii, 99, 173). It will
be easy for us to follow him, thanks to Fathers Allouez and Dablon,
who soon afterward made the same voyage, and have given us a
curious and circumstantial narrative of their itinerary (*Relation* of
1670, chap. xii; *id.* of 1671, 3rd part, chap. v)." This voyage was
up the Fox River to Lake Winnebago, thence up the upper Fox and
the Wolf Rivers to the Outagami village. Perrot also made a
journey to the Maskoutens and Miamis, who had fled for refuge to
the upper Fox River, above the Wolf. "It is to be believed that, in
the course of these few years, Perrot made still other voyages; but
the two which I have just narrated are the only ones on which the
old historians of Canada have furnished me any information. I will
content myself, therefore, with adding to what has gone before the
fact that when Perrot returned to the colony with the Ottawa fleet
[1670], he had already visited the greater number of the savage
tribes of the west; and that he had gained their confidence so far that
he persuaded them to do whatever he wished (Charlevoix, *Histoire*,
vol. i, 436). The Algonquins loved and esteemed him (Perrot,
119); and the various tribes of the bay honored him as their father
(La Potherie, *Histoire*, vol. ii, 173, 175). In a word, he was the
man best prepared in all New France for discharging the mission
which Monsieur de Courcelles was soon to entrust to him (Charlevoix, *ut supra*)."

"After this very inglorious campaign [1684] Perrot actually returned to the Puante River, in the seigniory of Becancourt, where
from 1681 (as the census of that year shows us) he had possessed a
dwelling and a land-grant of eighteen arpents. At that same time
Perrot had been married about ten years, since the eldest of his six
children was then fully nine years old. Although Perrot had inherited, in right of his wife, Madeleine Raclos, a considerable amount
of property, his affairs were none the less much embarrassed in the
present year 1684. We allow him to explain the matter himself, in
a letter to Monsieur de Saint Martin, one of his creditors, and
notary-royal at Cap de la Madeleine:

From the Puante River, this twentieth of August, 1684.
MONSIEUR: I have received your letter, by which I see that you
demand what is quite just. I would not have delayed so long to visit
you and all those to whom I am indebted, if I had brought in the peltries
which I left behind on account of the orders given me to come to the
war . . . if I had those in my possession, I would be bolder than I

am to go to find my creditors; but as I brought back nothing, even to pay for the merchandise [that I carried out], for fear of being punished for disobedience, I am ashamed. That will not prevent me from going down to Quebec to procure merchandise; if I bring back goods that suit you, you will dispose of them; if not, I will try to satisfy your claim in some other way, if I can. I am not the only one who has come down without bringing back anything. I expected to go to the Cap [de la Madeleine], in order to give you proof of what I am writing to you; but Monsieur de Villiers is sending me with some letters to Quebecq, which obliges me to give up going to see you until after my return. Believe me, I intend to give you satisfaction, or I could not do so. Your very humble servant,   N. PERROT.

In the course of the following years, the condition of affairs caused only more troubles for Perrot and for many others. The Iroquois closed all the passages, and no longer permitted the fleets of the Ottawas and the Canadian voyageurs to come down to the colony with their peltries, from which sprang universal poverty and misery. Monsieur de Champigny, intendant of New France, wrote in his despatch of August 9, 1688 (in the archives of the Marine): 'The merchants are still in a most deplorable condition; all their wealth has been in the woods for the last three or four years. It is impossible for them to avoid being considerably indebted in France; and, in a word, when the fur-trade fails for one year, very fortunate is he who has bread.' While awaiting a favorable opportunity for transporting to Montreal the produce of his trading, Perrot had deposited it in the buildings of St. François Xavier mission, at the Bay of Puans; but while he followed the Marquis de Denonville in his expedition against the Tsonnontouan Iroquois, a fire consumed the church, the adjoining buildings, and the 40,000 livres' worth of peltries which Perrot had left there (La Potherie, *Histoire*, vol. ii, 209)." [For Perrot's activities in 1685-1686, see volume i, note 171. – ED.]

On returning to the colony, Perrot endeavored to retrieve his ruinous losses of property by a new trading voyage to the west; and he obtained from Denonville the same office, with nearly the same authority, as that which La Barre had conferred on him. Probably in the autumn of 1687, he went to Green Bay, and thence to the upper Mississippi, to the fort which he had built there a few years before. While there, he traded with the Dakotas, and persuaded them to permit his taking possession of that region for France (1689). He returned to Montreal, on the way stopping at Michillimakinak and procuring the release of some Iroquois prisoners whom the Ottawas were about to burn at the stake; and the latter sent with him one of their chiefs to deliver the rescued captives to the governor. But soon after their arrival at Montreal an Iroquois army surprised (Aug. 25, 1689) the village of Lachine, massacred or captured its inhabitants, and ravaged Montreal Island. The French and the friendly Indians were overcome with fear, and the savages of the upper country were filled with contempt for the French, and the desire to protect themselves from danger by concluding a peace with the Iroquois and the English; knowing that this would be ruinous to the French colony, La Durantaye and the Jesuit missionaries at Michillimakinak labored to retain the Indians in the French alliance. Fortunately at this crisis, Count de Frontenac arrived at Quebec (Oct. 12, 1689), and immediately formed a plan to draw all the Algonquian tribes into an offensive alliance with the French against the Iroquois; to gain over to this the tribes of the northwest, he sent Perrot (May 22, 1690) with presents as his envoy to them – an undertaking in which the latter was successful. Frontenac sent armies against the Iroquois, into their own country, and thus broke up their previous mastery of the St. Lawrence route; so that in 1693 a fleet of two hundred Ottawa canoes brought down to Montreal 800,000 livres worth of peltries. In 1692, Perrot received orders to go to reside among the Miamis of the Marameg River, at the same time, however, apparently retaining his authority over the tribes about Green Bay; he was sent thither "on account of its being important to maintain that post against the new expeditions which the Iroquois might make in that quarter" (Letter of Callières, Oct. 27, 1695). Indeed, in that very year a band of Iroquois had endeavored to surprise the Miamis there; but the latter, with the aid of the French at the post (under command of Courtemanche) had repulsed the enemy. In the summer of the same year Perrot had gone to Montreal with chiefs of the various tribes under his control, who were received in audience by Frontenac. The governor urged the Miamis of the Marameg to unite with their tribesmen on the St. Joseph; under the influence of Frontenac and Perrot they seem to have consented, although somewhat reluctantly, to this removal. During the next few years Perrot had much to do with the western tribes, and encountered many adventures and even dangers. "The principal occupation of our author was, as before, to maintain harmony and peace among those tribes, always ready to tear one another in pieces, and to urge them to wage war against the Iroquois. That was a work as thankless as difficult, because it was hardly accomplished when it became necessary to begin it again on some new ground, so inconstant and fickle is the will of those peoples, whose 'wild young men, who are braves without discipline or any appearance of subordination, at the first glance or the first brandy debauch overthrow all the deliberations of the old men, who are no longer obeyed' (Letter of Denonville, May 8, 1686)." This fickleness was often displayed against even Perrot, whose property was seized by them, and who even was in danger of being burned at the stake by the Maskoutens (about 1693) and again by the Miamis (in 1696). In the latter case, chiefs from the other tribes offered their services to Frontenac to avenge the injuries of Perrot; but he knew their hatred to the Miamis, and discreetly declined this proposal. The governor was a firm friend of Perrot, and if he had lived would doubtless have enabled him to recoup his losses; but the death of Frontenac (November 28, 1698) deprived Perrot of a protector, and about the same time the court of France abolished the trading permits and ordered that the posts at Michillimakinak and St. Joseph be abandoned, and all the French soldiers and traders recalled to the colony (Letter of Champigny, Oct. 15, 1698; in archives of the Marine). As a result, Perrot was "completely ruined, and harassed by numerous creditors;" and his appeals to both the colonial and the royal governments were rejected – although Callières suggested that the latter grant a small pension to relieve the poverty of the unfortunate explorer, a request which seems to have been entirely ignored. But the same neglect was experienced by other faithful servants of the French cause – for instance, La Durantaye and Jolliet, who were reduced to the same extremity (see Raudot's "List of those interested in the Company of Canada," 1708; in archives of the Marine).

In the summer of 1701 Perrot was called to act as interpreter at a general conference of the Indian tribes that was held there. On this occasion those of the west who had been under his command entreated the governor to send him back to them, and displayed the utmost esteem and affection for him; this request was made by the Potawatomi chief, Ounanguissé, the Outagami chief, Noro, and the orator of the Ottawas and their allies, but was met only by vague promises, which were never fulfilled. See La Potherie, *Histoire*, vol. iv, 212-214, 257. The Marquis de Vaudreuil, who succeeded Callières as governor, was fortunately always a warm friend of Perrot and his family, and seems to have conferred on the former a command in the militia of the seigniories on the St. Lawrence, which carried with it a small salary and comparatively light duties. The leisure thus obtained by Perrot was spent largely in writing his various memoirs. He was still living in 1718, as is evident from his allusion at the end of chap. xxvii to Louvigny's expeditions (1716, 1717) to punish and afterward pacify the Outagamis. Further information regarding Perrot's later years is not available. "In his humble sphere, he always proved himself brave, loyal, and devoted; and as a writer he was, although without doubt unpolished and unskilful, yet honest – one who has in his memoirs known how to speak of himself without boasting, and of others without fawning, without jealousy, and without vilification." "The memoir that we have just published is the only one of all Perrot's writings which has reached us." From allusions therein, it is evident that he also wrote (1) a memoir on the Outagamis, addressed to Vaudreuil; and (2) several memoirs on the wars between the Iroquois and the western tribes, and on the various acts of treachery committed by the Indians, especially by the Hurons and Ottawas.

– TAILHAN.

An interesting and well-written sketch of Perrot's life forms no. 1 of the Parkman Club *Papers* (Milwaukee, 1896); it was prepared by Gardner P. Stickney. He has based it mainly on Tailhan's notes, but has collected other mention and minor details from Charlevoix, Parkman, Neill, and other writers. – ED.

APPENDIX B

[Here is presented information on various topics regarding Indian society, character, and religious beliefs, which seems more appropriately grouped here than scattered through the work, especially as some of the subjects are inconveniently long or general for footnotes. These articles are chiefly taken from the *Handbook of Amer. Indians*, vol. ii; the exceptions are obtained, as indicated, from excellent authorities. As will be noted, they are arranged in logical sequence, as far as possible. – ED.]

Social Organization

"North American tribes contained (1) subdivisions of a geographic or consanguineal character; (2) social and governmental classes or bodies, especially chiefs and councils, with particular powers and privileges; and (3) fraternities of a religious or semi-religious character, the last of which are especially treated under article 'Secret Societies.' Tribes may be divided broadly into those in which the organization was loose, the subdivisions being families or bands and descent being counted prevailingly from father to son; and those which were divided into clearly defined groups called gentes or clans, which were strictly exogamic and more often reckoned descent through the mother. Among the former may be placed the Eskimo," the Cree, Montagnais, and Cheyenne, of Algonquian tribes, the Kiowa, etc.; in the latter divisions are the Pueblos, Navaho, and the majority of tribes in the Atlantic and Gulf States, and some others. "Where clans exist the distinctive character of each is very strongly defined and a man can become a member only by birth, adoption, or transfer in infancy from his mother's to his father's clan, or vice versa. Each clan generally possessed some distinctive totem from which the majority of the persons belonging to it derived their names, certain rights, carvings, and ceremonies in common, and often the exclusive right to a tract of land. Although the well-defined caste system of the north Pacific coast, based on property and the institution of slavery, does not seem to have had a parallel elsewhere north of Mexico except perhaps among the

Natchez, bravery in war, wisdom in council, oratorical, poetical, or artistic talents, real or supposed psychic powers – in short, any variety of excellence whatever served in all Indian tribes to give one prominence among his fellows, and it is not strange that popular recognition of a man's ability sometimes reacted to the benefit of his descendants. Although it was always a position of great consequence, leadership in war was generally separate from and secondary to the civil chieftainship. Civil leadership and religious primacy were much more commonly combined. Among the Pueblos all three are united, forming a theocracy. Councils of a democratic, unconventional kind, in which wealthy persons or those of most use to the tribe had the greatest influence, were universal where no special form of council was established. . . The tribes possessing a well-defined clan system are divided into three groups – the north Pacific, southwestern, and eastern. . . Among the Plains Indians the Omaha had a highly organized social system. The tribe was divided into ten gentes called 'villages,' with descent through the father, each of which had one chief. Seven of these chiefs constituted a sort of oligarchy, and two of them, representing the greatest amount of wealth, exercised superior authority. The functions of these chiefs were entirely civil; they never headed war parties. Below them were two orders of warriors, from the higher of which men were selected to act as policemen during the buffalo hunt. Under all were those who had not yet attained to eminence. During the buffalo hunts and great ceremonials the tribe encamped in a regular circle with one opening, like most other plains tribes. In it each gens and even each family had its definite position. The two halves of this circle, composed of five clans each, had different names, but they do not appear to have corresponded to the phratries of more eastern Indians. A man was not permitted to marry into the gens of his father, and marriage into that of his mother was rare and strongly disapproved. Other plains tribes of the Siouan family probably were organized in much the same manner and reckoned descent similarly. The Dakota are traditionally reputed to have been divided into seven council fires, each of which was at one time divided into two or three major and a multitude of minor bands. Whatever their original condition may have been their organization is now much looser than that of the Omaha. . . The social organization of the western and northern Algonquian tribes is not well known. The Siksika [more commonly known as Blackfeet] have numerous subdivisions which have been called gentes; they are characterized by descent through the father, but would appear to be more truly local groups. Each had originally its own chief, and the council composed of these chiefs selected the chief of the tribe, their choice being governed rather by the character of the person than by his descent. The head chief's authority was made effective largely through the voluntary coöperation of several societies. The Chippewa, Potawatomi, Menominee, Miami, Shawnee, and Abnaki in historic times have had gentes, with paternal descent, which Morgan believed had developed from a material stage; but this view must be taken with caution, inasmuch as there never has been a question as to the form of descent among the Delawares, who were subjected to white influences at an earlier date than most of those supposed to have changed. . . The most advanced social organization north of the Pueblo country was probably that developed by the Iroquois confederated tribes. Each tribe consisted of two or more phratries, which in turn embraced one or more clans, named after various animals or objects, while each clan consisted of one or more kinship groups called *ohwachira*. When the tribes combined to form the confederacy called the Five Nations they were arranged in three phratries, of two, two, and one tribes respectively. There were originally forty-eight hereditary chieftainships in the five tribes, and subsequently the number was raised to fifty. Each chieftainship was held by some one *ohwachira*, and the selection of a person to fill it devolved on the child-bearing women of the clan to which it belonged, more particularly those of the *ohwachira* which owned it. The selection had to be confirmed afterward by the tribal and league councils successively. Along with each chief a vice-chief was elected, who sat in the tribal council with the chief proper, and also acted for a leader in time of war, but the chief only sat in the grand council of the confederacy."– J. R. SWANTON, in *Handbook Amer. Indians.*

Totems

"Totem" is a corruption by travelers and traders of the Chippewa *nind otem* or *kitotem*, meaning "my own family," "thy own family" – thence, by extension, "tribe," or "race." "The totem represented an emblem that was sacred in character and referred to one of the elements, a heavenly body, or some natural form. If an element, the device was symbolic; if an object, it might be represented realistically or by its known sign or symbol. An animal represented by the 'totem' was always generic; if a bear or an eagle, no particular bear or eagle was meant. The clan frequently took its name from the 'totem' and its members might be spoken of as Bear people, Eagle people, etc. Variants of the word 'totem' were used by tribes speaking languages belonging to the Algonquian stock, but to all other tribes the word was foreign and unknown." The use of this term is too often indiscriminate and incorrect, which has obscured its real meaning. "As the emblem of a family or clan, it had two aspects: (1) the religious, which concerned man's relations to the forces about him, and involved the origin of the emblem as well as the methods by which it was secured; and (2) the social, which pertained to man's relation to his fellow-men and the means by which an emblem became the hereditary mark of a family, a clan, or society. There were three classes of 'totems:' the individual, the society, and the clan 'totem.' Research indicates that the individual 'totem' was the fundamental." This personal "totem" was most often selected from the objects seen in dreams or visions, since there was a general belief that such an object became the medium of supernatural help in time of need, and for this purpose would furnish a man, in his dream, with a song or a peculiar call by which to summon it to his help. The religious societies were generally independent of the clan organization; but sometimes they were in close connection with the clan and the membership under its control. The influence of the "totem" idea was most developed in the clan, "where the emblem of the founder of a kinship group became the hereditary mark of the composite clan, with its fixed, obligatory duties on all members. . . The idea of supernatural power was attached to the clan 'totem.' This power, however, was not shown, as in the personal 'totem,' by according help to individuals, but was manifested in the punishment of forgetfulness of kinship. . . While homage was ceremonially rendered to the special power represented by the 'totem' of the clan or of the society, the 'totem' itself was not an object of worship. Nor was the object symbolized considered as the actual ancestor of the people; the members of the Bear clan did not believe they were descended from a bear, nor were they always prohibited from hunting the animal, although they might be forbidden to eat of its flesh or to touch certain parts of its body. The unification and strength of the clan and tribal structure depended largely on the restraining fear of supernatural punishment by the 'totemic' powers, a fear fostered by the vital belief in the potency of the personal 'totem.' "

– ALICE C. FLETCHER, in *Handbook Amer. Indians.*

Mode of Life

It is a popular fallacy that the Indians were generally nomadic, having no fixed place of abode; "the term nomadic is not, in fact, properly applicable to any Indian tribe." With some few exceptions, every tribe or group of tribes "laid claim to and dwelt within the limits of a certain tract or region, the boundaries of which were well understood, and were handed down by tradition and not ordinarily relinquished save to a superior force." There were some debatable areas, owned by none but claimed by all, over which many disputes and intertribal wars arose. "Most or all of the tribes east of the Mississippi except in the north, and some west of it, were to a greater or less extent agricultural and depended much for food on the products of their tillage. During the hunting season such tribes or villages broke up into small parties and dispersed over their domains more or less widely in search of game; or they visited the seashore for fish and shellfish. Only in this restricted sense may they be said to be nomadic." Even the plains Indians, who wandered far in hunting the buffalo, had a certain hold on their tribal territories and recognized the rights of their neighbors. The natives of the far north, owing to environment and geographical conditions, most nearly approached the nomadic life. – HENRY W. HENSHAW, in *Handbook Amer. Indians*, art. "Popular fallacies."

"Each North American tribe claimed a certain locality as its habitat, and dwelt in communities or villages about which stretched its hunting grounds. As all the inland people depended for food largely on the gathering of acorns, seeds, and roots, the catching of salmon when ascending the streams, or on hunting for meat and skin clothing, they camped in makeshift shelters or portable dwellings during a considerable part of the year. These dwellings were brush shelters, the mat house and birch-bark lodge of the forest tribes, and the skin tent of the plains. . . Hunting, visiting, or war parties were more or less organized. The leader was generally the head of a family or of a kindred group, or he was appointed to his office with certain ceremonies. He decided the length of a day's journey, and where the camp should be made at night. As all property, save a man's personal clothing, weapons, and riding horses, belonged to the woman, its care during a journey fell upon her. . . When a camping place was reached the mat houses were erected as was most convenient for the family group, but the skin tents were set up in a circle, near of kin being neighbors. If danger from enemies was apprehended, the ponies and other valuable possessions were kept within the space inclosed by the circle of tents. Long journeys were frequently undertaken for friendly visits or for intertribal ceremonies. . . When the tribes of the buffalo country went on their annual hunt, ceremonies attended every stage, from the initial rites (when the leader was chosen), throughout the journeyings, to the thanksgiving ceremony which closed the expedition. The long procession was escorted by warriors selected by the leader and the chiefs for their trustiness and valor. They acted as a police guard to prevent any straggling that might result in personal or tribal danger; and they prevented any private hunting, as it might stampede a herd that might be in the vicinity. When on the annual hunt the tribe camped in a circle and preserved its political divisions, and the circle was often a quarter of a mile or more in diameter. Sometimes the camp was in concentric circles, each circle representing a political group of kindred. . . The tribal circle, each segment composed of a clan, gens, or band, made a living picture of tribal organization and responsibilities. It impressed upon the beholder the relative position of kinship groups and their interdependence, both for the maintenance of order and government within and for defense against enemies from without; while the opening to the east and the position of the ceremonial tents recalled the religious rites and obligations by which the many parts were held together in a compact whole."

– ALICE C. FLETCHER, in *Handbook Amer. Indians.*

Mental and Moral Traits

"The mental functions of the Indian should be compared with those of whites reared and living under approximately similar circumstances. On closer observation the differences in the fundamental psychical manifestations between the two races are found to be small. No instincts not possessed by whites have developed in the Indian. His proficiency in tracking and concealment, his sense of direction, etc., are accounted for by his special training and practice, and are not found in the Indian youth who has not had such experience. The Indian lacks much of the ambition known to the white man, yet he shows more or less of the quality where his life affords a chance for it."

"The emotional life of the Indian is more moderate and ordinarily more free from extremes of nearly every nature, than that of the white person. The prevalent subjective state is that of content in well-being, with inclination to humor. Pleasurable emotions predominate, but seldom rise beyond the moderate; those of a painful nature are occasionally very pronounced. Maternal love is strong, especially during the earlier years of the child. Sexual love is rather simply organic, not of so intellectual an order as among whites; but this seems to be largely the result of views and customs governing sex relations and marriage. The social instinct and that of self-preservation are much like those of white people. Emotions of anger and hatred are infrequent and of normal character. Fear is rather easily aroused at all ages, in groups of children occasionally reaching a panic; but this is likewise due in large measure to peculiar beliefs and untrammeled imagination."

"Modesty, morality, and the sense of right and justice are as natural to the Indian as to the white man, but, as in other respects, are modified in the former by prevalent views and conditions of life. Transgressions of every character are less frequent in the Indian. Memory (of sense impressions as well as of mental acts proper) is generally fair. Where the faculty has been much exercised in one direction, as in religion, it acquires remarkable capacity in that particular. The young exhibit good memory for languages. The faculty of will is strongly developed. Intellectual activities proper are comparable with those of ordinary healthy whites, though on the whole, and excepting the sports, the mental processes are probably habitually slightly slower. Among many tribes lack of thrift, improvidence, absence of demonstrative manifestations, and the previously mentioned lack of ambition are observable; but these peculiarities must be charged largely, if not entirely, to differences in mental training and habits. The reasoning of the Indian and his ideation, though modified by his views, have often been shown to be excellent. His power of imitation, and even of invention, is good, as is his aptitude in several higher arts and in oratory. An Indian child reared under the care of whites, educated in the schools of civilization, and without having acquired the notions of its people, is habitually much like a white child trained in a similar degree under similar conditions." – ALES HRDLICKA, in *Handbook Amer. Indians*, art. "Physiology."

"The idea of the Indian, once popular, suggests a taciturn and stolid character, who smoked his pipe in silence and stalked reserved and dignified among his fellows. Unquestionably the Indian of the Atlantic slope differed in many respects from his kinsmen farther west; it may be that the forest Indian of the north and east imbibed something of the spirit of the primeval woods which, deep and gloomy, overspread much of his region. If so, he has no counterpart in the regions west of the Mississippi. On occasions of ceremony and religion the western Indian can be both dignified and solemn, as befits the occasion; but his nature, if not as bright and sunny as that of the Polynesian, is at least as far removed from moroseness as his disposition is from taciturnity. The Indian of the present day has at least a fair sense of humor and is by no means a stranger to jest, laughter, and even repartee." – HENRY W. HENSHAW, in *Handbook Amer. Indians*, art. "Popular fallacies."

"The specific question of psychological differences between Indians and other races is still an unsolved problem," on account of the lack of adequate data as a basis for conclusions. Some work has been done in the study and comparison of these differences, but the results are insufficient for definite general statements. Conflicting theories are in vogue among anthropologists – one that "the existence of cultural differences necessitates the existence of psychological differences;" another, that those "cultural differences are not due to psychological differences, but to causes entirely external, or outside of the conscious life," and "considers culture as the sum of habits into which the various groups of mankind have fallen." But thus far neither theory has been satisfactorily proved. "In conclusion, it appears that we have no satisfactory knowledge of the elemental psychological activities among Indians, because they have not been made the subjects of research by trained psychologists. On the other hand, it may be said that in all the larger aspects of mental life they are qualitatively similar to other races." – *Handbook Amer. Indians*, art. "Psychology."

Religious Beliefs

"Religious views and actions are not primarily connected with ethical concepts. Only in so far as in his religious relations to the outer world man endeavors to follow certain rules of conduct, in order to avoid evil effects, is a relation between primitive religion and ethics established. The religious concepts of the Indians may be described in two groups – those that concern the individual, and those that concern the social group, such as tribe and clan. The fundamental concept bearing upon the religious life of the individual is the belief in the existence of magic power, which may influence the life of man, and which in turn may be influenced by human activity. In this sense magic power must be understood as the wonderful qualities which are believed to exist in objects, animals, men, spirits, or deities, and which are superior to the natural qualities of man. This idea of magic power is one of the fundamental concepts that occurs among all Indian tribes. It is what is called *manito* by the Algonquian tribes; *wakanda*, by the Siouan tribes; *orenda*, by the Iroquois," etc. "The degree to which the magic power of nature is individualized differs considerably among various tribes. Although the belief in the powers of inanimate objects is common, we find in America that, on the whole, animals, particularly the larger ones, are most frequently considered as possessed of such magic power. Strong anthropomorphic individualization also occurs, which justifies us in calling these powers deities. It seems probable that among the majority of tribes besides the belief in the power of specific objects, a belief in a magic power that is only vaguely localized exists. In cases where this belief is pronounced, the notion sometimes approaches the concept of a deity or of a great spirit, which is hardly anthropomorphic in its character. This is the case, for instance, among the Tsimshian of British Columbia and among the Algonquian tribes of the great lakes, and also in the figure of the Tirawa of the Pawnee. . . The whole concept of the world – or, in other words, the mythology of each tribe – enters to a very great extent into their religious concepts and activities. The mythologies are highly specialized in different parts of North America; and, although a large number of myths are the common property of many American tribes, the general view of the world appears to be quite distinct in various parts of the continent." In the explanation of the world, the Indian view is quite different from that of the Semitic mind. The former "accepts the eternal existence of the world, and accounts for its specific form by the assumption that events which once happened in early times settled for once and all the form in which the same kind of event must continue to occur. For instance, when the bear produced the stripes of the chipmunk by scratching its back, this determined that all chipmunks were to have such stripes; or when an ancestor of a clan was taught a certain ceremony, that same ceremony must be performed by all future generations. This idea is not by any means confined to America, but is found among primitive peoples of other continents as well, and occurs even in Semitic cults."

In considering American mythologies five great areas may be distinguished: (1) The Eskimo area, its mythology characterized by many purely human hero-tales, and a very few traditions accounting for the origin of animals (and these mainly in human setting); (2) the North Pacific, "characterized by a large circle of transformer myths, in which the origin of many of the arts of man are accounted for, as well as the peculiarities of many animals; (3) the similar traditions of the western plateau and of the Mackenzie basin area, in which animal tales abound, many accounting for the present conditions of the world; (4) the Californian, "characterized by a stronger emphasis laid upon creation by will-power than is found in most other parts of the American continent;" and (5) the great plains, the eastern woodlands, and the arid southwest, where the tendency to "systematization of the myths under the influence of a highly developed ritual. This tendency is more sharply defined in the south than in the north and northeast," and has made most progress among the Pueblo and the Pawnee. "The religious concepts of the Indians deal largely with the relation of the individual to the magic power mentioned above, and are specialized in accordance with their general mythological concepts, which determine largely the degree to which the powers are personified as animals, spirits, or deities.

"Another group of religious concepts, which are not less important than the group heretofore discussed, refers to the relations of the individual to his internal states, so far as these are not controlled by the will, and are therefore considered as subject to external magic influences. Most important among these are dreams, sickness, and death. These may be produced by obsession, or by external forces which compel the soul to leave the body. In this sense the soul is considered by almost all the tribes as not subject to the individual will; it may be abstracted from the body by hostile forces, and it may be damaged and killed. The concept of the soul itself shows a great variety of forms. Very often the soul is identified with life, but we also find commonly the belief in a multiplicity of souls. . . The soul is also identified with the blood, the bones, the shadow, the nape of the neck. Based on these ideas is also the belief in the existence of the soul after death. Thus, in the belief of the Algonquian Indians of the great lakes, the souls of the deceased are believed to reside in the far west with the brother of the great culture-hero [Nanabozho]. Among the Kutenai the belief prevails that the souls will return at a later period, accompanying the culture-hero. Sometimes the land from which the ancestors of the tribe have sprung, which in the south is often conceived of as underground, is of equal importance.

"Since the belief in the existence of magic powers is very strong in the Indian mind, all his actions are regulated by the desire to retain the good-will of those friendly to him and to control those that are hostile." In order to secure the former, the strict observance of a great variety of proscriptions is needed, many of which fall under the designation of taboos — especially those of food and of work; also social. There are also found, all over the continent, numerous regulations intended to retain the good-will of the food animals, and which are essentially signs of respect shown to them; these are especially in vogue in their hunting. "Respectful behavior toward old people and generally decent conduct are also often counted among such required acts. Here also may be included the numerous customs of purification that are required in order to avoid the ill-will of the powers. These, however, may better be considered as a means of controlling magic power, which form a very large part of the religious observances of the American Indians."

"The Indian is not satisfied with the attempt to avoid the ill-will of the powers, but he tries also to make them subservient to his own needs. This may be attained in a variety of ways. Perhaps the most characteristic of all North American methods of gaining control over supernatural powers is that of the acquisition of one of them as a personal protector. Generally this process is called the acquiring of a manito; and the most common method of acquiring it is for the young man during the period of adolescence to purify himself by fasting, bathing, and vomiting, until his body is perfectly clean and acceptable to the supernatural beings. At the same time the youth works himself by these means, by dancing, and sometimes also by means of drugs, into a trance, in which he has a vision of the guardian spirit which is to protect him through life. These means of establishing communication with the spirit world are in very general use also at other periods of life. The magic power that man thus acquires may give him special abilities; it may make him a successful hunter, warrior, or shaman; or it may give him power to acquire wealth, success in gambling, or the love of women."

Magic power may also, in the belief of many tribes, be attained by inheritance; or it may be purchased; or it may be "transmitted by teaching and by bodily contact with a person who controls such powers." Another means of controlling the powers of nature is by prayer; also may be used charms or fetishes. "The charm is either believed to be the seat of magic power, or it may be a symbol of such power, and its action may be based on its symbolic significance; of the former kind are presumably many objects contained in the sacred bundles of certain Indians, which are believed to be possessed of sacred powers." Symbolic actions and divinations are also used for the same purpose.

"Still more potent means of influencing the powers are offerings and sacrifices. On the whole, these are not as strongly developed in

North America as they are in other parts of the world. In many regions human sacrifices were common – for instance, in Mexico and Yucatan – while in North America they are known only in rare instances, as among the Pawnee. However, many cases of torture, particularly of self-torture, must be reckoned here. Other bloody sacrifices are also rare in North America." On the other hand, sacrifices of tobacco smoke, of corn, and of parts of food, of small manufactured objects, and of symbolic objects, are very common."

Another method is "by incantations, which are in a way related to prayers, but which act rather through the magic influence of the words. . . In the same way that incantations are related to prayer, certain acts and charms are related to offerings. We find among almost all Indian tribes the custom of performing certain acts, which are neither symbolic nor offerings, nor other attempts to obtain the assistance of superior beings, but which are effective through their own potency. Such acts are the use of lucky objects intended to secure good fortune; or the peculiar treatment of animals, plants, and other objects, in order to bring about a change of weather. There is also found among most Indian tribes the idea that the supernatural powers, if offended by transgressions of rules of conduct, may be propitiated by punishment. Such punishment may consist in the removal of the offending individual, who may be killed by the members of the tribe, or the propitiation may be accomplished by milder forms of punishment. . . Other forms of punishment are based largely on the idea of purification by fasting, bathing, and vomiting."

Protection against disease is also sought by the help of superhuman powers. These practices have two distinct forms, according to the fundamental conception of disease. Disease is conceived of principally in two forms – either as due to the presence of a material object in the body of the patient, or as an effect of the absence of the soul from the body. The cure of disease is intrusted to the shamans or medicine-men, who obtain their powers generally by the assistance of guardian spirits, or who may be personally endowed with magic powers. It is their duty to discover the material disease which is located in the patient's body, and which they extract by sucking or pulling with the hands; or to go in pursuit of the absent soul, to recover it, and to restore it to the patient. Both of these forms of shamanism are found practically all over the continent;" but in some regions one of these theories of the cause of sickness predominates, in some the other.

"The belief that certain individuals can acquire control over the powers has also led to the opinion that they may be used to harm enemies. The possession of such control is not always beneficial, but may be used also for purposes of witchcraft. Hostile shamans may throw disease into the bodies of their enemies, or they may abduct their souls. They may do harm by sympathetic means, and control the will-power of others by the help of the supernatural means at their disposal. Witchcraft is everywhere considered as a crime, and is so punished."

"Besides those manifestations of religious belief that relate to the individual, religion has become closely associated with the social structure of the tribes; so that the ritualistic side of religion can be understood only in connection with the social organization of the Indian tribes. Even the fundamental traits of their social organization possess a religious import. This is true particularly of the clans, so far as they are characterized by totems. . . Also in cases where the clans have definite political functions, like those of the Omaha or the Iroquois, these functions are closely associated with religious concepts, partly in so far as their origin is ascribed to myths, partly in so far as the functions are associated with the performance of religious rites. The position of officials is also closely associated with definite religious concepts. Thus, the head of a clan at times is considered as the representative of the mythological ancestor of the clan, and as such is believed to be endowed with superior powers; or the position as officer in the tribe or clan entails the performance of certain definite religious functions. In this sense many of the political functions among Indian tribes are closely associated with what may be termed 'priestly functions.' The religious significance of social institutions is most clearly marked in cases where the tribe, or large parts of the tribe, join in the performance of certain ceremonies which are intended to serve partly a political, partly a religious end. Such acts are some of the intertribal ball-games," the sun-dance and the performances of the warrior societies of the plains, and the secret societies in so many tribes. "It is characteristic of rituals in many parts of the world that they tend to develop into a more or less dramatic representation of the myth from which the ritual is derived. For this reason the use of masks is a common feature of these rituals, in which certain individuals impersonate supernatural beings. . . It would seem that the whole system of religious beliefs and practices has developed the more systematically the more strictly the religious practices have come to be in the charge of priests. This tendency to systematization of religious beliefs may be observed particularly among the Pueblo and the Pawnee, but it also occurs in isolated cases in other parts of the continent; for instance, among the Bellacoola of British Columbia, and those Algonquian tribes that have the Midewiwin ceremony fully developed. In these cases we find that frequently an elaborate series of esoteric doctrines and practices exist, which are known to only a small portion of the tribe, while the mass of the people are familiar only with part of the ritual and with its exoteric features. For this reason we often find the religious beliefs and practices of the mass of a tribe rather heterogeneous as compared with the beliefs held by the priests. Among many of the tribes in which priests are found we find distinct esoteric societies, and it is not by any means rare that the doctrines of one society are not in accord with those of another. All this is clearly due to the fact that the religious ideas of the tribe are derived from many different sources, and have been brought into order at a later date by the priests charged with the keeping of the tribal rituals. . . It would seem that, on the whole, the import of the esoteric teachings decreases among the more northerly and northeasterly tribes of the continent."

"On the whole, the Indians incline strongly toward all forms of religious excitement. This is demonstrated not only by the exuberant development of ancient religious forms, but also by the frequency with which prophets have appeared among them, who taught new doctrines and new rites, based either on older religious beliefs, or on teachings partly of Christian, partly of Indian origin. Perhaps the best known of these forms of religion is the ghost-dance, which swept over a large part of the continent during the last years of the nineteenth century. But other prophets of similar type and of far-reaching influence were quite numerous. One of these was Tenskwatawa, the famous brother of Tecumseh; another, the seer Smohallah, who founded the sect of Shakers of the Pacific Coast; and even among the Eskimo such prophets have been known, particularly in Greenland." – FRANZ BOAS, in *Handbook Amer. Indians*, art. "Religion."

"In their endeavors to secure the help of the supernatural powers, the Indians, as well as other peoples, hold principally three methods: (1) The powers may be coerced by the strength of a ritualistic performance; (2) their help may be purchased by gifts in the form of sacrifices and offerings; or (3) they may be approached by prayer. Frequently the coercing ritualistic performance and the sacrifice are accompanied by prayers; or the prayer itself may take a ritualistic form, and thus attain coercive power.   In this case the prayer is called an incantation.   Prayers may either be spoken words, or they may be expressed by symbolic objects, which are placed so that they convey the wishes of the worshiper to the powers. . . Very often prayers accompany sacrifices. . . Prayers of this kind very commonly accompany the sacrifice of food to the souls of the deceased, as among the Algonquian tribes, Eskimo, and n.w. coast Indians.   The custom of expressing prayers by means of symbolic objects is found principally among the southwestern tribes.   ["The so-called prayer stick of the Kickapoo was a mnemonic device for Christian prayer." – WALTER HOUGH.]   Prayers are often preceded by ceremonial purification, fasting, the use of emetics and purgatives, which are intended to make the person praying agreeable to the powers.   Among the North American Indians the prayer cannot be considered as necessarily connected with sacrifice or as a substitute for sacrifice, since in a great many cases prayers for good luck, for success, for protection, or for the blessing of the powers, are offered quite independently of the idea of sacrifice.   While naturally material benefits are the object of prayer in by far the majority of cases, prayers for an abstract blessing and for ideal objects are not by any means absent. . . The Indians pray not only to those supernatural powers which are considered the protectors of man – like the personal guardians or the powers of nature – but also to the hostile powers who must be appeased."

– FRANZ BOAS, in *Handbook Amer. Indians*

Tawiskaron was "an imaginary man-being of the cosmogonic philosophy of the Iroquoian and other tribes, to whom was attributed the function of making and controlling the activities and phenomena of winter.   He was the Winter God, the Ice King, since his distinctive character is clearly defined in terms of the activities and phenomena of nature peculiar to this season.   As an earth-power he was one of the great primal man-beings belonging to the second cosmical period of the mythological philosophy of the Iroquoian, Algonquian, and perhaps other Indians."   According to the legends, he was a grandson of Awĕⁿ'ha'i (the Ataentsic of Huron mythology), or Mother Earth; and at his birth his body was composed of flint, and he caused the death of his mother by violently bursting through her armpit – a fault which he cast on his twin brother, Teharonhiawagon (or Jouskeha of the Hurons), who in consequence was hated by the grandmother. Teharonhiawagon was the embodiment or personification of life; he was the creator and maker of the animals, birds, trees, and plants, and finally of man. From his father of mysterious origin he had learned the art of fire-making, and that of agriculture, and how to build a house; and these arts he communicated to mankind. In all his beneficent endeavors he was opposed by Awĕⁿ'ha'i and Tawiskaron, who continually strove to thwart his plans; but by the counsels of his father and his superior magic power he was able to gain the ascendency over them and became (at a contest in playing the game of bowl) the ruler of the world. "The great and most important New Year ceremony among the Iroquois who still hold to their ancient faith and customs, at which is burned a purely white dog as a sacrifice, is held in honor of Teharonhiawagon for his works, blessings, and goodness, which have been enjoyed by the people." – J. N. B. HEWITT, ir Handbook Amer. Indians.

Tawiskaron is practically identical with Chakekenapok in Algonquian mythology, a younger brother of Nanabozho.

Prophets

"From time to time in every great tribe and every important crisis of Indian history we find certain men rising above the position of ordinary doctor, soothsayer, or ritual priest to take upon themselves an apostleship of reform and return to the uncorrupted ancestral belief and custom as the necessary means to save their people from impending destruction by decay or conquest. In some cases the teaching takes the form of a new Indian gospel, the revolutionary culmination of a long and silent development of the native religious thought. As the faithful disciples were usually promised the return of the earlier and happier conditions, the restoration of the diminished game, the expulsion of the alien intruder, and reunion in earthly existence with the priests who had preceded them to the spirit world – all to be brought about by direct supernatural interposition – the teachers have been called prophets. While all goes well with the tribe the religious feeling finds sufficient expression in the ordinary ritual forms of tribal usage, but when misfortune or destruction threaten the nation or the race, the larger emergency brings out the prophet, who strives to avert the disaster by molding his people to a common purpose through insistence upon the sacred character of his message and thus furnishes support to the chiefs in their plans for organized improvement or resistance. Thus it is found that almost every great Indian warlike combination has had its prophet messenger at the outset, and if all the facts could be known we should probably find the rule universal. Among the most noted of these aboriginal prophets and reformers within our area are: Popé, of the Pueblo revolt of 1680; the Delaware prophet of Pontiac's conspiracy, 1762; Tenskwatawa, the Shawnee prophet, 1805; Kanakuk, the Kickapoo reformer, 1827; Tavibo, the Paiute, 1870; Nakaidoklini, the Apache, 1881; Smohalla, the dreamer of the Columbia, 1870-1885; and Wovoka or Jack Wilson, the Paiute prophet of the Ghost Dance, 1889 and later." (Consult Mooney, "Ghost Dance Religion," in *14th Annual Report* of the Bureau of American Ethnology, part ii, 1896.) – JAMES MOONEY, in *Handbook Amer. Indians*.

The Shawnee Prophet

You are very well acquainted with the residence of the Shawnoe Prophet,[100] at or near the mouth of the Tipicanoe, we may date our difficulties with the Indians from the time he and his followers first

---

[100] Tenskwatawa, "the Shawnee Prophet," was a twin brother of Tecumseh. When quite a young man he apparently died; but when his friends assembled for the funeral he revived from his trance, and told them that he had returned from a visit to the spirit world. In November, 1805, when he was hardly more than thirty years of age, he called around him his tribesmen and their allies, and announced himself as the bearer of a new revelation from the Master of Life, which he had received in the spirit world. He denounced the witchcraft and juggleries of the medicine-men, and the "fire-water" obtained from the whites as poison and accursed; and warned his hearers of the misery and punishment which would follow all these evil practices. He advocated more respect for the aged, community of property, the cessation of intermarriages between the whites and Indian women; and urged the Indians to discard all clothing, tools, and customs introduced by the whites, and to return to their primitive mode of life. Then they would be received into Divine favor, and regain the happiness that they had known before the coming of the whites. He claimed that he had received power to cure all diseases and avert death in sickness or battle. This preaching aroused great excitement and a crusade against all who were supposed to practice witchcraft. The Prophet fixed his headquarters at Greenville, Ohio, where many persons came from various tribes of the northwest to learn the new doctrines. To lend these authority, he announced various dreams and revelations, and in 1806 predicted an eclipse of the sun; the fulfilment of this brought him great prestige, and enthusiastic acceptance as a true prophet. The movement spread far to the south and the northwest; it added many recruits to the British forces in the War of 1812, and occasioned the bloody Creek War of 1813. But the influence of the Prophet and his doctrines were destroyed by the battle of Tippecanoe; after the war came to an end Tenskwatawa received a pension from the British government and resided in Canada until 1826. Then he rejoined his tribe in Ohio, and soon afterward removed with them to Kansas; he died there in November,

settled at that place, not that I believe that his first intention was inimical to the views of the United States, but when he found, he had got such influence over the different Indians he immediately changed his discourse and from the instructions he occasionally received from the British, he was continually preaching up the necefsity of the Indians to have no intercourse with the Americans; as you will see in his form of prayers that he learnt to all his followers. I was informed by a very intelligent young man who has been often at the Prophet's village, and who has conversed with the Prophet and Tecumseh, he gave me the following history of the Prophet.

The Prophet with all his brothers are pure Indians of the Shawanoe nation, and when a boy, was a perfect vagabond and as he grew up he w^d not hunt and became a great drunkard. While he lived near Greenville in the State of Ohio, where spirituous liquor are plenty he was continually intoxicated; having observed some preachers [101] who lived in the vicinity of Greenville a preaching or rather the motions, etc., in preaching (as he cannot understand a word of English) it had such an effect on him, that one night he dremt that the Great Spirit found fault with his way of living, that he must leave of[f] drinking, and lead a new life, and also instruct all the red people the proper way of living. He immediately refrained from drinking any kind of spirituous liquor, and recommended it strongly to all the Indians far and near to follow his example, and laid down certain laws that was to guide the red people in future. I shall here give you as many of those laws or regulations as I can now remember, but I know I have forgot many.

1st Spirituous liquor was not to be tasted by any Indians on any account whatever.

2nd No Indian was to take more than one wife in future, but those who now had two three or more wives might keep them, but it would please the Great Spirit if they had only one wife.

3^d No Indian was to be runing after the women; if a man was single let him take a wife.

1837, at the present town of Argentine. "Although his personal appearance was marred by blindness in one eye, Tenskwatawa possessed a magnetic and powerful personality; and the religious fervor he created among the Indian tribes, unless we except that during the recent 'ghost dance' disturbance, has been equaled at no time since the beginning of white contact." — JAMES MOONEY, in *Handbook Amer. Indians.*

[101] These were Shaker missionaries to the Indians, according to Forsyth (see his sketch of Tecumseh and the Prophet in vol. IV of *Forsyth Papers*). — ED.

SHAWNEE PROPHET

4th If any married woman was to behave ill by not paying proper attention to her work, etc., the husband had a right to punish her with a rod, and as soon as the punishment was over, both husband and wife, was to look each other in the face and laugh, and to bear no ill will to each other for what had pafsed.

5th All Indian women who were living with whitemen was to be brought home to their friends and relations, and their children to be left with their fathers, so that the nations might become genuine Indians.

6th All medicine bags, and all kinds of medicine dances and songs were to exist no more; the medicine bags were to be destroyed in *presens* of the whole of the people collected for that purpose, and at the destroying of such medicine, etc., every one was to make open [102] confefsion to the Great Spirit in a loud voice of all the bad deeds that he or she had committed during their lifetime, and beg for forgivenefs as the Great Spirit was too good to refuse.

7th No Indian was to sell any of their provision to any white people, they might give a little as a present, as they were sure of getting in return the full value in something else.

8th No Indian was to eat any victuals that was cooked by a White person, or to eat any provisions raised by White people, as bread, beef, pork, fowls, etc.

9th No Indian must offer skins or furs or any thing else for sale, but ask to exchange them for such articles that they may want.

10th Every Indian was to consider the French, English, and Spaniards, as their fathers or friends, and to give them their hand, but they were not to know the Americans on any account, but to keep them at a distance.

11th All kind of white people's drefs, such as hats, coats, etc., were to be given to the first whiteman they met as also all dogs not of their own breed, and all cats were to be given back to white people.

12th The Indians were to endeavour to do without buying any merchandise as much as pofsible, by which means the game would become plenty, and then by means of bows and arrows, they could hunt and kill game as in former days, and live independent of all white people.

13th All Indians who refused to follow these regulations were to be considered as bad people and not worthy to live, and must be put to

---

[102] "Indians who have been present at some of these confessions, have repeated them to me, and certainly they were ridiculous in the extreme."

— T. Forsyth (marginal note).

death. (A Kickapoo Indian was actually burned in the spring of the year 1809 at the old Kickapoo Town for refusing to give up his medicine bag, and another old man and old woman was very near sharing the same fate at the same time and place).

14th The Indians in their prayers prayed to the earth, to be fruitful, also to the fish to be plenty, to the fire and sun, etc., and a certain dance was introduced simply for amusement, those prayers were repeated morning and evening, and they were taught that a diviation from these duties would offend the Great Spirit. There were many more regulations but I now have forgot them, but those above mentioned are the principal ones.

The Prophet had his disciples among every nation of Indians, from Detroit in Michigan Territory, to the Indians on the Missippi and [I] have since been informed, that, there were disciples of the Prophet, among all the Indians of the Missouri and as far north as Hudson Bay (see Tanner's narrative) always reserving the supreme authority to himself, viz, that he (the Prophet) might be considered the head of the whole of the different nations of Indians, as he only, could see and converse with the Great Spirit. As every nation was to have but one village, by which means they would be always together in case of danger. The Pottawatimie Indians in the course of one season got tired of this strict way of living, and declared off, and joined the main poque,[103] as he never would acknowledge the Prophet as his superiour, seeing perfectly that he the Prophet was seeking enfluence among the different Indian nations. Many Indians still follow the dictates of the Prophet in a great measure. The Prophet's plan in the first instance was to collect by fair means all the Indians he could, to live in the same village with him, and when he thought his party sufficiently strong, he would oblidge the others to come into measures by force, and when so assembled in great numbers, that he would be able to give laws to the white people. Tecumseh [104] has been heard to say,

---

[103] "The Main Poque was a pure Pottawatimie Indian, and a great juggler, and made the credulous Indians believe every thing he said, he had great influence among the Chipeways, Ottawas, Pottawatimies, Kicapoos, Sauks, Fox and other Indians. He died along Lake Michigan in summer of 1816."

                                        — T. FORSYTH (marginal note).
   See note 76 for sketch of this chief.— ED.

[104] Tecumseh (properly Tikamthi or Tecumtha) was a celebrated Shawnee chief, born in 1768 at the Shawnee village of Piqua (which was destroyed by the Kentuckians in 1780); his father and two brothers were killed in battle with the whites. "While still a young man Tecumseh distinguished himself

"We must not leave this place" (meaning Tipicanoe) [105] "we must remain stedfast here, to keep those people who wear hats, in check;" he also observed to the Indians, "no white man who walks on the earth, loves an Indian, the white people are made up with such materials, that they will always deceive us, even the British who says they love us, is because they may want our services, and as we yet want their goods, we must, therefore, shew them some kind of friendship." – THOMAS FORSYTH, in unpublished letter to Gen. William Clark (St. Louis, Dec. 23, 1812) ; in *Forsyth Papers*, vol. ix.

in the border wars of the period, but was noted also for his humane character, evinced by persuading his tribe to discontinue the practice of torturing prisoners. Together with his brother Tenskwatawa the Prophet, he was an ardent opponent of the advance of the white man, and denied the right of the government to make land purchases from any single tribe, on the ground that the territory, especially in the Ohio valley country, belonged to all the tribes in common. On the refusal of the government to recognize this principle, he undertook the formation of a great confederacy of all the western and southern tribes for the purpose of holding the Ohio River as the permanent boundary between the two races. In pursuance of this object he or his agents visited every tribe from Florida to the head of the Missouri River. While Tecumseh was organizing the work in the south his plans were brought to disastrous overthrow by the premature battle of Tippecanoe under the direction of the Prophet, Nov. 7, 1811." He fought for the British in the War of 1812, and was created by them a brigadier-general, having under his command some 2,000 warriors of the allied tribes. Finally, at the battle on Thames River (near the present Chatham, Ontario), the allied British and Indians were utterly defeated by General Harrison, Oct. 5, 1813; and in this contest Tecumseh was killed, being then in his forty-fifth year. He may be considered the most extraordinary Indian character in United States history. – JAMES MOONEY, in *Handbook Amer. Indians*.

[105] Tippecanoe was a noted village site on the west bank of the Wabash River, just below the mouth of Tippecanoe River, Indiana. "It was originally occupied by the Miami, the earliest known occupants of the region, and later by the Shawnee, who were in possession when it was attacked and destroyed by the Americans under Wilkinson in 1791, at which time it contained one hundred and twenty houses. It was soon after rebuilt and occupied by the Potawatomi, and finally on their invitation became the headquarters of Tecumseh and his brother the Prophet, with their followers, whence the name Prophetstown." Gen. W. H. Harrison marched against them with nine hundred men, and near the town his army was attacked by the Indians (Nov. 7, 1811), under command of the Prophet. The battle of Tippecanoe resulted in the complete defeat and dispersion of the Indians, with considerable loss on both sides. The site was reoccupied for a short time a few years later.
– JAMES MOONEY, in *Handbook Amer. Indians*.

The Kickapoo Prophet

Sometime last month (October, 1832) a party of Kicapoo Indians
were encamped near the River des Peres, and about a mile from my
place of residence (my farm). Curiosity led me to go and see them,
as I was formerly acquainted with some of their old people. I found
them to be the Prophet or Preachers [106] party, in going into their
camp I was much surprised to find their dogs so quiet and peaceable,
in every camp or lodge of every individual, a piece of flat wood hung
up about three inches broad and twelve or fifteen inches long on
which were burned with a hot iron (apparently) a number of straight
and crooked marks, this stick or board so marked they called their
Bible. Those Indians told me that they worked six days and the
seventh they done no kind of work, but prayed to the Great Spirit,
that no men of their community were allowed to have more than one
wife, that none, either young or old, male or female, were allowed
to paint themselves, that they never made, or intended to make, war,
against any people that they never stole, tell lies or do any thing bad,
that those who would not learn their prayers according to the direction
of the Preacher, he or she was punished with a whip by a man appointed for that purpose, that spirituous liquor was not to be tasted
by any one belonging to the community on pain of death but they
were to do unto all people, as they wished to be done by. The Kicapoo nation is divided into two parties, one party under the Prophet
or Preacher the other, (which is the largest party) are under their
chiefs now living west of this State (Mifsouri) where the party under
the Prophet is on their way to join them, and no doubt will try and
bring them all under his control. I should not be surprised, if this

---

106 This is evidently a reference to Kanakuk, a prophet who arose among
the Kickapoo after they ceded their lands (1819) to the United States, and
part of the tribe migrated to Spanish territory. Kanakuk exhorted the remainder of his people to remain in Illinois, to lead moral lives, to abandon
their old superstitions, to live in peace with one another and with the white
men, and to avoid all use of intoxicating liquors. Those of his people who
remained in Illinois accepted him as their chief, and "many of the Potawatomi
of Michigan became his disciples. He displayed a chart of the path, leading
through fire and water, which the virtuous must pursue to reach the 'happy
hunting grounds,' and furnished his followers with prayer-sticks [described
above by Forsyth] graven with religious symbols. When in the end the
Kickapoo were removed to Kansas he accompanied them and remained their
chief, still keeping drink away from them, until he died of smallpox in 1852."
(See Mooney's account in *Fourteenth Report* of Bureau of American Ethnology
[1896], 692-700.) — *Handbook Amer. Indians.*

preaching of the Prophet of the Kicapoo Indians, is the commencement of a religion which will take place among all the different Indian nations, who are, and are to be settled, in a country west of this State (Miſsouri) and my present impression is, that it ought to be encouraged by the government as it inculcates peace and good will to all men. I have been informed that the above party on their way to their place of destination, were seen punishing several of their people with a whip, for something they done wrong. – THOMAS FORSYTH (memorandum at end of vol. IX of *Forsyth Papers*).

The Winnebago Mescal-eaters

In this connection, the following note is of especial interest. It is furnished by Mr. Thomas R. Roddy (also known as "White Buffalo"). Among that tribe considerable progress has been made in late years by a "new religion," popularly designated as that of the "mescal-eaters," or the "mescal-button." Our readers are indeed fortunate in having this interesting account of its history and results, from so authoritative a source; it is sent to the editor by Mr. Roddy from Winnebago, Neb., under date of April 15, 1909. – ED.

I enclose a short history of the Mescal-eaters of the Winnebago tribe, as I know them from personal experience among them, and from conversations with the leading members of the cult. The name of Mescal-eaters is generally used, and its members call themselves by it, in their talk; but it is erroneous, as these people never used the mescal-bean in any form. This is a small red bean, nearly round, and similar in shape to the common navy bean; while what the Winnebagoes and many other tribes use is called "peyote," [107] which is a

[107] Peyote (a name of Nahuatl origin): a kind of cactus (*Lophophora williamsii*, Coulter; also named *Anhalonium lewinii*), found along the lower Rio Grande and in Mexico, which long has been used for ceremonial and medicinal purposes by the southern and Mexican tribes; it has been incorrectly confused by the whites with the maguey cactus, from which the intoxicant mescal is prepared. "The peyote plant resembles a radish in size and shape, the top only appearing above ground. From the center springs a beautiful white blossom, which is later displaced by a tuft of white down. North of the Rio Grande this top alone is used, being sliced and dried to form the so-called 'button.' In Mexico the whole plant is cut into slices, dried, and used in decoction, while the ceremony also is essentially different from that of the northern tribes." This plant has been examined and tested at Washington, and "tests thus far made indicate that it possesses varied and valuable medicinal properties, tending to confirm the idea of the Indians, who regard it almost as a panacea." Among the Mexican tribes, the chief feature of the ceremony is a

cactus growth, found in southern Texas and Mexico. It is a round, flat pod, one to two inches in diameter; it is used in their church services, being eaten and also made into tea, which is passed to the members at intervals during services. These services are usually held Saturday nights, beginning about eight o'clock, and lasting till about the same hour Sunday morning; and are of a very religious and solemn nature. God is their guide, and they use the Bible and quotations from it all through the services; they have short speeches by the members, singing of sacred songs, and playing on the small medicine drum; and they use the sacred gourd rattle, on which are traced drawings of Christ, the cross and crown, the shepherd's crook, and other religious emblems. The drawings or carvings are done with great skill and show the work of an artist. Each member on joining is presented with one of these musical gourds, which he uses during services. Speeches are usually made in their native Indian tongue, but when whites are present the speech is interpreted into the English language. On this reservation the membership is about three hundred, and they have a very comfortable church. When they visit where there is no church they erect a large cloth tepee, and hold services here for winning converts. Their altar is in the shape of a heart, about eight feet in length, and is built of cement; the members sit around this altar.

Medicine-eating can be traced back in this country about 200 years; it was first introduced by the Miskarora [i.e., Mescaleros], a tribe of old Mexico, among the Apaches and Timgas of Oklahoma – the Apaches introducing it among the Comanches, Kiowas, Cheyennes, Arapahoes, and Otoes. Twelve years ago the Otoes brought the new religion to the Winnebagoes and Omahas of Nebraska, where now about one-third of each tribe are members; and they are the most prosperous people of the tribe. In talking with Albert Hensley, one of the prominent leaders, he said: "The mescal was formerly used improperly, but since it has been used in connection with the Bible it is proving a great benefit to the Indians. Now we call our church the Union Church, instead of Mescal-eaters. Our ways may seem peculiar to

---

dance; but among the northern Plains tribes "it is rather a ceremony of prayer and quiet contemplation. It is usually performed as an invocation for the recovery of some sick person. . . The number of 'buttons' eaten by one individual during the night varies from ten to forty, and even more, the drug producing a sort of spiritual exaltation differing entirely from that produced by any other known drug, and apparently without any reaction." — JAMES MOONEY, in *Handbook Amer. Indians*.

some people, but our worship is earnest, and [we address] the same God as others do. We are doing this not to protect this medicine, but for God, as others do, and are not trying to deceive other Christian people. In doing so we would destroy ourselves and our God. Some try to stop our worshiping, but it is the work of God and cannot be stopped." Medicine-eating is praised highly by the members, and opposed as bitterly by the other faction. I have attended several of the meetings, and have also experienced the eating and drinking of the "peyote" medicine, with no bad effects. It is very surprising, the way the Indians have become familiar with the Bible, and how closely they try to follow the teachings of Jesus. By using the medicine in connection with the Bible, they are able to understand the Bible. Many members I have known twenty-five or thirty years, who formerly had been greatly addicted to the use of liquors and tobacco, and other vices; all have quit these bad habits and live for their religion. I cannot see wherein their minds have become impaired, as many talk and write, but I can see great improvements and advancement among the members. They are the best business men among this tribe, and their credit is good wherever they are known. John Rave, the leader, is one of the old-type Indians, of fine personal appearance, and has used the medicine twelve years; and any one would be pleased to engage him in conversation and hear his explanations of the Bible, and talk on the benefits and happiness enjoyed through this new religion. One wrong and misleading fact is the name "Mescal-eaters," which seems to cling to the minds of the general public. The Winnebagoes have the credit of being the first to use the Bible in conjunction with this medicine.

APPENDIX C

From a mass of correspondence incident to the preparation of the present work, the editor has selected the following extracts from letters, etc., written by persons who know from actual observation and experience the facts regarding what they state, and who are reliable and competent observers. Rev. Henry I. Westropp is a Jesuit missionary among the (Oglala) Sioux at Pine Ridge Agency, S. Dak. Franklin W. Calkins is the author of various books and magazine stories of Indian and frontier life; he has seen much of the Indians, and at one time lived among some of the Sioux and was adopted into their tribe. Rev. William Metzdorf (a secular priest), of St. Francis, Wis., was formerly a missionary among the Potawatomi of Kansas. Rev. J. Stucki is a Protestant missionary among the Winnebago of Wisconsin, at Black River Falls, Wis.; and Thomas R. Roddy is (as mentioned on page 281). These letters are used here, to give some idea of the character and present condition or status of the above tribes. – ED.

The Sioux

The Sioux have always been a religious-minded people, and it seems that even before the advent of the white men they believed in one God, whom they called the "Great Holy One" – great, as compared to a numerous band of other "holy ones" that they had. With such fruitful soil to work in, it was easy for the Christian missionary to sow the seed of the gospel. Their ideas of morality had always been strict, and these ideas still remain today. The Indian maidens are exceedingly bashful; they will run at the approach of a stranger, or, if that is impossible, hide their faces in their shawls; they dare not speak to any one in public, and at times refuse to answer even necessary questions. None of the Indians, as a rule, manifest their feelings in the way that white people do. Usually the Indian does not thank you for any benefit; he cannot blush, or if he does no one can see it; his code of honor is the contrary of the white man's, and his etiquette is very simple. This has led many to believe that he is taciturn, impassive, and unemotional; and yet nothing is more false. Conversation, social dinners, and smokes are the Indian's life. Two never talk at once; each one has his turn. Their inclination to curiosity may be estimated by the fact that they will recognize any one passing their house, a mile away, and perhaps tell him a year afterward what kind of a horse he was riding – something that they certainly could not do unless they were accustomed to scrutinize everything most curiously. When any one of their kindred is sick, they must travel miles and miles to show their sympathy; and if he dies, this event (as also his burial) is the occasion for all kinds of expressions of their sympathy and regret. To indicate this, they often cut their hair and dress in black for a year or more. Often they give away, at the death of a dear relative, all they possess – calico, food, blankets, ponies; and even the house is torn down. This idea of giving away everything, of doing "the big thing," is doubtless a beautiful trait, but it prevents progress. On the occasion of an Omaha dance or a Fourth of July celebration, the generous Sioux will stand up and give away anything and everything. An Indian can exercise no self-control in this respect; if he feels sad, he would give away the globe, if he owned it. In all his dealings he presents the figure of a grown-up child; and yet there is scarcely a white man who will not cheat this child wherever he can. It is a mistaken policy to treat them as grown-up persons. They have land, cattle, and everything imaginable issued to them; but as long as there is not an overseer with them to hold them down, and teach them how to use the land and implements they get, these are useless. Like a set of boys, when tired of work they run off and play; they cast everything aside, cattle, family, and all; they join a Buffalo Bill show, go off to another tribe on a visit, and so on. If one man gets a good start, there will be so many visitors around that he is scarcely to be envied. They are great visitors; that is their principal occupation. Their horses are run down to skin and bone, their places neglected, and everything thrown to the wind, so that they may go and visit their relatives, or other tribes. The weekly dance, the semi-monthly trip for rations, and trips to the store and the railroad, leave them but little remaining time for work. Under these circumstances, acquiring wealth or even supporting themselves is out of the question. Their miserable huts are hotbeds of disease; dirty clothes and blankets, ditto. Food of all and any kind, or none at all; carelessness in wet and cold seasons; lack of knowledge how to take care of themselves; lack of medical attendance – all these are working frightful havoc among them. Although they are scattered over so immense a territory, the missionary is doing what he can to teach them, and urging them to work and stay at home. He helps them out of his own pocketbook, tries to secure by foresight their seed in time, and procures for them the means to aid themselves; but this work is nothing to what it could be, since we so greatly lack the necessary means, ourselves living on charity. There is no reason why this great and noble tribe should not be saved, if we had the means. The missionary has great influence over them, and so has the religion which they embrace. The tribe ought to double its numbers every few years, for their fertility is great. The number of twins born among them surpasses belief, and every Indian woman gives birth to eight or ten children. Where are they? you ask; go find them in the graveyard.

There seems to be an impression in many quarters that the Indian is a liar and a thief; but nothing is farther from the truth. Indians are, like children, very unreliable, and I never take them too seriously. They are liable to say anything that comes into their heads, and their language is full of exaggerations. If they mean to say that a man laughed, or was frightened, or hungry, they will say that he died of laughter, or fright, or hunger. Burglary is unknown among them. When one of them leaves his tent, he puts a stick of wood in front of the flap, and no one will enter while he is gone. Knocking a man on the head for the sake of his money is unknown. If the Indian steals from the white man, he is practically taking back what belongs to him; and if, when at times he feels the gnawing pangs of hunger, he goes out and kills whatever cattle he may find, what wonder is it? Wilful murder is also very, very uncommon; and when Indians are brought before the courts their troubles are usually caused by drink, the worst enemy of these people. Drink is certainly the king of all the evils existing out here. The Indian will pawn his last shirt for a drink of "holy water," as he calls it. The Indians here (at Pine Ridge) being far removed from the railroad, liquor has not wrought such ravages here as among some other tribes; but unless the government takes strong measures against whisky-sellers the evil will be the same here as on other reservations – for the Indians are nothing else but children, and cannot resist a seducer.

– REVEREND HENRY I. WESTROPP, S.J., Pine Ridge, S. Dak.

You will find in my latest book, *The Wooing of Tokala*, a clear statement of my impressions regarding Indian character. Although this book is in the form of a novel, or story, it is primarily expository. In its dealings with Siouan sociology and, I may boldly add, psychology, it is endorsed by all educated Sioux, and by all its readers who have known the Sioux tongue and tribal life. It is in fact an intimate study of the Indians at first hand, and in it I have given conscientiously my best studies of the Dakota people. In the character of Tokala may be seen the chaste Sioux maiden – not at her best, because I haven't the ability to present her at her best; nor do I know of any one who is able to set forth fully the subtle *nuances* of Indian character. But I have in that book dealt as amply as I could with the moral character of the Dakota. Their standards of morality are very high, and their children are trained in accordance with these. When I lived among them there were only a very few disorderly or bad characters in the entire tribe; and these were regarded in precisely the same light as such persons are in any moral and well-regulated community of white people. – FRANKLIN WELLES CALKINS, Maine, Minn.

The Pottawatomi

Out on the bare prairies of Kansas I lived with the Pottawatomi Indians for four years, and became as one of their tribe; and what I here relate is based mostly on my own observations, or on traditions preserved in the tribe and told to me by the Indians. When the Pottawatomis first came into contact with the whites they occupied lands in southern Michigan and Wisconsin; about the time of the Revolutionary War they gradually left Michigan entirely and settled on their Wisconsin lands. About 1850 most of them went across the Mississippi, following the trail of the buffalo, and dispersed over the great western plains; a smaller number remained in the Wisconsin woods. Later, the government gave those of the plains a reservation on the Kansas River; but part of these lands were sold, and now the remnant of the tribe, about 1,200 in number, are living on their reservation in the northeastern corner of Kansas – besides a band who settled on the Pottawatomie reservation in Oklahoma, and those who now live on reservations in the northern part of Wisconsin. At times the latter Indians receive visits from their tribesmen in the south, who like to revisit their old Wisconsin home, which some of them still remember.

Their language is very like that of the Ojibwa, the Ottawas, and the Kickapoos; and its soft and harmonious, but brief and clear-cut, sounds tell us that we are dealing with a race of fine feeling, and manly but peaceable character. In many respects it is a beautiful language;

it is the very embodiment of system and regularity, and is very euphonic, with no harsh, grating sounds. The general rule is, that after each consonant a vowel follows; and when two or more consonants meet they readily combine and flow together. It is a language of verbs, almost four-fifths of its words being of that class; and it abounds in inflections, every phase of being, thought, or action being expressed by some termination. In it the letters n, f, l, r, v, x, y, z are lacking, except in words of foreign origin; and every written letter is pronounced. There are nine conjugations in this language, and each one can be used affirmatively, negatively, and dubitatively; moreover, a verb can be used to express any phase of thought. There is to-day a considerable literature in the Ojibwa language, including even a newspaper, the *Anishinabe Enamiad* (i.e., *The Catholic Indian*), which is published weekly by the missionaries in Harbor Springs, Mich., and is read by many of the Pottawatomis. I began the preparation of a Pottawatomi grammar, the first attempt at such a book (and in their dialect nothing has yet been published except a prayer-book); but I was called to another field, and did not finish it.

The idea that some people have of these Indians, that they are wild, cruel savages, or a race who can not be civilized, is entirely wrong and false. On the contrary, we find that with their bad habits – which I am sorry to say were taught to them mostly by white men – they have many very good qualities. If they are not quite as friendly toward the whites as we could wish, we must attribute this to the fact that they have not been treated right by the whites. The side of their life that I most admire is the quiet and peaceful family life. They very seldom quarrel in their homes, and the women do their work quietly and take care of their children, whom they love with greater affection than do many of the white women. I have never seen an Indian cruel to his children, and their patience with the faults of the children is astonishing. The curse of divorce is hardly known among them; they really believe in the indissolubility of the marriage bond, and, if the married pair have differences and become angered at each other, one of the two goes to stay with some neighbor until the other asks him or her to return and promises to be good again.

They dislike water, even for mere hygienic purposes, and their passion for strong drink has become proverbial; but they know their weakness, and I had in my congregation a great many Indians who belonged to the Temperance League and never touched a drop of any intoxicant. Their dislike for hard work is a characteristic which they

PECHECHO (Potawattomi)

have in common with many other races. But a peculiar feature which I often notice is hard to explain: the Indian man seems to have an abhorrence for sickness. If a member of his family is sick he usually leaves the house, goes to stay with some neighbor, and sends the neighbor's wife to his home to take care of his sick wife or child. Thus I often arrived at a sick-bed and found the poor family alone, because the neighbor had not yet come.

A very large part of the Pottawatomis are still heathens, and stick to their old religion with the same tenacity which the Christian converts show in their new faith. The former are less civilized, and never use the English language in their conversation, even when they are able to speak it. Naturally they sometimes show that they consider the Christians as renegades, and too great friends of the white men, and will not take part in any of their doings unless the whole tribe is interested in it. They believe in a Supreme Being, *Kitchi Manito*, the creator and benefactor of all mankind; they honor and adore him in the sun, and therefore they often call him *Kisis*, which means "the sun," or "month." They worship this God through their so-called dances, which are really religious ceremonies. Especially among this tribe, there are three great dances, each one lasting from two to three weeks: the first one, called the "green bean dance," is celebrated early in the summer, when the bean, one of their staple products, is ready for the table. The second, the most elaborate of all, the "green corn dance," [108] is celebrated when the corn is in its milk, in the right stage of growth to rejoice every Indian's heart. First, they all stack up as much hay as they need to feed their horses over winter, and as soon as the last haystack is completed they pack up their tents and travel to their dancing-ground, where they will stay until all celebrations are over. Later on, in the fall, they usually have a "Powou," a celebration corresponding to our Thanksgiving, the turkey being the central figure at the dancing-ground. This is a circular field prepared for that purpose; it is in the neighborhood of the chief's house, on the border of Big Soldier Creek, surrounded by trees and woods; the outer circle of this ground is raised a little, thus forming natural benches, which the women occupy. In the neighborhood a great dance-hall has been erected, built of boards; and in this they continue their dances, if storms or heavy rains interfere with the outdoor programme.

---

[108] Cf. the dance of this name (more commonly known as "busk") among the Creeks, their solemn annual festival, one of rejoicing over the first fruits of the year. See account of this feast in *Handbook Amer. Indians.* — ED.

They consider their dancing-ground a sacred place. For their great dances invitations are sent out to their relatives and to neighboring tribes; and thus many strangers are present on those occasions, as well as Pottawatomis from Wisconsin – who go to attend the ceremonies and also to draw money due them on allotments which they had received on the Kansas reservation. Catholics do not usually take part in these dances, except that some of the young fellows are drawn in when they hear the drums, and finally join in the dancing. These dancing feasts also include speeches, singing, and smoking – the latter being done with one pipe by perhaps a hundred persons; to this practice may be traced the spread of some diseases among them. They do not like to have their pictures taken, and any attempts to photograph them at these ceremonies have usually ended in the destruction of the camera. In the center of the dancing-ground is a large red cross, at the foot of which the eatables are deposited when they have their dinner. This cross is a peculiar feature in the Indian camps. I often inquired for its meaning, but could get no further information than that this custom was as old as the Indians. I think, however, that it is an old tradition of the Christian instruction which they received from the first missionaries among them, which they did not fully understand and have adopted into their ceremonial. At these feasts they thank the sun for the crops which he has given them, and the warm weather which has enabled these to grow, and they praise Kitchi Manito. On the last day they have a special ceremony over the sacred dog, which has been killed and cooked. Its skull is placed before the cross, and the meat is distributed among the dancers; singing their songs loudly, they dance around the skull, and finally jump over it. On one occasion, toward the end of the ceremony I saw an Indian step into the middle of the ring, and confess a crime which he had committed and for which the tribe had disowned him. He received pardon from the chief, and as a sign of reconciliation he was given a cup of milk by the chief, after which they crossed the pipes of peace. Outside of their dances the non-Christian Indians show hardly any sign of religion, except at their funerals. They place their dead in a sitting posture above the ground, the back of the corpse leaning against a stone or a tree. Others deposit their dead in hollow trees, which they cut off at the top, lowering the body into this hollow amidst plaintive songs and the monotonous beating of drums. I have seen such hollow trees that were actually filled with skeletons from top to bottom. Generally the body is only partly covered with logs or stones or earth.

They then tie a dog near the grave, to keep watch over it. If he is able to get loose before he starves to death, and goes home, it is considered a good omen, a sign that the deceased has arrived happily at the great hunting-grounds, and does not need the dog any more. Often, in passing by new graves, I made both dog and people happy, by cutting the rope.

No orphan asylums are needed among these people. If a mother loses one of her children she tries to soothe her sorrow by adopting an orphan or waif of about the same age; and all such children are well cared for. Such an adoption is a great feast for the tribe, the central figure being the adopted child; it is well dressed, and, according to the wealth of the new mother, receives many and fine presents. I always enjoyed these occasions, on account of the friendly and kind spirit which I always observed, and with which they treated me.

The Christians in this tribe were converted by the renowned Jesuit, Father Galligan, about fifty years ago; and although after his death they were left entirely to themselves, because no priest spoke their language, they adhered loyally to their adopted faith. Once or twice a week, throughout the long period of twenty-five years, groups of them met together, and said their prayers in common, and listened to the teaching of some of the older and better-instructed men. Their services consisted in reciting prayers and especially in singing the old religious songs, which had been translated for them into their language by Father Galligan and Bishop Báraga;[109] these gatherings lasted until a late hour, and were concluded by an elaborate meal. In this way the faith of the Christians was preserved, and, although many of them were poorly instructed, none of them fell away from their adopted faith; and when I first went to stay with them I found that they all were practical Catholics, and that they believed in their religion. The missionary who labors among them has no reason to complain about neglect of religious duty on the part of the Indians; and I could always point to them as exemplary church-goers. They receive the sacraments often, attend religious services regularly, and respond willingly to every demand of the priest. There is, of course, a little side-attraction connected with the divine services, as they all, after these are ended, partake of a sumptuous meal; thus every church

---

[109] Rev. (afterward Bishop) Frederic Báraga, a native of Austria, began a Catholic mission at La Pointe, on Chequamegon Bay, in 1835. He spent the rest of his life in missionary labors in northern Michigan and Wisconsin, dying in 1868. See Wis. *Hist. Colls.*, vol. xii, 445, 446, 451. — ED.

day is for them a kind of feast day. Peace, unity, and a spirit of good-fellowship prevail among them, and recall to us the love-feasts of the first Christians.

Among these Pottawatomis are persons, both of pure and of mixed blood, who are some of my best friends, and their friendship I appreciate as much as that of white people; and they are in every respect equal to our white men and women. Among them is the reverend Father Negauquetl, a full-blood Indian; he pursued his studies in the Sacred Heart College in Oklahoma and later at the Propaganda in Rome, where he was ordained a priest in 1905; and he is now working among his own people and the whites in the Indian Territory. He is the first Catholic priest of his race, and speaks both English and Italian perfectly, besides the different Indian dialects. Another is a Miss Blandin (now Mrs. Graham), the daughter of an English father and a full-blooded Indian mother; she is highly accomplished, an excellent musician, and a graduate from the University of Holton, Kans. Many of these Indians are highly esteemed by their white neighbors, and move in the best society. Along the two Soldier Creeks may be seen beautiful residences, with large barns, the property of wealthy Indians. The finest cattle and horses are shipped to market by them, and the checks that they sign are honored at any bank in Kansas. They dress in style and good taste, and they and their families appear in citizen clothes; they speak the English language well, and are in every respect true Americans. There is another but poorer class of Christians on that reservation who have no land of their own, and, not being able to acquire any land on the reservation, they rent land from other Indians. These are thrifty farmers, save their money, and are the best of Catholics. I wish that I could speak as highly of those who are non-Christians; their progress in civilization is slow, and most of them, at least the women, do not know the English language at all. They have struck a compromise in clothing, and appear only partly in citizen's dress; clinging to the blanket as if it were a part of their religion. Many years will be needed to civilize them fully, and it is to be feared that not many of them will be left for that; for every year diseases, especially consumption, erysipelas, and smallpox, carry many of them to the grave. The government makes great efforts to be just to the Indians, but even this fact is, I think, an explanation of their slow advance. Every Pottawatomi man, woman, and child receives from the government one hundred and sixty acres of land, and sometimes much more; as this is good hay land, it is rented, through the

O-CHEK-KA (Winnebago)

agent, for two dollars an acre, to white people, for cutting the hay. This secures to an Indian family – for instance, the father and mother, and five children – an income of about two thousand dollars, which is sufficient for them to live on without doing a stroke of work. If the Indian does not work, we cannot expect him to become a useful citizen; he needs both a teacher and a taskmaster, who will teach him at once the principles of Christianity and the love of labor, and show him that it is a blessing. Injustice, bloody persecutions, and wars of extermination did much to make the Indian that crafty and bloodthirsty savage whom we so often meet in story and history; but such is not his real nature. And now when truthful and sympathetic historians are looking up the records of the Indians, and studying their history, character, customs, and beliefs, we must deeply regret that in the past they were not given more sympathy and greater opportunities, and that the unfortunate conditions which tend to cause their extermination still continue. – Rev. WILLIAM METZDORF, St. Francis, Wis. (from an unpublished lecture given by him in Milwaukee, Jan. 21, 1907).

The Winnebago

As a rule, these Indians are very sociable among themselves, and with outsiders whom they have proved to be their friends. Toward strangers they are very reserved, and this may especially be said of the women. Very seldom a family lives alone; usually two or more families live close together. They are peaceable except when under the influence of liquor. They are hospitable even to excess. As a rule, diligence and cleanliness are not their strongest points; but their way of living (in tents), and their land being unfit for cultivation, will to some extent account for both. Their morals are not all one could wish, especially among the younger generation. "Firewater" is the great enemy of these Indians, and there are always unscrupulous whites who for the sake of gain will furnish it to them. Some of the Indians are bad, but there are also some who are highly deserving of respect, who might be pointed out as examples for others to follow. The greatest drawback to the elevation of these people is the poor soil on which they are located; they can not make their living on it, and are consequently compelled to scatter in all directions, in order to seek work by which to make a living; and thus they often come into contact with a class of whites whose influence is anything but edifying. The "new religion" (the use of the "mescal button") when first brought to these Indians found quite a number of adherents; but it seems to have lost ground gradually, and many of the Indians were very much opposed to it. – Rev. J. Stucki, Black River Falls, Wis.

The Wisconsin Winnebagoes have very poor sandy lands, and are not far advanced in farming, especially as they receive but little encouragement from the government or its employees. The Winnebagoes are naturally bright, intelligent people, more so than the average of Indian tribes; they are more intelligent than the ordinary white people, or the corn-eating natives of Nebraska. Those who live in Wisconsin earn their living by hunting and trapping, berry-picking, gathering ginseng, husking corn, digging potatoes, cutting wood, etc. Under the present methods, they waste considerable time waiting for the payment of the government annuities. I look for great advancement among the several tribes when the trust funds are paid, and the Indians are made to mingle more with the whites, and go out into the world to do the best they can; they will then reach the top of the ladder. Good education is all right for them if only they have something to do when their school days are over; but at the present day there is nothing for them except to go back to the wigwam. A Winnebago from Nebraska has recently won high honors in oratory at Yale University. In regard to the "mescal eating" among the Winnebagoes, those in Nebraska sent (in the summer of 1908) a delegation of about one hundred persons to Wisconsin, to introduce the new religion among their brothers there. They held three or four meetings, and made fifteen or twenty converts; but there was so much opposition to the movement that most persons held back from joining it.

– Thomas R. Roddy, Black River Falls, Wis.

BIBLIOGRAPHY

Documents forming the text of this work

BACQUEVILLE DE LA POTHERIE, CLAUDE CHARLES DE.   Histoire de l'Amerique Septentrionale (Paris, 1722).   4 vols.   Illustrated.

This work was approved by the royal censor at Paris in 1702, but was not published until 1716 — probably on account of the war between England and France (1701-1713), which only ended with the treaty of Utrecht, and the undesirability of publishing at that time a work regarding Canada, which was in danger of attack by the English. The edition of 1716 is mentioned by only Fevret de Fontette; the next one (1722), the edition best known to bibliographers, was issued at both Paris and Rouen; and a third edition appeared at Amsterdam in 1723. The work was published in four small volumes; it is the second of these, devoted to the history of the Indian tribes who were allies of the French in Canada, which is here presented (for the first time in English translation). A fourth edition was issued in Paris in 1753; a careful comparison shows that this is an exact reproduction of the 1722 edition, save for a few unimportant variations, chiefly in the color of the ink used on the title-pages. It is a curious fact that La Potherie's *Histoire* is not mentioned in the *Mémoires de Trevoux*, a publication of that period which aimed to record the names of all printed books relating to America. This information is chiefly obtained from the interesting paper of J. Edmond Roy on La Potherie and his works, in *Proceedings and Transactions* of the Royal Society of Canada, series ii, vol. iii, 27-41 — in which the reader will find fuller bibliographical details, and a brief synopsis of the *Histoire*.

It is of interest to note the gradual increase in the prices quoted by booksellers for this work. An early issue (undated) of Dufossé's *Americana* prices the *Histoire* (no. 13857) at twenty-five francs for edition of 1753; and later (no. 62174), at thirty-five francs, edition of 1722; while in his "new series" that of 1753, it is quoted at forty francs (nos. 15851 and 17181). In Chadenat's *Catalogues* may be noted the following: *Catalogue* 11 (1893), no. 11457, edition 1722, 40 francs; the same in *Catalogue* 22 (1898), no. 21991, edition "1722 or 1753;" for the same edition, in *Catalogue* 26 (1900), no. 26414, 50 francs (and in same catalogue the same price for the Amsterdam edition of 1723); in *Catalogue* 29 (1902), no. 29697, edition of 1722 (Paris, Nyon et Didot; "original edition of this very rare work"), 80 francs; the same price for the Amsterdam edition, in *Catalogue* 33 (1904), no. 34394; while in *Catalogue* 41 (1908), no. 44096, and *Catalogue* 44 (1910), no. 48816, the price is quoted at 125 francs.

PERROT, NICOLAS. Mémoire sur les mœurs coustumes et relligion des sauvages de l'Amérique septentrionale. Pub. pour la première fois par le R. P. J. Tailhan (Leipzig and Paris, 1864).

So much information in regard to Perrot's manuscript writings as was then available was collected by his editor, Father Tailhan, when he published the above work in 1864; for this, see his preface at the beginning of the *Mémoire*. Since then, no farther discoveries seem to have been made, unless the promised "Inventaire sommaire" of MM. Nicolas and Wirth, of Mss. in the archives of the Ministère des Colonies at Paris, has succeeded in unearthing some of the lost memoirs of Nicolas Perrot. It is more probable, however, that these writings were lost or destroyed (unless some duplicate copies found their way into the government archives) in their passage through many hands in the eighteenth century; for they were used by La Potherie, Charlevoix, and Colden, and possibly other writers — some of them being apparently preserved to us in La Potherie's second volume.

For prices on the *Mémoire*, the catalogues of the French booksellers should be consulted, as it is seldom offered by those in the United States. In Dufossé's *Bulletin de Bouquiniste* this book appears occasionally: no. 15180, at 12 francs; no. 36982, at 10 francs; and no. 60896, at 7.50 francs. Chadenat quoted it higher: from 10 to 12 francs in the years since 1890; and reaches 15 francs in *Catalogue* 43 (1909), no. 48011; while in two of his *Catalogues* — 23 (1899), no. 23659; and 41 (1908), no. 45118 — he mentions a copy of the *Mémoire* on large paper, printed from a large format in large quarto size, "a few copies only," quoted at 20 francs. O'Leary in *Catalogue* 11 (1907), quoted at $2.50 an unbound copy.

MARSTON, MAJOR MORRELL, U.S.A. Letter to Reverend Dr. Jedidiah Morse, Fort Armstrong, Ill., Nov., 1820. Ms.

This report on the Indian tribes in the district under Major Morrell's command was prepared by him in November, 1620, at the request of Rev. Dr. Jedidiah Morse, a special agent sent by the government to visit the Indian tribes of the United States and obtain all available information about their condition and needs for the use of the Indian Bureau in its dealings with them. Dr. Morse's report was published in 1822 (see title below), and is a most valuable document for the study of Indian history at that period; but it was long ago out of print, and is practically unknown to the general public. For the present work, the text of Marston's report is obtained not from the printed book, but from a copy of Marston's original Ms. which is preserved in the Draper Collection of the Wisconsin Historical Society; it is document no. 58 in vol. 1 of the Forsyth Papers (pressmark, "1 T 58"). The document is written, apparently by some copyist, on fifteen leaves of paper about foolscap size; the last paragraph and the subscription and signature are in Marston's autograph writing. The list of Indian tribes to which he alludes gives the names of each tribe in English, French, and ten Indian dialects; this paper has been by some oversight bound in the second volume of the Forsyth Papers.

FORSYTH, THOMAS. Manners and customs of the Sauk and Fox tribes of Indians. Ms., dated January 15, 1827.

This document is a memoir on the above-named tribes, written by the noted Indian agent, Thomas Forsyth, and sent by him to Gen. William Clark, then superintendent of Indian affairs; so far as is now known, it has never before been published. This manuscript, written throughout by Forsyth's own hand, is contained in volume IX of the Forsyth Papers (see preceding title); it fills thirty-four long pages, written in a small but very legible hand. It is followed by various other writings by Forsyth: miscellaneous memoranda, containing scraps of information (largely etymological) about tribal and place names in the northwest, bits of tribal history, etc.; a copy of a letter (dated St. Louis, Dec. 23, 1812) sent by Forsyth to Clark, which contains an interesting description of the region extending from Vincennes to Mackinaw and Green Bay, and from the Wisconsin and Mississippi Rivers to Lakes Erie and Huron; several anecdotes copied from printed books of the day; an interesting account of the Black Hawk War by Forsyth (whose official position, and contemporaneous residence in the region affected, render him a prime authority on that subject), entitled "Original causes of the trouble with a party of Sauk and Fox Indians under the direction or command of the Black Hawk, who was no chief;" and a note by him describing the religious character and practices of some Kickapoo Indians whom he encountered in Missouri, who were adherents of the noted "Kickapoo Prophet." The above letter of 1812 not only describes the topographical features of the region named, but enumerates and characterizes the various tribes inhabiting it, and gives an interesting sketch of the character and methods of the "Shawnee Prophet" and outline of the so-called "religion" inculcated by him among the Indians of the northwest.

General list of printed books and manuscript sources

ABEL, ANNIE HELOISE. The history of events resulting in Indian consolidation west of the Mississippi River (Washington, 1908).

In *Annual Report* of Amer. Hist. Association, 1906, vol. i, 233-454. Covers the period 1803-1840; at the end is a good bibliography of the subject, aiming to evaluate the various writings cited.

ADAMS, CHARLES F., editor. Memoirs of J. Q. Adams (Philadelphia, 1874-1877). 12 vols.

"Strictly speaking, this is an edition of J. Q. Adams's Diary, and is very valuable for tracing the United States Indian policy from 1825 to 1829." — ABEL.

ADAMS, HENRY. History of the United States of America, 1801-1817 (New York, 1889-1891). 9 vols.

ALLEN, JOEL A. History of the American bison (Washington, 1875).
In *Annual Report* of U.S. Geological and Geographical Survey of the
Territories, 1875, pp. 443-587.

AMERICAN ANTIQUARIAN AND ORIENTAL JOURNAL, 1878-1910. 32
vols. Illustrated.

Established (1878) at Ashtabula, O., by Stephen D. Peet, who remained
its editor until the close of 1910; now edited by J. O. Kinnaman. It has
been published successively at Beloit, Wis., Chicago, Salem, Mass., and
now (1911) at Benton Harbor, Mich. Contains many papers of archæological and ethnological value, by competent authorities; those concerning the old northwest are found chiefly in the earlier volumes. Among
them may be noted: Volume I, "Location of Indian tribes in the Northwest Territory at the date of its organization" (pp. 85-98). In recent
volumes: XXVI, S. D. Peet, "Races and religions in America" (pp. 345-360;
illustrated); Warren Upham, "Mounds built by the Sioux in Minnesota"
(pp. 217-222); XXVII, C. Staniland Wake, "Asiatic ideas among the North
American Indians" (pp. 153-161, 189-196); XXVIII, S. D. Peet, "The copper
age in America" (pp. 149-164), and "Pottery in its distribution and variety" (pp. 277-292); XXXI, J. O. Kinnaman, "Chippewa Legends" (pp.
96-101, 137-143).

AMERICAN ANTIQUARIAN SOCIETY. Transactions and collections
(Worcester, 1820; Cambridge, 1836). Vols. i, ii.

Largely devoted to Indian antiquities.

AMERICAN ARCHAEOLOGIST. Vols. I-II (Columbus, O., 1897-1898).
Illustrated.

AMERICAN BAPTIST HOME MISSIONARY SOCIETY. The Baptist home
mission monthly (New York, 1879-1910 +). Vols. 1-32. Illustrated.

AMERICAN BOARD OF COMMISSIONERS FOR FOREIGN MISSIONS. The
missionary herald (Boston, 1803-1910 +). Vols. 1-106. Illustrated (after 1865).

Begun under title of Massachusetts *Missionary Magazine*; united (June,
1809) with *The Panoplist*, begun three years before; after 1820 styled
The Missionary Herald.

AMERICAN FOLK-LORE SOCIETY. The journal of American folk-
lore (Boston and New York, 1888-1910 +). Vols. i-xxii.

Devoted mainly to folk-lore, but contains much other ethnological information; includes many articles and notes on our Indian tribes; its
editors and contributors include the leading authorities in its field. Notable papers in recent volumes: Volume XV — "Memorials of the Indian,"
A. F. Chamberlain; "Sac and Fox tales," Mrs. Mary Lasley (a daughter
of the noted chief Black Hawk); "Algonkian words in American English," A. F. Chamberlain. Volume XVIII — "Mythology of the Indian stocks

north of Mexico," A. F. Chamberlain; "The Algonkian Manitou," William Jones; "Who was the medicine-man?" Francis LaFlesche; "The Seneca White Dog Feast;" "Sioux Games," J. R. Walker (completed in the following volume). Volume XIX – "Ojibwa myths and traditions," Harlan I. Smith. Volume XX – "Some Dakota myths," Clark Wissler. Volume XXI – "The test-theme in N. American mythology," Robert H. Lowie.

AMERICAN HISTORICAL ASSOCIATION. Papers (New York, 1886-1891). 5 vols.

—— Annual reports, 1889-1907 (Washington, 1890-1908).

AMERICAN MISSIONARY ASSOCIATION. American missionary (New York, 1857-1910 +). Vols. 1-64. Illustrated (after 1899).

AMERICAN STATE PAPERS. Indian affairs, 1789-1827 (Washington, 1832-1834). 2 vols.

> Selected documents from the archives of the Indian Office, published under authority of Congress; highly valuable for the study of political relations between the Indians and United States, especially as some of the original documents from which these volumes are compiled are apparently no longer in existence.

ANNALES DE LA PROPAGATION DE LA FOI pour les provinces de Quebec et de Montreal (Montréal, 1877-1893). Nos. 1-50.

> Published by the Canadian branch (established 1836) of the Association de la Propagation de la Foi – a missionary society of world-wide membership in the Roman Catholic Church, which has published its *Annals* since 1827 (in various languages), as a successor to the well-known *Lettres édifiantes*. The Canadian *Annales* was a successor to *Rapport sur les missions du diocèse de Québec*, published at intervals from 1839 to 1874; both devoted chiefly to missions among the Indians.

ANTHROPOLOGICAL SOCIETY OF WASHINGTON. *American Anthropologist* (Washington, 1888-1898). 11 vols. Illustrated.

—— *Id.*, new series (New York, 1899-1911+). Vols. i-xiii.

> This valuable periodical is also the organ of the Amer. Ethnological Society, and its contributors include the leading scientists and thinkers in this branch of knowledge. Among notable papers in the new series are the following: Volume I, "Aboriginal American zoötechny," Otis T. Mason (pp. 45-81); III, "Rare books relating to the American Indians," Ainsworth R. Spofford (pp. 270-285); "Significance of certain Algonquian animal names," Alexander F. Chamberlain (pp. 669-683); "Aboriginal copper mines of the Isle Royale, Lake Superior," W. H. Holmes (pp. 684-696); VI, "Some principles of Algonquian word-formation;" William Jones (pp. 369-412); VII, "Popular fallacies respecting the Indian," Henry W. Henshaw (pp. 104-182); VIII, "Recent progress in American anthropology, 1902-1906" (pp. 441-558); X, "The tomahawk," papers by W. H. Holmes and W. R. Gerard (pp. 264-280); "Wooden bowls of the Algonquian Indians," C. C. Willoughby (pp. 423-504; illustrated); XI, "Tat-

tooing of the North American Indians," A. T. Sinclair (pp. 362-400);
"The various uses of buffalo hair by the Indians," D. I. Bushnell (pp.
401-425); XII, "Clan organization of the Winnebago," Paul Radin (pp.
209-219).

ARMSTRONG, BENJAMIN G.   Early life among the Indians (Ashland,
Wis., 1892).

> Reminiscences, dictated by Armstrong to Thos. P. Wentworth; relate
> chiefly to the Indians of northern Wisconsin, the treaties of 1835-1854, etc.

ARMSTRONG, PERRY A.   The Sauks and the Black Hawk War
(Springfield, Ill., 1887).   Illustrated.

> Compiled from the best printed sources, and from interviews with old
> pioneers, etc. Contains much information regarding the Sauk tribe, and
> biographical sketches of noted Indian chiefs.

—— The piasa, or, the devil among the Indians (Morris, Ill., 1887).

AUPAUMUT, HENDRICK.   Narrative of an embassy to the western
Indians (Philadelphia, 1826).

> "From the original manuscript, with prefatory remarks by Dr. B. H.
> Coates;" in *Memoirs* of the Penn. Historical Society, vol. ii, 61-131. The
> author was a chief of the N.Y. Stockbridge tribe, and was sent in 1792
> by the U.S. secretary of war on the mission above mentioned. He in-
> fluenced the western tribes against Tecumseh, and aided Gen. Harrison in
> the campaign wherein Tecumseh was defeated. In 1821 the Stockbridges
> removed to Wisconsin, and Aupaumut died there, some time after 1825.
> (Wis. *Hist. Collections*, vol. xv, 40, 41.)

AVERY, ELROY McK.   A history of the United States and its people,
from their earliest records to the present time (Cleveland, 1904-
1910+).   15 vols.   Illustrated.

> Its special feature is in the valuable and elegant illustrations which
> abound in every volume – maps and plans, portraits, views of historical
> scenes and buildings, reproductions of celebrated paintings, etc. Volumes
> I and IV are of interest in connection with the present work.

AYER, EDWARD E.   Collection of historical documents.

> One of the finest collections of Americana (both printed and Ms.) in the
> United States; it has long been in charge of the Newberry Library, Chicago.
> It includes most of the printed works of value relating to the Indians, and
> many manuscripts; among the latter are a considerable number relating
> to the Indians of the old northwest, especially as connected with the fur trade.

BARBER, EDWIN A.   Indian music.

—— Catlinite: its antiquity as a material for tobacco pipes.

> These articles appeared in the *Amer. Naturalist*, vol. xvii, 267-274 and
> 745-764 respectively.

BARROWS, WILLIAM.   The Indian's side of the Indian question (Boston, 1887).

BEACH, W. W. The Indian miscellany: containing papers on the history, antiquities, arts, languages, religions, traditions, and superstitions of the American aborigines (Albany, 1877).

Contains many valuable articles regarding the Indians; reprinted "from magazines and other ephemera," in order to preserve the information they contain.

BEAUCHAMP, REV. W. M. The Iroquois trail, or foot-prints of the Six Nations, in customs, traditions, and history (Fayetteville, N.Y., 1892).

Includes the "Sketches of Ancient History of the Six Nations" (Lewiston, N.Y., 1826) by David Cusick, a Tuscarora Indian; and notes and comments thereon by Beauchamp, long a missionary among the Iroquois, and an acknowledged authority on Iroquois lore, history, and antiquities.

—— [Various papers relating to the N.Y. Iroquois tribes – their history, arts and industries, etc.]

These are published as *Bulletins* of the N.Y. State Museum (1897-1907), nos. 16, 18, 32, 41, 50, 73, 78, 89, 108; they are valuable contributions to our knowledge of those tribes.

BECKWITH, HIRAM W. The Illinois and Indiana Indians (Chicago, 1884).

This is no. 27 of the *Fergus Hist. Series*; the author was a prominent antiquarian of Illinois.

BIGGS, W. Narrative, while he was a prisoner with the Kickapoo Indians (s.l., 1826).

BLACKBIRD, ANDREW J. History of the Ottawa and Chippewa Indians of Michigan; a grammar, and personal and family history of the author (Ypsilanti, Mich., 1887).

Written by an Indian chief well known in Southern Michigan.

BLACK HAWK. Life of Ma-ka-tai-me-she-kia-kiak (Boston, 1834).

This purports to be the story of his life, as dictated by him to Antoine Leclaire (a half-breed government interpreter), and edited by J. B. Patterson; not considered, by well-informed students, as altogether trustworthy.

BLANCHARD, RUFUS. Discovery and conquests of the Northwest, with the history of Chicago (Wheaton, Ill., 1879).

Written by a pioneer antiquarian, who did much to preserve records of early Chicago and Northwestern history; in that work the maps published by him made a prominent feature.

BLOOMFIELD, JULIA K. The Oneidas (New York, 1907). Illustrated.

Treats mainly of the missionary enterprises conducted among the Oneidas, especially those of the Protestant Episcopal Church on the Oneida reservation in Wisconsin.

BOYD, GEORGE. Papers, 1797-1846. Ms. 8 vols.

These papers are in the possession of the Wisconsin State Historical Society. Col. Boyd was U.S. Indian agent at Mackinac during 1818-1832, and at Green Bay 1832-1840.

BRINTON, DANIEL G. American hero-myths: a study in the native religions of the western continent (Philadelphia, 1882).

—— The American race: a linguistic classification and ethnographic description of the native tribes of North and South America (New York, 1891).

—— Essays of an Americanist (Philadelphia, 1890).

Classed under these heads: "ethnologic and archæologic; mythology and folk-lore; graphic systems, and literature; and linguistic."

—— Myths of the New World: a treatise on the symbolism and mythology of the red race of America (New York, 1868).

A third edition, revised, was issued at Philadelphia in 1896. The works of this able and scholarly investigator that are here mentioned are those of more general interest; besides these, he edited or wrote numerous others, of great value on certain special topics.

BROWER, J. V. Memoirs of explorations in the basin of the Mississippi (St. Paul, 1898-1903). 7 vols.

Written by a learned Minnesota antiquarian, long a prominent officer in the Minn. State Historical Society.

BRUNSON, REV. ALFRED. Journals and letter-books. Ms.

Brunson was a pioneer Methodist preacher in Wisconsin, and an Indian agent. These papers are in the possession of the Wisconsin Historical Society.

BUCK, DANIEL. Indian outbreaks (Mankato, Minn., 1904). Illustrated.

Written by a former judge of the Minnesota supreme court, a resident of that state since 1857. He claims "to treat all questions with judicial fairness," and says that "the Indian side of the trouble has been given a hearing" in his book.

BUREAU OF AMERICAN ETHNOLOGY. Annual reports to the secretary of the Smithsonian Institution (Washington, 1879-1908). 26 vols. Illustrated.

These publications contain monographs, written by the trained experts on the staff of the Bureau, on the history, character, mode of life, customs, mythology and religion, etc., of the North American Indians; and on various general and special aspects of the science of ethnology. They constitute a mass of data and scientific theory quite indispensable for the thorough study of these subjects, and of the utmost value to all students therein. Among the papers of especial interest for the field covered by this work are the following: "On the evolution of language . . . from the study of Indian languages," and "Wyandot government: a short study of tribal society," J. W. Powell (*First Report*); "Sign language among the N. American Indians," Garrick Mallery (*ibid*); "Animal carvings from mounds of the Mississippi valley," H. W. Henshaw, and "Art in shell of the ancient Americans," W. H. Holmes (*Second Report*); "On masks, labrets, and certain aboriginal customs," W. H. Dall, and "Omaha sociology," J. Owen Dorsey (*Third Report*); "Ancient pottery of the Mississippi valley," and "Origin and development of form and ornament in ceramic art," W. H. Holmes (*Fourth Report*); "Burial mounds of the northern section of the United States," Cyrus Thomas (*Fifth Report*); "A study of the textile art in its relation to the development of form and ornament," W. H. Holmes (*Sixth Report*); "Indian linguistic families of America north of Mexico," J. W. Powell, and "The Midē'wiwin or 'grand medicine society' of the Ojibwa," W. J. Hoffman (*Seventh Report*); "Picture writing of the American Indians," Garrick Mallery (*Tenth Report*); "A study of Siouan cults," J. Owen Dorsey (*Eleventh Report*); "The Menomini Indians," W. J. Hoffman, and "The Ghost-dance religion and the Sioux outbreak of 1890," James Mooney (*Fourteenth Report*); "The Siouan Indians," W. J. McGee, and "Siouan sociology," J. Owen Dorsey (*Fifteenth Report*); "Indian land cessions in the United States," C. C. Royce (*Eighteenth Report*); "The wild-rice gatherers of the upper lakes," A. E. Jenks (*Nineteenth Report*); "Iroquois cosmogony," J. N. B. Hewitt (*Twenty-first Report*); "American Indian games," Stewart Culin (*Twenty-fourth Report*).

BUREAU OF AMERICAN ETHNOLOGY. Bulletins (Washington, 1887-1910). 45 vols. Illustrated.

Of the same character as the papers in the *Reports*, save that they more often are bibliographical and linguistic in scope, or devoted to subjects of more limited interest. Among these are bibliographies of the Siouan, Iroquoian, and Algonquian languages, by J. C. Pilling (nos. 5, 6, and 13, respectively); "The problem of the Ohio mounds," and "Catalogue of prehistoric works east of the Rocky Mountains," Cyrus Thomas (nos. 8 and 12); "Handbook of the Indians north of Mexico," edited by Frederick W. Hodge (no. 30); "Tuberculosis among certain tribes of the United States" [among which are the Oglala Sioux and the Menomini], Ales Hrdlicka (no. 42).

BUREAU OF CATHOLIC INDIAN MISSIONS. Reports of Director (Washington, 1900-1910 +).

—— Annals of the Catholic Indian missions of America (Washington, 1878, 1880, 1881).

BURTON, C. M. Collections of documents relating to the early history of Michigan. Ms.

Mr. Burton, a resident of Detroit, has been collecting these documents during some forty years, "covering more than two centuries in the history of Michigan and the region of the Great Lakes." They include many originals, as well as many transcripts from French and Canadian archives; and consist of letters, diaries, military order-books, Indian and

French deeds and contracts, records of old Catholic churches, fur-trade accounts, etc. Of special interest regarding Indian affairs are the papers of LaMothe Cadillac, the founder of Detroit (published in the *Collections* of the Michigan Pioneer and Historical Society, vols. xxxiii and xxxiv); the Montreal papers, 1682-1804, copied from notarial records in Montreal; the papers of John Askin, a prominent fur-trader before 1812; and those of John R. Williams and William Woodbridge (for a time, superintendent of Indian affairs).

BURTON, FREDERICK R. American primitive music, with especial attention to the songs of the Ojibways (New York, 1909). Illustrated.

A careful study of Indian music, in both its technique and its meaning and use. Burton collected among the Ojibwas a large number of songs, which are here presented with their original words and music, and the story and meaning of each. At the end, twenty-eight of these are harmonized for pianoforte accompaniment, and have an English translation.

CALKINS, FRANKLIN W. The wooing of Tokala (New York and Chicago, 1907).

Although in the form of a story, this book was intended rather as a study of Indian character; it depicts life among a group of Dakota Indians, and "primitive conditions as they existed among the Sioux previous to and during the American Civil War." Adopted into one of their tribes, with whom he lived a considerable time, the author has obtained his material from personal experience and observation.

—— Indian tales (Chicago [1893]). Illustrated.

Accounts of various experiences of the author and other white persons among Indians in Iowa and Nebraska, 1860-1880.

CAMPBELL, HENRY C., and others. Wisconsin in three centuries, 1634-1905 (New York [1906]). 4 vols. Illustrated.

CANFIELD, W. W. The legends of the Iroquois told by "The Cornplanter" (New York, 1902).

A highly interesting collection of legends related, toward the end of the eighteenth century, by the noted Seneca chief Cornplanter to a white friend — whose notes of these conversations are here reproduced, with much information obtained from other prominent Iroquois chiefs, by Mr. Canfield.

CARR, LUCIEN. The food of certain American Indians, and their methods of preparing it (Worcester, 1895).

In *Proceedings* of Amer. Antiquarian Society, vol. x, part i.

—— Dress and ornaments of certain American Indians (Worcester, 1898).

Id., vol. xi, 381-454.

CARR, LUCIEN. The Mascoutins.

> *Proceedings* of American Antiquarian Society, vol. xiv, 448-462.

—— Mounds of the Mississippi Valley, historically considered (Frankfort, 1883).

> In *Memoirs* of Geol. Survey of Kentucky, vol. ii.

CARVER, JONATHAN. Travels through the interior parts of North America, 1766-1768 (London, 1778). Illustrated.

> An account of travels in the region of the Great Lakes and upper Mississippi River; it obtained great favor with the public, appearing, during some eighty years, in thirty editions and reissues, and in several foreign languages. Some parts of this narrative are plagiarized from Hennepin, Charlevoix, and other early writers, a fact which has caused Carver's veracity, and the genuineness of his account, to be discredited by some critics — even to the extent of supposing him to be illiterate, and incapable of writing such a book. The controversy is summarized by John T. Lee in his "Bibliography of Carver's Travels" (*Proceedings* of Wis. Hist. Soc., 1909, pp. 143-183); he adduces evidence to show that Carver must have been the author of the *Travels*, and a man of respectable character and education.

CASEY, M. P. Indian contract schools.

> In *Catholic World*, Aug., 1900.

CASS, LEWIS. Considerations on the present state of the Indians, and their removal to the west of the Mississippi.

—— Remarks on the policy and practice of the United States and Great Britain in their treatment of the Indians.

> These articles appeared in the *North Amer. Review*, January, 1830, and April, 1827, respectively.

CATLIN, GEORGE. Illustrations of the manners, customs, and condition of the North American Indians, with letters and notes written during eight years of travel and adventure, tenth edition (London, 1866). 2 vols. Illustrated.

> A work of prime importance, especially as it shows the Indian tribes of the west and south at a time (1832-1838) when they still retained much of their primitive mode of life. Catlin relates his adventures while traveling among them, and adds a wealth of information on their customs, character, beliefs, etc. — which are illustrated by three hundred and sixty drawings from his original paintings.

—— Adventures of the Ojibbeway and Ioway Indians in England, France, and Belgium, third edition (London, 1852). 2 vols. in 1. Illustrated.

> Catlin's "notes of eight years' travels and residence in Europe with his

North American Indian collection" — which contained nearly six hundred paintings, made by Catlin during eight years' residence among the Indian tribes; and included, besides many portraits, pictures of scenery, Indian villages, customs, games, religious ceremonies, etc., all from life; a catalogue of these appears at end of his vol. I. Catlin also exhibited in Europe many Indian curios — robes, weapons, ornaments, pipes, cradles, etc. During 1845-1846, he acted as interpreter and guide for some Indians (thirty-five in all) who had been carried to Europe for the purpose of public exhibition; and here he describes their novel experiences and the traits of character they displayed, this last being the chief value of his book.

CATON, J. D. The last of the Illinois, and a sketch of the Pottowatomies (Chicago, 1876).

No. 3 of *Fergus Historical Series.*

CHAMBERLAIN, ALEXANDER F. The contributions of the American Indian to civilization (Worcester, 1904).

In *Proceedings* of Amer. Antiquarian Society, vol. xvi, 91-126.

CHARLEVOIX, PIERRE F. X. DE. Histoire et description générale de la Nouvelle France, avec le Journal Historique d'un voyage fait par ordre du roi dans l'Amérique Septentrionnale (Paris, 1744). 3 vols.

A standard authority on early Canadian history, description of New France, and account of the Indian tribes therein. A translation of this valuable work was made by John G. Shea, with many excellent and scholarly annotations; published in six volumes (New York, 1866-1872). A reprint of Shea's edition appeared in New York, 1900, edited by Noah F. Morrison.

CHASE, LEVI B. Early Indian trails (Worcester, 1897).

In *Collections* of Worcester Society of Antiquities, vol. xiv, 105-125.

CHICAGO HISTORICAL SOCIETY. Collection of documents relating to the early history of Illinois. Ms.

A very large and valuable collection of documents (most of them originals) relating to the history of the northwest territory, and chiefly of Illinois. Notable among these are the papers of Gen. Henry Dearborn, Gov. Ninian Edwards, John Kinzie, and Pierre Ménard (the last two, noted Indian traders) ; and the transcripts from early records of Kaskaskia and Fort Chartres churches. Some of the Edwards papers were published in vol. iii (1884) of the *Collections* of this society.

CHIPPEWA ALLOTMENTS of lands, and timber contracts (Washington, 1889).

Senate Docs., Report no. 2710, 50th congress, second session. Report of "Select Committee on Indian Traders," containing evidence, documents, etc., proving gross mismanagement, abuses, and spoliation in the affairs of the Chippewa reservations in Wisconsin and Minnesota.

CHOUTEAU, AUGUSTE. Papers and correspondence, 1787-1819. Ms.

Chouteau was probably the most enterprising and influential of the pioneer fur-traders in the Missouri River Valley, and closely connected with the founding of St. Louis, of which event he left a manuscript account. The documents here mentioned are in the possession of the Mercantile Library, St. Louis.

CHRISTIAN JOURNAL, 1817-1830.　14 vols.

Edited by Bishop J. H. Hobart, and contains numerous papers relating to the Oneida Indians of Wisconsin.

CLARK, GEORGE ROGERS.　Letters, journals, etc., 1760-1859.　Ms. 65 vols.

This highly valuable collection of manuscripts is in the possession of the Wisconsin State Historical Society; it includes many early original documents, various subsidiary collections of papers, and a great deal of correspondence between L. C. Draper and the descendants of the Western pioneers.　Much of this matter relates to Clark's conquest of Illinois (1778), and his campaigns, soon afterward, to St. Louis and in the Wabash country. A selection from these papers is announced for this year (1911), in three volumes, edited by Prof. J. A. James of Northwestern University.

CLARK, W. P.　The Indian sign language (Philadelphia, 1885).

The author, an army officer, spent over six years among the Indian tribes, and acquired at first-hand the sign language and the explanations of it made by the Indians themselves.　To these he adds much valuable information regarding their customs, beliefs, superstitions, modes of life, etc.; and he writes in a spirit of appreciation for the abilities and good traits of those Indians who have not been demoralized by contact with the whites. He makes interesting comparisons between the Indian sign language and that taught in schools for deaf-mutes.　The book contains a map showing the Indian reservations, etc.

CLARK, WILLIAM.　Papers.　Ms.　29 vols.

This collection of documents contains the records of Clark and his successors in the office of superintendent of Indian affairs at St. Louis.　It is in the possession of the Kansas Historical Society.

CLARKE, PETER DOOYENTATE.　Origin and traditional history of the Wyandotts, etc., (Toronto, 1870).

In this little volume are collected the traditions of Wyandott (Huron) tribal history and legend, obtained from the few surviving ancients of that people by the author (himself a Wyandott); and much of this material is apparently not to be found elsewhere.

COLDEN, CADWALLADER.　The history of the five Indian nations depending on the province of New York (New York, 1727).

The above title refers only to Part I of Colden's work.　It was reprinted, but in a garbled form, in London, 1747 and 1750 — containing, however, Part II, of which a Ms. copy is preserved in the collections of the N.Y. State Historical Society.　The book was reprinted (1866) by J. G. Shea.

COLESON, A. Narrative of her captivity among the Sioux Indians (Philadelphia, 1864).

COLTON, C. Tour of the American lakes, and among the Indians of the Northwest Territory, in 1830 (London, 1833). 2 vols.

[CONDITION of Indian tribes in Montana and Dakota (Washington, 1884).]

> *Senate Report*, no. 283, 48th congress, first session. Report of a "Select Committee to examine into the condition of the Sioux and Crow Indians." Shows the destitution then prevailing among those tribes, and calls for government aid to them; also scores the management of the agency stores.

CONDITION OF THE INDIAN TRIBES: report of the Joint Special Committee appointed under joint resolution of March 3, 1865 (Washington, 1867).

> This report and its documentary appendix constitute a full survey of the status of the Indian tribes at that time. The committee (J. R. Doolittle, chairman) stated that the Indian population was rapidly decreasing, mainly through disease, vicious habits, and the loss of their old-time hunting grounds – all these causes being in large measure traceable to the encroachments, bad influence, and whiskey of the whites. The committee recommended that the Indian Bureau be retained in the Department of the Interior; and that more efficient government control and inspection be provided for Indian affairs.

CONGRÈS INTERNATIONAL DES AMÉRICANISTES. Comptes rendus, sessions 1-16. 1875-1910. Illustrated.

> The sessions of this learned body have been held biennially at various places since 1875 (at Nancy), the last one whose proceedings are yet published being at Vienna (1908). These volumes contain many articles relating to the Indian tribes of the central United States. Among these may be noted: Various articles on the mound-builders (second session, Luxemburg); Algic cosmogony (third session, Brussels); "sacred hunts" of the Indians (eighth session, Paris); "Contributions of American archæology to human history" (fourteenth session, Stuttgart); two papers on the Indians of the Mississippi, and one on customs and rites of the Iowa Foxes (fifteenth session, Quebec); "Types of dwellings and their distribution in Central North America" (sixteenth session, Vienna). The seventeenth session was held at Mexico City, September, 1910.

COPWAY, GEORGE. The traditional history and characteristic sketches of the Ojibway nation (London, 1850; Boston, 1851). Illustrated.

> The author (an Ojibwa chief, his Indian name Kah-ge-ga-gah-bowh) states that he has resided "six years among the pale-faces," and has attended school, twenty months in all, in Illinois. He recounts the traditions and legends of his people, describes their customs, beliefs, character, etc.; and shows their condition under British and American domination.

COPWAY, GEORGE. The organization of an Indian territory east of the Missouri River (New York, 1850).

> Copway urged Congress to erect a new Indian Territory, which should improve upon the old one by being set aside for northern bands only, and by providing at the outset for Indian self-government.

CORRESPONDENCE on the subject of the emigration of Indians, 1831-1833 (Washington, 1834). 5 vols.

> This is found in *Senate Documents*, vols. vii-xi, 23rd congress, first session (1833-1834).

COUES, ELLIOTT. The fur-bearing animals of North America (Boston, 1877).

CULIN, STEWART. American Indian games (Washington, 1905). Illustrated.

> In *Report* of Bureau Amer. Ethnology, 1902-1903.

CURTIS, EDWARD S. The North American Indian (New York, 1907-—). 20 vols., each accompanied by a portfolio of supplementary plates.

> This magnificent work (first begun in 1898) well carries out the author's aim, to present a true picture of Indian life in its natural surroundings and primitive, homely phases — especially in view of the rapid and often destructive changes therein which are taking place throughout the continent. The illustrations (most of which are 20x24 inches in size) are from photographs made by Curtis during his residence among the various tribes, and they are unusually accurate and artistic. They are accompanied by descriptive text and account of the author's experiences among the Indians, with which is combined much historical and ethnological information. He also records many Indian myths, related to him by the elders of the tribes, and much about their rites and ceremonies. The work is an interesting revelation of Indian life and character.

CURTIS, NATALIE, editor. The Indians' book; an offering by the American Indians of Indian lore, musical and narrative, to form a record of the songs and legends of their race (New York and London, 1907). Illustrated, chiefly from drawings made by Indians.

> Contains Indian songs, with original native music and words, English translation, and explanatory notes; some twenty tribes are thus represented, of whom the Winnebago and Dakota (and indirectly the Abenaki) belong to the subject of the present work. A valuable contribution to the literature of the Indians' higher life.

[CUTLER, JERVIS.] A topographical description of the state of Ohio, Indiana Territory, and Louisiana (Boston, 1812).

> "Comprehending the Ohio and Mississippi Rivers, and their principal tributary streams; the face of the country . . . and a concise account of the Indian tribes west of the Mississippi." By a U.S. army officer.

DAVIDSON, ALEXANDER, and Bernard Stuvé. A complete history of Illinois, 1673-1873 (Springfield, Ill., 1874).

DAVIDSON, J. N. In unnamed Wisconsin: studies in the history of the region between Lake Michigan and the Mississippi (Milwaukee, 1895).

DAVIS, ANDREW M. Indian games.

In *Bulletin* of Essex Institute, vol. xvii, 89-144.

DELLENBAUGH, FREDERICK S. The North-Americans of yesterday: a comparative study of North-American Indian life, customs, and products, on the theory of the ethnic unity of the race (New York, 1901). Illustrated.

A valuable and scholarly work, presenting the results of recent research in the languages, industries, mode of life, customs, beliefs, government, history, etc., of the North American tribes; contains a list of these, with the respective stocks to which they belong. Both text and the numerous fine illustrations are based largely on material in the Bureau of American Ethnology.

DENSMORE, FRANCES. Chippewa music (Washington, 1910). Illustrated.

A collection of songs, both ritual and social, in all numbering two hundred; the Indian words and English translation, with music, and full description of rites, customs, etc. This is *Bulletin* 45 of the Bureau of Amer. Ethnology.

DILLON, JOHN B. Decline of the Miami nation.

In *Publications* of Indiana Historical Society, vol. i, 121-143.

DODGE, CHARLES R. A descriptive catalogue of useful fiber plants of the world, including the structural and economic classifications of fibers (Washington, 1897).

Published by U.S. Department of Agriculture.

DODGE, RICHARD IRVING. Our wild Indians: thirty-three years' personal experience among the red men of the Great West (Hartford, Conn., 1883). Illustrated.

An interesting record of Indian customs and character, by an army officer; highly commended by his superior, Gen. W. T. Sherman, who nevertheless dissents from Dodge's estimate of Indian character. The author advocates military rather than civilian control for the tribes.

DOMINION OF CANADA. Report concerning Canadian archives (Ottawa, 1872-1910 +).

These reports contain many calendars of documents contained in the Dominion archives, and are indispensable to the student of Canadian history. Many of those documents relate to Indian affairs.

DONALDSON, THOMAS. The George Catlin Indian gallery in the United States National Museum; with memoir and statistics (Washington, 1885). Illustrated.

> In *Report* of Smithsonian Institution, 1885, part ii. A catalogue of the paintings and curios in the great Catlin collection, which was transferred to the Smithsonian Institution, 1879-1881. The pictures are arranged under the tribal names, each accompanied by extracts (narrative or descriptive) from Catlin's own books, an outline drawing from the same source, and much additional information furnished by Donaldson as editor.

—— The Six Nations of New York (Washington, 1892). Illustrated.

> An *Extra Bulletin*, Eleventh Census of the U.S. A valuable account of the Iroquois people in modern times, presenting not only statistics of population and property, but observations on their character, government, social conditions, mode of life, etc. Well illustrated with maps, portraits, etc.

DORMAN, RUSHTON M. The origin of primitive superstitions, and their development into the worship of spirits, and the doctrine of spiritual agency, among the aborigines of America (Philadelphia, 1881).

DORSEY, J. OWEN. Migrations of Siouan tribes.

> In *Amer. Naturalist*, vol. xx, 211-222.

—— [Papers on "Omaha sociology," "Siouan sociology," "A study of Siouan cults."]

> In *Reports* of Bureau of Amer. Ethnology: 1881-1882, pp. 311-370; 1893-1894, pp. 205-244; 1889-1890, pp. xliii-xlvii, 351-544, respectively.

DRAKE, BENJAMIN. Life of Tecumseh, and of his brother the Prophet, with a historical sketch of the Shawanoe Indians (Cincinnati, 1841).

> A plain narrative, based on letters written by Gen. Harrison to the War Department in 1809-1813, interviews with old pioneers, etc. Another edition was issued in 1852.

DRAKE, FRANCIS S. The Indian tribes of the United States (Philadelphia, 1884). 2 vols. Illustrated.

DRAKE, SAMUEL G. Biography and history of the Indians of North America (Boston, 1832). Illustrated.

> A popular work, but compiled from the best authorities of Drake's time. Other titles, used in some editions, were: "The book of the Indians," and "Aboriginal races of North America." Later editions contain many additions and corrections. A revision of the fifteenth (Phila., 1860) was issued in 1880 (New York).

DUNN, JACOB P. Indiana, a redemption from slavery (Boston, 1904).

> In *Amer. Commonwealths* series. This is a new and enlarged edition of his book first published in 1888. The author is secretary of the Indiana Historical Society, and a trained and careful investigator.

—— True Indian stories, with glossary of Indiana Indian names (Indianapolis, 1908).

> Narratives of military and other events in early Indiana history, relating to the Indians, and accounts of their leading chiefs.

EASTMAN, CHARLES A. Indian boyhood (New York, 1902). Illustrated.

> An interesting picture of Indian boys' life, as it records the experiences and impressions of the writer (a Sioux Indian) in boyhood and early youth.

—— The soul of the Indian: an interpretation (Boston, 1911).

> The author, writing as an Indian, aims "to paint the religious life of the typical American Indian as it was before he knew the white man." A valuable contribution to our data for a real understanding of the Indian character.

EASTMAN, CHARLES A. (Ohiyesa) and Elaine Goodale. Sioux folk tales retold (Boston, 1909). Illustrated.

EASTMAN, MARY H. The American aboriginal portfolio (Philadelphia, [1853]). Illustrated.

> Descriptive sketches of Indian life and customs, accompanied by handsome steel engravings from drawings by Capt. S. Eastman, U.S.A. (apparently the same plates as those in Schoolcraft's *Indian Tribes*).

—— Chicóra, and other regions of the conquerors and the conquered (Philadelphia, 1854). Illustrated.

> Sketches of Indian life, beliefs, etc.

—— Dahcotah, or, life and legends of the Sioux around Fort Snelling (New York, 1849). Illustrated.

> Written from intimate knowledge and direct observation of the Sioux Indians, who related many of their legends to the author (whose father and husband were army officers in the Northwest).

EDWARDS, NINIAN W. History of Illinois from 1778 to 1833, and life and times of Ninian Edwards (Springfield, Ill., 1870).

> Contains full account of the Black Hawk War, and many letters from high officials to Gov. Edwards.

EGGLESTON, EDWARD, and L. E. Seelye. Tecumseh and the Shawnee prophet (New York, 1878). Illustrated.

> Also includes sketches of Indian chiefs and American officers famous in

the frontier wars of Tecumseh's time. A popular narrative, but based on reliable authorities.

ELLIS, GEORGE E. The red man and the white man in North America (Boston, 1882).

Discusses traits of character of the Indians, their relations with the white people, missions, our policy toward the red men, their capacity for civilization, etc.

EMERSON, ELLEN RUSSELL. Indian myths, or legends, traditions, and symbols of the aborigines of America compared with those of other countries (Boston, 1884). Illustrated.

A valuable work, showing much research and learning.

EVARTS, JEREMIAH. Essays on the present crisis in the condition of the American Indians (Boston, 1829).

"These essays, twenty-four in number, were first published in the *National Intelligencer* under the pseudonym of 'William Penn.' They constitute a very fine exposition of the wrongs committed against the Indians and bear few traces of having been written from the absolutely missionary point of view." — ABEL.

——, editor. Speeches on the passage of the bill for the removal of the Indians, delivered in the Congress of the United States, April-May, 1830 (Boston, 1830).

FARRAND, LIVINGSTON. Basis of American history, 1500-1900 (New York, 1904). Illustrated.

This is volume II of *The American Nation: a history* (Albert B. Hart, editor.

FEATHERSTONHAUGH, G. W. A canoe voyage up the Minnay Sotor (London, 1847). 2 vols.

FIELD COLUMBIAN MUSEUM. Publications: anthropological series (Chicago, 1895-1905). Vols. i-ix.

FIELD, THOMAS W. An essay towards an Indian bibliography, being a catalogue of books relating to the history, antiquities, languages, customs, religion, war, literature, and origin of the American Indians, in the library of Thomas W. Field (New York, 1873).

FILLMORE, JOHN C. The harmonic structure of Indian music.

In *Amer. Anthropologist*, new series, vol. i, 297-318. The author was a professional musician, of long experience and fine taste.

—— A study of Omaha Indian music . . . with a report on the structural peculiarities of the music (Cambridge, 1893).

This paper, with another on Omaha music by Alice C. Fletcher, appeared in *Archæological and Ethnological Papers* of Peabody Museum, vol. i, no. 5.

FINLEY, JAMES B. Life among the Indians; or, personal reminiscences and historical incidents illustrative of Indian life and character (Cincinnati, 1868).

Written by a Methodist missionary among the Indians, chiefly the Wyandotts; contains much regarding the history of this tribe and others in their relations with the whites, from 1800 on.

—— History of the Wyandott mission at Upper Sandusky, Ohio (Cincinnati, 1840).

FLETCHER, ALICE C. A study of the Omaha tribe: the import of the totem.

In *Report* of Smithsonian Institution, 1897, pp. 577-586.

—— Indian education and civilization (Washington, 1888).

Published in *Ex. Docs.* no. 95, 48th congress, second session. A special report from the Bureau of Education; reviews missionary and educational work among the Indians from the earliest of such enterprises to the time of this report; gives abstracts of treaties with the tribe, and description, statistics, and other valuable data for each of the Indian reservations. A condensed and excellent book of reference for the subject.

—— Indian song and story from North America (Boston, 1900).

"Contains the music of the ghost, love, and other songs in the Omaha language." Miss Fletcher has made a specialty of Indian music, and has spent many years in the study of some of the plains tribes.

FORSYTH, THOMAS. Letter-books, memoirs, etc., 1804-1833. Ms. 9 vols.

These papers and books are in the possession of the Wisconsin Historical Society. They are all original documents (save two letter-books, which are transcripts from the originals), and concern the affairs of Forsyth's agency at Rock Island (1812-1830), the fur-trade, and the Indian tribes of that region; they include many letters from William Clark and Gov. Ninian Edwards, and much official correspondence, besides the two memoirs (by Forsyth and Marston) reproduced in the present volume.

FOWKE, GERARD. Archæological history of Ohio: the mound-builders and later Indians (Columbus, 1902).

—— Stone art (Washington, 1896).

In *Report* of Bureau of Amer. Ethnology, 1891-1892, pp. 47-178.

FRAZER, J. G. Totemism (Edinburgh, 1887).

FROBENIUS, LEO. The childhood of man: a popular account of the lives, customs, and thoughts of the primitive races (Philadelphia, 1909). Illustrated.

Based on the latest authorities, and shows extensive research. This edition is a translation from the German by the well-known ethnographer, A. H. Keane.

FULTON, A. R. The red men of Iowa (Des Moines, Ia., 1882). Illustrated.

    A history of the Indian tribes who resided in Iowa; sketches of chiefs; traditions, etc.; a general account of the Indian tribes and wars of the Northwest; etc. The material was obtained from writings of local historians, interviews with pioneers, etc.

GALE, GEORGE. The Upper Mississippi: or historical sketches of the mound-builders, the Indian tribes, and the progress of civilization in the Northwest; from A.D. 1600 to the present time (Chicago, 1867).

GALLATIN, ALBERT. A synopsis of the Indian tribes of North America.

    In *Transactions and Collections* of the Amer. Antiquarian Society, 1838, vol. ii.

GANNETT, HENRY. A gazetteer of Indian Territory (Washington, 1905).

    Issued as *Bulletin*, no. 248 of the U.S. Geological Survey.

GARLAND, HAMLIN. The red men's present needs.

    in *North American Review*, April, 1902.

GERARD, W. R. Plant names of Indian origin (New York, 1896).

    In *Garden and Forest*, vol. ix.

GREEN BAY AND PRAIRIE DU CHIEN PAPERS. Ms. 99 vols.

    Of similar character to the "Grignon, Lawe, and Porlier Papers," except that they relate to the regions of both Green Bay and Prairie du Chien. They were obtained from the estates of Morgan L. Martin, Green Bay (one of the most prominent among the early American pioneers in Wisconsin), and Hercules L. Dousman, of Prairie du Chien, a leading fur-trader (for some years a representative of the American Fur Company). This collection is in the possession of the Wisconsin Historical Society.

GRIFFIN, A. P. C. List of references on the relations of the Indians to the U.S. government (Washington, 1902). Ms.

    In library of Wisconsin State Historical Society.

GRIGNON, LAWE, and Porlier Papers, 1712-1873. Ms. 65 vols.

    This collection, consisting of letters, accounts, legal documents, etc., which had accumulated for a century and a half in the possession of the families bearing the above names, who were the chief factors in the fur-trade that centered in or passed through Green Bay, Wis., is now in the possession of the Wisconsin Historical Society. "A miscellaneous and highly valuable collection of letters and varied documents both in French and English — social, commercial, ecclesiastical, political, and military — throwing a flood of light on the early history of the region ranging from Mackinac to the upper Mississippi, and between Lake Superior and the Illinois country." — THWAITES.

GARNEAU, F. X. Histoire du Canada depuis sa découverte jusqu'a nos jours (Montréal, 1882).

> The above is the fourth edition. An English translation, annotated, was published by Andrew Bell, third edition (Montreal, 1866).

HADDON, ALFRED C. The study of man (New York, 1898). Illustrated.

> Treats of measurements and head-form in anthropology, the origin of some primitive vehicles, and the sources of various games and other amusements.

HAILMANN, WILLIAM N. Education of the Indian (St. Louis, 1904).

> No. 19 of *Monographs on Education in U.S.*, issued by the educational department of the Louisiana Purchase Exposition.

HAINES, ELIJAH M. The American Indian (Chicago, 1888). Illustrated.

> A popular cyclopedia of Indian ethnology; includes also chapters on relations between the red men and the whites, the history of the "Order of Red Men," Indian vocabularies, and the meaning of Indian geographical names; is based on the works of standard authorities.

HALE, HORATIO. Hiawatha and the Iroquois confederation: a study in anthropology (Salem, 1881).

—— Indian migrations as evidenced by language, comprising the Huron-Cherokee, Dakota, and other stocks (Chicago, 1883).

——, editor. The Iroquois Book of Rites (Philadelphia, 1883).

> From Ms. records made by the Indians themselves, containing the rituals used in their council meetings; Hale (who was an accomplished linguist and ethnologist) copied and translated, with the assistance of the most learned Iroquois chiefs, these rituals — to which he has added glossary, annotations, etc., and a critical introduction describing the organization, government and laws, traditions, character, policy, and language of the Iroquois peoples.

HARRISON, J. B. The latest studies on Indian reservations (Philadelphia, 1887).

> Published by the Indian Rights Association.

HARRISON, WILLIAM H. Aborigines of the Ohio Valley (Chicago, 1884).

> No. 26 of *Fergus Hist. Series.* This book also contains speeches by Miami chiefs in a council at Ft. Wayne, Sept. 4, 1811; and an account (from a Ms.) of the history, customs, etc., of the Northwestern Indians.

HARSHBERGER, J. W. Maize: a botanical and economic study (Philadelphia, 1893).

> *Contributions* of Botanical Laboratory of Univ. Pennsylvania, vol. i, no. 2.

HARVEY, HENRY. History of the Shawnee Indians, from the year 1681 to 1854, inclusive (Cincinnati, 1855).

The author was sent by the Society of Friends as a missionary among the Shawnees, and was with that tribe when they were obliged to surrender their homes and lands in Ohio (1832).

HEARD, ISAAC V. D. History of the Sioux war and massacres of 1862 and 1863 (New York, 1865). Illustrated.

Written by a member of Sibley's expedition against the Sioux in 1862, from first-hand sources of various kinds.

HEBBERD, S. S. History of Wisconsin under the dominion of France (Madison, Wis., 1890).

HENNEPIN, LOUIS. Description de la Louisiane. . . Les mœurs et la maniere de vivre des sauvages (Paris, 1683).

A translation of this work, with annotations, by J. G. Shea, was published at New York in 1880. A reprint of the English edition of 1698, edited by R. G. Thwaites, with numerous annotations, was issued in 1903, at Chicago.

HEWITT, J. N. B. Iroquois cosmogony (Washington, 1903).

In *Report* of Bureau of Amer. Ethnology, 1899-1900.

HODGE, FREDERICK W., editor. Handbook of American Indians north of Mexico: parts 1 and 2 (Washington, 1907 and 1910). Illustrated.

This is *Bulletin* no. 30, Bureau of Amer. Ethnology. This great work — actually begun in 1885, and its central idea conceived in 1873 — forms a most valuable Indian cyclopedia. It has been prepared by the trained specialists of the Bureau, aided by others from the various government bureaus and the great museums of the country; and it represents the latest data and the most reliable conclusions thus far reached by experts in American ethnology and archæology. "It has been the aim," says its editor, "to give a brief description of every linguistic stock, confederacy, tribe, sub-tribe, or tribal subdivision, and settlement known to history or even to tradition, as well as the origin and derivation of every name treated, whenever such is known." These tribal descriptions (including history, location, population, etc.) are followed by full bibliographical references to authorities for each variant of the tribal name. Special subjects, such as "Dreams and visions," "Food," "Pueblos," "War," are fully discussed by expert writers; and biographical sketches of noted Indians are furnished. At the end is a synonymy of all the names and variants mentioned in the articles on tribes; and a full bibliography of printed books and other sources. These occupy respectively one hundred and fifty-eight and forty-three pages of fine type, giving the information in the shortest form possible; and both these features will be prized for reference by students.

HOFFMAN, WALTER J. The Menomini Indians (Washington, 1896). Illustrated.

A valuable monograph on that tribe, written by a careful and trained ethnologist; he treats, with much detail, their history, government, cult societies, myths, and folk-tales, games and dances, dwellings and furniture, industries and occupations, food, etc. An extensive vocabulary of their language is added at the close. In the fourteenth *Report* of Bureau of Amer. Ethnology.

HOFFMAN, WALTER J. The Midē'wiwin or "grand medicine society" of the Ojibwa (Washington, 1891).

In *Report* of Bureau of Amer. Ethnology, 1885-1886, pp. 149-300. This paper is of special interest as describing the proceedings and ceremonies of an Indian secret society.

HOLMES, W. H. Aboriginal pottery of the eastern United States (Washington, 1903).

In *Report* of Bureau of Amer. Ethnology, 1898-1899. Other archæological papers by Holmes concerning the field of this work are published in the second, third, fourth, sixth, and thirteenth of the Bureau's *Reports*.

—— Sacred pipestone quarries of Minnesota, and ancient copper mines of Lake Superior.

In *Proceedings* of Amer. Assoc. for Advancement of Science, 1892, pp. 277-279.

——, and others. Arrows and arrow-makers: a symposium.

In *Amer. Anthropologist*, vol. iv, 45-74.

HORNADAY, WILLIAM F. The extermination of the American bison, with a sketch of its discovery and life history.

In *Report* of Smithsonian Institution, 1887, part ii, pp. 367-548.

HOUGH, FRANKLIN B., editor. Proceedings of the commissioners of Indian affairs, appointed by law for the extinguishment of Indian titles in the state of New York (Albany, 1861).

"Published from the original manuscript in the library of the Albany Institute."

HOUGH, WALTER. Fire-making apparatus in the United States National Museum (Washington, 1890).

In *Report* U.S. National Museum, 1888.

HOY, P. R. How and by whom were the copper implements made? (Racine, 1886).

HULBERT, ARCHER B. The historic highways of America (Cleveland, 1902-1903). 16 vols. Illustrated.

This series undertakes to show the intimate connection of America's history and development with the highways and waterways which connected the seaboard with the vast interior of this continent — traced successively by herds of buffalo, by Indian trade and migration, and by white pioneers, and followed in later years by the great transcontinental railroads. The following volumes are those of special interest for students of Indian history: I, "Paths of the mound-buildings Indians and great game animals;" II, "Indian thoroughfares;" and VII, "Portage paths: the keys to the continent."

HUNTER, JOHN DUNN. Manners and customs of several Indian tribes located west of the Mississippi (Philadelphia, 1823).

> Contains biographical sketch of the author, and account of his captivity among the Kickapoo Indians; description of Missouri and Arkansas territories, and their products; account of customs, mode of life, industries, character, etc., of Indians therein; and chapters on their materia medica, and practice of surgery and medicine.

—— The Indian sketch-book (Cincinnati, 1852).

ILLINOIS STATE HISTORICAL LIBRARY. Collections (Springfield, 1906-1910 +). Illustrated.

> These publications contain valuable original documents relating to the early history of Illinois, ably edited by experienced and scholarly investigators. The "Virginia Series" is useful for readers interested in the French element of Illinois history, and in the Indians; it includes "Cahokia records, 1778-1790," "Kaskaskia records" (for the same period), and "George Rogers Clark papers" – the last to be published (1911) in three volumes.

ILLINOIS STATE HISTORICAL SOCIETY. Transactions (Springfield, 1901-1910 +).

—— Journal (Springfield, 1908-1911+).

INDIAN AFFAIRS. Report on the fur trade (Washington, 1828).

> In Senate Committee *Reports*, 20th congress, second session.

—— Information in relation to the Superintendency of Indina Affairs in the Territory of Michigan, 1820-1821 (Washington, 1822).

> Contains accounts of Lewis Cass as superintendent, letters by him relating to the Indian tribes, etc.

INDIAN AFFAIRS, OFFICE OF (War Department). Reports (Washington, 1825-1848).

—— (Department of the Interior). Report of the Commissioner (Washington, 1849-1910 +).

> Both these series constitute an official record of Indian affairs, of prime value.

—— Records. Ms.

> These date from 1800 only, as in that year the earlier records were destroyed by fire; and since then various injuries and losses have occurred through removals, lack of proper facilities for their care, etc. Still, they constitute the most important materials extant for study of Indian history and affairs – in which much aid is rendered by the description of these rec-

ords contained in Van Tyne and Leland's *Guide to the Archives*, second edition (Washington, 1908), pp. 205-209.

INDIAN BIOGRAPHY. [Chronological list of famous American Indians, with biographies.]

In *National Cyclopedia of American Biography*, index vol., p. 169.

INDIAN BOARD for the emigration, preservation, and improvement of the aborigines of America. Documents and proceedings relating to the formation and progress of a board [for the purpose above stated], (New York, 1829).

INDIAN COMMISSIONERS, BOARD OF. Annual reports (Washington, 1870-1910 +).

—— Journal of the second annual conference with the representatives of the religious societies coöperating with the government, and reports of their work among the Indians (Washington, 1873).

INDIANS, LAWS RELATING TO. Laws of the colonial and state governments, relating to Indians and Indian affairs, 1633-1831 (Washington, 1832).

—— A compilation from the revised statutes of the United States; and acts of Congress . . . relating to Indian affairs, not embraced in or repealed by the revision of the United States statutes (Washington, 1875).

[INDIAN POLICY of the Government. Various articles in reviews and magazines, 1874-1882.]

In *Presbyterian Quarterly and Princeton Review*, July, 1875, Jan. and Oct., 1876; *Catholic World*, Oct. and Nov., 1877, Oct., 1881; *Methodist Quarterly Review*, July, 1877; *Nation*, July 20, 1876, Sept. 6, 1877, July 4 and Nov. 28, 1878, June 30, 1881; *North Amer. Review*, March, 1879, July, 1881, March, 1882; *Penn. Monthly*, March, 1879, Oct., 1880; *International Review*, June, 1879; *Harper's Magazine*, April, 1878, April, 1881; *Catholic Presbyterian*, April, 1881, Feb., 1882; *Amer. Law Review*, Jan., 1881; *Amer. Catholic Quarterly*, July, 1881. These are papers by able writers, on Pres. Grant's policy, the legal status of the Indians, their education at Hampton and Carlisle, and the "Indian problem" in general.

INDIAN RIGHTS ASSOCIATION. Annual report of the executive committee (Philadelphia, 1883-1911+).

—— Publications (Philadelphia, 1893-1909). 59 pamphlets.

Besides these, the Association has published other pamphlets, of occasional character.

INDIAN TERRITORY, GENERAL COUNCIL. Journal of annual session, 1873 (Lawrence, Kans., 1873).

This council, the fourth of its kind, sat during May 5-15, 1873; it was "composed of delegates duly elected from the Indian tribes legally resident" in Indian Territory.

INDIAN TREATIES, and laws and regulations relating to Indian affairs. Washington, 1826.

> Compiled by order of Secretary of War Calhoun, who ordered one hundred and fifty copies to be "printed for the use of the Department." Contains also a supplementary collection of treaties and other documents relative to Indian affairs, "to the end of the Twenty-first Congress" (i.e., to February, 1831).

—— Treaties between the United States of America and the several Indian tribes, from 1778 to 1837 (Washington, 1837).

> Published by the Commissioner of Indian Affairs. Under an alphabetical list of the tribes is a tabular enumeration of the treaties, with concise abstract of the provisions in each. This is followed by the full texts of the treaties, in chronological order. Some of the minor treaties can be found only here.

—— A compilation of all the treaties between the United States and the Indian tribes now in force as laws (Washington, 1873).

—— Indian affairs: laws and treaties (Washington, 1903, 1904).

> First edition, *Senate Document*, no. 452, 57th congress, first session; second edition, *Senate document*, no. 319, 58th congress, second session.

INGERSOLL, ERNEST. Wampum and its history (Philadelphia, 1883).

> In *Amer. Naturalist*, vol. xvii, 467-479.

INTERNATIONAL CONGRESS OF AMERICANISTS. [See Congrès Internationale des Americanistes.]

IOWA STATE HISTORICAL SOCIETY. Annals (Iowa City, 1863-1910 +). Illustrated.

JAMES, GEORGE WHARTON. Indian basketry (New York, 1901; Pasadena, Cal., 1902). Illustrated.

—— What the white race may learn from the Indian (Chicago, 1908). Illustrated.

> Valuable as calling attention, in vigorous and interesting style, to various admirable features in the mode of life, and the social, mental, and moral traits, of the Indian peoples. The author knows the Indians well from personal acquaintance and extensive observation, and well advocates the thesis stated in the title of his book.

JENKS, ALBERT E. The childhood of Ji-shib, the Ojibwa and . . . pen sketches (Madison, Wis., 1900).

JESUIT RELATIONS (Paris, 1640-1672; Quebec, 1869 [3 vols.]; Cleveland, 1896-1901 [73 vols.]).

> The annual reports sent by the Jesuit missionaries among the Indians

to their superiors in France; the original publications are rare and costly. The Quebec reprint was published by the Canadian government. The Cleveland reissue (edited by Reuben G. Thwaites and Emma Helen Blair), entitled *The Jesuit Relations and Allied Documents*, added to the original *Relations* many later ones, with letters and other documents written by the Jesuit missionaries; also portraits, maps, and other illustrations – the whole accompanied by a page-to-page English translation and copious annotations, bibliographical data, etc. These missionary reports have always been accepted as authorities of the first importance, on all matters relating to the Indians from Labrador to Minnesota, and from Hudson's Bay to the Ohio River; and they are especially valuable because they show, depicted by educated men, aboriginal life and character in their primitive conditions, as yet untouched or but slightly affected by contact with Europeans.

JOHNSON, ELIAS. Legends, traditions, and laws of the Iroquois, or Six Nations, and history of the Tuscarora Indians (Lockport, N.Y., 1881).

Written by a Tuscarora chief; although in rather desultory and scrappy form, contains considerable information of value.

JONES, REV. PETER. History of the Ojebway Indians; with especial reference to their conversion to Christianity (London [1862?]). Illustrated.

An Ojibwa chief by birth (his Indian name Kahkewàquonàby), and converted to the Christian faith in his youth, the author was a missionary among his people for more than twenty-five years, until his death (June 29, 1856). His account of the Ojibwas is descriptive, historical, and ethnological; and, like Copway's, contains valuable data regarding those tribes, especially authoritative as furnished by Ojibwas of high standing.

JONES, WILLIAM. Fox texts (Leyden, 1907).

Contains folk-tales (in history, mythology, tradition, etc.) collected by Jones (himself a Fox Indian) from the elders of his tribe; with English translations. "Among the best records of American folk-lore that are available." This is volume 1 of the *Publications* of the Amer. Ethnological Society of New York. The author, a trained and enthusiastic ethnologist, was slain (while in the prime of manhood) by hostile natives in Luzón, P.I., March 28, 1909.

KANSAS STATE HISTORICAL SOCIETY. Transactions (Topeka, 1881-1910 +). Vols. i-x. Illustrated.

KEANE, AUGUSTUS H. Man past and present (Cambridge, Eng., 1899). Illustrated.

An account of the various races of man, their origin, relations, and development; contains abundant references to the best authorities.

—— The world's people: a popular account of their bodily and mental characteristics, beliefs, traditions, and political and social institutions (London, 1908). Illustrated.

KEATING, WILLIAM H. Narrative of an expedition to the sources of the St. Peter's River, Lake Winnepeek, Lake of the Woods, etc., 1823 (Philadelphia, 1824). 2 vols. Illustrated.

This expedition was conducted by Major Stephen H. Long, sent by the War Department to explore the almost unknown wilderness of Northern Minnesota. "One of the earliest and best accounts of the Sioux and Chippeways that we have" (Eames). Volume II contains a comparative vocabulary of the Sauk, Sioux, Chippeway, and Cree languages.

KELTON, DWIGHT H. Indian names of places near the Great Lakes (Detroit, 1888).

KINGSFORD, WILLIAM. The history of Canada. Indexed. (Toronto, 1887-1898). 10 vols.

KINZIE, JULIETTE A. M. Wau-Bun, the "early day of the Northwest" (New York, 1856).

A new edition of this book, with an introduction and notes by R. G. Thwaites, has been published (Chicago, 1901). The author was wife of the noted Chicago early trader, John H. Kinzie; and her book throws much light on early Illinois history and Indian character.

KOHL, J. G. Kitchi-Gami: wanderings round Lake Superior (London, 1860).

"One of the most exhaustive and valuable treatises of Indian life ever written. It is wholly the result of personal experiences. Kohl lived intimately with the Indian tribes round Lake Superior, and endeavored to penetrate the thick veil of distrust, ignorance, and superstition of the tribes with whom he lived." — WILBERFORCE EAMES.

LAFITAU, J. F. Mœurs des sauvages Ameriquains, comparées aux mœurs des premiers temps (Paris, 1724). 2 vols. Illustrated.

A valuable early account of the Indian tribes; one of the standard authorities.

LA FLESCHE, FRANCIS. The middle five; Indian boys at school (Boston, 1900).

A story, drawn from actual experiences and persons, of the (mission) school life of some Omaha boys; written by one of them.

LAHONTAN, ARMAND LOUIS DE. Voyages dans l'Amerique septentrionale (Amsterdam, 1728). 2 vols. Illustrated.

An interesting account of travels in the interior of the North American continent, and of the savage tribes dwelling therein. The English edition of 1703 has been reprinted (Chicago, 1905), edited and annotated by R. G. Thwaites.

LAKE MOHONK [N.Y.] CONFERENCE of Friends of the Indian. Proceedings of first to twenty-seventh annual meetings (Boston, 1883-1910 +).

Since the acquisition of insular possessions by the United States, their inhabitants are added to the scope of this conference.

LAPHAM, INCREASE A. The antiquities of Wisconsin, as surveyed and described (Washington, 1885).

In *Contributions to Knowledge* of Smithsonian Institution, vol. vii. Lapham was a pioneer scientist of unusual ability and intellectual breadth.

—— A geographical and topographical description of Wisconsin; with brief sketches of its history . . . antiquities (Milwaukee, 1844).

—— The number, locality, and times of removal of the Indians of Wisconsin (Milwaukee, 1870).

LARIMER, MRS. S. L. The capture and escape; or, life among the Sioux (Philadelphia, 1870).

LE SUEUR, Pierre, and others. Early voyages up and down the Mississippi by Cavelier, St. Cosme, Le Sueur, Gravier, and Guignas (Albany, N.Y., 1861).

These narratives of early exploration were translated and annotated by J. G. Shea, in the above book.

LEUPP, FRANCIS E. The Indian and his problem (New York, 1910).

Of especial interest, as written by the late commissioner of Indian affairs; he has urged the abolition of the reservation system and of the Indian Office, the Indians to become citizens of the U.S., on the same footing as the whites.

LINCOLN, BENJAMIN. Journal of a treaty held in 1793 with the Indian tribes northwest of the Ohio by commissioners of the United States (Boston, 1836).

In *Collections* of the Massachusetts Historical Society, third ser., vol. v, 109-176.

LONG, J. Voyages and travels of an Indian interpreter and trader, describing the manners and customs of the North American Indians (London, 1791).

An early and valued account of the tribes in Canada and the region of the Great Lakes to the Mississippi River. Contains an extensive vocabulary of the Chippewa language, and other linguistic data. The author was in the service of the Hudson Bay Company, and traveled among the Indians for nineteen years. A French translation was published at Paris in 1794, and had another edition in 1810. This important work has been reprinted in Thwaites's *Early Western Travels*, vol. ii.

LUNDY, JOHN P. Zea maize, as it relates to the incipient civilization of Red Men all the world over.

In *Proceedings* of Phila. Numismatic and Antiquarian Society, 1883, pp. 15-22.

McCoy, Rev. Isaac.   Correspondence and journals, 1808-1847. Ms.

These documents are in possession of the Kansas Historical Society, and contain much information on "the actual removal of the Indians, especially of the northern tribes after 1830. McCoy surveyed, or superintended the survey, of several of the early reservations in Kansas, and located most of the tribes that went there. The government placed great reliance on him, and his truly kindly disposition toward the emigrants softened the rigor of the Jacksonian measures." — Abel.

—— The annual register of Indian affairs within the Indian (or Western) Territory (Shawanoe Baptist Mission, Ind. Ter., 1835-1837), nos. 1-4.

Contains valuable information about Indian Territory and the tribes settled therein; missions and schools among them, supported by various religious denominations.

—— History of Baptist Indian missions (New York, 1840).

Covers the period from 1818; is especially full regarding the Ottawas and Potawatomi.

McGuire, Joseph D.   Pipes and smoking customs of the American aborigines, based on material in the U.S. National Museum.

In *Report* of U.S. National Museum, 1897, part 1, pp. 351-645.

McKenney, Thomas L.   Sketches of a tour to the [Great] Lakes, of the character and customs of the Chippeway Indians, and of incidents connected with the treaty of Fond du Lac (Baltimore, 1827).   Illustrated.

The author was associated with Lewis Cass in negotiating the above treaty (Aug. 5, 1826), and belonged to the U.S. Indian Department. At the end of the volume are given the text of the treaty, a journal of the proceedings therein, and a Chippewa vocabulary; and the book has numerous illustrations. Gives interesting accounts of Indian life, and descriptions of the Lake region, as they appeared at that time.

—— Memoirs, official and personal, with sketches of travels among the Northern and Southern Indians; second edition, 2 vols. in 1 (New York, 1846).   Illustrated.

The author was U.S. superintendent of the Indian trade during 1816-1822, and later (1824-1830) chief of the Indian Bureau (the first to hold that post). Volume I recounts his experiences in these offices; volume II contains his reflections on the origin of the Indians, their claims on us for aid and justice, and a plan for their preservation and "the consolidation of peace between them and us."

—— and James Hall.   History of the Indian tribes of North America, with biographical sketches and anecdotes of the principal chiefs (Philadelphia, 1854). 3 vols. Illustrated.

A smaller reprint (in royal octavo) from the folio edition of 1848. Contains one hundred and twenty large and well-colored "portraits from the Indian Gallery in the Department of War, at Washington." Revised and enlarged by McKenney, who probably wrote the unsigned historical sketch of the Indian race in volume III; Hall contributed the "Essay on the history of the North American Indians," which follows. It contains one hundred and twenty large colored portraits of Indian chiefs, from the original paintings, mostly by an artist named King, who was employed by the government to paint portraits of the chiefs who visited Washington.

McKenney, Thomas L. and Matthew Irwin. The fur trade and factory system at Green Bay, 1816-1821.

In Wisconsin *Historical Collections*, vol. vii, 269-288.

McKenzie, Fayette A. The Indian in relation to the white population of the United States (Columbus, O., 1908).

Reviews the policy of the U.S. government toward the Indians, the political status of the latter, their lands and funds, education, missions, and other topics; contains much useful and recent information as to the advancement and present status of the Indians; and advocates the abolition of the reservation, final allotment of lands, Indian citizenship, provision of better training and opportunities on industrial lines, etc.

McLaughlin, James. My friend the Indian (Boston, 1910). Illustrated.

The author was Indian agent and inspector for many years.

McMaster, John B. A history of the people of the United States, 1783-1861 (New York, 1884-1900). 5 vols.

Mair, Charles. The American bison – its habits, methods of capture and economic use in the northwest, with reference to its threatened extinction and possible preservation.

In *Proceedings and Transactions* of Royal Society of Canada, first ser., vol. viii, sec. 2, pp. 93-108.

Mallery, Garrick. Sign language among North American Indians, compared with that among other peoples and deaf-mutes (Washington, 1881). Illustrated.

In Bureau of Amer. Ethnology, first *Report*, 263-552.

—— Picture-writing of the American Indians (Washington, 1893). Illustrated.

Bureau of American Ethnology, *Tenth Report*, 25-807.

Manypenny, George W. Our Indian wards (Cincinnati, 1880).

The author was commissioner of Indian affairs during 1853-1857, and chairman of the Sioux Commission of 1876. He recounts the history of the Indian peoples in their relations with the whites, from the time of the first encounter between the two races; contrasts the military with the civil administration of Indian affairs; and urges that justice, protection, and better industrial opportunities be furnished to these "our wards."

MARGRY, PIERRE. Découvertes et établissements des Français dans l'ouest et dans le sud de l'Amérique Septentrionale (1614-1754): mémoires et documents originaux (Paris, 1876-1886). 6 vols.

The following volumes are concerned with the northwest: I (1614-1684), explorations and discoveries on the Great Lakes, and the Ohio and Mississippi Rivers; V (1683-1724), formation of a chain of posts between the St. Lawrence and the Gulf of Mexico; VI (1679-1754), exploration of affluents of the Mississippi, and discovery of the Rocky Mountains.

MARSH, REV. CUTTING. Letters and journals, 1830-1856. Ms. 39 vols. and 55 letters.

These documents are deposited with the Wisconsin Historical Society. The author was a missionary of the American Board of Foreign Missions and of a Scottish missionary society, among the Stockbridge Indians of Wisconsin; and his papers relate chiefly to religious and educational matters. Marsh's reports to the Scottish Society for 1831-1848 have been published (nearly in full) in Wisconsin *Historical Collections*, vol. xv, 39-204.

MARTIN, HORACE F. Castorologia, or the history and traditions of the Canadian beaver (Montreal, 1892).

MASON, EDWARD G. Illinois in the 18th century (Chicago, 1881).

No. 12 in *Fergus Historical Series*.

—— Early Illinois (Chicago, 1889-1890). In 4 parts.

Nos. 31-34 of *Fergus Historical Series*. Is chiefly devoted to Menard, Todd, and Rocheblave papers.

MASON, OTIS T. Woman's share in primitive culture (New York, 1894). Illustrated.

—— The origins of inventions: study of industry among primitive people (London, 1895). Illustrated.

Valuable monographs by this distinguished writer (who was one of the foremost scientists in America, and curator of ethnology in the U.S. National Museum from 1884 until his death in 1908) are noted as follows: "Cradles of the American aborigines" (*Report* of Smithsonian Institution, 1887); "N. American bows, arrows, and quivers" (*id.*, 1893); "Migration and the food quest" (*id.*, 1894); "Influence of environment upon human industries or arts" (*id.*, 1895); "Aboriginal skin-dressing" (*Report* of U.S. National Museum, 1889); "Primitive travel and transportation" (*id.*, 1894); "Aboriginal American basketry" (*id.*, 1902). All these are abundantly illustrated.

MATSON, N. French and Indians of Illinois River (Princeton, Ill., 1874).

From old Mss., local traditions, etc., the author has gleaned interesting data regarding the Indian tribes in Illinois, and the early settlement of that region by the French.

MATSON, N.   Memories of Shaubena, with incidents relating to the early settlement of the West (Chicago, 1878 [second edition in 1880]).

A memoir of this noted Potawatomi chief, based largely on information furnished to the writer by Shaubena himself; contains also much information regarding the "Black Hawk War."

MICHIGAN PIONEER AND HISTORICAL SOCIETY.   Collections and researches (Lansing, 1887-1910 +).   Vols. 1-38.   Illustrated.

MICHILLIMACKINAC PARISH.   Register of baptisms and marriages, 1741-1821.   Ms.

The original of this important register is preserved in the parish church of St. Anne at Mackinac. At the beginning is an abstract of earlier entries dating back to 1695, copied from an old register which is now lost; there are also some records of burials, 1743-1806. A facsimile transcription of the volume is in the possession of the Wisconsin Historical Society, in whose *Collections* are published a translation of the entire document (vol. xviii, 469-514, and xix, 1-162).

MINNESOTA HISTORICAL SOCIETY.   Collections (St. Paul, 1850-1910 +).   Vols. i-xiv.   Illustrated.

Contain many important papers regarding the Indians of Minnesota. Notable among these are: "Dakota superstitions," G. H. Pond (1867, pp. 32-62); "History of the Ojibways," William W. Warren (of Ojibwa blood), and another account by Edward D. Neill, a scholarly and careful investigator (vol. v, 21-510); "Protestant missions in the Northwest," Stephen R. Riggs (vol. vi, 117-188); "A Sioux story of the war, 1862," Chief Big Eagle (pp. 382-400); "Prehistoric man at the headwaters of the Mississippi River," J. V. Brower (vol. viii, 232-269); "The Ojibways in Minnesota," Joseph A. Gilfillan (vol. ix, 55-128); several papers on history of missions in Minnesota (vol. x, 156-246); "The Dakotas or Sioux in Minnesota as they were in 1834," Samuel W. Pond (vol. xii, 319-501).

—— Documents relating to the early history of Minnesota.   Ms.

These collections contain many original manuscripts of great value for the history of the upper Mississippi region. Of especial interest are the papers of Henry H. Sibley, first governor of Minnesota; journals of Charles Larpenteur, Indian trader during forty years; letters received by Major Lawrence Taliaferro (dated 1813-1840) from prominent government officials; and papers connected with the Sioux outbreak in 1862.

MISSOURI HISTORICAL SOCIETY (St. Louis).   Documents relating to the early history of Missouri.   Ms.

A large and valuable collection, mainly concerned with the history of the region west of the Mississippi. Among them are a considerable number relating to the subject of the present work, especially as follows: On trade and Indian affairs in Upper Louisiana, prior to 1800; papers and letters connected with William Clark's official life; Stephen W. Kearny's journals of trips up the Mississippi (1820) and Missouri (1824); Sibley manuscripts (1803-1836), largely on Indian affairs; and the Sublette and Vasquez collections, containing hundreds of letters, business papers, etc., relating to the fur-trade during the first half of the nineteenth century.

MOONEY, JAMES. The ghost-dance religion and the Sioux outbreak of 1890 (Washington, 1896).

In Bureau of Amer. Ethnology, *Report* for 1892-1893, part ii, pp. 641-1110.

—— Mescal plant and ceremony (Detroit, 1896).

In *Therapeutic Gazette*, third ser., vol. xii. Cf. also papers by D. W. Prentiss and F. P. Morgan on same subject (*ibid.*).

MOOREHEAD, WARREN K. Fort Ancient, the great prehistoric earth-work of Warren County, Ohio (Cincinnati, 1890).

—— Primitive man in Ohio (New York, 1892).

—— Prehistoric implements (Cincinnati, 1900).

—— Tonda, a story of the Sioux (Cincinnati, 1904). Illustrated.

MORGAN, LEWIS H. League of the Ho-dé-no-sau-nee, or Iroquois (Rochester, N.Y., 1851). Illustrated.

This is a book of prime authority on the subject of the famous Iroquois League, and on the character, beliefs, customs, language, etc., of the tribes composing it. Morgan was adopted into the Seneca tribe, and made a careful study of the Iroquois peoples and their life. On a large map of the Iroquois country he shows all the villages and geographical features, with the Indian name of each — a table of these, with meanings in English, and identification of locality, appearing at end of volume.

—— Indian migrations.

In *North American Review*, Oct., 1869 and Jan., 1870; reprinted in Beach's *Ind. Miscellany*, 158-257.

—— Systems of consanguinity and affinity of the human family (Washington, 1871).

In *Contributions to Knowledge* of Smithsonian Institution, vol. xvii.

—— Houses and house-life of the American aborigines (Washington, 1881). Illustrated.

In *Contributions to Amer. Ethnology* of U.S. Geographical and Geological Survey, vol. iv.

—— Ancient society; or researches in the lines of human progress from savagery through barbarism to civilization (New York, 1878).

Morgan was a profound student of social evolution and the origins of civilization, and his books are valuable contributions to those subjects.

MORSE, REV. JEDEDIAH. A report to the Secretary of War of the United States, comprising a narrative of . . . the actual state of the Indian Tribes in our country (New Haven, 1822), [with map showing locations of the tribes].

> Pp. 11-96 are occupied with Dr. Morse's report to the secretary of war (then John C. Calhoun) on his mission from the government to ascertain the condition of the Indian tribes, performed in the summer of 1820. The rest of the volume (pp. 97-406) is devoted to numerous appendices illustrative of the subject — reports from missionaries, traders, civil and military officials; speeches by Indian chiefs; extracts from some printed works; descriptions of little-known regions; and statistical tables showing the condition of the tribes, the dealings of our government with them, the schools established for them, etc. It is a valuable collection of the best material obtainable at that time, and furnished by competent observers, mainly eyewitnesses of what they related.

NEILL, EDWARD DUFFIELD. The history of Minnesota; from the earliest French explorations to the present time (Minneapolis, 1878, 1882).

> First issued in 1858; both above editions (the third and fourth) revised and enlarged by adding much new material, to keep pace with later discovery and research. Written by a scholarly and able historian; contains much about the Indian tribes in Minnesota. The opening chapters of the first edition were reprinted as a separate (Phila., 1859) under the title Dahkotah Land, and Dahkotah Life.

—— History of the Ojebways and their connection with the fur traders.

> In Minn. Historical Society Collections, vol. v, 395-410.

NOBLE LIVES of a noble race (Odanah, Wis., 1909). Illustrated.

> Interesting as being mainly the work of the Indian children in the Franciscan industrial school at the Odanah mission. Contains also biographical sketches of missionaries and other friends of the Indians.

NORTH DAKOTA STATE HISTORICAL SOCIETY. Collections (Bismark, 1906-1910 +), vols. i-iii.

OGG, FREDERICK A. The opening of the Mississippi: a struggle for supremacy in the American interior (New York, 1904).

> A history of discovery, exploration, and contested rights of navigation on the Mississippi, prior to the end of the War of 1812-1815; gives special attention to the physiographic aspects of the history of the Mississippi basin, and the economic importance of the great river.

OHIO ARCHAEOLOGICAL AND HISTORICAL SOCIETY. Quarterly (Columbus, 1887-1910 +), vols. i-xix.

OTIS, ELWELL S. The Indian question (New York, 1878).

> An able and vigorous presentation of this subject from the standpoint of

an army officer. He shows that the Indian population is certainly not decreasing; reviews the policy of colonial and U.S. governments toward the Indian tribes, also the treaty system; regards the Indian as incapable of white civilization; and advocates military control of the reservations.

OWEN, MARY ALICIA. Folk-lore of the Musquakie Indians of North America (London, 1904). Illustrated.

> This is vol. 51 of *Publications* of the Folk-lore Society [of Great Britain]. A monograph on the folk-lore and customs of the Musquakie Indians of Iowa, better known as the Sauk and Foxes, by a lady who for many years has known these Indians personally and well. During this long acquaintance she collected a considerable quantity of specimens of their ceremonial implements and their beadwork, articles which represented their genuine native industries and their actual usages in ceremonials; this collection she presented to the Folk-lore Society, accompanied by careful descriptive notes and the above monograph. These writings are printed as above, and are illustrated by eight plates (two in colors) from photographs. A unique and important contribution to the history of those tribes.

PARKMAN, FRANCIS. The conspiracy of Pontiac and the Indian war after the conquest of Canada (Boston, 1870).

> The sixth edition, revised and enlarged.

—— La Salle and the discovery of the great West (Boston, 1879).

> The eleventh edition, revised and enlarged, of "Discovery of the great West."

—— The old régime in Canada (Boston, 1874).

—— A half-century of conflict (Boston, 1892). 2 vols.

> Covers the period 1700-1748; includes full account of the Fox War.

PARKMAN CLUB OF MILWAUKEE. Papers (Milwaukee, 1896-1897). 2 vols.

> A series of eighteen short monographs on various topics of Wisconsin and Northwestern history. Among them are: "Nicholas Perrot," G. P. Stickney (no. 1); "Voyages of Radisson and Groseilliers," Henry C. Campbell (no. 2); "Chevalier Henry de Tonty," Henry E. Legler (no. 3); "Aborigines of the Northwest," F. T. Terry (no. 4); "Jonathan Carver," J. G. Gregory (no. 5); "Eleazer Williams," W. W. Wight (no. 7); "Charles Langlade," M. E. McIntosh (no. 8); "Père René Menard," H. C. Campbell (no. 11); "George Rogers Clark and his Illinois campaign," Dan B. Starkey (no. 12); "The use of maize by Wisconsin Indians," G. P. Stickney (no. 13); "Claude Jean Allouez," J. S. La Boule (no. 17).

PEET, STEPHEN D. Myths and symbols, or aboriginal religions in America (Chicago, 1905). Illustrated.

> Discusses such subjects as Totemism and mythology; The serpent symbol in America; Sky worship; Phallic worship and fire worship; The rain god; Personal divinities and culture heroes; etc. Written by the editor (1878-1910) of the *American Antiquarian*.

PITEZEL, JOHN H. Lights and shades of missionary life during nine years spent in the region of Lake Superior (Cincinnati, 1857).

PITTMAN, PHILIP. The present state of the European settlements on the Mississippi; with a geographical description of that river, illustrated by plans and draughts (London, 1770).

> This important work, now exceedingly rare, has been reprinted by the A. H. Clark Co. (Cleveland, 1906), edited and annotated by F. H. Hodder. Pittman was a British military engineer, and gives an accurate account, written from personal observation of the Mississippi settlements just after the English occupation of that country as a result of the peace of 1763. An authority in early Western history, of the highest importance.

POKAGON, SIMON. O-gi-maw-kwe mit-i-gwä-ki – "Queen of the woods" (Hartford, Mich., 1899).

> A partly autobiographical story and a chapter on the Algonquin language, written by the noted Potawatomi chief Pokagon; to this the publisher (C. H. Engle) has added a biographical sketch and other data.

—— An Indian on the problems of his race.

> In *Amer. Review of Reviews*, Dec., 1895.

—— The future of the red man.

> In *Forum*, Aug., 1897.

POOLE, D. C. Among the Sioux of Dakota: eighteen months' experience as an Indian agent (New York, 1881).

> An interesting narrative by an army officer, of his experiences among the Sioux; he describes their character and mode of life, the difficulties arising from their relations with the white settlers, and the perplexities encountered in the administration of the agency system. Written in a spirit of fairness, and appreciation of the good traits in Indian character.

POWELL, JOHN W. The North American Indians (New York, 1894).

> In N. S. Shaler's *U.S. of America*, vol. i, 190-272.

—— Sketch of the mythology of the North American Indians (Washington, 1881).

> In *First Report* of Bureau Amer. Ethnology, 17-69.

—— Indian linguistic families of America north of Mexico (Washington, 1891).

> In *Seventh Report* of Bureau of American Ethnology, 7-142.

—— Technology, or the science of industries.

> In *Amer. Anthropologist*, new series, vol. i, 319-349.

—— American view of totemism (London, 1902).

> In *Man*, vol. ii, no. 75.

PRESBYTERIAN CHURCH in United States, General Assembly. The

church at home and abroad (Philadelphia, 1887-1898). Vols.
1-24. Illustrated.

PRESBYTERIAN CHURCH. Presbyterian monthly record (Philadelphia, 1850-1886). Vols. 1-37.

—— Woman's Board of Home Missions. The home mission
monthly (New York, 1887-1910 +). Vols. 1-24. Illustrated.

—— Women's Foreign Missionary Societies. Woman's work for
woman (Philadelphia, Chicago, and New York, 1871-1910 +).
Vols. 1-25.

> After 1904 styled *Woman's Work.*

PROTESTANT EPISCOPAL CHURCH, Board of Missions. The spirit
of missions (New York, 1836-1910 +). Vols. 1-75. Illustrated
(after 1873).

> In volume for 1874 is a map of the U.S., showing the Indian reserva-
> tions at that time.

RADISSON, PETER ESPRIT. Voyages of Peter Esprit Radisson, being
an account of his travels and experiences among the North American Indians, from 1652 to 1684 (Boston, 1885).

> Transcribed from original manuscripts in the Bodleian Library and the
> British Museum; edited by Gideon D. Scull; published by the Prince
> Society. Radisson and his companion, Médart des Groseilliers, explored the
> wilderness about Lakes Michigan and Superior (1654-1656), and spent a
> winter with the Sioux Indians in the vicinity of Lake Pepin (1659-1660) —
> perhaps the first white men to visit those lands; so these narratives are of
> special interest and value.

RAMSEY, ALEXANDER. Annual report of the superintendent of Indian affairs in Minnesota territory (Washington, 1849).

> Senate *Executive Document,* no. 1, 31st congress, first session.

RATZEL, FRIEDRICH. The history of mankind (London, 1896). 3
vols. Illustrated.

> Translated from the second German edition. A popular but reliable
> guide to anthropological and ethnological study; and gives a well-written
> and systematic account of the races of man throughout the world; and con-
> tains over one thousand one hundred illustrations of excellent quality,
> chiefly obtained from material in the great museums.

RAU, CHARLES. Ancient aboriginal trade in North America; and
North American stone implements (Washington, 1873).

> In *Report* of Smithsonian Institution, 1872, pp. 348-408.

REBOK, HORACE M. The last of the Mus-Qua-Kies and the Indian
Congress, 1898 (Dayton, O., 1900). Illustrated.

> A historical sketch of the Fox and Sac tribes.

REYNOLDS, JOHN. The pioneer history of Illinois, 1673-1818 (Chicago, 1887). Illustrated.

> First issued at Belleville, Ill., 1852; the second edition is much improved. The author was governor of Illinois during 1832-1834.

—— My own times, 1800-1855 (Chicago, 1879).

> A revised edition of an earlier publication by the Chicago Historical Society.

RIGGS, STEPHEN R. Táh-koo Wah-kán, or, the gospel among the Dakotas (Boston, 1869).

> A valuable account of the Dakota Sioux, their pagan customs, their native religious beliefs and worship, Protestant mission work among them, their outbreak in 1862 and its results. An appendix contains notes on their medical practices, and their songs and music. Written by a noted missionary, also remarkable for his linguistic ability; he compiled a Dakota grammar and dictionary (Washington, 1890; Dorsey's ed.), and, with his fellow-missionary Thomas S. Williamson, translated the entire Bible into that language — published at Cincinnati (1842), and later at New York (1871-1872, and 1880).

—— Mary and I: forty years with the Sioux (Chicago, [1880]).

> An interesting narrative of his experiences (1837-1877) as a missionary among the Sioux; mainly devoted to religious and educational work, but incidentally discloses considerable relating to Indian life and character.

RIGHT-HAND THUNDER. The Indian and white man; or, the Indian in self-defense (Indianapolis, 1880).

> Written by an Indian chief; edited by D. W. Risher.

ROBINSON, DOANE. Sioux Indians – a history (Cedar Rapids, Ia., 1908). Illustrated.

> A full and authoritative history, from the best original sources, of the Sioux of Dakota; written by the superintendent of the South Dakota Historical Society.

——, editor. The South Dakotan, a monthly magazine (Sioux Falls, S.Dak., 1900-1904).

ROOSEVELT, THEODORE. The winning of the West (New York, 1889-1896). 4 vols.

ROYAL SOCIETY OF CANADA. Proceedings and transactions (Ottawa, 1882-1910 +).

> Contains much valuable material regarding the Indian tribes of the northern and eastern United States, as well as numerous articles and papers on Canadian history, biography, etc.

ROYCE, CHARLES C. Indian land cessions in the United States (Washington, 1900).

> In the *Eighteenth Report* of Bureau of Amer. Ethnology, part ii. De-

scribes the policy toward the Indians of Spaniards, French, and English respectively, of the several English colonies, and of the United States; enumerates the treaties and acts of Congress authorizing allotments of land in severalty; and presents a schedule of land cessions (from 1784 to 1894), with descriptive and historical data and remarks for each, and maps.

ROYCE, CHARLES C. An inquiry into the identity and history of the Shawnee Indians.

> In *Amer. Antiquarian*, vol. iii, 177-189.

RUSH, BENJAMIN. An oration . . . containing an enquiry into the natural history of medicine among the Indians in North America, and a comparative view of their diseases and remedies, with those of civilized nations (Philadelphia, [1774]).

RUTTENBER, E. M. History of the Indian tribes of Hudson's River (Albany, N.Y., 1872). Illustrated.

> A reliable account, with numerous annotations, and careful citation of authorities, of the tribes along the Hudson, some of which are mentioned by Perrot and La Potherie as being more or less connected with the affairs of the western tribes.

SCHOOLCRAFT, HENRY R. Notes on the Iroquois; or contributions to American history, antiquities, and general ethnology (Albany, 1847). Illustrated.

> Largely historical and archeological; contains also several Iroquois traditions, a chapter on their language, and various miscellanies.

—— Oneota: or, characteristics of the red race of America (New York, 1845). Illustrated.

> "From original notes and manuscripts."

—— Algic researches (New York, 1839). 2 vols.

> "Comprising inquiries respecting the mental characteristics of the North American Indians."

—— Historical and statistical information respecting the history, condition and prospects of the Indian tribes of the United States (Philadelphia, 1851-1857). 6 vols. Illustrated.

> "Collected and prepared under the direction of the Bureau of Indian Affairs, per act of Congress of March 3d, 1847. Published by authority of Congress." Schoolcraft used not only his own extensive knowledge, and the unusual opportunities furnished by his marriage to an Indian woman of high rank; but the information and experience of many persons throughout the country who were conversant with Indian character and life, and several original Ms. accounts, previously unpublished. His work is a cyclopedia of the best information then available, much of which is not to be found elsewhere; and it contains much valuable material (also some of little importance) for the study of Indian ethnology, archæology, history, languages,

etc. The illustrations are largely steel engravings, mostly from drawings by Capt. S. Eastman, U.S.A.; and include many colored plates. In vol. vi, the title becomes "History of the Indian tribes of the United States," etc.

SCHOOLCRAFT, HENRY R. The American Indians, their history, condition and prospects, from original notes and manuscripts, new revised edition (Rochester, 1851).

—— Personal memoirs of a residence of thirty years with the Indian tribes on the American frontiers, with brief notices of passing events, facts, and opinions, A.D. 1812 to A.D. 1842 (Philadelphia, 1851).

SCHULTZ, J. W. My life as an Indian (New York, 1907).

SHARP, MRS. ABIGAIL G. History of the Spirit Lake massacre, and captivity of Miss Abbie Gardner (Des Moines, 1885).

SHEA, JOHN GILMARY. History of the Catholic missions among the Indian tribes of the United States, 1529-1854 (New York, 1855). Illustrated.

> A valuable work, by a leading authority in Catholic history. He relates the labors of Catholic missionaries — Spanish, French, and English, including even mention of the Northmen in Greenland and Vinland — in North America, with abundant reference to original authorities, and adds lists of the French missionaries.

—— Discovery and exploration of the Mississippi Valley: with the original narratives of Marquette, Allouez, Membré, Hennepin, and Anastase Douay (New York, 1853).

> Translations of above narratives (with annotations and biographical sketches) by Shea.

—— Historical sketch of the Tionontates, or Dinondadies, now called Wyandots.

> In *Historical Magazine*, vol. v.

—— History of the Catholic Church in the United States from the first attempted colonization to the present time (New York, 1886-1892). 4 vols.

SMITH, ERMINNIE A. Myths of the Iroquois (Washington, 1883).

> In *Second Report* of Bureau of Amer. Ethnology.

SMITH, GEN. THOMAS A. Letters, reports, and military orders, 1812-1818. Ms.

> This officer served in the War of 1812, and during 1815-1818 was at the head of the Western Military Department, with headquarters at St. Louis. His letters, orders, etc., despatched in his official capacity, and letters and reports from his subordinate officers at Forts Smith, Osage, Armstrong, and Crawford, constitute this valuable collection. It is in the possession of the State Historical Society of Missouri, at Columbia.

SMITHSONIAN INSTITUTION. Annual reports of the Boards of Regents (Washington, D.C., 1847-1910 +). Illustrated.

The appendices to these reports contain "miscellaneous memoirs of interest to collaborators and correspondents of the Institution, teachers, and others engaged in the promotion of knowledge." Among these are often found papers on archæological and ethnological subjects, written by experts, and largely based on material found in the National Museum. Among these may be noted, in recent reports, the following: Otis T. Mason, "Influence of Environment upon Human Industries or Arts" (1895); Thomas Wilson, "Prehistoric Art" (1896); Havelock Ellis, "Mescal, a new Artificial Paradise" (1897; reprinted from *Contemporary Review*, Jan., 1897); Alice C. Fletcher, "The Import of the Totem" [in the Omaha tribe], (1897); W. A. Phillips, "Stone Implements from the southern Shores of Lake Michigan" (1897); O. T. Mason, "Traps of the American Indians" (1901); W. H. Holmes, "Traces of Aboriginal Operations in an Iron Mine near Leslie, Mo." (1903); *id.*, "The Contributions of American Archeology to History" (1904); Georg Friederici, "Scalping in America" (1906).

—— Reports of the United States National Museum (Washington, 1883-1910 +). Illustrated.

In recent issues of these *Reports* are the following papers among those "describing and illustrating collections" in the Museum: J. D. McGuire, "Pipes and Smoking Customs of the American Aborigines" (1897); O. T. Mason, "The Man's Knife among the North American Indians" (1897); *id.*, "A Primitive Frame for Weaving narrow Fabrics" (1898); *id.*, "Aboriginal American Harpoons" (1900); *id.*, "Aboriginal American Basketry" (1902).

—— Smithsonian contributions to knowledge, vols. i-xxxiv (Washington, 1848-1910 +). Illustrated.

Notable articles therein: E. G. Squier, "Ancient Monuments of the Mississippi Valley" (vol. i); *id.*, "Aboriginal Monuments of the State of New York" (vol. ii); Charles Whittlesey, "Description of Ancient Works in Ohio" (vol. iii); I. A. Lapham, "The Antiquities of Wisconsin" (vol. vii); C. Whittlesey, "Ancient Mining on the shores of Lake Superior" (vol. xiii); Lewis H. Morgan, "Systems of Consanguinity and Affinity of the Human Family" (vol. xvii); Charles Rau, "The Archæological Collection of the U.S. National Museum" (vol. xxii); *id.*, "Prehistoric Fishing in Europe and North America" (vol. xxv).

SOCIETY FOR PROPAGATING THE GOSPEL among the Indians and others in North America, 1787-1887. [Boston, 1887.]

A centennial publication, containing historical sketches of the society, lists of officers, enumeration of its publications, etc. See the *Reports* and other matter issued by the society, for accounts of its work.

SOUTH DAKOTA STATE HISTORICAL SOCIETY. Historical collections (Aberdeen, 1902-1908+). Illustrated.

Vol. ii is devoted to a "History of the Sioux Indians," by Doane Robinson, secretary of the society.

SQUIER, E. G., and E. H. Davis. Ancient monuments of the Mississippi valley (Washington, 1848). Illustrations.

In *Contrib. to Knowledge* of Smithsonian Institution, vol. i.

STARR, FREDERICK. American Indians (Boston, 1899). Illustrated.

"Intended as a reading book for boys and girls in school," for which purpose it is admirable.

STEARNS, ROBERT E. C. Ethno-conchology: a study of primitive money.

In *Report* of Smithsonian Institution, 1887, part ii, pp. 297-334.

STEVENS, FRANK E. The Black Hawk War, including a review of Black Hawk's life (Chicago, 1903). Illustrated.

By far the most extensive and full account of the Black Hawk War, and of the life and deeds of that noted chief; based on the best printed sources, interviews, and correspondences and numerous original documents. Contains over three hundred portraits and views, of great historical value.

STEWARD, JOHN F. Lost Maramech and earliest Chicago: a history of the Foxes and of their downfall near the great village of Maramech (Chicago, 1903). Illustrated.

The story of the Fox tribe, as found in original sources, chiefly Mss. from Paris archives. This author locates at Maramech Hill (near the junction of Big Rock Creek with the Fox River of Illinois) the great battle of 1730, when the Fox tribe was almost exterminated.

STICKNEY, GARDNER P. Nicholas Perrot.

—— The use of maize by Wisconsin Indians.

Both these papers are in Parkman Club *Publications*, q.v.

—— Indian use of wild rice.

In *Amer. Anthropologist*, vol. ix, 115-121.

STITES, SARA H. Economics of the Iroquois (Bryn Mawr, Pa., 1905).

In *Monograph Series* of Bryn Mawr College, vol. i, no. 3.

STURTEVANT, LEWIS. Indian corn and the Indian (Philadelphia, 1885).

In *Amer. Naturalist*, vol. xix.

TANNER, JOHN. Narrative of captivity and adventures during thirty years' residence among the Indians in the interior of North America (New York, 1830).

"Prepared for the press by Edwin James, M.D." A detailed narrative of Tanner's experiences among the Indian tribes of the northwest; their customs and mode of life, etc. To this Dr. James has added much linguistic and ethnological information.

TAYLOR, EDWARD L. Monuments to historical Indian chiefs.

In *Publications* of Ohio State Archæological and Historical Society, vol. ix, 1-31, xi, 1-29.

TECUMSEH. Letters, notes, memoirs, etc., relating to Tecumseh, 1780-1840. Ms. 13 vols.

A collection by L. C. Draper of materials for an intended life of this great chief; includes much and valuable unpublished material regarding Tecumseh's life, travels among the various tribes, influence on his fellow-Indians, battles, etc. It is in the possession of the Wisconsin State Historical Society.

TEXTOR, LUCY E. Official relations between the United States and the Sioux Indians (Palo Alto, Cal., 1896).

Leland Stanford University *Publication.* Contains a full résumé of the Indian policy of the United States.

THOMAS, CYRUS. Indians of North America in historic times (Philadelphia, 1903). Illustrated.

In *History of North America* (Guy C. Lee, editor), vol. ii. Written "in conference with W. J. McGee."

—— Introduction to the study of North American archæology (Cincinnati, 1898; reprinted in 1903).

—— Burial mounds of the northern section of the United States (Washington, 1887).

In *Fifth Report*, Bureau of Amer. Ethnology.

—— Catalogue of prehistoric works east of the Rocky Mountains (Washington, 1891).

Bulletin 12, Bureau of Amer. Ethnology. A bibliography of the writings of this eminent scientist, prepared by himself a short time before his death, is published in *Amer. Anthropologist*, new series, vol. xii, 339-343.

THOMAS, WILLIAM I. Source book for social origins: ethnological materials, psychological standpoint, classified and annotated bibliographies for the interpretation of savage society (Chicago, 1909).

THWAITES, REUBEN G. France in America, 1497-1763 (New York, 1905).

This is vol. vii in *The American Nation* (A. B. Hart, editor).

—— The story of Wisconsin (Boston, 1899).

Revised and enlarged from edition of 1890.

—— Wisconsin: the Americanization of a French settlement (Boston, 1908).

THWAITES, REUBEN G.   How George Rogers Clark won the North-west, and other essays in Western history (Chicago, 1903).

—— Father Marquette (New York, 1902).

—— The story of the Black Hawk War (Madison, Wis., 1892).

In Wisconsin *Historical Collections*, vol. xii.

—— (editor).   Early western travels, 1748-1846 (Cleveland, 1904-1907).   32 vols.   Illustrated.

"A series of annotated reprints of some of the best and rarest contemporary volumes of travel, descriptive of the Aborigines and social and economic conditions in the Middle and Far West, during the period of early American settlement."   A most valuable contribution to American history, inasmuch as the works here reprinted are seldom found except in the large collections of Americana, and were thus accessible to but few students; and as this edition furnishes with them copious annotations and other aids to the reader, the results of modern research.   Among these writings are some that relate to the tribes considered in the present work, or to the history of the period which it covers; the more important of these are noted as follows:

Volume I.   Conrad Weiser's journal of a tour to the Ohio, 1748; George Croghan's letters and journals, 1750-1765; Charles F. Post's journals of Western tours, 1758-1759; Thomas Morris's *Journal of . . . experiences on the Maumee, 1764* (London, 1791).   [These documents are especially valuable because they furnish the history of English relations with the French and Indians upon the western borders during the last French War, and its sequel, Pontiac's conspiracy.   Two of the authors, Weiser and Croghan, were government Indian agents; the third, Post, was a Moravian missionary; and the fourth, Morris, was a British army officer.]

Volume II.   J. Long's *Voyages and travels of an Indian interpreter and trader* (London, 1791).   [The author spent twenty years in the fur-trade and among the northern tribes, and presents a graphic picture of Indian and Canadian life, and of conditions and methods in the fur-trade; also many vocabularies of Indian words, and observations on their analogies.]

Volume V.   John Bradbury's *Travels in the interior of America, in 1809-1811* (London, 1819).   [Bradbury was a zealous and indefatigable observer, and traveled through most of the regions of the Mississippi valley, and up the Missouri.   His book is one of the best existing authorities of this period.]

Volume VI.   H. M. Brackenridge's *Journal of a voyage up the River Missouri, 1811* (Baltimore, 1816).   [A reliable early authority.]

Volume VIII.   Estwick Evans's *Pedestrious tour . . . through the Western states and territories, 1818* (Concord, N.H., 1819).   [Evans traveled along Lake Erie to Detroit, and down the Ohio and Mississippi to the Gulf.]

Volume XIII.   Thomas Nuttall's *Journal of travels into the Arkansas Territory, 1819; with observations on the manners of the aborigines* (Philadelphia, 1821).   [The author was a scientist of high standing, who in the pursuit of knowledge traveled more than five thousand miles, through a region of which most was still the possession of wild Indian tribes; of these he has given minute and reliable accounts.]

Volumes XXII-XXV. Prince Maximilien's *Voyage in the interior of North America*, 1832-1834. English translati n (London, 1843). [An elaborate account – descriptive, historical, ethnological, and scientific – of the region between the Mississippi and the Rocky Mountains, and of the Indian tribes dwelling therein; magnificently illustrated by a special artist who accompanied the expedition.]

THWAITES, REUBEN G. (editor). [See also *Jesuit Relations*; and Wisconsin Historical Society, *Collections* and *Proceedings*.]

TURNER, FREDERICK J. The character and influence of the Indian trade in Wisconsin; a study of the trading post as an institution (Baltimore, 1891).

In *Johns Hopkins Univ. Studies*, vol. ix, 543-615. A revised and enlarged form of an address given before the Wisconsin Historical Society, Jan. 3, 1889 (printed in *Proceedings* of the society, 1889, pp. 52-98).

—— Rise of the new West, 1819-1829 (New York, 1906).

This is vol. xiv of *The American Nation* (A. B. Hart, editor).

—— The significance of the frontier in American history (Madison, Wis., 1893).

In *Proceedings* of Wis. Historical Society, 1893, pp. 79-112.

TYLOR, EDWARD B. Primitive culture: researches into the development of mythology, philosophy, religion, language, art, and custom (London, 1903). 2 vols.

First published in 1871; above is fourth edition, revised.

UPHAM, WARREN, and others. Minnesota in three centuries: 1655-1908 ([New York], 1908). 4 vols. Illustrated.

Written by the secretary and other members of the Minnesota Historical Society, largely from original material in the collections of that society.

U.S. DEPARTMENT OF THE INTERIOR. Statistics of Indian tribes, Indian agencies, and Indian schools of every character; corrected to January 1, 1899 (Washington, 1899).

—— Half-breed scrip. Chippewas of Lake Superior (Washington, 1874).

"The correspondence and action under the 7th clause of the second article of the treaty with the Chippewa Indians of Lake Superior and the Mississippi . . . concluded at La Pointe, Sept. 30, 1854," including also reports of government commissions appointed in 1871 and 1872.

VERWYST, REV. CHRYSOSTOMUS. Life and labors of Rt. Rev. Frederic Baraga (Milwaukee, 1900). Illustrated.

A carefully-prepared narrative (from original sources) of the noted Bishop Baraga's missionary labors among the Indian tribes in the northern peninsula of Michigan (1831-1867). Contains much valuable information about the Indians, their mode of life, character, beliefs, etc.; and includes sketches of earlier missionaries.

VERWYST, REV. CHRYSOSTOMUS. Missionary labors of Fathers Marquette, Menard, and Allouez, in the Lake Superior region (Milwaukee and Chicago, 1886).

WAKEFIELD, JOHN A. History of the war between the United States and the Sac and Fox Nations of Indians (Jacksonville, Ill., 1834; Chicago, 1908, Caxton Club reprint). Illustrated.

> A valuable contemporary account, by a militia officer engaged in that war. To the reprint are added useful notes and a sketch of Wakefield's life by the editor, Frank E. Stevens.

WALKER, FRANCIS A. The Indian question (Boston, 1874).

> The author was commissioner of Indian affairs, and discusses the Indian policy of the United States.

WARREN, WILLIAM W. History of the Ojibways, based upon traditions and oral statements (St. Paul, 1885).

> This account is contained in vol. v of the Minnesota Historical Society's *Collections*, 21-394.

WEBB, J. WATSON, editor. Altowan, or life and adventure in the Rocky Mountains (New York, 1846). 2 vols.

> Contains accounts of the mode of life, character, and traditions of the Winnebago and Potawatomi Indians.

WEBSTER, HUTTON. Primitive secret societies: a study in early politics and religion (New York, 1908).

> Shows painstaking research and compilation, and is "probably the best general work on the subject that has yet appeared, at least in English." It treats such topics as "The men's house," "The puberty institution," "The secret rites," "Development of tribal societies," "Clan ceremonies," "Magical fraternities," etc.

WHITE, E. E. Service on the Indian reservations (Little Rock, Ark., 1893).

> "The experiences of a special Indian agent while inspecting agencies and serving as agent for various tribes, including explanations of how the government service is conducted on the reservations; descriptions of agencies; anecdotes illustrating the habits, customs, and peculiarities of the Indians."

WILSON, DANIEL. Prehistoric man: researches into the origin of civilization in the Old and the New World, third edition (London, 1876). Illustrated.

> In *Proceedings* of Royal Society of Canada are the following papers by this author: "The Huron-Iroquois of Canada, a typical race of American aborigines" (vol. ii, sec. 2, pp. 55-106); "Paleolithic dexterity" (vol. iii, sec. 2, pp. 119-133); "Trade and commerce in the stone age" (vol. vii, sec. 2, pp. 59-87).

WILSON, FRAZER E. The treaty of Greenville (Piqua, O., 1894).
Illustrated.

>An official account of the treaty, together with the expeditions of St.
Clair and Wayne against the northwestern Indian tribes.

WILSON, THOMAS. Arrowpoints, spearheads, and knives of prehistoric times.

>In *Report* of U.S. National Museum, 1897, part 1, pp. 811-988.

—— Prehistoric art.

>In *Report* of U.S. National Museum, 1896, pp. 325-664.

—— Study of prehistoric anthropology.

>In *Report* of U.S. National Museum, 1888, pp. 597-671.

WINSOR, JUSTIN. Mississippi basin: the struggle in America between England and France, 1697-1763 (Boston and New York,
1895). Illustrated.

—— Narrative and critical history of America (Boston and N.Y.,
1889). 8 vols. Illustrated.

>Volume 1 is devoted largely to the aborigines of North America; and a
bibliography of that subject is given in pp. 413-444.

—— The westward movement: the colonies and the republic west of
the Alleghanies (Boston, 1897). Illustrated.

WISCONSIN fur-trade accounts, 1792-1875. Ms. 17 vols.

>These papers (in the possession of the Wisconsin State Historical So-
ciety) include invoices, claims, and other business documents, written in
both French and English, and refer to practically all the territory on the
map published with this book. They are concerned mainly with the operations of the Green Bay fur-traders, and to some extent those of Mackinac;
and include, besides, many military and government accounts.

WISCONSIN STATE HISTORICAL SOCIETY. Collections of the State
Historical Society of Wisconsin. Vols. i-xix (Madison, Wis.,
1855-1910 +).

>This series constitutes one of our most valuable sources for the history
of French occupation and of the Indian tribes of the northwest. It was
edited by Dr. Lyman C. Draper (1855-1888) and Dr. Reuben G. Thwaites
(since 1888), successively secretaries of the Wisconsin Historical Society,
and both widely known as authorities in the field of Wisconsin history and
in that of the Indian tribes of the state. It contains much original documentary material, often its first publication; papers and articles by many
specialists in those lines; reminiscences and narratives by old residents,
traders, missionaries, and others; reports of interviews with Indian chiefs,
etc. Many references have been made to the *Collections* in the annotations
to the present work. The following list of articles especially bearing on the
field of this work may be found therein:

>Volume 1 — Lieut. James Gorrell's journal, 1761-1763, pp. 24-48 (account

of the Indians, their commerce, relations with English, councils, etc.);
Charles Whittlesey's "Recollections," 1832, pp. 64-85 (Black Hawk War,
and other matter about Indians).

Volume II — James H. Lockwood's "Early Times in Wisconsin," (1812-
1832, pp. 130-195 (Indian trade, character, customs, relations with whites,
etc.); John Shaw's "Narrative," (1812-1816), pp. 204-229 (relations of Indians with whites); Papers on Winnebago and Black Hawk Wars (1827-
1832), pp. 329-414; "Advent of N.Y. Indians into Wisconsin" (1816-1838),
pp. 415-449.

Volume III — J. G. Shea's "Indian Tribes in Wisconsin," pp. 125-138.
Cass Mss. (documents from French archives, 1723-1727), pp. 139-177 (customs of Indians, relations with French); Alfred Brunson's "Ancient Mounds
in Crawford County," pp. 178-184 (followed by *résumé* of Lapham's *Antiquities of Wisconsin*); Augustin Grignon's "Recollections," 1745-1832, pp.
197-295 (Langlade, Indian trade and traders, sketches of Indian chiefs,
etc.); B. P. H. Witherell's "Reminiscences," pp. 297-337 (Tecumseh, War
of 1812, etc.); R. F. Morse's "Chippewas of Lake Superior," pp. 338-369.

Volume IV — John Y. Smith's "Origin of the American Indians," pp. 117-
152; Ebenezer Childs's "Recollections," pp. 156-185 (1820-1832; Indian
trade, Black Hawk, etc.); Alfred Brunson's "Early History of Wisconsin,
pp. 223-251 (Indian tribes, relations with whites); various papers relating
to New York Indians, pp. 291-334.

Volume V — "Canadian Documents," 1690-1730 (obtained from French
archives), pp. 64-122 (Fox War, etc.); Papers on the Winnebago War of
1827 (Lewis Cass, T. L. McKenney, and others), pp. 123-158, 178-204;
id., on the Black Hawk War, pp. 285-320; Notices of Chippewa chief Hole-
in-the-Day, pp. 376-416.

Volume VI — Forsyth's journal of a voyage up the Mississippi, 1819, pp.
188-219 (followed by a letter from him to Gen. William Clark); Moses
Meeker's "Early History of the Lead Region," pp. 271-296.

Volume VII — J. D. Butler's "Prehistoric Wisconsin," pp. 80-101; Joseph
Tassé's "Memoir of Charles de Langlade," pp. 123-187; J. T. de la Ronde's
"Narrative," (1828-1842), pp. 346-365; Henry Merrell's "Narrative,"
(1835-1840), pp. 382-399.

Volume VIII — Papers on implements and early mining of copper, pp. 140-
173; "The Pictured Cave of La Crosse Valley," pp. 174-187; Documents
relating to the French in the Northwest, 1737-1800, pp. 209-240; M. M.
Strong's "Indian Wars in Wisconsin," pp. 241-286.

Volume X — E. Crespel's account of De Lignery's expedition, 1728, pp.
47-53; French forts in Wisconsin (by E. D. Neill, L. C. Draper, and others),
pp. 54-63, 292-372; Lawe and Grignon papers, 1794-1821, pp. 90-140;
Papers of Thomas G. Anderson (British Indian agent), 1814-1821, pp. 142-
149; Papers on the Black Hawk War, pp. 150-229.

Volume XI — "Western State Papers," (documents relating to French,
English, and American domination), 1671-1787, pp. 26-63; Radisson's "Voyages" in Wisconsin, pp. 64-96; Papers from Canadian archives, 1778-1783,
pp. 97-212; Documents (by Dickson, Forsyth, and others) relating to Wisconsin in War of 1812, pp. 247-355.

Volume XII — Documents from Canadian archives, 1767-1814, pp. 23-132; Two papers on Indian trade, pp. 133-169; R. G. Thwaites's "Story of the Black Hawk War," pp. 217-265; Papers of Indian Agent Boyd, 1832, pp. 266-298; Moses Paquette's account of Wisconsin Winnebagoes, pp. 399-433.

Volume XIII — Documents relating to British occupation of Prairie du Chien in War of 1812, pp. 1-162; Early mining and use of lead (O. G. Libby and R. G. Thwaites), pp. 271-374; History of Chequamegon Bay (R. G. Thwaites and Rev. C. Verwyst), pp. 397-440.

Volume XIV — Elizabeth T. Baird's "Early Days on Mackinac Island," pp. 17-64; A. J. Turner's "History of Fort Winnebago," etc., pp. 65-117; Catholic missions to Indians, in nineteenth century, pp. 155-205.

Volume XV — "Some Wisconsin Indian Conveyances, 1793-1836," pp. 1-24; Mission to the Stockbridge Indians, 1825-1848, pp. 25-204.

Volumes XVI-XVII — Documents from the French archives, relating to the French régime in Wisconsin (1634-1748); many of these were hitherto unpublished, and they correct many errors and fill many gaps in northwestern history of that period.

Volume XVIII — Documents from the French, Canadian, and Spanish archives, relating to the domination of France (1743-1760) and England (1760-1800) in Wisconsin. Register of marriages in the parish of Michilimackinac, 1725-1821.

Volume XIX — Register of Mackinac baptisms, etc., 1695-1821, pp. 1-162; Journal of the fur-trader Malhiot, 1804-1805, pp. 163-233; The fur trade on the upper lakes, and in Wisconsin, 1778-1815, pp. 234-488 (from original sources in the Federal archives at Washington, the libraries of C. M. Burton and the Wis. Historical Society, etc.).

WISCONSIN STATE HISTORICAL SOCIETY.   Proceedings, at the annual meetings (Madison, 18—-1910 +).

Notable papers in recent years: "Indian agriculture in Southern Wisconsin," B. H. Hibbard (1904); "Historic sites on Green Bay," A. C. Neville, and "Printed narratives of Wisconsin travelers prior to 1800," Henry E. Legler (1905); "The habitat of the Winnebago, 1632-1832," P. V. Lawson, and "The Mascoutin Village [in central Wisconsin]," John J. Wood and Rev. Arthur E. Jones, S.J. (1906); "The Fox Indians during the French régime," Louise P. Kellogg (1907); "The old West," Frederick J. Turner (1908); "Indian Diplomacy and the opening of the Revolution in the West," James Alton James, and "Bibliography of Carver's *Travels*," John T. Lee (1909); "The relation of archæology and history," Carl R. Fish, and "A Menominee Indian payment in 1838," Gustave de Neveu (1910).

WOOD, NORMAN B.   Lives of famous Indian chiefs (Aurora, Ill. [1906]).   Illustrated.

BIOGRAPHICAL SKETCHES of nearly a score of renowned Indian chiefs, from Powhatan to Geronimo; also numerous anecdotes, stories, etc., designed to show the traits of the Indian character. The illustrations are unusually good — chiefly portraits, most of them from pictures in Field and National Museums.

YARROW, H. C. Introduction to the study of mortuary customs among the North American Indians (Washington, 1880).

A *Bulletin* of Smithsonian Institution.

—— A further contribution to the study of the mortuary customs of the North American Indians (Washington, 1881).

In *First Report* of Bureau of American Ethnology, pp. 87-203.

YOUNG, EGERTON R., compiler. Algonquin Indian tales (New York, [1903]). Illustrated.

Collected among the Ojibwa and other northern peoples, during some thirty years. A chief figure in them is the miraculous being Nanabozho.

ZITKALA-SA. Old Indian legends retold (Boston, 1901).

A delightful collection of Dakota stories told by an educated young woman of that people, and illustrated by Miss Angel de Cora, an artist belonging to the Winnebago tribe.

ADDENDA

ADDENDA

Doctor Paul Radin, of the Bureau of American Ethnology, has kindly revised the proofs for the second half of volume II and prepared the following additional matter. This courtesy was extended by Doctor Radin to the editor on account of the latter's serious illness and to avoid delay in publication.

The index was prepared by Gertrude M. Robertson.

Location of tribes

Amikwa: on the north shore of Lake Huron opposite Manitoulin, Indiana till 1672; scattered to French settlements afterwards, some of them going to Green Bay.

Chippewa: formerly along both shores of Lake Huron and Lake Superior across Minnesota to Turtle Mountains. In 1640, they were at the Sault. Since 1815 they have been settled in Michigan, Wisconsin, Minnesota, and North Dakota. *Villages* – Cheboygan and Thunder Bay in lower Michigan, Pawating and Ontonagon in Wisconsin.

Conestoga: an Iroquoian tribe on the Susquehanna River.

Delaware: the entire basin of the Delaware River, in eastern Pennsylvania and southeastern New York with most of Delaware and New Jersey.

Fox: Lake Winnebago and Fox River, with numerous villages along the same.

Huron: Lake Simcoe, south and east of Georgian Bay and afterwards along the St. Lawrence River. *Villages* – Andiata and Sandusky.

Illinois: formerly in southern Wisconsin and northern Illinois and sections of Iowa and Missouri, along western banks of the Mississippi as far as the Des Moines River.

Menominee: first at the Bay de Noque and Menominee River. In 1671 to 1852 on or near the Menominee and Fox Rivers. *Villages* – St. Francis and St. Michael.

Miami: in 1658 at St. Michael about the mouth of Green Bay. *Villages* – Little Turtle and Piankaskaw.

Mascoutin: beyond and south of Lake Huron and subsequently on the Fox River.

Mohawk: in the upper part of New York State.

Montagnais: on the St. Maurice River and eastward almost to the Atlantic Ocean.

Neutrals: north of Lake Erie.

Nippising: on Lake Nippising and Lake Nipigon.

Oneida: south of Lake Oneida.

Onondaga: in Onondaga County, New York.

Ottawa: on French River, Georgian Bay. *Villages* – Walpole Island and Michilimacinac.

Peoria: on some river west of Mississippi and above the mouth of the Wisconsin River, probably upper Iowa River.

Potawatomi: on the western shore of Lake Huron and south along the western shore of Lake Michigan. *Villages* – Milwaukee and Little Rock.

Sauk: the eastern peninsula of Michigan and south of it. *Village* – De pere Rapids, Wisconsin.

Shawnee: South Carolina, Pennsylvania, Tennessee, and Ohio.

Seneca: western New York between Lake Seneca and Genesee River.

Santee Sioux: near Lake Buadelower, Minnesota.

Teton Sioux: above the Falls of St. Anthony, Minnesota.

Winnebago: Green Bay and along the shores of the Fox River and Lake Winnebago. *Villages* – Red Banks and Doty Island.

Yankton Sioux: north of Mille Lac, Minnesota.

Addition to annotations

Volume II, page 192, line 13, "parties:" Schoolcraft in *Thirty years with the Indian tribes*, 215-216, gives an eloquent description of a party of Fox warriors. He says: "But no tribe attracted so intense a degree of interest as the Iowas and the Sacs and Foxes, tribes of radically diverse languages, yet united in a league against the Sioux. These tribes were encamped on the island or opposite coast. They came to the treaty ground armed and dressed as a war party. They were all armed with spears, clubs, guns, and knives. Many of the warriors had a long tuft of red horse hair tied to their elbows and bore a necklace of grizzly bears claws. Their head-dress consisted of red dyed horse-hair, tied in such a manner to the scalp-locks to present the shape of the decoration of a Roman helmet. The rest of the head was completely shaved and painted. A long iron-shod lance was carried in the hand. A species of baldric supported part of their arms. The azian, moccasin, and leggings constituted part of their arms. They were indeed nearly nude and painted. Often, the print of a hand in white clay, marked the back or shoulders. They bore flags of feathers. They beat drums. They uttered yells at definite points. They landed in compact ranks. They looked the very spirit of defiance. Their leader stood as a prince, majestic and frowning. The wild native pride of man, in the savage state, flushed by success in war and confident in the strength of his arm was never so fully depicted to my eyes. And the forest tribes of the continent may be challenged to have ever presented a spectacle of bold daring and martial prowess equal to their landing."

Additions to bibliography

Volume II, page 302, following line 15:

An interesting discovery regarding Perrot's memoir has been made by Mr. Wilberforce Eames of Lenox Library, New York City. This is, that the book had two issues in the same year, pages 221 and 222 being cancelled and cut out and replaced by another leaf which was pasted on the stub of the former. The changes in the two pages mentioned, were made in the second issue of the year. The differences between the two issues are for the most part in minor details. In some cases, the second issue omits details mentioned in the first issue, and vice versa. All these details relate to the distribution of the Illinois tribes.

Mr. Eames has courteously placed these facts and a transcript of the cancelled pages at the disposal of the editor.

Also the following additions to the alphabetical arrangement of the bibliography, volume II, pages 330-339:

LETTRES ÉDIFIANTES et curieuses écrites des missions étrangères; collected by C. le Gobien, J. B. du Halde, N. Maréchal and L. Patouillet and first published in Paris, 1776. Rearranged and edited by Y.M.M.T. de Querbeuf (Paris, 1780-1788), 14 vols.
    Only vols. iv and v relate to America.
LEWIS, J. O. The Aboriginal Portfolio (Philadelphia, 1835).
RADIN, PAUL. Winnebago tales; printed in *Journal of American Folklore*, 1909.
—— Clan organization of the Winnebago; printed in *American Anthropologist*, 1910.
—— The ritual and significance of the Winnebago medicine dance; printed in *Journal of American Folklore*, 1911.

INDEX

ABEL, ANNIE HELOISE: work cited, II, 303

Abnaki [Abenaki, Abenaquis], (tribe): I, 134, 185, *footnote*, 224, *footnote*, 364, *footnote*, II, 54, 82, 259; account, 54-55, *footnote*

Acadia [Accadia, Cadie]: I, 47, *footnote*, 197, 256, *footnote*, 348

Adams, Charles F: work cited, II, 303

Adams, Henry: work cited, II, 303

Adams, John Quincy: *Memoirs*, II, 303

Adario [Kondiaronk, Sastaretsi], (Tionontate chief): leads expedition against Iroquois, I, 253, *footnote*; cause of French massacre, 253, *footnote*; converted, 253, *footnote*

Adoption: see *Manners and customs*; *Captives*

Adornment (personal): see *Manners and customs*

Africa: I, 27, *footnote*

Agariata (an Iroquois): I, 307

Agniers: see *Mohawk*

Agriculture: see *Economic conditions*: industries, etc.

Alaska: I, 38, *footnote*, 81, *footnote*, 122, *footnote*; Kodiak, 171, *footnote*

Algeria: government, I, 26 and *footnote*

Algonkins [Algonquins]: I, 15, 26, 36, *footnote*, 65, *footnote*, 88, *footnote*, 147, *footnote*, 281, *footnote*, 288, *footnote*, 371, *footnote*, II, 252; location, I, 43, 148, 149, 177; driven to Mackinaw, 43, *footnote*; name applied to tribe, 43, *footnote*; characteristics, 197; courtship and mar-

riage, 67-74; hunters, 43; hunting expedition, 43-45; regard corn as treat, 102; esteem flesh of dogs, 53, *footnote*; government, 145, *footnote*; refuse to render justice, 46; worship Great Panther, 59; belief regarding souls, II, 208, *footnote*; compared to Dakotas, I, 161, *footnote*; allies of French, 203; offer services to Courcelles, 199. *Relations with Iroquois* — neighbors, I, 43; invite to winter with them, 43; hostile to, 306; attack, 151, 190-192; war against, 190-203; defeated by, 192-193; unwilling to free, 201

Alimibegon: I, 173

Allegheny [Alleghany] Mts: I, 122, *footnote*, 336, *footnote*

Allegheny River: I, 240, *footnote*, 336, *footnote*

Alliances: I, 309, 311, 317, II, 184, 189, 201; renewed, 33; periodical renewals, 190; significance of belts, 185; aids allies, I, 356-357. *Interrace* — of English and various tribes, II, 188; Indians and French, 135, *footnote*, 254; desirable with French, I, 347, II, 42; benefits from, with French, I, 356-357; renewed between French and Foxes, II, 62-64; Foxes oppose French, I, 185, *footnote*; between French, Miami, and Mascoutens, 332; between French and Potawatomi, 316; of all nations to avenge massacre of Illinois, 299-300. *Intertribal* — desired, II, 44, 92, 118; Miami wish to renew, 99; Algonkins form, I, 197; Assin-

Black Bass: name of Sauk clan, II, 191, *footnote*; name of Fox clan, 192
Blackbird, Andrew J: work cited, II, 307
Black Carp (family): I, 319
Blackfeet [Siksika], (Siouan tribe): I, 277, *footnote*, II, 258-259; blanket, standard of value, 149, *footnote*; hostile relations, I, 108, *footnote*
Black Hawk [Muc-it-tay Mish-she-ka-kake, Ma'katawimeshekä'kää], (subordinate chief of Sauk and Fox Indians): I, 301, *footnote*, II, 142, *footnote*, 193, *footnote*, 211, 303, 304, 307; account, 211, *footnote*; delivered up to U.S., I, 292, *footnote*; work on cited, II, 307
Black Hawk War: II, 142, *footnote*, 191, *footnote*, 211, *footnote*, 245, 303, 318, 334, 344, 350, 351; causes, I, 292, *footnote*, II, 181, *footnote*, 211, *footnote*, 294, *footnote*
Black River: I, 165 and *footnote*, 171, *footnote*, 172, 268 and *footnote*
Blair, E. H: II, 202, *footnote*, 328
Blanchard, Rufus: work cited, II, 307
Blandin, Miss — [Mrs. Graham]: II, 294
Blanket: I, 70, 78, 315, 334, II, 173, 176, 221, 285; Indians cling to, 294; mode of manufacture, 149, *footnote*; uses, 149, *footnote*; as sacrifice, I, 61, *footnote*; as wager, 97
Blondeau, Maurice: II, 153, *footnote*, 154, 198, *footnote*
Blondeau, Nicholas: II, 153, *footnote*
Bloomfield, Julia K: work cited, II, 307
Blue Chief (celebrated Sauk): II, 184
Boas, Franz [Francis, Frank]: quoted, I, 54-55, *footnote*, II, 208, *footnote*, 264-270
Bobé, Father: commends La Potherie's Ms., II, 134
Boisguillot, —: I, 244, *footnote*
Bow and arrows: see *Implements*; *Weapons*

Boyd, George: work cited, II, 308, 351
Brackenridge, H. M: *Journal*, II, 346
Bradbury, John: *Travels*, II, 346
Brebeuf, —: I, 81, *footnote*
Brinton, Daniel G: II, 152, *footnote*; work cited, 170, *footnote*, 308
British: II, 50, 59, 254, and *in footnotes on the following pages*, I, 205, 226, 261, 273, 288, II, 54, 136, 240, 241; Indian names for, II, 240-241, *footnote*; colonies, I, 25; regarded as friends, 352, II, 277; head of confederacy, 188; bribe with gifts, I, 267; try to win savages, 250-251, 250, *footnote*; intrigues, II, 135, *footnote*; secret connections, 79; gaining ascendancy, I, 261; dealings desirable, 259, *footnote*; desire peace, II, 42; defeated, 81, 82; cause trouble between French and Indians, I, 261, *footnote*; French try to prevent, from intruding, 256, *footnote*; Indians oppose, 156, *footnote*; conquest of Canada, 257, *footnote*; trade, 259, *footnote*, 261 and *footnote*, II, 22, 80, 81, 85, 95; trading-post, I, 246, *footnote*; sell Indians, 267 and *footnote*; arrested, 250; Cree friendly, 108, *footnote*; Hurons join, II, 22; relations with Iroquois, I, 267, II, 35, 95-96; relations with Ottawa, I, 267, II, 90, 106; with Potawatomi, I, 302; *footnote*; with Tecumseh, II, 279 and *footnote*
British Columbia: I, 122, *footnote*, 324, *footnote*, II, 265, 270
British Folk-lore Society: I, 294, *footnote*
Brochet (chief): II, 81
Brookes, Samuel M: II, 157, *footnote*
Brower, J. V: work cited, II, 308, 334
Brown, Adam (captive): II, 189, *footnote*
Brown, Charles E: I, 21, II, 152, *footnote*
Brulé [Bois-Brulés]: I, 109, *footnote*

De pere Rapids (Sauk village): II, 356

Des Moines River: II, 142, *footnote*, 147, 148, 200, 201, 211, *footnote*, 233, 355

Detroit (Mich.): I, 149, 250, 258, 261, 270, 271, II, 29, 146, 201, 278, 309, 346, and *in footnotes on following pages*, I, 153, 189, 256, 280, 316, 329, 351, II, 108, 140, 150, 184, 189, 244; plot against, I, 257, *footnote*

Detroit River: I, 237 and *footnote*

Devils: recognized as divinities, I, 48

Dhegiha (Siouan group): I, 278, *footnote*, II, 36, *footnote*

Dillon, John B: work cited, II, 316

Dionne, C. E: I, 308, *footnote*

Disease: II, 218-219; common, 294; epidemic, I, 354; sacrifice to avoid, 62, *footnote*; ceremony in connection with, II, 218-219, *footnote*, 219; protection sought from, 268; cure, I, 133, *footnote*, II, 234; causes great mortality, I, 242, 293, 340, 341, II, 37, *footnote*, 314; causes death of chief, I, 269 and *footnote*; among Mascoutens, II, 58; smallpox, I, 108, *footnote*, 364, *footnote*, 367, *footnote*, II, 280

District of Columbia: Georgetown, II, 150, *footnote*, 182, *footnote*; see *Washington*

Divorce: I, 303, II, 215; infrequent, 167, 288; for just cause, I, 64-65

Documentary History of New York: I, 200, *footnote*

Dodge, Charles R: work cited, II, 316

Dodge, Richard Irving: II, 316

Dog: II, 129, 275; used as comparison, I, 333, II, 17, 40, 72, 80, 215, 226; feasts, I, 53, 87, II, 125, 292; Sioux do not eat, I, 169; peaceable, II, 280; scent enemy, I, 180; dislike Indians, II, 103; symbol in dream, I, 356; sacrificed, 60 and *footnote*, 61, *footnote*, II, 272. *Uses —* drawing sleds, etc., I, 278, *footnote*; hunt-

ing, 108; pack-beast, 173, *footnote*; to watch near grave, II, 293

Donaldson, Thomas: work cited, II, 317

Dongan, — (Dutch governor): I, 200, *footnote*

Doolittle, J. R: II, 314

Dorman, Rushton M: work cited, II, 317

Dorsey, George A: quoted, II, 86

Dorsey, J. Owen: I, 185, *footnote*, 289, *footnote*; quoted, I, 367-368, *footnote*; work cited, II, 309, 317

Doty Island (Winnebago village): II, 356

Douglas County (Wis.): I, 279, *footnote*

Dousman, Hercules L: work cited, II, 321

Drake, Benjamin: work cited, II, 317

Drake, Francis S: work cited, II, 317

Drake, Samuel G: work cited, II, 317

Draper, Lyman C: II, 151, *footnote*, 313, 345, 349, 350; quoted, 153, *footnote*

Dreams: see *Beliefs and superstitions*

Dreuillette, Gabriel (Jesuit): I, 157, *footnote*, 165, *footnote*, 224; brief account, 224, *footnote*

Dubuque, Julien: II, 59, *footnote*

Ducks: I, 114, 304, II, 165

Du Lhut [Du Lhude], M. —: I, 244, *footnote*

Dunn, Jacob P: *Indiana*, II, 38, *footnote*, 318

Dutch: I, 226, *footnote*

Du Tisné, —: II, 108, *footnote*

EAGLE (name of Sauk clan): II, 163, 191, *footnote*, 211; marking of graves, 212

Eames, Wilberforce: II, 357; quoted, 329

Eastman, Charles A: work cited, II, 318

Eastman, Mary H: work cited, II, 318

Eastman, Capt. S., U.S.A: II, 318, 342

Finley, James B: work cited, II, 320

Fire: first, I, 38; two methods of making, 38, *footnote*; to obtain, 326; as signal, 366, II, 124; as gift, 64 and *footnote*

Fish, Carl R: work cited, II, 351

Fish: I, 90, 113, 220, 229, 261; used as sacrifice, I, 61, *footnote*; months names for, II, 116; see *Carp, Herring, Sturgeon, Trout, Whitefish*

Flemish Bastard (chief of Mohawks): I, 157 and *footnote*, 199; missionary killed by war party, 158; denies murder, 158; captured, 200; freed, 201; insolence, 202; punished, 202; begs for peace, 203

Fletcher, Alice C: quoted, II, 259-260, 261-262 and *in footnotes on following pages*, I, 51-52, 123, 125, II, 151, 206-207, 192, 235, 246, 325, 328; work cited, 319, 320, 343

Florida: I, 81, *footnote*, 305, *footnote*, II, 230, *footnote*, 279

Fontette, Fevret de: II, 301

Food: see *Economic conditions*: Food

Forsyth, Thomas (government agent): I, 14, 17, II, 137, 153, 193, 244, 245, 247, and *in footnotes on following pages*, I, 171, II, 141, 181, 187, 189, 197, 211, 240-241, 244, 277, 278; account, 244-245, *footnote; Manners and customs of Sauk and Fox Indians*, 183-244; article on Shawnee prophet, 273-279; scope and interest of work, I, 17; work cited, II, 303, 320, 350

Forsyth, Wm. (father of preceding): II, 244, *footnote*

Fort Armstrong (Rock Island, Ill): I, 14, 21, II, 137, 139, II, 148, 150, 342

Fort Chartres: I, 156, *footnote*

Fort Crawford: II, 342

Fort Edwards: II, 142 and *footnote*, 148, 177

Fort Frontenac: I, 25, 153, *footnote*, 239, 240; built, 227; Ottawas join French at, 232

Fort Leavenworth: I, 367, *footnote*

Fort Mackinaw: II, 157, *footnote*

Fort Madison: II, 150, *footnote*

Fort Nelson: I, 364, *footnote*

Fort Osage: II, 150, *footnote*, 342

Fortress Monroe: II, 211, *footnote*

Fort Richelieu: I, 142, *footnote*

Fort Sainte-Anne: I, 217, *footnote*

Fort St. Louis: I, 353, *footnote*

Fort Saint Peter: I, 162, *footnote*

Fort Smith: II, 342

Fowke, Gerard: quoted, I, 160, *footnote*; work cited, 320

Fox [Mus-quak-kie, Outagami, Renards], (Algonquian tribe): I, 14, 17, 27, 41, *footnote*, 188-189, 223, 245, 258, 260, 261, 268, 269, 270, 271, 294, 301, 316, 321, 344, 350, II, 20, 27, 28, 30, 34, 65, 71, 82-83, 99, 109, 122, 131, 144, 153, 154, 250, 251, and *in footnotes on following pages*, I, 171, 185, 238, 244, 269, 271, 291, 296, II, 17, 59, 108, 197, 203, 278; source of name, I, 294, *footnote*; clans enumerated, II, 192; division into bands, 156 and *footnote*; location, I, 294, *footnote*, II, 142, 355; land claimed, 147; form new village, I, 317; characteristics, 294, *footnote*, II, 187; general customs, 225-228; marriage customs, 165-167; hunting, 233-234; destitution, I, 318; beliefs regarding death, II, 174-175; transmigration, 175; trade, I, 319; annuities, II, 181-182 and *footnote*; suspicious of questions, 140-141; chiefs, 155-156; government by chiefs, 186; martial law, 163-164; chiefs urge Du Luth to visit, 29; invite Perrot to visit, 61; Perrot visits, 62-63; speech to, I, 354. *Wars*—II, 202, 288, *footnote*, 292, *footnote*; manner of raising war party, 157-158; neutral, 106; warriors described, 356-357; disposition of captives, 162; proposal to destroy, I, 266; disasters, 293-295;

compel Jesuits' aid, II, 55; advised to make peace, 205; relations with Chippewa, I, 357, 358, II, 27, 183; relations with Dakota, 34-35, 56, 66-67, 69-70, 97, 101, 111, 114-115, 117, 118; relations with French, I, 258, *footnote*, II, 17-18, 54, 55, 61-63, 65, 97, 126-127; with Iroquois, I, 227, II, 105, 110; with Mascoutens, 89, 105; with Miami, 123-124, 125, 126-127; with Ottawa, 124, 125; plots, 17-18, 54, 65; desire peace, 34-35, 101, 111

Fox: name of Sauk clan, II, 191, *footnote*; name of Fox clan, 192

Fox (animal): in creation myth, I, 36

Fox River: II, 146, 252, 344, 355, 356, and *in footnotes on following pages*, I, 155, 290, 294, 295, 316, 329, II, 57

Fox River Valley: I, 289, *footnote*

Fox-Wisconsin portage: II, 30 and *footnote*, 34, 65

Forum: II, 338

France: I, 15, 25, 76, 198, 220, 348, II, 250, 251, 253, 255, and *in footnotes on following pages*, I, 42, 256, 259, 261, 273, 316, 354, 367, II, 28, 43, 217; compels peace, I, 155, *footnote*; takes possession of Ottawa country, 222; overstocked with beaver pelts, 230, *footnote*; Limoux, I, 30, *footnote*

Frazer, J. G: work cited, II, 320

French: I, 15, 16, 76, 116, 172, 174, 175, 177, 198, 275, 306, and *in footnotes on following pages*, 63, 163, 277, 279, II, 47, 54; first white man in America, 240, *footnote*; Indian names for, 240-241, *footnote*; early settlers, I, 148, number in American settlements, 25; American possessions, 25, 26; colony aided by Perrot, 27; regarded as friends, II, 277; spread of name and glory, I, 348; deride superstitions, 64, 88; teach Indians, 134; humor savages, 135;

evil influence, 209, *footnote*, 263-264; soldiers commit murder, 204; use Indian slaves, 190, *footnote*; permit torture, 158; fail to keep assurances, 239; conquest over Indians, 178; make peace, 199; mediators, 308; negotiate peace, II, 136; voyage of discovery, I, 363-372; trade, 175, 176, 259, *footnote*, 319, 343 (see *Economic conditions*: trade); conspiracy against, 351-352, II, 54, 65; massacre, I, 259; reënforcements, 198; ordered to Michilimakinak, II, 65; return to Montreal, 104; cause tribes to continue to Montreal, I, 341; Canadians, 98-99, *footnote*. *Relations* – with English, II, 22, 81; alliance, I, 347, 356, II, 42, 189, *footnote*; with Indians, I, 147-148; with Algonkins, 150, 191; with Chippewa, 173, 358, II, 30; with Cree, I, 108, *footnote*; with Dakota, II, 117, 122; with Foxes, I, 185, *footnote*, 258, *footnote*, II, 62-64, 65, 70; with Hurons, I, 193, 257, *footnote*; with Illinois, 156, *footnote*; with Iroquois, 151, 190-192, 194, 199-203, 232-243, 334, II, 110, 254; with Mascoutens, I, 323-333, II, 65; with Miami, I, 322, 332, II, 13, 16, 70, 130; with Ottawa, I, 176, 222, II, 110; with Potawatomi, I, 149, *footnote*, 302-303, *footnote*, 316, 333, II, 251; with Sioux, I, 182; with Winnebago, 301; see *Perrot, Nicolas*

French and Indian War: I, 280, *footnote*, II, 244, *footnote*

French River: I, 43, 62, II, 356

Friederici, Georg: work cited, II, 343

Frobenius, Leo: work cited, II, 320

Frontenac, Louis de Buade de (gov. of Canada): I, 26, 66, 351, II, 50, 70, 88, 89, 94, 101, 104, 106, 109, 111-112, 132, 136, 254, 255, and *in footnotes on following pages*, I, 244, 256, 259, 261, 267, 269; relieves De

Menominee, I, 312; to Miami, 330, II, 17, 58; to Ottawa, I, 232. *Enumerated* — I, 87, II, 24; brandy, 24; captives, I, 349, II, 92, 104; collars, I, 253; food, 63, *footnote*, 71; of peltries, 254, ore, II, 59, 66; tobacco, I, 196, 238, *footnote*, 321, 362, 363, 365, II, 19, 50, 52, 57, 60, 77, 100, 112, 170, 238-239

Gilfillan, Joseph A: work cited, II, 334

Gode: I, 308; defined, 308, *footnote*

Goodale, Elaine: see *Eastman, Charles*, II, 318

Gorrell, James: *Journal*, II, 349

Government: in general, I, 145 and *footnote*; colonial, 271, *footnote*; federal, should encourage religion, II, 281; attitude recommended for U.S., 141, *footnote*; British attempts to make peace, 205; justice, I, 138-141; of gens, 320, *footnote*; by chiefs, II, 163-164, *footnote*, 186, 216-218; military, I, 120, II, 163-164, 192, *footnote*, 258, 262; tribal, I, 320, *footnote*, 332, II, 86, *footnote*, 163, 226, *footnote*

Goyogouins: see *Cayugas*

Graham, Mr. —: I, 150, *footnote*

Grand Calumet (island): I, 176, *footnote*

Grand [Great] Medicine Society: II, 224-225, 224, *footnote*

Grand River (Mich.): I, 241, *footnote*, 302, *footnote*, II, 184, 199, *footnote*

Gravier, Father: I, 40, *footnote*, 60, *footnote*, 89, *footnote*; quoted, 59, *footnote*; work cited, 69, *footnote*, 76, *footnote*, 169, *footnote*

Great Beaver: origin of tribes, I, 62-63

Great Britain: I, 281, *footnote*

Great Hare [Michabou, Ouisaketchak], (diety): I, 48; creates world, 32-36; creates man, 37; creates woman, 39-40; inspires making of bow, I, 38; gave different dialects, 41;

in dreams, 52; Montagnais belief, 36-37; Ottawa belief, 36, *footnote*

Great-Lake: name of Sauk clan, II, 191

Great Lakes: I, 159, II, 116, 184, 266, 309, 311, 330, 333, and *in footnotes on following pages*, I, 50, 171, 174, 246, 275, 278, 281, 287, 367, II, 190, 199

Great Lynx: name of Sauk clan, II, 191, *footnote*

Great Panther [Michipissy, Missibizi], (god of waters): worshiped, I, 59

Great Spirit [Geechee Manito-ah, Kee-shay-munitoo]: I, 299, 360, *footnote*, II, 114, 141, 142, 155, 156, 158, 161-162, 168, 179, 195, 203, *footnote*, 210, 235, 278, 280; beliefs concerning, 174, 222-223; confession to, 277; feasts, 169; 220-221; misconceptions, 222-223, *footnote*; reproves Tenskwatawa, 274; see *Manito, Mateomek, Messou, Nanabozho [Michabous]*

Green Bay [Bay of Puans, Bay of the Puants]: I, 254, 349, 354, 364, II, 28, 40, 74, 104, 110, 146, 177, 184, 201, 215, 250, 251, 253, 303, 308, 321, 349, 355, 356, and *in footnotes on following pages*, I, 48, 60, 103, 132, 149, 150, 153, 165, 189, 222, 244, 270, 277, 278, 290, 291, 302, 316, II, 30, 57, 140, 151, 184, 199; source of name, I, 288-289; described, 290-291; tides, 290, *footnote*

Green Bay and Prairie du Chien *Papers*: II, 321

Green Lake County (Wis.): I, 323, *footnote*, II, 227, *footnote*

Greenland: II, 270

Gregory, J. G: work cited, II, 337

Griffin, A. P. C: work cited, II, 321

Griffins: Indians pray to, I, 49

Grignon, Augustin: work cited, II, 350

Grignon, Lawe and Porlier *Papers*: cited, II, 321

Groseilliers, —: I, 168, *footnote*

Mississippi Valley: I, 25, 159, and *in footnotes on following pages,* 50, 66, 146, 169, 185, 246, 323, 324, 325, 332

Missouri (Siouan tribe): II, 200, and *in footnotes on following pages,* I, 156, 171, 277, 367, II, 108, 199

Missouri (state): II, 234, 280, 281, 303, 355, and *in footnotes on following pages,* I, 292, 295, 301, 367, II, 119, 146. *Cities* — Belle Fontaine, II, 150, *footnote*; St. Louis, I, 117, *footnote,* 292, *footnote,* II, 137, 146, 177, *footnote,* 181, *footnote,* 203, 244, 245, *footnote,* 313, 342

Missouri River: II, 142, 147, 148, 199, 205, 233, 234, 278, 335, and *in footnotes on following pages,* I, 117, 124, 160, 171, 277, 364, 367, II, 36, 199, 279, 292

Missouri River Valley: II, 313

Missouri State Historical Society: II, 342; *Documents,* 334

Moccasins: used as food, I, 229, *footnote*; peculiar to tribe, 328, *footnote*; gift to Perrot, II, 73

Mohawk [Agniers, Aniez, Annieronnon], (tribe of Iroquois confederation): I, 199, and *in footnotes on following pages,* 47, 157, 181, 199, 240, 371, II, 156; location, 356; courage, I, 147, *footnote*; demand peace, 200; French and allies wage war against, 202-203; beg for peace, 203; disclose treachery, 254; warn Seneca, 255

Mohawk River: II, 188

Mohegan (Algonquian tribe): adopt Pequot, II, 37-38, *footnote*

Moingwena [Moüingoüena], (Illinois tribe): I, 155, *footnote,* 295, *footnote*

Mo-ne-to-mack (Sauk chief): II, 155

Monroe, James: I, 14

Montagnais (Athapascan group): I, 197, 222, *footnote,* 281, *footnote,* II,

257; location, 356; myths, I, 36-37, *footnote*; creation belief, 40, *footnote*; abhor flesh of dogs, 53, *footnote*; bear feast, 131-132, *footnote*

Montana: I, 81, *footnote,* 364, *footnote,* II, 199, *footnote*; Missoula County, I, 123, *footnote*

Months: named from animals and fish: II, 115-116

Montreal (Que.): I, 25, 42, 157, 158, 188, 198, 201, 254, 261, 307, 309, 310, 313, 315, 317, 333, 334, 337, 343, 351, 357, II, 25, 42, 45, 46, 75, 79, 89, 96, 104, 106, 107, 109, 110, 136, 174, 251, 253, 254, 310, and *in footnotes on following pages,* I, 42, 148, 165, 171, 229, 238, 253, 259, II, 135; Mohawks settle in, I, 203; Ottawa go to, 210; Ottawa reach, 214; jurisdiction, 215; trade, 228; trip planned to, 336-339; ravaged by Iroquois, II, 254

Mooney, James: quoted, II, 272-273, and *in footnotes on following pages,* I, 43, 108, 270, 279-280, 282, 291, 294, 296, 303, 316-317, 327-328, 330, 339, 364, II, 26-27, 54-55, 77, 119-120, 156-157, 166, 184, 273-274, 278-279, 281-282; work cited, 309, 335

Moore, Clarence B: I, 324, *footnote*

Moorehead, Warren K: works cited, II, 335

Moose: I, 102, 110, *footnote,* 113 and *footnote,* 203, 280; origin of man, 37; as game, 44; form yards, 44, *footnote*; method of hunting, 107-108; great number killed, 221; October named for, II, 116

Morgan, F. P: II, 335

Morgan, Lewis H: II, 161, *footnote,* 191, *footnote*; work cited, 335, 343

Morris, Thomas: *Journal,* II, 346

Morse, Jedidiah: I, 14, II, 176, 181, *footnote,* 182 and *footnote,* 302; quoted, 177, *footnote*; letter of Morrell Marston to, 138-182; outline of work, 139-140, *footnote*

61, 83, 91, 107, 144, 153, 154, 183, 251, and *in footnotes on following pages*, I, 124, 238, 296, 303, II, 17, 59, 197, 203, 278; derivation of name, I, 291, *footnote*; account, II, 190-191, *footnote*; division into tribes, 163; division into bands, 156 and *footnote*; names of various clans, 190-191; location, I, 291, *footnote*, II, 147-148, 356; characteristics, I, 303, II, 187; suspicious of questions, 140-141; traditions show outside influence, I, 41, *footnote*; customs in general, II, 225-228; manner of procuring a wife, 165-167; of raising war party, 157-158; disposition of captives, 162; martial law, 163-164; chiefs, 157; described, 153-154; government by chiefs, 186; warrior bands, 192-194; warriors described, 356; brave meets with accident, 57; lodge, described, 191, *footnote*; hunting, 233-234; annuities, 181-182 and *footnote*; find traces of missionary, I, 172; attend council, 223; member desires war, 355; recommended attitude of government toward, II, 141, *footnote*; vocabulary and grammatical forms, 154; battle, 202; advised to make peace, 205. *Relations with* — French, II, 60, 97; Chippewa, 183; Dakota, 111; Foxes, 113-114, 122-123; Iroquois, 110, 133; Ottawa, 124

Sault Ste. Marie: I, 43, *footnote*, 178-179, 276, *footnote*, 302, *footnote*, 306, *footnote*, 354, II, 40, 355; Chippewa at, I, 109, *footnote*; Perrot summons chiefs, 222; Jesuit mission, 224, *footnote*; council, 225, *footnote*; general assembly, 343

Sauteurs: see *Chippewa*

Saxon [Sog-o-nosh, Sasenaugh]: II, 240, *footnote*

Scalping: I, 195, II, 26 and *footnote*; see *Dances*, scalp

Schoolcraft, Henry R: I, 39, *footnote*, 166, 318, 356; works cited, 341-342

Schultz, J. W: work cited, II, 342

Scioto River: I, 316, *footnote*, 336, *footnote*

Scotland: II, 139, *footnote*. *City* — Edinburgh, 153

Scull, Gideon D: II, 339

Sea: name of Sauk clan, II, 191, *footnote*

Seasons: II, 220; method of reckoning, etc., 116-117, *footnote*; feasts and other rites dependant upon, I, 62, *footnote*

Secret Societies: see *Religion*

Seelye, L. E: see *Eggleston, Edward*, II, 318

Seignelay, Marquis de: I, 250, *footnote*, 259, *footnote*; quoted, 243, *footnote*

Seneca [Sonnontoäns, Tsonnontouans, Tsonontouans], (Iroquoian tribe): I, 47, *footnote*, 148, 199, 240, 260, 280, *footnote*, II, 23, 58, 111, *footnote*, 134, 161, *footnote*, 335; meaning and scope of name, I, 240, *footnote*; location, II, 356; political history, I, 240, *footnote*; name of various bands, 240, *footnote*; Conestoga join, 226; Perrot to go against, 245; ruin Hurons 241, *footnote*; French and allies advance toward, 251; warned, 255; French and various tribes to go against, II, 16; adopt Tuscarora, 37, *footnote*; Ottawa to send message to, 44

Seneca Lake: I, 240, *footnote*

Serpent: pray to, I, 49; device of Wea, II, 120, *footnote*

Shakers (religious sect): II, 270

Shaman: I, 54, *footnote*, 133, *footnote*, II, 171, *footnote*, 208, 224, *footnote*, 267; see *Medicine-men*

Sharp, Mrs. Abigail G: work cited, II, 342

Shaubena [Potawatomi chief]: II, 334

Shaugawaumikong [Chagouamigon],

note; Seneca slow to abolish, 240, *footnote*; Illinois refrain from, 350-351; Ottawa plan against Sioux, 188-189; Ottawa continue, 252, II, 36; Ottawa persuaded, I, 250; between Potawatomi and Menominee, 310; between Sioux and Cree, 170; see *Black Hawk War, Conspiracy, Weapons*

War of 1812: II, 336, 342, 350, 351, and *in footnotes on following pages*, I, 288, 301, 316, II, 151, 189, 211, 245, 273, 279

Warren, Wm. H: work cited, II, 334, 348

Washington, D.C: I, 225, *footnote*, 289, *footnote*, II, 193, *footnote*, 198, *footnote*, 281, *footnote*

Washington, George: II, 150, *footnote*

Waupaca County (Wis.): I, 317, *footnote*

Wea [Oüaoüiartanons, Oüaouyartanons], (Miami subtribe): I, 296, *footnote*, 316, *footnote*, 317, *footnote*, II, 67 and *footnote*, 119, *footnote*, 120, *footnote*, 129, 130, 201; receive annuity, 181, *footnote*

Wealth: see *Economic conditions*

Weapons: I, 311, II, 62, 73, 206, *footnote*, 207, *footnote*, 209, 221, 261; deprived of, I, 120; placed on graves, 89; left with dead, 81; bow and arrows, 110, 138, 161, *footnote*, 180, 281, 321, 325, 344, II, 17, *footnote*, 20, 58, 77, 133, 164, 277; bucklers, I, 126; clubs, 126, 181, 191, 194, 195, 209, *footnote*, 259, *footnote*, 319, 325, 344, 345, 365, II, 17 and *footnote*, 20, 21, 29, 35, 37, 58, 64, 67, 85, 102, 118, 122, 133, 356; dagger, I, 352, II, 63; guns, I, 97, 110, 163, 189, 214, 238, 239, 246, 249, 259, *footnote*, 277, *footnote*, 307, 311, 312, 315, 330, 334, 342, 344, 345, II, 18, 19, 27, 28, 50, 56, 60, 89, 164, 176, 196, 203, *footnote*, 227, 236, 356; hatchet, I, 293, 307, 312, 319, 338,

365, II, 16, 36, 55, 64, 77, 89, 91, 173; knives, I, 209, *footnote*, 293, 307, II, 77, 93, 173, 356; lance, 17, *footnote*, 357; quivers, I, 344; spears, II, 356; sword, I, 214, 217, 342, 354, II, 55; tomahawk, I, 233 and *footnote*, 234, 239, 281, II, 180, *footnote*, 239

Webb, J. Watson: work cited, II, 348

Webster, Hutton: work cited, II, 348

Weiser, Conrad: *Journal*, II, 346

Wentworth, Thomas P: II, 306

West Indies: I, 259, *footnote*, 324, *footnote*, II, 38, *footnote*

Westropp, Henry I: II, 284; article on Sioux, 284-286

White, E. E: work cited, II, 348

Whitefish: I, 179, 275, *footnote*, 276, 282, *footnote*, 304; October named for, II, 116

Whites: see *Americans; British; Europeans; French; Interracial relations*

Whittlesey, Charles: work cited, II, 343, 350

Wight, W. W: work cited, II, 337

Wild-cats: I, 113

Wilkinson, James: II, 279, *footnote*

Williams, Eleazer: work on, cited, II, 337

Williams, John R: II, 310

Williamson, Thomas S: II, 340

Willoughby, C. C: work cited, II, 305

Wilson, Daniel: work cited, II, 348

Wilson, Frazer E: work cited, II, 349

Wilson, Thomas: works cited, II, 343, 349

Winnebago [Ho-tcan-ga-ra, Ochungara, Otchagra, Ouenibegons, Ouinipegous, Ouinipigou, Ouinipegs], (Siouan tribe): I, 18, 288, 306, 310, 312, 317, 366, II, 20, 76, 78, 82, 83, 229, 247, and *in footnotes on following pages*, I, 50, 89, 149, 162, 165, 277, 278, 302, 303, 321, 367, 371, II, 199, 211; source of name, I, 288-289, *footnote*; location, II, 356; characteristics, I, 293, 300-301, II,

The Late Emma Helen Blair

On account of the death of the editor whilst this work was in course of publication, we reprint below extracts from the two leading newspapers of her home city.

In the death of Emma Helen Blair at the Madison Sanitarium at 6:53 o'clock yesterday morning [September 25], Madison and the state lost one of the most remarkable women that Wisconsin has produced.

Miss Blair was born at Menasha, Wisconsin, September 12, 1851. From 1869 to 1871 she attended the high school at Westfield, Massachusetts. In 1871 she returned to Wisconsin and entered Ripon College, graduating in 1874. For two years she taught in public schools and then went to Milwaukee, where she spent nearly twenty years, chiefly engaged in journalistic work.

During the last few years of her residence in Milwaukee Miss Blair was the chief assistant for the Associated Charities, and thereby she gained an intimate knowledge of social and economic conditions. The interest she had developed in these matters led to her entering the State University in 1892, where during the following two years she took post graduate work in history, economics, and sociology. She later became a member of the library staff of the State Historical Society and assisted in the production of an annotated catalogue of the Society's famous collection of bound newspaper files, some 15,000 in number.

In 1894 Miss Blair began a most important work which introduced her to the favorable notice of many historical experts throughout the country. In that year she resigned from the library staff and began work as chief assistant to Dr. R. G. Thwaites in the editing and annotating of the famous *Jesuit Relations*, a stupendous historical undertaking in seventy-three volumes. After she completed her work on the *Jesuit Relations* she assisted in the editing of the well-known journal of Father Louis Hennepin and of the famous original journals of the Lewis and Clark expedition. In 1903 she began the editing of the long series of historical documents, entitled *The Philippine Islands, 1493-1898*, a work which appeared in fifty-five volumes. Her collaborator in this great undertaking was Dr. James A. Robertson, at present government librarian of the Philippines Library at Manila.

Miss Blair's final work, completed just previous to her last fatal illness, was the translation from the French, greatly enriched with her own historical notes, of Nicolas Perrot's celebrated Memoir on the habits and customs of the American Indians. His book has heretofore appeared only in French, and Miss Blair's translation will be a welcome contribution to the literature of western history. Nothing grieved her more in her final illness than the fear that she would not live to see the book in print on which she had spent so much time and thought.

Miss Blair became by dint of native ability and years of preparatory toil one of the most expert historical editors in this country. She had acquired a complete mastery of the French and Spanish languages. Her literary style was incisive, her historical judgment clear and accurate, and her knowledge of the details of typography quite unusual. In recognition of these qualities Ripon College and the State University honored her with degrees.

Despite her erudition Miss Blair was a woman of most modest demeanor and apparently quite unaware of the distinction into which her productions had brought her. Socially she was of a most charming disposition, kindly and sympathetic toward others, and ever ready to lend a helping hand. She was known and esteemed by a considerable body of fellow workers in the field of American History. The death of this remarkable woman brings genuine sorrow to many hearts. Her marked ability and rare personality were among the assets of literary Madison.—The Madison *Democrat*, Tuesday morning, September 26, 1911.

. . . Teaching, in which Miss Blair engaged after her graduation, did not satisfy her, and in 1877 she took a place on the staff of the Milwaukee *Christian Statesman*, her connection with which came to an end in 1884. Her learning and thoroughness soon caused her to be brought into service in the editing of historical documents. From 1896 to 1901 she was assistant editor, under Dr. R. G. Thwaites, of the *Jesuit Relations* and that important collection owes no little of its value to her vigilant accuracy, historical imagination, wide general knowledge, and fine sense of language.

She then took up several works independently, the most important being the vast collection of documents containing material for Philippine history, in fifty-five volumes, known as *The Philippine Islands, 1493-1898*. The motives which influenced Miss Blair to undertake this work were in a great measure philanthropic, for she hoped the full knowledge of historical conditions in the Islands would assist in solving the problems of governing them. It soon became evident that the people of the United States did not appreciate their new responsibilities so keenly as to make the monumental series a financial success; but the publisher and the editors would not give up and Miss Blair resolutely carried on the work begun with such high hopes. These disappointments and discouragements, coupled with more intimate personal anxieties, contributed no doubt to affect Miss Blair's naturally firm health and to promote the development of the malignant disease which caused her death. The work won the respect of scholars and the gratitude of the well informed.—The Wisconsin *State Journal*, Monday, September 25, 1911.